Also in the Variorum Collected Studies Series:

RICHARD M. FRANK, (Ed. Dimitri Gutas)
Philosophy, Theology and Mysticism in Medieval Islam
Texts and Studies on the Development and History of Kalām, Vol. I

NORMAN CALDER, (Ed. Jawid Mojaddedi and Andrew Rippin)
Interpretation and Jurisprudence in Medieval Islam

JULES JANSSENS
Ibn Sina and his Influence on the Arabic and Latin World

PATRICIA CRONE
From Kavad to al-Ghazali
Religion, Law and Political Thought in the Near East, c.600–c.1100

MICHAEL COOK
Studies in the Origins of Early Islamic Culture and Tradition

ANDREW RIPPIN
The Qur'an and its Interpretative Tradition

DIMITRI GUTAS
Greek Philosophers in the Arabic Tradition

M.J. KISTER
Concepts and Ideas at the Dawn of Islam

G.H.A. JUYNBOLL
Studies on the Origins and Uses of Islamic Hadith

GEORGE MAKDISI
Religion, Law and Learning in Classical Islam

FRANZ ROSENTHAL
Muslim Intellectual and Social History
A Collection of Essays

WILFERD MADELUNG
Religious Schools and Sects in Medieval Islam

VARIORUM COLLECTED STUDIES SERIES

Early Islamic Theology: The Muʿtazilites and al-Ashʿarī

Richard M. Frank

Early Islamic Theology: The Muʿtazilites and al-Ashʿarī

Texts and Studies on the Development and History of Kalām, Vol. II

Edited by Dimitri Gutas

ASHGATE
VARIORUM

Published in the Variorum Collected Studies Series by

Ashgate Publishing Limited
Gower House, Croft Road,
Aldershot, Hampshire
GU11 3HR
Great Britain

Ashgate Publishing Company
Suite 420
101 Cherry Street
Burlington, VT 05401–4405
USA

Ashgate website: http://www.ashgate.com

ISBN–13: 978–0–86078–978–9

British Library Cataloguing in Publication Data
Frank, Richard M.
Texts and studies on the development and history of kalām
Vol 2: Early Islamic theology : the Muʿtazilites and
al-Ashʿarī. – (Variorum collected studies series)
1. Islam – Doctrines – History
I. Title II. Gutas, Dimitri
297.2'09

ISBN–13: 978–0–86078–978–9

Library of Congress Control Number: 2006935669

The paper used in this publication meets the minimum requirements of the American National Standard for Information Sciences – Permanence of Paper for Printed Library Materials, ANSI Z39.48–1984. ∞ ™

Printed by TJ International Ltd, Padstow, Cornwall

VARIORUM COLLECTED STUDIES SERIES CS834

CONTENTS

This volume contains xii + 384 pages

FOREWORD

This is the second of three volumes reprinting the collected papers on Islamic subjects by Richard M. Frank, Professor Emeritus at the Catholic University of America. The first, published in 2005,[1] contains articles that study the lexical and intellectual context of Islamic theology (kalām) and explore its interactions with philosophy and mysticism. The present volume brings together studies on early kalām, the Muʿtazilites and the development of the thought of al-Ašʿarī, while the third will be devoted to articles on the Ašʿarites and the Ašʿarite tradition.[2]

The studies in the present collection represent an original attempt to make philosophical sense, and in particular understand the theoretical underpinnings, of what is in essence the great theological tradition in early Islam, the Muʿtazilite school of Baṣra. It opens with two pieces (I–II) on one of its greatest exponents, Abū l-Huḏayl al-ʿAllāf (whom some of his successors considered, perhaps rightly, as the real founder of kalām), continues with the masters of its classical period, the Ǧubbāʾīs, father and son, and their followers (III–V), and ends with their most famous, but rebel, student, al-Ašʿarī (VI–IX). The first selection, the classic short monograph describing the theological system of Abū l-Huḏayl, lays the foundation for those that follow, for it articulates Frank's original approach to understanding kalām. In sharp contrast to all previous studies in Western Islamic studies, which viewed kalām as "little more than a superficial and relatively unsophisticated way of stating and of arguing and defending one or another point of basic religious doctrine,"[3] Frank's monograph views the task of kalām as one "of discovering analytically and setting forth objectively in formal language the underlying structure of the created world as it manifested the *lógos*," the divine Word, "revealed in the *Koran*." In the performance of this

---

[1] *Philosophy, Theology and Mysticism in Medieval Islam. Texts and Studies on the Development and History of Kalām*, Vol. I, ed. Dimitri Gutas, Ashgate: Aldershot, 2005.

[2] A complete bibliography of Richard Frank's publications, compiled by James E. Montgomery and Monica Blanchard, is published in the volume, *Arabic Theology, Arabic Philosophy. From the Many to the One: Essays in Celebration of Richard M. Frank*, ed. by James E. Montgomery, Peeters: Leuven, 2006.

[3] R. Frank in his memoir "Yā Kalām," selection I in the first Variorum volume cited in the first note above, p. 3. The memoir provides indispensible orientation to the development of Frank's researches over the years.

task, the methods that were followed were deeply rational, and the goal of reason in this process was identified by Frank as being "not independently to uncover and make its own the truth of nature and its own existence," but

> to comprehend and verify out of its own experience of the world, through an analysis of the world, the truth which was already given to its pre-analytic understanding... . The initial assumption is not basically that the ultimate order of existence is of itself rationally and intelligibly ordered according to the norms of human reason, so that it may be discovered by and in the process of reflective thought, but rather that it manifests the creative Truth of God and that the underlying structure and coherence of this manifestation can be analytically described. This is important, for the kalām's initial and unreflected attitude towards the kind of truth to be attained and the place of reason in its attainment determined its method as well as its form and content. (I, p.7)

I cite at length Frank's statement of the goal and method of kalām because it describes kalām's very foundation and the basic and irreducible way in which it differs from philosophy. The accuracy of Frank's insight and his subsequent analysis of early kalām and the Aš'arite tradition can be gauged by how close it is to that of no less an authority than Ibn Ḫaldūn, who said the following on the subject:

> The theologians, following preponderantly this line of argument, for the most part deduced the existence and attributes of the Creator from the existing things and their conditions. Physical bodies, which are the subject of the philosophical study of physics, form part of these existing things. However, the philosophical study of them differs from the theological. The philosophers study bodies in so far as they move or are stationary. The theologians, on the other hand, study them in so far as they serve as an argument for the Agent. In the same way, the philosophical study of metaphysics studies existence as such and its attendant requirements that are due to itself. The theological study of metaphysics, on the other hand, is concerned with what exists in so far as it serves as argument for Him who causes existence. In general, to the theologians, the object of theology is to find out how the articles of faith, which the religious law has laid down as correct, can be proven with the help of rational arguments, so that innovations may be repulsed and doubts and misgivings concerning the articles of faith be removed.[4]

As research on both kalām and philosophy in the Islamic world proceeds with increasing intensity, it is important to keep in mind this distinction which has been very effectively delineated in Frank's incisive analyses of the formal structure and argumentation of kalām.

---

[4] Ibn Khaldūn, *Al-Muqaddimah*, ed. 'Abdassalām aš-Šaddādī, Casablanca, 2005, III, 35; translation adopted, with slight modifications, from Frank Rosenthal, *The Muqaddimah*, 2nd ed., Princeton, 1967, III, 52–3.

The next three studies (III–V) deal with classical Muʿtazilite teaching in the works of the Ǧubbāʾīs, mostly gleaned from one of the greatest manuscript finds of the twentieth century in the field of kalām, the *Muġnī* of the Qāḍī ʿAbd al-Ǧabbār. Frank's studies in this area culminated with his monograph on *Beings and their Attributes*, which should be consulted in connection with this set of articles.[5]

The final four pieces (VI–IX) form a unit of research. They discuss, among others, an issue already raised above, the role of reason in the procedures of kalām. Al-Ašʿarī tried to render precise his position on this subject vis-à-vis both the Muʿtazilites, whom he renounced, and the *ahl as-sunna*, with whose cause he identified (though on his own terms, for he clearly felt that *taqlīd* is to be condemned). These studies are based on a careful analysis of three of al-Ašʿarī's works in particular, his *Letter to the People of the Frontier* (*R. ilā ahl aṯ-ṯaġr*), *Flashes in Refutation of Heretics* (*K. al-Lumaʿ*), and *Exhortation to* [*Rational*] *Inquiry* (*K. al-ḥaṯṯ ʿalā l-baḥṯ*). The text of the last of these is also presented in a new edition (IX), in exemplary fashion. As is frequently the case with classical Arabic texts from the first four centuries of Islam, their transmission is rarely straightforward; those that were of importance in the ideological battles fought among various factions – as were the theological treatises written after al-Maʾmūn's *miḥna* came to an end – underwent different kinds of manipulation to fit a particular viewpoint. As a result, their manuscript transmission frequently showed signs of interpolation, emendation, or elaboration, and the creation of different recensions of the text. Al-Ašʿarī's *K. al-Ḥaṯṯ* happens to be one such text, as Frank discovered, and his detailed study of the manuscript tradition in elucidation of the various problems of transmission is a model of philological analysis. Philological accuracy is indispensable for all research whose primary sources are written, but especially so in the case of al-Ašʿarī, himself a very precise author. Frank's admonition with regard to the study of al-Ašʿarī, valid in any case for all the authors treated here, conveniently summarizes the import of this volume: "the more one studies the writing of al-Ašʿarī the more one is impressed with its acuteness and precision; nothing is extraneous ... This remarkable economy of his style requires that it be read very closely" (VIII, 149).

Once more it is a pleasant duty to express, also on behalf of the author, my sincere gratitude to all the publishers of the original articles for permission to reprint them in this collection, and in particular the Netherlands Institute for the Near East (NINO) and its director, Dr J.J. Roodenberg, whose generous consent enabled us to make once more widely accessible the monograph on

---

[5] *Beings and their Attributes. The Teaching of the Basrian School of the Muʿtazila in the Classical Period*, Albany, NY., 1978.

Abū l-Huḏayl. Dr John Smedley and Ashgate Publishing Limited are heartily to be thanked for including this volume in the Variorum Collected Studies Series. As before, the Viscusi Fund of the Department of Near Eastern Languages and Civilizations at Yale University gratefully provided moneys to defray some expenses relating to the preparation of the volume. I am particularly grateful to Mr Alexander Treiger who, in an already overburdened schedule of studies, found the time for the careful preparation of the index. And a final and heartfelt word of thanks must go to the author himself for the opportunity to be once more engaged with his inspirational work.

DIMITRI GUTAS

New Haven, CT
July 2006

ACKNOWLEDGEMENTS

Grateful acknowledgement is made to the following institutions, people and publishers for their kind permission to reproduce the essays included in this volume: The Netherlands Institute for the Near East and Dr J.J. Roodenberg, Leiden (for chapter I); *Le Muséon*, Revue d'Études Orientales, Editions Peeters, Louvain-la-Neuve (II, VI); Éditions Maisonneuve et Larose, Paris (III, VII); Régis Morelon, Director, Institut Dominicain d'Études Orientales, Cairo and Éditions Peeters, Leuven (IV, IX); Brill N.V. (Brill Academic Publishers), Leiden (V); The Royal Swedish Academy of Letters, History, and Antiquities, Stockholm (VIII).

PUBLISHER'S NOTE

The articles in this volume, as in all others in the Variorum Collected Studies Series, have not been given a new, continuous pagination. In order to avoid confusion, and to facilitate their use where these same studies have been referred to elsewhere, the original pagination has been maintained wherever possible.

Each article has been given a Roman number in order of appearance, as listed in the Contents. This number is repeated on each page and is quoted in the index entries.

I

THE METAPHYSICS OF CREATED BEING ACCORDING TO ABÛ L-HUDHAYL AL-'ALLÂF

A Philosophical Study of the Earliest Kalâm

I

TABLE OF CONTENTS

ABBREVIATIONS

abû Rašîd al-Nîsâbûrî, *K. al Masâ'il*	= Biram, Arthur, *die Atomistische Substanzlehre aus dem Buch der Streitfragen*, Berlin, 1902
Baqillânî, *Tamhîd*	= *al-Tamhîd fî l-radd 'alà l-mulḥida wal-mu'tazila*, ed. M. Khodeiri and M. abû Rîda, Cairo, 1367/1849
Farq	= 'Abd al-Qâhir al-Baġdâdî, *al-Farq bayn al-firaq*, ed. M. al-Kawthari, Cairo, 1367/1948
Fiṣal	= Ibn Ḥazm, *K. al-Fiṣal wal-Milal*, 5 vol's, Cairo, 1320
Gardet and Anawati, *Introduction*	= *Introduction à la théologie musulmane*, Paris, 1948
Ibn Taymîya, *Muwâfaqa*	= *Muwâfaqa ṣaḥîḥ al-manqûl li-ṣarîḥ al-ma'qûl*, ed. M. 'Abdalḥamîd and M. Faqî, 2 vol's, Cairo, 1370/1951
Intiṣâr	= abû l-Ḥusayn al-Khayyât, *K. al-Intiṣâr wal-radd 'alà Ibn al-Rawândî l-mulḥid*, republished and translated by A. Nader, Beyrouth, 1957
Maq.	= al-'Aš'arî, *Maqâlât al-'Islâmîyîn*, ed. H. Ritter, Istanbul, 1929-30
Milal	= al-Šahrastânî, *K. al-Milal wal-Niḥal*, ed. M. Badrân, 2 vol's, Cairo, 1327/1910-1375/1955
Nader, *Système*	= A. Nader, *le Système philosophique des Mu'tazila*, Beyrouth, 1956
Nihâya	= al-Šahrastânî, *Nihâyat al-'iqdâm fî 'ilm al-kalâm*, ed. A. Guillaume, Oxford, 1934
Pines, *Beitrage*	= S. Pines, *Beiträge zur islamischen Atomenlehre* Berlin, 1936
Pretzl, *Atomenlehre*	= Otto Pretzl, « die frühislamische Atomenlehre, » der Islam, 19 (1931), pp. 117-130
Pretzl, *Attributenlehre*	= *die frühislamische Attributenlehre* (Sitzbr. d. bayrischen Akad. d. Wiss., phil.-hist. Abteilung, 1940, 4) München, 1940

Razî, *K. al-'Arba'în*	=	Fakhruddîn al-Râzî, *K. al-'Arba'in fî' Usûl al-dîn*, Hyderabad, 1353
Râzî, *I'tiqâdât*	=	, *I'tiqâdât firaq al-muslimîn wal-muš-rikîn*, ed. A. al-Naššâr, Cairo, 1356/1938
Râzî, *Muḥaṣṣal*	=	, *Muḥaṣṣal 'afkâr al-mutaqaddimîn wal-muta'aḫḫirîn*, Cairo, 1323
Šarḥ al-Mawâqif	=	Ğurğânî, *Šarḥ al-Mawâqif*, ed. M. al-Na'sânî, 8 vol's, Cairo, 1325/1907
Tabṣîr	=	abû l-Muẓaffar al-Isfarâ'înî, *al-Tabṣîr fî l-dîn*, ed. M. al-Kawthari, Cairo, 1359/1940
Taftazânî	=	Sa'duddîn al-Taftazânî, *Šarḥ al-'aqâ'id al-nasafîya*, Cairo (Dâr 'Iḥyâ' al-Kutub al-'Arabîya, no date).
'Uṣûl	=	'Abd al-Qâhir al-Baġdâdî, *K. 'Uṣûl al-dîn*, Istanbul, 1346-1928

I. INTRODUCTION

Certainly one need make no apologies in justification of a study of abû l-Hudhayl al-'Allâf [1]. My purpose in this work, however, is somewhat broader than simply that of giving a detailed account or a synthetic doxography of his opinions on the 'questions' concerning creation, created being, and created beings, which were under so hot debate among various mu'tazilî authors in the 9th century. There are several more fundamental matters which must be studied before the significance and the meaning of a given author's thought and his particular views on a set of disputed questions can be evaluated and situated within the diversity of the whole mu'tazilî movement during its first phase, through abû 'Alî al-Ǧubbâ'î and before the kalâm's great bifurcation into the traditions which bear the names of his son, abû Hâšim and of his pupil, al-'Aš'arî. We must first gain some basic understanding of and sympathy with the universe which they sought to explain. What I shall try to do therefore is to give a description of this universe as it is seen through the system of abû l-Hudhayl.

First and above all we must understand, insofar as is possible across a great cultural and chronological chasm, the meaning which the author is trying to express, — the meaning of which the formulae are the formulation. We must try somehow to recapture for ourselves, out of the texts, something of the comprehension, the *lógos* of the world which expressed itself in this particular form and to restate for ourselves what the author meant to say. Indeed, if, beyond its undoubted social and political significance in the history of Islam, the earlier kalâm was more than a *vanitas et cura superflua*, that is, if it represents a really serious and meaningful attempt of the human mind to understand the ultimate structure of being, it constitutes a 'new thing', an epochal moment in the history of human thought, and is deserving of our most serious consideration. To understand it on this level however, we must see the world through it; that is, in order to understand the meaning of the kalâm and the significance of its statements about reality and the world as an historically defined expression of a genuine human experience of the world, we must somehow grasp the context of potential meaning from within which these statements arose and according to which intended that meaning which is theirs.

---

[1] For information concerning abû l-Hudhayl's life, etc., the reader may be refered generally to Nyberg's article on him in *EI*².

More than a few scholars, have taken the attitude that the early kalâm represents little more than a puerile and inept effort to defend the dogma of the *Koran*, that it is nothing more than a polemic apologetic, aggravated by certain differences of opinion on the part of the writers, for the dogmatic content of the Islamic revelation. But such an attitude assumes a kind of bad faith on the part of the authors; it presupposes that even from the beginning there is a complete disjunction between the data of faith and the data of reflective experience and that the mutakallimîn set about to 'defend' the literal content of the former without honestly taking the latter into consideration. Yet such an assumption of bad faith is ultimately simplistic. It does not ask whence and how comes the understanding of the content of the revelation. One may always, after all, whether explicitly or not, say *distinguo* and, at the beginning, the meaning of the *Koran* had itself to be made explicit and defined. In the time of abû l-Hudhayl Islamic dogma had not yet become formally defined in any area. Rather, it was taking form, beginning to take on the definitive configuration of its peculiar character in and among a number of diverse sciences, each of which was to form its own sub-traditions and make its particular contribution to the elaboration of this dogma.

Although from the outset the *Koran* was assumed by the faith of the believer to be the intelligible paradigm through which all being and meaning was revealed and to be known, its meaning had yet to be "worked out;" the exegesis of that meaning which it was felt to make manifest and to render intelligible in the general experience of the community (or that of a particular group, for Islam as a socio-cultural entity was already extremely complex) had yet to be made explicit in thematic understanding and defined [2]. Within such a situation the believer can only come to grasp the meaning of the *Koran* simultaneously with and in the understanding of the world of which he takes it to be the paradigm. Its potentiality of meaning for the believer — its potentiality to give meaning to human existence — is to be discovered within the horizons of a more general hermeneutic situation; since he understands it as a paradigm only within his total experience of the world, his understanding of the sense of the revelation

---

[2] I do not intend to enter here into the broader question of the place and rôle of the kalâm alongside of and in opposition to the other active disciplines (fiqh, ḥadîth, falsafa, etc.) which contributed to Islam's cultural self-elaboration as each, variously influenced by the others, in the common milieu made its own contribution to the evolution of the total tradition; nor, again, would I wish to exaggerate the place of the kalâm in the overall context of the growth of the Islamic tradition, for Islam was, almost from the beginning, an extremely diversified socio-cultural complex. Rather, abstracting from the complexity of the whole milieu, but remembering that it did form the larger, defining matrix, I should like to focus attention in the following remarks on the single problem of the kalâm as it elaborated, from within and into this matrix, a uniquely islamic metaphysics.

can only be brought forth thematically and made explicit from within the structured framework of a pre-predicative grasp of the totality of the world in which his human experience of the world in general and of the *Koran* in particular are given, simultaneously together. The revelation thus becomes the objectively meaningful paradigm through which the world is understood from within a non-objectified total experience which embraces, within a dialectically structured whole, both the *Koran* and the world. The meaningfulness and validity of the *Koran* as a paradigm had therefore to be first understood and set forth in grasping thematically the meaningful and intelligible coherence of the world which was given to human presence, as it was coherent and intelligible, within the paradigmatic framework of the revelation.

In the early period, when Islam's understanding of the meaning of the *Koran* as the model of the meaning and structure of its own existence had not yet been explicitly formulated and defined according to some kind of concensus of the group, there can be no question of a simple imposition of a dogmatic system upon the world and of the consciously arbitrary invention of a conceptual system which would "save the appearances" of the *Koran*, regardless of what non-sense (i.e., what violation of the lived sense of reality) might be perpetrated. Indeed, such an "apology" would be none at all, but would, on the contrary, constitute the believer's own demonstration to himself of the ultimate invalidity and incoherence of that very paradigm which his faith affirmed to make manifest the coherent meaning of all experience.

What kind of speculative system is the kalâm then? -what sort of an effort of the mind, to achieve what kind of understanding?

Unfortunately we have no statements concerning this matter which are attributable to the earliest muʿtazilî authors. The traditional attacks on speculation as such are of little help, for they represent, not simply rejections of particular conclusions regarding various points of dogma, but more fundamentally deprecate absolutely any attempt to dissolve or analyse the original compactness of the revealed and canonical sources of faith. For them, the purity and depth of faith is gained and maintained only in the immediate comprehending acceptance of its sources, wherein lies the only true knowledge (*ʿilm*), all else being vain opinion (*ẓann*). They can therefore only tell us what a part of the Muslim community knew the kalâm not to be.

Again, it must be remembered that particularly during its first period, what passes under the name of the kalâm was far from a homogeneous whole. The Muʿtazila, from the standpoint of its overall theology, does not in any way form a unified school or manifest a single concensus of teaching on any level; the "five theses" by which it is normally defined as a sect are significant chiefly from the standpoint of the heresiographer. The systems, for example, of abû l-Hudhayl, al-Naẓẓâm, and Mu'ammar are all three fundamentally incompatible with one another in terms of their basic outlook and understanding of the world. Our sources, too, are for the most part highly selective, their interest being all too often concerned with only those doctrines which are peculiar to an author and those in which he departs from some norm of orthodoxy. One must also keep in mind that the center of emphasis no doubt varied with different authors [3]; in the intellectual agitation of the time, the principal aim of some was indeed more speculative and theological than apologetic. Nevertheless, whatever the specific intellectual orientation of a particular author, there can be little doubt that the great majority of the Mu'tazila intended, on one plane or another, to define and validate the truth of Islam with the utmost fidelity to the revelation as they understood it. Nader's assumption of the contrary is untenable [4]. There is no evidence in the available texts which would show on the part of the early mu'tazilî writers anything but an effort to describe God and the universe systematically in conformity with a sincere understanding of the *Koran*. The fact that the individual would take to the discourse of rational understanding to defend and define the basic content of his faith indicates, of course, the presence of an apriori non-"traditionist" attitude already in his unreflected approach to the understanding of the revelation; he feels a need for one reason or another, for whatever explicit motive, to analyse the original compactness of his religious understanding into explicit and systematic formulation but this does not in any way indicate any impurity of his faith or denote a lack of sincerity and intellectual honesty in his effort to give a speculative account of Islam. One cannot "demonstrate" the existence of God or the truth of a particular position regarding human freedom and man's power of efficacious action without in some degree making explicit the underlying metaphysical structure of existence which gives coherence to the terms of the demonstration and according to which consequently it stands as a demonstration. *Per se*, the theological conclusions arrived at through the kalâm need not differ one iota from those of the tradition, though it must, of course, be admitted that formulation is very important; its statement is the ex-pression of a particular mode of understanding and it is at this level that the two diverge. Albeit the effort is to see and verify analytically the order of universal being in its concordance with the revelation, as understood by the particular author, the criterion whereby certainty is guaranteed, (that which is felt to be the ultimate ground of the proof as such) remains always the *Koran*, understood in one way

---

[3] Gardet and Anawati, *Introduction*, 47.

[4] *Cf. infra*, ch. V, n. 9.

or another within the overall horizon of possible meaning. In this way, abstracting from particular conclusions, the first and irreducible difference between the traditionists and the mutakallimîn concerns their attitude towards the very effort to understand and the possible validity of this effort. But there can be no apology without analysis and if the traditionist would "rationally" defend the meaning of the tradition and discursively establish the validity of the content of his faith according to the understanding of the world which is defined in his comprehension of the tradition, he is forced in some degree to abandon the injunction against analytic "speculation" (*al-ḫawḍ/al-naẓar*) in order to insist on the truth of the revelation precisely in its indissoluble compactness. There is, in fact, some evidence for the beginnings of a more "orthodox" speculation alongside the Muʿtazila prior to the time of al-'Ašʿarî [5].

From this standpoint then, the question of the kalâm in differentiation from the tradition is one of the degree or the rigidity with which one adheres to one or the other of the polar extremes and secondarily of the particular theological propositions ascribed to these extremes. To the extent that there could be, in the third century of the Hegira, a systematic speculative description of the structure of the universe which belonged to that central, native core of the islamic tradition, whose most conservative expression realised itself in the work of the traditionists, such a description is that of the earlier kalâm.

Still we must ask what — beyond the immediate, stated aim, which is that of an apologetic — kind of understanding is sought in establishing the theoretical foundations of the apology; what kind of knowledge of the basis of its own validity does it assume possible? What is the order of the truth which it seeks in establishing the foundation of its dogmatic assertions? From the outset it is apparent that the kalâm differs radically from Christian theology, even though this too was ostensibly apologetic in its first beginnings [6]. The kalâm did not seek to penetrate rationally into the mysteries of God and His creation, for that part of Islam which was represented by the earlier kalâm was not, like Christianity, the inheritor of the Greek assumption that human reason, of its own innate powers, could uncover ever more of the truth and render it intelligible through and within its own light nor that there was a truth "naturally" inherent in things and in the order of the world as world; faith did not seek understanding in the sense of a further penetration into what was revealed or hope to uncover the truth and order of created existence according to the light of human intelligence. The importance

[5] *Cf.* Schacht, *New Sources for the history of Muhammedan Theology*, Studia Islamica 1 (1953), 33.
[6] *Cf.* Gardet and Anawati, *op. cit.*, 313 and generally *ibid.*, 303ff and Gilson, *l'Esprit de la philosophie médiévale* [2] (Paris, 1948), 17ff.

given to human understanding and the demands of reason varied somewhat, both explicitly and implicitly, from author to author, but the early kalâm as such, though having in some aspects the appearance of a kind of rationalism [7], was not philosophical or theological in the sense formally assigned these terms in Western thought.

The kalâm was nevertheless, no matter how understood, a speculative science and as such its aim was understanding: truth. The question is, in a sense, the nature of the truth sought; it is, so to speak, not ἀλήθεια but rather *al-ḥaqq*. Here we must keep in mind that the *Koran* is a most singular book in a number of respects. Conspicuous among them is that, in the way in which it argues, pleads, and makes its threats and promises, it makes, in a certain sense, a kind of direct appeal, in a great number of passages, to a rational level of understanding. It contains remarkably few archetypal figures which of themselves, as they stand in the text, demand to be understood symbolically or allegorically. Unlike the Old or New Testament, the "history" which the *Koran* contains is not — and cannot be — presented as the constitutive historical past of the community to which the prophet addressed his message; it is not presented in such a way that it must be taken up in understanding as the ordered historical past of the believer in his present faith but rather, events are cited often as almost random examples of faith and disbelief, piety and wickedness, and of how God has dealt with men in the past. Again, the *Koran* gives frequently a very bold and almost conceptually elaborated picture of God's dominion over creation in a form culturally and psychologically little removed from the fundamental, unreflected world-view of a significent part of the milieu of the earliest mutakallimîn.

God "created the heavens and the earth *bil-ḥaqq*; [8]" this *Truth* underlies and permeates all creation. All creation, again, stands as a "token" (*'âya*) or vast complex of innumerable "tokens" of God's omnipotent power and dominion. However, the *Koran*, as His Word addressed to man in human language, revealing and self-revealing, is the only token which explains itself, speaking to the hearer in articulate self-expression; it is ultimately the supreme *'âya* and the key which opens the only sure way to seeing and comprehending the true meaning of every other of God's tokens. It was this, I think, *viz.*, the fact that the *Koran* was its own articulate and self-interpreting token of God's Being and creative omnipotence, which forced itself of itself into his understanding, making all other tokens

---

[7] *Cf. infra*, ch II, n. 31 and ch. IV, n. 7.

[8] *Koran*, 14.22, 15.85, *et alibi*; *cf.* also the interpretation of this by Ibn Ḥanbal (*Radd 'alà l-zanâdiqa wal-ğahmîya* [Darulfünun Ilahiyat Fakültesi Mecmuasi, 1927] 321) and al-'Aš'arî (*K. al-Luma'* [ed. McCarthy in *The Theology of al-Ash'ari*, Beyrouth, 1953] §115).

visible and intelligible in its light, that the Prophet took as the *'i'ǧâz* : its being its own compelling, self-sufficient evidence of its own validity and truth. So also the *Koran* remained for Islam, even though the *'i'ǧâz* came to be taken in a literary sense, the paradigmatic *'âya* for the understanding of all Being. It revealed not merely the order of the world and the being of creatures in their createdness but also, as the Word of the source of all Truth and existence, manifested the ultimate truth of creation : the meaning of creation and of the existence of creatures as a relationship to the Creator (*al-Ḥaqq*).

The task of the kalâm then, whether as apologetic or as speculation for its own sake, could neither be to penetrate into the revelation in such wise as to go beyond it and probe the mystery of God (*al-ġayb*) [9] nor to penetrate with the natural light of human reason into creation; the revelation as the expressed Word of God was of itself absolute while on the other hand, creation could have of itself no meaning to yield save its very createdness, the true understanding, of which (*al-'ilm*) was to be had with certainty only through the revelation. The task, then, was one of seeing reflectively and of systematically understanding the Truth of creation that was revealed paradigmatically in the *Koran* — of discovering analytically and setting forth objectively in formal language the underlying structure of the created world as it manifested the *lógos* revealed in the *Koran*. In this way then, the goal of reason was not independently to uncover and make its own the truth of nature and its own existence [10], for this it already posessed. Rather it was to discover, in the reflective contemplation of reality, the metaphysical structure of being, whose truth was the created manifestation of *the* Truth; it was to comprehend and *verify* out of its own experience of the world, through an analysis of the world, the truth which was already given to its preanalytic understanding, how the revealed paradigm was reflected in material creation, in order to validate thematically the believer's understanding of the revelation. The initial assumption is not basically that the ultimate order of existence is of itself rationally and intelligibly ordered according to the norms of human reason, so that it may be discovered by and in the process of reflective thought, but rather that it manifests the creative Truth of God and that the underlying structure and coherence of this manifestation can be analytically described. This is important, for the kalâm's initial and unreflected attitude towards the kind of truth to be attained and the place of reason in its attainment determined its method as well as its form and content. The place of reason is to bring to rational, systematic expression the truth of the paradigm as trans-

---

9 Taking *al-ġayb* as the non-present, the non-phenomenal: that aspect of the Creator which remains completely transcendent and which He does not make manifest to man.

10 Contemplation (*θεωρία*) is not valued as such in the kalâm; *cf. infra*, ch. III n. 31.

cendent it underlies the multiple variety of discrete and individual events which make up the world. As was pointed out above, this does not mean in any way at all that there was a rude imposition of a pre-fabricated koranic model of the structure of created being upon the reality given in immediate experience, apart from and despite the "evidence" of such experience.

The necessity to question was not eliminated in the light of the revelation. In a sense, indeed, the revelation makes known that aspect of being which is not given to immediate reflection, *viz.*, its createdness from the point of view of the Creator, while leaving yet to be posed the question of the nature of created being as such, and it is to this that the kalâm had first to address itself, even as an apologetic, in order to make explicit the ground of its theological understanding. The primal question indeed, is that of being-created [11]. To the extent that he consciously puts out to describe the ultimate metaphysical structure of being in general, abû l-Hudhayl, for example, does in fact, albeit without an explicit "question" or philosophical doubt, set forth and attempt to answer the primeval question of all metaphysics: "why does anything at all exist rather than nothing? [12]" The kalâm is in this way an *universalis consideratio de veritate* [13] and by this fact has gone far beyond any simple primitivity or naïveté.

We must not be misled in our appreciation and understanding of the kalâm by its form and vocabulary on the basis of our being "accustomed to regard the Greek way of thinking as obligatory [14]." If there is no abstract term for *being* but rather it is always spoken of as a being-created (*ḫalq*) and the modes of being are the modes of being-created, this is no prima facie evidence of "primitivity" [15] but rather an indication that the central problem was, in fact, that of the nature of created being in its being created. So also we must keep in mind that if one finds no terms in the work of abû l-Hudhayl and the first generations of the Mu'tazila for "essence", such terms were nevertheless available; they were used by al-Kindî and can hardly have been totally unknown to abû l-Hudhayl and his contemporaries. If, then, the mutakallimîn refused them, the refusal must have a significance which is to be sought in the structure of the world of which they

---

11 Significantly there is no word in the earliest kalâm for God's being, for this is transcendent and altogether beyond the grasp of human understanding. *There is no univocal sense of Being.*

12 Martin Heidegger, *Einführung in die Metaphysik*² (Tübingen, 1958), lff, citing Leibniz.

13 St. Thomas Aquinas, *In Metaphysica* III, *lect.* 1, §343, cited by K. Rahner *Geist in Welt*² (München, 1957), 73.

14 Bruno Snell, *The Discovery of the Mind* (Harvard, 1953) introduction, p. 1.

15 It is considered by Pretzl to be so; *Attributenlehre*, 55.

sought to give an account. One does not choose a philosophical or theological terminology as he might a pair of socks. It is formed and taken up in the act of reflective consciousness which poses the question, in the act of posing the question; the possibility of a meaningful answer is given already in the form of the question as it, posed thematically within a total context of possible meaning. Any indifference regarding the terminology can only stand in direct proportion to an indifference of disengagement from the existential demand of the question.

To speak therefore of the "absolutely primitive and unscientific way of thinking of the founders" of the kalâm [16], or to see in the early kalâm an inadequate "compromise between revealed religion and a poorly understood and somewhat naïvely handled pre-aristotelian philosophy [17]," or to find beneath its surface "fragmentary accounts of substance [18]" is to alienate it from itself and to judge it in terms of what it was not and did not mean to be. It is, in short, to demand that the structure and the horizon of the experience of being out of which arose the kalâm, ought to have been other than they were and that it ought to have taken up, or even wanted to take up, more exactly systems of thought which lay somehow in the margins of its past but in such a way that they were not and could not be existentially present to Islam [19].

What I wish to suggest therefore is that the chief problem is one of understanding; first and above all we must grasp philosophically the philosophical content of the kalâm. We must get somehow behind the rethoric of its expression in order to see in and through the formulae the way in which reality revealed itself to a certain historically and culturally determined modality of human presence to the world and to understand its validity as a statement of the truth of human experience. It is only after this has been done that we can begin to make a valid and intelligent appraisal of the kalâm's debt to previous systems of thought and to understand it fully in the history of its own evolution, in itself and in the larger islamic context.

---

16 Pretzl, *Attributenlehre*, 8; *cf. infra* ch IV, n. 8 and ch. II, 46.

17 Nyberg, *'Amr ibn 'Ubeid et Ibn al-Rawendi, deux réprouvés*, in *Classicisme et Déclin culturel dans l'histoire de l'Islam* (Paris, 1957), 131.

18 Fakhry, *Islamic Occasionalism and its Critique by Averroës and Aquinas* (London, 1958), 35; *cf. infra*, ch. IV, n. 5.

19 I cannot here go into the question of the falsafa; it began to reach its full and final form later than the kalâm and, as it developed, its real debt to earlier islamic thought was enormous, much more so than is often allowed. For all its appearances, the lógos of the system of Avicenna, *i.e.*, its most basic orientation in what makes it unique, can only be understood from within the islamic tradition which preceded it, not that of classical antiquity.

Remarkably little has been done towards the study and exposition of the early kalâm as a serious theological and metaphysical system; most of the work has been philological. Pines' *Beiträge zur islamischen Atomenlehre* contains yet the best description of certain aspects of the early kalâm but the scope of the work does not carry it much beyond the exteriority of the formulae and it remains fundamentally a doxography. Again Pretzl in his *Frühislamische Atomenlehre* and later in his *Frühislamische Attributenlehre* attempts with some success to penetrate deeper into the philosophical structure of the kalâm, but his work suffers from his explicit conviction that the early kalâm was absolutely naïve and simplistic and a preoccupation with finding the extra-islamic origins of certain of its elements. More recently Albert Nader has undertaken to study the philosophical and theological content of the mu'tazilî kalâm in his *Système philosophique des Mu'tazila*, a work which covers almost the entire range of mu'tazilî speculation in considerable and excellently documented detail. Finally, Majid Fakhry in the first section of his *Islamic Occasionalism* devotes a special chapter to the "metaphysics of atoms and accidents" but his discussion remains on a doxographic level without his treating the problems philosophically. The most penetrating insights into the meaning and intent of the early kalâm remain, I think, to be found in Massignon's *Passion d'al-Hallaj*, even though the treatment there is highly abbreviated and frequently somewhat gnomic. [20]

What I hope to do therefore in this work is to outline briefly the metaphysics of created being as it is found in the available fragments of the work of abû l-Hudhayl. It is best to deal with a single author since it is only within a unified system that any part of the whole manifests its validity and truth and carries whatever conviction it may have as a coherent vision of the totality. Whatever may have been their verbal agreement on the five theses, we can no more validly describe a single and unified concensus about the fundamental and detailed structure of being in the varied systems of the Mu'tazila than we can lump together the Dominicans, Augustinians, and Franciscans of the middle ages and say simply that "the scholastics say...," for there are between diverse authors, basic and fundamental differences of view which are nigh absolutely incompatible and great cataclysms of speculative thought hang often on a split hair.

The reasons for the choice of abû l-Hudhayl are obvious. The Mu'tazilî kalâm was, we must recall, for a century the only developed native theology in Islam and it forms, particularly in the school of Baṣra, the direct forerunner of most of the later kalâm. Allowing then for the typically mu'tazilî theological positions

---

20 There is a work, *Abû l-Hudayl -al-'Allâf* (Cairo, 1369/1949) by 'Alî M. al-Ghurâbî, but it is totally inadequate and needs no further consideration.

and for a number of doctrines which are unique to his thought, even within the Mu'tazila, the work of abû l-Hudhayl stands at the very beginning of what was to become one of the mainstreams of islamic speculation. Certainly a good deal of serious and systematic thought preceded the founding of the great schools of the 9th century. Already in the time of the Caliph 'Abd al-Malik, fragmentary though our information be, we can discern in Ghaylân of Damascus, Ma'bad al-Ğuhanî, Ğa'd ibn Dirham, and perhaps Wâṣil ibn 'Aṭâ' [21] the serious beginnings of later theological speculation, just as one can see beneath the homiletic fragments of al-Ḥasan al-Baṣrî a thorough foundation and outline of much of the thought of al-Muḥâsibî. The real significance and historical influence of the neoplatonist Ğahm b. Ṣafwân has yet to be assessed [22]. The system of abû l-Hudhayl however, remains the first which we can see clearly and it would seem most probable that it was first in his work that the kalâm discovered the form which it sought and began to take on its definitive shape [23]. In his understanding of the metaphysical structure of created being we shall expect therefore to find Islam's earliest complete, systematic account of the universal order of being which it felt to underlie its world. Islam formed the milieu of an historically new and unique experience of being and we should expect to find in the work of abû l-Hudhayl one of the purest and most spontaneous transcriptions of certain aspects of this experience, as it was understood in those circles which sought to understand it analytically. The question of how the world is to be understood is still a question; the problem of understanding had not yet been lost and forgotten in the process of dealing with the already elaborated mechanics of its solution and turned into a debate over the terms of the account rather than the structure of the reality to be accounted for.

To the extent then that we are able to grasp the meaning of abû l-Hudhayl we may hope to gain some insight into the order of potential meaning out of which

---

21 To me it would seem probable that the propaganda of Wâṣil b. 'Aṭâ' was almost entirely political (cf. Watt, *Political attitudes of the Mu'tazila*, JRAS 1963, 52ff and Pellat, *le Milieu Basrien et la formation de Ğâḥiẓ* (Paris, 1953), 176) and the theological theses attributed to him (*e.g., Milal*, 84ff) may in great part be simply the projection of mu'tazilî doctrine back upon the quasi eponymous founder. We have no clear cause to speak of abû l-Hudhayl's having a "theology inherited from the school of Wâṣil" (Nyberg, art. *abû l-Hudhayl* in *EI*²) for the background is certainly more complex than this; *cf.* n. 23.

22 Cf. R.M. Frank, *The neoplatonism of Ğahm b. Ṣafwân*, le Muséon, 78, (1965), pp. 395 ff.

23 Nyberg suggests (*E I*² *art. cit.*) that it was abû l-Hudhayl who introduced atomism into islamic theology. Certainly he is the earliest author within the horizon of our present knowledge by whom a thorough atomism is elaborated. In my opinion however, it is too thoroughly articulated in the work of abû l-Hudhayl and too expertly treated in terms of its basic problems to have been original with him; further I cannot agree with Nyberg (*ibid.*) that he was naïve as a thinker.

the kalâm was generated and understand the experience and the truth which it meant to manifest.

I shall here restrict myself insofar as is possible to the metaphysics of the system, avoiding those questions which are purely theological as well as those which concern abû l-Hudhayl's position on the troubles which divided the early Muslim political community. Thus the "five theses" which are commonly used to define the Mu'tazila, viz., the Unity of God (*al-tawḥîd*), God's Justice (*al-'adl*), the promise and the threat of punishment and reward in the next life (*al-wa'd wal-wa'îd*), the "intermediate position" (*al-manzila bayn al-manzilatayn*), and the obligation to fraternal correction (*al-'amr bil-ma'rûf wal-nahy 'an al-munkar*) will not be treated at all. So also the question of the createdness of the *Koran* will be omitted and, finally, that of man's power to effect his own acts (*al-qudra*) will be considered, not in terms of God's justice, but only insofar as it constitutes a determinative element in the stucture of human existence and forms a point of indetermination in creation.

In the discussion of the texts I have tried to avoid logical abstractions and such terms as "essence" which are basically foreign to the system, hoping to maintain the focus, like that of the author, as concrete as possible. Wherever practical within the limits of clarity and English usage I have tried to retain the author's terminology. Thus "thing" (*šay'*) has been used in almost all places instead of "being" (*ens/Seiendes*) and the term "substance" rigorously avoided, since it carries, out of its history in Western philosophical thought, a whole set of connotations which have no place in abû l-Hudhayl's thought. "Accident" I have retained to render '*araḍ*, always in quotation marks, since I could find no really suitable term in English.

Allâh al-Musta'ân

II. THE BEING OF THE CREATED COMPOSITE

A. *The Thing as a Composite*

The things that make up the created world are corporeal bodies which are ultimately composed of "atoms" and their inhering "accidents.[1]" Body exists as such through the creation of the "accidents" of composition (*ta'lîf*), juxtaposition (*iǧtimâ'*), contiguity (*mumâssa*), and conjunction (*muǧâma'a*) in the "atoms". It has its specific configuration as being such a body and in being that particular body which it is, with its particular attributes and accidents, through God's creation in its "atoms" of those specific "accidents" of composition, etc., as they are determined in the individual instance, together with such other "accidents" as determine and define every particular property, attribute, and state which may qualify the being of the thing at a given moment. In the composite, each "accident" inheres separately in the individual "atoms," as many as may belong to it [2]. The reality of the thing, then, in its being what it is, consists in the presence (*wuǧûd*) of the total complex of its separate "accidents" in their inherence in the atoms" which belong to it, as their substrate.

The unity of the thing, therefore, in its being that thing which it is, is constituted by its being a body and it is for this reason that "accidents" are said to inhere or to occur (*ḥalla, ḥadaṯa*) in bodies (*'aǧsâm*), although strictly speaking the corporality and the specific configuration of the individual body are themselves the results of the inherence of the created "accidents" of composition, conjunction, etc., in the specific multitude of "indivisible parts" or "atoms" that form the substrate. In this way, the oneness of the thing is that of an agglomerate sum; its basic constitutive units are the "atoms," each with its inherent "accidents," and it is constituted as a unity, in its being a thing, by the mutual adherence together of its "parts" in spatial isolation from and exclusion of others which are

---

1 On the ontology of the composite in the composition of "atoms" and "accidents" *cf, infra* ch. IV. It must constantly be borne in mind that the term "accident" is not here taken in the usual, Aristotelian sense; rather it is a quite distinct concept which is to be understood and defined from within the system.

2 That is, the "accidents" adhere separately in each individual "atom" of the thing, but a single "accident" may, in some cases, belong only to a part of the whole, adhering only, thus, in a particular set of "atoms;" *cf. Maq.*, 319 and 330.

not part of the specific composite. Its oneness consists, thus, in one sense, in its spatial unity alone. From another standpoint however, the unity of the thing in the spatial conjunction of its parts is not a mere conjunction and nothing more, for to the extent that the "composition" which founds the oneness of a particular body is grounded in a unique and separate act of creation which determines it as this body and this thing, its unity in being itself and its distinctness and separation from every other thing is quite absolute [3]. Considered in itself, however, it is a unity of a multitude of discrete parts whose cohesion in forming and determining the thing as a specific thing is founded in the actuality of a particular set of "accidents" which the parts share together, each in its individualty. The thing is thus constituted and defined as a thing, in the wholeness and unity of its being what it is, through the created inherence of a set of specific "accidents" in a particulate substrate. The foundation of its existence in the world (*i.e.*, in space or "place" — *makân*) as that thing which it is, is the composition and conjunction of its "parts" or "atoms" as a body and it is therefore by the thing's being such a body that it is defined. However, although the body, in its spatial, composite unity (the "composition of parts") forms the material ground of the possibility of the being of most other "accidents" in the thing [4], it does not, as such, in any way constitute an intrinsic principle which specifically determines the existence of the particular set of other attributes or "accidents" that may inhere in it [5]. That is, while the composite substrate forms, in the composition of its "atoms," the possibility of the existence of other "accidents," it is not otherwise, in and of itself, the cause of the inherence, in its parts, of any specific set of "accidents," for each "accident" is created by God, in the body, as He wills. There can, thus, be no question of "essences," for there is no intrinsic principle according to which there must exist in a given material body one or another single "accident" or specific complex of "accidents," which, in their total, common inherence in the unified substrate, constitute the total character or nature of a particular existent thing. Although the real presence of certain "accidents" does, in several cases, constitute the immediate possibility of the presence of certain others,

---

3 This is a separate question which will be treated in ch. V.

4 With several exceptions (*viz.*, movement, rest, contiguity, isolation, and *kawn*) all those "accidents" which may belong to a thing can adhere *only* in a composit substrate, not in a single "atom," (*cf.* references cited *infra*, ch. IV, n. 17); *i.e.*, their being is to inhere in a composit plurality of "atoms" (an extended body) even though they inhere separately in each "atom."

5 In the later kalâm, the "accident" of "being in place" (*taḥayyuz* : the act of being actually existent in a specific location in the world) is taken as the principle of individuation (*cf.* for example abû Rašîd al-Nîsâbûrî, *Kitâb al-Masâ'il*, 6f). For abû l-Hudhayl however, that a thing exist at all is that it exist in a place (i.e., a defined substrate), since it has, in itself, no being at all outside that of its reality in the world (*cf. infra*, esp. ch. V, n. 9). There is, therefore, no question of an "essential" unity of the thing in being that which it is, apart from its actual existence in the world in the spatial unity of its substrate.

one "accident" does not arise from another as a necessary consequent from its principle [6]. Each separate "accident" which contributes to the total being of a thing in its being what it is at a specific moment, is the object of a separate and independent act of creation.

The being of the thing is then that it exist as a specific composit totality, but its existence as such a totality is that it be a sum, created so in each of its elements. It has no essence, nature, or intrinsic principle, by and of itself in its being what it is, that determines the individual qualities and attributes which characterize its being that which it is. It exists, thus, simply as a composite whole (*ğumla*) of a finite number of discrete elements (the separate "atoms," each with its own compliment of "accidents") to which a given name is applied [7]. In short, the specific attributes and properties which make up its total being, in its being that which it is, have no common principle of their unified inherence together in the thing, other than the creative act of the divine will which made the body a body and the several "accidents" to exist in it.

---

6 There may be several exceptions to this principle, as he would seem to have "length" (*viz.*, extension in space) arise directly as a function or consequent of the "accident" of composition (*cf. infra*, ch. IV, nn. 13f) and to hold that motion and rest are consequent directly upon *kawn* (*cf. infra* ch. II, n. 17). Generally however, each "accident" is considered ontologically separate and independent of every other, forming a distinct and separate object of God's creative power. Thus he says that God may suspend a heavy stone in the air for a period of time "without creating an act of falling or descending" and may conjoin fire and cotton "without there occuring an act of burning" (*Maq.*, 312; *cf.* also *infra*, ch. III, n. 12). In order, thus, to maintain the distinctness and independence of the separate "accidents," abû l-Hudhayl (as well as a number of other early mu'tazilî authors) consistently avoids stating directly that the actual presence (*wuğûd*) in the thing of one "accident" is the condition of the possibility of the presence of another, but rather reverses the formulation; for example, he says that "it is impossible that God conjoin [in the same substrate] the power of effective action, the act of knowing, the act of willing, and death, just as it is impossible that He conjoin life and death" (*Maq.*, 568). Though he thus, in a way, maintains the logical distinctness of these "accidents" and seeks to affirm their ontological independence of one another, he has nevertheless effectively stated that life is the condition of the existence of *qudra*, etc., given his definition of the contrary as that which exists when its contrary does not (*Maq.*, 376). This is in noteworthy contrast to later formulations which make, for example, life the condition (*šarṭ*) of these "accidents" (*cf.* for example, *'Uṣûl*, 28ff and 105) and represents a radically different view from that which speaks of them as "consequents" (*tawâbi'*) of life, as *Šarḥ al-Mawâqif*, 4, 184: وقالت المعتزلة باسرهم توابع الحياة كالعلم والقدرة والارادة وسائر ما يشترط فى قيامه بمحله الحياة (*cf.* also *ibid.* 2, 215).

7 الجملة التى وقع عليه اسم ... (*Maq.*, 329). Names are given to those things (*entia*) which are perceived in their existence as distinct entities, God being the author of perception (*cf. infra* ch III, nn. 11f) and so the guarantor of the reality of the named (*cf.* also the *Koran, Sûrat al-'Insân* (76), v. 1 and the remarks of Massignon *Passion*, 549). On the use of *ğumla* for the whole thing insofar as it is a body, *cf.* also *Farq*, 79: الجزء الذى قامت به الحركة هو المتحرك دون غيره من اجزاء الجملة.

B. *Becoming*

Strictly speaking, abû l-Hudhayl does not recognize becoming or the process of change in the sense in which western thought generally gives these words; *i.e.*, he does not know the *coming-to-be* of a thing out of something which was not it nor admit of alteration or change as a continuous process of becoming, such as the *metabolai* which are treated by Aristotle in *Physics* V or the "motions" (*ḥarakât*) listed by his contemporary, al-Kindî in his *Risâla fî l-ʿilla al-garîba lil-kawn wal-fasâd* [8]. However, albeit he does not know the categories of coming-to-be and passing-away in one sense, things do in fact come to be and thereafter undergo change while remaining themselves what they are and this fact the system must and does account for in its own way. The ontology of the becoming of things is one of the foremost problems of the system.

The initial coming-to-be of a thing is "its being made to be or its being created after its not being," God's "initiation of its existence after its non-existence, for the first time [9]." We may thus speak of an absolute coming-to-be as of the total composite of the thing in the initial "composition" of its body, together with such other "accidents" as may simultaneously be created in it. In this same way, we may also speak of the initial creation of the existence of but a single "accident" which "comes to be in the body" (*yaḥdutu fî l-ǧism*), as for example, whiteness or an act of perception on the part of man. In the coming-to-be of the whole composite as in the coming-to-be of a single "accident," considered from one aspect, the cases are ontologically identical, in that they represent, in one case

---

[8] *Cf. Rasâ'il al-Kindî*, ed. M. abû Rîda, 1 (Cairo, 1369/1950), pp. 214ff, in which he treats (pp. 216ff) motions which are مكانية وربوبية واضمحلالية واستحالية. The terms *kawn* and *fasâd* as they are used by al-Kindî and the falâsifa meaning "coming-to-be" and "passing-away" do not occur in abû l-Hudhayl or the other early kalâm authors. Again, where abû l-Hudhayl uses the term "creation" (*ḫalq*) and the "initiation (of existence)" (*ibtidâ'*), al-Kindî uses تهوى (*op. cit.*, 161f) which is possibly derived from Syriac ܐܝܬܗܘܝ, though the editor (preface, p. 21) considers it to be taken from the pronoun هو (without taking into account that the term هوية is probably in the translations, a transcription of Syriac ܗܘܝܐ; cf R. Frank, *The origin of the Arabic philosophical term* انية, Cahiers de Byrsa, 6 (1956), 188, n. 4). Al-Kindî also uses for this *'ibdâʿ* (*op.cit.*, 165, where it is defined) and *ta'yîs* (*ibid.*, 183). With al-Kindî, as with the falâsifa generally, the concepts are altogether different from those of the kalâm, as he speaks (*ibid.*, 217) of حركة... اما ذاتية وعرضية and of *fasâd* as انتقال عن عينه الى عين اخرى (*ibid.*), where abû l-Hudhayl would use *fanâ'* or *buṭlân*.

[9] *Maq.*, 363f, *et alibi*.

as in the other, the coming-to-be of "accidents" in their being created in the substrate [10].

Abû l-Hudhayl does speak of an "accident" of "becoming" (*kawn*, pl., *'akwân*), wherein he does recognise a kind of continuous process, *viz.*, a defined process of becoming in time and place from "this" to "that." In this sense, it is a specific becoming through time, in space and direction. We must keep in mind however that the objects of God's will are realised simultaneously with the act of His willing [11], so that individual "accidents" are complete and perfect as they are created in the thing at the moment of their creation. Within the system then, the ontological reality and being of a thing, in all the states of its being, whatever successive alterations of state it may undergo, lie not in any continuum of progression or process, marked and measured by the act of a given state, but in the discrete acts of the perfected realisation, through creation, of the "accidents" whose actuality *is* these states. He conceives the succession of states not as moments which the mind notes and designates by name as "points" along a line of continuous becoming but rather the apparent, ontic continuity of being in becoming is a line which the mind plots through the points which are the moments of the realisation of the successive states in the actuality of a succession of ontologically discrete "accidents" in the thing. To this we shall return shortly.

The being of a thing in movement or rest [12] (and so, consequently, also the being of movement and rest as "accidents") does not consist in the duration in being and becoming through and between two points of time in space [13]. Rather, the reality of movement lies in the final and perfect realisation of its "passage" between two particular moments (*waqtân*) in specifically designated points in space, as the reality of "rest" is the perfected actuality of being in the same place in the second moment [14]. *Kawn*, on the other hand, is a "becoming in space"

---

10 On the creation of the "atoms" or the substrate as such, cf. ch. IV.

11 *Maq.*, 418.

12 Diverse types of movement and rest are listed in *Maq.*, 345, 361, *et alibi.*

13 The term "space" of course is not used by the author, nor does the term *ḫalâ'* (the void) occur in any of the fragments. He would, however, seem to conceive of a kind of space as a homogeneous milieu of potential local existence; note that he says (*Maq.*, 323) that a thing may "move from nothing to nothing," for place is defined by the presence of the thing — a single atom or a body in the defined multitude of its atoms.

14 *Cf.* the references cited *infra*, n. 17. Abû l-Hudhayl's conception of time is obscure and one cannot tell to what extent his thought on the subject was elaborated. Like all other created things, time is an "accident" but since it cannot belong to the corporeal being as inherent in it and a part of its reality, it does not occur in any substrate (*Maq.*, 367 and 369), i. e., it is immaterial. (On "accidents" not in substrates, *cf.* also *infra*, ch. V, concerning the act of creation). Time is created by God in discrete

and as such is "distinct from motion, rest, and contiguities;" [15] it is, we might say, the extended moment of being in space, whose reality is the realisation of spatio-temporal directionality, relative to and within two specifically defined limits of before and after and, if movement is involved, of here and there [16]. The act and reality of *kawn*, therefore, as a "becoming in space" is other than the realised act (in abû l-Hudhayl's terminology, "accident") of motion or rest which may be involved in such a becoming, as its term [17]. Within the paradigmatic framework of a universe wherein all being is realised in discrete "quanta," abû l-Hudhayl thus conceives *al-kawn* as the act of being temporally located in space, as this act is distinct from the perfected actuality of movement or rest, etc. [18]

As such then, *al-kawn* is, within its own real termini, a single indivisible act ("accident"), realised in the thing, whose unity is constituted between the spatio-

---

units and "accidents" are divided (*inqasama*) in their being according to the single moments of time (*Maq.*, 319), motion occuring in discrete acts in each time (*waqt, zamân*) (*ibid.*). The sources unfortunately do not furnish us with the information by which its relation to the being of things can be fully analysed.

[15] *Cf. Maq.*, 325, 351, and 355; he is no doubt using "contiguity" (*mumâssa*) here to imply also the "accidents" of juxtaposition, separation, etc. Abû l-Hudhayl's position in this differs from that of most other authors, who take *kawn* as a general term embracing motion and rest, etc. (e.g., Nazzâm (*Maq.*, 351), Muḥammad b. Šabîb (*ibid.*, 354), al-Ġubbâ'î (*ibid.*, 352, 355), *et al.*). Later, with both the Mu'tazila and the 'Ašâ'ira, *al-'akwân* is used almost universally to indicate the "accidents" classed under *ḥaraka, sukûn, iǧtimâʿ*, and *iftirâq*.

[16] Massignon notes (*Passion*, 560) that "'Allâf et 'Ash'arî ont donné une coloration matérialiste, spatialisation, au mot *kawn* en le liant par un nexus à l'atome qui y surgie;" in this he would seem to be taking the word in the wrong sense of "becoming," *viz.*, as a coming to be out of something. At any rate, his equation (*ibid.*) *kawn* = *'ayn* = *makân* (following *Šarḥ al--Mawâqif*, 5, 7ff?) is not applicable to abû l-Hudhayl, albeit he cites him. Much more exact is the statement of Pretzl (*Attributenlehre*, 47) that the *'akwân* are the "Seinsweisen des Dinges im Raum," although here too, since he is discussing the use of the term in the majority of the Mu'tazila, what he has to say is not fully applicable to abû l-Hudhayl. Nader's rendering of *kawn* by the word *génération* (*Système*, 170ff, passim) is misleading.

[17] *Cf.* references cited *supra*, n. 15. It is thus that he says (*Maq.*, 325) that "the body, at the moment of God's creating it is كَائِنٌ لَامُتَحَرِّكٌ وَلَاسَاكِنْ (*cf.* also the remarks of Ġurǧânî and Siyâlkûtî in *Šarḥ al-Mawâqif* 2, 216 and 6, 166 and also *infra*, ch. IV, n. 17). As the term *kawn* is used in the few fragments in which it occurs in context (*cf.* esp. *Maq.*, 237 and 350f) it seems at first somewhat obscure, though if it be taken as I have here defined it, the meaning is clear enough; what he is saying in these two passages is simply that if a man effect, in "the first moment," a *kawn* (*viz.*, an act of spatially oriented becoming) towards the right, the movement, at the instant of its realisation "in the second moment" will be to the right, etc. Al-Baġdâdî, who is not the most perceptive of our sources, says (*'Uṣûl*, 40f) that despite his efforts, abû l-Hudhayl was unable himself to make sense of this distinction between *kawn*, motion, rest, etc.; *cf.* the same kind of polemic, *ibid.*, 92 and 134.

[18] *Cf. supra*, n. 6, concerning the ontological separateness of "accidents."

temporal limits which define the indivisible discreteness of its being [19]. As an "accident," although again it is the realisation in the thing of the extension of being-between two points of time in space, it remains in itself ontologically distinct from movement and rest and most importantly, though a kind of becoming in the unity of its being-between its temporal and spatial termini, it is altogether distinct from the existence of the thing as the ground of its reality and from its being in its continuation and perdurance in existence (*al-baqâ'*) [20].

Motion or movement (*al-ḥaraka*) is a created "accident" which "comes to be in a body" or some part of a body [21]. Although movement is a thing's "transference from the first place and its departure from it", [22] it is not a "becoming" (*kawn*), as was noted, but an "accident" which comes to be in the thing as a completion or perfected act of *having moved*. This is not in any way to say that abû l-Hudhayl does not consider the act of a body's passing from one point to another in space as continuous along its path; he expressly rejects any notion of a "quantum leap [23]." The problem is rather that in discussing the "accident" of movement, he is not treating of the fact of traversing a trajectory through space, as this constitutes a continuous event, but of movement as a moment in the being of a thing, which qualifies and defines the thing as being in a place other than that in which it was in the previous instant. That is, the focus of the discussion is on movement in the ontology of the thing as a composite of "accidents" and "atoms" not on motion as a physical event. Thus conceived, movement is *in* the thing, its reality consisting in the perfection of the being of the thing in its being "in the second place" at the first moment of its being there [24]. Movement, thus,

---

19 Concerning the kind of thought which underlies this view of things, cf, the remarks of Henri Bergson *Matter and Memory* (N.Y., Anchor Books, 1959), 203f and *Evolution Créatrice*[86] (Paris, 1959), 303ff; *n.b.* also the remarks of J.P. Sartre on the concept of the "instant," in *l'Etre et le Néant*[55] (Paris, 1957), 544.

20 Cf. *infra*, ch. V.

21 *Maq.*, 321f and *Farq*, 79; since the thing is one in the unity of its body, we say that the thing has moved and the movement is attributed to the whole composit, even though only a part of it may move (*Maq.*, 319); al Baġdâdî (*Farq, loc.cit.*), either for polemical reasons or through ignorance, distorts the intention of abû l-Hudhayl in this point.

22 *Maq.*, 355.

23 *Maq.*, 321.

24 The "accident" belongs to the "second moment," for its reality in being is the perfection of its actualisation; thus he says (*Maq.*, 233) : وهو يفعل فى الاول والفعل واقع فى الثانى لان الاول وقت يفعل والثانى وقت فعل (*cf.* also *Milal*, 73f, *Šarḥ al-Mawâqif* 6, 100). This statement should not be dismissed as a simple play on the aspects of the Arabic verb, through some simplistic understanding of the relationship between language and perception.

has its being as a discrete moment ("accident") in the reality of the thing [25]. It can have no perdurance or continuance in existence (*baqâ'*) [26] since it is terminated in its coming to be at the very instant of its actualisation as an "accident," when the thing of which it is the perfection either comes to rest or goes on to a second movement. Thus also a single "atom" may have only a single motion at a time, although a single body may be moved in its several parts simultaneously by more than one agent, in which case we speak of a single movement of the body as a whole [27].

While motion has no duration whatsoever, other "accidents" may endure (*qad tabqà*) through a period of time or, more strictly, over a succession of moments. The body (*ǧism*) may endure through the perdurance of the "accidents" of "composition," etc., together with a number of other "accidents" which determine certain more or less permanent characteristics of its being that thing which it is, *e.g.*, color, life, etc. [28] There is thus, according to abû l-Hudhayl, a real continuity of being in a thing, in the perdurance in existence (*baqâ'*) of a particular set of "accidents" over and through the passing into and out of existence of others. We say that "an 'accident' comes to be in a body" since the body, in its corporeal actuality, remains stable in its existence through the perdurance of the "accident" of composition, which is the basis of its being a body [29] and is modified in the states of its being by the coming to be of a new "accident" and the annihilation of the contrary, which it supplants [30].

In this respect, then, body is conceived as the basic, stable or quasi permanent foundation of the being of things in their real presence in the world and the basis of their continuity of being in their existence. We must remember however that

---

25 Motion, like all other "accidents" which belong to a substrate, "comes to be" (*ḥadaṯa*) in the thing (*Maq.*, 355) and inheres (*ḥalla*) in it (*Maq.*, 319). According to Nader (*Système*, 175ff), abû l-Hudhayl speaks of the "penetration" of motion into the body through the activity of the agent. The expression is not, I think, altogether exact if one takes into account the fact that abû l-Hudhayl is not primarily discussing the physical event in, the same way that he does not mean by *qudra* or *istiṭâ'a*, as "accidents" belonging to man, the mere ability to cause the transfer of physical energy to a material object (*cf. infra*, ch. III, n. 22). Nader's statement (*ibid.*, 177) that, for abû l-Hudhayl, movement is an *écoulement* involves the same misunderstanding.

26 *Maq.*, 358, *et alibi.*

27 *Maq.*, 319; thus he says (*ibid.*) that "accidents" are divided according to time, place, and agent, *i.e.*, that each one is distinct as the product of a single agent (*fâ'il*), inhering in a single "atom" (*cf. supra*), at a particular moment.

28 *Cf. Maq.*, 358f, *Šarḥ al-Mawâqif* 5, 27 and 38f, *'Uṣûl*, 50f.

29 He speaks of *baqâ' al-ǧism*, *Maq.*, *loc. cit.*; on its being in the act of composition (*ta'lîf*), *cf. infra*, ch. IV, 2.

30 *Cf.* his definition of contraries, *Maq.*, 376, *cit. supra*, n.6.

the "body", which constitutes the unity of the thing in its being and its continuity in being in identity with itself, is not "corporality" or an abstract principle of the thing's being, but is always to be understood as the specific, real individual body, qualified by its particular dimensions and configuration and such other enduring "accidents" as may have been brought to actuality in it, while its act of existence and the permanence in existence of whatever enduring "accidents" may belong to it, for so long as each may individually perdure, is grounded in God's act of creation and His further maintaining the several "accidents" in being. That is, the thing, as that which continues in existence, identical with itself, through change, is the created composite of undifferentiated, indivisible parts, in which adheres a given set of enduring "accidents." However, since each "accident" which inheres in the corporeal composite is ontologically distinct and independent of every other in its created inherence, there is no principle intrinsic to the particular complex of "accidents" which formally constitutes the being of the thing in the unity of its being that which it is. Each corporeal thing is ontologically unique in its being a particular agglomerate sum of "accidents," the object of a particular act or series of acts of creation. A thing is, therefore, pragmatically defined or *named* as being a body having such a particular set of attributes [31]. As such, however, things do have a permanence in being and a continuity in their identity with themselves over the successive changes which come to be in them.

The becoming of a thing, as its initial coming-into-existence, is the absolute initiation of its being in an act of creation which has no ontological continuity with any preceding being. On the other hand, its becoming, in the sense of the alteration and change of certain of its particular "accidents" is a kind of progress in the thing of a series of discrete and discontinuous states whose actualisation in being is achieved through the immediate activity of an outside agent in the creation of particular "accidents" and the simultaneous annihilation of their contraries in the thing. In the case of the creation of these "accidents" there is a continuity of being in the thing, nevertheless, with its existence in its previous states, in that each new "accident" does in fact supplant its contrary. In each case, the contrary, in a certain sense, underlies the real possibility of the realisation of a given "accident," so that in their alternate inherence in the composite thing the actualisation of a given "accident" is, in a sense, founded in a potentiality of the thing, represented by its prior state as qualified by the inherence of the contrary

---

[31] *Cf.* for example, the definition of man, *Maq.*, 329. There is a remarkable similarity to modern biological definitions of species (*viz.*, a list of physical characteristics) and Massignon is quite right in speaking of "un positivisme tranchant, et un matérialisme implicite, (qui) amenaient donc à refuser absolument toute existence aux idées générales." (*Passion*, 553).

"accident [32]." On the other hand, the real potentiality lies in the possibility of an act of creation which in no way is dependent upon the thing, so that strictly speaking we cannot say that the actualisation of a new "accident" arises from a "potency" essentially belonging to the thing in which it comes to inhere. The actualisation of a new "accident" in the thing can only be said to conform to the "nature" or character of the thing in that the act of creation, which was the initiation of its existence as a whole determined it and endowed it with a certain finite complex of "accidents" which thereafter, according to the will of the Creator, form the proximate basis for subsequent change in its being a "body" and in those "accidents" which form its more or less permanent attributes as such and such a thing, together with others which give way to their contraries in the process of change. The "potentiality" of the thing is wholly dependent upon an "arbitrary" act of creation just as the realisation of the new "accident" in the thing depends upon another. The given "accident" is annihilated by the agent which causes the inherence of its contrary [33].

By virtue of its being that which it is, the thing has no intrinsic principle or "nature" (φύσις) by which changes and alterations are originated from within it [34], but rather it exists, in and of itself, only as capable of being changed [35]. It exists in the world as the created locus of the possibility of the realisation of another act of creation. We cannot, in a sense, properly say that it *has* of itself a potentiality but only that it is the possible object of the potentiality of an extrinsic agent — that it is *maqdûr ʿalayhi* [36], for the passive potentiality which may be predicated of it has no being save in correlation to the actual power of

---

[32] In view of this and considering the ontological place of the body in the total composite, one might be tempted to take the body as "substance," comparing abû l-Hudhayl's statement that "bodies are not contrary to one another" (*Maq.*, 376) with that of Aristotle (*Metaphysics*, 1068a, 10f) that οὐσία has no contrary. This cannot be done, however, for several reasons; most importantly, the formal reality of the thing, according to abû l-Hudhayl, is the "accidents" since, other than "accidents", the thing is not anything. Further, the reasons for which Aristotle holds that οὐσία has no contrary (*cf.* St Thomas Aquinas, *in Meta.* XI, *lect.* xii, §§2378-84) are altogether different from those for which abû l-Hudhayl says that bodies are not contrary to one another. "Accidents" are contrary to one another *per se* (*Maq.*, 359, *et alibi*) and contrary succeeds contrary in the individual parts of the substrate, while body arises through the "accident" of composition (*ta'lîf*) as it inheres in the "atoms" and ceases to be with the annihilation of *ta'lîf* and the creation of the "accident" of disjunction (*iftirâq*) or isolation (*infirâd*) in the individual "atoms." However, *cf. infra* ch. IV, nn. 14 and 21.

[33] *I.e.*, the contrary does not itself annihilate its contrary, *Maq.*, 376.

[34] Concerning φύσις, *cf.* the remarkable discussion of M. Heidegger, *Einführung in die Metaphysik*, 10ff.

[35] Man forms an exception to this; *v. infra*, ch. III.

[36] There is no term for passive potentiality as a quality belonging to the thing or as a fact of its existence. *Qudra*, indeed, is used in some contexts in a way seemingly parallel to that of Greek δύναμις as in the statement لان الفعل اذا خرج من القدرة خرج منه ضده بخروجه (*Intiṣâr*, 17), but here, as always, *qudra* is a positive and distinct attribute of the agent who is *qâdir*.

an agent to act upon it; with the absence of a specifically defined potentiality (*qudra*) on the part of an agent which is present to the thing, it has *no* possibility of change [37].

In sum, though there be a real continuity and stability of the thing in its being, through the permanence of certain "accidents" which collectively make up, in the unity of the body, the formal reality of its being, its being in the alteration of states which it may undergo consists ontologically in a "progress" through discrete and discontinuous stages in that one "accident" is altogether annihilated and another created in its place. Since the ontological potentiality and the cause of the actualisation of change in no way reside in any inherent "nature" of the thing, but only in the factic presence of a given complex of specific "accidents," the being of the thing is ontologically complete and perfect at any given moment with the created actuality of the "accidents" that have been realised in it. Becoming, as change, is ontologically a progress through extrinsically determined, discontinuous stages, in each of which the being of the thing is completely and exhaustively realised.

C. *The Finitude of Created Being*

All created being is composite (*ḏû 'ab'âḍ*) according to abû l-Hudhayl, and as such is finite [38], in contrast to God, the Eternal, Who is infinite in the absolute simplicity of His Being [39]. In the composite material creature, we have always to deal with a finite whole or totality (*kull, ǧamî'*), for corporeal being exists, in the unity of the composite, as a finite sum of elements. It has its being as a defined aggregate of discrete, indivisible parts in which inheres a determinate set of distinct "accidents," while each "accident" inheres separately in the individual "atoms," complete and undivided in its actuality. A "being-at-rest" (*sukûn*) may endure two moments, but the act of being at rest is, in itself, as it inheres in the thing, one and undivided in each "atom" in which it inheres and, inhering in the whole, constitutes a single and undivided act in the total composite which is the thing in its unity as a composite. At every level, no matter how considered, the being of the thing is defined and constituted as the unified whole or sum of a multitude of discrete elements. At any given instant its being is complete and perfect in the created actuality of the total sum of its "accidents," and its history, to the extent that we may legitimately speak of such, is the sum of the discrete moments of its existence: the total of those "accidents" that

---

37 *Cf. infra* concerning the ultimate termination of all change, esp. nn. 42ff.

38 وجب ان يكون المحدث ذا غاية ونهاية وان له كلا وجميعا (*Intiṣâr*, 16); وجدت المحدثات ذات ابعاض وماكان كذلك فواجب ان يكون له كل وجميع (*ibid.*).

39 Cf. *ibid.* and *infra*, ch. III, nn. 45f.

have belonged to it as having been created in the specific body which is the thing, from the moment of God's initiation of its existence. Its entire being, from the beginning to the end, taken at any point, is in every respect the finite sum of a determined multitude of discrete elements. With the exception of man (a matter with which we shall deal in the following section), a thing, in its being, is never in any way more than it is at any given moment of its existence. It has, of itself and by virtue of its being what it is, no inherent principle of change or transcendence towards any state or act beyond the totality of the "accidents" which define the totality of its being in the immediate moment. Whatever potentiality to change it may be considered to have belongs, as was pointed out, properly to the agent who may effect the change and its remaining in existence, beyond the immediate moment, is itself subject to God's causing it to remain.

The indefinite and the infinite have no part in created being [40]. Those things which are are completely defined in the created perfection of their "accidents" at any given instant and if we would speak of the possibility of being as the possibility of continued existence and change in those things which are, or of the initiation of the existence of hitherto non-existent things, or generally of the possibility of the future in the world, then we must speak of the actually existing potentiality (*qudra*) in reference to which the possibles are possible, *viz.*, God's creative power.

Considered in itself, as one with God's being, His Power is infinite [41]; considered, on the other hand, as directed to its objects in creation, it is "limited" by the number and character of those things to which it is actually directed, that is, those which are from eternity determined and defined in His Foreknowledge of what He will create [42]. In this way then, even in the ground of its existence, the possible exists not as an infinite potentiality of creation which shall progressively be defined (whether unto a term or not is not here in question) by its realisation and actualisation nor as the absolute possibility of what God might have willed to create, but only of those particular events which are foreordained, already determined and defined in His foreknowledge. Strictly, therefore, we should not speak of the possible objects of God's creative activity but only of those particular objects which have not yet been realised and those whose alloted time (*'ağal*) has not yet come [43].

---

40 On the way in which this is true of man, cf. *infra*, ch. III, 3.

41 *Cf. Intiṣâr*, 80; the question of the Divine Attributes is beyond the scope of the present study; generally, cf. *ibid.*, 59; *Maq.*, 165, 177, 484ff, *et alibi*, *Milal*, 71 etc.

42 *Cf. Maq.*, 163 and the references in the following note.

43 On the general understanding of *al-'ağal* as determined by God, *cf. Maq.*, 257, *Fiṣal* 3, 84, and *Šarḥ al Mawâqif* 8, 170f; cf. also *infra*, ch. III, n. 39.

For abû l-Hudhayl thus, the being of created things and of all creation exists always and forever as a finite whole : a completed whole in what has been, of what is actually present in the world, or as the defined totality of what shall be brought to existence. There is nothing, in fact, whose being, actual and potential, is not defined as a *whole* (*ǧamîʿ*, *kull*) in every respect. The possible in general, insofar as it is a real possible, and the totality of all possibles, as all those acts which God will ever create, must form a finite sum, defined in God's foreknowledge [44].

In consistency with his system then, he concludes, though with some hesitency [45], that "everything which shall be will one day be described as having been" and consequently one must affirm, he says, that there is "a finite whole and totality of what has been and what shall be [46]." Any kind of infinitude of created being is unthinkable. There is a fixed, finite limit to the real possibles as determined in God's knowledge, his *maqdûrât*, and so there must come a moment when all the possibles have been realised and there is nothing whatsoever left "in potency." Even God's power and potentiality to create new things, insofar as it is correlative to its object, is exhausted with the completion in creation of the totality of those things which are defined in His knowledge as the real objects of His power [47].

This principle he applies rigorously. That the material world, which we know

---

44 *Cf. Intiṣâr*, 16 and 90f, *Maq.*, 163 and 485.

45 He is said to have given up or repented of his speculation on this topic (though not necessarily to have recanted !); *Intiṣâr*, 16f, 20f and 92.

46 فان قلتم ان كل الاعراض غيركل الاجسام اقررتم بالكل للاجسام والاعراض... فكل ما يكون سيوصف يوما ما بان قدكان...فقد اقررتم بكل لما كان وما يكون (*al-Intiṣâr*, 20; Nader in translating this "vous généraliserez alors pour les corps et pour les accidents..., pour tout ce qui était et ce qui est" has missed the point entirely). It would seem that abû l-Hudhayl was led to this conclusion and to affirm its theological consequents primarily by the logic of his system — the consistency of created being as discrete and finite (*cf. Intiṣâr*, 16f and 20f). The argument that to allow an infinity on one end (*i.e.*, the future) would necessitate positing an infinite past (*Intiṣar*, 18f, *Farq*, 74, *Milal*, 73) takes on a special quality within this particular system. *Cf.* also the argument used by al-Khayyâṭ in his apology for this particular doctrine of abû l-Hudhayl (*Intiṣâr*, 56) that if there were no term to the acts of the blessed they would have then to be rewarded anew on the basis of their actions in paradise (*cf.* also *Farq*, 75); this is important in that it demands, implicitly at least, an existential *Vollendung* to human existence (*cf. infra*).

47 "...because the things which are objects of [God's] power at present have not all come forth into existence, but when all created beings have come forth into existence and not one of them remains unrealised, dependent upon the power (*qudra*) of its maker, it will be impossible to say that the agent of the act is capable (*yaqdur*) of producing another like it since there will be nothing like it in the power [of the agent], all acts having come forth into existence," *Intiṣar*, 20; *cf.* also generally, *ibid.*, 15ff, esp. 17ff.

(*al-dunyâ*), shall come to an end on the Day of Judgement designated in God's design, is common Islamic doctrine. Beyond this however, the acts of the blessed and the damned in the next life also constitute moments in the reality of created being and to put the term of the being of things at the end of the world is to put none at all. Thus, to the scandal of a great number of Muslim thinkers, abû l-Hudhayl insists that there must also be a term to the acts and movements (the "becomings and movements") of the blessed and the damned — a term in which all created being is ultimately consummated [48]. Unlike Ğahm b. Ṣafwân, he does not say that all created being, and with it thus the pleasures of the blessed and the pains of the damned, will be annihilated [49], but rather all these shall, at a given moment, be commanded by God to "remain." Thus, as even in created things certain "accidents" may endure, their endurance being a single and undivided act, so also the "permanent and fixed remaining" of the actuality and being of those in the next life must constitute a single, perpetual moment of existence wherein they remain [50]. All existence thus finds its *Endung* and *Vollendung* in the divine command in which it terminates. All created existence is summed up in the moment of one eternal act. In this, it should be noted, the being of each individual remains; there is no confusion. Rather, the being of each individual is complete and fulfilled in the totality of his reward or punishment. In a sense, this totality of actuality transcends the momentary completeness of being in the moments of its existence in this world, for in this final moment of "rest," there is not the permanent realisation of merely a single moment but rather of all the possible pleasures and rewards of the blessed and all the possible pains and punishments of the damned [51]. Again, though we have not the explicit texts to determine exactly how he conceived it, we may say that in these pleasures or pains, in each case, was concretised as reward or punishment, God's judgement of the whole earthly life of each individual, so that in a sense this terminal and enduring moment collects, ratifies, and totalises the existence of each individual [52] and in a single act seals for eternity the whole sum of all existence from Adam to the end of the world.

---

[48] *Cf. Maq.*, 358f, *'Uṣûl*, 50f, 94, and 238, and the references cited below.

[49] He has nevertheless been accused eristically of having said that they will terminate in annihilation (*fanâ'*); *cf.*, for example, *Intiṣâr*, 17ff and *Farq*, 73f.

[50] وصاروا فى الجنة باقين بقاء دائما ساكنين سكونا باقيا ثابتا لا يفنى ولا يزول ولا ينفد ولا يبيد (*Intiṣâr*, 17) and كان يزعم ان الجنة والنار ومافيها باقيتان لا تفنيان ولا تبيدان ابدا (*Ibid*, 18) Generally, cf. *ibid.*, 15-21 and 56f, *Maq.*, 163 and 485, *Farq*, 74f, and *Milal*, 73.

[51] He insists that there is a perfection, not a stonelike inactivity in this final "remaining" (*Intiṣâr*, 56f) and says (*ibid.*, 17) that "when the blessed arrive at the last of their movements (to which we have affirmed that there is a finite, numerical totality) all pleasures will be summed up in them." (*cf.* also, *ibid.*, 18 and *Farq*, 74).

[52] *Cf. Intiṣâr*, 56f and *supra*, n. 46.

III. MAN

A. *General Remarks*

Man, like all other created beings, is a corporeal complex of created "accidents," each of which is separate and distinct from the other and from the body by which the individual is defined [1]. In this way, man is said to have both "soul" (*nafs*) and "spirit" (*rûḥ*) [2] and is described as living (*ḥayy*), though his life is an "accident" identified neither with soul nor spirit [3] and is other than the individual in the totality of his being himself (*ġayruhu*) [4]. So also, he is capable of producing acts through free choice (*qâdir, mustaṭî'*) though this capacity (*qudra,* or *istiṭâ'a*) is other than the will (*'irâda*); it does not consist in "bodily health and well-being" [5] and is distinct from life [6] and, like life, is other than the person himself (*ġayruhu*) [7]. Again, he has, as "accidents," five senses, "distinct from the body and the soul [8]" and intelligence or mind (*'aql*), a kind of "sense" (*ḥiss*) which is at once its contents and "the capacity for the aquisition of knowledge [9]." However, the senses are "distinct from the body and the soul; the act of perception (*'idrâk*) is an internal

---

1 *Cf.* the definition of man in *Maq.*, 329 and *Fiṣal* 5, 65.

2 The place of both *nafs* and *rûḥ* in the system is obscure, since they are hardly discussed at all in the fragments. *Nafs* is held to be an "accident" (*Fiṣal* 5, 74), distinct from the senses and the body (*Maq.*, 339) and from *rûḥ* (*ibid.*, 337). He says that it may be taken from the body during sleep (*ibid.*, where also *Koran* 39.42 is cited), but does not otherwise, in the available texts, discuss it. It would be important to know if he in any way identified *nafs* with ego consciousness or with the passions (*cf. Koran* 5.33, 50.15, and 12.53). *Rûḥ* likewise "may be taken from him during sleep" (*Maq.*, 337); he is, however, uncertain whether it is a "body" (*i.e.*, a distinct organ and separate complex of " atoms ") or an "accident" (*ibid.*, 402) i.e., a function of the body or of a part of the body. From an analysis of human existence as it is construed by abû l-Hudhayl one might, with some justification, question whether *nafs* and *rûḥ* played any really significant rôle within the system; on the other hand it must be acknowledged that our sources are highly selective, being interested only in certain subjects and in these citing often only extreme positions (*i.e.*, those not generally held).

3 *Maq.*, 337; though distinct from life it nevertheless disappears at death by "going out if it is a body or being annihilated if it is an 'accident'" (*Maq.*, 402).

4 *Maq.*, 229.

5 *Ibid.*, and *Milal,* 73f.

6 *Cf.* references cited above.

7 *Maq.*, 229; in a sense the expression *ḥayy mustaṭî'* forms a kind of definition, parallel to the *ḥayy nâṭiq* of the falâsifa.

8 *Maq.*, 339; *i.e.*, neither is it a function of the organs of sense nor an act of the "soul."

9 *Maq.*, 480.

act of knowing (*'ilm al-qalb*) which is altogether independent of the physical states of the body and the operations of the organs of sense [11]. It is an act which distinguishes and knows objects and things [12], created directly in the heart by God [13]. Within this, the basis of unity and cohesion being the spatio-temporal cohesion of the "atoms" as a unified body, in which all these diverse and independent "accidents" occur through the will of the Creator, man appears, like other creatures, as a hollow, material aggregate which has no existential unity of interiority and forms no individual, self-centering locus of conscious being in the world [14].

However, though defined as a body having a given configuration in which adheres a complex of distinct and separately created "accidents," man, unlike any other creature [15], has the power of realising his own acts (whether interior or exterior) through conscious choice. To this extent then, he is fundamentally a moral being — one whose being is to produce his own acts and be judged ultimately in his individual and personal responsibility for them. From the standpoint of this investigation, the most important point is that ontologically, in contrast to other created "things," which, as was pointed out above, are in no sense any more than they are, being complete in the finitude of their being at each moment of their existence, man, in being a willing agent (*muḫtâr, mustaṭî'*), has within himself, as a permanent attribute of his being [17], a principle of transcendence : his being insofar as he is *qâdir, mustaṭî'*, is oriented out of the present into the future in the potentiality (*qudra*) of his own acting into the future. We must examine this in some detail, for the thought of abû l-Hudhayl on this point is far from simple.

---

11 *Maq.*, 569 and 312 (top); perception is "*necessary knowledge*" (*'ilm al-iḍṭirâr*), *ibid.*

12 *Cf. Maq.*, 361 and further see *infra*, n. 25. There are a number of things involved in this thesis; on the one hand perception and knowledge are distinguished from the states of the body in accordance with the system's general tendency to make all "accidents" separate and independent of one another (*v. supra*); beyond this however, in insisting that the physical states of the organs of sense and the act of perception and knowing (*'ilm*) are totally independent of one another as they take place in the living person, abû l-Hudhayl is, within the limits of his own terminology, saying that the act of perception, as a human act involving a kind of knowing, transcends the mere functioning of any set of organs (the physiologist's electrical discharges, if you will). The completeness with which he separates the two acts, of course, creates other problems.

13 *Maq.*, 569, 410 and 312. Since man, as the perceiver, does not determine according to his own free choice the content of the act of perception, he cannot be said to be the agent or maker (*fâ'il*) of the act; *cf. infra*. Also involved here is the theological question of the vision (*ru'ya*) of God in the next life.

14 *Cf.* Massignon, *Passion*, 480f and *infra*.

15 We have not to do here with angels or *ǧinn*; none of the available texts mention them.

17 *Cf. infra*, n. 33. The system recognises, it should be noted again, no such thing as an "essential" attribute and *al-istiṭâ'a* disappears finally in the next life; *cf. infra*.

B. *The Structure of the Act*

In the terminology of abû l-Hudhayl, the power of realising an act (*al-qudra, al-istiṭâ'a*) is not in any wise simply the inherent power of acting through a release of physical energy on the part of a conscious agent, not the mere availability of raw force to achieve or effect some act. On the contrary, it is the potentiality of effecting a deliberately chosen end; *al-istiṭâ'a* (or *al-qudra*) only *exists* where there is the real possibility of unconstrained choice on the part of a free agent and vice-versa there can be no act of the will (*'irâda*) save where there exists the real potentiality of effecting its object [18]. Any act on the part of man, which is not freely determined in an act of the will is neither his nor, indeed, is its execution said to be wrought by his power of action, but on the contrary must be God's; *i.e.*, involuntary action or inaction on the part of a human agent is not his. It does not arise through any act of his will nor is it realised through his *qudra* but is in every respect God's [19]. In other words, to the extent that action is not a deliberate, unconstrained projection of his own potentiality from within a present situation into the future, man in no wise transcends his momentary state (is not *qâdir*) but rather is moved by external forces through a series of discrete moments in which his being, like that of non-human, material creation, is exhaustively determined, without his intervention and participation as a moral being [20]. Thus, will and *qudra* are what we should term the basic faculties of moral (i.e., properly *human*) action and are accordingly oriented into the future. In man the act of the will and the intention to act always precede the exterior

---

18 *I.e., al-istiṭâ'a* always involves a set of contraries (*diḍḍân*) and the possibility of performing the specific act or leaving it undone; *cf. Intiṣâr*, 17f and 20, and also *infra*, nn. 34 and 37.

19 It is thus that he only ascribes to man those acts the nature (*kayfîya*) of which he understands : كل ما يتولد عن فعله مما يعلم كيفيته فهو فعله *Maq.*, 402; (*cf.* also *ibid.*, 374 and 378, *Milal*, 74 and on the expression *mâ ya'lam* (*ya'rif*) *kayfîyatahu*, *cf.* also *'Uṣûl*, 234, which is discussed *infra*, III, n. 51). That event or action whose nature or character is unknown cannot, as such, be intended or willed. Fakhry (*op.cit.*, 44) seems not to have understood this "sublte distinction." N.B., that there is no act or event therefore which is not the direct and immediate result of some willed intention (albeit the secondary *fi'l mutawallad* on the part of the human agent may in a sense be unintended); the actualisation of the being of a thing (its being brought into being as that thing which it is in the fulness of its being) is primarily attributable only to the agent who knows and intends its being so, to the extent and in so far as he knows and intends it. This notion of a specific, knowing intentionality underlying all events and things is a basic assumption of the kalâm from abû l-Hudhayl through al-Râzî and Šahrastânî, etc., and forms the basis of most of the traditional proofs for the existence of God. Secondary causes are not necessarily excluded in this scheme; rather they are not true or primary causes in that they do not determine the being of the result in a knowing intention which exhausitively embraces its every aspect, as does God.

20 *Cf. Intiṣâr,* 17 (bottom).

actualisation of their object [21]; it is because he conceives *al-qudra* as a potentiality to initiate an event in the world — a nexus between will and action, rather than as simply the raw force or power whereby movement is transmitted to things, that abû l-Hudhayl insists that in the case of exteriorised activity, *qudra* always precedes the realisation of the act [22]. Man's act is *his* and proceeds from his human power to act only to the exent it is the result of a prior intention of the will.

The world and its structure — the perception of things and man's awareness of himself as among and different from them, as the total potential field of action, are given in the act of the intelligence (*'aql*), which includes the data of perception and innate knowledge (*'ilm iḍṭirâr, 'ilm ḍurûrî*) as well as that knowlege which is acquired through thought and reflection (*'ilm iktisâb, 'ilm iḫtiyâr*) [23]. Given to adult understanding [24] is not merely the raw perception of the phenomenal present but with this is given also the perception of the objective moral good and evil of things [25] and the basis of a natural knowledge of God, together with an

---

21 *Maq.*, 418 *et alibi*; it is unlike God's act of willing, which is simultaneous with the realisation of its object (*ibid.*), for human acts in no way resemble those of the Creator (*Maq.*, 551). Man's internal acts are, however, simultaneous with the act of his will; *cf. Milal*, 73 and *Šarḥ al-Mawâqif* 6,100.

22 *Intiṣâr*, 60f, *Maq.*, 232, *Farq*, 77, *Fiṣal* 3, 22. Human *qudra* does not strictly necessitate its effect (*'awǧaba l-fi'l*), *Maq.*, 415. Man has, in fact, the power only to initiate motion and rest (*Maq.*, 311f, 350f, 431) and so cannot himself produce or effect, for example, bodily strength (*quwwa*), life, or a corporeal body (*Maq.*, 403; *cf.* also *infra.*, n. 51). It is within this framework that he says that the power to act precedes the act. "Accidents" other than motion and rest result from (*tawallada 'an*) these, in some instances, and are attributed to the person (*yunsabu 'ilayhi*, *Intiṣar*, 60) as the one morally responsible while what cannot "result from motion, rest, and the conjunction and disjunction which arise therefrom" (*Maq.*, 311f) but does follow upon the act is produced by God, as for example, the perception and understanding of one's action or discourse on the part of another (*cf. Maq.*, 402, 410 and *Milal*, 74). We need not here go into the detail of the problem of *tawallud* and the physical limits of human action, since that lies beyond the aim of the present considerations; what is here important is that *al-qudra/al-istiṭâ'a* forms, whitin man, the basis of the possibility of effecting his will and so of his moral action in the world. Concerning *tawallud* and the range of man's power to act, besides the above references, *n.b.*, *Intiṣâr*, 122.

23 *Cf.* the references cited above, nn. 9 and 11. Al-Baġdâdî's statement (*Farq*, 78 and *'Uṣûl*, 32) that sense knowledge (*'ulûm al-ḥawâss*) is, according to abû l-Hudhayl, freely acquired (*'ilm iḫtiyâr wa-ktisâb*) is to be taken in a different sense if it is not simply contrary to the explicit statement of al-'Aš'arî.

24 He recognized "stages" in the growth of the mind (in terms of the growth of its contents: its *ma'lûmât* or *'ulûm*), moral responsibility becoming complete only at maturity (*al-bulûġ*) when the intelligence reached its perfection (*kamâl*), *cf. Maq.*, 480, *Farq*, 78; the broadest implications of all this for revealed and "natural" law (*cf.* the following notes) and the detail of his moral thought I shall not deal with here; on this, cf. *Farq*, *loc.cit.* and *'Uṣûl* 258 and 260.

25 يعلم حسن الحسن وقبح القبيح, *Milal*, 74. Thus it is, since there is objective good and evil perceivable in things, that actions are objectively good or evil and accordingly abû l-Hudhayl speaks of

innate moral demand of conscience that this basis be elaborated in thought and the good persued and evil avoided [26]. Nevertheless, though the world is thus given [27] to present awareness [28] as an objectively structured field of possible action, the act of perception does not of itself contain any appeal to action. That is, the act of perception and understanding, even though containing the objective moral good and evil inherent in the potential of what is perceived, does not of itself transcend the facticity of the given and does not, therefore, constitute for the perceiver an existential situation. Motivation is not given in the act of "knowing," whether in raw perception or reflective consideration, even though the moral potential of the possible actions be given [29]. The factic presence of what is given in perception is constituted as a situation when some possible action (positive or negative) therein occurs to the mind in its immediate potentiality as desirable (*ḫaṭara*), and it is upon the situation as a potential act occuring to the mind that the will must act. The act of perception is created immediately by God so that the presence of consciousness to its own potentiality in the world, like man's material existence in space, belongs to him at any given moment as it is given in the form of a created "accident." Further, the occurance to the mind the of potentiality of the situation as desirable or repugnant in terms of specific acts (*al-ḫâṭir*) is also initiated from without, either by God or by Satan [30]. It is then the givenness of the existential situation, as it presents the immediate possibility of a specific act, that the intelligence (*'aql*) must examine reflectively (*tafakkara*), forming and determining its purpose and intent in terms of moral

---

unintentional obedience (*ṭâ'a*) or disobedience (*ma'ṣiya*) to God's commands, even on the part of the unbeliever, where there can be no desire of "drawing near to God" (*al-taqarrub 'ilà llâh*); *cf*. *Intiṣâr* 57ff, *Farq* 75f, and *Milal*, 74f.

26 *Cf*. *Farq*, 78 and 75f; it is in these terms thus that he is able to speak of a kind of "natural law" (*taklîf qabl wurûd al-sam'*), *cf*. *Milal*, 74.

27 We shall have, of course, to include in the objectively given the self of the perceiver as it forms, in the state of its givenness at the moment, an object of possible action, as for example the possibility of an interior act (*fi'l-qalb*) — *e.g.*, an act of knowing or of scheming constitutes as possible goal of action.

28 It may be in this sense of the immediate perception of the present (*'idrâk* = *'ilm*) that abû l-Hudhayl said that "acts of knowing (*'ulum*) do not endure" (*Šarḥ al-Mawâqif* 5, 38f); unfortunately, however, while Siyâlkûtî and Čelebî in treating this passage comment (*ibid.*) on this thesis as it is held by the two Ğubbâ'îs, neither gives any further detail or the position of abû l-Hudhayl.

29 This is the clear sense of *Maq.*, 429, 1 - 3 (where the author opposes this position to that of al-Naẓẓâm and Ğa'far b. Ḥarb, who say that there is no perception without a *ḫaṭir*); *cf*. also *Milal*, 84.

30 *Cf*. *Maq.*, 429 and *'Uṣûl*, 27; as every act is objectively good or bad (*i.e.*, one of obedience or disobedience to the divine law), so also the double source of motivation or inclination, which must be from without. Man is not himself the conscious agent of his own first impulse of attraction or aversion to a given object, nor can things, which neither in themselves nor in their being perceived transcend in any way the givenness of their being at the moment, be the source of an act. *Cf*. also Massignon, *Passion* 492 and *infra*, n. 32.

good and evil which are objectively contained in the elements of the situation [31]. Finally, it is upon the known as given in the product of present perception, prior knowledge, and reflection that the will makes its decision whether to perform the specific act or not [32].

C. *The Being of Man: Givenness and Transcendence*

Man thus as *mustaṭî'*, has the capacity of transcending his own present. However, this freedom of transcendence is highly contingent, although his being is not bounded completely in the finite term of the moment. The fact of his freedom, first, is given him as an inescapable component of the structure of his being; i.e., *al-istiṭâ'a* is given by a divine act of creation so that man cannot choose to be *mustaṭî'* and cannot therefore escape the ultimate judgement of himself in his acts. Again, although *al-istiṭâ'a* is a permanent element ("accident") of his being [33] which covers thus categories of acts, the real possibility of its actualisation is only given within the terms of a specific situation which cannot be willed;

---

31 On the importance of intelligence (*'aql*) in Islamic moral thought, *cf.* Gardet and Anawati, *Introduction*, 347ff; reflection, according to abû l-Hudhayl, does not necessarily produce motivation to the act but elaborates the potentiality of the situation in terms of the given potential so as to establish intent, which becomes the actual motive or intention through the act of the will. Again, though the question of the nature of faith and the ultimate perfection of action in the intended act of obedience to God (*Maq.*, 266f) is a theological question into which we need not enter here, it should be noted in passing that within the general framework of abû l-Hudhayl's thought, contemplation is not valued but rather intellect (*'aql*) is oriented almost totally towards action; *i.e.*, though the highest priority is given to the recognition and knowledge of God (*ma'rifat Allâh*) the place of this knowledge in man's existence is to direct his actions as faith (*cf. Maq., loc.cit*). "This world is a place of action": ان ابا الهذيل يزعم ان الدنيا دار عمل وامر ونهي ومحنة (*Intiṣâr*, 56). πρᾶξις takes complete precedence over θεωρία. Man's self-possession and self-totalisation lies in action not knowing (*cf. infra*). On this world as *dâr 'amal*, *cf.* also the remarks of al-Ḥasan al-Baṣrî in *Hilyat al-'Awliyâ'* (Cairo, 1357-1938) 2, 140 and the remarks on his attitude by Ibn Sîrîn (for whom salvation was by grace alone), *ibid.*, 270.

32 He does not describe the structure of the act of the will; i.e., he does not discuss the actualisation of its decision as a choice in any of the available texts. *Al-ḫâṭir* is clearly not the act of the individual to whom it occurs; it "happens to him" and consequently an external agent must be assigned. On the other hand, by definition, within the system, the act of the will, to the extent that it is a free decision, is preëminently *the* human act. The problem is that the author could not give man an infinite regression of acts of the will and at the same time could not make God the agent, since this would destroy utterly the concept of human freedom. It is for this reason that Ibn Taymîya says (*Muwâfaqa* 1, 206f) that "the Basra school of the qadarî mu'tazila end up having to say that the act of the will on the part of the creature takes place without an agent and so they deny the agent of the act of the will even while affirming that it has a final cause."

33 *Maq.*, 230; cf. also *Intiṣâr*, 61f.

its actuality is entirely contingent upon the givenness of a situation which defines the specific possibility of the act. [34]

As was noted above, man's existence within the situation, his perception of the objective reality of the situation, and his initial reaction to it as a situation (*al-ẖâṭir*) are not subject to his free choice. Human freedom, then, is a freedom only to evaluate the possibility of acting within the determinations of a situation whose objective structure in its presence to consciousness is given. Within these limits of determination, man, in his freedom to determine his own acts, constitutes an element of indetermination in the world. The actuality of *al-istiṭâ'a* precedes the act so that his being in its potentiality of self-determination is an indeterminate to-be-determined in that the actuality of its being within a given moment is the projection of itself into the future : its actuality of itself as potentially acting or not acting [35].

We cannot, therefore, say of man that his being, like that of other created things, is complete and exhausted in the finiteness of its being, what it is at any given moment. Within the system however [36], the range of indetermination which exists in the world in the being of man is quite narrow. Although *al-istiṭâ'a*, in being an "enduring 'accident'," is a general potentiality to act, its actuality arises only within defined situations in immediate reference to a single pair of contraries (*cf.* note 34). His potentiality of transcendence is therefore in no way one of a creative spontaneity but one only of a choice between two alternatives which arise within a defined objective context. Not only is this context exteriorily defined insofar as it is present to the awareness of the human agent, but furthermore the moral potentiality of the context is also preordained and determined independently of the agent, since although the possibility of acting lies within the power of the agent, the good and evil of his potential act lie within the elements of the context. Man's freedom of self-determination in action is thus minimal;

---

34 Since its reality is always limited and determined as the capacity to perform a single particular act or not, it is said to terminate with the first moment of the realisation of the act (تفنى مع اول وجود الفعل *Fiṣal* 3, 22; cf. also *Intiṣâr*, 20).

35 *Cf. Šarḥ al-Mawâqif* 6, 100 and references cited *supra*, n. 22.

36 This is a kind of "extrapolation," for the matter is not discussed directly in any of the fragments. We cannot avoid the question however, especially given the importance of the idea of the total finitude of creation within the system, as it is witnessed by the author's insistence on the ultimate termination of all movement and change. Given his thesis of the discrete finitude of all created being, which has already been outlined, we can determine with relative certainty the general sense of the finitude of human existence as abû l-Hudhayl understands it.

his existence is in no respect one of a creative interiority of spontaneous contingency [37].

Again, consciousness is present to the world and so to its own potentiality as a potentiality to act in the world, in the temporal series of its acts of perception, each of which is a discrete "accident" created by God, complete in itself, and separate from the others. So also the concomittant act of knowing, though it may contain the past as the present reality of a given possibility, is discrete and complete in its own actuality. We have then a transcendence always from one discrete moment, created by God, to another, *viz.*, that of the realisation of the act [38]. Finally, as the individual's general potentiality to act is realised in a series of isolated moments, the series itself is finite and is ultimately exhausted in a terminus (*'ağal*) which is foreordained by God [39], so that we might say that as an enduring attribute of the person, *al-istiṭâ'a* is given him by God who knows from eternity the detail of its eventual actualisation, as a kind of quantum, finite from the outset.

D. *The Unity of the Person*

In the preceding section we have seen that abû l-Hudhayl has elaborated an extremely subtle analysis of the structure of the human act. We must however ask what is and wherein lies the unity of consciousness as the existential unity of the person in his being one and identical with himself. To what extent must we say that for abû l-Hudhayl man is ultimately no more than an "inert carcass," an "aggregate of atoms [40]?"

It must be noted at the outset that in defining man as a material body [41], abû l-Hudhayl does not mean to say that he is the "atoms;" the body as a human body, the locus of the being of whatever "accidents" may define the concrete reality of an individual in time and place, exists through and in the complex

---

37 We have here an almost classical exposition of that legalistic conception of human freedom which is, in a sense, no freedom at all and which, in the words of Berdyaev "humiliates man rather than exalts him".

38 The nature of human existence as abû l-Hudhayl understands it is thus not in any way a perpetual *Sorge* or *Sich-vorweg-schon-sein-in-einer-Welt* (*cf.* Heidegger, *Sein und Zeit*, § 41, pp. 191ff) — a constantly self-determining indeterminate, but rather a self-determining determinate of this to that.

39 *Cf. Maq.*, 257, *Fiṣal* 3, 84, *Milal*, 75; he insists on this in order to maintain the absolute finitude of the totality of created being, both actual and potential, *i.e.*, both as it is contained in God's foreknowledge and as it is and has been realised in the world.

40 Massignon, *Passion*, 480f.

41 *Fiṣal* 5, 65.

of "accidents" which determine the basic materiality (conjunction, etc.) together with those others which determine its specific characteristics, color, etc. Man is the individual in the concrete reality of his material presence in the world [42] and the reality of the "atoms" in their being a substrate for this particular "body" is that of the aggregate of their "accidents." The person, in final analysis, is the totality of his "accidents" at a given moment within their unity of inherence in the body which is itself, in its own reality as a body, a function of a set of defined "accidents." The question then, of the existential unity of the person is one of the oneness of interiority within a complex of "accidents [43]." The problem concerning the ontological oneness of the person arises from the fact that abû l-Hudhayl does not posit or describe a unified and self-totalising act (such as the "soul" in classical and medieval thought) whose being is the reality of the person and through which the body is his living corporeal actuality, but rather he posits the body as an aggregate of undifferentiated "atoms" in which adheres a complex of ontologically distinct "accidents" whose sum within the spatially united substrate constitutes the being of the person.

The question of the ontological oneness of things as bodies, in the spatio-temporal unity of their parts, has been outlined above. So also, as with other created beings, the oneness and density of the human person is, for abû l-Hudhayl, the oneness of the composite totality which is constituted in and by the body; again however, this is not merely an accidental conjunction and juxtaposition in space of the elements of the particulate substrate, but of the living body in its reality as bearing all those permanent "accidents" and functions which adhere in it. In this way man remains always a composite unity; though living and capable of acting, he is not himself the act of his living and his power of acting [44], for such an absolute unity and infinity of self-identity belongs to God alone, the Absolute (*al-Ṣamad*) [45], Who knows and "Whose act of knowing is himself," and Who lives and "Whose life is himself," etc., "like to whom there is none [46]." The act

---

42 *Maq.*, 329.

43 *Cf. infra.*

44 *Cf. supra*, n. 7.

45 On the use of *Ṣamad*, *cf.* for example, the remarks of al-Isfarâ'înî in the preface to his *Tabṣîr* (p.9) ان الصمد هو الذى لا جوف له وهذا يتضمن نفى النهاية; *cf.* also Massignon, *op. cit.*, 645, n. 3 and the references there cited.

46 هو عالم بعلم هو هو وهو قادر بقدرة هي هو, etc., *Maq.*, 165, 484, *et alibi* and *cf.* also *Intiṣâr*, 80 (§70) where *Koran* 42.11 is also cited. The author's treatment of the problem of the *tawḥîd* is remarkably refined and I find it difficult to admit that the discussion of the divine attributes in the early kalâm is no more than "ein mit Schlauheit und Pfiffigkeit geführter Streit um Worte" which was absolutely fruitless (Pretzl, *Attributenlehre*, 35).

and reality of the body in its being a human body is not life and its functions (as it is with Aristotle and the Scholastics); this is not merely that *al-qudra* is distinct from the health and well-being of the body, that the act of perception is distinct from the organs of sense, etc., through the fact that these functions transcend the given states and arrangement of the raw materiality of the body, but rather that those attributes do not belong to it by any intrinsic principle of its being. The elements of his being, though constitutive of the totality in its being what it is, do not properly belong to it in virtue of its being, in itself, that thing which it is, but only through the gratuitous and arbitrary act of the Creator. Although there is a most intimate functional interrelationship between perception, knowledge, thought, and will in the structure of the act and although each and all of these "accidents" is, in its created actuality, founded immediately upon the presence of life in the body, there is no intrinsic basis for their presence in the body. The sole cause and principle of their actual presence in the whole is the will and the action of the Creator. Of and in himself, man does not within himself bear the principle of his own being and the fore structure of his existence. His presence in the world, through the composite unity of the body, together with the structure of the reality of this presence in terms of the "accidents" which constitute it, are determined from without, there being no formal principle of his being by which he is what he is.

We cannot say, however, simply that the person is nothing more than a mere aggregate of unrelated "accidents" adhering in an assemblage of undifferentiated "atoms." The unity of the living body is not simply that of a merely accidental conglomeration of indivisible parts or a simple, exterior juxtaposition of elements in space. First, it has the ontological unity of its being-created a single, unified body; the union of parts in their constitution of a created body forms, as has been noted, a unity different from that of a simple contiguity of independent parts [47]. Life, again, albeit a distinct "accident," adheres in and infuses (*ḥalla*) the body in the entirety of its "parts" and, insofar as the living body is the reality of the person, it is constitutive of the being of the body in its being the locus of consciousness, will, and the power to act, since these cannot exist apart from the living body [48]. Within the living body, *al-qudra*, in its intimate functional

---

[47] *Cf. supra*, ch. II. This abû l-Hudhayl does not state directly but besides its being almost necessary to the consistency of the system, his holding that man cannot make "bodies," though he can cause motion and the "accidents" consequent thereon (*cf. supra*, n. 22) leaves little doubt.

[48] That is, *'irâda*, *'ilm* (and so also *'idrâk*), and *qudra* (*istiṭâ'a*) may not exist save in the living, individual body — "may not coexist with death" (*Maq.*, 232 and 313), cf. *supra*, ch. II, n. 6. For comparative purposes it were well to recall at this point that in the Aristotelian and Scholastic systems (in contrast to those of the neo-platonists) the person is the reality of his corporeal existence; "anima est actus totius corporis" (St. Thomas Aquinas, *Comm. in Lib. de Anima*, II, lect, ii, §242) and "non oportet quaerere si ex anima et corpore fit unum... ... forma per se unitur materiae, sicut actus ejus;

relationship of interdependence with perception, knowledge, thought, will, etc., is an "accident" by which the whole body, in all its "parts" is *qâdir mustaṭî'* and so has the free disposition of its own efficacious action. That is, although the particulate or granular quality of the body remains, in the substrate, it is the totality of the parts, as a human individual, which acts [49]; it is the whole, finally, that, in the oneness of its being-created this individual person, is ultimately to be judged "on the last day," in terms of his disposition of himself through his power of self-determination in action. *Al-qudra* is, as we have seen, the power of self-possession and self-determination in moral action of the person in his being "this body which he is" and it is himself, as solely responsible for himself in his action, who is re-created identical with himself in the re-creation of the body at the last judgement.

In the resurrection God will create anew (*marratan 'uḫrà*) the human person in identity with himself as that person which he was created "the first time" (*'awwala marratin*) [50]. The several "accidents" which, together adhering in the unity of the body were that person, are re-created according to the Divine purpose into that corporeal unity whose reality in its unity is the person [51], In sum, there

---

et idem est materiam uniri formae quod materiam esse in actu" (*ibid*, II, *lect.* 1, §234; cf also *Quaestiones disputatae, de Anima, Quaest.* 10f and note the remarks of K. Rahner, *Zur Theologie des Todes* (Freiburg, 1958), pp. 20ff. This position, of course, is quite different from that of abû l-Hudhayl, but the essential materiality of life in the organic unity of the body as the reality of the living creature is common to both positions.

49 *Cf. Maq.*, 330: كان ابو الهذيل يقول ان كل بعض من ابعاض الجسد فاعل على الانفراد ولا انه فاعل مع غيره ولكنه يقول الفاعل هو هذه الابعاض; cf. *Koran* 41.19ff.

50 *Maq.*, 363f.

51 Massignon, speaking of abû l-Hudhayl (*Passion*, 481), states that the resurrection is the simple "reunion of the atoms;" this, however, cannot be the case since it is the "accidents" which constitute the reality of the thing. Though we have no adequate discussion of the topic, this is nevertheless quite clear in his treatment (*Maq.*, 374) of the question of what "accidents" are susceptible of being re-created identical with themselves (of being *mu'âda*). The simple recongregation of a given multitude of undifferentiated and absolutely qualitiless "atoms" cannot reconstitute a "thing" in its being that which it was, no matter what it be, for it is not the mere juxtaposition of parts which is the cause of their being those things which they are. It is for this reason that man cannot himself make a corporeal body or cause life to exist in one (*Maq.*, 403) and even God cannot give him this power (*ibid.*, 378). He cannot, in short, himself be the agent of precisely those "accidents" which make a thing be that thing which it is. It is in this context alone that we can understand the curious statement attributed to abû l-Hudhayl in *'Uṣûl*, 234: كل ماعرف كيفيته من الاعراض فلا يجوز ان يعاد وكل مالا اعرف كيفيته فجائز ان يعاد; that is, only those "accidents" whose nature (*kayfîya*) man does *not* know are capable of being recreated, for man can know and effect only motion and rest (and indirectly by *tawallud* those "accidents" of juxtaposition and separation which are directly consequent upon them — *Maq.*, 311 and 378), *viz.*, those which are by definition not constitutive of the thing in its being that which it is; *cf. supra, nn.* 19 and 21.

is, as it were, in man a disunity of interiority and a unity of exteriority. Within, he is a composite of distinct "accidents" whose unity has its being in their created presence in the body; life itself, the created possibility of the existence of the person in the body is a distinct component of his being and *al-qudra*, which is in a sense a unifying power of self-possession in the body, like life and his very existence, is not properly his own, but like every other element in the structure of his being is grounded in an exteriorly determined act of creation. On the other hand, man is ontologically constituted as one and a unity in the material unity of the body through the transcendent act of creation and God's will which determine his being in being a single, individual person. He is one and identical with himself through a oneness and existence which is not his in any way, out of elements which are not himself.

IV. "ATOM" AND "ACCIDENT" IN THE STRUCTURE OF MATERIAL REALITY

A. *General Remarks*

There can be little question of the "reality" or "concreteness" of "atoms" for abû l-Hudhayl. He says, for example, that a mustardseed (*ḫardala*) could, in theory, be divided (God could divide it) in half and each half in half and so forth until one arrived at an "indivisible part [1]." Again, he holds that these "parts" can exist separately in isolation (*infirâd*) [2] and further states that it would be possible to perceive an "indivisible part" were God to create such an act of perception in us [3].

Created reality can be exhaustively divided into the two categories of "atom" and "accident [4]", but we must be careful as to how we understand the statement that other than the undifferentiated "atoms" everything is "accident." It is especially misleading to take the terms *ǧawhar* ("atom") and *ʿaraḍ* ("accident"), since they have been used by the translators and falâsifa as equivalents of the Greek *οὐσία* and *συμβεβηκός* (Syriac, ܓܕܫܐ), and think of them as "substance" and "accident" as these terms have been used in the Aristotelian tradition [5].

---

1 Maq., 314.

2 *Cf. Maq.*, *ibid* and p. 311: يجوز على الجوهر الواحد الذى لا ينقسم اذا انفرد ما يجوز على الاجسام من الحركة والسكون ومايتولد عنها من الجامعة والمفارقة وسائر ما يتولد عنها.

3 *Maq.*, 315.

4 *Cf. Intiṣâr*, 20f and *infra*, n. 6.

5 There would seem to be some question as to whether abû l-Hudhayl did actually use the term *ǧawhar* or not (*cf.* Pines, *Beiträge*, 3f), while it is certain that he did use the expression *al-ǧuz'u lladî lâ yataǧazza'u/yanqasimu*. At any rate, though the definition of the atom or *ǧawhar* as that which bears "accidents" (*'aʿrâḍ*) is, in a sense, one with that of the Aristotelian *οὐσία* or the scholastic *substantia*, the concepts have little else in common (but *cf. infra*, n. 21). So also, the basic understanding of "accident" in the early kalâm, whatever may be the use of the term *ʿaraḍ* in the translations and the writings of the falâsifa and later mutakallimîn, is entirely different from what it is in the systems of classical antiquity and the latin literature of the middle ages. Fakhry, for example, (*op.cit.*, 34) ignores this fact and, taking *ǧawhar* and *ʿaraḍ* as would be equivalents *in meaning* of "substance" and "accident" in the Aristotelian systems, is unable to understand the position of al-Ǧubbâ'î and, failing therefore to see the coherence of meaning of the terms within their own proper context, ends up by speaking of "fragmentary accounts of substance" (*ibid.*, 35) which underlie the early kalâm.

Certainly for abû l-Hudhayl and most of the early Mu'tazila the basic unit of phenomenal being is body — the bodies (*'aǧsâm*) of things. Ultimately, all created being is corporeal, being made up of material bodies with their various "accidents :" qualities, attributes, states, etc. [6]. In this same sense, then, we can quite correctly speak of a basic, implicit materialism in the earlier kalâm [7]. In considering the "atoms" as the basic unit of "things" in their corporeal reality however, we must take care not to lend to them functions which they do not have in the system. Above all, the "atoms" of the early kalâm play no real rôle in the explanation of the physical properties of things; of and in themselves they are altogether qualitiless and absolutely inert, so that we must carefully refrain from seeing in them the atoms of classical systems and from finding in the "materialism" of early Islamic speculation any parallels to modern "materialistic" systems wherein the natures and properties of things are constituted by the nature of matter in and of itself [8]. In the kalâm, the "natures" of things cannot be explained

From a purely philological point of view he has overlooked the fact that the principal origins of both the concept and the term (ǧawhar = "atom" = οὐσία) are unquestionably stoic (*cf.* references, *infra*, n. 14; Pretzl's attempt to find an Indian origin [*Atomenlehre*, 126ff, *Attributenlehre*, 7f] is not convincing [cf. Pines, *Beiträge*, 122f]). Even this quasi historical equivalence, it should be noted, cannot justify the use of "substance" to translate "*ǧawhar*" in the kalâm since, beside the erroneously prejudicial resonance of the term in normal European usage, Muslim authors had no awareness of the common origin of the divergent uses of the word οὐσία in the ancient traditions but rather, in typical Arab fashion, took the usages of the term in the kalâm and the falsafa as simply two distinct meanings (*cf.* for example, the remarks of Taftazânî, *op. cit.*, 62). It is worth noting that the concept οὐσία, as it is understood by Aristotle finds no real equivalent anywhere in the mainstream of Islamic thought (Averroës being marginal), for the concept of the real in its self-subsistent identity with its own being, which is the very center of Aristotle's metaphysics, is reduced by Avicenna and the later mutakallimîn who were influenced by him to a mere "possible essence which when it exists concretely in the world is not in a substrate" (*cf.*, the discussion of Taftazânî, *loc.cit.* and *Šarḥ al-Mawâqif* 5, 10) while the metaphysical system is built chiefly on the notions of "essence" (*ḏât*) and quiddity (*mâhîya*), the possible and the necessary etc.,

6 Cf. Massignon, *Passion*, 549. This is not simply that they are "objets déterminables que le Coran isole" (*ibid.*) but that they are *objects*, *i.e.*, phenomenal objects of our immediate perception, which have color, movement, etc. It is for this reason that we find the common tendency, when real totalities and their qualities and attributes are in question (as opposed to a discussion of the *ǧawâhir* as such) to oppose "accident" and "body" rather than "accident" and "atom". (*Cf.* for example, *Intiṣâr*, 20f, where abû l-Hudhayl is cited, or *Maq.*, 345, where "motion, rest, standing, reclining," etc., are listed as "accidents, not bodies," *et alibi*). Body (*ǧism*) is not, strictly, itself an "accident" but rather as a kind of function of "accidents"; *cf. infra*.

7 Massignon, *op.cit.*, 553.

8 Pretzl, prejudiced by non-islamic systems, is determined that an atomism ought to be a "Naturerklärung" (*Atomenlehre*, 122ff) and finding himself unable to deal therefore with the qualitiless inertia of the *ǧawâhir* concludes to the primitivity of the kalâm (*cf. supra*, ch. 1). His problem is fundamentally that he wants to find within the composite itself an inherent principle which would explain the *nature* of the thing as that which persists in existence (*op.cit.*, 123). The fact is, however, that the denial of

in terms of their materiality at the level at which this materiality coincides with their atomic substrate.

In brief, the "atom" in the early kalâm is a constitutive element or principle in the *ontological* structure of created beings; it is not meant to give any explanation of the ontic structure or of the physical properties of phenomenal reality [9]. It is important to keep these two things distinct, for the system, as a genuine attempt of the mind to understand itself and the world, is comprehensible only in this way. The birth, "canonisation," and the longevity of this unique type of atomism in Islamic thought is founded precisely in the fact that it did render a truly coherent and intelligible explanation of the ontological or metaphysical structure of being as it was given to an experience paradigmatically moulded in Islam [10].

B. *The "Accidents" as the Reality of the Thing*

All phenomenal being, according to abû l-Hudhayl, is "accident" for the primary objects of our perception are palpable, composite bodies and the "accidents" which inhere in them : configuration, density, color, motion, etc [11]. Most important, bodies themselves, the basic constitutive units of created beings, are themselves in their being bodies, constituted by the "accidents" of composition (*ta'lîf*), conjunction (*iǧtimâ'*), contiguity (*mumâssa*), etc. [12]; that is, extended dimensionality or, more exactly in the terms of the system, the reality of dimension as such or real extension in space, by which a body is constituted as a body, has its reality and its being in the "accidents" of composition and conjunction and is not

---

the existence of any "nature" as an inherent principle of being and activity belonging properly and essentially to created things in and of themselves is a fundamental *apriori* for most of the kalâm; the importance of this assumption for our understanding of the kalâm has been noted above.

9 Arguments against the notion of "prime matter" (*hayûlà*) which ostensibly base themselves on ontic properties of material objects are no more indicative that the *ǧawâhir* are to be taken as physical "atoms" than do the counter arguments (those of Avicenna, for example), which show the same polemic base, indicate that *hayûlà* or *materia prima* is not a purely metaphysical concept. Given the very nature of the questions, ontic matter and ontological *materia* or *ǧawâhir* are not always kept completely distinct in the works of many ancient and medieval authors, though it is clear nevertheless that most major writers were quite well aware of the distinction. The same is true of abû l-Hudhayl's speculation about the contiguity of six "atoms" (*Maq.*, 302f and *Šarḥ al-Mawâqif* 6, 294).

10 It is to be noted that even later when the kalâm takes on a much more sophisticated dress, *viz.* the terminology of the falsafa, these basic theses, remain, restated but unchanged in their essential.

11 الاجسام ترى وكذلك الحركات والسكون والالوان والاجتماع والافتراق والقيام والقعود والاضطجاع وان الانسان يرى الحركة اذا راى الشيء متحركا (*Maq.*, 361).

12 *Cf. Maq.*, 302f, *et alibi.*

constituted as such simply by the atoms as atoms [13]. The specific dimensionality and configuration which belong to a thing and which determine and constitute the corporeal body whereby the thing is defined as such, is, in this way, the specific and particular "accidents" of length, etc., which arise "in the atoms" through the creation of the "accident" of composition, etc. All further attributes, properties, etc., which may belong to and define a thing are "accidents" which may be said to inhere in the specific body, not however as inhering in the body as such but rather as inhering separately and collectively in the "atoms" which make up the body as that body which it is. The formal reality of things is therefore "accident." The corporality of their materiality as also their every property, attribute, and accident, not only the material density and palpability of the body, but also the reality of its movements, as was noted above, is that of the realisation of an "accident." Al-Ǧuwaynî, therefore is quite correct in saying that the "*mulḥida*", (viz., the falâsifa) call the *ǧawâhir* ("atoms") by the term *hayûlà* (Greek, ὕλη: prime matter) and "accidents" by the term *ṣûra* ("form," Greek εἶδος) [14]. The "atoms" are in no sense the thing, but rather its reality in being that thing which it is and so also of its being the kind of thing which it is, is the reality of its being a particular aggregate of permanent and transitory "accidents" and its substantiality in existence is the substantiality in existence of the particular aggregate of created "accidents." To be such a thing is to be such a complex of "accidents."

C. *The Atom*

What then is the being of the "indivisible part"? There is no question of its reality within the ontological structure of things as abû l-Hudhayl conceives it, but we must examine the nature of this reality. It is, most simply, by definition a "substrate" (*maḥall*) for the realisation of "accidents" in the world. It is not, as was mentioned above, the "things," for their reality is that of their bodies and all of the "accidents" which adhere in them, permanent and transient. Again, the "atoms" are not, of themselves, in any way real bodies, for body, as such,

---

13 As has been pointed out by Pines (*Beitrage*, 5f) "atoms" are not bodies (*Maq.*, 307); rather "two things neither of which are long are conjoined and there arises a single length" [one long thing or something long] (*Maq.*, 315), body being that which is extended in three dimensions (*ibid.*, and 302f, 306). It is thus that Ibn Taymîya says that body arises as a function of "accidents": الاجسام هى مستلزمة للاعراض (*Muwâfaqa* 1, 186).

14 *'Iršâd*, 23: الجواهر فى اصطلاحهم تسمى الهيولى والاعراض تسمى صورة. Like certain other aspects of the kalâm, this finds an almost exact parallel in the teaching of the Stoa; cf. Max Pohlenz, *die Stoa* (Göttingen, 1948) 1, 66 and also Paul Kraus, *Jabir ibn Hayyan* 2 (Mémoires de l'Institut d'Egypte, 45, Cairo, 1942), 170.

arises as a function of the creation of the particular "accidents" of composition, etc., in a set of "atoms" together with the other "accidents" which qualify its corporeal nature. Ultimately then, the atoms form "points" for the localisation of being, the place or locus of the realisation of "accidents." In the constitution of a body, the simple and unmodified composition of "indivisible parts" forms a kind of skeleton of dimensionality and materiality: a structured framework of the *quanta of potential existence.* Thus, in a very strict sense, the atoms form the *materia prima* of beings in a system in which all being is realised in discrete and discontinuous units in space, — in atomistic quanta of single "things." [15]

The "atom" has no actuality, in one sense, apart from "accidents." Even God, the author holds, cannot strip it completely of them [16]. The minimum "accidents" are those which may inhere in a single isolated "atom" : movement, rest, contiguity, isolation, and *kawn* [17]. Within the categories of the system, these are no more than the basic "accidents" which, in their actuality constitute the reality of the presence of the "atoms" as defined, real points of possible existence in space [18]. They form, we should say, by their inherence therein, the reality of the spatial existence of the "atom" as a possible locus of other "accidents." Considered in itself, the "atoms" form a kind of absolute base for the potentiality of the *maqdûr 'alayhi* in its existence in the world.

However, the "atom" is an ontological reality distinct in itself, in that it is the stable substrate of a fluctuating multiplicity of momentary and enduring "accidents." Abû l-Hudhayl will not reduce the entire being of things to the "accidents" as do Ibrâhîm al-Naǧǧâr and Ḍirâr b. 'Amr [19], but insists on the reality of the substrate as the ontological, material base of the being of things. As that which

---

15 *Cf.* Gardet and Anawati, *Introduction,* 325 ("...la vision traditionelle que l'Islam s'est fait du monde : vision essentiellement discontinue."). The "atoms" at this early period were not, probably, considered as mathematical points, however; *cf.* Pines, *Beiträge,* 5f.

16 *Maq,* 311.

17 *Cf. Maq.,* 303, 311, 314f, *et alibi* and also *Maq.,* 325, *Šarḥ al-Mawâqif* 6, 166 (قال الجوهر فى اول زمان حدوثه كائن لا متحرك ولاساكن) and 2, 216 (though abû l-Hudhayl is not here mentioned by name, his position on the matter is cited); regarding *kawn* as an "accident" distinct from movement, rest, etc., and its relationship to these, cf. *supra,* ch. II, 2.

18 It is this difficulty of defining the *ǧawhar* as something (beyond the fact that it has a name) in itself which gave rise to the protracted debate over its nature, which is almost classically stated by al-Šaḥḥâm, abû 'Abdallâh al-Baṣrî, and Ibn 'Ayyâš, who, in the words of Ǧurǧanî, say that الجوهرية نفس التحيز (*Šarḥ al-Mawâqif* 2, 217; on the latter two *cf.* also abû Rašîd al-Nîsâbûrî, *K. al-Masâ'il,* 12). In the final analysis these basic "accidents", most particularly those of contiguity and isolation, hold here a place analogous to that of the *ṣûra ǧismîya* or *forma corporeitatis* in the system of Avicenna.

19 *Cf. Tabṣîr,* 62f; *Maq.,* 317f and 305f.

persists through successive changes in the creation and annihilation of "accidents," it has a permanence in existence which the great majority of "accidents" do not have. In and of itself however, it cannot be said in any way to have any higher degree of being or greater ontological substantiality than the "accidents," for it too has its being in the same way as the "accidents," through an act of creation, and whatever permanence in existence it has, again, lies in God's causing it to endure, as is also the case with the "accidents." Real things, which make up the world, bodies and their "accidents," exist only as composites of "atoms" and "accidents," within which the constituent parts are all alike dependent in the act of their existence upon God's immediate creation [20]. Neither the *ǧawhar* nor the *'araḍ* has the ground of its being strictly in the other. Given the history of the term, we may not therefore, properly apply to *ǧawhar* and *'araḍ*, in the kalâm, the terms "substance" and "accident"; to do so is to prejudice, most erroneously, the real meaning of the terms as the authors have used them. Indeed, it is utterly incorrect to say that in the system of abû l-Hudhayl substantial reality lies entirely or primarily in the "atoms." [21].

The being of all things and their substantiality in being lies in their being-created, for this is the ground of the totality of their being. We must, therefore, inquire briefly into the ultimate ontological structure of things in their being-created, if we are to discover and understand the nature of existence and the being of things as it is seen by abû l-Hudhayl.

---

[20] *Cf. Maq.*, 363 and *infra*, ch. V.

[21] One may, of course, apply the term "substance" to the *ǧawâhir* if it be done quite strictly within the limits, say, which Aristotle will allow for the application of the term οὐσία to ὕλη (*n.b.*, *Metaphysics* Z, ch.3, esp. 1029a, 10ff), as indeed the stoics used it.

V. THE BEING OF THE THING

In the period of abû l-Hudhayl the kalâm had not yet taken on the formally abstract vocabulary of Being which is found in the falsafa and the later kalâm, particularly from the beginning of the eleventh century. Here, on the contrary, the vocabulary of Being and Existence is that of creation (*ḫalq*), the initiation of a thing's existence (*al-ibtidâ'*), its continuation in existence (*al-baqâ'*), and the total cessation of its existence (*al-fanâ'*), as has been noted by Pretzl. [1] This fact, however, in no way impeded the incisiveness or the clarity of his thought nor obscured his vision in seeking to uncover and bring to light the ontological structure of created existence, nor, I should insist, indicates any naïveté whatsoever on the part of abû l-Hudhayl or of the other major islamic authors who used the same terminology [2]. Quite on the contrary, in the case of abû l-Hudhayl, despite the limited number of our texts and the biased selection of our sources, one can discern in his handling of the conceptual apparatus which he uses, a highly nuanced precision in his thinking and a remarkable penetration and insight into the most basic problems of metaphysics.

The being of a thing, which is the act by which it exists, is its being-created (*ḫalquhu, takwînuhu*). In a sense we might say that all created existence is event (*ḥâdiṯ, wâqi'*): that it be, i.e., that it "happen," occur in the real world (*ḥadaṯa, waqa'a*) is that it be created (*maḫlûq, muḥdaṯ*) and its reality in being is constituted by and grounded in its being-created. The formal reality of the thing, as was noted above, is the structured complex of its "accidents" so that its reality in being what it is consists in and is grounded in the actuality of the sum of its "accidents," as they adhere in the "substrate." Its substantiality in its being itself is the substantiality of the "accidents" in their inherence in their corporeal substrate. The thing *is* its "accidents" — *is* the complex of "accidents" which is it; its reality in being is the reality of the being of the specific "accidents" in the body as they form the aggregate sum which is the thing. Abû l-Hudhayl says then that from one standpoint "composition" (*ta'lîf*) is "the thing's being created composed," as also "length" is "the thing's being created long" or "color" is "the thing's being created colored [3]." Nothing could be more explicit. In the total complex of

---

1 Pretzl, *Attributenlehre*, 55.

2 *Cf. ibid.*; Pines (*Beiträge*, 19) speaks of an "inadequate conceptual apparatus; "cf. supra, ch.I.

3 *Cf. Maq.*, 366 and 511, *cit, infra*, n. 12.

"accidents" which is, in its aggregate totality, the formal being of the thing, its being such a thing or this kind of thing which it is (the *Sosein*) is constituted by and *is* the actuality of its being-created [4]. The act of being, then, by which it exists, which is its being-created, founds at once the reality of its existence and the plenitude of its being in being that thing which it is. There is no question here of a formal "essence" distinct from the actual existence of the thing; we have not to do with abstract "essences" (*ḏawât*) or quiddities (*mâhiyât*) and their createdness (*maǧ'ûlîya*) or intrinsic potentiality (*'imkân ḏâtî*) to be factually present (*wuǧûd*) in the world or to the mind, as in the later kalâm and the falsafa [5].

Prior to its actual existence in the world, a thing simply is not and in itself has no being whatsoever, save in that it is known by God as an object of His omnipotence (i.e., that it is *min maqdûrâtihi*), whose reality in being lies in the realisation of a particular act of His creation. Of and in itself it cannot be said to have any being at all; we cannot say that it potentially *is* or exists itself as a possible, for its being is its being-created and the potentiality of its actual existence consists entirely and unconditionally in God's eternal power-to-create. Prior to the actualisation of the being-created of the thing through the realisation of the act of God's creation, we cannot strictly say the thing potentially exists, *viz.*, that *it*

---

4 *Cf.* Taftazânî, *op. cit.* 87 and the remarks of al-Isfarâ'înî in the margins of the same (p. 89), who complains that in this way abû l-Hudhayl makes the act of creation subsist in the creature (*qâ'im bil-mukawwan*).

5 We keep in mind that the refusal by the early mutakallimîn to speak of "essences" cannot be considered as fortuitous, as was indicated in the preface; the concepts and the terms were "physically" available. This concentration on the concrete thing (*šay'*) and its ontological structure in the order of creation on the part of the early mutakallimîn and their almost total exclusion of any consideration of the logical structure of being, defines and expresses a specific attitude towards reality which most sharply differentiates it from the later writers (*cf.* the remarks of Gardet and Anawati in *Introduction*, 75f, though they do not treat the great mu'tazilî authors of the 11th century). This is not, I should again emphasise, any indication that the problems are not in fact known to the earlier authors, but rather that they took a specific stand on the whole question and analysed the order of being as it was manifested in its appearance within the world defined by that stand. Even in dealing with later authors, particularly in their discussion of their earliest predecessors, one must be quite careful to ascertain whether in using the term *ḏât* ("essence") the author means "essence" as a universal or, as is frequently the case, the individual thing considered in its essential nature in being that thing which it is. The origins of the technical use of the term *ḏât* probably arose out of the common بذاته and as a technical term may well be connected with the Syriac ܟܝܢܐ (*cf.*, بذاته = ܒܟܝܢܬܗ.) Nevertheless, it should be noted the roots of the distinction in the later kalâm and the falsafa, between *ḏât*/*mâhîya* and *wuǧûd*, are grounded in the kalâm, as has been noted by a number of authors (*cf.* Quadri, *la Philosophie arabe* (Paris, 1947) 102 and reference to Carra de Vaux, Gilson, *l'Etre et l'Essence* (Paris, 1948), 67, Gardet, *la Pensée religeuse d'Avicenne* (Paris, 1951), 45 and reference n. 2) albeit Goichon (*The Philosopher of Being* in *Avicenna Memorial Volume* (Calcutta, 1956) would find its origins in Aristotle and a passage of Plotinus (on which, *cf.* Roland-Gosselin, *de Ente et Essentia* [Paris, 1948], p. xix).

is a potential existent but properly only that there exists God's potentiality or power-to-create. Since abû l-Hudhayl recognises no "essence" or quiddity, there can be no question of potentiality which would reside in a kind of paradigm and which would belong to it as such and whose being would be the being of the "essence" wherefore we should be able to speak of the essential potentiality which belongs to the essence by virtue of its being itself, of itself, that essence which it is in itself, so that consequently the possibility of the thing would be grounded in the thing itself as the possibility of the essence to be realised and defined in the concrete, spatio-temporal existence of the individual.

The Mu'tazila is not infrequently accused of holding just such a position. The thesis, however, which is held by some mu'tazilî authors with a certain variety of detail and diversity of formulation, that the *thing*, prior to its actual, material existence in creation (*al-šay' al-ma'dûm*, *i.e.*, when it is not present in the world) is "something fixed and determined" (*šay' ṯâbit mutaqarrir*) in its createdness, is said to have been introduced into the kalâm by abû Ya'qûb al-Šaḥḥâm, a disciple of abû l-Hudhayl's [6], whereafter it was held by most of the principals of the Baṣra school [7]. The whole debate on this question, as it was later carried on, frequently in a purely abstract terminology of universals and "essences," begins in the question of the status of the particular, individual thing (whether a single *ǧawhar*, "accident," or a composite whole which exists as a single *thing*) as it is known eternally and intended by God as "this particular creature" and in the problem of the identity and self-continuity of the individual human person in the particularity of his unique individuality over the hiatus between death and the resurrection — a particular defined individual as a single person who has been defined in his own existence as the totality of his lived life, whom God will re-create in his total individuality and judge as such "on the last day [8]." Despite the paucity of fragments and the fact that we have no texts ascribed to abû l-Hudhayl which treat directly and explicitly the question of the being of the possible and its status in being prior to its created presence in the material world or, more exactly, its status in its non-presence-in-the-world (*al-'adam*), in that it is that thing which is to be created (*creandum*) itself that which it shall be, we can nevertheless glean from what little information is given in the sources and out of the general consistency of the system a reasonably clear conception

---

[6] *Cf. Nihâya*, 150 and *Milal*, 76.

[7] *Cf.* the list in Râzî's *Muḥaṣṣal*, 37f.

[8] Among others, *cf.* the remarks of Râzî in *K. al-'Arba'în*, 63 and generally the whole chapter. This is a complex problem whose treatment is far from simplistic in those writers who adhere to the thesis and the position of each must be studied in the contextual matrix of the particular system. *Cf.* also the following note.

of how he understood the possibility of existence of that which is not. The possibility of the existence, as the potentiality of a thing which materially exists in the world to continued existence and alteration has already been outlined in part above. Things, according to abû l-Hudhayl, discrete and individual, which exist, can be said to *be* and to have *their* existence only in the reality of their being themselves in themselves and identical with themselves in the actuality of their being-created, but, as was pointed out above, this, insofar as it is a real possibility, resides solely and unconditionally in God's power of creation. We cannot properly say that the thing *is* potentially existent in the state of its non-presence-in-the-world, but only that God's potentiality to create what He knows as the object of His power-to-create *is* and that this power, as such, is constitutive of itself in its reality and so also of the possibility of its objects. The objects, in themselves, have no being and are not themselves in themselves their own potentiality. A thing can itself be said to *be* only in its being a created being (*šay' maḫlûq*) in its being-created; *i.e.*, it exists itself in being, in itself, that thing which it is, only in the actuality of the realised act of its being-created (*ḫalquhu*). Considered in itself it has no being at all save in the created existence of the material composite which takes place (*ḥadaṯa*) in the concrete dimensions of time and place. [9] In this way then, a thing's being, in its being

---

[9] Cf. Râzî, *Muḥaṣṣal*, 34. The very statement of abû l-Hudhayl that "color" is the "thing's being created colored" etc., (*cf. infra*) is indicative. Nader, however (*Système*, 130) says that abû l-Hudhayl, al-Ka'bî and his disciples of the Baghdad school, held that "le néant possible d'exister" was something stable and fixed, etc. His citations to the *Šarḥ al-Mawâqif* I could not check, having no access to the edition from which he draws his citations (*viz.*, that of Constantinople, 1286); on the other hand, Ǧurǧânî does quite clearly and explicitly say in this work (ed. Cairo, 1325, vol. 2 p., 190) that *except for* abû l-Hudhayl, abû l-Husayn al-Baṣrî, and al-Ka'bî and his disciples of the Baghdad school, the Mu'tazila held that the thing, prior to its existence (*i.e.*, considered as a possible in the state of its non-existence as its non-presence-in-the-world), is something fixed and determined, etc.; in this he follows the same statement (though without reference to al-Ka'bî and his followers) in the *Nihâya* of Šahrastânî (*loc.cit.*). (Abû l-Ḥusayn Muḥammad b. 'Alî al-Basrî was a disciple of the Qâdî 'Abd al-Ǧabbâr, who broke with his master on this point; *cf.* Râzî, *I'tiqâdât*, 45 and also his *K. al-'Arba'în*, 53f and 59, Ibn al-Murtaḍà, *Ṭabaqât al-Mu'tazila*, [ed. S. Diwald-Wilzer, Wiesbaden, 1961] 118f. *Milal*, 130f and Ǧurǧânî, *op.cit.*, 2, 212f, who notes that his position on this point was similar to that of the Aš'arites) The habit common to many authors of ascribing, without qualification, the position of al-Balḫî to the Mu'tazila *in toto*, even though a number of mu'tazilî writers (besides those mentioned, *e.g.*, Hišâm al-Fuwaṭî — *cf. Maq.*, 158 and *Fiṣal* 5, 42) did not adhere to such a thesis, would arise from polemical considerations and from the fact that by the late 11th century the only surviving mu'tazilî schools were those of abû Hâšim and abû l-Ḥusayn al-Baṣrî, the latter in all probability being of little importance; as for our chief earlier sources, abû l-Ḥusayn, given the time of his activity, would hardly have been known to al-Baġdâdî, Ibn Ḥazm, or al-Isfarâ'înî.

It should be noted that the whole problem, especially insofar as one is concerned with the interpretation of the statements of earlier writers, is rendered difficult in great part because of the polemical way in which it is treated by many of our "orthodox" sources; it is set forth, for example, in the *Nihâya*

what it is, is altogether constituted by and grounded in the fact *that it is*, viz., the reality of its being-created. Apart from the terminology and considering the thing (*ens*) only in the concrete reality of its being itself in its being-created, we find in abû l-Hudhayl's conception of the existent thing an understanding analogous to the Aristotelian *οὐσία*, in that the thing's being what it is (*τὸ τί ἐστι*) is one with the fact it is (*ὅτι ἐστι, τὸ εἶναι*) [10]. The reality of the thing is the being-created of the "accidents" as they are the thing in their inherence in the "substrate," and its formal reality, in being that thing which it is, is not in any way separable from the reality of its spatio-temporal existence in being-created.

It should be said in passing that this restriction of the being and reality of the thing to its being and reality as it exists concretely in the world is not due to any inadequacy in the language and the terminology available to the author, i.e., to the fact that the terms for being and existence are "creation," "perdurance in existence," etc., for the problem of the reality and being of a thing as it is known by God as a possible or as a determined object of His power is discussed with considerable refinement by other authors using the same terminology [11]. The thing however, is not the ground of its own existence. This is not simply that the thing's being what it is is distinct from the fact that it actually exists; this is a fundamentally logical distinction with which abû l-Hudhayl does not concern himself. On the contrary, while it is identical with its being as its being-created (*ẖalq*), "that act of creation which is the thing's being-created that which it is" is itself "created" (*maẖlûq*) [12]. Being-created (*ẖalq*) is other than its ground

---

(150ff) or the *K. al-'Arba'in* (*loc. cit.*) in the form of a quasi debate in which the thesis that the "*šay' ma'dûm*" is "something" i.e., a being, is expounded in its most extreme form, *viz.*, as implying the eternity of "essences" and so of "things" in themselves, since it was precisely this which the opponents of the thesis felt to be the fundamental danger inherent in it. In his failure to study the texts carefully and to take all this into consideration, Nader completely misinterprets the facts (*Système*, 135) and contrary to all the evidence ends up by saying "n'est pas là un subterfuge auquel ont eu recours les mu'tazila pour dissimuler leur croyance à l'étérnité du monde... ?" ! Ǧurǧânî, though expressing himself in abstract terms which are basically foreign to the earlier kalâm, quite correctly notes in his discussion of the "createdness of quiddities" that the argument in this subject between the Mu'tazila and the 'Ašâ'ira is purely terminological (*cf. Šarḥ al-Mawâqif* 2,213 and 3, 40ff [*maqṣad* 6 : الماهيات الممكنة هل هي مجعولة], esp., 48ff; *cf.* also the remarks of Siyâlkûtî, *ibid.*, 2, 189 and 3, 46f) and carefully refers in his discussion to "the opinion ascribed to the Mu'tazila" (*ibid.*, 3, 50; this remark is picked up and discussed by Siyâlkûtî, *ibid.*, 3. 45 and also at 2, 198).

10 *Cf.* generally, Gilson, *l'Etre et l'Essence*, 46ff.

11 *Cf.*, for example, *Maq.*, 158f, *et alibi*.

12 قال ابو الهذيل الخلق الذى هو تاليف والذى هو لون والذى هو طول والذى هو كذا مخلوق فى الحقيقة (*Maq.*, 366); وخلق الله سبحانه للشىء مؤلفا الذى هو تاليف وخلقه للشىء ملونا الذى هو لون وخلقه للشىء طويلا الذى هو طول مخلوق فى الحقيقة *ibid.*, 511. *cf.* also the same statement, attributed to the 'aṣḥâb abî l-Hudhayl, *ibid.*, 189f.

which is the act of creation (*ḫalq*)! Abû l-Hudhayl has not simply taken the term *al-ḫalq* twice, once as active and once as passive, to play a game with the word but has analysed, rather, the density of that nexus which is most eloquently expressed in the absoluteness of the *maṣdar* [13], *viz.*, that point where the being of the thing as a being-created is the realisation of the act of creation. The ground of the thing's reality in its being-created and the actuality of its existence is the act of creation (*ḫalq*), but "the creation of a thing is other than the thing [14]." On the one hand, thus, it is one with the fullness of its own being, insofar as this is the reality of its being-created; that is, it is identical in its being what it is with the reality of its own existence, in that this act of existence is its being-created, while on the other hand, its being-created, as created is not its own self-sufficient and self-subsistent ground.

Viewed from this standpoint, whether in the initiation of its existence (*ibtidâ'uhu*), its continuance in existence (*baqâ'uhu*), or its passing totally out of existence (*fanâ'uhu*), the being of a thing, as the ground of its actuality, is the realisation of the act of the agent (*fâ'il qâdir*) [15] or Creator and so is distinct from it. "The initiation of existence is other than the thing initiated [16]" and "the perdurance of a thing in existence is other than that which perdures [17]". "In this way then, the ground of the existence of the thing in the act of its existence in the world is, insofar as it "belongs" to the agent and is the act of the Creator, distinct from the thing which exists, present in the world [18]. The creation which is the being-

---

13 Throughout this discussion it must be carefully borne in mind that the *maṣdar* or infinitive indicates, of itself, the event or act in a most stark and absolute way, without any direct reference to either agent or object (and so without being of itself either active or passive) or any notion of time relative to the speaker (*cf.* generally the remarks of Miskawayh in *al-Kitâb* [ed. Derenbourg, Paris, 1881], 79f). This semantic compactness of absoluteness of the form is very important. If, indeed, the beginnings of the kalâm represent an epochal moment in the history of human thought, there can be little doubt that certain elements of the linguistic structure of Arabic, such as the density of the *maṣdar*, played an important rôle therein. One must beware of pushing such a thesis too far, but on the other hand, there can be little question but that had the linguistic structure been other than it was, certain facts of the problems treated would perforce have been differently seen, stated, and treated. Linguistic differentiation is an irreducible source of variety and fecundity in the history of speculative thought and the fruitfulness of the work of the early mutakallimîn both for Islam and eventually, through the great falâsifa, for the West, lay thus in part in some of the unique qualities of the Arabic language and in what Heidegger has called "die Nennkraft des Wortes" (*Holzwege*³ [Frankfurt a/M., 1957], 35); *cf.* also the remarks of Gilson, *op. cit.*, 11.

14 خلق الشيء غيره *Maq.*, 366.

15 *Cf.* supra on the thing as *al-maqdûr 'alayhi*.

16 كان ثبت الابتداء غير المبتدا *Maq,*. 364.

17 البقاء غير الباقي, *Maq.*, 366.

18 That is, we must take "the thing which perdures" (*al-bâqî*) or "the thing created" (= "*that which results from*" the act of creation [*mâ waqa'a 'an al-qawl*]) as the thing in its being "this thing which it is."

created of the thing, in its being that thing, and which is "strictly speaking created" (*fî l-ḥaqîqati maḫlûq*) is founded in ("results from" — *waqaʿa ʿan*) [19] a simultaneous act of creation (*ḫalq*) [20] which "can only metaphorically be termed created [21]." For abû l-Hudhayl the being of a thing (*ḫalquhu*), in the reality of its existence in the world, is totally grounded in the act of God's will (*'irâda*) and in the act of creation which is "His saying 'be' (*kun*)" [22], as also its continuance in existence lies in God's saying "endure" (*ibqa*) and its passing out of existence in His saying "cease to exist" (*ifna*) [23]. "The thing created is that which results from God's saying 'be'." The ground of its being as the act of creation which is this "Be", because of its association with the reality, in time, of the thing which exists through, it can thus metaphorically be said to "become" and even to be created, but in itself, it is distinct from the thing and the temporality and spatiality of the world. As God's act of willing the thing and commanding it to *be*, the act of existence is strictly speaking uncreated [24] and forms no part of the created world; it is immaterial, "not in any place" (*lâ fî makân*) [25]. The author does not insist that the act of existence which is God's creative act (*al-ḫalq*, *al-baqâ'*, etc.) does not "occur" (*ḥadaṯa*) or have its actuality "in a place" or in a substrate (*maḥall*) — *viz.*, in the thing — merely in order to avoid having "an accident inhere in an accident" as has been suggested [26]. To exist in space is to inhere in

---

19 كل ذلك مخلوق فى الحقيقة (*Maq.*, 541) معنى مخلوق انه وقع عن ارادة من الله وهو واقع عن قول وارادة (*ibid.*, 366), *cf also ibid.*, 511.

20 والخلق مع المخلوق فى حاله *Maq.*, 363.

21 *Cf. Maq.*, 366 and 511.

22 خلق الله للشيء [الذى] هو تكوينه بعد ان لم يكن هو غيره وهو ارادته وقوله له كن ... وابتداء الله الشيء بعد ان لم يكن هو خلقه له وهو غيره (*Maq.*, 363f.); cf. also *ibid.*, 541 : انه واقع عن ارادة من الله وقوله له كن.

23 والبقاء غير الباقى والفناء غير الفانى والبقاء قول الله عز وجل للشيء ابق والفناء قوله افن *Maq.*, 366, *cf.* also *Farq*, 76, §5 and ان البقاء هو قول الله عز وجل للشيء ابقه وكذلك فى بقاء الجسم وفى بقاء كل ما يبقى من الاعراض *Maq.*, 359.

24 The term *ḥâdit* is used of it, for example, in *Farq*, *loc. cit.* and *'Uṣûl*, 51 and 106 (*cf.* also *Šarḥ al-Mawâqif* 5, 8f); *i.e.*, as being simultaneous with the thing it is not strictly *qadîm*, although it remains nevertheless strictly uncreated: ليس بمخلوق فى الحقيقة وانما يقال له مخلوق فى المجاز (*Maq.*, 510f)

25 *Maq.*, 363; *cf.* also *ibid.*, 369 and 189f and *Farq*, 76, *'Uṣûl*, 106. The use of the term *ʿaraḍ* (*Maq.*, 369) for this act of God's Will and His act of creation, if it was actually used by abû l-Hudhayl alongside *ḥâdiṯ* (*ibid.*, *cf.* also *supra*) is probably due in part to the lack of any other category in which to put it, since all being, other than that of God Himself, is ex-haustively divided by *ʿaraḍ* and *ǧawhar* (cf. Čelebî in *Šarḥ al-Mawâqif* 4, 99).

26 Cf. Pines, *Beiträge*, 25; on the question of the inherence of an "accident" in an "accident", *cf.* also *supra*.

a substrate (*ǧism*, *maḥall*, *ǧawhar*, etc.) and is consequently to be a creature. To say that the act was part of or inhered in the creature would be to involve one's self in the infinite regression of Mu'ammar's "*ma'ânî*" or to make the creature identical with the ultimate ground of its own being [27], while to make it inhere in some substrate of its own, *i.e.*, to give it an existence of its own as a material creature would make no sense at all [28]. In sum, to adapt a statement of Heidegger's "Sein kann nicht *sein*. Würde es sein bliebe es nicht mehr sein, sondern wäre ein Seiendes [29]." The ultimate ground of being cannot belong to the creature and cannot itself be created.

From one standpoint then, that the thing exist is identical with its being that particular, defined thing which it is and as such, we can say that the thing is itself subsistent in its own being; it is itself the being-created which is it. This act of existence, however, which is the reality of its being-created cannot be identical with the ultimate ground of its being, precisely insofar as it is the fullness of the thing in the concreteness of its being created. In itself, the thing is a being-created and this being constitutes its reality in the fullest content of its being. Though from one standpoint it is thus subsistent in its own being, it is, on the other hand, altogether contingent and dependent upon the act of creation which is the ultimate ground of its being. Again, we must keep in mind that the question here is not of the contingency of an "essence" in its real presence in the world, but of the being which is the reality of the thing in being, the *esse* which is the *perfectio entis*. Thus also, in itself and of itself, though subsistent in the world in its being-created, it remains an aggregate of "accidents" whose unity in being consists in the spatial conjunction of its parts (*'aǧzâ'* or *ǧawâhir*) or its body, together in isolation from other things. Considered, however in the act which created the juxtaposition and composition in space, which is the unity of the thing and the creation in the corporeal composite of all the other "accidents" which inhere in it, its unity is complete and perfect in its being that thing which it is;

---

27 It is precisely this of which al-Taftazânî complains (*op. cit. supra*, n. 4) concerning abû l-Hudhayl's statement that the being-created of the thing is its being that which it is, as is noted by 'Isâmuddîn al-Isfarâ'înî (*cit. ibid.*)

28 Fakhry seems not to have understood this completely when he says (*op. cit.*, 47) that "both abû l-Hudhayl and al-Jubbâ'î... further maintained the exceptional thesis that God could create an accident in no substratum..." He does note (*ibid.*) that such a thesis "was doubtless an expedient for interpreting their theological notion of the creation and the annihilation of the universe," but failed to grasp the real sense of this "expediency" having taken the statement of *Farq*, 76 at face value without analysing its meaning in terms of abû l-Hudhayl's context or taking into account the polemical nature of al-Baġdâdî's account.

29 *Kants These über das Sein* (Frankfurt a/M., 1963), 35.

its ontological density, in the ground of its existence, in being itself the totality of that which it is, is that of a true unity.

In the same way, as was pointed out above, the thing cannot strictly be said to be its own potentiality. Its potentiality resides rather in the potentiality (*qudra*) of the source of its being. Of and in itself it has not, strictly speaking, either its own actuality in existence or its own potentiality but is ever a creature subject to the power of its creator — *maḫlûq maqdûr ʿalayhi.*

To sum up then, the thing is itself subsistent in its own being, which is the principle of the total content of its being that thing which it is in the actuality of its being, but this being is a being-created which is altogether contingent upon an act of creation which is uncreated and totally independent of the thing and of any worldly contingency. In the scholastic terminology, it is from one aspect an *ens subsistens*, whose *esse* is the principle of its total reality (*perfectio essendi*), but its *esse*, as the act of that reality which it is, being an *esse creatum* is not *per se subsistens* but is itself grounded in an uncreated act which is *per se subsistens, viz.*, God's Will and Creative Command. We have thus in abû l-Hudhayl an understanding of the ontology of the created thing (the *ens creatum* and its *esse creatum*) which is in some ways more akin to St. Thomas' understanding of the relation between *esse* and *essentia* than to Avicenna's conception which is one of the difference rather between *quidditas* and *existentia* [30]. For abû l-Hudhayl the question is not that of the mere factual state of being present in the world or in the mind as this state constitutes the factic mode of existence of a determined thing but rather of the ontological structure of reality at a far more basic level.

---

30 On this question generally and the difference between the two points of view (which are not by necessity mutually exclusive) *cf.* the excellent discussion of E. Coreth, *die Metaphysik*² (Innsbruck, 1964) §25, pp. 180ff, esp. *Zusatz* 1 pp. 187ff, where he treats of the difference between the positions of St. Thomas and Suarez.

II

THE DIVINE ATTRIBUTES ACCORDING TO THE TEACHING OF ABU L-HUDHAYL AL-'ALLAF *

Abû l-Hudhayl al-'Allâf, who died sometime about 841 at well beyond the commonly allotted three score years and ten, was not only the first of the great Mu'tazilite masters but was, in a real sense, the founder of the classical Mu'tazilite tradition. His lifetime spans the period in which most of the fundamental traditions of Islam were created out of the initial chaos of its quest for self-identity within the bewildering intellectual and religious diversity of the civilisations of which it made itself heir when it came forth in conquest from the more sheltered confines of its birthplace. Abû l-Hudhayl was witness to the foundation of the institutions of 'Abbasid rule, the acme of its power and the beginnings of its lapse into decline. He saw the establishment of the four great schools of law and the concomitant rise of traditionism as well as the beginnings of the ṣufi tradition.

In the historical context of this period, the kalâm — the *discourse* on the principles of Islamic dogma — was of great importance, not merely in terms of the questions of the Imamate and the definition of who is a believer (and so a member of the community of faith), but more importantly to define the essential dogmas (τὰ δοκοῦντα) as such and to give an account of the community's belief and fix the sense of the revelation. The kalâm served as an apologetic and as the vehicle for formulating and defining the content of Islam's faith. We read of disputes (and it was the dispute — *al-munâẓara* — that gave the kalâm its characteristic form of literary expression) between the early mutakallimîn and the dualists, Jews, and Christians, but there were also disputes between the mutakallimîn themselves and formally organised sessions to discuss points of theology (the *maǧâlis an-naẓar*) and it is to these, no doubt, that the Muslim practice of theology chiefly owes its development, for it was here that the questions of what it means to call God creator, of what is the nature of the world and of the created as created, and what is the nature of

* This study was begun under a grant from the American Council of Learned societies for which the author is most grateful.

revelation as revelation and of the « speech of God » as speech and as God's had to be elaborated so that the believer might have a satisfying thematic understanding of his own belief.

The teaching of abû l-Hudhayl concerning the divine attributes, which I propose to examine in the pages that follow, is important from several standpoints. It is not only very early in date — perhaps the earliest system of which we have sufficient information to gain a reasonably comprehensive view — but it lies as the foundation of the theology that, developed and refined in successive generations of abû l-Hudhayl's disciples, was to become the predominant and most influential among all the branches of the Muʿtazila. The system presents itself as one that is highly articulated and strikingly original in many aspects though containing, at the same time, a number of difficulties and knots that would have to be worked out by the succeeding generations of the school. Given the early, almost pioneering character of his work, this is to be expected. The great surge of Islam's eager assimilation and adaptation of the thought and sciences of past ages and other peoples was begun and all kinds of materials, pagan and Christian, were becoming progressively available, orally and in writing. Muslim thought and doctrine was yet plastic as it sought to build itself and achieve understanding of itself through systems and elements of systems not yet fully adapted to an Islamic context. Although abû l-Hudhayl's thought is thoroughly and unequivocally Islamic in almost every respect, one yet sees quite clearly that he was unable to arrive at a complete integration of the system, for to certain of its elements there cling still some shreds of the diverse origins from which they were taken. For the historian, the examination of the system in the author's attempt to integrate it is instructive in two ways : as it sheds some light on the character of the sources of his doctrine as he tried to build a new and Islamic theology and as the comparison of abû l-Hudhayl's thought with that of his followers reveals, in their treatment of the master's teaching, the primary direction of the school's (and with it, in a sense, Islam's) evolution in the specific topics that presented them the greatest difficulty. It is because of this dual interest that I have digressed once or twice in what follows from the strictly circumscribed subject of the doctrine of abû l-Hudhayl, most particularly in taking up one patristic source that bears a remarkable similarity not merely to the thought of abû l-Hudhayl but more clearly to that, better documented, of the later masters of the school.

It were best to begin with the examination of several passages of al-Aš'arî's *Maqâlât al-Islâmîyîn* in which he outlines the basic teaching of abû l-Hudhayl concerning the nature of God's essential attributes.

Abû l-Hudhayl said : « He is knowing in an act of knowing that is He and is *qâdir* in a power of efficient causality that is He and is living in a life that is He » and he spoke in similar fashion concerning His hearing, seeing, eternity, might, majesty, glory, grandeur, and concerning His other essential attributes. Further he used to say : « When I say 'God is knowing', I affirm that He has an act of knowing that is God and deny that there is ignorance in God and indicate that there is something known [by Him] that has come to be or will come to be; when I say *qâdir*, I deny that there is any incapability of efficient causation in God and affirm that He has a power of efficient causality that is God and indicate that there is something subject to [His] power of efficient causality; when I say 'God has life' I affirm that He has a life that is God and deny that there is non-life in God » [1].

Their master, abû l-Hudhayl al-'Allâf said : « The creator's act of knowing is He and so also His power of efficient causality, His hearing, His seeing, and His wisdom ». He spoke in similar fashion concerning His other essential attributes and asserted that when he asserted that the Creator is knowing he affirmed the reality of an act of knowing that is God, denied that there is ignorance in God, and indicated that there is something known [by Him] that has come to be or will come to be; and that when he asserted that the Creator is *qâdir*, he affirmed the reality of a power of efficient causality that is God, denied that there is any incapability of causation in God and indicated that there is something subject to [His] power of efficient causality that has come to be or will come to be. So also concerning the rest of the essential attributes, he spoke using the same formula. When some one would say to him, « Tell us about God's act of knowing that is He; do you hold that it is His power of efficient causality ?,» he would say no to this proposition, though when asked « Is it distinct, then, from His power of efficient causality ? », he would refuse this proposition too, albeit this is the kind of thing he refused to allow from his opponents (viz., their statement that God's act of knowing is not said to be God nor is it said to be distinct from Him) [2]. Whenever some one said to him, « When you say that God's knowing is God, then say that God (the Exalted) is an act of knowing », he disagreed and would not say that He is an act of knowing, despite his saying that God's knowing is God [3]. When some one said to abû l-Hudhayl, « Do you say that God has an act of knowing ? », he would reply : « I say that He has an act of knowing that is He and that He is knowing in an act of knowing that is He ». He spoke in the same way concerning the other essential attributes. Thus abû l-Hudhayl denied the

[1] *Maqâlât al-Islâmîyîn* (ed. H. Ritter, Istanbul, 1929-30), 165.

[2] The opponents al-Aš'arî has in mind would seem to be Ibn Kullâb and his followers in that Ibn Kullâb is specifically named in an exactly parallel context later in the same work (p. 177); J. van Ess, however, suggests (*Ibn Kullâb und die Miḥna, Oriens* 18-19 [1967], 112f.) that Hišâm b. al-Ḥakam may well be a more likely candidate.

[3] *Maqâlât*, 484; cf. generally *ibid.*, 177 and al-Baġdâdî, *Uṣûl ad-Dîn* (Istanbul, 1346/1928), 90f.

act of knowing insofar as some one might mistake him to have affirmed it to be [ontologically distinct], since in fact he affirmed the reality of the Creator alone. He used to say : « The meaning of the proposition 'God is knowing' is that of the proposition 'He is *qâdir*' and the meaning of the proposition 'He is living' is 'He is *qâdir*'. » This follows necessarily since he did not affirm the reality of any attributes belonging to the Creator which are not He and he affirmed only the reality of the Creator alone [4]. When some one would ask him how the attributes differ so that one says 'knowing' and says '*qâdir*' and says 'living', he replied : « Because the object of the act of knowing differs from the object of the power of efficient causality » [5].

Even from a superficial reading of these texts it is plain to see that abû l-Hudhayl's conception of God and His attributes is akin to and, in its formulation, fundamentally derivative of the quasi neoplatonic theology long current among Christian theologians. He does not wish to understand the oneness of God in the radical terms of the neoplatonic One but rather his model is, so to speak, that of Mind, for the act of Mind is thought, life, etc., and within the unity of its being, Mind determines, in the act of its knowing, the being of all beings. Its « attributes are in it all one (*ma'an*), not separately or in distinct places... and therefore it is called by the name of each one of them » [6]. His teaching, in brief, would appear to be a fairly straightforward equivalent to common neoplatonic doctrine or its Christian adaptations; he is, in fact, specifically accused of having borrowed his teaching from Greek sources. Al-Aš'arî says that « abû l-Hudhayl took this doctrine from Aristotle, as Aristotle says in one of his works that the Creator is entirely an act of knowing, entirely a power of efficient causality, entirely an act of living, entirely an act of hearing, and entirely an act of seeing. He improved the

[4] This statement needs to be qualified in terms of abû l-Hudhayl's conception of God's will, on which see below.

[5] *Maqâlât*, 485f.

[6] *Theology of Aristotle* (ed. A. Badawi, Cairo, 1955), 71, 6f., reading *tusammà* for *yusammà* in line 7 with Dieterici's text (Leipzig, 1882, p. 61, 1); the error (or variant) is noted neither by Thillet (*Arabica* 5 [1958], 61 and 65) nor by Lewis in his review in *Oriens* 10 (1957), 395ff. In its own context the citation is only marginally pertinent to the present discussion but the parallelism of formulation is significant given that there are other grounds for establishing some kind of relationship between abû l-Hudhayl and the *Theology* (see below).

formulation, according to his own notion, and so said 'His act of knowing is He and His power of efficient causality is He' » [7].

Whether the assertion of abû l-Hudhayl's dependence on this source is original with al-Aš'arî or not is immaterial. Eager interest in the thought and sciences of antiquity and the translation of ancient writers began almost at the outset of the 'Abbasid age and there is good evidence that among the contemporaries of abû l-Hudhayl knowledge of Aristotle and discussion of his doctrines were not uncommon. Ibn al-Murtaḍà says that abû l-Hudhayl investigated the works of Aristotle [8] and among his contemporaries an-Naẓẓâm is reported to have made a detailed rebuttal of one of his works [9] and Ḍirâr b. 'Amr to have written a work in refutation of the Aristotelian conceptions of *οὐσία* and *τὸ κατὰ συμβεβηκός* [10]. Even so, though a part of the organon was early put into Arabic by the son of Ibn al-Muqaffa', the work of translating the corpus of philosophical works did not begin in full earnest until the reign of al-Ma'mûn, which is well after the formative period of abû l-Hudhayl's theology, so that the precise form and manner in which the earliest mutakallimîn got their Aristotle is somewhat uncertain [11]. It is clear, at any rate, that while some of their Aristotle was genuine some was spurious. Now although al-Aš'arî's citation of Aristotle belongs to this latter category, as has been pointed out [12], it does nevertheless have some significance for the background of abû l-Hudhayl's teaching even if, perhaps, indirectly. Whatever may be the remote origins of this citation, it

[7] *Maqâlât*, 485. It is curious to note that Ibn ar-Râwandî is cited by al-Ḫayyâṭ (*al-Intiṣâr* [reprinted by A. Nader, Beyrouth, 1957], 59) as saying that « not one person of all mankind was so brash as to say this before him ».

[8] *Ṭabaqât al-Mu'tazila*, ed. S. Diwald-Wilzer (Wiesbaden, 1961), 44.

[9] *Ibid.*, 50, cited by J. van Ess in *Ḍirâr ibn 'Amr und die Cahmîya, Der Islam* 43 (1967), 256, q.v.

[10] Ibn an-Nadîm, *al-Fihrist* (ap. J. Fück, in *Professor Muhammad Shafi Presentation Volume*, Lahore, 1955), 69, nº 14.

[11] Cf. van Ess, *op. cit.*, 261.

[12] Cf. H. Wolfson, *Philosophical Implications of the Problem of Divine Attributes in the Kalam*, *JAOS* 79 (1959), 78, who wants (cf. *ibid.*, 44) to find the source of the citation in the *Metaphysics* but offers no convincing evidence to support his hypothesis and O. Pretzl, *Die frühislamische Attributenlehre* (*SBAW* 1940, 4), 13 (cited by van Ess in *Oriens* 18-19, 112), who suggests that the pseudo-Aristotelian *Theology* might be the work that al-Aš'arî has in mind; his German citation is, however, either incorrect or represents a distorted paraphrase of the passage cited above, n. 6, by which he inserted the term *Allâh* for *'aql*.

is clear from the introduction of the nouns « hearing » (*sam'*) and « seeing » (*baṣar*) that, in its present form it stems from an Islamic source, either from the work of a Muslim author or from one that has been adapted to an Islamic topology, even though it is most probable that al-Aš'arî believes the attribution to Aristotle to be correct. In form and content the citation bears a remarkable similarity to formulae that are attributed in several sources to the ǧahmîya. For example, Aḥmad b. Ḥanbal reports that they hold that God « is entirely face, entirely light, entirely power » [13] to which list one manuscript significantly adds the phrase « and entirely an act of knowing » (*huwa kulluhu 'ilm*) [14]. Ad-Dârimî, again, in his *Radd 'alà l-ǧahmîya* gives a fuller form of the same thing : « His act of hearing, His act of seeing, and His act of knowing, in their opinion, are but a single thing, so that to their way of thinking the act of hearing is not distinct from the act of seeing nor is the act of seeing distinct from the act of hearing, nor is the act of knowing distinct from the act of seeing. He is, in their opinion, entirely an act of hearing, an act of seeing, and an act of knowing » [15]. In one place, finally — though the context is clearly polemical — al-Aš'arî identifies, by implication at least, the teaching of abû l-Hudhayl with that of the ǧahmîya [16].

Several years ago I suggested that fundamentally the ǧahmîya represent a primitive attempt to found a neoplatonic school of Islamic theology and also that although the evidence is admittedly tenuous, there is some ground on which to offer an hypothesis that they are

[13] *Radd 'alà l-ǧahmîya* in *Darulfünun Ilahiyat Mecmuasi* V-VI (1927), 315, 10f. (translated in SEAL, *Muslim Theology* [London, 1964], 98).

[14] Cf. S. PINES, *Beiträge zur islamischen Atomenlehre* (Berlin, 1936), 125, n. 1.

[15] Ed. G. VITESTAM (Lund-Leiden, 1960), 39; on the parallel in the *Radd* of Ibn Ḥanbal, cf. *ibid.*, Introduction, p. 21, n. 3 and concerning the problem of the interpretation of these statements within the general context of the teaching of the ǧahmîya, cf. my *The Neoplatonism of Ǧahm ibn Ṣafwân*, *Le Museon* 78 (1965), 417ff. In connection with the citation of al-Aš'arî mentioned above (n. 7), Pretzl (*loc. cit.*) suggests also a possible parallel in Xenophanes, viz., DIEHLS, fr. 24 : *οὗλος ὁρᾷ οὗλος νοεῖ, οὗλος δὲ τ'ἀκούει* (which he paraphrases, « Er ist ganz Auge, ganz Verstand, ganz Ohr »); there is, however, no genuine parallelism here and even if there were a verbal parallelism one would have to take it as purely fortuitous, for Xenophanes is far too remote to have any proximate historical significance for the kalâm. Whatever the sources for the diverse theories of the first generations of mutakallimîn, they had to come from current, active school traditions.

[16] *Al-Ibâna* (Cairo, n.d.), 39f.

somehow connected with the sources out of which came the Arabic Plotinus tradition and with it the *Theology of Aristotle*[17]. This work, it is obvious, could not — at least in the form in which we have it — have played any role in the formation of abû l-Hudhayl's thought, for he was an extremely old man when the translation of Ibn Nâʿima al-Ḥimṣî was published. Nor, on the other hand, can one speak with much confidence of any direct ǧahmî influence on him, even though it has been frequently stated that the ǧahmîya had a profound influence on the formation of Muʿtazilite theology[18], for unless one were prepared to assert that they were the sole purveyors of neoplatonic or neoplatonizing doctrine and formulae accessible to Muslim thinkers prior to the 9th century, some more concrete evidence of such influence will have to be adduced. We have, unfortunately, very little firm historical information at all concerning the ǧahmîya[19]. That the handful of reports we have seem to reflect a reasonably coherent doctrine of identifiable character would, at least, point to a master — most probably Ǧahm — and surely a number, no matter how small, of disciples who spread his teaching sufficiently to provoke the explicit condemnation of abû Ḥanîfa, Ibn Ḥanbal, and generations of the latter's followers. The school — to the extent that one may legitimately refer to such — was short lived, but whatever its spread and whatever its influence, they belong to the period of abû l-Hudhayl's formation.

Within all this the exact place and character of the ǧahmîya are tantalizingly ambiguous; some elements of their terminology and their seemingly thoroughgoing neoplatonism would appear surely to indicate some possible connection with the first beginnings of the Arabic Plotinus tradition and it is, thus, not insignificant that al-Ašʿarî attributes, in the passage cited above, a characteristically ǧahmî statement to Aristotle. On the other hand, however, one gets the impression that the ǧahmîya (at least that group indicated by the sources) were interested not in philosophy but in theology; i.e.,

[17] *Le Museon* 78 (1965), 395-7.

[18] Cf. Pines, *loc. cit.*; Wolfson, *op. cit.*, 75; Seal, *op. cit.*, 47f.; Nyberg, art. *Muʿtazila* in *EI*, and also H. Laoust, *Classification des sectes dans le* Farq *d'al-Baghdadi*, *REI* 29 (1961), 20. For a most careful appreciation of Ǧahm's relation to the beginnings of the Muʿtazilite kalâm, see van Ess in *Der Islam* 43, 241-279 and 44, 1-70.

[19] Cf. *ibid.*; W.M. Watt in *JRAS* 1963, 38ff.; *Le Muséon* 78, 395ff., and W. Madelung, *Der Imam al-Qâsim ibn Ibrâhîm und die Glaubenslehre der Zaiditen* (Berlin, 1965), 18ff., and index.

in what might be dubbed a neoplatonically oriented kalâm [20]. Significantly, in this connection, M.S. Seale has suggested that there are identifiable origenistic elements in the teaching of the ǧahmîya [21], and in regard to the formula « he is entirely... » (*huwa kulluhu...*) employed in the pseudo-Aristotelian source which al-Aš'arî believes to have been used by abû l-Hudhayl, it may be noted that Origen speaks, in one place, of « *natura illa simplex et tota mens* » [22]. This is particularly interesting since there are several strikingly near parallels between certain positions of Origen and abû l-Hudhayl (see below) but even so the significance of this formula remains at best minimal since it is not uncommon. For example, whereas the ǧahmîya, following a thoroughly « Greek » or neoplatonic reasoning, reject the notion that God has any will (*irâda* = βούλησις) [23], we find in Theodoret the statement that « God is entirely will » [24]; both of these conceptions are equally opposed to the teaching of abû l-Hudhayl. At this point, then, we can only say that though al-Aš'arî had, no doubt, a definite source in mind when he asserted that abû l-Hudhayl's conception of God's essential attributes derived from an « Aristotelian » work, his statement is based on outright conjecture. Very little is known concerning abû l-Hudhayl's theological background [25] and to seek

[20] It is worth pointing out in this connection that a christianized form of the *Enneades* may well have been in circulation. We find, for example, a number of citations of Plotinus, embedded without acknowledgement and modified where needed to suit a Christian context, in the glosses of John of Scythopolis (mid-6th century, cf. K. KRUMBACHER, *Geschichte der byzantinischen Literatur*² [München, 1897], p. 56) to the pseudo-Dionysian treatise *On the Divine Names*, of which a goodly number of Syriac copies are yet extant; cf. for example, the longish citation in Br. Mus. ms. Syr. Add. 12151, fol. 115R° 16-31 = III 8, 2, 6-31 of the *Enneades* and the paraphrase in fol. 114V° 31-38 of I 8, 12-13, 7. These glosses have been assimilated into the commentary of Maximus the Confessor from which they can be extracted with the aid of the Syriac.

[21] *Op. cit.*, see index s. Origen; see also infra n. 85.

[22] *De Principiis* I, 1, 6 (ed. KOETSCHAU, *CGS* 5, p. 21, 17f.).

[23] Cf. *Le Muséon* 78 (1965), 414, n. 82 and 423f.

[24] *Quaestiones et responsiones ad orthodoxos*, Q. 144 (*PG* 6, 1396D) : ... καὶ τὸ ἁπλοῦν ... καὶ ὅλον βουλή ἐστι καὶ ὅλον βουλὴν ἔχον ἐστιν. On the attribution of this work to Theodoret, cf. P. CANIVET, *Théodoret de Cyr, Thérapeutique...* I (*Sources Chrétiennes*, 57, Paris, 1958), 25, n. 6.

[25] For information on his biography, cf. Nyberg's article « abû l-Hudhayl » in *EI*²; he is reported to have studied with a certain 'Uthmân aṭ-Ṭawîl who, in turn, was a disciple of Wâṣil b. 'Aṭâ', but of 'Uthmân's teaching nothing is known and little is certain concerning that of Wâṣil, in that most reports are late and, one suspects, represent fundamentally the teachings of classical Mu'tazilite dogma projected back upon the « founder » of the sect; cf. generally, VAN ESS, *op. cit.*, 11f.

sources by grasping at the straws of too easily paralleled formulae is fruitless. A close examination of the system will reveal several possible origins, more or less identifiable as to their general character, for certain of abû l-Hudhayl's teaching but what is more revealing for the history of the kalâm is to discover how the diverse elements of the system were combined, with a high degree of originality, into a new and Muslim theology.

To return, then, to the fragments, it would seem reasonably clear that abû l-Hudhayl's aim in the passages cited above was to describe God as absolutely one in the perfect unity of His being, so that, although we speak of the perfections or attributes of His being and predicate them of Him as truly belonging to Him, what is signified by the attribute is precisely God Himself in the perfection which is His being: *nomina significant substantiam divinam et praedicantur de Deo substantialiter* [26]. In brief, he wanted to affirm the ontological reality of the attributes which the *Koran* gives to God (which God gives Himself, in Muslim terms) without implying any division or plurality in His being. Thus « he affirmed the reality of God alone » in such a way that the statements « God is knowing », « is *qâdir* », etc., have the same meaning [27], in that they do not refer to the presence in Him of distinct and separate perfections or acts (*ma'ânî*) but to God Himself. The attributes or perfections of God are distinguished by their objects that we distinguish [28]. Insofar as the difference (*iḫtilâf*) belongs to the objects and not to God, the distinction of perfections would be simply *ad modum intelligendi* [29]. That this is the sense of his position would seem confirmed by the fact that, with the exception of God's act of willing and the creative command 'Be', which are immediately connected with the temporality of the genesis of created beings, abû l-Hudhayl appears to have made all the divine attributes eternal perfections of God's being, including His hearing and seeing [30] and even, it seems, His mercy, beneficence,

[26] St. Thomas Aquinas, *Summa Theologica* I, 13, art. 3, corp.

[27] *Maqâlât*, 486, cited above.

[28] *Ibid.*, 486.

[29] On the problem of sameness and difference according to abû l-Hudhayl see below, n. 79.

[30] « The sense of my saying 'hearing' (*samî'*) is that I affirm an act of hearing that is God and deny deafness in God... », *Maqâlât*, 174; cf. also *ibid.*, 165 and 484. Ibn Ḥazm (*Fiṣal* [Cairo, 1321] 4, 193, 7) says, without qualification, that abû l-Hudhayl denied that God is *samî' baṣîr*, but this is clearly erroneous. Pazdawî (*Uṣûl ad-dîn* [ed. H. Linns,

etc. [31], which later followers of the school tended to consider, in one way or another, as « attributes of action » because of their correlation to the temporality of creation. The complete identity of these perfections with God's being, again, would seem significantly to be emphasised by the inclusion among the attributes identical with God, in the lists given by al-Aš'arî, of His majesty (*'azama*), might (*'izza*),

Cairo, 1383/1963], 31) says that he affirmed these attributes but does not differentiate his position from that of al-Ǧubbâ'î and abû Hâšim.

[31] Šahrastânî, in the *Milal* (ed. M. Badran, Cairo, 1328/1910 - 1375/1955, p. 75f.) lists, along with *samî'* and *baṣîr*, as eternal attributes *ġafûr*, *raḥîm*, *muḥsin*, *ḫâliq*, *râziq*, etc., and if *lam yazal samî'an* implies an attribute identical with God's being, so also will be the case the with the others. The list does not contain *murîd* since this he held to be temporal (cf. *infra*); the inclusion of *ḫâliq* is curious. Šahrastânî goes on to say, however, that abû l-Hudhayl qualified his position concerning the eternity of these attributes saying that « from eternity God is seeing and hearing in the sense that from eternity He will hear and will see [*sayasma'u wa-sayubṣiru*] and so also with the attributes of forgiveness, etc. » Al-Aš'arî records a somewhat similar report from Ǧa'far b. Ḥarb (*Maqâlât*, 173 and 486), according to whom abû l-Hudhayl did not say that God « is hearing and seeing from eternity in the sense 'he sees and hears' [*yasma'u wa-yubṣiru*] since that would require the actuality of the being of the seen and the heard » but al-Aš'arî goes on to say that in his opinion the report is erroneous. The thesis reported by Ǧa'far b. Ḥarb is somewhat similar to that held by al-Ǧubbâ'î, viz., that God is said to be eternally *samî' baṣîr* but not *sâmi' mubṣir* since the latter terms are transitive and imply the actuality of their concrete objects which cannot be eternal, in contrast to the former adjectives which are intransitive and imply only the ability to hear (cf. *Maqâlât*, 175., 'Abd al-Ǧabbâr, *Šarḥ al-uṣûl al-ḫamsa* [ed. A. Ousman, Cairo, 1384/1965] 167f., and also *al-Muġnî* 12 [ed. I. Madkour, Cairo, n.d.], 59, 10-15 and al-Baġdâdî, *op. cit.*, 97). — Ǧa'far b. Ḥarb, as a younger contemporary who had close contacts with abû l-Hudhayl, ought to be a fairly reliable source and it is noteworthy that neither he nor Šahrastânî indicates that abû l-Hudhayl made any distinction of terms as al-Ǧubbâ'î did. This is significant in that it would appear that abû l-Hudhayl made a consistent effort to keep as far as possible always within the strict verbal terms of the revelation in interpreting the divine attributes (see below) and it may be, therefore, that these reports reflect something of the teaching of the school before al-Ǧubbâ'î's elaboration of a much freer approach to the question of the divine names. On the other hand, al-Aš'arî is an exceptionally accurate reporter and while recounting fully the teaching of al-Ǧubbâ'î on this subject, he does explicitly state that he does not feel that the report of Ǧa'far b. Ḥarb can be substantiated. Again, one notes that in his lists of the attributes which abû l-Hudhayl held to be substantially identical with God, including *sam'* and *baṣar*, al-Aš'arî mentions none of the attributes normally identified as attributes of action (*ṣifât al-fi'l*) which Šahrastânî gives in his list. The silence of 'Abd al-Ǧabbâr on the subject is inconclusive and in the final ananysis one can only say that it is not possible, on the basis of present information, to clarify the detail of abû l-Hudhayl's teaching regarding these attributes.

glory (*ǧalâl*), etc. [32], and more especially His eternity (*qidam*) [33] which would seem predicated, at least implicitly, of the other attributes. In this way, though he follows al-Aš'arî's conjecture of dependence upon a Greek source, Šahrastânî would seem to be essentially correct in saying that abû l-Hudhayl « simply picked up this doctrine from the philosophers who believe that His essence is one, containing no plurality in any way whatsoever and that the attributes are not, besides the essence, determinant perfections (*ma'ânî*) subsistent in His essence, but rather are His essence itself » [34].

God's being will, then, be identical with His attributes or perfections, as in the Aristotelian formula *οὐσία = ἐνέργεια*. The divine essence, being one in the unity of its perfections, all the perfections that we distinguish will, in reality, be one in that each is perfectly coextensive with the act of God's being, so that His power is His knowing, etc.; in scholastic terms, *in Deo est idem potentia, et essentia... et intellectus, et sapentia, et justitia* [35]. The logic of this is seen clearly enough by abû l-Hudhayl's opponents. Šahrastânî says polemically that « these attributes are aspects (*wuǧûh*) of the Essence, precisely equivalent of the hypostases of the Christians » [36] and most of his non-mu'tazilite opponents accuse him of teaching, implicitly at least, that God is an act of knowing (*'ilm*) or an act of *qudra* and that His knowing is identical with His power, etc. [37]. Both of these theses, however (sc. that the perfections are completely

[32] *Maqâlât*, 165, 177. Note that the ǧahmîya held that God's *'aẓama* is created (*muḥdaṯ*); cf. *Le Muséon* 78, 418.

[33] *Maqâlât*, 165 and 180; on this and the significant absence of the term *wuǧûd* from the lists see below.

[34] *Op. cit.*, 71.

[35] Aquinas, *op. cit.* I, 25, a5 *ad* 1; such a thesis is explicitly allowed by Ibn Ḥazm (*op. cit.*, 3, 129; cf. also *ibid.*, 148f.).

[36] *Milal*, 72; he adds, following 'Abd al-Ǧabbâr (*Šarḥ al-uṣûl al-ḫamsa*, 183) that the thesis is equivalent to abû Hâšim's explanation of the divine attributes as « states » (*aḥwâl*) of God's being. Šahrastânî's polemical accusation that abû l-Hudhayl's conception is essentially that of abû Hâšim and that the two are equivalent to the Christian notion of hypostases (*aqânîm*) is interesting in that it does reflect certain Christian apologetic arguments; cf. e.g., Ibn Zur'a's use of the term *ḥâl* in arguing that in God one may distinguish *ṯalâṯatu 'aḥwâl* in P. Sbath, *Vingt traités philosophiques et apologétiques d'auteurs chrétiens* (Cairo, 1929), p. 9 and 13 (on the work, written in 979, cf. Graf, *GCAL* 2, 252f.).

[37] *Intiṣâr*, 59 (on which see below), *Ibâna*, 35, *Maqâlât*, 484, *al-Baǧdâdî, al-Farq bayn al-firaq* (ed. M. Abd al-Hamid, Cairo, n.d.), 127 and *Uṣûl* 91; cf. also Ibn Ḥazm, *op. cit.*, 2, 129ff. (*cit. infra*).

identical with the being of God Himself and with each other and that He is these perfections), abû l-Hudhayl specifically denies. He says on the one hand, without qualification, that it is erroneous to say that God is an act of knowing (*ʿilm* = νόησις) or is the power of efficient causality (*qudra* = δύναμις)[38], despite the fact that he holds that « when one says that God is *qâdir*, he has affirmed the reality of a power of efficient causality that is God », etc. The problem then is what precisely does he mean : what is he trying to say and, more importantly perhaps, what is he trying to avoid ?

The meaning of the formulae must be taken out of the whole theological system which gives them what meaning they have and in which the specific structure of the problem which they are meant to answer is defined. We tend, as it were « naturally », to read abû l-Hudhayl's statements on the divine attributes against and in terms of the background of patristic thought. The result of such a native prejudice, however, may vitiate the effort of study if it is not approached with the utmost caution, for the two systems are opposed in some of their primary assumptions. This becomes immediately apparent as soon as one begins to try to place the formula concerning the divine attributes in the context of the whole system. Most basically, in terms of the present investigation, according to abû l-Hudhayl (and most of the kalâm), the rational knowledge of God is not and cannot be had through the consideration of the nature of mind but only through the consideration of the nature of the createdness of the material world. That is, where the Aristotelian and neoplatonic traditions — variously merged in late antiquity and in most of the Christian theologians — seek to achieve a discursive understanding of God and His attributes through the consideration of the nature of the immaterial that is mind, abû l-Hudhayl refuses the notion that there is any immaterial being other than God and consequently must seek to establish his analysis of the attributes from a primary understanding of God as creator. Again, though the radical materialism of the kalâm appears in many respects Stoic in inspiration and attitude[39], man does not, in the teaching of abû l-Hudhayl, contain within himself any element or reason that shares in or imitates the divine and which by introspective reflection would yield an in-

[38] *Intiṣâr, loc. cit.* and *Maqâlât, loc. cit.*

[39] Cf. J. van Ess, *op. cit.*, 256ff. and, on the term kalâm itself, his *Erkenntnislehre des ʿAḍudaddin al-Īcī* (Wiesbaden, 1966), 56ff.

tuition of the nature of God. There are traces, as it were, of the concept of the immanent *logos* in abû l-Hudhayl's assertion that a direct knowledge of God is given in the immediate evidence of creation [40] but the tracks lead away in a contrary direction. The creator is absolutely transcendent and consequently is in no way subject to immediate perception or intuition; He is the non-phenomenal (*al-ġâ'ib*) par excellence, who, if He is to be known by reason, can be known only through the evidence (*dalîl* = σημεῖον) [41] of the phenomenal (*aš-šâhid*) [42] which is material. The implications of this conception, which are still in process of being worked out in the thought of abû l-Hudhayl, have a profound effect on the whole system as they determine the method of rational analysis and set the theoretical limits of its achievement. The effect of this orientation is seen immediately in abû l-Hudhayl's explication of the statement « God is knowing », for our primary evidence that God knows is the order of His works, whence one may make immediately the affirmation that since He is an agent « there is something known by Him that has come to be or will come to be ». Here already one stands in complete opposition to Aristotle's conception of a god that knows naught save himself. This formula, however, is but a minimal statement of what it means to say that God is knowing; within the context of the system the matter is far more complex.

In the material order, i.e., among created beings of which we have direct perception and knowledge, the attributes or accidents that belong to a being constitute, in a sense, the formal reality of its being :

[40] Cf. al-Baġdâdî, *Farq*, 129 and *Uṣûl*, 32, 258, and 260 and VAN Ess, *op. cit.*, 160f.

[41] Cf. *ibid.*, 359f.

[42] One notes in the context of the present discussion that al-Ǧubbâ'î held that the act of knowing is itself perceived (*mudrak*) and known in an immediate intuition (*wuǧûd*) (*al-Muġnî* 12, 23) and defines the knower as one « from whom the realisation of a well-ordered act is possible when he is capable of bringing it to being and is physically competent (*qâdirun ʿalayhi maʿa s-salâma*; *ibid.*, 14) for otherwise there would be no way of affirming that God is knowing. (On the notion of *fiʿl muḥkam*, cf. *ibid.* 16 [ed. A. AL-KHOULI, Cairo, 1380/1960], 191 and 207.) Note that the « phenomenal » (*šâhid*) is not exclusively what is subject to direct perception but includes that whose reality is secondarily manifest in phenomena; one can thus speak of the essential properties of atoms (*ǧawâhir*) as something known *fî š-šâhid* (cf. e.g., al-Bâqillânî, *at-Tamhîd* [ed. R. McCARTHY, Beyrouth, 1957], 77, 8 = § 136). The « phenomenal » thus (i.e., what is manifest to sense) is frequently used in the sense of world-immanent : that which is directly perceptible or which manifests itself as contained in the material perceptible as opposed to the immaterial and world-transcendent (*al-ġâ'ib*). Cf. also *al-Muġni* 12, 434.

the content and fullness of its being in being that reality that it is [43]. The perfections (*ṣifât/aʿrâḍ*) are the actuality of its being in being. On the other hand, however, the beings that we most readily identify as such — a man, for instance, an animal or the like — have not any essential unity of being beyond the material unity of the body. That is, it is not ontologically unified in its being in such a way as to subsist as a *being* (οὐσία) essentially and « by nature » one in the actuality and operation of its primary properties. On the contrary, its being is that of a composite (*ǧumla*) : a specific arrangements of atoms conjoined and juxtaposed in space together with a complex set of accidents which inhere in them, not « by nature » as essential properties belonging to its being, but simply as created in them [44]. The acts or perfections of a being do not belong to it as to the being of a unified reality (οὐσία) as properties of a single essence (τὸ τί ἦν εἶναι) but the plurality of accidents remains a plurality inherent in a plurality of accidentally conjoined atoms. Man, thus for example, is a complex of atoms whose conjunction is created in a particular configuration. Life is an accident and so also is the act of knowing; and although the latter cannot, according to abû l-Hudhayl, persist in the body without the former, it is, even in man, nevertheless considered as an ontologically distinct and separate attribute, created by God [45]. Here in such a framework there is no central and essential reality such as the « soul » which is the principle of life in the body and whose perfection is mind, the perfection of which is, in turn, the act of knowing; there is no inherent « principle of life » such as the ψυχή which determines the essential « nature » (φῦσις) of the organism with its form, natural faculties, and operations, but rather God

[43] Cf. my *Metaphysics of Created Being according to abû l-Hudhayl al-ʿAllâf* (*Uitgaven van het Nederlands historisch-archaeologisch Instituut te Istanbul*, 21), 41 ff.

[44] *Ibid.*, 15, n. 6 and 36f. and, in general 34ff. It should be noted that this view of the fundamental ontological structure of the material existant does not exclude a notion of the consistent operation of « natural » or physical factors in the real processes of the world; there is, in fact, no little evidence that reasonably comprehensive theories concerning the purely physical and, if you will, chemical aspects of the material world were articulated in kalam circles on the basis of inherited scientific tradition. Some of this has been indicated in the article of van Ess cited above. The subject deserves serious attention if we are to gain a view of the comprehensiveness of the kalâm. The kalâm is first and foremost a theology and was not created as a rational physics or metaphysics (cf. *Metaphycs of Created Being* 40, n. 8 and VAN Ess, *op. cit.*, 268) but as a rational theology it must rest on an elaborated philosophical basis.

[45] Cf. *Metaphysics of Created Being*, *loc. cit. supra* n. 43.

creates and annihilates life in the body as an ontologically independant attribute. Although the act of knowing « cannot coexist with non-life » it subsists as an independant accident in the heart.

Such a system simply does not offer a framework in which one can say that thought is the actuality of mind which is itself the essential perfection of the knower, for thought or the act of knowing (*'ilm*) is an accident or determinant perfection (*'araḍ/ma'nà*) that comes to inhere in a particular part or organ of a substrate of atoms which in their created juxtaposition and conjunction constitute the body (*ǧism*) that is the individual. The act of knowing, in brief, is not the perfection or act (*ἐνέργεια*) of the knower in the essential unity of his being, for there is no essential unity to the composite that is the body. It is, to be sure, a perfection of the reality of the composite but it bears no intrinsic, essential relationship to the being of the total composite. The only proof that God is knowing is that His works are well ordered [46].

Exactly how abû l-Hudhayl understood the structure of the act of knowing (*'ilm*) is uncertain. Al-Ǧubbâ'î is quoted as saying in his *Masâ'il al-Ḫalâf* that abû l-Hudhayl held that the act of knowing is conviction (*i'tiqâd*) [47]; probably « the conviction that the thing is as it really is » [48]. 'Abd al-Ǧabbâr, however, even in giving the citation of al-Ǧubbâ'î seems uncertain and he remarks elsewhere that abû l-Hudhayl held that « the act of knowing is generically distinct and is not conviction » [49]. In any event, it would appear absolutely certain that he did not conceive the act of knowing as identical with the actuality of its own content, i.e., that he did not hold that *νόησις* is *τὸ νοούμενον*. If, like al-Ǧubbâ'î, he held that the act of knowing is conviction there is no question on the matter [50]. If he held (an

46 Cf. *al-Muġnî* 7 (ed. I. AL-ABYARI, Cairo, 1380/1961), 64f. and n. 42 above.

47 *al-Muġnî* 12, 25.

48 *I'tiqâdu š-šay'i 'alà mâ huwa bihi*; this definition is attributed to al-Ǧubbâ'î *ibid.*, 13, *ult.* and in *Maqâlât* 523, 14 and al-Baġdâdî, *Uṣûl*, 4.

49 *Šarḥ al-uṣûl al-ḫamsa*, 188.

50 On the problem of the application of the term *i'tiqâd* to God, cf. VAN ESS, *Erkenntnislehre*, 74. The statement of al-Ǧubbâ'î that the act of knowing is known as such by an immediate intuition given in the act itself (*al-Muġnî* 12, 46) does not imply that he felt that on any level the object known (*ma'lûm*) is essentially identical in its being known with the act of knowing. The passage (p. 45f.) deals not with the knowing of the act of knowing but with the question of whether the knowledge that the act of knowing is a knowing (i.e., not *mere* conviction, opinion, or ignorance) is a distinct act of knowing or not. Al-Ǧubbâ'î holds that just as one who wills is aware of his act of

earlier position?) that *'ilm* is a generically distinct accident, then we cannot, on the basis of present information, be certain of precisely how he understood it. In all events, it is clear enough that the system does not offer any place for a general conception of mind as an entity whose actuality is its act and whose act is the actuality in it of its object as known, and even less of the conception that the act of mind (*ἐνέργεια νοῦ*) is life, *δύναμις*, etc.

Accordingly we do not find in the system of abû l-Hudhayl or in those of his followers, the notion that God is the sole adequate object of His own knowing. God has knowledge of « the totality of things » (*ašyâ'* = *ὄντα*) but His knowing of creatures is conceived as a knowing of « objects » and abû l-Hudhayl does not reckon God as a part of this totality [51]. God knows all things and He knows Himself. The sources — admittedly inadequate — do not report that he equated God's knowledge of Himself with the fact that His knowledge is Himself as this is done in the Christian or hellenistic tradition which his formulae seem to reflect. Abû l-Hudhayl insists that God's knowledge is infinite insofar as it is identical with Himself [52] and that it is infinite in that He knows Himself [53] but the two propositions are nowhere explicitly combined. Though it is plain that the school's doctrine could not readily accomodate an Aristotelian or neo-platonic conception of the nature of mind, exactly how they did conceive the ontology of God's knowing Himself is not at all clear. The question, as a matter of fact, is seldom discussed, even in the classical period of the kalâm, albeit the problem is present in theses reported from a number of early authorities and despite the fact that there seems to have been a considerable reaction to the neoplatonic thesis, pur-

willing in an immediate intuition or perception (*idrâk*) (*ibid.*, p. 5; cf. also 23, cit. *supra* n. 42), so also the knowledge that the act of knowing is an act of knowing (i.e., objectively true) is an immediate intuition without the intervention of a second act (as is held by abû Hâšim and some of his followers). *'Ilm* is of the same category as ignorance (*ǧahl*; *ibid.*, p. 121) and, like it, is of an object. Similarly, note that al-Ǧubbâ'î allows that under certain circumstances one may say that *'ilm* = *wuǧûd*, as one is said to know (*'arafa*) the whereabouts of his errant camel, so that God may be, he says, said to be eternally *wâǧid* of things in that he knows them (*ibid.*, p. 17; correct *wâḥid* to *wâǧid* and *yḥd* to *yaǧid* in lines 9f.); cf. also *ibid.* 5 (ed. EL-KHODEIRI, Cairo, 1958), 222f. Note finally that abû l-Hudhayl defines understanding or recognition (*al-ma'rifa*) as forming a process of reasoning (*istidlâl*) (*ibid.* 12, 25).

[51] *Intiṣâr*, 91f.

[52] *Ibid.*, 80.

[53] *Ibid.*, 16.

portedly held by Muʿammar, that God cannot know Himself since this would introduce the duality of knower and known into the divine being [54]. In any case, it would seem reasonably certain that abû l-Hudhayl conceived God's knowing — whatever other qualifications he may have made—as a knowing of objects, just as we know objects [55].

Though he held that God knows creatures as objects abû l-Hudhayl plainly did not feel that this knowledge produces any kind of plurality in God. He does, it is true, speak of things as « in » God's knowledge [56] but strictly they are not *in* His knowledge as νοητά that are constitutive of it. The object in its being-known does not, within the system, constitute the actuality of the act of knowing, because it has no being as intelligible but only as object, an object whose reality is extrinsic to the being of the knower. Creatures, therefore, as such, do not share in God's eternity and do not, in their being known, constitute an ontological plurality in the act of knowing that is God [57].

54 Cf. *ibid.*, 45, al-Baġdâdî, *Farq*, 155 and *Uṣûl*, 95, Ibn Ḥazm, *op. cit.*, 4, 194, and *Milal*, 100; cf. also my remarks in *JAOS* 87 (1967) 259, n. 52.

55 Though there were many variations in the description of God's knowing as the school tradition evolved, this univocal conception of knowing as a knowing of objects would appear constant. Thus ʿAbd al-Ğabbâr, while making a number of distinctions between the knowing of God who knows by His essence (*li-nafsihi*) and that of the human knower who knows by a finite and discrete act of knowing (*bi-ʿilm*), says (*al-Muġni* 6/2 [ed. G. Anawati, Cairo, n.d.], 117, 10ff.) that « God is related to the object of His knowing as knowers are related... and His state [as knower] must be like the state of the human knower ». So also he speaks of God's knowledge of Himself as « detailed » in opposition to our general knowledge of Him (*al-Muḥît bit-taklîf* [ed. U. Azmi, Cairo, n. d.], 159, 17ff.; cf. also *ibid.*, 193; the former passage seems to be paraphrased in Paris ms. ar. 1252, fol. 21R°). The actual and apparent differences between the teaching of abû l-Hudhayl, al-Ğubbâ'î, abû Hâšim, and the Qâḍî on this matter will have to be taken up in another place.

56 Cf. e.g., *Intiṣâr*, 16, lines 8ff and 19ff. and on the problem of the expression *fî l-ʿilm* and *fî l-qudra*, cf. *infra*.

57 It was abû Yaʿqûb aš-Šaḥḥâm, a disciple of abû l-Hudhayl's, who was first to introduce explicitly into the Baṣra school the thesis of the reality of the possible (cf. my *Remarks on the Early Development of the kalâm* in *Atti del III Congresso di Studi Arabi e Islamici* [Naples, 1967], 324ff. and references). For abû l-Hudhayl the possible is strictly a pure non-being. Nevertheless it is quite clear that he did not — for how could he? — completely escape the problem of having some kind of *θεῖα παραδείγματα*, that are in some way *of God* and eternal with his knowledge (see below). Throughout the long history of the kalâm this was a most acute problem and it appears to have arisen even at the very earliest beginning of Islamic speculation. The ğahmîya, it would seem, may have held the thesis of the « createdness » of God's knowledge not simply to escape the problem of duality in the absolute oneness of God (cf. *Le Muséon* 78, 408ff.) but equally perhaps to insist that the being of creatures, even as they are contained in

Such, at any rate, would seem to be the way in which abû l-Hudhayl understood the matter.

The situation with God's power (*qudra*) is parallel to this in his teaching; it is infinite in that it is God, even though the totality of its objects, as those things which He will really create, constitutes a finite sum [58]. The objects (*maqdurâtuhu*) thus are not « contained in it » as constitutive of it in such a way as to limit it, for it is not identical or coextensive with them. The limit (*ġâya, nihâya*), fixed in God's knowledge of what He will create, belongs to the being of the things (the realities — *ašyâ* — whose being is a being-created) that come to be, not to God.

Still we must ask what precisely he intends in refusing to allow that God is an act of knowing or is the reality of His power of efficient causality. He refuses also, as was seen above, to say without qualification that God's knowing is His power, even though they would seem to be one and the same in that they are God. He says, rather, that they are neither identical with one another nor are they distinct (*ġayr*) from one another [59]. The difference (*iḫtilâf*) between God's

the divine act of knowing, is absolutely created (*muḥdaṯ*). This would appear to be rather explicit in the teaching of Hišâm b. al-Ḥakam (d. before 800) who held that « it is impossible that God, by His own being, know entities (*ašyâ'*) eternally » but that He knows them only after He has created them since there is no knowledge save of an actually existent object (*ma'lûmun mawǧûd*) (cf. *Maqâlât*, 37 and 493f.). It is conceivable (though highly uncertain) that by *ma'lûmun mawǧûd* he meant the object as it is present to the mind and not necessarily as it exists concretely in the world. In any event, he nicely avoids the problems that arise concerning the eternity of God's knowledge in relation to the createdness of its objects as known by insisting that one cannot say either that God's knowledge is generated (*muḥdaṯ*) or that it is eternal (i.e., eternal and so necessary or created and so temporally contingent), as he avoids thus the notion of its temporality but not that it is in some way derivative. The chief and most important sense of his position is that the being of created beings, even as they are known by God, is ontologically created and absolutely dependent upon God as the creator. The same problem is apparent in the teaching of Hišâm al-Fuwaṭî (d. 833), at one time a disciple of abû l-Hudhayl's, who, though allowing that God is eternally knowing, hesitated to say that God knows creatures eternally (*ibid.*, 488f.). (N.b. also the citations of the doctrine of « Šayṭân aṭ-Ṭâq », *ibid.*, 37f.) The problem here is not simply one of the eternity of the world that some (the so-called *azalîya*) would derive from the eternity of God's knowledge (cf. VAN Ess, *Die Gedankenwelt des Ḥariṯ al-Muḥāsibī* [Bonn, 1961], 175) but rather that of the eternal necessity of the possible *per se*.

[58] Cf. *Intiṣâr*, 80; on the finitude of the possibles see below.

[59] *Maqâlât*, 177, 15ff and 484, 11ff. The formula *lâ huwa wa-lâ ġayruhu* is old and is found already with Hišâm b. al-Ḥakam, as van Ess has pointed out (*Oriens* 18-19, 111ff.) and resembles trinitarian formulae (v. *ibid.*, 119).

knowing and his power is grounded in the real difference of their proper objects [60]; but he does not mean by this to say that the distinction between the attributes is simply *quoad nos*. God's knowledge is not a completely closed act of self-knowing; it is also a knowing of objects as objects and to the extent that it is correlated to those objects it is not absolutely coextensive with His power. Likewise, in that His knowing is not simply and exclusively a knowing of Himself, identical with Himself, abû l-Hudhayl denies, against the thesis of the ǧahmîya and the pseudo-Aristotle cited above, that God is an act of knowing [61]. Analogously then he predicates all the other attributes of God in the same way.

Thus though he denied the reality of the attributes as something « eternal with God » [62] or as distinct subsistent acts « in God », he did nonetheless affirm them as ontologically real perfections *of* God that are predicated of him *substantialiter* [63]. Nor are they merely the divine essence and no more. Šahrastânî describes his position in contrast to that of al-Ǧubbâ'î this way : « The difference between saying 'knowing *per se*, not by an act of knowing' and saying 'knowing by an act of knowing that is His essence' is that the former is a denial of the attribute while the latter is the affirmation of the reality of an essence which is itself an attribute or the affirmation of the reality of an attribute that is itself an essence » [64]. Thus, although abû l-Hudhayl affirmed the proper, entitative reality only of God Himself in the unity of His being, he does not arrive at the point of negating the positive ontological character of the attributes as predicated of Him. One notes, for example, the difference between his position and that of an-Naẓẓâm, for where the latter allows that the statement « God is knowing » is simply a denial that God is ignorant and holds that the distinction of the attributes is based exclusively and entirely

60 *Maqâlât*, 486, 5f.

61 *Ibid.*, 484, *ult.* and *Intiṣâr* 59 (2d. line from bottom).

62 Cf. *ibid.*, 60, 2 (here of God's « face »); the problem involves also the concept of « eternal attributes » (*ṣifât qadîma*) on which see below.

63 The terminology here is important : *qad ṯabbata 'ilman huwa llâh*, etc. (*Maqâlât*, 484, 7ff. and 165, 8ff.); as an ontologically distinct reality he affirmed only God Himself (*lam yuṯbit 'illâ llâh*, *ibid.*, 486, 1-2).

64 *Milal*, 72; al-Ḫayyâṭ (*op. cit.*, 59, 20) said that abû l-Hudhayl allowed that God is knowing *per se* (*bi-nafsihi*) and 'Abd al-Ǧabbâr likewise (*Šarḥ al-uṣûl al-ḫamsa*, 183, 1-3) sees no more than a verbal distinction between the two positions. The distinction does, however, prove significant within the evolution of the school's doctrine from abû l-Hudhayl through abû Hâšim.

on the distinction of the qualities that are negated (sc. *ǧahl*, *'aǧz*, etc.) [65] abû l-Hudhayl holds that the statement, far from being a mere negation of ignorance in God, is the affirmation of the actuality of God's knowing and of the positive content of His knowledge (sc. created reality and Himself). He steers a path, thus, between the two extremes formed by those who, like an-Naẓẓâm and Ḍirâr, denied the positive actuality of the attributes and those who affirmed them as eternal and subsistent in God [66].

The wording of abû l-Hudhayl's formulae, which from the remains seems carefully consistent, is itself of significance for our understanding of his intention and attitude towards the problem of the attributes. From the evidence of the earliest sources, the *Kitâb al-Intiṣâr* of al-Ḫayyâṭ and the *Maqâlât al-Islâmîyîn* of al-Aš'arî which, besides showing a consistent pattern of expression that must reflect substantially abû l-Hudhayl's own usage, give a number of appar-

[65] Cf. e.g., *Maqâlât*, 487 and note 'Abd al-Ǧabbâr's polemic against this kind of « negative theology » in *al-Muġnî* 6/1 (ed. A.F. AL-AHWANI, Cairo, 1382/1962), 70, 13ff. The same kind of doctrine was held by Ḍirâr b. 'Amr (cf. *Maqâlât*, 166 and 281 and generally VAN ESS, in *Der Islam* 43, 277ff.).

[66] Because of his conception that the attribute that inheres or subsists in a being is ontologically a distinct entity, abû l-Hudhayl felt that to speak of God's knowing by an eternal act of knowing that is subsistent in Him was to imply not simply a division in God but the existence of an hypostasis or second eternal being along with God (*ṣifatun lahu qadîmatun ma'ahu*, *Intiṣâr*, 60, 2). This position al-Ḫayyâṭ attributes to the so-called *Nâbita*, an ultra-orthodox, anti-ši'ite and anti-mu'tazilite group, connected with the ḥanbalites (cf. D. SOURDEL, in *SI* 13 [1950], 6). Among them he meant, no doubt, to include Ibn Kullâb, whom al-Aš'arî mentions as an opponent of abû l-Hudhayl's (cf. *supra*, n. 2), who held that God's attributes are subsistent (*qâ'ima*) in Him (cf. VAN ESS, in *Oriens* 18-19, 110ff.) and eternal. Ibn Kullâb seeks to avoid the unpleasant conclusions of the Mu'tazila in part by insisting that the divine attributes are eternal not of themselves but only by virtue of the eternity of God (cf. *al-Muġnî* 7, 4, Br.Mus. ms. ar. 8613, fol. 112R°, and al-Ǧuwaynî, *aš-Šâmil* [ed. H. KLOPFER, Cairo, 1383/1963], 46f.; and on his understanding of *qidam*, cf. VAN ESS, *op. citt.*, 122f. and *infra*); thus he prefers the formula *lam yazal qadîman bi-'asmâ'ihi wa-ṣifâtihi* (*Maqâlât*, 546 — the term *qadîm* is omitted in the same formula, *ibid.*, 169 but this changes the sense not a bit) which is used also by Ibn Ḥanbal, who condemns the expression « *Allâh wa-nûruhu, Allâh wa-qudratuhu* », etc., as involving hypostases (*op. cit.*, 323, 1ff.). This becomes the standard « orthodox » formulation and is used in the *Fiqh Akbar* II (Hyderabad, 1373/1953, p. 1). It is interesting to note that in contrast to Ibn Kullâb, al-Aš'arî, who is extremely precise in his language, does not hesitate to speak of the eternity (*qidam*) of God's knowledge in the *Luma'* (§ 20) though otherwise, both in that work and in the *Risâla ilà ahl aṯ-ṯaġr* he seems to avoid even the use of the adjective *qadîm* as qualifiying an attribute.

ently direct citations, it would appear that he conscienciously avoided any terms for God's essence or being. The use of the term *nafs*, which from an early period is often used interchangeably with *ḏât*, is excluded here because of abû l-Hudhayl's understanding of it an as attribute [67]. The term *ḏât*, however, was certainly available — it is used by Ibn Kullâb and an-Naẓẓâm [68] — but nowhere do we find, for example, the formula *huwa 'âlimun bi-'ilmin huwa ḏâtuhu*; in all cases, rather, he uses either the pronoun *huwa* or the name *Allâh* [69]. Again, other than to refer to God's act of willing, which he conceives as a kind of temporal hypostasis, one finds no occurance of the terms *wuǧûd* or *mawǧûd* in reference to God nor, moreover, does he seem to use the word *šay'* of God. This cannot be attributed to a primitive stage of development of the technical vocabulary at this period of the kalâm, for a complex tradition of speculation was already established, and the technical terminology, although it was to undergo considerable refinement in the following century, was quite developed. Abû l-Hudhayl himself, in fact, employed these terms in treating other topics. Ibn Kullâb (d. ca. 854), it should be noted, evidently went to considerable lengths to elaborate the question of the application of the terms *šay'* and *mawǧûd* to God and the problem could hardly have been unknown to abû l-Hudhayl. As was noted above, abû l-Hudhayl seems to have excluded God from the totality of beings indicated in the expression « God is *bi-kulli šay'in 'alîm* »; again, he says that « one being (*šay'*) differs from another being *per se* (*bi-nafsihi*) or resembles it and corresponds to it *per se*, but would not say that the Creator differs from the world (*yuḫâlifu l-'âlam*) » [70]. All this would tend to indicate that abû l-Hudhayl conceived God's being

67 On *nafs* as an attribute see below. He does use the expression *bi-nafsihi* in connection with material beings (cf. *Maqâlât*, 351, 8 and below). Al-Ḫayyâṭ says in one passage (cf. n. 64 above) that abû l-Hudhayl allowed that God is knowing *bi-nafsihi* but this is purely interpretative. Again al-Aš'arî, in speaking of abû l-Hudhayl, mentions « the attributes by which He is described *li-nafsihi* » (*op. cit.*, 165, 7, 484, 7, and 188, 12) but here he is classing the attributes and speaking for himself, not quoting abû l-Hudhayl.

68 For an-Naẓẓâm, cf. e.g., *ibid.*, 166 and 486f. and on Ibn Kullâb see below.

69 Šahrastânî (*op. cit.*, 71) gives the formula *'ilmuhu ḏâtuhu* but this is interpretative; in similar fashion al-Baġdâdî (*Uṣûl*, 91) has *'ilmu llâhi huwa nafsuhu*, but this is altogether impossible since *nafs* is treated separately as an attribute itself (see below). Elsewhere (cf. *Farq*, 127) his formulations follow those of al-Ḫayyâṭ and al-Aš'arî as do those of 'Abd al-Ǧabbâr, al-Isfarâ'înî (*Tabṣîr* [ed. AL-KAWTHARI, Cairo, 1359/1940], 42, and Ibn al-Ǧawzî (*Talbîs* [Cairo, 1379/1050], 83).

70 Cf. infra, n. 79.

as utterly ἐπέκεινα τῆς οὐσίας somewhat after the manner of the ğahmîya [71] and the neoplatonising sources that appear to inderlie some of his thought. Unfortunately the paucity of documentation forbids our drawing any firm conclusions, particularly since, had he expressly disallowed the use of the terms *šay'* and *mawğûd* of God, one would expect that this would have been reported in that he would be the sole mu'tazilite authority to do so.

The general structure of abû l-Hudhayl's understanding of the attributes can be clearly seen in its contrast with that of Ibn Kullâb. According to Ibn Kullâb, God exists, eternal in His attributes, which are subsistent in Him (*qâ'imatun bihi*), distinct from Him and each other but yet not distinct (*lâ huwa wa-lâ ġayruhu*). He says further, however, that God's « essence » (*ḏât*) is He and His Self (*nafs*) is He and that He is existent not through an act of being and a being (*šay'*) though not through an act or perfection that is the ground of His being a being [72]. Abû l-Hudhayl on the contrary, while avoiding any radical negation of the attributes such as that of an-Naẓẓâm or Ḍirâr, does not divide and classify them. In his conception, the divine unity is more compact; God's self (*nafs*) is He as His eternity (*qidam*) is He [73], as He is one and identical with Himself, and so also His knowledge, power, grandeur, etc., are likewise God Himself. The exclusion of the term *šay'* and the absence of the word *wuğûd* in the lists, as was mentioned above, may indicate that he felt that God's transcendence precluded the application of these terms. Beyond this, however, it is notable, in regard to his omission of these terms, that no attribute is listed, with the sole exception of *qadîm* (an early and almost universal innovation), which has not a basis in the Koran [74]. From reading the citations given by al-Aš'arî and al-Ḫayyâṭ one has

[71] Cf. *Le Muséon* 78, 398-402.

[72] ذاته هى هو ونفسه هى هو وهو موجود لا بوجود وشىء لا بمعنى له كان شيئا (*Maqâlât*, 169f.; cf. also *supra* n. 66). Whether or not he treated *qidam* as a distinct attribute or put it in a class with *wuğûd* is somewhat uncertain; significantly the term does not occur in the lists of attributes that are given by al-Aš'arî but the statement of 'Abd al-Ğabbâr (*loc. cit.*), on the other hand, would indicate that he did consider it a subsistent attribute. The followers of Ibn Kullâb are reported to have disagreed as to whether God is *qadîmun bi-qidam* (*Maqâlât*, 547) and also as to whether He is *Allâh bi-'ilâhîya* (*ibid.*, 178); cf. generally VAN ESS, *op. cit.*, 122f.

[73] Cf. *Maqâlât*, 165 and 177, *cit. supra*.

[74] On *nafs*, cf. e.g., *Koran* 6, 12 and 54 and note also the remarks of al-Ḫayyâṭ (*op. cit.*, 59f.) regarding *wağh*; on *qadîm* as an innovation, cf. Ibn Ḥazm, *op. cit.*, 2, 151f. and *al-Muġnî* 5, 179.

the distinct impression that abû l-Hudhayl made a considerable effort to keep his fundamental formulations as much as possible within the language of the revelation and to handle them in such a way that the conceptual framework was not forcibly imposed upon a rude adaptation of the sacred text but would adhere closely, insofar as was possible, to it. It is to *Allâh* that « the most beautiful Names » belong (7.180) : « *Allâh*, there is no God but *HE* » (3.2). Thus it is that abû l-Hudhayl predicates all the attributes of *Allâh*, the absoluteness of whose being is given in the *Huwa* [75], and will not predicate God of the attributes (*Allâhu ʿilmun*, etc.) or the attributes of one another. This same tendency is manifest too, I think, in his treatment of God's will and His speech, even though there (perhaps only because the sources give fuller information) the speculative character of his thought would seen more elaborate.

GOD'S POWER AND THE FINITUDE OF THE POSSIBLES

Now although abû l-Hudhayl did try to keep as much as possible to the terms of the *Koran* in listing the attributes and, even though following a somewhat modified neoplatonising model, in describing the unity of the divine being in these attributes, the operative considerations in the elaboration of his thought are thoroughly rational or philosophical in character and his consistent application of the major assumptions of his system (at least up to a very late point in his long carreer) gave rise to several assertions that were quite problematic and, as such, were almost universally rejected by his contemporaries and successors. One of the most notable of these is the thesis that ultimately there must come a term to the production of new being, a moment in which the acts and movements of the blessed and the danmed will be consumated in a permanent state that is the sum of the blessedness and damnation of each [76]. The creation of new being, he insists, cannot continue indefinitely; « there is a finite totality, limit, and whole to those things that shall come to be and to those that shall not come to be which are subject to God's power

[75] On *Allâh* as the supreme name, cf. G. Anawati, *Le nom suprême de Dieu* in *Atti del III Congresso di Studi arabi e islamici*, 11ff.

[76] Cf. my *Metaphysics of Created Being*, 25f. and refs.

of efficient causality and are known to Him, just as there is a finite totality and whole of what has come to be» [77].

His argument for this thesis is outlined briefly by al-Ḫayyâṭ [78];

The thesis which abû l-Hudhayl argued is that contingent beings (*al-'ašyâ'u l-muḥdaṯa*) have a whole, totality, and limit at which they terminate in their being known and subject to the power of efficient causality. This is because the eternal differs from the contingent [79]; since, according to him, the eternal is not finite

[77] *Maqâlât*, 485; cf. also *ibid.*, 163 where *mâ lâ yakûn* is omitted. N.b. that he does not say that created being comes to an end in annihilation as did the ǧahmîya but that no new being is produced. Thus he says regarding the limit of what is subject to God's power, that « if the one who asks means 'is what God has the power to create finite and limited in its being known and subject to [His] power and counted ?' yes; not one being of it escapes Him nor is He incapable [of creating a single being] of it; but if the one who asks means that it has a term and limit at which it ceases to exist and ends altogether, then no» (*Intiṣâr*, 16, 8ff.).

[78] *Ibid.*, 16f.; cf. also 20f., 90ff. and *infra*.

[79] The sense of this is clear but the expression *li-muḫâlifati l-qadîmi lil-muḥdaṯ* is troublesome; it would seem to be interpretative (and not incorrectly so) on the part of al-Ḫayyâṭ, to the extent that abû l-Hudhayl is reported to have rejected the expression « God differs from (*ḫâlafa*) creation» (cf. *Maqâlât*, 351, 9), although he did allow that one say that He is « unlike» (*ḫalâf*) to creation (cf. al-Bâqillânî, *Tamhîd* § 425, p. 253 and al-Ǧuwaynî, *Šâmil* 1, 206, 1 — in contrast to *Fiṣal* 4, 193 where it is said that he denied that God is *ḫalâfun li-ḫalqihi*). His treatment of the terms *ḫâlafa*, *iḫtalafa*, and *ḫalâf* appears to be grewsomely tangled in the sources, particularly in the report of al-Aš'arî (*Maqâlât*, 350f.). What he held would seem to be something like this : strictly speaking one should not say that one accident resembles (*tušbih*) another since two similar beings (*muštabihân*) are similar by a being-similar (*bi-štibâh*) (*ibid.*, 350, 9f.); in the same way two beings that are dissimilar (*muḫtalifân*) are so by a being-dissimilar (*bi-ḫtilâf*) (*ibid.*, 351, 6). Nevertheless, one may say (*qad yuqâl*) that one motion is the like (*šibh*) of another (*ibid.*, 350, 11) and, as two movements may be said to be alike, so too black and white may be said to be unlikes (*ḫalâfân*) (*Šâmil* 1, 186, 17). (Note that he denied that one movement may be unlike [*ḫalâf*] another [*Maqâlât*, 351, 4f.]; this is probably that he held that all motion is intrinsically similar by definition, a thesis he most likely insisted upon in opposition to the contrary which would involve the possibility of eternal circular motion as opposed to rectilinear motion). Strictly speaking, things that differ (*ḫâlafa*) are those in which unlikes (*ḫalâfân*) inhere, so that the terms *muḫâlif* and *muḫtalif* are properly applicable only to a corporeal composite in reference to the substrate that forms its corporeality (cf. *Tamhîd*, *loc. cit.* and *Šâmil* 1, 186 and 206; the former gives only the term *muḫâlif* while the latter gives *muḫtalif* also). That the differing composites, however, are dissimilar is not immediately grounded in the inherent « unlikes» (*ḫalâfân*) (*Maqâlât*, 351, 6f.) but rather in the actuality of being-dissimilar (*bi-ḫtilâf*). Quite clearly the basic source of this tangle of distinctions is abû l-Hudhayl's tendency, noted above, to find an ontologically real and discrete perfection or accident underlying every aspect of the being of a composite and the parallel thesis that only the individual accidents and atoms are ontologically real entities (a problem

or limited and in no way has either part or whole, the contingent must be finite and limited and have a whole and totality. He said : « Contingent beings exist as composed of parts (*ḏâtu 'ab'âḍ*) and whatever is thus must necessarily have a whole and totality. If it were possible that there be parts without a whole, it would be possible that there be a whole or totality without parts and since the latter is impossible so also is the former ». As further evidence of this he adduced the words of God (the Mighty, the Glorious) that « God has power over every thing » (16. 76) and « knows every thing » (2. 28 *et pass.*), « comprehends every thing » (41. 54), and His saying « and He has counted every thing by number » (72. 28). He said : « It is established through the revealed word of God (the Mighty, the Glorious) that there is a whole to beings and He has affirmed that He Himself knows it and comprehends it. Now enumeration and comprehension can only be of the finite and limited ».

This thesis was rejected almost universally. Arguing against it Ibn Ḥazm says that out of ignorance of both the kalâm and the nature of beings, abû l-Hudhayl believed that « what has not come forth into actuality is subject to number, and this is a shameful error, since that which has not come forth into actuality is not a being (*šay'*) and cannot be subject to number » [80]. Abû l-Hudhayl's point

which the school did not find a genuinely satisfactory solution to until abû Hâšim introduced the theory of « states »); accidents have no secondary perfections and, on the other hand, the atoms are ontologically distinct from the accidents and cannot properly be said to differ by virtue of the inherence of disparate accidents, even though this may be said to be the basis of the actuality of their « being-dissimilar ». This, at least, would seem plausible and consistent with his general understanding of the metaphysics of atoms and accidents. Several citations, however, remain perplexing; al-Aš'arî reports — according to the reading of the text (*op. cit.*, 351, 5f.) — that « he did not assert that accidents are not dissimilar because he held that the dissimilar is dissimilar by virtue of a being-dissimilar » ! If this sentence really makes sense (i.e., if one is not to omit one of the negatives), the clarification of his reasoning will have to await the (alas unlikely) discovery of further and more detailed information. Likewise there is a difficulty in the statement reported several lines further on in the same passage to the effect that « he asserted that one thing differs from another (*yuḫâlif*) or is similar to it (*yušbihuhu*) or conforms to it (*yuwâfiquhu*) *per se* », for this would seem in clean contradiction to the information given by al-Aš'arî himself as well as by al-Bâqillânî and the Imâm al-Ḥaramayn, mentioned above. It is possible that he here refers to « unlikes » (*ḫalâfân*), etc., and that the author is simply paraphrasing and interpreting, but without further information any conclusion (including the above suggestion !) would be hazardous.

[80] *Op. cit.*, 4, 84; cf. also *ibid.*, p. 1, 15f. which he there cites and also 3, 90f.; Ibn Ḥazm affirms (*ibid.*, 2, 130, 162 *et alibi*; cf. also R. Arnaldez, *Grammaire et théologie chez Ibn Ḥazm de Cordoue* [Paris, 1956], 287) that God knows the reality of every being in an eternal knowing, but he does not discuss the problem, raised by abû l-Hudhayl, of the actuality of the being of the possible in God's knowledge in that He knows *ab aeterno* the perfection of its being.

is, however, that God knows « what has come to be and shall come to be » in the perfection of the being of each. God, the Eternal (*qadîm*) [81] is altogether immaterial, absolute in the compactness of His being so that one can speak neither of part nor of whole. Material being, in contrast, consists exclusively of the ontological « quanta » or absolutely discrete entities that are atoms and accidents, the totality or sum of which, at every moment, forms a finite integer as the sum of a finite number of discrete parts. Given the ontological discreteness of the atoms and accidents and that, of those that ever shall come to be (i.e., that God knows He will create), there is none but that shall inevitably come to be, the totality must be finite since it is impossible to know an infinite totality of discrete elements [82].

This bears a certain parallelism with the teaching of Origen who says :

Πεπερασμένην γὰρ εἶναι καὶ τὴν δύναμιν τοῦ θεοῦ λεκτέον, καὶ μὴ προφάσει εὐφημίας τὴν περιγραφὴν αὐτῆς περιαιρετέον· ἐὰν γὰρ ᾖ ἄπειρος ἡ θεῖα δύναμις, ἀνάγκη αὐτὴν μηδὲ ἑαυτὴν νοεῖν · τῇ γὰρ φύσει τὸ ἄπειρον ἀπερίληπτον. πεποίηκε τοίνυν τοσαῦτα, ὅσων ἠδύνατο περιδράξασθαι καὶ ἔχειν ὑπὸ χεῖρα καὶ συγκρατεῖν ὑπὸ τὴν ἑαυτοῦ πρόνοιαν · ὥσπερ καὶ τοσαύτην ὕλην κατεσκεύασεν, ὅσην ἠδύνατο διακοσμῆσαι. [83]

and later in the same work :

Μηδεὶς δὲ προσκοπτέτω τῷ λόγῳ, εἰ μέτρα ἐπιτίθεμεν καὶ τῇ τοῦ θεοῦ δυνάμει · ἄπειρα γὰρ περιλαβεῖν τῇ φύσει ἀδύνατον τυγχάνει.

[81] God's being eternal (*qadîm*) becomes, for al-Ǧubbâ'î, the chief of His attributes that is the key to all the others (as it is also, in a sense, for al-Aš'arî) but whether the development of this thesis can be projected back as far as abû l-Hudhayl is doubtful.

[82] His insistence on the ontological discreteness of the atoms and accidents as the ground for the conclusion is very succinctly put in an argument quoted by al-Ḫayyâṭ (*op. cit.*, 20, 18ff.); « if you say that some accidents are bodies and that some bodies are accidents you have passed not simply beyond the pail of common sense but have gone beyond hopeless nonsense; if you say that all accidents are other than all bodies, then you have affirmed that there is a whole to bodies and accidents.... Tell me then concerning all that has come to be and exist : is there a single element of it that is described as not being ? If you say 'no' — as you must — then one replies that all that shall be will one day be described as having been ».

[83] *De Principiis* II 9, 1 (*GCS* 5, 164), cited by E. de Faye, *Origène* 3 (Paris, 1928), 34; like abû l-Hudhayl, Origen goes on to cite scripture to confirm his thesis, saying, in the translation of Rufinus, « porro autem sicut et scriptura dicit 'numero et mensura universa' condidit » (*Wis.* 11, 20).

ἅπαξ δὲ πεπερασμένων ὄντων, ὧν περιδράττεται αὐτὸς ὁ θεὸς ἀνάγκη ὅρον εἶναι μέχρι πόσων πεπερασμένων διαρκεῖ [84].

There is here a seeming parallelism whose likelihood would appear enhanced by the analogy of abû l-Hudhayl's conception of the final, consummated state of the blessed and Origen's ἀποκατάστασις, [85]. Though none, I think, would deny that some origenistic elements may lie in the formative background of abû l-Hudhayl's thought, the parallelism between their understanding of the finitude of creation and the limit of God's power is not altogether strict. There are a number of significant differences that are illustrative of abû l-Hudhayl's orientation. The ἀποκατάστασις, for Origen, is not necessitated by the finitude of creation; indeed, creation is, he holds, eternal since it is unthinkable that there have been a moment before which God was not creating [86]. Like abû l-Hudhayl he says that an infinite creation is impossible and God's power finite since the infinite cannot be grasped by mind and God's providence cannot comprehend it, but his basic attitude is quite different from that of the Muʿtazilite master. Following a good Greek tradition, he feels that perfection lies not in the unlimited but in the finite; God Himself is finite or limited and His power could not even comprehend itself, were it not so. « For Origen it is not a matter of limiting the omnipotence of God but of explaining it : it is because God is omnipotent that He has created all that he could » [87]. It is the « measure » found in

[84] *De Pr.* IV 4, 8 (p. 359).

[85] The similarity of their thought on the final state of the blessed was pointed out by M. Seal (*op. cit.*, 70ff.) though he distorts the teaching of abû l-Hudhayl in order to draw a closer parallelism than exists (cf. van Ess in *Bibliotheca Orientalis* 23 [1966], 103).

[86] Cf. G. Bardy, art. *Origène* in *DTC* 11, coll. 1529f.; the Muʿtazila was extremely careful to avoid the notion of necessary creation and that any such notion be implied by the attribute *ǧawâd* (cf. ʿAbd al-Ǧabbâr, *al-Muḥîṭ bit-taklîf*, 74, 8ff. and L. Gardet, *Dieu et la Destinée de l'homme* [Paris, 1967], 35); al-Ǧubbâ'î is more careful to exclude from this attribute the notion of any kind of necessity (cf. *al-Muġnî* 14 [ed. M. el-Siqa, Cairo, 13851/965], 45ff). That Origen conceived an endless series of ἀποκαταστάσεις (cf. J. Quasten, *Patrology* 2, 98f.) need not concern us here.

[87] Cf. Bardy, *op. cit.*, 1530 and Faye, *op. cit.* 1, 35; H. Langerbeck, in *JHS* 77 (1957), 72 and *Aufsätze zur Gnosis* (*AAWG* 3/69, 1967), 161 suggests that Origen follows closely an Aristotelian line of thought according to which will (βούλημα), because of its correlation to the πρακτά, cannot be infinite so that God, who creates by willing, cannot be infinite. This conception is in noteworthy contrast both to the teaching of abû l-Hudhayl and to that of ʿAbd al-Ǧabbâr who holds that though God knows an infinity of individuals and though His power is infinite, there cannot be an infinity

beings and the perfection of the world that Origen sees as the primary evidence for its createdness [88].

For abû l-Hudhayl the finitude of creation is necessitated by the discrete character of the ultimate ontological elements of created being. God's knowledge embraces the infinite that is Himself [89]; thus it is not the infinite *per se* that is ἀπερίληπτον and incapable of actuality, but an infinite whole of discrete parts — an infinity of discrete elements. It is the very nature of material being that excludes thus the possibility of an eternal sequence of creatures, whether in the past or in the future. Al-Ḫayyâṭ reports that against his rather numerous Muslim opponents abû l-Hudhayl insisted that his position was true « lest he be led, as he saw it, to have to acknowledge the validity of the position of those who hold that the world is eternal (the *dahrîya*); it is as if he said : 'know that the thesis of the dahrîya is valid and correct to the extent that the thesis — valid according to your understanding — that one being succedes another endlessly is valid and correct » [90]. A like line of reasoning is reported by the same author in a form that merits some brief attention : Asked why he held this position and what was his proof,

« he replied that if it were possible that He realise one new being after another endlessly, it would not be excluded that one being precede another without any beginning. And if this were possible we should (as he saw it) have no way of affirming the fact of the temporal contingency of body and along with our denial of its temporal contingency, we should have to deny its creator, since He is not known by sense but only by His acts » [91].

In showing that it is metaphysically impossible that God's speech be eternal, 'Abd al-Ǧabbâr gives a number of arguments, among them that,

« Since to allow the possibility of an eternal speech of the [same] type as this [phenomenal] speech would require that one allow the possibility of an eternal

of acts of willing (cf. e.g., *al-Muġnî* 6/2, 98, 12f.); here, as with abû l-Hudhayl, the infinity is excluded because an infinity of discrete entities cannot exist simultaneously, but since creation will continue indefinitely, God's acts of willing, according to the Qâḍî, will continue infinitely in the infinite future (*ibid.*, 193f.); cf. also n. 106 below.

[88] *In Gen. Comm.* 7, 20 (*PG* 12, 49b), translated and discussed in Bardy, *op. cit.*, coll. 1527f.

[89] Cf. *Intiṣâr*, 16, 5; 91, 2ff. and esp. 91, 17ff.

[90] *Ibid.*, 19, 21ff.; cf. also *al-Muḥîṭ bit-taklîf*, 116, 17ff. The same argument is set forth in a direct citation from abû l-Hudhayl's *K. al-Qawâlib* in *Farq*, 124.

[91] *Intiṣâr*, 18, 18ff.

body of the [same] type as these bodies. To allow this, however, would void the method by which the temporal contingency of bodies is known. This would mean that the knowledge of the Eternal (be He exalted) — not just of His speech — would be altogether impossible. It would require that one allow the possibility of eternal motions of the [same] type as temporally contingent motions and the affirmation of the reality of perfections of the [same] type as accidents, all of which were eternal along with Him and herein would lie the invalidity of the method of knowing the temporal contingency of accidents and bodies and [of knowing] the Eternal » [92].

Again, the same author, arguing in another place that we have an immediate and true intuition of the intention (*qaṣd*) of a person who performs an act and thereby of his agency, says:

« If the matter were not as we have stated it, one could not know that it is possible that something that is in motion be at rest rather than as it is, since we depend, in this, exclusively on the fact that were it not for the free decision of the mover he would remain at rest. If this method were not possible, the knowledge of the temporal contingency of bodies, etc., would be impossible » [93].

In this second passage the Qâḍî brings up the fundamental kalâm principle that voluntary, self-directed intention underlies the generation of all being. He says, in effect, that the basis of our knowledge of the nature of material body and its inalienable properties of motion, rest, etc. (the so-called *akwân*) rests on the intuition of this principle and that to deny the principle is to deny that the world reveals itself to understanding as it truly is and, consequently, to give up all hope of any rational knowledge of reality. Against the charge that his assertion that we have an intuition of the agent's intention is simply conjecture or opinion (*ẓann*) and not knowledge, he says that this cannot be since the one who claims this will have to say that all knowledge of phenomena is mere opinion [94]. Likewise in the first passage, his argument is that to allow the possibility of an eternal speech or word is implicitly to deny the truth of the way the world reveals itself to human understanding; considering material being, as it is phenomenally available (i.e., as *šâhid*), the mind finds that its ultimate ontological structure excludes the possiblity of its being eternal and if this conclusion is false, then all reasoning about the world is invalid. That the world does reveal itself as it truly is and so gives evidence of the creator is a primary postulate; man is under

[92] *Al-Muġnî* 7, 85, 16ff.; cf. also *al-Muḥîṭ bit-taklîf*, 116, 17ff.

[93] *Al-Muġnî* 8 (ed. T. AL-TAWIL and S. ZAYED, Cairo, n.d.), 9, 19-22.

[94] *Ibid.*, 11. 1-2.

moral obligation to speculation and is to seek the knowledge of God [95], and since God is all-wise it is inconceivable that He would vitiate the phenomenal basis of rational enquiry [96].

In these terms, then, abû l-Hudhayl's perspective in the several arguments that the sources report his giving in support of the temporal finitude of the world becomes somewhat clearer. The dahrîya argue that every body that we have observed with its temporal attributes (sc. motion and the other *akwân*) is preceded in time by other temporal attributes; body is, therefore, eternal and every motion preceded by another motion eternally [97]. Against this, abû l-Hudhayl argues that an analysis of the ultimate ontological structure of corporeal being demands its temporal contingency [98] and as a second argument, dependant in part on the first and involving the knowledge and power of a willing agent, that an infinite creation of corporeal beings is impossible. The argument that to allow an infinite succession of beings into the future would involve the affirmation of an infinite series also into the past, however, is primarily directed against the Muslim opponents of his thesis that there is a finite term to creation. This is evident from the citations of al-Ḫayyâṭ. As is the case with ʿAbd al-Ǧabbâr in the citations given above, the essence of his argument is that if we allow the possibility of an infinite series of created beings in the future, then the nature of corporeal being does not exclude an infinite series in the opposite direction and our rational understanding of the nature of material creation is erroneous [99].

He went beyond this, however; the possible too, he held, is limited. « There is a finite totality, limit, and whole to those things that shall

[95] Cf. van Ess, *Erkenntnislehre*, 303ff.

[96] Cf. *al-Muġnî* 16 (ed. A. al-Khouli, Cairo, 1380/1960), 185, 16f.

[97] Cf. Ibn al-Muṭahhar al-Maqdisî, *K. al-Bad' wat-ta'rîḫ*, ed. M. Huart, I (Paris, 1899), 131, 1ff.

[98] Cf. *Šarḥ al-uṣûl al-ḫamsa*, 95ff. and regarding the later elaboration of the argument within the school, see also *al-Muḥîṭ bit-taklîf*, 40ff. Note that abû l-Hudhayl insists on a kind of ontological « isotropy » of corporeal being, i.e., that all bodies of which we have no direct experience must be ontologically identical to those of which we do have direct knowledge (cf. *al-Muġnî* 12, 99 and for the similar position of ʿAbd al-Ǧabbâr, cf. *al-Muḥîṭ*, 41, 22ff.), in part, probably, against the notion that the celestial bodies are ontologically different from terrestrial ones (cf. also n. 79 above).

[99] Abû l-Hudhayl's argument in reply to an objection of the dahrîya, cited from his *K. al-Qawâlib* by al-Baġdâdî (cf. *supra* n. 90) must — at least as stated — rest ultimately on the « four theses » (for which see *Šarḥ al-uṣûl al-ḫamsa*, 95 and *al-Muḥîṭ*, 38, 14ff.) and a similar process of reasoning.

come to be and *to those that shall not come to be which are subject to God's power of efficient causality and are known to Him*». Within the context of the system this thesis is fully consistent. From one standpoint one could argue in the same way he does in the case of what God will create; viz., that God knows all the discrete individual beings that He could create and that this sum of discrete parts must also be finite since there cannot be an infinite integer. It appears from the sources, however, that abû l-Hudhayl's understanding of the finitude of the possibles was rather more elaborate than this.

One must be careful, in formulating the problem, to keep within the conceptual structure of the author's thought, for the term « the possible » may be ambivalent. For abû l-Hudhayl, as for the later followers of his school and most of the early kalâm, there is no potency in beings; strictly speaking, no being, considered in itself, has any potentiality to become other than it is. We can speak of potentiality only in reference to the efficient causality (*qudra*) of an agent who is capable of bringing it into existence or annihilating it or, in the case of a composite (*ǧumla*), of effecting the realisation of a new accident within its material substrate or some part of it; but matter (the atom as substrate) cannot properly be said to constitute the prior potentiality of the realisation of new being [100]. Again, abû l-Hudhayl holds that prior to its actual, material presence (*wuǧûd*) in the world, a thing simply is not; the « essence » cannot be said to constitute itself its possibility [101], for it has no being at all.

[100] Against this thesis Avicenna argues (*K. al-Išârât wat-tanbîhât* [ed. J. Forget, Leiden, 1892], 151) that the possibility (*'imkân*) of the possible, considered in itself, lies in the substrate (*mawḍû'*) and not in the power of the efficient cause; his argument, however, has little force from the standpoint of the kalâm since he follows a basically Aristotelian notion of potentiality according to which it is the possibility of becoming other (of othering one's self or of being othered) whereas, in the atomistic ontology of the kalâm, one cannot strictly speak of a γένεσις or μεταβολή as these terms are understood in the Greek tradition. Rather one has to do with discrete ontological « quanta », so to speak (atoms and accidents) that are absolute in the sense that they can be described only in terms of the two discrete states of existence and non-existence; being is realised from non-being through the agent's power of efficient causality, whether it be of the atom or accident. Cf. generally my *Metaphysics of Created Being*, 21ff.

[101] In this too Avicenna argues against the kalâm; cf. *Ilâhîyât aš-šifâ'* (ed. G. Anawati and S. Zayed, Cairo, 1960), 181. Cf. also the debates over this matter between Faḫr ad-Dîn ar-Râzî and several followers of the Mâturîdî school in his *Munâẓarât* (ed. F. Kholeif, Beyrouth, 1966), Qq. 3-4, pp. 17ff. and my comments in *Bibliotheca Orientalis* 25 (1968) 230ff.

Created being, thus, considered in itself, has no prior potentiality, for its potentiality resides exclusively in the agent's power of efficient causality; i.e., its possibility is the possibility (*ǧawâz*) that the agent bring it into being. The possible, therefore, as that which can come to be, is spoken of as « that which is subject to the agent's power of efficient causality » (*maqdûruhu*) and is, in a sense, contained in its possibility, « in the power of efficient causality » (*fî l-qudra*) and in the agent's knowledge of what he can or will create (*fî l-ʿilm*). The possible, strictly speaking, is therefore what is really subject to God's efficient causality and, as the possible that will come to be, is, from eternity, coextensive with what He knows He will actually create.

Now the power (*qudra*) to bring a given thing to being is also the power to realise the contrary and furthermore, so long as the power remains without impediment, the power to realise a similar act. From this standpoint, God's power can be considered to embrace an indefinite number of future contingents. Viewed however from God's standpoint, the beings that He will create and the totality of those things that shall come to be are precisely defined and delimited « in His knowledge of them, His power to create them and His ennumerating them » [102], and, within this perspective, the pos-

[102] *Intiṣâr*, 16, 9; note that this series of terms (*fî l-ʿilmi bihi wal-qudrati ʿalayhi wal-iḥṣâʾi lahu*) can be rendered actively as here or passively as above; on this see below. — Manifest in this is a tendency that continues through the later evolution of the school (particularly in treating the efficient causality of the created agent; cf. infra n. 106) to understand *qudra* in terms of discrete quanta or parts (*aǧzâʾ*) each of which is correlated (*mutaʿalliq*) to the (possible or effected) realisation of one part of an act. Thus, for example, ʿAbd al-Ǧabbâr, arguing that a thing may not be directly subject to and realised through the *qudra* of two agents, says that through a single quantum of power of efficient causality (*quadratun wâḥida*) an agent can effect but a single part in a single substrate (i.e., atom) in a single moment (*al-Muġnî* 8, 76, 16ff. and generally *ibid.*, p. 106f, and vol. 16, 50 and 13, 236, 7ff.; a similar conception is held by the ašʿarites: cf. e.g., al-Bâqillânî, *Tamhîd* § 490) and that although the agent may have two quanta of efficient power (*qudratayn*) relative to a particular effect, as a single, discrete quantum, the effect is subject (*maqdûr*) to only one (*al-Muġnî* 8, 130, 1ff.). Following this tendency, abû Hâšim sees a distinct « state » (*ḥâl*) in God's knowing each discrete thing He knows and « there is a distinct state of His being *qâdir* correlated to each *maqdûr* which is not said to be the state of His being *qâdir* over another *maqdûr* » (al-Baġdâdî, Uṣûl, 92, 6-9). One can in like manner speak of *aǧzâʾu l-kalâm* (e.g., *al-Muġnî* 7, 23f.) or *aǧzâʾu n-naẓar* (e.g., *ibid.*, 12, 276, 5-7 or 117 *et alibi*) and that to omit the first « part » entails the omission of all successive « parts » (*ibid.*, 450ff. generally and esp. p. 459, 465 — citing abû Hâšim — and 482ff.).

sibles that will not come to be are strictly the contraries of those beings that shall come to be. This is clear in abû l-Hudhayl's conception of the termination of the possibles at the consummation of all being:

He asserted that when God has effected their perdurance (*baqâ'ahum*) and their state of rest (*sukûnahum*) it will be altogether impossible to say that he has the power of efficient causality to effect in them what he has effected and to realise in them what he has realised. Rather, before he had created their perduring and the actuality of being-at-rest in them, he was capable (*qâdir*) of creating perdurance and of creating the act of being-at-rest as well as of their contraries, but when he has created for them life, perdurance, and rest, it will be impossible to say that God has the power of effecting the life that He has effected or the rest that He has effected or the perdurance that He has already brought into being or of their contraries (sc., non-being, motion, and death), since when the act proceeds out of the power of efficient causality, its contrary goes out of it too in its going forth [103].

When then abû l-Hudhayl speaks of these things « that shall not come to be » the frame of reference is strictly that of the reality that has come to be or that shall come to be, as for example, the classical case of the « possibility » of abû Lahab's having believed and therefore having been saved in consequence of his belief [104]. The possibles, in this perspective, as the non-realised contraries of the real or its non-realisation, constitute a series whose terms correspond precisely to those of the real and since the latter is finite and precisely delimited in God's knowledge, thay too must be so. Within this framework the « possible » which assumes a different creation as the context of its possibility is in fact excluded from all real possibility of existence; it is, so to speak, twice removed from being *maqdûr 'alayhi* in the power of efficient causality upon which the true possibility of being depends or to which it is correlated. For abû l-Hudhayl the possible, as that which the real (that which has come to be or shall come to be) could have been or could be, must be finite, correlated to the finite series constituted by the sum of entities (atoms and accidents) that shall be. The limitation, it should be noted however, is not determined by the materiality of the real; i.e., the possible is not limited through the concrete limitations of materiality as such, considered in terms of the determinations of a particular time and place, or by the nature of the material, for potentiality — the possibility of the realisation

103 *Intiṣâr*, 17, 12-18.

104 Cf. for example, *al-Muġnî* 6/1, 141.

of new being — resides exclusively in the efficient causality of the agent.

Even though he evidently grounded the impossibility of an infinity of possibles on the impossibility of an infinite sum of discrete elements, the conclusion was nonetheless that God's power is limited and though His knowing is infinite He cannot know an infinity of beings [105]. It is not merely the totality of what shall be that is limited but the possible too, and it is this, more than anything else, I think, that stirred up a barrage of opposition even from some of abû l-Hudhayl's own disciples [106] and that ultimately led to his own abandonment of the thesis [107].

[105] Ibn ar-Râwandî attacked abû l-Hudhayl as having held that God's knowledge is finite (*Intiṣâr*, 16, 2f. and 90f.) in reply to which al-Ḫayyâṭ insists (*ibid.*, 16 and 91f.) that insofar as God's knowledge is Humself it is, according to abû l-Hudhayl, infinite and insofar as He knows Himself His knowing is infinite (in contrast to the position of Origen, cited above); al-Aš'arî is careful in his wording to state that the limit belongs to God's knowing what shall come to be and shall not come to be (*Maqâlât*, 485). With this it is interesting to contrast the position of St. Thomas Aquinas who says that given the supposition that the world and generation continue eternally, God knows not merely the infinity of individuals that will exist in each species but knows too, as possibles, an infinity of species, each of them with an infinity of possible individuals (*De veritate* Q. 20, a 4, *ad* 1).

[106] Ǧa'far b. Ḥarb (d. 236/850), originally a disciple of abû l-Hudhayl's who later became a disciple of abû Mûsâ al-Murdâr at Baghdad (cf. art. *Dja'far b. Ḥarb*, by A. Nader in *EI*²) attacked the notion of the finitude of creation in his *K. al-Masâ'il fî n-na'îm* (cf. *Intiṣâr*, 91 and also 57, 14) and wrote another work entitled *Tawbîḫ abî l-Hudhayl* (cf. *Farq*, 122). Al-Murdâr, who was known as the « monk of the Mu'tazila » because of his asceticism (cf. *Ṭabaqât al-Mu'tazila*, 70f.; R. Brunschvig in *Arabica* 9 [1962], p. 350, and H. Laoust, *Les schismes dans l'Islam* [Paris, 1965], 105), is reported to have written a voluminous work against abû l-Hudhayl and especially to have attacked his notion of the ultimate termination of creation (*Farq*, 122f.); another work against him *Fî n-na'îm* is reported to have been written by Hišâm al-Fuwaṭî (*Fihrist ap.* Fück, *op. cit.*, 69, nº 9) and Bišr b. al-Mu'tamir wrote also a work against him (cf. *ibid.*, 59) and accused him of *nifâq* (*ibid.*). — The contrast between the position of abû l-Hudhayl and the later doctrine of the school according to which the power of God is absolutely without limit is seen clearly in the teaching of 'Abd al-Ǧabbâr : the possibles subject to God's efficient causality are, he says, infinite for any given category of accidents in a single substrate (*maḥall*) at any single moment of time while that which is subject to the efficient causality of a human agent is finite. That the possible which is subject to the human agent's power of efficient causality is finite is not, however, due to the limitation of the particular material object that is presented to the agent as the locus of the realisation of his act but it is, rather, determined in terms of the specific (quantitative; cf. *supra* n. 102) measure of his particular power that is correlated to the object; cf. *al-Muġnî* 4 (ed. M. Hilmi and A. al-Ghanimi, Cairo, n.d.), 277 and with

Abû l-Hudhayl's position and its inherent difficulty becomes quite manifest in his reported treatment of an objection to his conception of the finitude of the possibles raised by al-Murdâr during a dispute that took place in the house of Thumâma b. al-Ašras, a student of abû l-Hudhayl's who died in 828 [108]. The objection, as stated by Ibn ar-Râwandî, is that the realisation of an act in another does not become impossible on the part of one from whom its realisation is possible at a given time unless there intervenes a change in the potential agent, « just as when a hard stone breaks something by virtue of its hardness and weight, it does not become impossible for it to break something similar without some change in it and some deficiency that overtakes its very being » [109]. According to al-Ḫayyâṭ, abû l-Hudhayl treated this objection in the following way :

He asserted that one speaks of the agent today just as of the stone in the example : no agent performs an act save that his realising a similar act is possible (*ǧâ'iz*) until his state is changed from one of having the power of efficient causality and the absence of any impediment to one of the incapacity for efficient causation and being impeded (*mina l-qudrati wat-taḫliyati 'ilà l-'aǧzi wal-man'*). At that moment he becomes incapable of the act of which he was capable (*kâna mumkinan lahu*) because of the incapacity for efficient causation that arose, since the things that are today subject to the power of efficient causality (*al-'ašyâ'u l-maqdûru 'alayhâ*, i.e., the possibles) have not all been brought forth into being. When, however, all contingent beings (*al-muḥdaṯâtu kulluhâ*) have come into existence and not one of them remains non-existent and dependent upon the agent's power of efficient causality, it will be impossible to say that the agent of the act has the power (*yaqduru*) to realise a similar act, since there is no similar [act] in the power of efficient causality, all acts having come into existence. One speaks of the stone in the same way : when today something is broken by it, it is fit to break a similar object, exactly as today it is possible that the agent who realises an act realise one like it. The situation of the stone with regard to its being used to break something when all contingent beings have come into existence and not one remains

specific reference to the problems involved in abû l-Hudhayl's position cf. *al-Muḥîṭ bit-taklîf*, 116, 17ff.; cf. also *al-Muġnî* 7, 55, 3-6; 14, 277, 6-7 and 15, 38, 20f. as well as *al-Muḥîṭ*, 159 which is quoted above, n. 55.

[107] Cf. *Intiṣâr*, 21, 6ff. and 92, 3ff.; al-Ḫayyâṭ in making his apologia for this teaching tries to affirm that abû l-Hudhayl was not absolutely convinced of the validity of the position and did not take it very seriously (*lam yakun yatadayyanu bihi wa-lâ ya'taqidu*, *ibid.*, 91, 9) but investigated it only for the sake of speculation (cf. *ibid.*, 18, *ult.* f., 57, 12f. and 92,3); al-Baġdâdî, however, the explicitly takes up this claim of al-Ḫayyâṭ's (*Farq*, 123f.), rather effectively shows that he did hold it quite firmly at one time.

[108] Cf. Laoust, *loc. cit.*, and *Ṭabaqât al-Mu'tazila*, 64 and also Ibn an-Nadîm ap. Fück, *op. cit.*, 63.

[109] *Intiṣâr*, 19, 17-20.

subject to the power of efficient causality will become that of the agent in the same moment: it will be impossible that something be broken by it, just as it will be impossible that the agent, at that moment, realise any further act (*šay'an siwâhu*) [110].

Thus, when the end of the creation of new being, eternally fixed in God's knowledge, has arrived, He will be altogether incapable of creating even one more thing, even though His power is infinite in itself. Ǧa'far b. Ḥarb — not without reason — felt that abû l-Hudhayl's doctrine tended to lead towards that of the dahrîya, i.e., to the thesis that God is not free [111]. As we shall see, however, in what follows, abû l-Hudhayl quite explicity held that God is essentially free, so that the fixed finitude of the possible is contingent in its determination.

Connected with this and unquestionably among the teaching of abû l-Hudhayl that Ǧa'far b. Ḥarb shied away from is his conception of whether or not God can do what is unjust or wrong. According to al-Aš'arî's report « abû l-Hudhayl said that wrong, injustice and lying lie within the power of God and He has the power to do injustice and wrong and to lie but has not done this because of His wisdom and mercy. It is impossible that He do any of this » [112]. He further reports that « when someone said to him, 'But if God were to do wrong', he would reply, 'It is impossible that He do it' » [113]. That he says both *yaqduru 'alà l-ǧûr* and *'alà 'an yaǧûr* is noteworthy; clearly he wishes to deny the distinction made by 'Abbâd b. Sulaymân who would allow that injustice lies within the power of God but said He has not the power to do it. He said that « to bring into being what He knows will be lies within the power of God but one does not say that He has the power not to bring it into being and one does not say of that which we know will not be that He has the power to bring it into being, eventhough it is said to lie within His power » [114].

110 *Ibid.*, 20, 5-15.

111 *Farq*, 122; cp. the discussion in *al-Muġnî* 14, 61, 3ff.

112 *Maqâlât*, 555: ان الله سبحانه يقدر على الظلم والجور والكذب وعلى ان يجور ويظلم ويكذب فلم يفعل ذلك لحكمته ورحمته ومحال ان يفعل شيئا من ذلك

113 *Ibid.*, 556, 7-8.

114 *Muġnî* 6/1, 127f.: قال عباد ان ما علم الله انه يكون يقدر على تكوينه ولا يقال يقدر على ان لا يكونه وما نعلم انه لا يكون لا يقدر على ان يكونه وان قيل انه يقدر عليه; 'Abbâd (d. 250/864) was a disciple of Hišâm b. 'Amr al-Fuwaṭî (d. before 218/833), a pupil of abû l-Hudhayl, and the two

ʿAbd al-Ǧabbâr takes exception to al-Ašʿarî's statement that abû l-Hudhayl held that it is impossible (*muḥâl*) that God do injustice and says that « the doctrine of abû l-Hudhayl, together with most of his disciples, and that of abû ʿAlî [al-Ǧubbâ'î] and abû Hâšim is that God is described as having within His power to do that which, were He to do it, would be wrongdoing and lying, even though He does not do this because of His knowledge of its being evil and His being incapable of deriving any benefit from doing it (*bi-stiġnâ'ihi ʿanhu*); they treated the problem of His power to do what He knows will not be in the same way. It is reported, however, of abû l-Hudhayl that he said, 'It is impossible (*yastaḥîl*) that God do wrong even though it lies within His power,' but this is improbable and self-contradictory » [115]. The Qâḍî would appear to be correct in saying that the teaching of the three masters of the Baṣra school is substantially the same [116], but it is also plain that abû l-Hudhayl did in fact employ the term « impossible » (*muḥâl* or *mustaḥîl*), the implications of which disturbed ʿAbd al-Ǧabbâr and probably Ǧaʿfar b. Ḥarb as well [117]. Asked what if God does the injustice and wrong which lie within His power, he replied, according to al-Ašʿarî, « It is impossible (*muḥâl*) that the Creator do this, since that would not happen save on the basis of a deficiency in the Creator » [118].

It is instructive to compare this with the teaching of Origen:

> *δύναται δὲ καθ' ἡμᾶς πάντα ὁ θεός, ἅπερ δυνάμενος τοῦ θεὸς εἶναι καὶ τοῦ ἀγαθὸς εἶναι καὶ σοφὸς εἶναι οὐκ ἐξίσταται · ὁ δὲ Κέλσος φησιν ὡς μὴ νοήσας, πῶς λέγεται ὁ θεὸς πάντα δύνασθαι, ὅτι οὐκ ἐθελήσει οὐδὲν ἄδικον, διδοὺς ὅτι δύναται μὲν καὶ τὸ ἄδικον, οὐ θέλει δέ. ἡμεῖς δέ φαμεν ὅτι, ὥσπερ οὐ δύναται τὸ πεφυκὸς γλυκαίνειν τῷ γλυκὺ τυγχάνειν πικράζειν παρὰ τὴν αὐτοῦ μόνην αἰτίαν,*

are reported (*Maqâlât*, 202f. and 558) as having held an identical position regarding the proposition « if God were to do what is wrong »; the distinction between *yaqduru ʿalà fiʿl* and *ʿalà 'an yafʿal* undoubtedly goes back to the beginnings of the school. Finally, the distinction of « what we know will not be » is simply made in terms of our capability of speaking of the possible that surely will never come to be, which must be based on revelation (cf. e.g., *supra* n. 104).

115 *Al-Muġnî* 6/1, 128; cf. also *ibid.*, 6/2, 138, 12ff.

116 Cf. the reports of the teaching of al-Ǧubbâ'î and abû Hâšim, *ibid.*, 6/1, 150f. and n.b. the distinctions made p. 137, 10-13; and see also *ibid.* 14, 187f. Al-Ǧubbâ'î's conception of the problems here involved, which is quite complex, especially in the rhetoric of his exposition, I hope to deal with in a subsequent study.

117 On his teaching, cf. e.g., *Maqâlât*, 556f.

118 *Ibid.*, 200, 12ff.; cf. also Ibn al-Muṭahhar al-Maqdisî, *op. cit.* 1, 107, 5-7.

οὐδὲ τὸ πεφυκὸς φωτίζειν τῷ εἶναι φῶς σκοτίζειν, οὕτως οὐδ' ὁ θεὸς δύναται ἀδικεῖν · ἐναντίον γάρ ἐστιν αὐτοῦ τῇ θεότητι καὶ τῇ κατ' αὐτὴν πάσῃ δυνάμει ἡ τοῦ ἀδικεῖν δύναμις. εἰ δέ τι τῶν ὄντων δύναται ἀδικεῖν τῷ καὶ πρὸς τὸ ἀδικεῖν πεφυκέναι δύναται ἀδικεῖν, οὐκ ἔχον ἐν τῇ φύσει τὸ μηδαμῶς δύνασθαι ἀδικεῖν [119].

From one standpoint the attitudes of abû l-Hudhayl and Origen are quite parallel : both assert that it is impossible that God do evil since it is contrary to His « nature » or divinity to do so. There is, however, a marked difference in the attitude of the Muʿtazilite master, an orientation that is directed clearly (and especially in the context of the later elaboration of the problem within the school) away from the thoroughly « Greek » attitude of Origen. Abû l-Hudhayl will not allow even the position of an-Naẓẓâm, according to whom God has not the power to do evil since it is impossible that He have the power to do that which from eternity He knows He will not do [120]. In part, no doubt, one has here to do with abû l-Hudhayl's conception of the nature of the power of efficient causality as embracing both the object and its contrary [121] and the insistence, so important a factor in the evolution of the school's doctrine on many a theological question, of reasoning by strict analogy from the phenomenal to the non-phenomenal. Much more important, however, in shaping the direction of his thought is his conviction — in conformity with the fundamental insight of the *Koran* — that there can be no intrinsic restriction on the power of God and His freedom. His insistence that the hypothesis « if God were to do evil » is altogether impossible since God would have to be other than He is in such an event, is quite parallel to Origen's argument that God cannot do evil since if He did evil He would not be God [122]. The crucial difference, though, is that abû l-Hudhayl will not in any way accept the notion that God is constrained by His « nature » and can do only that which it is His nature to do. The objective impossibility that He do what He

[119] *Contra Celsus* III, 70, 8-20, ed. Borret, vol. 2 (*Sources Chrétiennes*, 136, Paris, 1968), p. 160; cf. also *ibid.* V, 23 and Faye, *op. cit.* 3, 33 and Bardy, *op. cit.*, col. 1518.

[120] *Al-Muġnî* 6/1, 141; cf. also *Farq*, 131 and 133f. and also the fictitious debate recorded *ibid.*, 199. Abû l-Hudhayl wrote a work against an-Naẓẓam on this subject (cf. Ibn an-Nadîm *ap.* Fück, *op. cit.*, p. 58, nº 27).

[121] *Intiṣâr*, 16, 16; cp. *Maqâlât*, 577, 5f.

[122] *Op. cit.* V, 23 : *φαμεν δὲ ὅτι οὐ δύναται αἰσχρὰ ὁ θεός, ἐπεὶ ἔσται ὁ θεὸς δυνάμενος μὴ εἶναι θεός · εἰ γὰρ αἰσχρόν τι δρᾷ θεὸς, οὐκ ἔστι θεός.* Cf. also the references cited by Borret, *op. cit.*, 160, n. 1.

knows from eternity He will not do [123] does not imply any intrinsic compulsion of His nature or limitation on His power. Rather, he says that God does not do evil or injustice because of His wisdom and mercy; He has created mankind out of no need (*ḥâǧa*) on His part but only for the sake of their well-being. That He do evil is inconceivable because of His absolute self-sufficiency (*ġinà*) and the total absence in Him of any deficiency (*naqṣ*) by virtue of which it would be possible for Him to derive some benefit from any creature [124].

Even with the lamentable absence of fuller documentation certain aspects of abû l-Hudhayl's position are reasonably clear. He is fundamentally opposed to the basis of Origen's argument, even though his thought on this question would appear more akin to it in some respects than is the fully elaborated doctrine of his successors in the Baṣra school, in that he holds that it is really impossible (*muḥâl*) that God do evil since otherwise His being would be other than it is [125].

The same problem is raised in terms of the question of whether God could have made creation more salutory (*aṣlaḥ*) for mankind than it is. Abû l-Hudhayl holds that « God has not the power to do what is more salutory than what He has done » but here he conceives a maximisation of what is best within the framework of creation and not a limitation that is intrinsic to God's power. God has the power to create what is equally salutory and, too, what is less so, but since He creates from no need but, in His wisdom, only for the well-being of His creatures, He does what is morally most fitting (*awlà*) and it is in this sense that it is impossible (*lâ yaǧûz*) that He omit what is most salutory [126]. By insisting that God could do other than He

[123] This is clearly implied in his insistence on the impossibility (*istiḥâla*) of any further creation when the term fixed in God's knowledge has been reached.

[124] Cf. *Šarḥ at-uṣûl al-ḫamsa*, 307, 12ff., *Maqâlât*, 577, 2f. and the references cited above nn. 115 and 118.

[125] 'Abd al-Ǧabbâr insists that not only does God's having the power to do evil not indicate that His being may become other than it is (i.e., that He be *ǧâhil muḥtâǧ* rather than *ġanîy 'âlim*) but that the actual occurance of such an event, though it would be an indication (*dalâla*) of same such deficiency in His being, could not necessitate the reality of such (*al-Mugnî* 6/1, 140f.; cf. also the distinctions made *ibid.*, 137, vol. 15, 176, 12ff, and vol. 16, 59f.).

[126] *Maqâlât*, 576f. Ibn Ḥazm (*op. cit.* 4, 193) says that abû l-Hudhayl's teaching is the same as that of an-Naẓẓâm, but here again (cf. *supra* n. 120) where an-Naẓẓâm asserts that God does not have the power to do other than He does (*Maqâlât*, 576), abû l-Hudhayl, because of the way he understands the nature of God's power, insists that He can.

does but what would be equally salutory, abû l-Hudhayl avoids the implication that because of His unbounded generosity (*ǧûd*) He is constrained by His nature in such wise that He cannot do other than He does [127].

GOD'S SPEECH AND HIS WILL

In the matter of God's word — or, more properly, His Speech (*kalâm*) — abû l-Hudhayl distinguishes two altogether different senses : the creative « Be » (*kun*) and the revelation, addressed to men. The *Koran* (and implicitly the other revelations as they were given to each prophet) is a created discourse ontologically having the same basic properties as human speech. Distinct from the uttered sound (*ṣawt*) and having the property of perdurance (*al-baqâ'*) [128], speech is ontologically a distinct entity that subsists as an accident in a substrate. The elements which constitute speech (viz., *al-ḥurûf* : the letters or elements of articulation) are distinct from the sound of the voice and speech is essentially the reality of these elements as they embody meaning [129] : to speak is to articulate meaning and

---

[127] That he employs the expression *laysa bi-baḫîl* in the passage cited by al-Aš'arî (*Maqâlât*, 577, 3) rather than *ǧawâd* may be significant in terms of his avoidance of this conclusion; cf. also the references to 'Abd al-Ǧabbâr, *supra* n. 86.

[128] Cf. *al-Muḥîṭ bit-taklîf*, 327, 14ff., *al-Muġnî* 7, 191, 11-13, and *Maqâlât*, 432; concerning abû l-Hudhayl's treatment of « perdurance » cf. my *Metaphysics of Created Being*, 20f. and 50f.

[129] Cf. *al-Muġnî* 7, 7, 15ff. (which tells the teaching of al-Ǧubbâ'î but may be taken as valid for abû l-Hudhayl too, since the doctrine of the two was essentially the same on this point according to both the Qâḍî [e.g., *al-Muḥîṭ*, *loc. cit.*] and al-Aš'arî [*op. cit.*, 599]; in *al-Muġnî*, *loc. cit.*, lines 19-20 one should read *yqwl* for *nqwl* in both places and should introduce *ġyr* following *huwa* in line 19). According to al-Aš'arî (*op. cit.*, 604, 14f.) al-Ǧubbâ'î held that « a single phoneme [*ḥarf*] may constitute speech ; he justified this by citing the teaching of the philologians that speech is a noun, verb, or particle that gives meaning» (reading *bi-ma'nan* for *li-ma'nan*). One report (Paris, Bibl. Nat., ms. arabe 1252, fol. 30R°, 15) has it that al-Ǧubbâ'î taught that speech is « meaning that subsists in the elements of articulation » (*ma'nan qâ'imun bil-ḥurûf*). The unknown author (whose doctrine on this matter is identical with that of the later Baṣra school; n. that his initial definition of speech [fol. 30R°, 6f.] is verbatim that given in *Šarḥ al-uṣûl al-ḫamsa*, 529, 8f.) contrasts this with the teaching of al-Aš'arî (*al-kalâmu ma'nan qâ'imun bi-ḏâti l-mutakallim* [line 9]; the same formula is given in 'Abd al-Ǧabbâr, *op. cit.*, 528, 1). The formula attributed to al-Ǧubbâ'î is quite problematic however, in that it directly implies a situation in which one accident inheres in another, a thesis that neither he nor abû l-Hudhayl would have found tolerable. It is conceivable that the author has simply garbled some such statement as that found in al-Aš'arî's *Maqâlât*

the being of speech is that of the elements of articulation (*al-ḥurûf*). His position is, in the words of ʿAbd al-Ǧabbâr, that speech « has existence in the existence of another and, by sharing the substrate, characterises this other in its being in the substrate » [130]. That is, speech (sc. the *ḥurûf*) is ontologically an accident that has its existence through subsisting in an ordered substrate; its presence (*wuǧûd*) in the substrate is dependent upon the presence of another accident, viz., the order of the material substrate (*maḥall*), as for example, it may subsist in air (*al-hawâ'* — already a complex composite) by virtue of the ordering of the air as sound (*ṣawt*) and the air, then, or the sound, in consequence of the presence of the elements of articulation, is characterised as speech.

The nature of the *ḥurûf*, however, unlike that of most other accidents, is such that their actuality in being is not bound to the presence of only one kind of ordered substrate. On the contrary, according to the particular vehicle or substrate, they may exist in several modes, as sounded, as written, or as held in memory [131]. For this reason then, in contrast to other material accidents, speech may exist simultaneously in a plurality of substrates since the immediate condition of its presence in the individual substrate is not the actuality of the

(*loc. cit.*), but such a misleading use of the technical language of the kalâm is altogether improbable. Al-Ǧubbâ'î (and abû l-Hudhayl too) held that speech *is* the *ḥurûf* as meaningful; that he defined speech as the *ḥurûf* is plain enough from the citations given above as also from *al-Muǵnî* 16, 54 (cited in the following note; cf. also *al-Muḥîṭ*, 307, 1f. and 330, 4ff.); consequently it is more likely, I should think, that the formula given in the Paris ms. is so construed in order to follow al-Ǧubbâ'î's conception that the elements of articulation (*ḥurûf*), as the structured reality that is speech, are ontologically distinct and separable from the sound which is the condition of their actuality as subsistent in the air, without having to take the trouble to redefine or explain his conception of the *ḥurûf* in its difference from that of his followers (cf. n. 131).

130 *Al-Muǵnî* 16, 54, 1ff.; again here, he mentions only al-Ǧubbâ'î, but the same thesis — less succinctly expressed — is attributed to abû l-Hudhayl in *al-Muḥîṭ*, 327; cf. also references n. 132, below.

131 *Al-Muḥîṭ*, *loc. cit.*, *al-Muǵnî* 7, 187 (*cit. infra*), *Maqâlât*, 192 and 598f. This contrasts with the doctrine of the later school (e.g., ʿAbd al-Ǧabbâr) which, though defining speech as the *ḥurûf*, considered them as uttered phonemes and so insisted that their actuality consists only as « divided sounds » (*aṣwâtun muqaṭṭaʿa*) : « speech cannot be ordered phonemes (*ḥurûfun manẓûma*) unless they are divided sounds ». (*al-Muǵnî* 7, 7, 11f.); ʿAbd al-Ǧabbâr says, consequently, in the same passage, that it would have been better for al-Ǧubbâ'î to have restricted the definition of speech simply to the *ḥurûf* without trying to make it altogether other than the sound (cf. also *Muḥîṭ*, 307, 1ff. and 330, 4ff.).

specific mode of ubication (i.e., one of the *akwân*) but the structuring or actuality of the substrate as sound, writing, or memory, which do not constitute a set of contraries [132]. Speech, thus, exists in several modalities without losing its distinct ontological identity as speech and is not, strictly speaking, subject to local motion [133]. In this way, a given utterance maintains its own ontological identity under whatever varying mode of existence it may occur. In however many times and places it may be repeated, it remains the speech of the speaker who first initiated its being; ontologically, abû l-Hudhayl says, « the retelling is the thing retold itself » (*al-ḥikâyatu ʿaynu l-maḥkî*) so that a discourse repeated *is* in the strictest sense the original speech of the one who initiated its being [134]. The existence of speech, like that of all other material accidents, is subsistent in a substrate (*maḥall*), so that its being is dependent upon its actuality in the substrate, but so long as a given statement subsists in some substrate — in memory or in writing — it perdures in existence (*yabqâ*). It ceases to exist only if all the substrates in which it subsists cease to exist.

Abû l-Hudhayl, thus, held that the *Koran* was primevally created by God in « The Cherished Tablet » and that this discourse itself exists as recited, written, and retained in the hearts of men, without losing its integrity or identity with itself. Strictly speaking, the Word of God that is the revelation is not world-transcendent. It is a material

[132] Cf. *al-Muġnî* 7, 187 (reading *wlkn* for *wlkḏb* in line 9) and 8, 147, 13ff. (omitting *lâ* after *li'annahu* in line 14). This whole construction sits most awkwardly within the general metaphysics of the system. Al-Ǧubbâ'î is reported (*al-Muḥîṭ*, 328, 3ff.) to have felt constrained to modify his doctrine on the basis of a difficulty involving the intention of the one who repeats the statement of another (cf. also *ibid.*, 330), but this was insufficient to make the thing coherent and consistent within the system. It should be noted that the passage of Šahrastânî's *Milal* (p. 119, 9ff.) cited by J. Bouman (*Le conflit autour du Coran et la solution d'al-Bâqillânî* [Amsterdam, 1959], 26, n. 116) and V. Cremonesi (*Un' antico documento Ibâḍita sul Corano creato, Studi Magrebini* 1 [1966], 146, n. 59) cannot reflect the genuine taching of al-Ǧubbâ'î.

[133] *Maqâlât*, 192 and 598f.; n.b. also the argument of al-Ǧubbâ'î reported in *al-Muḥîṭ*, 313, 4ff. and cf. also *Farq*, 184.

[134] *Muḥîṭ*, 327; al-Ǧubbâ'î is reported to have argued that speech, though repeated by another speaker, remains always that of the original speaker (*al-mubtadi'u bihi*) since another cannot « initiate its being in such wise that it be simultaneously the speech of the one who initiated its being and that of the one who intends to repeat his speech » (*al-Muġnî* 7, 188, 15f.; cf. also *al-Muḥîṭ*, *loc. cit.*, and *Maqâlât*, 599; all three of these reports are attributed directly and, it would appear, exclusively to al-Ǧubbâ'î, but the reasoning of abû l-Hudhayl, to judge from his teaching concerning the *Koran* [see *Maqâlât*, 589f. and below] must surely have been somewhat similar).

being as are all beings save God Himself, and if God were to destroy *all* the substrates in which the *Koran* has its existence, it would cease to exist as speech [135]. As speech, the Word of God is contingent upon His will, as is all material being, but the revelation is not, for this reason, a « mere » creature. Like all speech, it is the speech of the one who originated it and the *Koran* — the Arabic words and phrases, these *âyât* — is the articulate speech of God [136], the Eternal

135 *Maqâlât*, 192 and esp. 598f.; he does not mention the existence of the revelation in God's knowing; what lies behind this is probably that God's knowledge cannot be termed memory (*ḥafẓ*); in memory, speech is retained as speech, fully articulated in its material parts. As speech, thus, i.e., as a complex accident composed of parts ordered in space and time, it cannot subsist in God. — There is really no ambiguity concerning the ontological status of the « Cherished Tablet » as Bouman suggests (*op. cit.*, 18) and clearly no ground for seeing in it a transcendent and incorruptible recepticle as does Cremonesi (*op. cit.*, 141; cf. also the remarks of W. M. WATT in *Early Discussions about the Qur'an, MW* 40 [1950], 97, n. 51, which seem to lean towards the same prejudice concerning the « Tablet »); it is material (i.e., is composed of atoms in which God's speech subsists as an accident) and therefore must be world-immanent like all other material creatures. Its special or « transcendent » character derives exclusively from the holiness of the Speech of God — the « mighty scripture » that would humble a mountain (59.21) — for whose being it is the primal locus.

136 This thesis was supported by texts of the *Koran* itself (cf. *al-Muġnî* 7, 188) identical to those used by the Aš'arîtes and the Ḥanbalites to uphold their own (opposing) theses. Bouman (*loc. cit.*) says that in failing to distinguish sharply between the divine and human speech « ce fondateur de la théologie mu'tazilite a ouvert un chemin que ses successeurs n'ont pas tardé à suivre et dont les graves conséquences étaient la contingence et la relativité de la forme humaine, c.à.d. arabe du Coran ». The implication of « relativity » in the verbal text of the revelation is, however, one of the very things that the Baṣra school sought to avoid (cf. e.g., *al-Muḥîṭ*, 323, 3ff. and also 325 and 329); the position of abû l-Hudhayl in making the word of God the articulate words of the *Koran* that we hear and read would seem, in part at least, to avoid some of the ambiguities of the positions of the aš'arîs and some of the ḥanbalites, for whom the true word of God, as transcendent, is not *per se* articulated in a particular linguistic form but, on the contrary, is above all language, the particular material articulation being, consequently, an accidental verbal ex-pression of or allusion to the true Speech. This position, which seems to derive from Ibn Kullâb (cf. WATT, *op. cit.*, 96 and VAN Ess in *Oriens* 18-19, 103f.), is quite explicit for the aš'arites and would seem inescapable within some ḥanbalite formulations; cf. e.g., al-Bâqillânî, *al-Inṣâf* (ed. M. al-Kawthari, Cairo, 1369/1950), 94f., *at-Tamhîd*, 251, 5f. (§ 423), al-Baġdâdî, *Uṣûl*, 107, 2f., and ad-Dârimî, *ar-Radd 'alà Bišr al-Marîsî l-'anîd* (ed. M. AL-FAQI, Cairo, 1357), 124. Similarly Bouman's statement concerning the teaching of al-Ǧubbâ'î that « the Arabic of the *Koran* is no more than a human expression of the revelation » falls wide of the mark, for far from being a verbal expression (*'ibâra*) of or allusion (*amâra*) to something that is the true revelation (that contained in the « Cherished Tablet » or whatever), the verbal form of the *Koran*, recited, written, or memorized, *is* the revelation itself. This is absolutely clear even in the brief reports of al-Aš'arî.

Creator, available to human perception and understanding. It is as available in the materiality of its being in the form of language that the verses constitute *âyât*: signs of God's power and omnipotence. When one hears the *Koran* recited, what he hears is, in the strictest sense, the speech of God; not a « copy » or imitation, but the very Speech of God, « a glorious lection, in a cherished tablet » (85.21f) which is essentially inimitable and irreproducible. « If mankind and the jinns combine to reproduce the like of this lection, they will not produce its like ». (17.88). Here again, as in the case of the essential attributes, the teaching of abû l-Hudhayl manifests a notable effort to keep the literal sense of the revelation, even though in the process there arise a number of serious difficulties in terms of the consistency of the underlying metaphysics of his system.

It is in order to retain the dogmatic content of the revelation that, to the scandal of more « orthodox » thinkers, abû l-Hudhayl « divides » God's speech. Whereas the Word addressed to men that consists in the announcement of commands, prohibitions, and informations — the Speech that is recited, written, and retained — exists in the world as an object available to sense, God's creative command that brings beings to Being cannot be ontologically no more than a creature. The creative « Be » and the divine act of willing constitute together God's act of creation [137]. Because of their unique correlation to the temporality of the creature whose being they effect, however, they differ significantly from the other attributes. Al-Aš'arî summarises abû l-Hudhayl's teaching concerning God's will and creative utterance thus :

> Abû l-Hudhayl said : « The creation of a being, which is the act of bringing it into being after it was not, is distinct from it. It is His willing it and His saying to it 'Be'. The act of creation is temporally simultaneous with the thing created. It is not possible that God create a being that He does not will and to which He does not say 'Be' ». He affirmed the reality of the act of creation of the accident as distinct from it and likewise the creation of the atom. He held that the act of creation that is an act of willing and speaking is immaterial... God's willing a thing is distinct from it and His willing faith is other than His commanding it [138].

[137] On the relationship of the act of creation to the creature, cf. my *Metaphysics of Created Being*, 45ff.

[138] *Maqâlât*, 363f.; God's commanding faith, etc., is the verbal command and a part of the created revelation (cf. *al-Muġnî* 6/2, 4 and *Milal*, 72, which is cited by Cremonesi, *op. cit.*, 140).

The creation which is composition or which is color or which is length, and all that is thus, is created in the strict sense and takes place through an act of speaking and an act of willing, while the creation that is an act of speaking and an act of willing is, in the strict sense, not created but is termed created only in a metaphorical sense [139].

Abû l-Hudhayl said: « God's act of willing a thing's coming to be is distinct from the thing that is brought into being; it exists immaterially. His willing faith is distinct from it and from His commanding it and is [un-]created ». He did not make the act of willing identical with that of commanding or with judgement or report. Muḥammad ibn 'Abd al-Wahhâb al-Ǧubbâ'î adhered to the same doctrine save that abû l-Hudhayl held that the act of willing something's coming-to-be and the act of saying to it 'Be' are the act of creating the thing... Abû l-Hudhayl did not affirm that the act of creation is created [140].

These texts present several immediate problems. One notes first that whereas al-Aš'arî says in the first citation that according to abû l-Hudhayl « it is not possible that God create a being... to which He does not say 'Be' », 'Abd al-Ǧabbâr asserts that he held what seems to be a position quite to the contrary : « Know, he says, that the doctrine of our master abû l-Hudhayl is that when He (the Exalted) wishes to create a being (*al-'iḥdâṯ*), He creates its being simply by saying 'Be' (and so also in the re-creation of a being or its annihilation). This, however, does not entail what these determinists claim, viz., that it follows necessarily that He cannot create the being of a 'Be' save by means of another 'Be' and so on endlessly. His intention in this is, rather, that when He (the Exalted) wishes some act, He realises it simply by saying this utterance to it, not that it does not lie within His power to create its being except by this means » [141]. The opposition of the two reports, nonetheless, may be only apparent, for we have quite clearly in the two texts a difference of terminology exactly paralleling that which abû l-Hudhayl uses in treating the problem of the possibility of God's doing evil, discussed above. It is most probable, thus, that he taught that though it lies in God's power to create (*yaqduru 'alà l-ḫalq*) without the utterance *kun*, it is nevertheless impossible (*muḥâl, ġayr ǧâ'iz*) that He do so since He knows eternally that He will create through the creative « Be ». The « Be »,

139 *Maqâlât*, 366 (cf. also *ibid.*, 511); on the distinction of two meanings of the term creation (*ḫalq*), cf. my *Metaphysics of Created Being, loc. cit.*

140 *Maqâlât*, 510 (cf. also the report concerning his disciples, *ibid.*, 189f); the insertion of the negative *ġayr* in line 5, suggested by the editor, is clearly necessary in view of the consistency of the other reports.

141 *Šarḥ al-uṣûl al-ḫamsa*, 562.

thus, is, as ʿAbd al-Ğabbâr indicates, a kind of instrument or means (*tarîqa*)[142] that springs immediately from God's essential power of efficient causality (*qudra*). Still, the ontological status of the creative command and of God's will remains somewhat problematic.

The terminology occuring in the sources that report abû l-Hudhayl's doctrine concerning God's creative command and will varies notably. Al-Ašʿarî, in the passages just cited, says once (363, 14) simply that he held that God's act of willing is « immaterial » (*lâ fî makân*) but in the other (510, 4) that it « exists (*tûğad*) immaterially », as also in a nother passage he reports that abû l-Hudhayl allowed the « existence (*wuğûd*) of accidents not in a body and of temporally contingent beings immaterially »[143]. Al-Baġdâdî, on the other hand, in conformance with what seems to have become fairly common usage[144], says in both his *Farq bayn al-firaq* and the *Uṣûl ad-dîn* that abû l-Hudhayl held that God's creative command « comes to be [in time] immaterially » (*ḥâdiṯ lâ fî maḥall*). This vocabulary unquestionably reflects the later usage of the Baṣra school. However, although the term *ḥâdiṯ* is used, for example, in the works of ʿAbd al-Ğabbâr[145], the term *muḥdaṯ* is by far more common and would seem to be preferred from the time of al-Ğubbâ'î[146]. The course of this variation of terminology and formulation is instructive for our present problem as it contrasts with the apparent usage and the the context of abû l-Hudhayl.

Dividing the two horns of the problem as it is debated, ʿAbd al-Ğabbâr ever and again repeats the pair of formulae : « God's act of willing is temporally generated » (*muḥdaṯa*) and « it exists immaterially »

[142] *Ibid.*, line 8.

[143] *Maqâlât*, 369, 13.

[144] *Farq*, 127 and *Uṣûl*, 106; Cremonesi (*op. cit.*, 140, n. 33) thinks that the presence of the term *ḥâdiṯ* does not truly reflect the thought of abû l-Hudhayl but is introduced polemically by al-Baġdâdî. Šahrastânî, in treating this question (*Milal*, 72), employs no verbal adjective though in speaking of the doctrine of al-Ğubbâ'î says that he affirmed *'irâdatan ḥâdiṯatan lâ fî maḥall* (*ibid.*, 118; cf. also *Nihâya* [ed. A. Guillaume, Oxford, 1934], 248) and similarly al-Ğuwaynî says that the Baṣra school of the Muʿtazila asserted that He is willing *bi-'irâdatin ḥâdiṯatin lâ fî maḥall* (*Iršâd* [ed. M. Moussa and A. ʿAbd el-Hamid, Cairo, 1369/1950], 94).

[145] E.g., *al-Muḥîṭ*, 276ff.

[146] Cf. generally *al-Muġnî* 6/2, 140ff. and 149ff., *et pass.*, *Šarḥ al-uṣûl al-Ḫamsa*, 440ff. (and also *al-Muḥîṭ*, e.g. 277, 12). Concerning al-Ğubbâ'î, cf. *al-Muġnî* 6/2, 143, 1 and also al-Ašʿarî, *Ibâna*, 44, where both *muḥdaṯ* and *maḫlûq* occur in a polemical context aimed most directly, it would appear, at his master.

(*tûğadu lâ fî maḥall*)[147]. The sense of neither of these two formulae, however, as they are understood by the Qâdî, can in any way be read into the teaching of abû l-Hudhayl. ʿAbd al-Ğabbâr, following al-Ğubbâ'î and abû Hâšim, takes the act of the will (*irâda*) as an act (*fiʿl*) done, whether in God or in man, so that the term *muḥdaṯa* is to be taken quite strictly in its passive sense. This, however, cannot be so read in the teaching of abû l-Hudhayl, according to which God's act of the will « is not, strictly speaking, created »; for him the terms *maḫlûq* and *muḥdaṯ* are equivalent[148] whence the use of the term *muḥdaṯ* is excluded. On the other hand, ʿAbd al-Ğabbâr's (following abû Hâšim's) use of the term *tûğad* (or *mawğûda*) quite strictly reflects a distinction belonging to the theory of « states » or *aḥwâl* : God's act of the will (*irâda*), though immaterial, is an entitative perfection (*maʿnà*) that has *being* and, in its being, as the act and perfection of God, is the cause (*ʿilla*) of a state which, though having no existence (*wuğûd*) as an entity, « becomes » or « arises » (*tağaddad*) and constitutes a non-entitative attribute (*ṣifa*) of God[149]. Abû l-Hudhayl's use of the term « exist » quite obviously cannot reflect this kind of distinction. Now al-Ašʿarî reports that the disciples of abû l-Hudhayl disgareed as to the « locus » of God's act of willing; according to one position « God's act of the will subsists in Him immaterially » (is *qâ'imatun bihi lâ fî makân*) while the other holds that « God's act of the will exists (is *mawğûda*) immaterially, without saying that it is subsistent in God (The Exalted) »[150].

Despite the assertion of Ibn ʿAyyâš that Ğaʿfar b. Ḥarb, who was at one time a disciple of abû l-Hudhayl, was the first to teach that God's act of willing « exists immaterially »[151], there is, I feel, little question that this was the position of the master. Al-Ašʿarî in no way qualifies his reports of abû l-Hudhayl's teaching on this matter[152]

[147] E.g., *al-Muğnî* 6/2, 3 and *loc. cit.* supra n. 146 et *pass.*, *Šarḥ al-uṣûl al-ḫamsa*, *loc. cit.*, *et alibi.*

[148] *Maqâlât*, 541.

[149] Cf. e.g., *al-Muḥîṭ*, 276, 17ff.; on the distinction of terms *wuğûd*, *tağaddada* and *maʿnà*/*ʿaraḍ* and *ṣifa*/*ḥâl*, see my *Abû Hâšim's Theory of 'States'* in *Acts of the Fourth Congress of Arabic and Islamic Studies.*

[150] *Maqâlât*, 190, 2ff.

[151] Cf. *al-Muğnî* 6/2, 4 (and on Ğaʿfar b. Ḥarb, *supra* n. 106); in the same place he reports the contrary assertion by aṣ-Ṣâhib al-Ğalîl (whom I take to be the wezir Ibn ʿAbbâd, who was known as aṣ-Ṣâhib al-Kâfî more commonly).

[152] Cf. also *Maqâlât*, 369, 14ff, where again al-Ašʿarî says that according to abû l-Hudhayl God's will has its being immaterially.

and ʿAbd al-Ǧabbâr, who reports the assertion of Ibn ʿAyyâš, does not himself seem convinced of its validity. In either case, at any rate, God's will — as also His creative command — is conceived as a kind of temporal hypostasis, an hypostasis, as it were, of His knowledge and power as these bear on the production of created being. In the one case as in the other, it is the very temporality of God's willing, as it is immediately correlated with the temporal realisation of its object, that requires that it be somehow other than God Himself as He is, in Himself, absolute in the Oneness and eternity of His being. The thesis that His act of the will is subsistent in Him was not acceptable to the school in that the basic conception of the nature of God's being excluded the notion of subsistent perfections (as held, for example, by Ibn Kullâb) of any kind, and, I should think, *a fortiori* any temporal and contingent act.

The significance of the expression *mawǧûda lâ fî makân* is this: God's « essence » in the unity of His essential attributes is not subject to temporal perfections; i.e., it cannot form a substrate for an entitatively separable perfection or act. All reality other than the divine essence consists of atoms or accidents so that God's act of willing, as something that is temporally contingent, must, for want of another category of being, be an accident (ʿ*arad̩*) [153]. It would seem likely that abû l-Hudhayl simply used the term *mawǧûda* to describe God's act of willing because he did not want to imply the passive notion of generation inherent in *muḥdaṯa* and implied, perhaps, in *ḥâdiṯa*, since he did not conceive it as properly speaking created or generated. On the other hand, the use may be more pregnant; as was noted above, it would seem that in contrast to others of his contemporaries, he avoided the application of the terms *wuǧûd*, *mawǧûd*, etc., to God's essence and it is therefore possible that he used the term *mawǧûda* of God's will in a very strict sense to designate its existence as something distinct from His essence. Because of the extremely fragmentary character of the available data this question cannot be resolved. Whatever may be the solution to the terminological problem however, it is nonetheless quite plain that we have here to do with a kind of hypostasis, temporal and contingent, yet uncreated.

Because of the very nature of the question one can, with little or no difficulty, find almost any number of patristic parallels — particularly involving the hypostasis of the Logos — with abû l-Hud-

[153] Cf. *ibid.*

hayl's teaching concerning the act of God's will; but precisely because of the topical inevitability of such quasi parallels, it is impossible to establish any historical connection or to say that Christian trinitarian speculation had any direct influence on his teaching. That Origen several times says that the Son proceeds from the Father just as the will proceeds from the mind [154] may be worth noting, in view of the apparent near parallels of some of his thought with that of abû l-Hudhayl mentioned above, but it would be fruitless to persue this. Of quite another order, however, is the parallelism of the little tract, spuriously attributed to St. Justin the Martyr, that goes under the title *Quaestiones Christianae ad Graecos*, for in this work, which concerns itself almost entirely with the temporality of creation and the freedom of God's action, we find a most striking and unequivocal similarity to the thought of abû l-Hudhayl and his successors in the Baṣra school of the Mu'tazila. That this similarity arises from any direct dependence is not to be affirmed without some better evidence than I have discovered, but that the *Quaestiones Christianae* or some similar and parallel material — originating perhaps from the School of Antioch [155] — was current and available together with the other non-islamic materials which contributed to the earliest formation of the kalâm is hardly to be denied. It is, to be sure, possible that

[154] E.g., *de Pr.* I, 2, 6 (p. 35, ll. 4 and 16) and notably I, 2, 9 : Intelligenda est ergo virtus dei, qua viget qua omnia visibilia et invisibilia vel instituit vel continet vel gubernat, qua ad omnia sufficiens est, quorum providentiam gerit, quibus velut unita omnibus adest. Huius ergo totius virtutis tantae et tam immensae vapor et, ut ita dixerim, vigor ipse in propria subsistentia effectus quamvis ex ipsa virtute velut ex mente procedat, tamen et ipsa voluntas dei nihilominus dei virtus efficitur. Efficitur ergo voluntas altera in sua proprietate subsistens, ut ait sermo scripturae, 'vapor quidam' primae et ingenitae 'virtutis dei' hoc quidem quod est inde trahens (p. 40, 2-10).

[155] The author and date of the work (which has been very little studied) are equally unknown. A. Harnack attempted in his *Diodor von Tarsus* (*TU*, N.F. 6, 4, Leipzig, 1901) to show that the *Quaestiones Christianae* together with three other works likewise attributed to Justin (viz., *Quaestiones et Responsiones ad Orthodoxos*, *Quaestiones Graecae ad Christianos*, and *Confutatio dogmatum Arsitotelis*) belonged to Diodorus, but the subsequent studies of F.X. Funk and others (cf. Quasten, *Patrology* 3, 548f. and *supra* n. 24) demonstrated conclusively that the *Quaestiones et Responsiones* was the work of Theodoret and brought the attribution of the others once again into total uncertainty. Most authorities seem to feel that they belong to the mid-5th century and originated in the school of Antioch (cf. G. Bardy, in *Rev. Bibl.* 1933, p. 212). Harnack points out that the term « Greeks » to indicate pagan philosophy dates chiefly from the 5th century (*op. cit.*, 49). They are, at any rate, known to Photius (v. *ibid.*) and so can at least be located within the period with which we are here concerned.

just as one finds a number of significant parallels between the kalâm and the later Latin scholasticism, the clear parallelism between the doctrine of the Mu'tazila concerning God's will and that found in the *Quaestiones Christianae* may simply represent a case of spontaneous convergence, for Muslims and Christians had alike to answer the problem (or threat) posed by « the Greeks » and the solution given by the Mu'tazila, like that of the unknown author of the *Quaestiones*, is one of a limited number of reasonable choices. In any event, because of its manifest similarity to the thought of abû l-Hudhayl, both in its premises and in the basic character of its conclusions, the teaching of the *Quaestiones Christianae* deserves to be cited in some detail.

The initial point of departure in arguing against the « Greek » attitude towards the understanding of the divine activity and God's being shows an orientation fundamentally akin to that of the kalâm. Against the « philosophical » thesis that, because of the absolute oneness and immutability of God's essence, His activity must likewise be eternal and immutable, the author of the *Quaestiones Christianae* contends that rather than begin solely by the abstract consideration of the divine essence and the presumption of its *natural* activity, one must commence the inquiry into how God creates with the consideration of creation and its nature and, doing this, he concludes that it cannot be by His essence and the necessity of His being that God creates but by willing the existence of what He creates. Thus he says :

εἰ ἄπειρα μὲν δύναται ποιεῖν ὁ θεός, ἀλλὰ τῷ βούλεσθαι · ὁ θεος δὲ διάφορα μὲν εἶναι οὐ δύναται · ἓν γάρ ἐστι, καὶ ἁπλοῦν, καὶ μονοειδές · διάφορα δὲ βούλεται · οὐκ ἄρα τῷ εἶναι ποιεῖ, ἀλλὰ τῷ βούλεσθαι [156].

and subsequently he argues more fully that if God did not create by an act of the will (*βουλήσει* = *bil-'irâda*), the world would not exist as it does :

Εἰ οὐ ποιεῖ τις βουλήσει ἃ καὶ μὴ βουλόμενος ἐποίει, πῶς οὖν βούλησει τὸν κόσμον ἐποίησεν ὁ θεὸς, ὃν καὶ μὴ βουλόμενος ποιεῖν, ἐξ ἀνάγκης ἐποίει ; Εἰ ἓν μὲν τῇ οὐσίᾳ ὁ θεός, ἄπειρος δὲ τῇ δυνάμει · τὰ δὲ συνυφιστάμενα αὐτῷ μήτε ἓν κατὰ τὴν οὐσίαν αὐτοῦ, μήτε ἄπειρα κατὰ τὴν δύναμιν αὐτοῦ, οὐδ' ἄρα συνυφίσταται αὐτῷ. Ὁ

[156] *PG* 6, 1436D.

θεὸς ἀεὶ τέλειός ἐστιν, ἀεὶ δυνατός ἐστιν · καὶ ἐν αὐτῷ μὲν πρότερον καὶ ὕστερον οὐδέν · ἐν δὲ τοῖς ἔργοις αὐτοῦ ἐστιν ἀμφότερα [157].

On this basis he insists, then, significantly that because God's acts are realised in the world and in time, the dialectic that would argue that God's acts are timeless and that past and future are in no way relative to God is fatuous, since the predicates « has done », « did », « does » and « will do » are clearly valid; His acts occur in the world and in a temporal sequence, and so he argues :

εἰ δὲ ταῦτα κείμενα ἐπὶ τοῦ θεοῦ, σημαντικά τε καὶ θετικὰ γίνονται τοῦ πάντα τὰ ποιήματα τοῦ θεοῦ ἔγχρονα εἶναι παρ' αὐτῷ, δῆλον ὅτι ἀτόπως ὑπέθηκε τὸ μηδὲν ἔγχρονον αὐτῷ [158]*... ἔλεγχος γίνεται τοῦ μὴ ὀρθῶς εἰρῆσθαι τὸ οὐδὲν ἔγχρονον παρὰ τῷ θεῷ τὸ παρεληλυθὸς ἐν τῷ ἐνεστῶτι, καὶ τὸ μέλλον ἐν τῷ ἤδη γεγονέναι· ἅτινα ἐστι ἔγχρονα · καὶ εἰ ἐνήλλαξε τὸν τρόπον τοῦ πῶς ἔστι παρὰ τῷ θεῷ τὰ τοῦ χρόνου μέρη, ἀλλ' ὅμως δέδωκεν εἶναι παρ' αὐτῷ τὸ παρεληλυθός* [159].

If the temporal sequence of God's activity is denied, we cannot even speak of God as « acting » or even as creator (*ποιητής*) [160].

One notes here that in contrast to a more « philosophical » train of thought, according to which God uses angels or immaterial intelligences as the intermediate agents of creation and His activity involving the world, while He Himself remains altogether remote from the cosmus and the temporality of material being, this text, like the one cited immediately above, implies that God continues to act in the world. Like the masters of the Baṣra school of the Muʿtazila, the author of the *Quaestiones Christianae* refuses to conceive God as absolutely unrelated to the temporality of creation. He will not, that is, say that God's being is totally atemporal in every aspect. Quite to the contrary, God acts or creates in time (*ποιεῖ ἐν χρόνῳ*) [161] and since God's act, which results immediately in the realisation of the being He creates, is temporal, His act of the will which is the immediate cause of the being of the creature must itself be temporal.

εἰ ἔγχρονον τὸ γενέσθαι ἔγχρονον καὶ τὸ ποιεῖσθαι · ἰσοδύναμα γάρ. Ἀδύνατον γὰρ ἐν τῷ ποιεῖν τὸν ποιοῦντα μὴ γίνεσθαι τὸ ποιούμενον ...

157 *Ibid.*, 1441Af.; cf. also 1417Df.

158 *Ibid.*, 1420A; n.b. also 1413, § 6.

159 *Ibid.*, 1420D; cf. generally Q. 3, 1417ff.

160 *Ibid.*, 1420BC : *τῶν γὰρ ῥημάτων τῶν χρονικῶν ἔμφασιν δηλούντων καὶ ἐχόντων, ἐκ τῆς ἐνεργείας τοῦ θεοῦ ἀναιρουμένων, εὑρηθήσεται ὁ θεὸς ἀνενέργετος · διὸ οὔτε ποιητής.*

161 *Ibid.*, 1420B.

῾Ο θεὸς εἰ τῷ εἶναι ποιεῖ, ἀναγκαστικῶς ποιεῖ ἃ ποιεῖ · εἰ δὲ τῷ βούλεσθαι ποιεῖ, αὐθεντικῶς ποιεῖ · αὐθεντικῶς δὲ ποιῶν, ὅσα βούλεται καὶ οἷα βούλεται, καὶ ὅτε βούλεται ποιεῖ [162].

The reasoning here is very much that of the *mutakallimîn* of the Baṣra school. God's act of the will stands in an immediate and determinate correlation to His act (it is *muta'alliqa bil-fi'l*, in kalâm terms). His activity is not the essentially and eternally determined outflowing of the superabundance of His nature [163], but is a contingent act, whose actuality is temporally simultaneous with its effect. As in the systems of abû l-Hudhayl and the followers of his school, God's act of the will (*βούλεσθαι*) is not thus determinant of and so prior to His eternal knowledge of what He will create, but rather is the effective and decisive activity whereby the act is realised at the moment of its coming to be.

Consequently then, as do the masters of the Baṣra school (though making a distinction that they will not), he concludes that God's will (*βουλή*), of which His act of willing (*βούλεσθαι*) is the actuality (*ἐνέργεια*), must be other than His essence. Here again the parallelism of reasoning is remarkable : this follows, he argues, from the fact that in contrast to God's essence which is eternal in its perfection and cannot be other than it is, His acts of willing need not exist; His acts of willing could be other than they are and creation either another and different creation or altogether non-existent. Thus he says :

Εἰ ἄλλο τὸ ὑπάρχειν καὶ ἄλλο τὸ ἐνυπάρχειν · καὶ ὑπάρχει μὲν τοῦ θεοῦ ἡ οὐσία, ἐνυπάρχει δὲ τῇ οὐσίᾳ ἡ βουλή· ἄλλη ἄρα ἡ οὐσία τοῦ θεοῦ καὶ ἄλλη ἡ βουλή. Εἰ ἡ μὲν βουλὴ τοῦ θεοῦ ἐκ τῆς οὐσίας, ἡ δὲ οὐσία οὐκ ἐκ τῆς βουλῆς, ἄλλη ἄρα ἡ οὐσία τοῦ θεοῦ καὶ ἄλλη ἡ βουλή. ῾Η οὐσία τοῦ θεοῦ τὸ μὴ εἶναι οὐσία οὐ δέχεται · ἡ δὲ βουλὴ τοῦ θεοῦ δέχεται τὸ μὴ βούλεσθαι· οἷον ἐβόυλετο ὁ θεὸς ποιῆσαι ἕνα ἥλιον, δεύτερον ἥλιον οὐκ ἐβούλετο ποιῆσαι [164].

God's acts that flow from His power are not infinite but are temporally variable and contingent and consequently it is not His power, which is infinite and eternal, that determines the realisation of the act but His willing. As does abû l-Hudhayl, the author of the *Quaes-*

[162] *Ibid.*, 1433f.; cf. also 1441B.

[163] Cf. the problem concerning the attribute *ǧûd* noted above, n. 127.

[164] *Ibid.*, 1432A (and cf. also *Quaestiones Graecae ad Christianos*, *ibid.*, 1472Cf.). N.b. that the wording of this passage could easily serve as the basis of the diasagreement between the disciples of abû l-Hudhayl mentioned above n. 150. On the distinction of *βούλεσθαι* and *βουλή* as the former is the actuality of the latter, cf. 1432D.

tiones associates thus God's power and knowledge with His essence as infinite and unchangeable while His acts are contingent and finite. Two passages are worth citing at length to illustrate this parallelism :

Καὶ εἰ ἔστι μὲν ἡ τοῦ θεοῦ δύναμις ἄπειρος, ὥσπερ οὖν καὶ ἔστι, πεπερασμένα δὲ τὰ ἔργα αὐτοῦ, πῶς οὐκ ἔστιν ὁ θεὸς καθ' ἃς ἔχει μὲν δυνάμεις, μὴ ἐνεργῶν δὲ κατ' αὐτάς, οὐ φθαρτὸς τῇ ἐνεργείᾳ, κατὰ τὴν κρῖσιν τοῦ ἀποκριναμένου; Εἰ δε καθ' ἃς ἔχει δυνάμεις, καὶ μὴ ἐνεργῶν κατ' αὐτάς, φθαρτὸς οὐκ ἔστιν, οὐδὲ ἄρα, παυσαμένης τῆς ἐνεργείας τοῦ θεοῦ τῆς τὸν κόσμον παραγούσης, φθείρεται θεὸς τῇ ἐνεργείᾳ. Ὅσον δὴ καὶ βούλεται, καὶ οὐχ ὅσον δύναται · καὶ οὐ ποιεῖ φθαρτὸν τὸν θεὸν ἡ τῆς ἐνεργείας συστολή · οὐδὲ ἄρα ὅταν συστέλλῃ τὴν ἐνέργειαν, κατὰ μεταβολὴν συστέλλει τῆς δυνάμεως · ἀλλ' ἔστι μὲν ἡ δύναμις τοῦ θεοῦ ἀεὶ ἀμετάβλητος, κέχρηται δὲ ταῖς ἐνεργείαις ἐφ' ὅσον βούλεται. Οὐ γὰρ ἐνεργεῖ θεὸς καθάπερ ἐνεργοῦσιν οἱ ἐν τῷ ἐνεργεῖν τὸ εἶναι ἔχοντες, καὶ παυσαμένης τῆς ἐνεργείας παύονται καὶ αὐτοὶ τοῦ εἶναι, οἷον τὸ πῦρ καὶ ἡ χιών [165].

Τὸ μὲν πῶς συμβέβηκε τῷ πυρὶ ἡ θερμότης, ὡς βούλεται λέγειν ὁ ἀποκρινάμενος, λεγέτω. Οὐ γὰρ περὶ τοῦ πῶς αὐτῷ συμβέβηκεν ἡ θερμότης νῦν ἐστι τὸ ζητούμενον, ἀλλὰ περὶ τῆς ἀβουλήτου ἐνεργείας, καθ' ἣν τῷ εἶναι ἐνεργεῖ. Τὸ βούλεσθαι ἢ οὐσία ἐστιν, ἢ πρόσεστι τῇ οὐσίᾳ. Ἀλλ' εἰ οὐσία ἐστὶ, οὐκ ἔστιν ὁ βουλόμενος · εἰ δὲ πρόσεστι τῇ οὐσίᾳ, ἐξ ἀνάγκης ἄλλο καὶ ἄλλο ἐστίν · οὐκ ἔστι γὰρ τὸ ὂν καὶ τὸ παρὸν ταὐτόν. Εἰ πολλὰ μὲν βούλεται ὁ θεός, πολλὰ δὲ οὐκ ἔστιν, οὐκ ἄρα ταὐτὸν παρὰ τῷ θεῷ τὸ εἶναι τῷ βούλεσθαι. Ὁ θεὸς, εἰ ὅσα μὲν βούλεται ποιεῖν, δύναται ποιεῖν · οὐχ ὅσα δὲ δύναται ποιεῖν, βούλεται ποιεῖν · οὐ ταὐτὸν ἄρα παρ' αὐτῷ τὸ εἶναι τῷ βούλεσθαι. Ὁ θεὸς εἰ ἓν μὲν ἔστι, καὶ ἁπλοῦν καὶ μονοειδές · πολλά δὲ βούλεται καὶ πολλὰ οὐ βούλεται · οἷον βούλεται μὲν τῇ ποικιλλίᾳ πολλὰ εἶναι τὰ ὄντα, ἄπειρα δὲ αὐτὰ εἶναι τῷ πλήθει οὐ βούλεται [166].

Because of the way in which the subjects involved in the questions are handled one cannot be absolutely certain of precisely how the author may have treated the detail of the ontology of God's act of willing, but from the evidence of this tract we can see a number of apparent constructs which are closely akin to the teaching of the Baṣra school. He says that God's act of creating (ποίησις) is His activity in the thing created [167] and this act of creation is itself generated

[165] *Ibid.*, 1425Af.

[166] *Ibid.*, 1433B.

[167] *Ibid.*, 1433C : Ἀδύνατον γὰρ ποιητὸν ἀγέννητον ... ἡ ποίησις ἐνέργειά ἐστι τοῦ ποιοῦντος ἐν τῷ ποιουμένῳ.

or created [168]. The act of creation, however, which is temporal and generated, is dependent upon and comes to be through God's act of willing (*βουλήσει, τῷ βούλεσθαι*). Now though he says that the terms « created » and « uncreated » are altogether opposed to one another [169], the author of the *Quaestiones Christianae* nowhere says into which category God's act of willing is to be classed. It may be that he simply dodged the issue, but even by his silence, we may assume that he did not wish to say that it is created (*γεννητόν*). God's will is the act which is the ground of the creation of the creature, i.e., of its being-created. Thus while the creation of the thing (*ποίησις*) is an act (*ἐνέργεια*) of God « in the thing created », the act of willing, through which the act of creating takes place, is also an act (*ἐνέργεια*), viz., the actuality of God's will which is other than His essence [170]; but as the ground of the creation of the thing it must in some way be prior to it. Again, God is a subsistent being (*ἐνυπόστατον*) but as His act of willing, though temporal in its being and other than He in His essence, is non-subsistent in its actuality (*ἀνυπόστατον*) [171].

As there are a number of clear similarities in this to the teaching of the kalâm, there are also not insignificant differences, the most obvious of which arise from the opposition of the fundamentally « Aristotelian » character of the philosophical system that underlies the thought of the author of the *Quaestiones Christianae* to that which forms the framework of abû l-Hudhayl's teaching. These differences themselves are instructive, however, in that they reveal something of the way in which the early kalâm adapted some of the sources out of which the mutakallimîn of the period were attempting to create a coherent system of theological thought that was congenial to Islam's sense of its own understanding of the world and its revelation. Specifically, the conception that God's act of willing is *ἀνυπόστατον* is a fair equivalent of abû l-Hudhayl's considering it as belonging to the category of accidents, insofar as it is a perfection or act of God, whose essence is self-subsistent. In the one case as in the other it must

[168] *Ibid.*, 1437A : *Ὁ θεὸς οἰκίαν οὐκ ἐποίησεν, ἀλλ' ἐποίησε τὸν ἄνθρωπον, καὶ δέδωκεν αὐτῷ δύναμιν ποιητικὴν τῆς οἰκίας. Οὐδὲν οὖν τούτων ἀγεννήτως παρὰ τῷ θεῷ, οὔτε ἡ ποίησις τοῦ ἀνθρώπου οὔτε ἡ δόσις τῆς δυνάμεως.*

[169] *Ibid.*, 1433C : *μαχόμενα ὀνόματα τὸ ἀγέννητον καὶ τὸ ποιητόν.*

[170] *Ibid.*, 1432C : *ὥσπερ τὸ κινεῖσθαι ἐνέργειά ἐστι κινήσεως, οὕτω καὶ τὸ βούλεσθαι βουλῆς ἐστὶν ἐνέργεια.*

[171] *Ibid.*, 1432D : *ἄλλο τὸ ἐνυπόστατον καὶ ἄλλο τὸ ἀνυπόστατον · καὶ θεὸς μὲν ἐκεῖνο, τὸ βούλεσθαι δὲ τοῦτο.*

be other than His knowledge, power, etc., which are His essence, for God cannot will His own being nor is His being that He will [172]. On the other hand, however, the categories ἐνυπόστατον and ἀνυπόστατον really are not applicable in abû l-Hudhayl's metaphysical system, for the Aristotelian conception of οὐσία can find no proper place in it; and this is of considerable consequence in the resulting schema. The material body, as a composite of atoms and accidents is not a unity in being as a subsistent entity, but on the contrary the individual atoms and the separate accidents are each, singly, entities (*ḏawât*, *mawǧûdât*, *ašyâ'*), ontologically distinct and real. In so far as the atoms constitute the substrate of material beings, the formal reality of any being is the accidents [173], and consequently any being outside God that is not material will have to fall into the category of « accident» (*'araḍ*), « an accident in no substrate ». Thus, just as abû l-Hudhayl will not say that God's act of willing is subsistent in Him (*qâ'imatun bihi*), the author of the *Quaestiones Christianae* avoids saying that it is an act of God (ἐνέργεια θεοῦ) which might imply its being an act of His essence, but holds rather that it is the actuality of His will, that is other than His essence; but nevertheless, taking each set of assertions within the contexts of their proper systems, abû l-Hudhayl's statement that God's act of willing « exists » (*tûǧad*) or is « existent » (*mawǧûda*) tends much more to make it a kind of real hypostasis, than to say that it is an act that, though other than God's essence, is ἀνυπόστατον. Both authors, however, begin with a similar preoccupation, sc. to explain how God's acts can be diversified and, in a sense, arbitrary, against the pagan conception that would make His action one of unchangeable necessity, and both follow a single basic pattern of reasoning.

Abû l-Hudhayl takes God's act of willing, together with His creative utterance, « Be » as His act of creating, which, as the immediate ground of the being of created being is, strictly speaking, uncreated even though, as a kind of temporal hypostasis of His creative power, it may metaphorically be termed created. The act of creation which is, so to speak, « in the thing created » is, on the other hand, its being-created and this, he holds, is its being in being what it is at the moment of its creation [174]. He conceives, thus, only two basic terms in the

[172] *PG* 6, 1432f.; this argument is quite common in the later Baṣra school; cf. e.g., *al-Muġnî* 6/2, 185f. and *Šarḥ al-uṣûl al-ḫamsa*, 440.

[173] Cf. my *Metaphysics of Created Being*, p. 42, n. 14.

[174] Cf. *ibid.*, 48ff.

act of creation: God's temporal but uncreated act of will and command and the actuality of being of the thing created in its being-created.

Here too, in his retention of the distinct character of God's act of willing and the creative « Be », abû l-Hudhayl adheres closely to the text of the *Koran*, against the doctrine of an-Naẓẓâm, for example, who held that to will is, for God, simply that He create what He creates [175]. Abû l-Hudhayl, however, does more than merely maintain the appearances of the revealed text. The sense of God's creating by willing is that creation (i.e., the world) is essentially contingent in its every aspect, as opposed to the notion of creation without will and choice, according to which it must be necessary and essentially imperishable [176]. Likewise, according to the understanding of abû l-Hudhayl and his successors, to identify God's will with His power of efficient causality, as would seem to be basically the position of an-Naẓẓâm, implies an absence of freedom and an absolute limitation on His freedom and power [177], just as to make it an essential and eternal attribute would tend to imply the eternal necessity of God's acts and that « He wills every being that can be willed », a dismal conclusion that al-Aš'arî was willing to accept [178] and which the doctrine of the Baṣra school is constructed precisely to oppose.

[175] Cf. *Maqâlât*, 190, 509f., and also 365.

[176] Cf. e.g., Proclus, *In Parmenidem* (ed. V. Cousin, Paris, 1864), 786, 19ff.

[177] Cf. e.g., *al-Muġnî* 6/1, 141, *cit. supra* n. 120.

[178] Cf. *al-Luma'*, §§ 65 and 49 and also al-Baġdâdî, *Uṣûl*, 154f; on the conjunction of God's will and His foreknowledge according to the Aš'arites cf. also *Ibâna* 9 and 44, al-Bâqillânî, *at-Tamhîd*, § 477, and the comments of 'Abd al-Ǧabbâr in *al-Muġnî* 13 (ed. A. Afifi, Cairo, 1382/1962), 141 *et alibi pass.*

III

SEVERAL FUNDAMENTAL ASSUMPTIONS OF THE BAṢRA SCHOOL OF THE MU'TAZILA

In an excellent article recently published, M. G. Vajda makes the following remark: "L'existence d'une conscience morale universelle était pour des théologiens comme 'Abd al-Ǧabbâr une évidence irréfragable et ne pouvait aucunement faire problème." (1) The reality, indeed, of universally binding moral principles that are known to all men is one of the primary ordering or operative assumptions on which the Baṣra School of the Mu'tazila based the entire of their theology. What I propose to do here is to examine in outline and very briefly where and how this assumption fits into the system, for although the fact of such universal moral consciousness is taken as given, it is not given simply, but complexly understood in terms of the nature of man and the nature of God. For the sake of convenience I have taken nearly all of the material for the following exposition from the *Muġnî* of the Qâḍî 'Abd al-Ǧabbâr, but treated thus in abstract the outline is valid for the school, at least from the time of al-Ǧubbâ'î. Again, attempting to maintain both brevity and unity of focus I have omitted several problems in what follows or mentioned them only by way of allusion but I hope that with this the matter will be nowhere muddled.

(1) "De l'universalité de la loi morale selon Yûsuf al-Baṣîr", *REJ* 128 (1969), p. 176.

Life is defined in terms of perception: the living being is perceiving or sentient *(al-ḥayy=al-mudrik)* and it is perception that distinguishes the living being from the non-living. ([1]) This implies a fundamental outward orientation of the living being, an orientation towards the world and some form of action. ([2]) Knowledge *('ilm)* for the Mu'tazila is a knowing of objects. It is a grasp of and conviction about the being, character, states, situations, and circumstances of things and events; ([3]) and intelligence *('aql)*, consisting in an accumulated aggregate of universally common knowledge, whose perfection *(kamâl)* is attained in mature experience ([4]), is directed essen-

(1) Cf. *M(ugnt)* 13, p. 239, 19, p. 240, 2;11, p. 335, 13 ff.; 16, 43, 1 f., *et alibi.* The living being is strictly conceived as a structured unity of material parts (cf. esp. *M* 11, pp. 327-338, 348-352, 357 f., and 367-70); it is not identified with any single component, whether a material organ, "spirit", or what ever else (cf. generally *ibid.*, pp. 312-367). On the strictness with which the living individual is identified with the specific material parts that constitute his being, cf. e. g., *ibid.*, p. 467. "Desire" *(šahwa)* which directs the creatures perception towards its objects (cf. *ibid.*, pp. 72 ff.) is here assumed.

(2) In discussing the minimal conditions for the being of sentient being *(ibid.)*, the Qâḍî notes that perception without an object would be pointless (*'abaṯ*, and so inconceivable since God would not perform a useless act; see below) and suggests that as a minimum the living creature might have only some material part *(ba'ḍ)* or some accident inherent in such a part as the sole object of its perception. This, however, in no way vitiates the thesis that perception and thereby life is primarily oriented towards the world and defines a stance towards objects as actual or potential objects of action. The difference between this and the position of the Aristotelian and Platonic traditions is clear enough.

(3) Knowledge *('ilm)* is generally taken by Abû Hâšim and his followers as a conviction *(i'tiqâd)* that entails a secure sense of certainty *(yaqtaḍî sukûna n-nafs;* cf. generally *M* 12, 13 ff., and concerning *sukûn an-nafs, ibid.*, 106 ff. and 199-204); it is a conviction that the thing is as it really is (*'alà mâ huwa bihî;* cf. e. g., *M* 11, p. 5, 6; p. 70, 11; 12, p. 13, *ult.*; and 15, p. 111, 11 f.). Cf. also J. van Ess, *Die Erkenntnislehre des 'Aḍudaddîn al-Icî* (Wiesbaden, 1966), pp. 71 ff. God's knowledge too the school seems to have conceived as a knowing of objects (cf. my comments in *le Muséon* 82 (1969) pp. 465-468); the matter is important and needs serious and detailed investigation.

(4) Intelligence *('aql)* (which belongs ontologically to the category of conviction —cf. *Šarḥ al-'uṣûl al-ḫamsa*, ed. A. Ousman, Cairo, 1965/1384, p. 90) is defined generally as a sum or aggregate *(ǧumla)* of specific knowledge *('ulûm maḫṣûṣa— though not bil-tafṣîl)*, both intuitive (including the knowledge of common perceptibles, cf. *M* 11, p. 380, 11 ff., and the basic moral principles, cf. *ibid.*, pp. 198 f. and 384 ff.) and acquired, which forms the basis for inquiry, reasoning, judgement, and action. It is, in short, *al-'ilm bi-ǧumal al-'a'yân wal-'awṣâf wal-'aḥkâm*

tially and primarily towards action (1), specifically towards those actions which are morally good and best in terms of achieving benefit and well-being and avoiding harm. (2)

Besides intelligence: man is also endowed by God with an autonomous power of efficient causality *(qudra)* by which he is, within given limits and under specific conditions, the originating author of his own acts, for by virtue of his autonomous power of efficient causality he has within himself, as a quality of his own being, the ground of the possibility of his acts. It can be said, therefore, that man "by nature" (constitutionally) is an autonomous agent who seeks his own good through action.

In order to maintain the integrity of man's autonomy as a moral agent, the Mu'tazila assume that he is endowed with a native capacity to discover and know what is good and what is evil in the realm of human activity. That is, in the maturity or full actuality of his intelligence *(kamâl 'aqlihi)* he is given the general moral principles through which, on the basis of other general and specific knowledge, he may rationally determine the good or evil of specific actions. In sum, then, man is conceived as having an innate desire to seek his own good, an innate power to act, and an innate understanding of the fundamental criteria of good and evil. It is the "natural" desire to discover and achieve what is best for his own action that, manifesting itself as an anxiety or fearful concern *(ḫauf)* to avoid what may be only apparently beneficial and discover what is ultimately and most truly beneficial to do, that the Mu'tazila consider the foundation and essence of "the obligation

(*M* 15, p. 25, 7 f.). Cf. *M* 11, pp. 375, 17 ff., p. 379, 13 ff., *et alibi pass.* On the etymology, cf. al-Aš'arî, *Maqâlât al-Islâmîyîn* (ed. Ritter, Istanbul, 1929-30) pp. 480 f. and 526, *M* 5, pp. 226 f., 11, pp. 386 f., and 12, pp. 16 f. It is because of intelligence that man's knowledge of the perceptibles differs from that of animals; cf. *M* 12, p. 161.

(1) *'Aql* is specifically defined (*M* 11, 375 *et alibi*) not in terms of action in general but in the context of the *taklîf* since beings lacking intelligence (sc. animals, children, the insane, etc.) are not subject to *taklîf* (cf. e. g., *M* 12, pp. 297 f., 14, pp. 298 and 444 f.). On this matter see below.

(2) *Al-intifâ'* and *al-manfa'a* are defined in terms of pleasure *(iltiḏâḏ)* and happiness *(surûr)*; cf. *M* 11, pp. 78-84 and *Šarḥ al-'uṣûl al-ḫamsa*, p. 80.

to enquire" *(wuǧûb an-naẓar)* into the nature and ground of being in general. Because of his concern for his own well-being the individual must enquire into how he may fare well and avoid what he fears and so also, on the basis of his immediate understanding of good and evil and out of concern for his well-being, he is drawn to an ultimate concern which is to know the ultimate conditions of his being. ([1]) This initial state of anxiety is inalienable from one who has intelligence. ([2]) From this perspective, then, man is viewed as having an inalienable orientation towards God, as the source of his being and the locus of his ultimate good. ([3])

The good of action—what is good to do or to be sought through action ([4])—is measured in terms of the good of man as a knowing, creative agent, i.e., of the individual person who projects and effects his own weal or woe through his autonomous power of efficient causality. The context of human action, the world, is most particularly characterized by the presence of others; it is a context of a plurality of free knowing agents, each of whom seeks his own good in action and interaction. The fact and sense of well-being are had, thus, within the context of the presence and action of other free intelligent agents and are variously dependent upon them as also the action of each individual is, in diverse ways and degrees, mutually conditioned by and dependent upon that of others. Within this inter-subjective context of action, in which each individual seeks naturally his own well-being, intelligence has an immediate intuition of the fundamental principles of moral good and evil,

(1) *M* 12, p. 366, 3 ff.

(2) Intelligence knows intuitively the (moral) necessity of avoiding harm and in the absence of a true and authentic feeling of certitude *(sukûn an-nafs)* doubt and the occurence of anxiety are inevitable (cf. *M* 15, p. 352, ult. f. and 12, p. 195, 8 ff., and generally *ibid.*, pp. 358 ff. (esp. 361 f.), 430-433 *et alibi*). That intelligence is bound, through its grasp of basic moral principles, to the *taklîf* is not of concern in the immediate context but will be taken up later.

(3) God is, in a real sense, the ultimate and true object of the innate "obligation to enquire" but He is not the "ben de l'intelletto" as conceived by the Patristic or Scholastic traditions since knowledge is differently conceived and the good does not lie in contemplation.

(4) Action *(fi'l)* here equally includes interior and exterior acts *(af'âl al-qulûb* and *af'âl al-ǧawâriḥ)*.

including that of moral obligation in terms of the intrinsic "right" of other autonomous agents each to seek his own well-being. It knows intuitively those types of action that are blameworthy: the evil *(al-qabîḥ)*, whose performance is blameworthy and the obligatory *(al-wâgib)* whose omission is blameworthy, as also of the good (*al-ḥasan*, which may be done simply for its own sake) (1), the merely permissible *(al-mubâḥ)*, etc.

Since sense experience is the apparent foundation of all knowledge (2), it would seem that the basis of moral judgements is experience within the intersubjective context of the human world. (3) Quite to the contrary, however, the knowledge of the general principles of the evil and the obligatory, of the praiseworthy and blameworthy in human acts, depends not on the experience of association with intelligent men *(muḫâlaṭat al-'uqalâ')* but is given directly in an immediate intuition of the intelligence. (4) Though somehow inseparable from the intersubjective context, these principles are neither derived

(1) The criteria of these classifications of acts as discussed in pt. 6 of the *Muġnî* are given in some detail, with translations of important passages in the article of Vajda cited above. That the good *(al-ḥasan)* may be done simply for its own sake is extremely important within the Mu'tazilite system as is noted by the Qâḍî (*M* 6/1, p. 210, 4) in a passage that is translated and discussed by Vajda (*op. cit.*, 179 f.). The central importance of the first argument given by 'Abd al-Ǧabbâr is that without this thesis one must hold either that God cannot act at all or that He must act by the necessity of His nature and can act only according to that necessity. It is directed, thus, primarily against the philosophers who, as so often, are referred to as *al-mulḥida* (line 12). The Mu'tazila, not altogether without reason, see a parallel implication in the Aš'arite thesis that God is *murîd li-nafsihi*.

(2) Cf. e. g., *M* 12, p. 58, 4-5 and also pp. 59 ff. and 161-163.

(3) Cf. *M* 16, p. 299, 17-19.

(4) Cf. *M* 11, pp. 483 f. The universal principles of moral judgement belong by direct intuition to the maturity of the intelligence *(kamâl al-'aql)* and are thus known necessarily *(bi-ḍṭirâr)* by all intelligent men; *ibid.*, 198 f. (Generally cf. concerning *al-qabâ'iḥ al-'aqliya*, *M* 14, pp. 154 ff., *al-wâǧibât al-'aqlîya*, pp. 161 ff., and *al-muḥassanât al-'aqlîya*, pp. 171 ff.) Thus the classical kalâm of the Baṣra school of the Mu'tazila conceives, in its own way, the possibility of a kind of *solitarius autodidactus*, as through the knowledge of these principles, the other innate data of intelligence and the process of reasoning, human understanding will (or can) by its own autonomous efforts attain a knowledge of God and the principles of the revelation *(see below)*.

from it nor given by it as such. Rather, they are an intrinsic constituent of intelligence and, as such, in some way an essential property of the autonomous agent, in that his autonomy and freedom do not lie exclusively in the power of efficient causality but are correlated also to his knowing of his act and his judgement of the secondary aspect *(waǧh)* (1) that may qualify it as morally good or evil. (2) This is of central importance to the whole complex of the Mu'tazilite position. As the original, ontological possibility of action *(ṣiḥḥat al-fi'l)* is grounded in the power of efficient causality *(qudra)* (3) which is an attribute of the human agent, at the disposal of his intention *(qaṣd)* and free choice *(iḫtiyâr)*, so that he is truly an autonomous agent, so the knowledge and judgement of the acts whose possibility lies within his power of efficient causality are also his as an attribute that belongs to him properly as a human individual, so that he is truly responsible as an autonomous agent.

Knowledge and the understanding of the universal moral principles are taken together with the power of efficient causality as essential characteristics or attributes of the autonomous agent (whether man, in whom they are contingent attributes or God, who is knowing and *qâdir* by His very being, which

(1) The *waǧh* of an action is understood as analogous to the "state" *(ḥâl)* of a corporeal being; cf. *M* 8, p. 74; 11, p. 267, 13-15; p. 270, 1-3; p. 169, 18 ff.; 14, p. 22, 3-10, and pp. 242 f. and also p. 11, n. 2; and on the *ḥâl*, cf. my article, "Abû Hâšim's theory of 'States'" in the *Acts of the Fourth Congress of Arabic and Islamic Studies*.

(2) The correlation of these two is particularly clear in the thesis of the necessity of both *tamkîn* and *'aql* for the validity of the *taklîf* (cf. *M* 11, pp. 371 ff. *et alibi pass.*). In terms of the present context, man is given as *mukallaf*, i. e., *ḥayy qâdir 'âlim murîd*. I assume of course the usual conditions of *at-taḫliya, salâmat al-binya*, etc.

(3) N. b. that action *(fi'l)* involves a true production of being *('îǧâd, 'iḥdâṯ)* so that the ontological possibility of action entails (limited, to be sure, for the human agent who is not *qâdir li-nafsihi)* the possibility of being as such. It is in the last analysis because of their complete rejection of this thesis while trying nevertheless to describe a "created" (i. e., ultimately contingent) universe that Avicenna and the *falâsifa* could only conceive a completely deterministic universe.

is eternal and necessary). (1) The principles of moral judgement are, in this way, coeval with mind and prior to action. Mind judges the act in its possibility, prior to its realisation or non-realisation; the act is known and judged as good, wrong, obligatory, or whatever, in the immediate but not yet determinate possibility of its being done or left undone. The universal moral principles are given, as it were, already with the possibility of action in general; not with the acts as pure possibles *(maqdûrât)* grounded in the power of efficient causality (2), but in the being of the autonomous agent *(al-fâ'il al-qâdir)*, in accordance with whose "necessary knowledge" (3) the possibles must be judged in the concrete particularity of their immediate possibility. The agent knows by an innate and necessary knowledge that injustice *(ẓulm)* is wrong, that to express gratitude to one who has freely bestowed a favor *(šukr al-mun'im)* is obligatory, and that to direct a wayfarer *('irsâl aḍ-ḍâll)* is good. These specific qualifications can be

(1) Though following the common use of the language as defined by the philologists *(ahl al-luġa)* the formal definition of man is normally given in terms of his being a material or corporeal composite *(ǧumla)* or individual *(šaḫṣ)* having a unique configuration (cf. e. g., *M* 7, p. 13, 8 and generally *M* 11, pp. 358 ff., and for the beginnings of the school, al-Aš'arî's *Maqâlât*, p. 329, 9-12), he is nonetheless conceived as "essentially" *ḥayy qâdir* (cf. e. g., *M* 11, p. 312, 4-5, p. 345, 3, and p. 358, 18). Intelligence and the knowledge of the characteristics of acts *('aḥwâl al-'af'âl, 'aḥkâm al-'af'âl)* are seen generally as necessary specifically in terms of the *taklîf*, as the latter is entailed by the former (see below; though the *taklîf* does not, as such, add to an act any quality that it does not have anyway, cf. e. g., *M* 11, p. 503), but even so, intelligence is inalienably linked to the real nature of man, for it is intelligence that distinguishes him from dumb animals (*al-bahâ'im;* cf. *M* 14, p. 116, 4 ff. and p. 7, n. 1 above).

(2) *Qudra* grounds the sheer possibility of being *(wuǧûd, ḥudûṯ)*, while the moral qualification *(ṣifa* or *ḥukm;* note that the latter term is not restricted to this use and need not imply any kind of extrinsic "judgement") of the act depends upon the manner (*waǧh;* cf. p. 10, n. 1) or circumstantial state *(ḥâl)* of its occurrence. (Note that the act of willing is an act: *fi'l*). The *waǧh* (or *ḥâl*) is not bound to the essential nature (or ontological category: *ǧins*) of the act and so is not entailed in its being as such, but on the contrary is a secondary or accidental qualification *(ṣifa zâ'ida);* cf. e. g., *M* 14, p. 242, 16 ff., 8, p. 171, 12 ff., 11, p. 529, 9 ff., *et alibi*. It depends fundamentally on the knowing intention of the agent, so that moral qualification is entailed in every conscious act of the knowing agent; cf. e. g., *M* 11, p. 63, 9 ff.; 6/2, p. 338, 8 f., and generally 6/1, pp. 70 ff.

(3) We may conveniently take "necessity" here doubly, both of man's *'ilm ḍarûrî* and of God's eternal knowledge (on which see below).

seen as determined by the nature of the autonomous agent in terms of the intersubjective context of activity. More than this, however, the agent alone, simply through his being a knowing agent *(qâdir 'âlim)* constitutes a "moral situation"; i.e., because he is a knowing agent, he can have no act that is without some moral qualification. (1) He knows by a necessary knowledge that the pointless act *(al-'abaṯ)* is morally wrong. (2) Thus it is that before the gratuitous initiation of creation, God knew the moral qualifications of His possible acts. (3)

Man is not a necessary being nor is any aspect of his being, strictly speaking, necessary. God, indeed, could have remained forever inactive, creating nothing. (4) Creating man, He need not have created him as he is; i.e., as an intelligent, autonomous agent. (5) Nonetheless, though created by an altogether gratuitous act of God *(tafaḍḍulan)*, man stands as a kind of absolute in the quasi-unconditionality of the created actuality in which he *is* and exists as a knowing, autonomous agent. God eternally knows the universal moral principles that determine what is good and what is wrong and though He can suffer no diminishment and can derive no benefit, God's actions are yet subject to praise and blame under the same universal conditions as are those of men. (6) Furthermore, having created man, God enters into an intersubjective context with His creature. The relationships involved in this context (which are discussed in numerous contexts. especially those involving the *taklîf* and the relation of the *mukallaf* to the *mukallif*) are far from simple. What is most important from the standpoint of the present considerations is that albeit God enters this context as a knowing moral agent whose acts are subject to judgement under the same universal criteria as are man's, He remains altogether world-transcendent and essentially, therefore, apart from the immediate interhuman

(1) See the references at the end of n. 2, previous page.
(2) Cf. e. g., *M* 11, p. 64, 7 f., p. 191, 3-4, and 13, p. 126, 3-5.
(3) Cf. generally *M* 11, pp. 68 ff.
(4) Cf. *M* 11, p. 99, 5-9.
(5) Cf. *M* 11, p. 73, 8 ff. and 15, p. 64, 17-19.
(6) Cf. *M* 8, pp. 174 f., 11, p. 507, 2-6, *et alibi pass.;* v. also p. 14, n. 3.

context of action but, at the same time, nevertheless, dominates and determines that context entirely and absolutely in that, through His initial and continuing creation, He determines and produces all the elements of the world that are not directly subject to human causality. God is the creator of the living being, of his desire, and of his power of efficient causality; He is the creator of his knowledge of the perceptibles that he perceives (1), just as He is creator of all "necessary knowledge", both that which belongs to the mature intelligence *(kamâl al-'aql)* and is universally common to all intelligent men and that which is gained through specific experience and learning. (2) God is directly responsible, thus, for the basis of all motivation to action (3) and for the actuality of that which leads man to seek God, viz., the desire, knowledge, and fearful concern that impel man to seek the locus of his ultimate well-being (4), as also He furnishes the material evidence that will lead to the knowledge thus sought and the possibility of understanding them. (5) From the human standpoint, the knowledge of the universal principles of moral judgement is given in God's arbitrary and gratuitous act of creating the intelligence *('ikmâl al-'aql)* (6); and intelligence knows them in the context of the

(1) Cf. e. g., *M* 11, p. 495, 10-12; God can create directly *(ibtidâ'an)* a true and proper knowledge of perceptibles even in the absence of the normal modes of perception (sc. the senses) whereby the perceptibles are offered to understanding, as for example He can create a genuine knowledge of color in one who is blind (cf. e. g., *M* 5, p. 167, 12 f.).

(2) Cf. e. g., *M* 14, p. 128, 8 ff.; on the kinds of necessary knowledge, cf. *M* 8, p. 6, 10-12 and on the universality of what is known *fî kamâl al-'aql, M* 11, p. 328, 14 f., 16, p. 284, 12 f., and regarding what is only had *bil-'âda*, cf. e. g., *M* 15, pp. 353 f. and 16, pp. 27 f. See also p. 9, n. 4.

(3) The motive *(ad-dâ'î)* is the reason for which the act is performed (cf. *M* 15, p. 35, 7 f.) and as such is a state of the agent rather than of the object or act (cf. *M* 6/1, p. 187, 14); it is taken generally to be the "knowledge, conviction, or opinion" (cf. *M* 13, p. 91, 2 f., 8, p. 52, 14 f.) of the desired object as the agent is aware of his desire (cf. *M* 11, p. 119, 16 ff.). Vajda (*op. cit.*, p. 192, n. 3) notes the semantic parallelism between *ad-dâ'î* (and *aṣ-ṣârif*) and the terminology of Aristotle in the *Rhetoric* A, 5, but the parallelism, in the full context of the system is most likely, I should think, only verbal.

(4) Cf. *M* 11, p. 210, 5-11 and generally 12, pp. 386 ff.

(5) Cf. *M* 11, pp. 408 f., p. 142, 13 ff., 16, p. 289, 14 f., *et alibi*.

(6) The term *'âqil*, simply for semantic and etymological reasons, is not applied to God; cf. *M* 5, pp. 226 f. and 11, p. 386, 7-11.

world, whose creation is likewise gratuitous. In this created act of knowing, however, they are known as necessary, universal, irreducible, and underivable. It is upon this absolute and universal character of the fundamental principles that the Baṣra School bases its thesis of God's justice. ([1])

The essential good and aim of human action, the basic nature of moral good and evil, arise as given in the nature of the autonomous, knowing, and intending agent. They are, as it were, given in the givenness of such agents. That God will to impose on man *(kallafa)* an obligation in fulfilment of which he is offered the reward of paradise beyond this life and failing which he is threatened with the pains of hell hereafter is considered a distinct act, separate from the initial creation of man: a gratuitous act done purely for the benefit of the creature. ([2]) God might have chosen to create man initially in the heavenly paradise, in which case there would have been no *taklîf*. ([3]) Since, however, He chose to create man as He did in this world, the *taklîf* is necessarily entailed in God's endowing man with intelligence, though it remains nonetheless secondary in that intelligence is its prior condition. ([4]) The created, intelligent agent is, thus, *mukallaf* by his very nature as intelligent and this original state of his being under conditioned moral obligation *(at-taklîf al-'aqlî)* constitutes a kind of "natural *taklîf*" arising directly from the being of the created intelligence and grounded ultimately in God's eternal knowing; in God's own nature, therefore.

Now this "natural *taklîf*" requires that the agent be rewarded

(1) Without the assertion of such universality, they feel, the thesis cannot be rationally supported in any form; cf. e. g., *M* 11, p. 60, 5 f.

(2) Cf. e. g., *M* 11, pp. 134 ff. (and for the "three manners of conferring benefit" mentioned there, v. *ibid.*, pp. 81 ff.) and pp. 184 ff.; see also p. 9, n. 1.

(3) On this question cf. *M* 11, pp. 71 f., pp. 518 f.; 14, pp. 137 f., *et alibi;* for the beginning of the school tradition, cf. also al-Aš'arî, *op. cit.*, p. 249, 1-3.

(4) Cf. *M* 11, p. 178, 14 ff., p. 298, 7 ff. (generally, pp. 297 ff.), and 13, p. 424, 10 ff. (though in some passages the matter may, for specific reasons, be viewed from the opposite side; cf. e. g., *M* 11, p. 68, 14 ff.). The gratuitous creation of the conditions renders the *taklîf* (and so also the reward: *ṯawâb*) morally obligatory on God; cf. *M* 14, p. 67, 17 ff. (read *ta'rîḍ* for *at-ta'wîḍ*, line 21), 13, pp. 419 f., and generally 11, p. 484 ff.

for certain acts, compensated for suffering, etc., even without God's specific command and prohibition (1), but since in actuality there must be specific rewards (and punishments) for specific actions and since intelligence alone gives only general and universal moral principles, there must be, in addition to the "natural *taklîf*", a further *taklîf* wherein God explicitly lays down and informs man of, the specific conditions of his obligations and potential rewards; i.e., the "natural *taklîf*" *(at-taklîf al-'aqlî*—or simply *al-'aql)* requires the revelation and the *šarî'a (at-taklîf as-sam'î)*. (2) Just as the creation of intelligence in man entails the "natural *taklîf*" it further requires because of the "natural *taklîf*" the imposition of the revealed *taklîf*. (3) Again here, although morally necessary on God's part, the revealed law is gratuitous, first in the gratuitous character of the original creation of the conditions from which its moral necessity arises (4) and secondly as the specific stipulations and rewards are in no wise necessarily determined. (5) Particular requirements and stipulations of the revealed law may vary according to the specific nature of the creature on whom they are imposed, as man differs from the angels (6); for men, the revelation normally requires language (7) and its details may be variable for different cultural traditions and times and places. (8)

Though the imposition of the *taklîf* is, in a true sense, ultimately arbitrary and gratuitous on God's part, He must (i.e., is morally bound) nonetheless impose it in accordance with the established nature of his creature and the world He has made. It must be a good in terms of the natural good of

(1) Cf. e. g., *M* 11, pp. 175 ff.
(2) Cf. e. g., *M* 15, p. 44, 12 ff.
(3) Cf. *M* 15, p. 114, 7-12.
(4) Cf. n. 2 above and *M* 12, 376 f.
(5) Cf. *M* 13, p. 187, 11 ff., 14, p. 91, 12 ff., *et pass.*
(6) Cf. *M* 11, p. 241, 12-17.
(7) Cf. *M* 5, p. 170, 11 ff.
(8) Cf. *M* 11, p. 394, 1 ff. and generally the treatment of the possibility and fact of the *nasḫ* in vol. 16, pp. 49 ff., and in terms of the present discussion, particularly pp. 84 ff.

the subject upon whom it is imposed. That is, since the good which is the natural aim of human action and the moral conditions of human activity are knowable by human reason, the reward offered under the *taklîf*, as also the punishments threatened and the specific prescriptions of the revealed law must be intelligible and understandable *(ma'qûla)* to human reason, for if God is not to violate the autonomy of his servants and thereby, in effect, render the *taklîf* morally reprehensible (1), the *taklîf* must be offered as a freely given option which the mature intelligence may grasp as a good and may freely accept or reject. Were its prescriptions incomprehensible as good and obligatory within the terms of the good and morally obligatory known innately to human intelligence, its imposition would not conform to the prior and essential norms that are binding on man and God alike. In short, the conditions and prescriptions of the *šarî'a* must conform to the conditions of human knowing and the principles of moral good and evil inherent in created intelligence. (2)

Here again, the determinant element seems, from one standpoint, to be the nature of man as an autonomous, intelligent agent. (3) He contains within himself, by his very nature, as it were, the conditions of the necessity of the *taklîf* and the moral principles that must govern the specific actuality of its promulgation and imposition by God. The human agent, however, is created, brought to being by the free choice of the divine will; his power of efficient causality and his intelligence depend directly and entirely upon God's creation. M. Gardet

(1) Cf. *M* 11, pp. 391 ff. and generally pp. 367 ff.

(2) Cf. e. g., *M* 11, pp. 530 f., 12, pp. 235 f., and generally 15, pp. 97-105; the prescriptions of the *šarî'a* are *maṣlaḥa* or *'alṭâf fî l-'aqlîyât;* cf. *M* 13, p. 48, 7 ff., p. 164, 9 ff., p. 418, 10 ff., *et alibi pass.*

(3) This sense of *autonomy* is made keenly apparent in the thesis that the recognition of the validity of the *taklîf* as a good rests on a prior knowledge of God and His nature (cf. e. g. *M* 4, pp. 174 f., 12, p. 275, 5 ff., p. 326, 9 ff., *et alibi*) and that this knowledge must be freely and autonomously attained by human reason reflecting on the evidences(*'adilla;* cf. references p. 13, n. 5) of creation ; i. e., for the moral validity of the *taklîf*, the initial knowledge of God must be attained by the free exercise of man's own reflection (*naẓar*, of which he is himself *qâdir*), not *iḍṭirân* (cf. e. g., *M* 12, p. 513, 3 ff., *Mutašâbih al-Qur'ân* 1, 25, 5 ff.).

has suggested that in the Mu'tazilite doctrine one finds "a good and evil conceived as human good and evil carried to infinity, imposing themselves on God like an extrinsic law." (1) To an extent this appears to be certainly so. From another perspective, however, one might suggest that the effort was to make the thing go the other way. That is, the universal moral principles are conceived as essentially and inseparably bound to the nature of the autonomous knowing agent *(al-qâdir al-'âlim)* and so inderivably to the nature of God Himself who is *qâdir* and *'âlim* by his very being *(li-nafsihi, li-ḏâtihi).* They are incumbent upon man because and insofar as, through God's creative act, he is such an agent. (2) Though created and totally dependent for his being upon God's gratuitous act, man yet remains a kind of absolute, since God who is *qâdir 'âlim* by His very being is (howbeit the Mu'tazila would never never use the phrase) the exemplar: God who is autonomous in an infinite power such that there can be no other like it and in whose infinite knowledge the universal principles of moral judgement are given eternally. (3)

There appears to me to be in all of this a general pattern of distinctive but yet discernibly Stoic cut; but that must be the

(1) Louis Gardet, *Dieu et la destinée de l'homme* (Paris, 1967), p. 98.

(2) They are based on principles inherent in intelligence *('uṣûlun fî l-'aql)* and not upon any *'îǧâb mûǧib;* cf. e. g., *M* 14, pp. 22 f. (reading *al-'aql* for *al-fi'l*, p. 22, line 19), 12, p. 487, 11 ff., 8, pp. 206 ff. *et alibi.*

(3) It is worth noting that it is because of their conception of God's infinite power and His eternal knowledge of the universal principles of moral judgement that the Mu'tazila are required, by the very consistency of their system, to treat a number of questions in terms of what appears, at first glance, to be the most nit-picking kind of casuistry, as for example in the arguments that are reported to have prompted the rift between al-Aš'arî and his master, abû 'Alî al-Ǧubbâ'î (cf. *M* 11, pp. 229 ff. and pp. 249 ff.; 14, pp. 140 ff. *et alibi*) or those involving the *maṣlaḥa* that *must* be found in God's causing pain and illness, etc., to humans and animals (cf. e. g., the chapters on *al-'iwaḍ* in *M* 13, pp. 387 ff.); for if God is absolutely all-powerful creating directly and intentionally all things that do not depend upon the causality of men and morally obliged by the universal principles of moral judgement, He must be directly responsible for all such natural events; hence a thesis that would allow a general providence within which some things went awry and misfortune and suffering would befall some simply within the system's operating for the general good of the whole would be inconsistent and so untenable.

subject of another inquiry. Within the Islamic context one might conclude by noting that God is, within this perspective (which is common to most of the kalâm), viewed as essentially an agent: an agent who acts and whose activity is directed outside Himself, not in the contemplation and knowing of Himself. This is in marked contrast to the doctrine of Avicenna and the *falâsifa* (and even more so that of Aristotle), but whereas the self-contemplation of the philosophers' First Cause entails the creation of the world by the absolute necessity of its being, the Mu'tazila see the activity of God, whose nature is that of an autonomous agent *(ḥayy*, *qâdir*, *'âlim*, *samî'*, *baṣîr)*, as absolutely free and unconstrained.

IV

AL-MA'DŪM WAL-MAWJŪD

the Non-Existent, the Existent, and the Possible in the Teaching of Abū Hāshim and his Followers*

From an early period in the development of Islamic theology the question of the nature and status of the possible and the non-existent (*al-ma'dūm*) was a topic of heated debate that not infrequently manifested itself in squalls of conflicting formulae.[1] The sense of the theses upheld and attacked, i.e., the participants'

* This article was prepared in 1973 for inclusion in a volume of studies whose appearance has proved impossible. Some of the problems here raised I have subsequently treated from a somewhat different perspective in my *Beings and their Attributes* (Albany, 1978) to which the reader may be referred for additional references.

The following abbreviations are used in the notes that follow:

M:	'Abd al-Jabbār: *al-Moghnī fī abwāb al-tawhīd wal-'adl*, several editors, Cairo, 1958–1965.
Mas:	Abū Rashīd al-Nīsābūrī, *Kitāb masā'il al-khilāf bayn al-Baṣrīyīn wal-Baghdādīyīn*, Ms. Berlin 5125 = Glaser 12.
Mas (B):	The first part of the same work published by A. Biram, Berlin, 1902.
MQ:	'Abd al-Jabbār, *Motashābih al-Qor'ān*, ed. M. Zarzour, 2 volumes, Cairo, n.d.
Moh:	*al-Majmū' al-moḥīṭ bil-taklīf*, ed. U. Azmi, Cairo, n.d.
SU5:	*Sharh al-oṣūl al-khamsa*, ed. A. Ousman, Cairo, 1384/1965.
ZS:	Abū Rashīd al-Nīsābūrī, *Ziyādāt al-Sharḥ*, an extensive fragment of the first part of the work published by M. Abū Rida under the title *Fī l-tawḥīd*, Cairo, 1969.

1. Cf. generally Joseph van Ess, *die Erkenntnislehre des 'Aḍudaddīn al-Ijī* (Wiesbaden, 1966), 192 ff. T.J. de Boer considered the discussions concerning the non-existent to be simple "dialectic quibbling"; cf. *The History of Philosophy in Islam* (London, 1903, reprinted N.Y., 1967), 55.

understanding of the issues under debate and expressed in their various formulations, is sometimes not altogether plain to see; because of the paucity and the doxographic character of much of the available data concerning many authorities, particularly those of the earliest period, any interpretation of the statements attributed to them must be in part conjectural, while for others the foundation of the understanding has not been fully laid; i.e., there has been no adequate study such as to set forth the theoretical systems that form the framework and context of the specific theses and arguments.

For the major schools of *kalām* in its classical period, viz., the "orthodox" schools of Abū l-Hasan al-Ash'arī (d. 324/935) and Abū Mansūr al-Mātorīdī (d. 333/944) and the Mo'tazilite traditions that follow Abū Hāshim al-Jobbā'ī (d. 321/933) and Abū l-Qāsim al-Ka'bī (d. 319/931), as well as the Shi'ite theologies that are directly dependent upon these, the divergence of doctrine on the question of the non-existent is often defined in terms of the question of whether the "non-existent", i.e., the object of which "non-existent" is understood to be predicated, is or is not posited as a real, not merely mental, object, an entity ("something": *shay'*) and one finds the Mo'tazila for the most part affirming the proposition[2] and the Ash'arites on the whole, together with al-Mātorīdī, denying it categorically[3] and insisting that to hold such a doctrine is, in effect, to hold that there are beings that are eternal along side and independantly of God[4].

---

2. Though the thesis is often attributed to the Mo'tazila without qualification, a number of them did not hold it; cf. van Ess, *loc. cit.* and also R. Frank, *The Metaphysics of Created Being According to Abū l-Hodhayl al-'Allāf* (Istanbul, 1966), 48, n. 9. The position of al-Ka'bī offers some difficulty (pending a more thorough study of the matter) for though some authorities, e.g., al-Baghdādī (cf. *al-Farq bayn al-Firaq*, ed. M. 'Abd al-Ḥamīd, Cairo, n.d., 179f.) imply quite clearly that he held the *ma'dūm* to be "something"; others, e.g., al-Jowaynī (cf. *al-Shāmil*, ed. A. an-Nashār, Alexandria, 1969, 125) and al-Jorjānī (*Sharḥ al-mawāqif*, Cairo, 1325, vol. 2, 190; cf. also the lengthy discussion in the Imāmī work contained in Paris, ms. ar. 1252, foll. 7R° ff.) say that he did not.

3. Cf., e.g., al-Bāqillānī, *K. al-Tamhīd* (ed. R. McCarthy, Beyrouth, 1957), § 329 and al-Jowaynī, *op. cit.*, 124; cf. also Ibn Ḥazm, *al-Fiṣal* (Cairo, 1321) 3, 118.

4. Cf., e.g., al-Jowaynī, *op. cit.*. 127f.; Fakhroddīn al-Rāzī, *K. al-Arba'īn* (Hyderabad, 1353), 150ff. and *al-Moḥaṣṣal* (Cairo, 1323), 35, as well as al-Ṭūsī's comments *ibid.*, 38, n. I. Al-Mātorīdī makes the same charge in *K. al-Tawḥīd* (ed. F. Kholeif, Beyrouth, 1971), 86ff. and 242ff. as does also, for example, the Ḥanbalite Abū Muhammad al-Tamīmī in an *'aqīda* that has manifest Ash'arite leanings, in Ibn abī Ya'lā, *Tabaqāt al-Ḥanābila* (Cairo, 1371/1052) 2, 267, where he declares the thesis that the *ma'dūm* is "something" to be *kofr*.

In order to come to an understanding of the debate and the significance of the question for Islamic theology in general one must first have some clear grasp of the specific doctrines of the several schools and their leading authorities. Apart from this, the terms of the formulae of the polemics are but sound and fury without significance or meaning and the attempt to interpret them likely to produce a result more fancy than fact.[5] Quite apart from divergences in the use of vocabulary, even careful and fulsome analysis of doctrines given in the works of their opponents are likely to be misleading, for any complete and formed theoretical system tends, by its own internal coherence, to exclude alien constructs of differing systems as such and "refutations" of opposing formulations and theses, though they may well (and most often, in fact, do) come to grips with the fundamental issue, do not necessarily touch the main point and intent of the opponent's assertions since these are inextricably bound into the whole system with its own peculiar ordering point of view and perspective.[6] What I propose, therefore, to do in the following pages is to set forth in some detail the doctrine concerning the being of the possible among several of the most important masters of one of the major schools, namely that of the followers of Abū Hāshim in the Baṣrian tradition of the Mo'tazila, as these are given in the available works of the Qāḍī abū l-Ḥasan 'Abd al-Jabbār al-Hamadānī (d. 415/1025) and his disciple Abū Rashīd al-Nīsābūrī[7].

5. It has been suggested, for example, that the source of the Mo'tazilite assertion that the non-existent is "something" lies in their failure to distinguish "being" and "essence" (cf. A.J. Wensinck, *The Muslim Creed*, Cambridge, 1932, 166f.) or that the Mo'tazila really held that the world is eternal and simply sought to hide their real doctrine beneath the cloak of abstruse argumentation (A. Nader, cf. *le Système philosophique des Mo'tazila*, Beyrouth, 1956, 135f.) or that the *kalām* understanding of the *ma'dūm* reflects Platonic "ideas" concerning "ante mundane matter" somehow under the influence of Plotinus (cf. H.A. Wolfson, "The Kalam Problem of Non-Existence and Saadia's Second Theory of Creation", *JQR* 36 [1945–46], 381).

6. Thus, for example, Miskawayh, a follower of the doctrines of the *falāsifa*, observing the debate of the *motakallimīn* concerning the *ma'dūm* altogether from the outside (i.e., from a complete commitment to another and different speculative tradition) sees the whole thing as merely a naive failure "to affirm the reality of intelligible forms" (*al-ṣowar al-'aqliyya*); cf. *al-Hawāmil wal-Shawāmil*, ed. A. Amin and A. Saqar, Cairo, 1370/1951, 343–345.

7. We shall, in effect, focus quite narrowly on the treatment of the problem by these two authors for though not the direct disciples of Abū Hāshim they appear to follow his teaching concerning the ontology of the existent and the possible quite closely. That is (even aside from the fact that it is their works that are preserved and available!) it is clear that Abū Isḥāq ibn 'Ayyāsh and Abū 'Abdallāh, his direct disciples and the masters of 'Abd al-

In that one says that a thing is "non-existent" (*ma'dūm*) "insofar as it is not existent" (*mawjūd*),[8] the expression *ma'dūm* (as also the verbal noun, *'adam:* "non-existence" or "being non-existent") is found used of "what existed (*wojida*) at one time and subsequently, at another, was non-existent" (*'odima*),[9] of "what has not come to be" (*lam yaḥdoth*),[10] as well as for the non-existent whose existence is altogether impossible (*al-mostaḥīl wojūdoho*) — whose non-existence is necessary (*wajaba 'adamoho*)[11] — as, for example, something whose existence would entail a contradiction in terms (sc., whose existence

---

Jabbār, departed in some significant respects from the teaching Abū Hāshim in elaborating their understanding of these questions while 'Abd al-Jabbar (closely followed by Abū Rashīd), because, it would seem, of some major difficulties generated in the specific innovations of his masters, returned to the fundamental teaching of Abū Hāshim. Whatever innovations, apart from the introduction of some new vocabulary, the Qāḍī may have made in the doctrine of Abū Hāshim is quite difficult to determine in the absence of any of the writings of Abū Hāshim himself. That neither 'Abd al-Jabbār nor Abū Rashīd cite Abū Hāshim as holding any opinion contrary to their own concerning these questions would, in any event, indicate that they at least considered themselves to be thoroughly in agreement with his teaching. Again, it is quite difficult to say if there are any significant differences between 'Abd al-Jabbār and Abū Rashīd in their treatment of these problems because of the nature of the sources, i.e., that one must cull and collect the evidences of their thought on the issues involved from various and scattered contexts that, for the most part, seldom concern themselves primarily with the problem of the ontology of the existent or the possible as such and particularly because the first sections of the *Moghnī* of 'Abd al-Jabbār which would contain extensive material that is not only parallel to but most likely the source for much of what is found in Abū Rashīd's *Ziyādāt al-Sharḥ* and the first part of his *K. al-Masā'il* has apparently not survived.

The comparison of the doctrine of Abū Hāshim and his Baṣrian successors with those of the *falāsifa* is quite beyond the scope of the present study; it might be noted here, however, simply for the purpose of chronological orientation, that Abū Hāshim (277/890–321/933), though slightly younger, is a virtual contemporary of al-Fārābī, who died a relatively old man in 339/950, while the *Moghnī* of 'Abd al-Jabbār, written over a twenty years period extending from A.H. 360 to 380 (cf. *M* 20/2, 257), was completed when Avicenna was ten years old.

8. *Min ḥaytho lam yakon mawjūdan*: *M* 6/2, 77, 2; cf. also, e.g., *ibid.*, 135, 6f.; *M* 8, 74, 17 and 102, 17; and 4, 230, 11f.

9. E.g., *SU* 5, 176, 13f.

10. E.g., *M* 6/1, 9 *ult.* f. (where read *bi-'an lā yakūna* for *wa-'in lam yakon* and *taqūlūna* etc., for *yaqūlūna*, etc,; note also that there is apparently a lacuna in the preceding context, most probably by homoiotel. with *al-qabīḥ* in 1. 13).

11. *M* 6/2, 135, 8.

would entail its being other than what it is: *qalb al-jins*)[12] or a second eternal (= necessary) being along with God. Strictly, however, the expression *maʿdūm* is not applied so broadly; "it is defined as the known that is non-existent".[13] That whose being is altogether impossible is not really an object of knowing (*maʿlūm*) but is purely imaginary and a knowledge of it is "a knowing that has no object" (*ʿilm lā maʿlūm laho*);[14] i.e., it is "a knowing that has no object that can be properly said to have either non-existence or existence"[15]: a knowing "that is not correlated to any object that can be described as existent or non-existent".[16] Thus for Abū Hāshim and his followers the *maʿdūm* is somehow a real individual object of knowing, something to which the knowing has a real (*fī l-ḥaqīqa*) relationship and conversely what is not "known", i.e., is not and cannot be properly an object of knowing, is not said to be *maʿdūm*.[17] Again, in that the act of knowing, as a knowing of the known, "is related to it as it really is",[18] the knowledge of the *maʿdūm* is not a knowledge simply of its existence (*wojūd*), i.e., of the actuality of its existence, potential or past (as it really was or

12. Cf., e.g., *M* 11, 452, 13f.
13. *Al-maʿlūm alladhī laysa bi-mawjūdin*: *SU* 5, 176, 17; or as "the known that has not the attribute of existence" (or, more precisely within the terms of the system, "the attribute of being-existent"): *al-maʿlūm alladhī laysat laho ṣifat al-wojūd* (*Moḥ*, 356, 18f.). Note ʿAbd al-Jabbār's rejection of *ʿal-montafī'* as a strict synonym of *ʿal-maʿdūm'* on the grounds that it is properly used only of what has once been and is no longer existent (*SU* 5, 176). It should furthermore be noted that the expression *intafā*, according to his usage, is also applied to the "attributes" (*ṣifāt*), which, belonging to the category of "states" (*aḥwāl*), cannot be said properly to exist since they are the states of the existent (*v. infra*).
14. *M* 4, 247, 3f., citing al-Jubbāʾī and Abū Hāshim.
15. *Lā maʿlūma laho yoshār ilayhi bi-ʿadamin wa-lā wojūd*, *ibid.*, still citing "the Two Masters"; cf. also 248, 11.
16. *Ghayra motaʿalliqin bi-maʿlūmin yūṣaf bi-'annaho mawjūdin aw-maʿdūm*: *Mas* fol. 174v° 5f. In having an imaginary object or content the act of knowing (*ʿilm*) is said to have a "quasi correlation" to the imagined object, "to have the character of something that is correlated [to something else albeit strictly speaking it is not] (lit., to be *fī ḥokni l-motaʿalliq*) (e.g., *M* 4, 248, 11; the same expression is used also, for example, of the motivation towards or the will to perform an impossible or unattainable action which, beyond the scope of the subject's power of causation, lacks possibility (*ṣiḥḥat al-wojūd*) and so is unreal. This is contrasted to "attributes that are not correlated to another in any way at all": *lā tataʿallaq bi-ghayrin aṣlan* [e.g., *M* 4, 248, 12; cf. *Mas* fol. 174v° 13 *alibi*] such as "life". The whole question of relation (*taʿalloq*) in the system requires study.).
17. Cf. *SU* 5, 176f.
18. *Yataʿallaq al-ʿilm bil-shay'i ʿalā mā howa bihi*: cf. e.g., *M* 6/1, 188, 61; 11, 5, 6; 11, 159, *& alibi pass.*

would be as existent) but a knowledge of a non-existent entity as and insofar as it is non-existent "in the moment of its non-existence" (*fī ḥāl 'adamihi*).[19] From one standpoint, therefore, the *ma'dūm* is the real that was and is no longer and may come to exist in the future.[20] Now, insofar as concerns the subject of the present inquiry, the status and reality of the once but now no more existent was a topic of scant concern for the theologians of the *kalām*; the problem was, rather, that of the possible and it would seem clear enough that in introducing into the Baṣrian School of the Mo'tazila the thesis that "the non-existent is an entity" (*al-ma'dūm shay'*) Abū Ya'qūb al-Shaḥḥām was solely concerned with the question of the possible.[21] Accordingly, the later masters of the school identify the *ma'dūm* quite strictly with the possible. "There is no basis on which we can say of a thing that it is non-existent when it has never come to be at all save insofar as it has not come to be though its coming to be is possible" (*min ḥaytho lam yoḥdath ma'a jawāzi ḥodūthihi*).[22] The possible—the *ma'dūm*—in this sense is not, however, understood simply as that which is now actually possible but, on the contrary, the "non-existent" embraces the totality of all possibles: "there is no non-existent but that its existence is possible or was possible".[23] This includes both that which was possible and once existed as well as the non-existent possible that though once possible is now no longer possible (as, for example, the now no longer possibly existent contrary of the

19. Cf., e.g., *SU* 5, 554f. (which is directed against the Ash'arites) and *Mas* (B), 20f.; see also below, n. 89.

20. Thus S. van den Bergh in *Averroes Tahafut al-Tahafut* (Oxford, 1954) 2, 4, *ad* 3, 6 and van Ess, *op. cit.*, 198.

21. Cf., e.g., al-Ash'arī, *Maqālāt al-Islāmīyīn* (ed. H. Ritter, Istanbul, 1929–30), 162 and my remarks in *Atti del III Congresso degli Studi arabi e islamici* (*Ravello*, 1966) (Naples, 1967), 324f. Van Ess (*op. cit.*, 193) cf. also *die Gedankenwelt des Ḥārith al-Muḥāsibī* [Born, 1961], 175) suggests that al-Shaḥḥām took his position as a compromise between that of a group whom al-Ash'arī dubs *al-azaliyya* and that of Hishām b. al-Ḥakam (on which cf. also *le Muséon* 82 [1969], 467, n. 57).

22. *M* 4, 255, 17f., i.e., though the possibility of its being (past or present) is posited; cf. also *ibid.*, 247, 12f. and ZS, 193, 11ff.

23. *Lā ma'dūma illā wa-yaṣiḥḥ wojūdoho 'aw-kāna yaṣiḥḥ wojūdoho; Mas*, fol. 174v° 16f. (on which see below). Concerning the definition see also n. 85 below. It should be kept in mind that the Baṣrians in speaking about the possibles do not consider the question as merely one concerning possible, future instantiations of one or more classes of being, but rather in terms of single individuals that are known (posited) as particular individuals in God's infinite knowledge.

possible that came to be).[24]

Before proceeding to discuss the question of the ground of the possibility of the possible and the ontological status and character of the *ma'dūm* as non-existent it is necessary to outline briefly the ontology of the existent (*mawjūd*) and its various attributes (*ṣifāt*) and characteristics (*aḥkām*) and the nature and role of existence (*al-wojūd*) itself as these are understood in the analysis of Abū Hāshim and his followers.[25]

Though the expressions *mawjūd* (existent) and *wojūd* (existence), etc., are frequently used in the texts with the sense simply of factually "being found" (*wojida*) present in or to something, as of a material body's being concretely present or at hand in the world or of an accident's concrete, entitative presence as inhering in its material subject or substrate, the notion of being or existence as signified by the expression *al-wojūd* is the subject of an elaborate ontological analysis within the Baṣrian tradition. According to 'Abd al-Jabbār, the term *mawjūd* (existent) cannot be defined by any expression that is clearer "since we have, in the presence of perceivable reality, an immediate even if only general knowledge of the existent".[26] Thus, for material beings, "the sense of this expression [sc., '*mawjūd*'] is that [the entity so described] is characterised by a state having which the conditions of the actuality of those characteristics [*aḥkām*] that specifically characterise the existent are realised, e.g., the possibility of its being seen or its being related to another,[27] its being inherent in a substrate or its being a substrate of inherence, etc."[28] Elsewhere he describes it as "that which is specifically characterised by an attribute given which [its] attributes

24. Cf., e.g., *M* 8, 102, 14–16.

25. In order to be fully complete the discussion of the nature of "existence" (*al-wojūd*) as conceived by Abū Hāshim and his successors would have to be elaborated in the context of a full discussion of their understanding of the nature of attributes (*ṣifāt*) as such and the conception of "states" (*aḥwāl*) in general (note that *ḥāl* is a categorial expression covering *ṣifāt* and *aḥkām*), something that is beyond the scope of the present writing. For a general outline of the matter see my *Beings and their Attributes*, Albany, 1978.

26. *Moḥ.* 139, 2f.; it is thus that he rejects the definition of Abū 'Abdallāh on the grounds that the terms of the definition are more obscure than the term defined (and anyhow are not used by him in that sense!): *SU* 5, 175f.

27. *Ta'alloqoho bi-ghayrihi*; note in regard to the above discussion of the real relation of knowing to its object even when this is *ma'dūm* that the latter is not said to be *mota'alliq bil-'ilm* but rather *mota'allaq bihi*.

28. *M* 5, 232, 3–5. See also my *Beings and their Attributes*, pp. 58ff. *et alibi*.

and characteristics are manifested";[29] that is, it is specifically characterised by the attribute of existence (*ṣifat al-wojūd*). Our grasp of the specific attributes is given in the actuality of the thing's existence and vice-versa; neither are the specifically characteristic attributes given to our knowledge and understanding apart from the actuality of the thing's existence wherein they become manifest (*taẓhar*) nor is its existence known and available to understanding apart from the grasp of the characteristic attributes that are manifested through it.[30]

Existence is the "ground (*aṣl*) of [the actuality of] all other attributes in any being (*dhāt*)";[31] it is their "condition" (*sharṭ*): the condition that is the ground of their actuality (*al-moṣaḥḥiḥ*). It is the ground of the actuality (*ḥoṣūl*) and the manifestation (*ẓohūr*) in being of the "essential attributes" of every being, sc., of those attributes that it has—that belong to it (are *min ḥaqqihi*)—"by virtue of the way it is in itself" (*li-mā howa 'alayhi fī dhātihi/nafsihi*), "that are entailed by 'the Attribute of the Essence'" (*al-moqtaḍāt 'an sifati l-dhāt*) and "flow immediatly from it" *al-ṣādirat 'anhā*).[32] "The attribute of existence is that through which the manifestation (*ẓohūr*) of the essential attributes is realised so that the former is the condition of the actuality (*al-mosahhih*) of the latter... and thus in the case of every existent it is by virtue of its existence (*li-ajli wojūdihi*) that the attribute that is entailed by the Attribute of the Essence is manifest and it is by virtue of its existence [sc., of the existent] that we know how it is in itself

---

29. *Ḥadd al-mawjūd annaho l-mokhtaṣṣ bi-ṣifatin taẓhar 'indahā l-ṣifāt wal-aḥkām*: *SU* 5, 176, 5 f. (This definition and the whole passage *SU* 5, 175 f. are found repeated almost verbatim in the text of al-Farzadhī published by Abū Rīda in the appendix to *ZS*, pp. 571 f.) "Characteristic" is maybe not an altogether felicitous rendering of *ḥokm* (p. *aḥkām*) in this usage; it does, however, render the sense quite accurately for most contexts and I can at this point think of no better English equivalent.

30. Cf. *M* 7, 153, 3–6. See also *Bings and their Attributes* p. 62.

31. ZS, 46, 1.

32. Regarding the technical terminology see *Beings and their Attributes*, p. 80, n. 1. It will be sufficient here to note that there is some fluctuation and betimes apparent inconsistency in the use of some expressions to denote the "Essential attributes", (sc., those that are *li-mā howa 'alayhi fī dhātihi/nafsihi* = *al-moqtaḍāt 'ammā howa 'alayhi.../'ani l-dhāt, l-nafs* = *al-ṣādirāt 'ammā...*, & c.) as for these one finds not infrequently the shorter or abbreviated expression *al-ṣifāt al-nafsiyya* (originally a quite strict equivalent) and *al-ṣifāt al-dhātiyya* as well as *ṣifāt al-dhāt/l-nafs*, even though *ṣifat al-dhāt* (sometimes *al-ṣifat al-dhātiyya*) is formally distinguished as the "Attribute of the Essence". In what follows I have rendered the former as "essential attribute(s)" and the latter as the "Attribute of the Essence". On the distinction as well as the sense of the term *dhāt*, see below.

(*mā howa 'alayhi fī dhātihi*)".[33] Thus, to cite the most frequently employed example, the "essential attribute" of the atom (*al-jawhar*) is "to occupy space" (*al-taḥayyoz*) and it is through and by virtue of its existence (*wojūd*) that this attribute is realised and becomes manifest;[34] its existence is inseparable from the actuality of this attribute[35] and it is by this that it is known, identified, and defined (sc., as that which, when it exists, occupies space).[36] Similarly, God's "essential attributes", according to Abū Hāshim and his followers, are entailed by His "Attribute of the Essence" and belong to him "by virtue of the way He is in Himself"[37] so that in the ontological analysis of the school, in God too the actuality of the "essential attributes" by which His being is distinct and distinguished from all other being may be said to be grounded in His existence. "There is no class of being but that when it exists it has some attribute by which it is distinguished from others."[38] Existence (*al-wojūd*), thus, is a univocal concept for the Baṣrian Mo'tazila of the classical period; "the attribute of existence is a single attribute in existent beings."[39]

These attributes (viz., the "essential attributes") which a thing has "by virtue of the way it is in itself" (*li-mā howa 'alayhi fī dhātihi*) are those by which it is distinguished and so are the immediate ground of its being-similar *tamāthol* to another or its being-different (*ikhtilāf*) from it and by which, consequently, it is known as being that which it is. As was indicated in the citation above, however, these attributes arise from the "Attribute of the Essence" (*ṣifat al-dhāt*)—are entailed (*moqtaḍā*) by it given the existence of the "Essence"/ thing-itself" (*dhāt*).[40] The "essential attributes", thus, and the "Attribute of the

33. *Moḥ*, 142, 12ff.

34. Cf., e.g., *M* 12, 61, 10ff.; *Moḥ*, 142, 15f. (*q.v.* generally).

35. Cf., e.g., *SU* 5, 112, 7f. = 538, 5ff.; this frequently repeated formulation is attributed to Abū Hāshim in *ZS*, 76, 1–3.

36. Cf., e.g., *M* 5, 219, 17f.

37. Cf., e.g., the citation of Abū Hāshim in *Moḥ*, 172, 4–6, *SU* 5, 182, 15 and below concerning God's existence (*wojūd*) as an "essential attribute". See also *Beings and their Attributes*, p. 82, n. 17.

38. *Lā jinsa illā wa-taḥṣol laho 'inda l-wojūd ṣifa bāna bihā min ghayrih: M* 8, 22, 17.

39. *Moḥ*, 141, 24f. (*q.v.* & *sqq.*) and *Mas* (*B*), 13, 5f. (cf. also n. 54 below).

40. "Essence"/thing-itself: *dhāt*; the fundamental meaning of the term may be built up out of the context of the discussion. Though "thing-itself" or "essence" may be quite accurate equivalents of *dhāt* in most contexts one should beware of specific overtones that they may carry over from their long and varied use in the philosophical systems of the Western

Essence" are ontologically distinct.[41] In the case of the atom, for example, to occupy space, i.e., the attribute of occupying space: "its being occupying-space" (*kawnoho motaḥayyizan*), is distinct from its being an atom (*kawnoho jawharan*). Abū Hāshim and the Masters of the Baṣra School who follow his teaching closely do not look upon this as a purely logical distinction. That the atom occupy space is, as was noted above, conditioned by the actuality of its existence and as conditioned depends upon the realisation of the condition (viz., existence: *al-wojūd* as *moṣaḥḥiḥ*). The atom's being an atom, however, is not so conditioned. Abū Hāshim's formulation is significant; he speaks not of the "essence"/thing-itself (*dhāt*) simply but of the "Attribute of the Essence" (*ṣifat al-dhāt*): the thing-itself's being as it is in itself (*mā howa 'alayhi fī dhātihi*); that is to say, its being itself identical with itself in itself—its predicability of itself as being itself. This attribute is not grounded in something else but is irreducible.[42] It is the ground

---

tradition. *Al-dhāt* is most strictly the "thing-itself" or the "self (of the thing)" (wherefore in most contexts it is practically interchangeable with *al-nafs* as "self") and so is employed for the thing's "self" as it is in itself and what it is in itself in being itself (thus "essence", if you will), as also it may be used simply for the thing in its being "an entity" (*tóde ti* = *shay'*; cf. below, n. 47): a single unitary being that is itself the subject of knowing and predication as a single or unitary being or entity. The term, thus, is used often loosely of any proper subject of proper attribution or predication (e.g., a living being insofar as it is a single "totality": *jomla*) but is strictly applied (in the realm of created beings) to the atoms (*al-jawāhir*) and accidents (*al-a'rāḍ*) (thus the *ma'dūm* is said to fall under two categories, sc., atoms and accidents: *Mas* (*B*), 21 f.) for within the system these alone (apart from God) are truly said to be entities as unitary beings. All else (viz., bodies—*ajsām*—with their various properties and among them living bodies) is composite, made up of atoms and their inherent accidents. Living bodies as such have a kind of unity of being and are qualified by some states in their wholeness as totalities but this unity is not a true unity; they have, rather, simply the character of being one thing (not being so in the strict sense: *fī l-ḥaqīqa*: they are, that is, *fī ḥokmi l-shay'i l-wāḥid* (e.g., *M* 11, 334 & *alibi*), *bi-manzilati l-shay'i l-wāḥid* (e.g., *ibid.*, 302 & *alibi*) and "have a character in some respects like that of a thing-itself" (*fī l-ḥokmi kal-dhāt*: *M* 4, 312, 19). For the detailed examination of this question see. *Being and their Attributes* pp. 43 and 10ff.

41. For the explicit statement of the distinction, which originates in the teaching of Abū Hāshim, cf., e.g., *Moḥ*, 107, 23ff. and 172, 2ff.; *M* 4, 250, 14ff.; *ZS*, 489, 12ff. (where read *thābita* for *thāniya*, 1. 12); *Mas* (*B*), 13, 2ff. (where read *li-'adami ma'nan* for *li-'adamin 'alā wajh*); *Moḥ*, 142, 14f. (cited above n. 33) and *SU* 5, 93, 6f. Note that the formula *mā howa 'alayhi fī dhātihi* by implication indicates a "state" (sc., *kawnoho 'alā ḥalin fī dhātihi*); regarding this, see below.

42. It is not *'an shay'in* (*ZS*, 489, 12f.) and one can validly assign no ground for it (cf. *ibid.*, 287, 11f., cited below n. 94). For the example of the "atom" cf. generally *Mas* (*B*), 12ff.

(*aṣl*) of whatever other attributes it may have. "The atom's being an atom cannot be by virtue of the way it is in itself because there is here no other attribute to which one may point and say that on its account it is an atom, for what we mean [by the atom's being an atom] is the ground of its attributes."[43]

Again, the sole ground of the intelligibility of a thing-itself—i.e., the ground of its intelligibility for us—is the "Attribute of the Essence": its being itself identical with itself,[44] for it is the ground of the "essential attributes" which constitute the mode of the manifestation of the thing-itself in the actuality of its existence and, consequently, its accessibility to perception and knowledge through and in the actuality of its existence (*wojūd*). "The thing-itself must perforce be characterised by some attribute by which it is distinct (*tatamayyaz*)[45] from others and this attribute must perforce have some characteristic [sc., the "essential attribute (s)"] through which it becomes manifest (*taẓhar*). Now this characteristic is, so to speak, its "true nature" (*kal-ḥaqīqati lahā*) and must have the condition of existence."[46] Although it is the thing-itself that we know (it is defined as "that which may be known and of which predications may

---

Note that all attributes or states (*ṣifa*, strictly, is a *ḥāl*) are properly rendered in the form *kawn al-shay'*... "the thing's being thus or so." The act of knowing is not an attribute (*ṣifa*) in the terms of Abū Hāshim and his followers; rather it is, in the corporeal knower, an entitative accident (*'araḍ*) that, inhering in the subject, is the reason or cause (*ma'nā*, *'illa*) of the actuality of the attribute (*ṣifa*) which is the knower's being knowing (*kawn al-'ālimi 'āliman*). The "states" (*aḥwāl*) are ontologically real as states or modalities of the being of the existent and their predication of it (of the existent "thing-itself" or living totality) is a statement of the way it concretely and really is as so qualified (*mawṣūf*). It should be noted, however, that for the authors with whom we are here concerned, the expression *kawn/kā'in* in this usage (and so also *thobūt/thābit*, which 'Abd al-Jabbār takes sometimes as synonymous, cf. e.g., *SU* 5, 176) does not necessarily denote or imply the actuality of a true state of being, i.e., that the subject is ontically real as having existence being really in such a state. Thus, though Abū Hāshim will say that "the atom is an atom even when it is non-existent" (*al-jawhar yakūn jawharan fī ḥāl 'adamihi*: *Mas* (*B*), 12, 6f.; cf. also *ibid.*, 18, 19ff. cited in the following note) the use of the expression *yakūn* (is) implies no real state of being as existence or existent.

43. *Mas* (*B*), 18, 19ff.; cf. also *Moḥ*, 61, 8ff.

44. Cf. *SU* 5, 108, 10f. The non-existent is not directly accessible to human knowing cf. n. 84 below.

45. Sc., the "Attribute of the Essence". On this "distinctiveness" see below.

46. *Mas* fol. 17V° 17–19. "True nature": *al-ḥaqīqa* were more accurately paraphrased as "what it really is", that is, that which we most fundamentally and essentially understand and refer to when we name the thing.

be made"[47]), it is known through and in terms of the manifest "essential attributes" that are entailed by (*moqtaḍiya 'an*) the "Attribute of the Essence." The "Attribute of the Essence", however, remains undisolved in its self-identity and so inaccessible in itself as it presents no analysable terms. It is itself itself. Thus the "Attribute of the Essence" is said to be "restricted" (*maqṣūra*) to the "essence"/ thing-itself[48] because the thing-itself in itself is not predicable of anything other than itself. Only as existent, with and in the actuality and manifestation of its "essential attributes", does it become thus and so and thereby, in existence (*'inda l-wojūd*), directly accessible to our knowing and possessed of attributes (*ṣifāt, awṣāf*) which may be predicated of it as true states (*aḥwāl*) of its being.

As the "Attribute of the Essence" is prior to the "essential attributes" of which it is the ground, so also it is prior to existence: the thing-itself's being existent. The actuality of the "essential attributes" and their manifestation are conditional (*mashrūṭ*) in that they depend upon the actuality of the existence of the thing-itself (*wojūd al-dhāt*) as the "condition of their actuality" (*moṣaḥḥiḥ*), but the thing-itself's being itself identical with itself is not grounded in something else or conditioned by anything, for it is impossible that the thing cease to be identical with itself.[49] The identity of the thing-itself with itself—its predicability of itself—remains true even in its non-existence: when it is *ma'dūm*.[50]

The "Attribute of the Essence" is the absolute or unconditioned ground of all other attributes that a thing may have in being that which it is. The "essential attributes" that flow immediately and necessarily from the "Attribute of the Essence" when the thing-itself is existent are necessitated as such not by the condition of their actuality (sc., by existence as *moṣaḥḥiḥ*) but in "by the thing-itself's being as it is in itself" (*li-mā howa 'alayhi fī dhātihi/nafsihi*). The "Attribute of the Essence" is "that whose effect is greater and stronger than the effect of conditions (*shorūṭ*) and factors that fulfill the condition of actuality (*toṣaḥḥiḥ*),

---

47. *Al-dhāt mā yaṣiḥḥ 'an yo'lama wa-yokhbara 'anho*: e.g., *Mas* (*B*), 19, 12f. Attributes (*ṣifāt*) as states (*aḥwāl*), though we may speak of their characteristics (*aḥkām*), are not properly speaking objects of our knowing and our predication; rather it is the thing (*shay'* = *dhāt*) which we know as being in such or such a state that may, thus, be predicated of it. See also below n. 85.

48. Cf., e.g., *Moḥ*, 61, 9 and 197, 3; *Mas* (*B*), 19, 5–9 and 21, 5–8 and the following note.

49. *Ḫorūj dhāt 'an ṣifatihā l-maqṣūrati 'alayhā idhā lam takon mashrūṭatin bi-sharṭin lā yaṣiḥḥ*: *Moḥ*, 197, 2f.; cf. also *SU* 5, 108, 9–14 and generally *ZS*, 192 ff. Cf. also n. 42 above.

50. Cf. *ZS*. *loc. cit.* and the discussion in *Mas* (*B*), 12 ff. On the character of this reality of the thing *fī 'adamihi* and that it is not a state (*ḥāl*) of the *ma'dūm* see below.

i.e., [it is] that which effects the attribute by way of necessity (*to'aththir fī l-ṣifati bi-ṭarīqati l-ījāb*), so that the atom, by virtue of the way it is [in itself] effects its occupying space when it exists and so similarly with black;[51] for this reason that which is entailed [*al-moqtaḍā*, sc., that which is entailed by the "Attribute of the Essence" given existence] differs specifically [from the characteristic, manifest attribute(s) of another thing] not because of any difference specific to existence itself."[52] As the condition may (as is the case with all created beings) arise (*tajaddada*) and be present at one time and disappear and be absent (*zāla, intafā*) at another, so these attributes whose actuality is conditional upon its presence may contingently appear at one time and be absent at another. The "Attribute of the Essence", however, which is not so conditioned, is not subject to this contingency.[53]

Existence (*al-wojūd*) is univocal: "the attribute of existence is the same in all existent beings."[54] "Existence" can be neither more nor less[55] and God, insofar as He is considered simply in His being-existent (i.e., as *mawjūd*), shares this attribute with all other existents.[56] Existence as the condition of the actuality of a being's "essential attributes" is only analogously the ground of their being (*yajrī majrā l-aṣli fīhā*).[57] It is the "Attribute of the Essence" that is the absolute ground of whatever attributes and characteristics a thing may have including the manner in which it belongs to it to exist when it exists: *wajho stiḥqāqihi lil-wojūd*. That is, it is "the way the thing is in itself" that determines the possibility of the possible (*jawāz/ṣiḥḥat al-wojūd*): that it may exist and may not exist, its existence being contingent upon the action of an agent (*fāʿil*) who effects its existence, and the necessity of the necessarily existent (*wojūb al-wojūd*): the

---

51. For the example see, e.g., *Moḥ*, 107, 8 ff., 188 f., & *alibi pass.*

52. *Moḥ*, 142, 18–20 cf. also *Moḥ*, 206, 6 ff. and the argument in *ZS*, 177 f.

53. Cf., e.g., *Mas (B)*, 21, 1 ff. (where read *motajaddida* for *mtḥddh* in 11, 9 f., 16 and 19), *ibid.*, 13, 5–7 and the text cited in the previous note. On the use of the expression *tajaddada* and its distinction from *ḥodūth* and *wojūd* see my "Abū Hāshim's Theory of 'States'" pp. 93 f.

54. *Ṣifat al-wojūd wāḥidaton fī l-dhawāti l-mawjūda: Moḥ*, 141, 24 f.; cf. generally *ibid.*, 142, 11–20 and also *Mas (B)*, 13, 5 f.; *M* 4, 84, 1 ff.; 7, 87, 17 ff., & *alibi pass.* and note especially *Moḥ*, 143, 11–17. On the predication of *mawjūd* of God cf. also *M* 5, 292 ff.

55. *Al-wojūd lā yaṣiḥḥ fīhi tazāyod: M* 9, 116, 1 f.

56. Cf. *ZS*, 546 f.: *al-qadīm yoshārik sā'ira l-mawjūdāti fī l-wojūd*; and *M* 11, 433, 5 f.

57. Cf., e.g., *Moḥ*, 147, 12 f. It is in this sense that one may say that to be contingent (i.e., possible: not necessary) and to be eternal (i.e., necessary) are modalities of existence and so are "posterior to existence" (*al-ḥodūth wal-qidam yatbaʿāni l-wojūd: M* 7, 153, 4).

unconditioned necessity of that whose non-existence is impossible.[58] Thus, according to the analysis of Abū Hāshim and his followers, that the eternal (*al-qadīm* = God) exist (i.e., its being-existent: *kawnoho mawjūdan*) is an "essential attribute": it is existent "because of the way it is in itself" (*li-mā howa 'alayhi fī dhātihi*);[59] but the way it is in itself (sc., the eternal's being eternal), as the "Attribute of the Essence",[60] "is unconditioned by anything else" (*ghayr mashrūṭatin bi-'amrin siwāhā*). The "Attribute of the Essence" sc., "to be eternal, is existence itself" (*kawnoho qadīman nafs al-wojūd*),[61] i.e., is to exist necessarily. God's existence is absolutely unconditioned in its necessity.

That the *ma'dūm* is identified with the possible has been noted above (nn. 21 f.). The possibility of the possible is the possibility of existence (*jawāz/ ṣiḥḥat al-wojūd*): the possibility of the thing-itself which is non-existent (*al-dhāt al-ma'dūma*) to exist and existing to manifest "by virtue of the way it is in itself," its essential attributes and properties. There is no intermediate between existence and non-existence; the thing-itself is either existent (*mawjūda*), manifesting its "essential attributes", or it is non-existent (*ma'dūma*).[62] The system does not recognize any becoming according to which a thing-itself may be said to be in one respect and in another not to be. Change (*al-taghayyor*) is predicated only of composites (sc., bodies: *ajsām*, including the living in their quasi unity as *jomal*: totalities) whose change is, in reality, a becoming-other (*taghāyor*) as some of their constituent elements cease to exist (*zāla, intafā, 'odima*) and are replaced by others with the consequent alteration (alternation) of particular states, either of the material substrate (*maḥall*) as such or, in some instances of the living "totality" as a whole.[63] Again, since the ontologically real components

58. Cf. *M* 11, 433, 2–9.

59. Cf., e.g., *M* 11, 423, 14f.; *SU* 5, 182, 12–15 (where the reference to "the four attributes" is to the primary "essential attributes": existent, living, *qādir*, and knowing); *ZS*, 459f. (where *'an al-ṣifati dhātiyya* is to be understood after *moqtadan* in the 2d line from the bottom of p. 459) and particularly 195, 9ff.

60. Cf., e.g., *M* 4, 250, 14ff.; 7, 84, 15f. (where read *fa-mā* for *mimmā*); *SU* 5, 107, 7ff. On the identification of the eternal as the necessary cf. my "Philosophy and the kalām, a Perspective from one Problem" in *Islamic Philosophical Theology* (ed. P. Morewedge, N.Y., forthcoming).

61. Cf. *Moḥ*, 61, 8ff.

62. Cf., e.g., *M* 6/1, 10, 11f.

63. Cf., e.g., *ZS* 567, 7ff.; *M* 6/2, 107, 7ff. and 199, 4ff. (where read *al-taghayyor* for *al-taghyīr* in 11, 6 and 9); and 11, 427f. The attributes (*ṣifāt*) and characteristics (*aḥkām*) may be

of material being consist exclusively in the atoms (*jawāhir*) and the accidents (*aʿrāḍ*) that inhere in them, both of which as entitative realities (i.e., things-themselves) either exist, manifesting their "essential attributes" or are non-existent, one can speak of the possibility of existence only in two respects. That is, of the three modes of potentiality commonly recognized in medieval thought, viz., the thing's potentiality in the potentiality of matter: that the matter is capable of receiving the perfection (whether as an accidental form or as a substantial form), its potentiality in the power of the agent (*in virtute agentis*) to produce it, and its potentiality in itself (*quia termini non sunt discohaerentes = potentia in intellectu*), the Baṣrian tradition of the Moʿtazila recognizes only the last two: the intrinsic possibility of the *maʿdūm* to become existent and the power of the autonomous agent to cause it to exist.

The sole cause of the existence (*wojūd*) of beings whose being is possible, sc., of things-themselves (*dhawāt*) whose existence is not necessary, is, according to the Baṣrian School, the power of efficient causality (*qodra*) of the autonomous agent (*al-qādir = katexoúsios*).[64] Accordingly, the *maʿdūm*, as that whose existence is possible (*mā yaṣiḥḥ/yajūz wojūdoho*) is identified with the *maqdūr* [*ʿalayhi*]: the object of the autonomous agent's power of efficient causation or, more properly speaking in the strict terms of the analysis, that which is reated as its object to the state (*ḥal*) of the autonomous agent in his having the power of efficient causality to effect its existence (*kawnoho qādiran ʿalayhi*, i.e., *ʿalā ījādihi*). "There is no way to assert the reality of the non-existent [i.e., that a thing-itself is, in fact, *maʿdūm*] save as that which is correlated to the state of the autonomous agent."[65]

---

said to be possible as one may speak of the possibility of their becoming or arising (*tajaddod*) or their actuality (*ḥoṣūl*), but this is reduced to the possibility of the being of things-themselves (*dhawāt*) (sc., to the possibility of the existence, *wojūd*) either of the things-themselves as the immediate ground of their "essential attributes" or of the accidents [*aʿrāḍ*] as *maʿānī*, i.e., insofar as by their inherence in the atoms [*jawāhir*] as substrate [*maḥall*] they are the causes of the attributes and characteristics as states (*aḥwāl*) of the subject whether the material substrate alone or of the living *jomla*) and of the agent's action.

64. On the forms of causality recognized by the school and that of the autonomous agent (*al-fāʿil al-qādir*) in particular see my "Philosophy and the Kalām," The equivalence *'exousía = qodra* and *istiṭāʿa* is found also in the translation literature; cf., e.g., the Arabic version of Alexander of Aphrodisias *Perì toũ 'eph' 'emīn* (*Scripta Minora II/1: de Anima*, pp. 172–4) in A. Badawi, *Commentaires sur Aristote perdus en grec et autres épîtres*, Beyrouth, 1971, pp. 80–82.

65. *Lā ṭarīqa li-'ithbāti l-maʿdūmi 'illā mā yataʿallaq bi-ḥāli l-qādir: Moḥ*, 117, 11f. Thus "it

God's power of efficient causality is infinite and unrestricted in itself and so extends to an infinite number of classes of beings (*'ajnās*)[66] and to an infinity of individuals in each and every class.[67] It is the ultimate ground of the possibility of all possibles (*maqdūrāt*) as such (i.e., of their being *maqdūrāt*), for the possibility of the realisation of the act of any created agent, whether man, jinnī, or angel, derives from God's having created in him the power of autonomous action and causation (*iqdāroho laho*), a gratuitous act whose possibility and actuality are grounded in God's autonomous power (*'exousía*). Again, it is the nature of the autonomous agent's power of efficient causality (*al-qodra: kawn al-qādiri qādiran*) that it does not necessitate the existence of its object[68]—i.e., it is not determined to a single object—but extends to the contrary and an indeterminate number of individuals in whatever class (*jins*) of beings.[69] It is, thus the ground of alternati-

belongs to that which is not subject to the agent's power of causation that its existence is impossible just as it belongs to what is subject to the agent's power of causation that its existence is possible": *M* 8, 116. For the definition of the *maqdūr* as that to which the agent's power of efficient causality is correlated (i.e., it is possible that he effect its existence: *wojūd*) cf., e.g., *M* 8, 75, 16f. (where read *tajaddod* for *thdd* in l. 12); 9, 80, 1f.; 15, 197, 9; and *Moḥ*, 356, 23. The definition of the autonomous agent is reciprocal; "it belongs to the autonomous agent that to effect the existence of the object of his power of efficient causality (*ījād maqdūrihi*) is possible on his part without his having any relationship to it beyond his being *qādir 'alayhi*" (*M* 9, 22, 8ff.) (the sense of the reference to "no other relationship beyond his being *qādir 'alayhi*" is that even though other states [e.g., those involved in the acts of willing, intending, or knowing] may indeed be correlated to and determinant of the manner or mode of the occurence/coming-to-be of the act [*wajh woqū'ihi/ḥidūthuhi*] and so determinant of some real aspects or modalities of the act or the being that is made to exist, nonetheless the occurence/coming-to-be [*woqū'/ḥodūth* = *tajaddod al-wojūd*] as such and in itself is correlated to and depends exclusively upon the agent's being-*qādir*, so that the function and efficacity of any other state is grounded in and is subordinate to that of his being-*qādir*); cf. also, e.g., *M* 4, 306, 15ff., 331, 3–5; 8, 109, 3ff.; 9, 134, 23f.; *Moḥ*, 161, 9f. and 359, 2f.; & *alibi*.

66. Q 1, 50; *M* 6/1, 129 *ult.* f. Note that although the English word "genus" is correct to render Arabic *jins* as this word is used in the literature of the *falsafa* it would be quite misleading to render it thus in the *kalām* literature.

67. Cf., e.g., *M* 4, 277ff.; 6/1, 162ff.; 11, 453f.; 7, 55, 3ff.; *SU* 5, 155f. and 317, 1ff.; *Moḥ*, 115, 1ff.; *Mas* fol. 183 V°; *ZS*, 256ff. and 268; & *alibi iass.* The thesis, insofar as it insists that at any instant God has the "power" (*qodra*) to create more than He has, sc., an indeterminate number at any instant (cf., e.g., *M* 6/1, 136, 4f.), is directed in part, at least, against the position of Abū l-Hodhayl, on which cf. *le Muséon* 82 (1969), 473ff.

68. Cf., e.g., *M* 9, 50, 4 and generally my "Philosophy and the Kalām".

69. Cf. reference above. We need not, for the purposes of the present study, enter into the question of the specific restrictions of the created agent's power of efficient causality

ves in the action of the agent (and so the ground of his freedom and autonomy) and so of the infinitude of alternatives in the unrestricted power of the eternal agent (apart from which one could not speak of the possible but rather only of the necessary and the impossible); it is the ultimate ground of the possibility of the possible insofar as its possibility is the possibility on the part of the autonomous agent that it be made to exist. Besides the possibility of what will be (sc., what the eternal agent knows will come to be through the efficacious power of His unnecessitated act), it is the ground of the possibility of what has not come to be and is now excluded from actual possibility through the factic necessity of what has been and what is.[70] It is the ground of the possibility of creation as such: of its possibility and its non-necessity — that it can and in fact does exist but need not have existed at all — and that no individual creature need exist or have existed; it is possible (God might have: it lies within His Allmight) that He have created nothing at all[71] or that he have created a different universe (e.g., it is possible that it consist of a greater quantity of matter: *jawāhir*;[72] any given event [action or existent] might have taken place earlier or later or in another place;[73] mankind might have been created initially in the state and place of the blessed of the life to come and there have been, therefore, no obligation involving reward and punishment: no *taklīf*;[74] the revealed law need not be specifically as it is;[75] God could increase His benefits and graces towards mankind[76]). So

---

(*tajānus maqdūrāti l-qodar*; on this see *Beings and their Attributes*, p. 164, n. 8).

70. Cf., e.g., *M* 9, 119; the thing remains *ma'dūm* as having been possible (*jā'iz al-wojūd* and *maqdūr*); cf. above nn. 23f. and the following references. Similarly, that a thing's being made to exist be impossible as precluded (*mamnū'*) by some "impediment" (*man'*) relative to it (i.e., to the *maqdūr* as such) does not imply its being thereby excluded from its relation to the agent in his having the power of efficient causality to produce it; he remains *qādir 'alayhi* (cf., e.g., *M* 4, 330ff. and *Moḥ*, 195). The thing remains, thus, possible in itself and possible in the power of the autonomous agent. In this way even though material creation ("bodies") cannot exist *ab aeterno* for reasons intrinsic to the nature of material being as such, its possibility nonetheless is eternal in God's eternally having, by virtue of the way He is in Himself, an unrestricted and unconditioned power of efficient causality (cf., e.g., *M* 4, *loc. cit.*) and in that its possibility as possible in itself is also unconditioned and perpetual.

71. Cf., e.g., *M* 11, 99, 7f., 112ff.; 14, 110ff. and my "Philosophy and the Kalām".

72. E.g., *ZS*, 257, 1ff.

73. Cf. *M* 8, 112 11ff. (where insert *aḥad* after *fa'l* in 1. 10).

74. E.g., *M* 14, 137ff.

75. E.g., *M* 15, 137f.

76. Cf., e.g., *M* 11, 154, 5ff., 256, 12ff.; & *alibi pass.* This is directed against the teaching of the *falāsifa* and that of Bishr b. al-Mo'tamir (cf., e.g., *M* 6/2, 2, 11f.) and Abū l-Qāsim al-

also it is the ground of the possibility of the possible that will not ever come to be: that which God knows He will never bring to be[77] and that which cannot under any circumstances come to be, e.g., that act which, if God were to perform it, would be morally wrong: injustice or lying or the like on His part, for though His performing such an act is in fact impossible (*lā yajūz*) because of His wisdom and His *autárkeia (ghinā)*, it is nevertheless possible (*yaṣiḥḥ wojūdoho*) in that it falls within His power of efficient causality, for the thing itself is not impossible in itself and God's power of efficient causality, in itself, is unrestricted.[78]

The infinite and indeterminate power of God. thus, is the ground of the possibility of whatever is possible (*maqdūr*). Logically, however, the intrinsic possibility of the thing-itself considered in itself—that its terms are not incompatible with its existence—is prior to its possibility in the power of the agent. "The possibility of the realisation of existence is prior to the possibility of the autonomous agent's having the power to effect its existence, so that the im-

---

Ka'bī (cf., e.g., *M* 14, 55 and *ZS* 269f.) and generally the "*aṣḥāb al-'aṣlaḥ*" (sc., those who hold that God must and can only do that which is absolutely "for the best" in respect of His creatures), in whose doctrines the Baṣrians see not merely a restriction of God's power but the implication of the inherent necessity and determinism in His action.

77. Cf., e.g., *M* 11, 4 ff. (where read *anna 'ilma l-'ālim* for *anna l-'ālim* p. 5, 1. 5) and 6/2, 205 ff. Note however that God's foreknowledge as such does not exclude the possibility (*ṣiḥḥa*) of what will not be nor necessitate the being of what will be (cf., e.g., *M* 11, 70, 14ff., 159, 11ff., 277, 10ff., and the references above).

In this general context one may raise the question of the autonomous action of the created agent (whose possible act likewise includes what he will not do) in that the system categorically refuses to subordinate the autonomous act of the human agent directly to God's act—i.e., to make the action or inaction of the created agent directly dependent upon God's action or will—so that they do hold, in a sense, that there are two sources of the autonomous or free initiation of action and being (*iḥdāth*) against the Ash'arite conception of the created or contingent power of efficient causality (*al-qodra l-moḥdatha*) which is fully coordinated to and coherent with the latter's notion of continuous creation); however, even though the created agent's power of efficient causality is relatively autonomous in the agent, being the ground of his freedom, it yet exists (*tūjad*, i.e., the separate quanta of power—*qodar*—have entitative existence as accidents materially present in the corporeal agent) only through God's having created it so and consequently the ultimate ground of the possibility of the possibles whose possibility is immediately grounded in their relation to the power of the created agent lies in God's being-*qādir* by virtue of the way He is in Himself.

78. Cf., e.g., *M* 6/1, 129ff., 135ff., and 149f.; 15, 176, 11ff.; 16, 59ff.; *Moḥ*, 220, 24ff. and 247. Cf. also *le Muséon* 82 (1969), 486f. (where read "we know" for "He knows" p. 486, l. 28).

possibility of the former renders the latter impossible".[79] "The thing's being made to exist through the action of the autonomous agent is, as it were, derivative of the possibility of its existence in itself" (*kal-far'i 'alā ṣiḥḥati wojūdihi fī nafsihi*).[80] This insistence upon the priority of the thing-itself as possible in itself is frequent enough in the texts.[81] It remains, therefore, to examine what they have to say about this priority, i.e., concerning the nature and status of the thing-itself (*dhāt*) as *ma'dūm* and as, in itself, it is related to the power of the autonomous agent.

We have noted above that the thing-itself (*al-dhāt*) in the "Attribute of the Essence" (*ṣifat al-dhāt*) is prior to the actuality of its existence as the ontological ground of the characteristic and essential attributes that are realised and manifested when it exists: those that, given the existence of the thing-itself, flow immediately from the "Attribute of the Essence" — from the "Essence"/thing-itself because of the way it is in itself. The thing-itself, considered in this respect, is essentially prior to the action of the agent who causes its existence (*al-mūjid, al-moḥdith*), for the agent's power of efficient causation is only to bring the thing to existence (*iḥdāthoho*): to effect its existence = make it existent (*ījādoho*),[82]

79. *Ṣiḥḥat al-ḥodūthi tatba'ohā ṣiḥḥat kawni l-qādiri qādiran 'alayhi fa-stiḥālatoho dhālika: M* 8, 72, 5f.

80. *M* 11, 94, 15ff.

81. Cf. also, e.g., *M* 8, 68, 14f. and 109, 3f.; 9, 134, 21ff.; *Moḥ*, 356, 23f., *& alibi*.

82. Note that within the system this thesis, sc., that the power of efficient causality is the power to realise the existence of something (*al-qodra 'alā l-ījād*) and this alone (cf., e.g., *M* 8, 63ff.) has as its corollary that the power of causation cannot be a power of causing non-existence: the power of annihilation (*al-qodra 'alā l-i'dām/al-ifnā'*) (cf. generally, e.g., *M* 8, *loc. cit.* and especially 65ff. and 74ff.—where read *tatajaddad* for *tḥdd* on p. 75, 12). Since the school holds no doctrine of continuous creation (i.e., of God's continually maintaining in existence the being that continue to exist after the moment of their initial coming to be), neither after the manner of Abū l-Qāsim al-Ka'bī of the Baghdad School of the Mo'tazilla nor after that of the Ash'arites, the possibility of the non-existence of matter (i.e., the atoms) once it has come to exist, that is, if and how God can cause it to cease to exist, becomes a major subject of discussion and debate. The solution offered is that the atom must have some contrary (*ḍidd*) which God can create and which created would cause the annihilation of all matter (since it cannot be specific to a particular substrate); cf. generally *M* 11, 442–451 and *Mas (B)*, 69ff. and 74ff. This position, that beings whose nature it is to continue in existence (*min ḥaqqihā 'an tabqā*), once made to exist, are independant of the agent who caused them to exist so that the continuation of the world in existence requires no action on God's part, fits consistently and coherently with their notion that the action of the created agent in generating the being of his own acts is fully independant of God's action (*v. supra* n. 77).

and is not the power to determine and make it be that which it is.[83] The essential identity of the thing-itself with itself in being that which it is (e.g., that black be black or that the atom be an atom, to cite the most common examples) and consequently also the essential and characteristic attributes that, upon existence, derive immediately and necessarily from the way it is in itself, are not determinable by the agent. The non-existent (*al-ma'dūm*) which is the thing-itself that in itself may exist is thus "something" (*shay'* = *tóde ti*), for in that it is a specific thing-itself that in itself may be made to exist and that, as such, has a real correlation to the autonomous agent's power of efficient causality, there is no circumstance under which it is not true that "it may be known[84] and that true predications may be made of it;" it is "something", that is to say, a (particular) entity that is a true correlate (*mota'allaq bihi*) of our knowing![85] As a thing-itself) (*dhāt*), the *ma'dūm* is known not simply in general (*'alā jomla*) but specifically (*'alā l-tafṣīl*) in its proper characteristics.[86] It is known and distinguishable (*motamayyiz*) in its otherness (that it is *ghayr*) from what is other as in its similarity and difference in relation to what is similar and different;[87] so also the possibles in their specific identity as possibles are distinguishable (*motamayyiz*) from and different (*mokhālif*) from God[88] and as possibles they are distinguishable from that whose existence is not possible at all.[89]

---

83. Cf., e.g., *M* 8, 63 ff. (esp. 68 ff.) (where read *al-a'rād* for *ighr'ḍ*: 64, 16; *khabaran* for *jbr'*: 66, 13; *bi-motajaddid* for *bothdd*: 67, 7: *al-taḥayyoz* for *'ltkhyr*: 68, 19; *yataḥayyaz* for *ytkhyr*: 68, 20; *motaḥayyizan* for *mtkhyr*: 68, 21; *al-'araḍ* for *'lghrḍ*: 68, 19–21; and *khabaran* for *jbr'*: 70, 3); *ZS*, 50 ff., 201 ff. and 320 ff.; *Moḥ*, 64, 1 ff.; *& alibi pass.*

84. It is known to God whose knowing embraces all knowables and can be known by us, though we have no knowledge of future contingents (cf., e.g., *M* 11, 161, 11 ff.; 15, 57, 14 ff.; and 13, 337, 14 f.) and consequently no direct knowledge of the *ma'dūm* (sc., the particular possible) (cf., e.g., *M* 8, 7, 14 f. and 75, 8 f.).

85. The terms *dhāt*, thus, and *shay'* are defined by precisely the same formula (on whose stoic origins cf. van den Bergh, *op.cit.*, 2, 4, *ad* 3, 6 cf. also Sībawayh, *al-Kitāb*, ed. A. Harun, Cairo, 1385/1966, 1, 22 = Būlāq p. 7); cf., e.g., *M* 5, 251, 3 f. (where read *al-kalām* for *'lkl'*, 1. 3) and *Mas (B)*, 19, 11–13 (cited above n. 47); cf. also *SU* 5, 108 (cited above n. 44) and concerning *ta'alloq al-'ilmi bihi*; see also above.

86. Cf., e.g., *ZS*, 191 f.; *Mas (B)*, 21, 15–20 and *Mas* fol. 174 V°, 16 ff. (cited above nn. 23 and 46).

87. For the use of these terms to describe the *ma'dūm* see, e.g., *Mas (B)*, 21; *M* 7, 128, 11 f. (where insert *lā* after *sā'iri mā*, 1. 12); 8, 268; *ZS*, 226 f., *& alibi.*

88. Cf. *Mas (B)*, 21, 9–14.

89. Cf., e.g., *ZS*, 193, 11–13. It is thus that 'Abd al-Jabbār and Abū Rashīd insist against Ibn

The *ma'dūm* as such — insofar as it is *ma'dūm* — is simply possible; both its existence and its non-existence are equally possible; i.e., neither is necessary and neither impossible. The non-existents (*al-ma'dūmāt*) "whatever their individual and specific dissimilarity [among themselves as thing-themselves] all have in common that their existence is possible and their non-existence is possible."[90] Though the coming-to-be (*ḥodūth*) and existence (*wojūd*) of the non-existent are conditioned, i.e., contingent upon the action of the autonomous agent (*al-qādir*), its non-existence (*'adam*) — i.e., its continued non-existence: *istimrār 'adamihi*—as such, is not derived or conditioned (*mashrūṭ*).[91] Of itself the possible "remains non-existent" (*baqiya/istamarra ma'dūman*) so long as it is not made to exist through the autonomous agent's power of efficient causation.[92] "The thing-itself entails the possibility of existence and this alone."[93] That the thing-itself be itself and itself that which it is irreducible and unconditioned; that is, the "Attribute of the Essence," "the way a thing-itself is in itself must be absolute and no ground for it can be validly assigned."[94] One cannot ask why a thing is what it is.

But what is the reality of the thing-itself as a non-existent possible? Non-existence (*al-'adam*), i.e., "the non-existent's being non-existent" (*kawn al-ma'dūmi ma'dūman*) is not a state (*ḥāl*) or attribute (*ṣifa*) of the thing-itself. That is, to say that the *ma'dūm* is non-existent is not to assert that the thing-itself *is* actually and in fact in any state of being or is qualified by an attribute as is the case when we say that a thing is existent (*mawjūd*), i.e., that it has actually and in fact the state or attribute of being-existent (*kawnoho mawjūdan*), for non-existence is not in actuality and fact a state or attribute (it is not *ṣifa thābita*) but

---

'Ayyāsh that even though our knowledge of non-existence and the non-existent derives from a knowledge of the existent (v. below), our knowledge of the thing-itself that it is non-existent and possible is not a knowledge of it as it would or may or will exist (a knowledge of "an expected attribute", thus) but of it as non-existent in its non-existence; cf. *SU* 5, 554f.; *Mas (B)*, 12 and 20f.; and *ZS*, 191f.

90. *ZS*, 227, 1f.; cf. also *Mas (B)*, 65, 7; *M* 6/2, 135, 8.

91. Cf. *ZS*, 193, 14–16; *SU* 5, 343, 11ff. (where read *al-'adam* for *al-qidam* in 1. 11) and *Mas* fol. 52 V°.

92. Cf. *M* 4, 255, 3f. and *Mas (B)*, 65, 6ff. (on which page read *al-ma'ānī* for *'lmgh'ny* in 1. 4; *yothbat* for *ythyt* and *ba'd* for *bo'd* in 1. 16).

93. *M* 4, 270, 13f.: *al-ladhī taqtaḍīhi l-dhāt ṣiḥḥat al-wojūdi faqaṭ.*

94. *ZS*, 287, 11f.: *'inna mā howa 'alayhi l-shay' fī dhātihi yajib lā li-wajhin bal bi-'ayyi shay'in 'ollila fasad.*

is simply "the absence of the attribute of being-existent" (*zawāl ṣifati l-wojūd*).[95] To say that a thing is non-existent is the negation (*nafy*) of a state or attribute (viz., that of being-existent); it does not imply that there is in fact (*thobūt*) a contrary state (as, by contrast, to say that a body is-not in motion implies that it is in fact in the state of being-at-rest).[96] Similarly, "its being subject to the power of an agent that can effect its existence" (*kawnoho maqdūran 'alayhi*) does not imply or require that there is in fact some state or attribute by which it is specifically qualified and which (since non-existence is the negation of existence and the agent's power of efficient causation is the power to effect the existence of the non-existent that is the correlative object of his power) would be the contrary (*ḍidd*) of existence (*wojūd*).[97] The meaning of the statement that a thing-itself is non-existent is given only in the understanding of the absence of the state of being-existent;[98] i.e., the non-existent is not distinguishable from the existent as having an attribute but rather by the fact that the existent has a state of being in virtue of which it is distinguishable from the non-existent, sc., its being existent,[99] a state that is given to our immediate apprehension as and in the manifest actuality of the "essential attributes." The reality of the non-existent

---

95. Cf. *Moḥ*, 353, 18f. and *ZS*, 228, 10–19 (citing 'Abd al-Jabbār), and the references below.

96. Cf. *M* 6/1, 9f. (on which cf. n. 10 above); 5, 74f.; *ZS*, 245; and *Mas (B)*, 72, 1 ff. and 74f.

97. Cf. *M* 8, 75, 14 ff. Abū Rashīd argues (*Mas (B)*, 71, 6 ff.) that if the non-existent, as such, had a state (*ḥāl*) in being non-existent the state would have to be "Essential" (*li-dhātihi*), i.e., would belong to the "essence"/thing-itself as such, since the possible is non-existent *ab aeterno (fī mā lam yazal)* in itself as possible; thus, since the eternal as such is unconditionally necessary, non-existence as a real state of the thing-itself would be necessary as eternal and consequently the existence of the *ma'dūm* would be altogether impossible. The thesis that non-existence (*al-'adam*) is not a state is, again, bound to the thesis that the power of efficient causality is not a power of making something non-existence (*'alā l-'i'dām*) for it is only a power to effect the actualisation of "a contingent accident" (*ṣifa motajaddida*), sc., coming-to-be (*al-ḥodūth* = *tajaddod al-wojūd*); cf. generally n. 82 above and references there cited. *Al-'adam* is sometimes loosely referred to as *ṣifa motajaddida* (e.g., *Mas*, fol. 52 V°) as one says of that which having been existent ceased to be existent that it has passed from being-existent to being-nonexistent, but strictly speaking it is not such; cf., e.g., *Moḥ*, 353, 18 ff.

98. Cf. *M* 4, 230, 11–14; cf. also *M* 8, 74f. Thus the knowledge of existence (what it is to be existent) is the basis (*aṣl*) of that of non-existence (*al-'adam*): *Mas (B)*, 71, 17f.; cp. also 'Abd al-Jabbār's definition of the non-existent cited above; see also n. 89.

99. *Fa'amma mofāraqat al-ma'dūmi lil-mawjūdi fa-li-'anna lil-mawjūdi ḥālam bi-kawnihi mawjūdan bāna bi-hā mina l-ma'dūmi wa-'in lam yakon lil-ma'dūmi bi-kawnihi ma'dūman ḥālon*: *M* 6/1 54, 12f. (on which page read *al-binya* for *'ltubh* in 1. 10); cf. also *M* 6/2, 135, 6f. and 5, 230, 11 ff., as well as n. 38 above.

(*al-ma'dūm*) is, thus, the reality or fact of its possibility (*thobūt al-jawāz*).[100] "The thing-itself entails the possibility of existence and this alone." In the "Attribute of the Essence" the thing-itself that is-not existent can only be predicated of itself but not as itself being in any way. As and insofar as it is non-existent it is-not (*laysa*) and 'is-not' is the denial of an attribute or state. Non-existence, thus, is a negation (*nafy*) but not, as the Ash'arites would have it, a pure negation (*nafy ṣirf*), for the possibility of the possible is in fact real (*thābit*) and for this reason it is distinguishable from the purely imaginary as something (*tóde ti*) that is really and in fact correlated to the agent's power of efficient causation and, thereby, a real object of knowing.[101] The individual non-existent is posited as an entity only as it is known to be *maqdūr 'alayhi*.

The possible considered in itself is absolute; its essential identity with itself (sc., the "Attribute of the Essence"), as the unconditioned ground of its possibility, is absolute. It is inconceivable that the thing cease to be the possible that it is in itself.[102] The language of the masters of the Baṣrian Mo'tazila may appear often (and it is this that so agitated some of their opponents) to set the "things-themselves" (i.e., the possible *dhawāt*) up as realities, i.e., as somehow concretely having in their being possibles a being of their own along side and independantly of God's being, as for example Abū Rashīd will say that the non-existent (*al-ma'dūm*) in its "Attribute of the Essence"—its predicability of itself as it is identical with itself—is perpetual (*abadan*)[103] as he will say that God's power of efficient causality is perpetual.[104] The possibility of the thing-itself is, as was noted above, logically prior to its possibility in the agent's power of efficient causation but as regards the real possibility of the thing's coming to exist—its being actually and in fact possible that it come to be existent—the two are coordinate and reciprocal; the impossibility of the agent's causing it to exist (the impossibility of its being made to exist on the part of the autonomous agent) entails the impossibility that it exist at all as conversely the impossibility of its

100. Cf. *SU* 5, 209, 19ff. (where read *mūjidin* for *mawjūdin*, l. 19 and *al-mūjid* for *al-mawjūd* in the last line). The formula *al-ma'dūm thābit* I have not found used by any of the Baṣrian Mo'tazilites.

101. Cf., e.g., *M* 4, 247, 13f. and *Moḥ* 117, 11f., cited above. Non-existence is, thus, a kind of "*stéresis* viewed as something positive" as van den Bergh suggests (*op. cit.*, 2, 47, *ad* 61, 7) but the masters of the Baṣrian Mo'tazila would find the formulation there altogether intolerable in its implications.

102. Cf., e.g., *ZS*, 194, 5ff., 195, 4ff., 287, and above.

103. Cf., e.g., *ZS*, 194, 9 (and generally 193ff.); v. also n. 70 above.

104. Cf., e.g., *ZS*, 268, 10.

existence in itself entails the impossibility of its existence at all.[105] Thus Abū Rashīd explicitly refuses to ground the possibility of the possible as it is possible in itself in the agent's power of efficient causality;[106] nor, within the terms of the system, can it be grounded in God's knowledge, for the essential identity of the possible with itself in itself, as the unconditioned ground of its possibility, is the prior condition of its relationship (*ta'alloq*) to knowing as an object of knowing: an object that can be said to exist or to be non-existent. To say, however, that the non-existent possible is "an entity" (*shay'*) is not for Abū Hāshim and his followers, an affirmation of its being a concrete reality; [107] as we noted above what is "real" as being a fact or "really the case" (*thābit*) is simply its possibility. In its being non-existent it has, of itself, properly speaking, no being (no *ṣifa,* no *ḥāl* whatsoever); insofar as it is *ma'dūm* one can say properly only that the thing-itself is-not existent (*laysa bi-mawjūd*) and that it is possible that it be existent. But this fact: that its coming-to-be, its becoming existent, is possible is given only as one knows that it is in fact the potential object of the agent's power of efficient causation; "there is no way to assert the reality of the non-existent save as that which is correlated to the state of the autonomous agent."[108] According to the analysis of the system, as we have seen, one says of a thing that it is non-existent only insofar as it is-not existent though its existence is possible. It is, therefore, only insofar as a thing-itself's coming to be and being existent are possible, not logically and ideally only but really and in fact, that our predication of it as non-existent is other than merely ideal or imaginary. It is only insofar as its existence is really and in fact possible (*thābit al-jawāz*) that the non-existent is other than a purely imaginary object of our knowledge and predication and only, therefore, thus that it can properly be said to be "an entity" (*shay'*) and a "thing-itself" (*dhāt*). In the realm of the real, the possible is the *maqdūr 'alayhi* and the reality of its possibility consists in its correlation to the state of the autonomous agent in his being *qādir 'alayhi*; the non-existence (*'adam*) of the agent entails the impossibility of the relation (*yoḥīl al-ta'alloq*)[109] and consequently "if one could not imagine the existence of some autonomous

---

105. Cf., e.g., *M* 4, 331, 5–11 and above.
106. Cf., *ZS*, 287, 6 ff.; the argument for the counter position is set forth more fully on p. 284.
107. "Our saying *shay'* [entity] is not an assertion of existence (*laysa bi-'ithāt*) for it is used of the non-existent just as it is of the existent": *M* 5, 251, 3 f. (on which seen n. 85 above).
108. *M* 4, 247, 13 f. and the references above nn. 22 and 65.
109. Cf., e.g., *SU* 5, 177, 15 ff. and *Moḥ*, 139 f. as well as *Mas* fol. 139 R°, 14 ff.

agent it would not be possible to describe anything as possibly existent."[110]

Such, in sum, is the basic analysis of Abū Hāshim and his followers in the Baṣrian School of the Mo'tazila concerning the nature of the non-existent possible. A number of important questions remain to be raised, including the general implications of their teaching within the larger contexts of their theology, that of other *kalām* systems and of Islamic philosophical thought generally. It is hoped that the present outline will, at any rate, serve somewhat to enlighten the continuing discussion and investigation of these issues.

---

110. *Moḥ*, 365, 13f.: *law lam yotaṣawwar wojūd qādirin mina l-qādirīn la-mā ṣaḥḥa wasf shay'in mina l-'ashyā'i bi-ṣiḥḥati l-ḥodūth.*

V

ABU HASHIM'S THEORY OF «STATES»

ITS STRUCTURE AND FUNCTION

The question of the real structure and significance of the theory of the *aḥwāl* or «states» first introduced into the kalām by al-Jubbā'ī's son, abū Hāšim, has long constituted a real, if not always explicit, problem for students of Islamic theology. Many years age now, Max Horten tried to lay the question to rest in his article «Die Modus-Theorie des abu Haschim» (1) based chiefly on Šahrastānī's *Kitāb al-Milal wan-Niḥal* and the *Muḥaṣṣal* of Rāzī, and this article continues to be cited, even today, as authority on the subject. He describes the *ḥāl* as «die bestimmte Daseinsform oder Erscheinungsform des Wesens» and explicates this statement saying that it is «ein *Inhaerens*, da er zum Wesen hinzukommt. Wenn er nun dem Wesen näher steht, so müssen die ferner stehenden Akzidenzien zunächst in dem Modus, und erst indirekt, durch Vermittelung des Modus, in dem Wesen inhärieren» (2). Reading this, one immediately senses a difficulty;

---

(1) *ZDMG* 63 (1909), 303ff. A number of other scholars have discussed the problem but with little positive result for the most part; the chapter on the *aḥwāl*, for example, in 0. Pretzl's *Die frühislamische Attributenlehre* (*SBAW* 1940, 4, pp. 51-4) approaches the matter but does not carry through to the point of contact, while A. S. Tritton in his *Muslim Theology* (London, 1947) makes no attempt to understand the concept but says (p. 150) that abu Hāšim was «a child in philosophy»! A. Nader's chapter on the subject in his *Le système philosophique des Mu'tazila* (Beyrouth, 1956, pp. 211-216) shows an almost absolute failure to grasp the basic terms of the texts. L. Gardet, likewise, erroneously identifies the theory of «states» as a «sort of conceptualism» in his article on abu Hāšim in *EI*[2] (*s.* al-Djubba'i), following Massignon (cf. *Passion*, 555f. and 571).

(2) Horten, *op. cit.*, pp. 303-4.

Horten has here, following his own errant paraphrase of Šahrastānī, conceived the problem in Scholastic terms which are altogether alien to the earlier kalām and which are in no way reflected in the section of the *Milal wan-Niḥal* which he cites. Again, on a quite superficial level, the *ḥāl* does not «inhere» *(ḥalla)* in a subject, for this is the property of accidents *(a'rāḍ)* alone. Starting from this position one can get nowhere in the direction of a description of the theory that will conform to the evidence of the texts. The question is difficult, however, the evidence not always unambiguously lucid and more recently, in a brief discussion of the *ḥāl*, Joseph van Ess, who is perhaps the foremost authority on the kalām, suggests that the theory is no longer to be reconstructed with certainty (3). On the other hand, S. van den Bergh, in a note to his translation of Averroes' *Tahāfut al-Tahāfut*, manages, with considerable insight, given the evidence available at the time of his writing, to strike very close to the center of the theory (4).

The difficulty which has long stood in the way of an adequate description of the theory of the *aḥwāl* has been the insufficiency of texts, i.e., of texts of authors who accepted the theory and made explicit use of it. The polemical passages of Rāzī or Šahrastānī — even the long and eloquent discourse on the subject in the *Nihāyat al-Iqdām* (5) — are really quite obscure when one does not know beforehand the structure of the theory as propounded by its adherents, for to allow that it might make sense was the last thing that these authors wanted to grant. Now finally, however, with the publication of a major part of the *Muġnī* of the Qāḍī 'Abd al-Jabbār al-Hamadānī, as well as his *Šarḥ al-uṣūl al-ḫamsa* and the *Muḥīṭ bit-taklīf*, we have a great deal

(3) *Die Erkenntnislehre des 'Aḍudaddīn al-Īcī* (Wiesbaden, 1966), 206.

(4) *Averroes' Tahafut al-Tahafut* (Oxford, 1954), 2, 4 (especially lines 12-17). His suggestion that the term *ḥāl* is a translation of Greek πως ἔχον is, I feel, not really substantiated; that the kalām is akin to and in significant respects descended from Stoic thinking has long been recognised. The evidence, however, would seem to point to the theory of the *aḥwāl*'s having been introduced by abu Hāšim independently of the kalām's primitive sources. That there are some (but by no means throughly consistent) analogies between the Stoic πως ἔχον and the *ḥāl* would seem rather to be evidence of parallel solutions to parallel problems than a direct borrowing. The suggestion *(ibid.)* that the term *ma'nà* represents Greek λεκτόν has, insofar as it relates to the problem of the *ḥāl*, absolutely no basis in the kalām usage (see below) and that the term *aḥkām* represents Greek νοήματα is, at best, problematic (both this and the term *ḥaqīqa* need serious study).

(5) Ed. A. Quillaume, Oxford, 1934, pp. 131ff.

of text in which the theory, even if it is not set forth explicitly for its own sake, is put to considerable use and, in a number of passages, made sufficiently clear for us to get a quite precise notion of exactly how it was employed and what problems it was meant to solve (6).

What I wish to do here, then, is to outline the theory on the basis of a number of passages drawn mostly from the writings of ʻAbd al-Jabbār and to indicate briefly how it came to arise in the school of al-Jubbā'ī and how it was used. Once the fundamental structure of the theory and its characteristic vocabulary are made clear, the detail of its use is fairly easy to work out.

Initially it may be best to recall several of the school's basic concepts of the ontological structure of material beings. The ultimate real ontological elements of material creation are two: atoms *(jawāhir)* and accidents *(aʻrāḍ)*. The qualitiless atoms, as a kind of particulate or granular *materia prima*, constitute the material substrate in which the accidents inhere; their reality is that of the ontologically real locus of the being of the accidents that inhere in them (7). The accidents, on the other hand, constitute the formal reality of beings: the defined and specific content of their being. By their inherence in the substrate *(maḥall)* of atoms, they determine the being of the composite in its being what it is. They form, in the strictest sense, the thing as it exists, complete and perfect in the totality of its perfections. Movement, for example, is the cause of the atom's being in motion and also the perfection of its being insofar as it is moved. The presence of color in the substrate is the reality and actuality of the thing's being colored (8).

---

(6) Van Ess remarks (*op. cit.*, 208) that the term *ḥāl* is not frequently used and suggests in his article «Ibn Kullāb und die Miḥna» (*Oriens* 18-19 [1965-66] p. 137) that it appears that none of the disciples of abū Hāšim accepted the theory. In actual fact, however, it was taken up by most, if not all the most important masters of the Baṣra school in the following generations (e.g., by abū ʻAbdallāh, abū Rašīd, Ibn ʻAyyāš, and ʻAbd al-Jabbār) even if they did not all use it in exactly the same way in all areas of their thought (see below). The difficulty arises because the term *ḥāl* is not the only term for the concept (see below) and is not inevitably used when the theory is in play or alluded to, but once the theory is reconstructed and its typical vocabulary clearly recognised, its omnipresence in the later writings of the school becomes manifest.

(7) Cf. generally R. FRANK, *The Metaphysics of Created Being according to abû l-Hudhayl al-ʻAllâf* (Istanbul, 1966) 34ff. and esp. 42-44. The parallel in the Stoic conception of *οὐσία* (= *τὸ ἄποιον ὑποκείμενον*) is remarkable; cf. E. WEIL, «Remarques sur le Matérialisme des Stoïciens» in *Mélanges Alexandre Koyré* 2 (Paris, 1964), 561.

(8) Cf. generally Frank, *op. cit.*, 13ff. and 39ff.; again the analogy with basic Stoic conceptions is notable; cf. e.g., Weil, *op. cit.*, 564. Albeit they are distinguished

Most important to the present investigation is that atoms and the accidents are ontologically distinct from one another; they have their being as distinct entities *(ašyā'* or *ḏawāt)*, created by God in a particular act of creation which is the ground of the being of each separately. So also, the accidents are ontologically separate and distinct from one another. According to the school of al-Jubbā'ī, life is the condition of the existence of the act of knowing, but nonetheless, the act of knowing *('ilm)* is not an aspect or perfection of life, but is a distinct perfection or accident that inheres in the material substrate of the living body as a discrete and separate entity. It is an existing reality *(šay'un mawjūd)*, having its own being *(wujūd)* as such. The whole being — man, for example — is held to be a composite *(jumla)*, made up of a particular finite set of discrete atoms and accidents.

The problem, then, out of which the theory of the *aḥwāl* arose, was this: an accident comes to inhere *(ḥuduṯa/ḥalla fī)* in a particular

---

when one speaks of the immaterial (i.e., God),both *'araḍ* and *ma'nà* appear to be used without significant distinction to designate the ontologically discrete, inherent perfections of material bodies. The latter, which seems to become more prevalent in later authors, has, however, been the source of no little confusion because of attempts to render it, according to its common non-technical sense, as «idea» (e.g., Horten, *op. cit.*, 305, n. 2 [where he talks of «was in der geistigen Welt eine Idee...»], M. Allard, *le Probleme des attributs divins dans la doctrine d'al-Aš'arî* [Beyrouth, 1965] 149, van den Bergh, *loc. cit.*) or as «concept» (Nader, *op. cit.*, xv, H. Laoust in *REI* 34 [1966], Cahier I, 53) and the like. The term *ma'nà*, however, in the specialised sense of a perfection or accident that is the cause of a thing's being-so, would seem to have been almost as common as *'araḍ* from the very earliest period of the kalām; e.g., for Hišām b. al-Ḥakam (cf. al-Aš'arī, *Maqālāt* [ed. H. Ritter, Istanbul, 1929-30] 345), abū l-Hudhayl (cf. 'Abd al-Jabbār, *al-Muġnī* 5 [ed. M. el-Khodeiri, Cairo, 1958] 55), Ibn Kullāb (al-Aš'arī, *op. cit.*, 170 *et alibi*), al-Aš'arī (*K. al-Luma'*, § 25), 'Abd al-Jabbār *(op. cit., passim)*, al-Baġdādī (*al-Farq bayn al-Firaq* [ed. M. Badr, Cairo, 1328/1910] 311f.), etc. On the question generally, cf. Pretzl, *op. cit.*, 38ff. and my «Al-Ma'nà, some reflections...» *JAOS* 87 (1967) 248ff. In this article I suggested that the term, in its origin, probably represents an equivalent of Greek *αἰτία* used in this special sense; it would seem that the notion of the *λόγος σπερματικός* also may well lie in the background (for certain aspects of the analogy cf. Weil, *op. cit.*, 561ff.); it is to be noted that *ma'nà*, insofar as it is used in distinction from *'araḍ* is almost inevitably used to designate the accident as the cause *('illa)* of some effect in the subject. It is perhaps significant for the background of this term that Origen commonly uses the term *αἰτία* in the sense of "property" (cf. M. Borret, *Origène, Contre Celse* 2; *Sources Chrétiennes* 136, Paris, 1968, p. 160, n. 1). In any event it is amply clear from many typical passages (cf. e.g., *al-Muġnī* 9, 53, 22ff. and 59, 17ff., *et alibi pass.*) that one has not to do with any kind of conceptualism or the like.

part or organ of a body, but the perfection, of which it is the cause *('illa)* is attributed to the whole *(jumla)*. What, however, is the meaning of the proposition that one man differs from another in that he is «knowing» and the other «ignorant», when the only real entities are the separate bodies (i.e., the composite substrates) and the act of knowing *('ilm)* inhering in the one and the act of ignorance *(jahl)* in the other? That is, when the composite, which is the individual man, is not ontologically one but is a created composite of many ontologically discrete elements, we can say that the body of the one is spatially separate from that of the other and that the accident of knowing is different from that of ignorance, but we have no way, within the metaphysics of the system, of saying that the one composite, considered in its entirety, differs ontologically from the other, for the accidents in question belong only to the single organs (here the heart) which are the substrate, while the unity of the whole is essentially «accidental» i.e., the whole *(jumla)* is created such by God but is not *One* as unified in being a single being (*essentia* or *οὐσία*, in the strict sense) (9). The accidents *(ā'raḍ/ma'ānī)*, in brief, and the atoms *(jawāhir/ajzā')* have being *(wujūd)* and are entitites or beings *(ašyā'/ /ḏawāt)*, but the composite, strictly speaking, is not ontologically *a being;* the composite unity of the body consists in the union of parts through the inherence of the accidents of conjunction *(ijtimā')* and contiguity *(mumāssa)* and its various parts are qualified according to the determination of the particular accidents that occur in them, separately in each; each one of these exists, having its own essential

(9) For a statement of the problem, cf. *Farq*, 180f. (and also below, n. 22); Horten *(op. cit.)* notes this aspect of the problem (cf. also van Ess, *Erkenntnislehre*, 206) while Pretzl *(loc. cit.)* sees quite correctly that it is, in part at least, the origin of the problem; neither, however, notes that the «sameness» and «difference» involved in the *aḥwāl* are not those discussed in terms of the atoms and accidents; that is, the sameness and otherness or difference (*tamāṯul*, *iḫtilāf*, etc.) of ontologically real and discrete «beings» (viz., atoms and accidents) are not those of composites with their qualities and attributes *(ṣifāt)*. (N.B. that while the terms *'araḍ* and *ma'nà* are used of accidents as ontologically real and distinct perfections inherent in a substrate, the terms *ṣifa* and *ḥukm* are chiefly used of the *aḥwāl* and other derived attributes by authors who follow the theory of the «states»). One does not use the terms *iḫtilāf* and *tamāṯul* of composites *(jumal)*, which are not properly existent beings (see below); rather one uses *fāraqa* (cf., e.g., *Farq*, *loc. cit.*, *Muġnī* 7 [ed. I. Ibyari, Cairo, 1380/1961] 82 and 157, and n. 29 *infra)*. If one will speak of the problem of «universals» as involved in the theory of the *aḥwāl* (e.g., Horten, *op. cit.*, 304) he must beware of abandoning the grounds of the kalām's own conception of the problem.

character and being in being what it is. The composite, however, is and remains a composite of discrete entities. The unifying act is that of the accident of conjunction which inheres separately in the various atoms or parts, joining them together into a composite whole, but there is no unifying act (ἐντελέχεια) such as the «soul», for example, that constitutes the whole as ontologically a single being.

How then does one say that the whole (the composite) lives or knows, sees or acts? Ontologically what does this mean insofar as it refers to the composite? Now, as was mentioned above, the composite has a kind of unity in its being created *a* body *(jismun wāḥid);* it is a unity grounded in the accidents of conjunction and composition which is so created by God and so exists as a single thing, different, so to speak, from a mere conglomerate (10). In terms of this unity, therefore, abū Hāšim said that although the accident of knowing inheres only in the heart, it is the cause *('illa)* (11) of a «state» *(ḥāl)* or attribute *(ṣifa)* that belongs to the entire composite, viz., that of its «being knowing» *(kawnuhu 'āliman)*. That is, the accident of knowing comes to be *(ḥadaṯa)* inherent *(ḥāll)* in a particular part (or a defined group of atoms that constitute its *maḥall:* sc., the heart) of the whole and the whole composite, in the unity of its being-composed, becomes truly qualified *(mawṣūf)* as knowing *('ālim)*. Its being-knowing *(kawnuhu 'āliman)*, however, is not itself an ontological reality; it is «a 'state' which the being is in through an inherent causal determinant» *(ḥālun huwa 'alayhā li-ma'nan)*. This, in essence, is the theory of the *aḥwāl*, at least insofar as it concerns material beings and states that are dependant upon ontologically distinct, inherent acts.

In this way «accidents are divided into several types: those which qualify the substrate [*maḥall*] and necessitate its having a 'state' [*ḥāl*] (e.g., the *akwān)*, those that qualify the substrate without necessitating its having a 'state' (e.g., colors), those that qualify the composite [*jumla*] and necessitate its having a 'state' without, however, having any effect [*ta'ṯīr*] on the substrate at all (e.g., the act of the will and the act of conviction), and those that necessitate its having a 'state' and which have an effect on the substrate (e.g., life and *qadra*)» (12). What is meant here — and we need not go into the specific argument of the context,

---

(10) Cf. *Metaphysics of Created Being...*, 13ff.

(11) On the use of the term, cf. *JAOS* 87, 250ff. and below.

(12) 'Abd al-Jabbār, *al-Muġnī* 6/2 (ed. G. Anawati, Cairo, nd) 162, 3-7; cp. *al-Muġni* 9, 87, 18ff., where in an identical passage the author uses, instead of *ḥāl*, the term *ḥukm*, a more general term like *ṣifa*.

sc., whether the act of the will can exist immaterially *(lā fī maḥall)* (13) — is quite simple; some accidents qualify only their own immediate substrate (i.e., only those atoms in which they inhere), either without producing any result beyond their own inherence (colors) or by causing a state exclusively in the atoms in which they inhere, as motion (14) which effects only those atoms that are moved, in that these alone, within the entire composite, have the state of being-in-motion *(kawnuhā mutaḥarrika);* others, on the contrary, bring about a state that qualifies the entire composite; of these, some are, so to speak, static (e. g., knowing) while others have a direct effect on the composite in that they effect states that are the condition for the realisation of other perfections that follow consequent upon them, as life is the condition of the presence of the acts of knowing, willing, etc. (15).

The theory may not be always directly and specifically mentioned in the texts, but is nonetheless at least implicit as «'knowledge' [*'ilm*] may be mentioned in the sense of that whereby one becomes knowing [i.e., the accident of *'ilm*] or it may be mentioned in the sense of one's being-knowing, as when we say that so-and-so's knowledge of grammar is greater than his knowledge of established usage, since what we mean by the latter is his state and condition [*ḥāluhu wa-mā huwa 'alayhi*], not the act itself [*nafsu l-ma'nà*]» (16). Again, there is considerable disagreement among the principal authorities concerning the application of the theory to specific problems involving specific attributes *(ṣifāt)*. Concerning inattentiveness or unawareness *(as-sahw)*, abū Hāšim's position was ambiguous; he seems to have held at one time that it was a distinct and real act *(ma'nà)* that excludes the act of knowing, essentially effecting only the immediate substrate *(maḥall)* inhering in which it precludes the realisation of the act of knowing, and at another time to have felt that it is a strict contrary to *'ilm*, effecting thus a state

---

(13) Cfr. generally *ibid.*, 160ff.; the passage cited is part of an objection to the theory, held by the school from the time of abū l-Hudhayl, that God's will *(irāda)* is a temporal but immaterial act; for 'Abd al-Jabbār's reply, cf. *ibid.*, 173, ad. 9.

(14) Cf. *Muġnī* 6/1 (ed. A. Ahwani, Cairo, 1382/1964) 198: انما نقول فى الحركة انها هى العلة فى كون المتحرك متحركا دون جسم المتحرك.

(15) Cfr., e.g., al-Baġdādī, *Uṣūl ad-Dīn* (Istanbul, 1346-1928) 28ff. and below, or, for the fact that *sahw*, according to abū Hāšim, depends upon the presence of life, cf. *Muġnī* 6/2, 62.

(16) *Mugnī* 14 (ed. M. el-Saqa, Cairo, 1385/1965) 33, 13-15.

of the composite (17). 'Abd al-Jabbār, on the other hand, and Ibn 'Ayyāš, held that it is, in reality, a privation which, as such «qualifies the living [body] and is contrary to that which does necessitate a state of the composite and so is analogous to it in necessitating the state of the composite» (18).

Acts or accidents that cause states of the whole living body are properly predicated of the whole and distinguish the whole as such. That is to say, as inherent accidents *(a'rāḍ/ma'ānī)*, they belong to the substrate *(maḥall)* and a part *(ba'ḍ)* of the whole, but as attributes *(ṣifāt)* they are predicated of the whole. Thus «to describe the one who wills as willing indicates his being distinguished by a state [*ḥāl*], because of his being in which, acts take place by him in a specific way» (19). In brief, though we say that the act of willing inheres in a specific part of the composite, we use the term «willing» *(murīd)* not of the part that is its immediate substrate, but of the man and the entire composite that is the man is distinguished by his being in such and such a state from another who is in a given state. Otherwise we should have to say that it was the immediate substrate of the act of willing (sc., the individual parts of the heart) that come to be willing by the inherence of the accident (20). In this way then, «the knower's being described as knowing is not at all taken from the act of knowing, but indicates his being qualified by a state on account of which he is distinguished from other composites» (21). The state, in sum, is of the entire composite and our attribution of the state to the composite does not strictly refer to the accident which is its cause, for by the attribute *(ṣifa)* the composite is distinguished from another, not the specific accident and its immediate substrate from another.

The state *(ḥāl)*, however, has no Being; it is not ontologically an entity, for in the material order, the only ontologically real beings are the atoms and the accidents. Thus 'Abd al-Jabbār says, «The

---

(17) *Ibid.*, 7, 44, 6ff. and 6/2, 16ff.; for al-Jubbā'ī's understanding of *sahw*, cf. *ibid.* 12 (ed. I. Madkour, Cairo, nd) 212.

(18) *Ibid.*, 7, 44f. and 6/2, 63 *(ult.)*; for the operation of the theory of states caused by *ma'ānī* generally, cf. *ibid.*, 7, 44-47.

(19) *Ibid.*, 6/2, 294f.

(20) Cf. *ibid.*, 158f.: ولو صح لوجب ان يكون محل الارادة هو المريد بها وهذا يؤدي الى ان يكون القلب بل كل جزء منه مريد. Cf. also *ibid.*, 163 and *al-Muḥīṭ bit-Taklīf* (ed. O. Azmi, Cairo nd) 189, bottom.

(21) *Muġnī* 7, 157, 15f.; cf. also 'Abd al-Jabbār, *Šarḥ al-usūl al-ḫamsa* (ed. A. Ousman, Cairo, 1384-1965) 207f.

qādir is the living composite, but that which exists is each separate part of it; that which exists is not, strictly speaking, the *qādir* nor is the *qādir*, strictly speaking, the thing which exists» (22), for the only things which can be said strictly to have being *(wujūd)* or to come into being *(ḥadaṯa)* are the atoms and accidents (23). To handle this distinction, those who adhere to the theory of «states» introduce a specialisation of terms: of those things that are ontologically real entities, one uses *wujūd* and *ḥudūṯ*, but of the states *(aḥwāl)* and secondary attributes *(ṣifāt zā'ida)* one uses the term *tajaddud*. This distinction is somewhat difficult to manage in English since almost any term that will reflect the «becoming» character of *tajaddada* must perforce imply a coming *to be*, and accordingly imply the sense of existence that the specialised terminology would avoid. For the present discussion I would propose to use «being» and «existence» for *wujûd* and its derivatives, «coming-to-be» for *ḥudūṯ* with its derivitaves, and «becoming» for *tajaddud*. The distinction, then, is made thus: «That which comes-to-be is that which exists after its non-existence, while that which has no existence but becomes is said to be becoming but not coming-to-be» (24). Coming-to-be *(al-ḥudūṯ)*, thus, is defined as «the becoming of existence» *(tajaddudu l-wujūd)* for existence is itself a state. Becoming *(tajaddud)* is a more general term indicating a temporal newness of actuality and so may be used of that which has being having come into being *(al-mawjūd al-ḥādit/muḥdaṯ)*. Thus in a passage which is quite illustrative of the usage, 'Abd al-Jabbār, speaking of the *akwān*, says: «The attributes that result from these accidents become, wherefore that which produces them must become. Accordingly, when their becoming is established, their coming-to-be is established, since by coming-to-be we mean no more than the becoming

---

(22) القادر هو الجملة الحية والموجود كل بعض منه فليس الموجود فى الحقيقة هو القادر ولا القادر فى الحقيقة هو الموجود *Muḥīṭ*, 139; in the same way one says that the agent *(al-fā'il)* is the composite, not a part of it (cf. *Muġnī*, 7, 21; and note the analysis in *al-Muġnī* 8, 150f. and esp. 155).

(23) Cf. e.g., *Muḥîṭ*, 36: بل الحوادث لا تخرج من ان تكون جواهر او اعراضا.

(24) الحادث هو الموجود بعد عدمه واما ما لا وجود له وتجدد فيقال له تجدد ولا يقال له حدوث ... This citation (alas) stands haplessly in my notes without any indication of where, in the work of Abd al-Jabbār, it was found; with chagrin I beg the reader's indulgence.

of existence» (25). Thus it is, too, that the act of the will is said to be something that is made to come-to-be *(muḥdaṭa)* while the state of «being willing» *(kawnuhu murīdan)* is *mutajaddid*, for the act of willing is a *ma'nà* that produces the state in the composite (26). Finally, if the «state» has no existence as a real ontological entity, neither can it be said to be non-existent *(ma'dūm)*, for «we affirm that a thing is non-existent only insofar as it is not actually existent [*mawjūd*]» (27) and since, even in its becoming, the state of the composite does not come-to-be so as to be existent, it cannot properly be said to be non-existent either in its actuality or before its becoming (28).

The state, in this way, is not something existent, but it is, rather, the actuality of the body or composite, as it is in such-and-such a state *('alà ḥāl)*; so also the state is not, strictly speaking, itself an object of our knowing. That is, the «state» is «not known in isolation but it is only the reality as being in the states that is known» (29). The proper and immediate objects of our knowing are realities — normally composite bodies and their constituent parts that are ontological

---

(25) ان هذه الصفات الصادرة عن هذه المعانى متجددة فيجب فى المؤثر فيها الموجب لها ان يكون متجددا فاذا ثبت تجددها ثبت حدوثها لانا. لا نعنى بالحدوث اكثر من تجدد الوجود *Šarḥ al-uṣūl al-ḫamsa*, 110; with the last phrase, cf. *Muġnī* 6/1, 234, 14.

(26) Cf. *ibid.* 6/2, 140, esp. lines 14-17; the one who is *murīd* is in this «state» by a cause *('illa)* which distinguishes him as being thus rather than otherwise (cf. *ibid.*, p. 6, 8ff.). Thus it is that 'Abd al-Jabbār argues that *al-ḫāṭir* is an entitative accident *(ma'nà)* because it is «*'amrun ḥâdiṭ*» (*ibid.*, 12, 404) and in the same way, the state cannot arise through *tawallud* «since this is characteristic of things that come-to-be. When something comes-to-be as consequent of, and according to [the coming-to-be of] another, [that other] must be what generates it [*muwallid lahu*]; but this is impossible in the case of the states which become but are not characterised by coming-to-be» (*ibid.*, 78).

(27) *Ibid.*, 6/2, 77; cf. also 6/1, 70f.

(28) One must be careful with the terminology; the «state», thus, does not have an intermediate position between the existent *(al-mawjūd)* and the non-existent *(al-ma'dûm)* or between existence and non-existence (van den Bergh, *op. cit.*, 4f. and van Ess, *op. cit.*, 207), for its being not existent *(ġayr mawjūd)* is of a different order. The problem of the non-existent *(ma'dūm)* (especially as it involves the possible) is one of the most difficult for the kalām throughout its history, but the question of the ontological status of the «states» is quite distinct (and uncomplicated). Much of the confusion is due to the purposeful obfuscation of the polemicists.

(29) *Šarḥ al-uṣūl al-ḫamsa*, 184: فانها عندنا غير معلومة بانفرادها وانما الذات عليها تعلم ففارق احدهما الاخر. Cf. also *ibid.*, 366; he attributes this thesis to abū Hāšim.

entities. We have an intuition of the «state» but it is, properly speaking, a knowledge of the reality which is the composite, viz., a knowledge of the body as being in such a state.

One must not, simply because the «state» or *ḥâl* is said to be not existent *(ġayr mawjūd)*, underestimate its real importance in the metaphysical structure of composite beings. The composite body, it is true, is strictly composite; i.e., it is a composite of ontologically discrete elements — both atoms and accidents — and each and every moment of its being is perfect and complete as measured by the completeness in being of each of its constituent elements. Each atom and each accident is absolute and complete in its being and since the being of the composite is the whole formed by the totality of these elements, its being is likewise perfect in them at any given moment of its existence. To whatever extent that we can speak of change or becoming (*μεταβολή*, *taġayyur*) we refer to the composite in its wholeness and, in a true sense, indicate its becoming other *(taġāyur)*, in that it becomes another composite through the discrete substitution or one (or several) entitative accidents *(ma'ānī)* for another within the whole (30). Now whereas within the earlier systems of abū l-Hudhayl or al-Jubbā'ī, one can say little more than this, the notion of «states» furnishes a coherent way of describing the alterations of the composite as belonging to it in its wholeness, for with the substitution of one accident for another, the whole composite undergoes a change while remaining the same composite through the underlying identity to the body as substrate (31).

More than this, however, the function of the «states», in the metaphysical system, permeates all levels of material being. The accidents are, indeed, the real ontological cause of the states of the composite, but, considered from another perspective, it is the states themselves that are of primary interest in many of the most important aspects of created beings. «The act is possible on the part of the agent because of his *being qādir*, not because of the accident of *qudra*, even though the accident of *qudra* is the cause of his being *qādir*» (32). It is, thus, in a real sense, the state that constitutes the actuality of the

---

(30) Cf. *Mugnī* 6/2, 107: وقد قال شيخنا ابو هاشم ان الشى. الواحد لا يجوز ان يكون متغيرا كما لا يجوز ان يكون متغايرا وانما يقال ذلك فى الجملة فتوصف بانها متغايرة متغيرة. Cf. also *ibid.*, 199, 10-13.

(31) Cf. *Metaphysics of Created being*, *loc. cit. supra*, n. 10.

(32) *Muġnī* 12, 33; cf. also ibid. 8, 148, 15ff.

composite, not the accidents *(ma'ānī)* that are the causes *('ilal)* of the states. It is, for example, not the accident of life *(al-ḥayāt)* in its existence as an accident inhering in the substrate, that is the immediate ground or condition of the possibility of the presence in the body of the accidents of knowing, will, etc., but rather the condition *(šarṭ)* is «the body's being living» *(kawnuhu ḥayyan)* (33).

The attributes represented by the states are divided into two categories: one is of those states whose becoming *(tajaddud)* is caused *(mu'allal)* by a cause inherent in the substrate (viz., a *ma'nà*) whence they are called *ma'nawīya*. The other consists in those states or attributes that arise immediately by virtue of the essential character of the thing *(li-mā huwa 'alayhi fī nafsihi/ḏātihi)* and these are consequently termed *nafsīya* (34). Ubication *(at-taḥayyuz)* is an inalienable state of the atom, its essential «principle» which it has «by virtue of its being as it is in itself» *(li-mā huwa 'alayhi fī ḏātihi)* (35). To be an atom *(jawhar)*, according to Ibn 'Ayyāš, is ubication (36). Given the condition *(šarṭ)*, therefore, of existence *(wujūd)* — itself a state — the *akwān* are inalienable and inevitable accidents of the atom (37), since the existence of the atom is, as it were, implicit *(muḍamman)* in that of the *kawn* (38). The states involved in the real existence of the atom are, in this way, essentially linked: given the essential state, which is *taḥayyuz*, and the condition of existence, the state of «being in a position» *(kawnuhu kā'inan fī jiha)* arises *(tajaddad)* immediately by virtue of the accident (viz., the specific *kawn*). Thus the essential *(nafsī)* attribute or state of ubication is the immediate principle *(aṣl)* of the inherence of the accident *(ma'nà)* which is the cause *('illa)*

---

(33) *Muḥīṭ*, 133f. (cf. generally 131ff. and n. 43 below).

(34) Cf., e.g., al-Juwaynî, *Iršâd* (ed. M. Moussa and A. Abd el-Hamid, Cairo, 1950) 30f. and also al-Jurjâni, *Šarḥ al-Mawāqif* (Cairo, 1325/1907) 5, 2f. Allard (*op. cit.*, 386ff.) discusses the distinction but does not mention the basis of the terminology or its application to created beings. Tritton (*op. cit.*, 186) refers to the former as «conceptual» (cf. also Nader, *loc. cit.*) and to the latter as «personal».

(35) Cf. abū Rašīd an-Nisābūrī, *K. al-Masā'il* (*Die atomistische Substanzlehre*, ed. A. Biram, Berlin, 1902), p. 18 (of text; see generally pp. 18ff.); on the use of the expression, note that one can speak similarly of the *jins* of an accident: e.g., *ḥukmun yajibu li-jinsihā aw-li-mā hiya 'alayhi fī jinsihâ* (cf. *Muġnī* 7, 30). On the use of the infinitive *taḥayyuz* to indicate the *ḥāl*, cf. the similar use of *taḥarruk* in *Muḥīṭ*, 45, 7.

(36) Cf. *Šarḥ al-Mawāqif* 2, 217.

(37) Cf. *Muḥīṭ*, 38ff and *Šarḥ al-uṣūl al-ḫamsa*, 95ff.

(38) *Muġnī* 6/1, 164f.

of the derived *(ma'nawī)* state, sc., its being in a position *(jiha)* or place *(makān)*. For example, the coming-to-be *(ḥudūṯ)* of movement *(ḥaraka* = one of the *akwān)* in the atom is the immediate cause of the state that consists in its «being» in one place *(kawnuhu kā'inan fī makān)* after it was in another; the principle *(aṣl)* which is the ground of the actualisation of this state, is the *essential state* (or attribute) of the atom (39). «The possibility of its passage through positions is a property of its ubication» (40).

The only ontologically entitative realities involved in this are the ubiquitous atom and accident (41). The interrelation between the two, however, and their basic properties as well as those of the composite are discussed almost entirely in terms of three states, viz., *taḥayyuz* (the essential state of the atom), *wujūd* (the state of its actuality and the condition of the presence of the accidents) and *al-kawnu fī jiha* (the state which is grounded in the first, essential state upon the condition of the actuality of the second) (42). This central and, indeed, essential role of the «states» is an absolutely essential part of the metaphysics of the school of abū Hāšim. 'Abd al-Jabbār, for example, says that the relationship between the state of a «body's being alive» *(kawnuhu ḥayyan)* to the presence of the accidents of knowledge, will, *qudra* etc., is identical to that of the state of ubication to the substrate's *(maḥall)* functioning as a substrate; i.e., the one is the principle *(aṣl)* of the other in both instances (43).

There is no need, within the scope of the present paper, to go further into the detail of how the theory was applied to the metaphysics of created beings (44), for what has been said is enough to make clear its basic structure and, I should hope, to show that by no means was it an abstruse construction concocted *ad hoc* to solve one or two difficulties concerning the divine attributes and the problem of universals (45).

(39) Cf. *Muḥīt*, 41.

(40) *Ibid.*, 39: من حكم تحيزه صحة تنقله في الجهات

(41) Cf. *supra*, n. 23.

(42) Cf. abū Rašīd, *op. cit.*, 3, 14 and *Šarḥ al-uṣūl al-ḫamsa*, 97 (bottom).

(43) *Muḥīṭ*, 133.

(44) Note, for example, that the «ways» *(wujūh)* in which an act or event may take place *(waqa'a)* are understood analogously as states (cf. *Muġnī* 8, 74, 4-6; 11, 276, 13-15; 14, 22 *et alibi passim*).

(45) Horten, *op. cit.*, 303. This same misunderstanding is shared by Maimonides who seems to have had as much difficulty with the notion as later generations of scholars; cf. A. Altmann, "Essence and Existence in Maimonides", *Bul. of the John Rylands Library* 35 (1952-53), 29ff.

The theory, to a considerable extent, was developed in order to give an analytic explanation of the nature and function of the atoms and accidents as they constitute the ultimate ontological principles of created beings — to give a fuller and more adequate account of the metaphysical structure of created bodies than was possible in the systems of abū l-Hudhayl and al-Jubbā'ī.

The theory is, nevertheless, of central importance to the understanding of the divine attributes as this is worked out by abū Hāšim and his followers (though abū 'Abdallāh al-Baṣrī does not seem to have applied it to this problem) (46). The problems here involved are extremely complex and must be examined in the context of the whole development of the theology of the divine attributes in the Baṣra school from the time of abū l-Hudhayl. Pending the completion of such a study, however (the second part of which I hope to bring to publication in the near future), we can here indicate in outline the structure of the question and how abū Hāšim handled it in terms of the theory of states.

So long as all speculative knowledge of God (and hence also the analytic understanding of the content of the revelation) is based exclusively on reasoning from the phenomenal and world-immanent *(aš-šāhid)* to the world-transcendent *(al-ġā'ib)* and all being other than God is material, all reasoning about God is extremely difficult. For example, the basis of knowing (47) in a corporeal being is an accident, viz., the act of knowing *('ilm)*. Accordingly, abū l-Hudhayl says that «God is knowing through an act of knowing that is He» (48) but he refused to allow that God is an act of knowing or that the several attributes were each simply identical with the other in the identity of God's being (49). Al-Jubbā'ī, then, eliminated the act and said only that «God is knowing *per se*» (50). This, however, tends to preclude the analogy *(qiyâsu l-ġā'ibi 'alà š-šāhid)*, for the only

---

(46) Cf. *Muḥīṭ*, 107.

(47) There is no need here for any discussion of God's will; this for abū Hāšim, as for 'Abd al-Jabbār, is an incorporeal act *(ma'nan lā fī maḥall)* which is the cause of the state of God's being willing; the analogy with created being is here plain enough.

(48) Cf., e.g., *Maqālāt*, 165 and *Šarḥ al-uṣūl al-ḫamsa*, 183. The present discussion is rather grossly oversimplified; for the detail see R. Frank "The Divine Attributes according to the Teaching of abu l-Hudhayl al-'Allaf", *le Muséon* 82 (1969), 453f.

(49) *Maqālāt*, 484f.

(50) Cf., e.g., *ibid.*, 522, *Muḥīṭ*, 107, and *Šarḥ al-uṣūl al-ḫamsa*, 182.

knowers that we have direct experience of are «knowing through an act of knowing» *(ālimūna bi-ʻilmin)*, an accident. Abū Hāšim, then, facing the problem in this form (with all its concomitant implications), attempted to solve it in this way: that the one who knows know (i.e., that he be knowing) is a state. In the case of the created (i.e., corporeal) knower, it is not the substrate (i.e., the atoms of the heart) that knows through the inherent accident but rather the living composite *(al-jumlatu l-ḥayya)*. The actuality of his knowing — i.e., that he be knowing — is a state that arises through the coming-to-be of a cause *(maʻnà = ʻaraḍ)*, sc., the act of knowing, which inheres in the heart. His state, thus, is an attribute determined by an ontologically distinct, inherent cause; it is *ṣifatun maʻnawīya* in the technical jargon. God, however, being altogether immaterial, is not the subject of acts or perfections that are founded in inherent accidents. Nonetheless his actuality as knowing *(kawnuhu ʻāliman)* is analogous to that of the created knower insofar as to be knowing is, in the one case as in the other, a state of a being according to which it knows. God's being knowing, in contrast to that of the corporeal knower, is a state that belongs to him by his «essence» *(li-mā huwa ʻalayhi fī nafsihi)* (51). To be knowing, then, is of the essence of God; it belongs to him to know as to have place in space *(taḥayyuz)* belongs to the atom. ʻAbd al-Jabbār will, in many instances, say that God is *qādir* or knowing *li-nafsihi* (52), using, as it were, the expression of al-Jubbā'ī, for God is essentially knowing, but in the stricter terminology — as he remarks — the proper expression is *li-mâ huwa ʻalyhi fî nafsihi* (53). The act of knowing, as a state *(ḥāl)*, introduces no plurality into God's being, since it is not existant *(mawjūd)* in its own right as an ontologically distinct perfection. If one will speak, then, of the state's having «a certain unreality» or the like, it should nevertheless not be forgot

(51) Cf., e.g., *ibid.*, and *Muḥīṭ, loc. cit.;* the author *(ibid.)* sees no really significant difference between the doctrine of al-Jubbā'ī and that of abū Hāšim. What he seems to mean is that the notion of the *ḥāl* is, in a sense, implied in al-Jubbā'ī's statement that the formula «God is knowing» means that there are objects known to him and that he is بخلاف ما لا يجوز ان يعلم (cf., e.g., *Maqālāt*, 542). Šahrastānī asserts (*K. al-Milal wan-Niḥal* [ed. M. Badran, Cairo, 1910-55] 72) that abū l-Hudhayl's position is essentially that of abū Hāšim. On the surface this may appear plausible, but nevertheless it needs to be examined critically, especially in view of the polemical context.

(52) Cf., e.g., *Muġnī* 7, 62.

(53) Cf. *Muḥīṭ*, 107 (last two lines).

that it is a genuinely «real» aspect, quality, or qualification *(ṣifa, iḫtiṣāṣ, ḥukm)* of the being to which it belongs. God's essential attributes are no less real states than are those of a material being; i.e., that a state be *nafsīya* does not diminish its actuality as a state of that to which it belongs and make it less a state than one that results from an ontologically distinct act inherent in a material body.

What I have given here is but an abstract or outline of the question. The theory must ultimately be studied in the live contexts of its actual use by the several authors who employed it, for it is only there that its real significance for the history of the kalām may be seen and understood.

VI

ELEMENTS IN THE DEVELOPMENT OF THE TEACHING OF AL-ASH'ARI

In preparing the critical edition of al-Aš'arī's *al-Ḥaṯṯ 'alā l-baḥṯ* (commonly known under the spurious title *Risālat istiḥsān al-ḫawḍ fī 'ilm al-kalām*) it was my intention to append to the analysis of the text a discussion of the place of this work within the corpus of al-Aš'arī's writings, insofar as this is determinable within the limits of the few of them which are available[1]. The treatment of the problem required, however, much more space than anticipated, wherefore it seemed appropriate to publish the study separately here. What I have to present, thus, is a view of a few selected aspects and elements of al-Aš'arī's thought that are witnessed in his surviving works as these may be evidential of the course and character of his theology. The present study is by no means exhaustive, even within this narrowly defined perspective. It is hoped, that the examination of these one or two problems may serve to give a clearer perspective on others.

The development and direction of al-Aš'arī's thought after his «conversion» has never been adequately examined. The problem not only remains obscure, but has become somewhat acute since the attribution of *al-Ḥaṯṯ* to al-Aš'arī has been denied by Prof. Makdisi in a lengthy study which appeared in *Studia Islamica*[2]. Here he proposes a somewhat radical reëvaluation of the generally accepted view concerning the origin and the basic character of what we commonly recognize as al-Aš'arite theology. Although Makdisi's thesis is no longer tenable in its opposition to the more commonly accepted view, it is nonetheless interesting for the questions it raises and a brief examination of his reasoning will serve to bring out the principal difficulties which must be confronted and dealt with in any treatment of the problem.

Basing himself on the *Ibāna fī 'uṣūl ad-diyānah* and on the traditionalist

[1] The text, together with a structural analysis appeared in *MIDEO*, 18 (1988), p. 83-152. The present study was completed in 1984, but certain problems prevented its immediate publication. Because of the limitation of time, only a small number of essential corrections and emendations have been made to the original study. Concerning several matters further detail pertinent to the present study may be found in our *Knowledge and Taqlīd, the Foundations of Religious Belief in Classical Ash'arism*, in *JAOS*, 109 (1989), p. 38-62 and *The Science of Kalām*, forthcoming.

[2] *Ash'arī and the Ash'arites in Islamic Religious History*, in *Studia Islamica*, 17 (1962), p. 37-80 and 18 (1963), p. 19-39; in what follows I shall refer to these as «MAKDISI I» and «MAKDISI II» respectively. Concerning the original title of the work, etc., see the introduction to the edition.

position set out in al-Aš'arī's *Maqālāt*, to which the author proclaims his own adherence, Makdisi concludes that *al-Ḥaṯṯ* cannot be an authentic work of al-Aš'arī, but quite to the contrary belongs likely to a period no earlier than that of al-Subkī (d. 771/1370). There is no need, I think, to review all of Makdisi's meticulous discusion of the issue. Given, however, the importance of the question and the seriousness with which he argues his thesis, it will be appropriate to consider his principal arguments. The matter is especially important in view of the significance of Makdisi's position for our understanding of the basic intentionality of al-Aš'arī's post-conversion teaching and, consequently, for his place in the school tradition that bears his name.

Accepting the authenticity of the *Ibānah* and of the statement made towards the end of the first part of *Maqālāt* that the author adheres to the doctrine of the traditionalists (*'aṣḥāb al-ḥadīṯ*), Makdisi sees al-Aš'arī as having been converted not simply from the doctrines of his Mu'tazilite master, al-Ǧubbā'ī to an orthodoxy whose basic elements were generally those of the traditionalists, but to have done so entirely in the spirit of the more radical traditionalism of the Ḥanbalites[3]. *Al-Ḥaṯṯ* is, however, plainly a thoroughgoing and uncompromising polemic in favor of the practice of systematic theology (*kalām*) against its traditionalist opponents. Reading, then, the *Ḥaṯṯ* and the *Ibānah* under the assumption that the foregoing description of al-Aš'arī's conversion is correct, Makdisi finds the two works altogether irreconcilable one with the other. He reasons in part as follows:

Now Ash'arī could have been a rationalist, who then became a traditionalist. Or a traditionalist, and later a rationalist. But he could not have been both at one and the same time. There is nothing inconsistent in an Ash'arī who was a traditionalist using *reason* in defense of orthodoxy. There would definitely be something inconsistent in an Ash'arī who was a traditionalist using *kalām* in

[3] Makdisi consistently distinguishes between the «traditionists» (*al-muḥaddiṯūn*) and the «traditionalists» (*'ahl al-ḥadīṯ, 'aṣḥāb al-ḥadīṯ*), the latter representing a dogmatic or theological attitude and doctrine concerning the tradition, while the former simply names those whose work consists in establishing the validity of the texts (*matn*) and their *isnāds* and in transmitting them. The distinction is certainly useful, even though the texts do not themselves always make it so neatly. The expressions '*'ahl al-ḥadīṯ*' and '*'aṣḥāb al-ḥadīṯ*' are commonly employed to designate *muḥaddiṯīn* (traditionists), as for example al-Bayhaqī may be classed among the *muḥaddiṯīn* a traditionist, but not as a traditionalist in Makdisi's sense; he was an Aš'arite, though not a *mutakallim*, i.e., not a specialist in systematic theology (*kalām*), al-Baghdādī, thus, speaks (*Uṣūl*, p. 254,16f.) of «the early *ahl al-hadīṯ* who were *mutakallimūn*, such as 'Abdallāh b. Sa'īd (Ibn Kullāb), al-Ḥāriṯ al-Muḥāsibī ... and al-Qalānisī». None of the individuals mentioned was a traditionalist in Makdisi's sense and two of them, ibn Kullāb and al-Qalānisī, were specialists in *kalām*. One notes also Ibn Fūrak's division of the *aṣḥāb al-hadīṯ* into traditionists (*muḥaddiṯīn*) and theological exegetes, amongst whom he obviously includes himself (see n. 15 below).

defense of orthodoxy. For between reason and rationalist *kalām* there was a difference. It was *all* the difference between Muslim traditionalism and Muslim rationalism. The traditionalists made use of reason in order to understand what they considered as the legitimate sources of theology: scripture and tradition. What they could not understand they left as it stood in the sources; they did not make use of reason to interpret the sources metaphorically. On the other hand, the rationalists advocated the use of reason on scripture and tradition; and all that they deemed to contradict the dictates of reason they interpreted metaphorically in order to bring it into harmony with reason[4].

He concludes, then (*ibid.*, p. 23), that «the theologian who wrote the *Ibānah* could not have written *Istiḥsān al-khawḍ* [sc., *al-Ḥaṯṯ*] and claim allegiance to both lines of thought at one and the same time. For the latter work is a refutation of all that for which the former stands»[5]. The distinction between the rational and logical formalism of *kalām* and the traditionalist's manner of treating the canonical sources of theological doctrine is essentially sound; the conclusion, however, remains questionable *prima facie*, for in order to affirm it one has not only to deny the validity of the ascription of *al-Ḥaṯṯ* to al-Aš'arī, but also that of the *Luma'* as well, to do which would be wholly implausible[6].

The conception of the argument Makdisi makes in the passage cited above is clear enough and with it his problem. He begins by making an absolute dichotomy between Muslim «rationalism» and Muslim traditionalism and goes on then to equate rationalism and *kalām*, speaking first of «rationalist *kalām*» and then of *kalām* simply; *kalām* as such, all *kalām*, is rationalistic. The thesis, like the dialectical move, betrays a Ḥanbalite prejudice. If one identifies *kalām* exclusively with the Mu'tazila, then certainly the unqualified equation of *kalām* with rationalism

[4] Makdisi II, p. 22.

[5] Thus he says (*ibid.*, p. 20) that the common view of al-Aš'arī ascribes to him a «two faced position» and requires that he have had «a 'double' or a split personality» (*ibid.*, I, p. 43, citing Wensinck, who asks, «Or is Ash'arī a man with two faces»: *The Muslim Creed*, p. 91).

[6] Makdisi remarks (II, p. 30 f.) that «Whatever works are attributed to Ash'arī, we will always have the problem not only of determining their authenticity as to authorship, but also of determining whether they belong to the pre-conversion, or post-conversion period of his life». Curiously, he nowhere mentions *al-Luma'* which is not only a work plainly written after his conversion, but was moreover one of the most popular of all his writings. It is listed in Ibn an-Nadīm's *Fihrist* (Cairo, 1348, p. 257), which was composed in 388/987-8; commentaries were written on it by al-Bāqillānī (d. 403/1013) and Ibn Fūrak (d. 406/1015) and a refutation of it (*Naqḍ al-Luma'*) by the great Mu'tazilite master, 'Abd al-Ǧabbār; the *Šāmil of* al-Ǧuwaynī is, in fact, a *taḥrīr on* al-Bāqillānī's *Šarḥ al-Luma'* (cf. *Šāmil* [1981], p. 3). It is frequently cited, moreover, by later Aš'arite authors alongside other of al-Aš'arī's writings which have not survived. It should be kept in mind that there were two versions of the *al-Luma'*, of which the extant text represents the shorter.

has some de facto validity, for the earlier Mu'tazilite masters held that the mind's autonomous judgement, based on purely rational principles and axioms is the sole arbiter of what must be or what may be true in theology and their theology is, in this and in other respects, rationalistic in the proper sense of the term. If, on the other hand, one hears '*kalām*' more broadly as a general expression for systematic or speculative theology, then the simple identification of *kalām* and rationalism as the same and coëxtensive is not analytically true and may not be valid at all. Any process of reasoning and any attempt to attain logically controlled, conceptual understanding in matters of theology must proceed from some set of theoretical presuppositions, basic assumptions and principles, explicit and implicit, but these need not in any way presuppose, include or embrance rationalism in the sense implied by Makdisi. One must grant, in brief, that between the traditionalist fundamentalism of ibn Ḥanbal and the leading masters of the Ḥanbalite school on the one side and the «rationalistic *kalām*» of the Mu'tazila on the other, there may be some third and it is, in fact, this third, «intermediate way» to which the al-Aš'arites lay claim[7].

Our question is, then, (1) whether the teaching of al-Aš'arī as witnessed in the available sources may be said to represent such an intermediate position and (2) how *al-Ibānah* and *al-Ḥaṯṯ*, taken together with the other of his extant writings may be seen as coherent among themselves in presenting such a position. An affirmative answer to the first part of the question would seem easy enough to reach and to justify. The second is more complex, since it involves the detail of a set of texts of different character and form, written at different times. What I propose to do here is to look briefly at al-Aš'arī's conception of the authority of the Koran and the hadîth and at his understanding of the place and function of reason with respect to these theological sources and then to review a very limited number of questions to see how they are treated by al-Aš'arī in his available writings and as his teaching is witnessed by later masters of his school. This will not only resolve the immediate question, but will serve to elucidate some aspects of the historical controversy concerning the validity of *kalām*. More importantly, perhaps, it will furnish a basis on which to make some suggestions

[7] Cf., e.g., GARDET and ANAWATI, p. 52 ff. and ALLARD, *Problème*, p. 73 ff. (It should be noted, however that Fr. Allard underestimated the conceptual discipline and logical formalism of al-Aš'arī's *kalām*). This notion of a *via media* originates with the Aš'arites' own conception of their theology; cf., e.g., the statement of the Qāḍī abū l-Ma'ālī 'Azīzī b. 'Abd al-Malik cited in IBN 'ASĀKIR, p. 149 f. For the identification of ibn 'Abd al-Malik (d. 494/1100) see ALLARD, *Problème*, p. 72, n. 1 and MAKDISI, *Ibn 'Aqīl*, p. 369.

concerning the evolution of al-Aš'arī's thought from the time of his conversion. With the exception of that of the ontological status of the Koran as «God's speaking», the several questions which we shall examine include none of the major topics universally treated in the Aš'arite compendia. They are, rather, secondary questions which the radical traditionalists tended to employ as a kind of litmus by which to test the orthodoxy others, holding their own treatment of the source texts as the measure and norm. Accordingly, we may use al-Aš'arī's treatment of several of these questions as a probe to assess the relative conformity or non-conformity of his theology, both in its form and in its content, to that of the Ḥanbalite traditionalists[8].

Al-Aš'arī's understanding of the role of reason with respect to the canonical sources of theological knowledge, the Koran and the Tradition, is most clearly and explicitly set forth in his *Risāla ilā ahl aṯ-ṯaghr bi-Bāb al-Abwāb*, a work written shortly after his conversion[9]. In this

[8] In what follows I shall, for each topic, look first at what al-Aš'arī himself has to say, following this, in each case, with one or two citations of later Aš'arites and then with citations of Ḥanbalite masters who were more or less contemporary with al-Aš'arī. The views of the Aš'arite masters of the classical period will help both to clarify the terminology and the sense of al-Aš'arī's statements and to manifest the unity and continuity of the school's teaching in the two centuries following the death of the founder. (Occasionally, for the sake of clarifying the use and intension of a term, I have included citations of the sufis, al-Ǧunayd [d. 298/910] and al-Ḥallāǧ [d. 309/922]. These are, in nearly every case, taken from the dogmatic preface to al-Qušayrī's *Risālah* and as so placed belong properly to an Aš'arite context. Besides illustrating the significance of several concepts examined in the present study these serve also to show that the contexts of Aš'arite *kalām* and of some of the leading sufi masters are not mutually exclusive but are, on the contrary, complementary to one another and that in those areas where they overlap or coïncide, both vocabulary and concept are the same or analogous. This is of considerable importance for the reading and understanding of the texts of both traditions, if one is to see the unity of sunnī religious life and thought and not to disolve them historically into a collection of disparate literary traditions). The citations of contemporary Ḥanbalite masters will help to elucidate the controversy between the two schools as it appeared from the Aš'arite side and will further manifest the character and intention of al-Aš'arī's teaching by showing it against the foil of a part of the historical background to which it was sympathetic but unavoidably opposed. One should not take it that the great Ḥanbalite teachers were unthinking «fundamentalists» who read the revealed text in a grossly literal fashion. Far from it. The theological sense and significance of their position is too complex, however, to go into here, nor is that necessary. For the purposes of our present inquiry, the main point is that for al-Aš'arī and others the attitude of the Ḥanbalites tended to foster a materially literalist, understanding of the text.

[9] Al-Aš'arī's teaching concerning the relationship of reason and revelation as it is presented in this work was examined in some detail in our *Al-Aš'arī's Conception of the Nature and Role of Speculative Reasoning in Theology*, in *Proceedings of the Vth Congress of Arabic and Islamic Studies*, ed. G. VITESTAM, Stockholm/Leiden, 1975, p. 136-154. I shall not repeat the detail of that study here, but rather will summarise it, focusing on the question at hand. There is no reason to doubt the authenticity of *aṯ-Ṯaghr* as a work of al-Aš'arī; see the remarks in ALLARD, *Problème*, p. 53 ff. and ours, *op. cit.*, p. 148, n. 8.

work he claims that in order to bring his followers to the fullness of belief the Prophet led them systematically through four stages of understanding. These are set forth explicitly at the outset (p. 81,21 ff.) and are followed in detail through the first half of the work (p. 81-91), and may be said to govern its overall structure. The four stages are these: the Prophet, by means of «conclusive arguments» and «demonstrations from evidence» brought his hearers to understand (1) that they and the world are contingent beings whose existence depends upon an uncreated (i.e., eternal) creator, (2) that there is only one eternal being and that, while not similar to any created entity, He is endowed with the attributes of life, knowledge, the power to act, will, speech, sight, and hearing, and is capable of communicating with His creatures, (3) that Muhammad is truly the Apostle of God, and finally (4) that given the truth of (1)-(3), all men are obliged to believe all that God teaches through the scripture and the words of His Prophet and to do all that He commands to do. «The means of their knowing this is the intelligence *(al-'aql)* which was made their instrument of discrimination» (p. 101,9 f.). Nowhere does al-Aš'arī suggest, as do his Mu'tazilite contemporaries, that even in the total absence of prophetic revelation prudent men can and should, motivated by a natural concern to know the context and the conditions of their ultimate well-being, come to a knowledge of the contingency of the world, the nature of God, and the obligation of men to worship Him and to live righteously. He insists, rather, that the Prophet called the attention of his hearers to these matters and made them aware *(nabbaha)* of the issue, showing them step by step how to achieve a reasoned knowledge of God and of their relationship to Him[10]. The basic method of his instruction, however, was founded on drawing conclusions rationally by means of logical rules from manifest evidence. The terms '*dalla, yadullu, dalālah*' (to show by evidence) and '*istidlāl*' (inference) occur no less than fifty one times in the first half of *aṯ-Ṯaghr*. Since the teaching of the Prophet, his demonstrations and arguments, are intrinsically clearer, less open to doubt and to challenge by counter arguments, than are those of the hellenising «philosophers», one ought to follow the way or method (*ṭarīqah*) of the Prophet; one must learn to use the reports (*'aḫbār*) of the Prophet's teaching as demonstrations (p. 90 f.). It is for this reason

[10] Thus, where for the Mu'tazila the moral obligation to undertake this inquiry is essentially prior to the revelation, for al-Aš'arī it is posterior; the inquiry leading to a validly founded belief in God is provoked by the activity of the Prophet and is known to be ethically obligatory only after the initial process is completed, i.e., when the authority of God's command is fully recognised.

that the pious ancestors (*as-salaf*) «adhered to the Scripture and the Sunna and sought to grasp the truth of whatever they were called to know through them» (p. 90,15). The fuller and more explicit form of the arguments and assertions of scripture is set forth in *kalām*. He says, for example,

[The Muslims] are agreed that He (the Mighty, the Glorious) is not similar to any entity belonging to the world; God (the Mighty, the Glorious) calls attention to this (*nabbaha*) where He says, «No one is like to Him» (Q 112,4). This is so simply because if He were similar to any of His creatures, then [either] (1) it would follow that the contingency of existence and the need for a cause of the realisation of contingency which this implies as belonging to those of His creatures to which He is similar must belong to Him, or (2) it would follow that those of His creatures which He resembles must be eternal [i.e., exist necessarily]. But it can be demonstrated that (a) the existence of every creature is contingent and (b) that it is impossible that [any creature] be eternal, as we have shown above. That He (the Mighty, the Glorious) is not similar to His creatures does not negate His existence, since the means of asserting the reality of His being is not the direct apperception of Him, but rather that He is as reason demands on the basis of the evidence of His acts[11].

Al-Aš'arī's attitude towards the Koran and the Sunna is made altogether clear where, commenting on the great efforts of later generations of Muslims to collect hadîths «in order that they might have certitude (*yaqîn*) concerning what they hold as true» he notes that

The most zealous of them used to travel to distant lands seeking a single word (*kalimah*) that might reach them from the Apostle (God's prayer and peace be upon him), eager to know the Truth to the fullest and seeking the sound demonstrations (*al-'adillatu ṣ-ṣaḥīḥah*) concerning it so that their minds might be at ease[12] in the religion they profess. In this way they are separated from those whom God rebukes for their binding themselves uncritically to the authority of those of their leaders whom they revere without any rational evidence (*dalālah*) which requires this[13].

This passage occurs in the final section of the first part of the work where, having outlined the order, form, and basic content of what he considers to be the Prophet's teaching and before beginning the properly dogmatic section of the work[14], he stops to discuss the value of

[11] P. 93,16-22, reading *lil-laḏī* for *al-laḏī* in line 19; cp. AL-AŠ'ARĪ, *al-Luma'*, § 7.

[12] Note that the phrase «their minds might be at ease» (*taskuna nufūsuhum*) reflects al-Ǧubbā'ī's definition of knowing (*'ilm*) in the strict sense. This would tend to confirm the very early date for this work. Concerning the origin of the expression, see our remarks in *Bi. Or.*, 35 (1978), p. 365b.

[13] *Aṯ-Ṯaghr*, p. 91,9-12, reading *'aǧadduhum* for *'ḥdhm* in line 9 and *taqtaḍī* for *yaqtaḍī* in line 12.

[14] *Bābu ḏikri mā 'aǧma'a 'alayhi s-salafu mina l-'uṣūli l-latī nubbihū bil-'adillatī 'alayhā*...: p. 93,8; with this cp. the statement of al-Isfarā'īnī quoted in n. 23 below.

the reports of the Prophet's sayings as they bear on the basic dogmas presented in the four stages of the Prophet's teaching. Several points should be noted with regard to what he has to say here. First, the original acceptance of the truth of the teaching of the Koran and of the Prophet is achieved in a rational judgement based on logically reasoned argumentation. The preëminent value of the authenticated reports of the Prophet's teaching lies precisely in the fact that they present the truth of the doctrine set out in the four stages. Given one's critically achieved recognition of the divine origin of the Scripture and of the Prophet's own teaching, his binding himself thus to the authority of the Koran and the authenticated reports of what the Prophet said and did does not constitute *taqlīd*, the uncritical acquiescence to the opinion or judgement of another. In binding himself thus to the authority of the Scripture and the Sunna one does not submit to the judgement and the views of men but to the instruction of God. This acceptance of the authority of the Koran and the Sunna, moreover, does not retrospectively anul one's rational understanding of their content with regard to the most basic religious dogmas (the *'uṣūl ad-dīn*) nor does it dispense him from the appropriate application of the rational principles employed in his original assent (*taṣdīq*) when he comes to consider those teachings of the Koran and of the Prophet which are such that they must be accepted on faith alone.

According to al-Aš'arī's principles, then, there is nothing inconsistent in one's unqualified acceptance of the preëminent authority of the Koran and the Tradition and in his recognising the value of *kalām* nor is there any inconsistency in his associating his own doctrine with that of the *'aṣḥāb al-ḥadīṯ*. Ibn Fūrak, in his *Bayān muškil al-'aḥādīṯ*, says[15] that the *'aṣḥāb al-ḥadīṯ* are divided into two groups (*firqatān*), (1) *'ahl an-naqli war-riwāyah*, sc., «those whose concern is focused chiefly on the transmission of the *sunan* and who are strongly motivated to detail the courses of their transmission and to compile their *'isnāds* ...» and (2) «those who are primarily concerned with validly establishing the methods of reflective inquiry (*an-naẓar*), the rules of reasoning, and the explanation of how the secondary dogmas (*al-furū'*) are derived from those that are primary (*al-'uṣūl*) ...». It is altogether clear from the immediate context and from the author's procedure in the course of the book that for him the second group of the *'aṣḥāb al-ḥadīṯ* accomplish their task of clarifying the true sense of those reports which apparently attribute the properties and characteristics of creatures to God (*tūhimu*

[15] *Bayān* (1941), § 3, p. 9 f.

ẓawāhiruhā t-tašbīh) by employing the method and the principles of *kalām*. They are, in brief, *mutakallimūn*. The contention of the Ḥanbalites to the contrary, viz., that one cannot possibly be a «traditionalist» (*min 'aṣḥābi s-sunnah, min 'ahli l-ḥadīt*) and practice *kalām*, is founded in part on a difference as to what is meant by the word '*sunnah*'. Where al-Aš'arī and his school regard the Sunna (the *hadîth*) first and primarily as a body of texts which present the authentic teaching of the Prophet and which, as texts, must be studied, understood, and interpreted, the Ḥanbalites sometimes speak of «*sunnah*» meaning not simply the texts but the texts taken integrally with their own interpretation of them. They refer, that is, to their interpretation of the texts as «*sunnah*»[16]. This attitude is conspicuous in the formulation which states that religious truth is accessible through the canonical sources but that

Religious truth (*ad-dīn*) consists simply in the Scripture of God (the Mighty, the Glorious) and in traditions and *sunnas* and in valid transmissions of firm and acknowledged traditions ... by trustworthy men, one of which affirms the other until they reach back to God's Apostle (God be gracious to him) and the Successors to his Companions (God be gracious to them) and the Successors of the Successors and after them those religious authorities who are recognised and are to be imitated, who cleave to the Sunna and depend upon the traditions[17].

Al-Aš'arī's condemnation of *taqlīd*, at the end of the last cited passage of *aṯ-Ṯaghr* should be noted. The hadîth is valued as presenting the authoritative teaching of the Prophet: what he said. The Companions and other transmitters of the reports have, like later experts in hadîth, no independant authority nor, consequently, does their interpretation — or any one else's — concerning the theological meaning or implication of what is said in the reports have any autonomous authority. The rejection of *taqlīd*, in matters of theology is common for the al-Aš'arīte tradition. Al-Bāqillānī says, «I do not think that *taqlīd*, has any valid function with regard to the basic dogmas of Islam; what is to be followed is the rationally probative evidence, not the fellows of one's own school»[18].

[16] This is very clear in *Ṭabaqāt*, I, p. 242,4 ff. where '*sunan*' refers not to the texts but to dogmas; cf. also, e.g., *ibid.*, II, p. 31,20 f. Compare this with the common Aš'arite contention that the Koran and the Tradition are together with consensus and reason the sources of theological knowledge.

[17] *Ṭabaqāt*, I, p. 31,4-6.

[18] *Lam 'ara lit-taqlīdi fī 'uṣūli t-tawḥīdi waǧhan, wad-dalīlu huwa l-muttaba'u dūna 'aṣḥābi l-maḏhab*; cited in *Šarḥ al-Iršād*, f. 112ᵛ. The expressions '*dalīl*' and '*dalālah*' are complex in their meaning and their connotations and accordingly are employed in several ways so that it is impossible adequately to render them by one and the same English word or phrase in all contexts. Basically, '*dalīl*' describes something (properly an entity, but

We need not here go into the detail of the teaching of the al-Aš'arites concerning *taqlīd*, in matters of religious doctrine; rather we shall simply present abū Isḥāq al-Isfarā'īnī's outline of the matter from an *'aqīdah* of his[19]. After listing twenty five articles which, he says, must by universal agreement be believed (*i'taqada*) if one is to be a Believing Muslim (*mu'min*), he goes on to make the following remarks:

When a person believes this the literalists[20] say that he truly has Belief

sometimes loosely a state of affairs) as and insofar as it indicates, points to (*dalla, yadullu 'alā*), and is evidential of, something else (either intrinsic or extrinsic to itself). '*Dalālah*' is the *maṣdar* of '*dalla, yadullu*' (and so too of the verbal adjectives, '*dāll*' and '*dalīl*') and thus designates the *dalīl*'s being evidential or the *dalīl* as an evidencing. What is evidential, however, is evidential only to a questioning or enquiring consciousness which grasps its presence not simply as and insofar as it is what it is but as pointing beyond itself to another (sc., to the *madlūl 'alayhī*: what is evidenced). '*Dalīl*' and '*dalālah*' may, thus, be employed to describe a thing as an evidence (as evidential) and may also be used to name the mind's grasp of it as evidential and so may name the explicit intention in which it is grasped, sc., the thematically posited and formulated minor premise. Finally, then, '*dalīl*' and '*dalālah*' (the latter more properly, since it is a *maṣdar* or *nomen actionis*) may be employed to designate the argument or demonstration in which the conclusion to the reality of what is evidenced in the evidential object and implied in the premises is drawn or shown. Contextually, thus, '*dalīl*' and '*dalālah*' may refer (1) to the (evidential) object or state of affairs as evidence or (2) to the premise in which the intentional grasp of the object as the consequent to an antecedent (and so as evidential) is formally presented, or (3) to the demonstration as a whole and may also (and frequently does) refer (4) to all of these as they come together in the *dalālah* or, to put it another way, as the *dalālah* (the evidencing) is variously realised in each and completely in all taken together. J. van Ess has suggested (*The Logical Structure of Islamic Theology*, in *Logic in Classical Islamic Culture*, ed. G. von Grünebaum, Wiesbaden, 1970, p. 26 f.) that '*dalīl*' is an equivalent of Greek 'σημεῖον' as used by the Stoics. The evidence for this is strong and the thesis doubtless correct. One should note, however, that whatever may be the phylogenetic origin of the particular use, these words had a life and a diversified history of their own within *kalām* and the broader context of Muslim Arabic and so acquired a richness and complexity which does not follow any Greek source.

[19] *al-Isfarā'īnī*, p. 135 f. On the question generally see our, *Knowledge and Taqlīd* (cf. above n. 1).

[20] «Literalists»: *'ahl aẓ-ẓāhir*. Similarly, al-Baghdādī says (*Uṣūl*, p. 254,15 f.) that this position (which he adopts as his own) is held by «aš-Šāfi'ī, al-Awzā'ī, aṯ-Ṯawrī, abū Ḥanīfa, Ahmad b. Ḥanbal, and the literalists, as well as the early traditionalist *mutakallimūn*», (amongst whom he includes ibn Kullāb and al-Qalānisī). «The literalists» does not here refer to the juridical school commonly known as the Ẓāhiriyya. Al-Isfarā'īnī contrasts their position to that of the «expert theologians» (on which name, see below) and al-Baghdādī to that of al-Aš'arī (presented *op. cit.*, p. 255,1-7). That in Aš'arite contexts the expression '*'ahl aẓ-ẓāhir*' refers to the «fundamentalist» or literalist jurists and traditionalists is clear enough. In discussing al-Bāqillānī's teaching concerning the valid and essential role of formal reasoning (*an-naẓar*) in theology (explicitly against the Sumaniyya, the Bāṭiniyya, and the Imāmiyya) al-Anṣārī remarks (*Ghunyah*, f. 3r,16 f.) that «so also the literalists (*'aṣḥāb aẓ-ẓāhir*) hold that religious truth (*ad-dīn*) is accessible exclusively in the Scripture, the Sunna, and in the sayings of the leading religious authorities of earlier generations (*'a'immatu s-salaf*)». Likewise in another passage (*ibid.*, f. 30v,2 ff.) he says, «God transcends being in places and spatial positions; our teaching in this matter is opposed, however, by the Muṯbita and the Karrāmiyya and some of the

('*īmān*)[21]: that he is one of those on whose behalf the Prophet will intercede and he will ultimately achieve paradise. The expert theologians[22], however, say that this is not the case until his belief (*i'tiqād*) in what we have set forth becomes, as we have explained, a real knowing (*ma'rifah*) and he thus belong to the number of those who know (*al-'ārifūn*) and be no longer counted among those who simply repeat the statements of others (*al-muqallidūn*). If *taqlīd*, is allowable, it is allowable only according to the judgement of the expert theologians. They, however, are universally agreed that it [sc., *taqlīd*] is not allowable. What is requisite in this matter is that he know ('*arafa*) each item of what we have presented on the basis of the evidence for it (*bi-dalīlihī*). For each one there is in the Scripture and the Sunna something to make one cognisant of its truth in a way that is conceptually and evidentially probative[23].

[The expert theologians] differ, however, as to the reason for which his belief (*i'tiqād*) on the basis of *taqlīd* is not knowledge ('*ilm*). Some of them say that

literalists ('*ahl aẓ-ẓāhir*); some of these people say that He is continguous to the uppermost surface of the Throne and that it is possible that His state alter and that He move from one place to another...». Again, al-Ǧuwaynī says (*Iršād*, p. 128) that «the Ḥašwiyya who adhere to the literal sense of the texts, take the position that God's speaking consists of syllables and sounds (*ḥurūfun wa-'aṣwāt*; cp. *al-Ḥaṯṯ*, § 2.321) and assert categorically that the sounds and intonations made by the reciters are the very speaking of God...»; in al-Anṣārī's Commentary (*Šarḥ al-Iršād*, f. 113ᵛ,4 f.) and in his *Ghunyah* (f. 86ᵛ,20 f.) this passage has «the literalists» in place of «who adhere to...» (*al-muntamūna 'ilā ẓ-ẓāhir*). On the question see n. 79 below. Cp. also the use of '*ẓāhirī*' in AL-GHAZĀLĪ, *Munqiḏ*, p. 80,2.

[21] «He truly has (religious) Belief»: *istaḥaqqa l-'īmān*. Parallel to this expression we find in al-Baghdādī (*Uṣūl*, p. 255,3) *yastaḥiqqu sma l-mu'min*; that is to say, he has the attribute «Belief» and so truly «deserves» the title «Believer», since it is the attribute which is the truth of the description, its ontological basis: what is «named» (*al-musammā*) — implied and asserted and referred to — by 'Believer' and 'Believes' is the noun (sc., the *maṣdar*) 'Belief' and the attribute named and referred to by it.

[22] «The expert theologians», i.e., the most rigorous: '*ahl at-taḥqīq*. The expression is ambivalently resonant in this context: is the term underlying the denominative '*at-taḥqīq*' '*al-ḥaqq*' (what is right, true, the fact) or is it '*al-ḥaqīqah*' (the true and the strict sense of the words we use to talk about reality and about God as they are most formally and rigorously to be understood)? In most contexts it is the former (sc., «those who verify»), but here one tends to hear the latter. In one passage of *Ghunyah* (f. 13ᵛ f.) al-Anṣārī divides the Aš'arites ('*aṣḥābuhnā*) into two classes, sc., '*ahl at-taḥqīq* (those who employ terms rigorously according to their strictest meaning and reference) and *al-muqtaṣidūn* (those who employ them in a somewhat looser way, closer to that of ordinary speech). Similarly al-Qušayrī defines '*al-wāḥid*' in *Taḥbīr* (p. 87, where omit *ḥaqīqah* following *al-wāḥid* and read *qasīm* for *qism* with *MS Yeni Cami*, no. 705, f. 108ᵛ), giving «its strict definition according to '*ahl at-taḥqīq*» and in his *Risālah* (4, p. 48,5 f.) explains the meaning of '*ʿāǧiz*' «according to the *muḥaqqiqīn*» (= '*ahl at-taḥqīq*), though in a way contrary to that which is most common among the Aš'arites (concerning which, cf. our remarks in *Journal of Religious Ethics*, 11 [1983], p. 211, n. 23). With reference to the question immediately under discussion in al-Anṣārī's *Ghunyah* (*loc. cit.*), viewed from the author's perspective the former class will include al-Bāqillānī and al-Ǧuwaynī and the latter Ibn Fūrak and al-Qušayrī. Al-Isfarā'īnī in our present context is not dividing the Aš'arites but rather is distinguishing the teaching of the majority of them from that of the literalists.

[23] *Li-kullin tanbīhun mina l-kitābi was-sunnati 'alā taḥqīqi l-'uqūli wal-'adillah*. With this cp. *aṯ-Ṯaghr*, p. 93,8, cited in n. 14 above. This is the main point of *al-Ḥaṯṯ*, § 2.2.

this is so simply because he does not know (*'alima*) that those on whom he depends in his *taqlīd* are infallible[24] and are not in error. Others say that this is not so, since he [sc., the *muqallid*] is in a position analogous to that of a person to whom doubt occurs and who cannot avert to anything pertinent to it so as to free himself from it. They go on to say, however, that if God graciously rids him of the doubt, purifies his belief (*i'tiqād*) and frees it from the evil suggestion (*al-waswās*) that befell it, then this is knowledge on his part and valid religious Belief (*'imānun ṣaḥīḥ*). When he believes (*i'taqada*) that the object of his belief is as in fact it is and does so with conclusiveness, then in the proper sense of the word he is one who knows (*'alima*).

The [expert theologians] are agreed that what authenticates his belief (*i'tiqād*) as knowledge (*ma'rifah*) is a single proof (*dalīlun wāḥid*) for each question, [given which proof] he does not need to go deeply into the matter and to be capable of dealing with disputed questions and their responses, for when a doubt occurs to him he dispels it with the proof which he has.

What the author is saying here is basically this: one becomes a Believer (*mu'min*) when he assents to the basic articles of Muslim Belief. To Believe (to be a Believer: *al-'īmān*) is, according to commonly accepted lexical definition, to hold that these articles are true (*at-taṣdīq*). Accordingly, the literalists hold that any one who believes and says that they are true (*ṣaddaqa*) is, by definition a Believer. The «expert theologians», however, sc., those who take the meaning and implications of the words seriously into consideration and employ them rigorously, insist that the unreflected and uncritical acquiescence to, and the mere repetition of, the statements and opinions of others does not constitute a valid judgement; one who has not, with some degree of clarity at least, seen that a given proposition is in fact true cannot himself say that it (or that the statement of it) is true. His statement, «it is true that SP» (or «'SP' is true») is unfounded and so empty. He cannot affirm it «conclusively» in his own voice. Confronted with even a flimsy and spurious argument (*šubbah*) for the contrary, he must deny what he previously affirmed. It is always possible that God, by a special intervention, raise the mere belief (*al-i'tiqād*) of one who is *muqallid* to the level of knowledge, but this is not what occurs in the normal course of events. The fact is then that one must in some way and to some extent consider the matter and must himself see that the facts are as proposed before assenting to the given statement of them as true:

[24] «Infallible»: *ma'ṣūm*; the word normally means that the individual so described does not (would not or cannot) err either ethically by deceiving or by unintentionally making a false statement. In the present context the former sense alone would seem intended, given the «*yuḫṭi'u*» (is in error) which follows it. Concerning the connotational differences between '*ma'rifah*' and '*'ilm*' in the present context and the several connotations of '*i'tiqād*', see our *Knowledge and Taqlīd*, p. 41, n. 15 and p. 54, n. 38 (cf. above n. 1).

knowing (*al-ma'rifah*) formally precedes the holding as true (*at-taṣdīq*) which constitutes valid religious Belief[25].

At the beginning of his *Risālah* al-Qušayrī condemns *taqlīd* in unequivocal terms:

The Masters of this group of people (sc., the sufis) have constructed the foundations of their religious life on valid principles (*'uṣūlun ṣaḥīḥah*) regarding theology, by virtue of which they have safegarded their basic beliefs (*'aqā'iduhum*) from innovations and have professed their beliefs in a doctrine of God's uniqueness in which He is neither likened to creatures nor stripped of His attributes...; they have carefully elaborated the fundamental dogmas of their beliefs (*'uṣūlu l-'aqā'id*) by clear proofs and plain evidence. As abū Muḥammad al-Ǧarīrī [a follower of al-Ǧunayd, d. A.H. 311] said: «The foot of the Deceiver will slip into the abyss of ruin with those who do not really know God's uniqueness through some of its phenomenal evidences», by which he means that those who rely on *taqlīd* and have not reflected on the evidences (*dalā'il*) of God's uniqueness have fallen away from the ways of salvation (*sunanu n-naǧāh*) into the bonds of perdition[26].

Al-Aš'arī's condemnation of *taqlīd* in *aṯ-Ṯaghr* is most likely aimed at the Mu'tazila[27]. It remains, however, that the statement is unqualified and so, in the absence of any contextual evidence to the contrary, must be read as universal: to bind one's self uncritically to the judgements and opinions of others in matters of theology is rejected. That al-Aš'arī in some contexts (e.g., *al-Ibānah*), including perhaps the present one, directs his condemnation of *taqlīd* polemically against the Mu'tazila is in no way inconsistent with his directing it against others in other contexts, viz., against the Ḥanbalites in *al-Ḥaṯṯ*. What he says in *aṯ-Ṯaghr* quite plainly excludes the attitude of an extremist such as the Ḥanbalite, al-Barbahārī, against whom *al-Ḥaṯṯ* is chiefly directed, i.e., against a thesis that «the true religion (*ad-dīn*) is *taqlīd* and *taqlīd* is to the Companions of the Apostle of God»[28].

[25] Thus «the first of the stages is knowing, then certainty (*al-yaqīn*), then assent (*at-taṣdīq*)...»: AL-QUŠAYRĪ, *Risālah*, 3, p. 77,3 f. Al-'Arūsī explains the meaning of 'knowing' insofar as it is the first stage, identifying it with «the formal reasoning and the reflection which leads to knowing» (p. 77); with this, cp. the statement of al-Bāqillānī translated below, in n. 67. Thus at the end of his *Luma'* al-Qušayrī says, «these are the dogmas which one has to know (*lā budda min ma'rifatihā*): p. 63,6. It is in this sense that al-Aš'arī speaks of the obligation of all Muslims to treat questions in terms of «the set of principles commonly agreed upon by means of intelligence, sense perception, and what is given in immediate intuition» (*al-Ḥaṯṯ*, § 2.313).

[26] *Risālah*, 1, p. 40 ff.; cp. also his *R. aš-Šikāyah*, Karachi, 1384/1964, p. 43 (= SUBKĪ, 3, p. 419 f.). The opening section of the al-Qušayrī's *Risālah* is in essence an Aš'arite *'aqīdah*, even though, given the context, it is not cast in formal, Aš'arite terms as is *Fuṣūl fī l-'uṣūl*, for example.

[27] This is contextually plausible in *aṯ-Ṯaghr*; it is explicit in *Ibānah*, p. 6,21 ff.

[28] *Ṭabaqāt*, 2, p. 29, *ult.*, q.v. ff.; cp. also *ibid.*, p. 38 f. Concerning the attitude of the Ḥanbalites, note also the remarks of 'Abd al-Wahhāb al-Warrāq (d. A.H. 250-1): «Ahmad

According to al-Aš'arī, then, certain fundamental theological truths which form the basis of Belief are (or may be) known rationally, e.g., that the world exists as a gratuitous action of God, that He is eternal and endowed with at least seven basic attributes which are neither identical with His essential being nor distinct from it, etc. There are other religious truths, however, knowledge of which is possible only by report (*sam'an*), sc., through information furnished in the Koran or in the teaching of the Prophet, for example, the existence of paradise and hell, the resurrection to come, the future intercession of the Prophet on behalf of the Believers, that God will be «visibly» manifest to the believers in the life to come, etc. In addition to such dogmas, the Koran and the Tradition also contain descriptions of God the significance of which is not in every case clear and unambiguous, since what they appear to indicate cannot, on the one hand, be discovered or independantly verified by reason and, on the other hand, cannot be readily understood in terms of those dogmas which are known with clarity. Concerning these al-Aš'arī says (*aṯ-Ṯaghr*, p. 106,15-18):

[The Muslims] are agreed that one must affirm the truth of everything which the Prophet gave them in God's Scripture and in all of the Sunna whose transmission is authenticated and that one is obliged to act in accord with his judgement and to affirm the truth of the text of what is problematic and ambiguous (*muškiluhu wa-mutašābihuhū*) and, while believing in the text, to remand to God anything whose interpretation he does not understand. This obtains only with regard to that in which they are obliged (*kullifū*) to believe in a general way, without full cognitive clarity[29].

What he means by this is that, for some of these descriptions of God, one believes in the truth of what the text intends (sc., what God means to assert) while having only an uncertain or indistinct grasp of what is meant, not an understanding which can be expressed in clear and exact

[ibn Ḥanbal] is our leader (*'imām*); he is one of those *who are deep rooted in knowledge* (Q 3,7) and when I stand before God and He asks me, 'Whom did you imitate?', I shall say, 'Ahmad ibn Ḥanbal'» (*ibid.*, 1, p. 210,21-23) and similarly, «Since the Prophet said, 'Refer it to one who knows it', we refer it to Ahmad ibn Ḥanbal» (*ibid.*, p. 211,9). One is bound directly not to the authority of the revealed sources, but to their reading by the founder of the school. It should be noted, however, that not all the Ḥanbaliṭes were always content with *taqlīd*, at least not with its practice in all situations. Ibn 'Aqīl speaks against it in at least one context; cf. MAKDISI, *Ibn 'Aqīl*, p. 524. The definition of *taqlīd* there cited, sc., «*ta'ẓīmu r-riğāli wa-tarku l-'adillah*» is notably similar to that given by al-Aš'arī in *aṯ-Ṯaghr*: «... fī taqlīdihī li-man yu'*aẓẓimu min sādatihī bi-ghayri dalālatin taqtaḍī ḏalika*». (Note that the reference of '*ḏālika*' in al-Aš'arī's statement is ambiguous; it could refer either to the thesis which one adopts by *taqlīd* or it could refer to the practice of *taqlīd* itself).

[29] With this cp. AL-QUŠAYRĪ, *Luma'*, p. 60,2 ff.

terms so as to present an unambivalent account of what is referred to. Such a reading of the text is sometimes said to be «*bi-lā kayf*»: «without any how». The expression «*bi-lā kayf*» itself, however, is ambivalent and has to be examined. It has most commonly been understood by scholars to mean simply that one reads the text and acknowledges that what it says is true «without asking questions» or «without further comment»[30]. This seems, indeed, to be the way many of the traditionalists and most all the Ḥanbalite contemporaries of al-Aš'arī normally employ it. «One does not make comparisons ...; one affirms the truth of the report of God's Apostle without any how and without any commentary (*bi-lā kayfa wa-bi-lā šarḥ*) and without saying 'why?' or 'how?'»[31]. It might appear on first reading that al-Aš'arī means only this and no more when he says (*aṯ-Ṯaghr*, p. 98,8 f.),

> [The Muslims] are agreed that one describes God (He is exalted) by every description by which He has described Himself and by which His Prophet has described Him, without raising any objection and without howing it (*min ghayri 'tirādin wa-lā takyīf*).

The latter phrase, however, says much more than a mere «without further comment». Generally, and in the usage of the Aš'arites always, '*bi-lā kayf*' has other, more formal connotations. It means that one does not attribute physical attributes to God; he does not, that is, ascribe to God the characteristics and properties of creatures.

> One does not say 'how?' with regard to the object of our worship, for 'how?' is employed to ask about the physical constitution (*hay'ah*) and the condition [of a thing]; the Creator (be He praised) has, however, no physical constitution and no condition[32].

Thus, in discussing a tradition which speaks of God's «finger» Ibn Fūrak says that the text cannot mean that God has bodily members,

[30] Cf., e.g., WENSINCK, index, *s.v.* and GARDET and ANAWATI, index, *s.v.*

[31] AL-BARBAHĀRĪ in *Ṭabaqāt*, 2 p. 19,14 f. For this use of '*bi-lā kayf*' cf. also AD-DĀRIMĪ, p. 39,9 f. and AL-BAYHAQĪ, p. 408,8 f. and 14 f. and p. 409,1 ff. Note that al-Bayhaqī in these passages is not speaking in his own voice but is quoting the words and opinions of others. He is an Aš'arite and his own treatment of what it means to assert something «*bi-lā kayf*» conforms fully to that of the Aš'arite school (see the citations below). The Aš'arism of al-Bayhaqī is discussed in J.-C. VADET, *Tradition islamique et aš'arisme dans le 'Livre des noms et attributs divins' d'al-Bayhaqī*, in *BEO*, 33, p. 253-269, but one has the impression that the author is not altogether familiar with the theology of the Aš'arite school, either in its conception or in its formal vocabulary.

[32] AL-QUŠAYRĪ, *Fuṣūl*, § 16. The lexicographers commonly understand '*kayfa*' as an interrogative particle used basically to enquire after the state (*ḥāl*) of a thing (e.g., IBN FĀRIS, *Maqāyīs al-lughah*, *s.v.*); appropriate answers to 'how?' describe the physical state of a thing, e.g., 'well' or 'healthy' (cf. e.g., AL-MUBARRAD, *al-Muqtaḍab*, 2, ed. A. M. 'ADĪMA, Cairo, 1386, p. 311).

«since it conveys the true meaning and does not convey a sense of *kayf* and *tašbīh*»[33]. To ask concerning how (*kayfa*) a thing is assumes its having an attribute or property which answers to the «how?», sc., a *kayfiyyah*. To be describable and distinguishable in terms of physical characteristics — to have such distinguishing characteristics — is to have a *kayfiyyah*[34]. «Form entails *kayfiyyah*»[35] and conversely «*kayfiyyah* entails physical disposition and configuration»[36]. According to the Aš'arites, however,

[33] *Bayān* (1943), p. 102,12: *lā tufīdu l-kayfa wat-tašbīh*; cp. «... how can this be, when the being described has no how and no where and the mind cannot liken it to anything» (... *bi-lā kayfa wa-lā ḥayṯu wa-lā yumaṯṯiluhu l-'uqūl*): *Ghunyah*, f. 16v,14; with this compare the formulation of al-Ǧunayd in the text cited below, n. 39.

[34] According to the grammarians, the most basic forms of questions is that which requires an answer 'yes' or 'no'. Interrogative particles such as '*kam*' (how much, how many) and the like allow one to avoid a lengthy series of questions in order to elicit a single, positive response (cf. AZ-ZAǦǦĀǦ, *Mā yanṣarif wa-mā lā yanṣarif*, ed. H. M. QARĀ'A, Cairo, 1391/1971, p. 88 and *Bayān* [1943], p. 60). One has not, thus to ask «is he well?», «is he worse?», «is it round?», and the like, but simply «how is he/it?». The «how» anticipates an answer which describes the subject as having a given physical property or disposition and thus presumes, and by implication asserts, that it is such as to have physical properties and dispositions. The class of properties and dispositions answering to '*kayfa*' is termed '*al-kayfiyyah*', the latter word being related to the former as a *maṣdar* to the corresponding descriptive term, e.g., as '*'ilm*' is related to '*ya'lamu*' or to '*'ālim*' and to '*ma'lūm*'. That '*kayfiyyah*' is to be understood as a *maṣdar* (not as an abstract noun), cf., e.g., AZ-ZAǦǦĀǦĪ, *al-Īḍāḥ fī 'ilal an-naḥw*, ed. M. AL-MUBĀRAK, Beyrouth, 1393/1973, p. 58 f. and AL-FARRĀ', *Ma'ānī l-Qur'ān*, ed. A. I. SALABĪ, 3, Cairo, 1972, p. 137.

[35] *Aṣ-ṣūratu taqtaḍī l-kayfiyyah*: AL-BAYHAQĪ, p. 296,16, q.v. ff. (Concerning the sense of '*ṣūrah*' see the following note.) This use of '*kayfiyyah*' antedates al-Aš'arī and his school. In his *Ta'wīl muḫtalif al-ḥadīṯ* ibn Qutayba says, concerning texts which describe God as visible to the blessed and which describe Him as having created Adam «in His (own) form» (*ṣūrah*), that «we believe in [the truth of] this without asserting [that He is qualified by] either a *kayfiyyah* or by any spatial boundary' (*lā naqūlu fīhi bi-kayfiyyatin wa-lā ḥadd*): p. 141,1 and 150,7 f. (For the association of spatial delimitation and *kayfiyyah* see also the citations of ibn 'Abd al-Malik below.) For this sense of '*kayfiyyah*', cf. also, e.g., the statement of al-Māturīdī, «... *bi-lā kayfa*, since *kayfiyyah* belongs to something that has a shape» (... *'iḏi l-kayfiyyatu takūnu li-ḏī ṣūrah*): *Kitāb at-Tawḥīd*, ed. F. KHOLEIF, Beyrouth, 1970, p. 85.

One has to recognise thus in the classical kalām texts several lexically distinct formal uses of '*kayfiyyah*': (1) a thing's being such that it has physical properties, (2) a physical property or attribute, (3) the «how it is» that one must know in order to do it or make it, and (4) the mode of the actuality of an attribute or state (in the analysis of abū Hāšim and his followers). These uses of '*kayfiyyah*' are heard, within the semantic context of these texts, as directly implied by '*kayfa*' and by '*kayyafa, yukayyifu*' (on which see below) and so are distinct from and independant of '*al-kayfiyyah*' which is found as the translation equivalent of Greek 'ποιότης'; it is heard, that is, as a *maṣdar* which refers to and names the disposition or property that is semantically and logically implied by '*kayfa*' and by the denominative '*kayyafa*'.

[36] *Al-kayfiyyatu taqtaḍī l-hay'ata wat-tašakkul*: *Ghunyah*, f. 106v,8. «*al-hay'atu wat-tašakkul*» here represents a conceptual analysis of the sense of '*ṣurāh*' (form, shape) as used in the text cited in the preceding note. This richer sense of '*ṣūrah*' is consonant with

God transcends whatever qualities are evidential of temporal contingency that creatures, human or other, may have. No imagining can picture Him nor can any understanding measure Him. Any being which might be thought of as like Him and which has any physical property (*lahu kayfiyyah*) (and this is an attribute of created entities) is such that He can create beings like it in a single instant[37].

The Aš'arites and others thus commonly employ '*kayyafa, yukayyifu*', as in the passage of *at-Taghr* which we just cited, with the sense «to ascribe physical properties to» a being, i.e., to describe it as having, or to assert that it has, a *kayfiyyah*. «We predicate the name of God as it stands in the text without attributing physical properties to Him and without likening Him to creatures» (*bi-lā takyīfin wa-lā tašbīhi*)[38]. Similarly, al-Ǧunayd (d. 298/910) says that there are no beings which are either like God or contrary to Him, i.e., He belongs to no kind or class of entities; He is not described as «similar to anything or as having physical attributes or as having shape or as being comparable to anything»[39]. «Everything in the world which has physical attributes (*kullu mā fī l-'ālami mina l-mukayyafāt*) is created ...»[40]. To say how a thing is, in sum, is to assign it to some class of created beings by attributing to it the properties that are distinctive of that class (*ǧins*)[41].

its ordinary usage. Ibn Fāris (*Maqāyīs al-lughah, s.v.*), «The *ṣūrah* of any created being is the form [disposition/nature] of its physical constitution (*hay'atu ḫilqatihī*)». (Note the loaded resonance between '*maḫlūq*' and '*ḫilqah*' here.) Thus *Koran* 6,9 («If We had made him an angel, We should have made him a man») is glossed, «i.e., in the form (*ṣūrah*) of a man, since they are incapable of beholding the form of angels»: AL-FARRĀ', *op. cit.* (see above n. 34), 1, p. 328; cf. also Muqātil b. SULAYMĀN, *Tafsīr*, 1, ed. A. M. ŠEHĀTA, Cairo, n.d., p. 365.

[37] AL-QUŠAYRĪ, *Luma'*, p. 60,17-20. (in the translation of this passage [*ibid.*, p. 68] I inadvertantly dropped the *ka-ḏālika*. The account of *al-kayfiyyah* in the note [*ibid.*, p. 72, n. 8] is erroneous). A closely analogous passage occurs in al-Qušayrī's *Mu'taqad*, but without the phrase «*mimmā lahū kayfiyyatun wa-hya min ṣifāti l-maḫlūqāt*»; it reads, «... He is neither a body nor an atom nor a corporeal individual (*šaḫṣ*) nor a being that has shape (*ḏū ṣūrah*); no understanding can measure Him nor can any imagining picture Him; any being which might be thought of as like him is such that He can create the like of it»: *MS Murat Buhari*, no. 210, f. 74ᵛ,9-12.

[38] AL-BAYHAQĪ, p. 336 f. (a portion of this passage is translated below); similarly he says (*ibid.*, p. 410,4) that «al-Aš'arī did not conceive God's sitting on the Throne in physical terms» (*lam yukayyifi l-istiwā'a*); cf. also *ibid.*, p. 452,19 f.

[39] Cited in *Risālah*, 1, p. 45 and 4, p. 43: ... *bi-lā tašbīhin wa-lā takyīfin wa-lā taṣwīrin wa-lā tamṯīl* .... For the classical kalām, every creature (every being other than God) is corporeal: to be some kind of thing is to be corporeal and to have corporeal properties is to belong to some class (*ǧins*) of things.

[40] Abū l-Ma'ālī b. 'Abd al-Malik, cited in IBN 'ASĀKIR, p. 150,19 f.

[41] God does not belong to any class (*ǧins*) of things (*Tamhīd*, § 446, p. 263,15 f.) and so is not such that He can be distinguished from others of the same class by some manifest characteristics (*lā ǧinsa lahū fa-yatamayyaza bi-'amāratin 'an 'aškālihī*: AL-QUŠAYRĪ, 1, p. 66,32 f.). Thus al-Ḥallāǧ is quoted as saying that whoever enquires after the class of

Whereas the literalist traditionalists say that they read the revealed texts «without any how», the polemic of the Aš'arites refers to them as the «*mukayyifah*»: those who ascribe physical properties to God and so liken Him to creatures[42].

The Ḥašwiyya, who attribute material qualities to God, say that He will be visible [to the blessed in the next life] having physical properties and spatial limits (*yurā mukayyafan maḥdūdan*) just like all other visible entities..., [whereas al-Aš'arī] says that He shall be seen without entering into anything and without spatial limits and without being qualified by physical properties (*min ghayri ḥulūlin wa-lā ḥudūdin wa-lā takyīf*)[43].

To say that God is not similar to creatures, is, in short, to say that His being cannot be conceived or imagined[44]. Our understanding, what we can conceptually or imaginatively grasp, is limited to the phenomenal world (*aš-šāhid*) and it is for this reason that the Aš'arites insist that we may validly describe God only by those descriptions by which He has described Himself. To ask 'how?' — to posit a *kayfiyyah* in (or of) God — is, in brief, to employ logical forms (*al-qiyās*) in a way that is does not take into account the nature of the subject term.

something posits its having characteristics which distinguish it as a member of a particular class (*man kāna lahu ğinsun ṭālibuhu mukayyif*: cited *ibid.*, p. 46,3-5: *Aḫbār al-Ḥallāğ*, no. 13,5; the personal '*man*' belongs to the context). With this one should note the citation of al-Ḥallāğ in AL-KALĀBĀḎĪ, p. 34 f.: *fa-'in qulta kayfa, fa-qadi ḥtağaba 'ani l-waṣfi bil-kayfiyyati ḏātuhū ..., wa-'in qulta mā huwa, fa-qad bāyana l-'ašyā huwiyyatuhū*: «If you say 'how?', His Being is veiled beyond being described as having any physical characteristics...; and if you say 'What is He?', His being-He is distinct from things». Al-Ḥallāğ thus denies absolutely that God has any *kayfiyyah*; if the words we employ to describe God are understood as they are understood when we use them to speak of created entities, then the description is inconsistent and so untrue. His being is «veiled», beyond any such description. (The «veil» here reflects the use of the word in several hadīths.) Al-Ḥallāğ allows, however, that a *huwiyyah* belongs to God, i.e., that He is such as to be designated by the third person pronoun, '*huwa*', which is used as the subject term of a descriptive sentence. The being of God by virtue of which He may be designated by '*huwa*' is not, however, the same as the being by virtue of which creatures are such as to be designated by '*huwa*', for He belongs to no class of entities. One cannot, therefore, rightly ask «What is He?» (*mā huwa*), for though the 'He' may be properly employed, the 'what' cannot. The Being which is designated by the 'He' here is such that it cannot be described by a predicate of the form 'is a ...', which is assumed by the 'what?' of the question. (To what extent does ibn Ḥanbal's intention in the formula [*Radd*, p. 105,12 f.], «*'innahu šay'un lā kal-'ašyā'*» approach this one of al-Ḥallāğ?). '*Huwiyyah*' here is a *maṣdar*, formed like '*kayfiyyah*'. For the use of '*huwiyyah*', cp. e.g., AL-GHAZĀLĪ, *Maqṣad*, p. 18,6, where he speaks of being the referent of '*huwa*' (i.e., of a subject term) and of being other (*al-ghayriyyah*).

[42] IBN 'ASĀKIR, p. 149, where note the sequence, «*al-ḥašwiyyatu l-muğassimatu wal-mukayyifatu wal-muḥaddidatu ...*»; see generally *ibid.*, p. 149 f.

[43] Ibn 'Abd al-Mālik, cited *ibid.*, p. 149,17-20; cf. also the citation of al-Ḥallāğ in AL-KALĀBĀḎĪ, p. 35,8: *laysa li-ḏātihi takyīf.*

[44] Cf. the statement of al-Isfarā'īnī: *lā yušbihu šay'an mina l-maḫlūqāti wa-taḥqīquhū 'annahu lā yutaṣawwaru fī l-wahmi wa-mā dūnahu yaqbalu hāḏihi ṣ-ṣifah*: *'Aqīdah*, § II,4.

For the Aš'arites, thus, as for many others, to understand the descriptions of God which occur in the revealed texts *bi-lā kayf* is to read them with *tanzīh*, i.e., with the understanding that God's being transcends description by any expression as that expression is commonly used in talking about the world and the things of our normal experience. «God may be described only by what is appropriate to Him» (*Ta'wīl*, f. 118ʳ,5). When, then a descriptive term is equivocal in meaning it must be understood and predicated in a way that is appropriate to the particular subject[45].

What al-Aš'arī means, then in the passage of *aṯ-Ṯaghr* which we are considering is not that one does not, or should not, try to think about the meaning of the text, but rather that he should neither argue with the language of the revealed text nor take it literally according to the everyday sense and connotation of the words. One must, in brief, avoid *ta'ṭīl* (the denial of God's having distinct attributes) and *tašbīh* (the conception of His attributes as similar to those of creatures). If one wishes, or needs (e.g., against the errors of *ta'ṭīl* and *tašbīh*), to clarify the sense of the revealed text, this cannot be accomplished by *taqlīd*. Employing, rather, rational principles and the truths achieved in the primary dogmas of theology, one may (or must) make appropriate distinctions and form a judgement of what the report may plausibly assert and, concomitantly, about what it cannot assert, while continuing to recognise that the ultimate meaning (what God is really saying and talking about) is simply not to be discovered with absolute certainty, at least not in this life.

After completing his discussion of God's seven primary attributes, al-Aš'arī proceeds in *aṯ-Ṯaghr* (p. 96,20 ff.) to take up several of the problematic descriptions of God which are found in the Koran and the Tradition. We should note that with regard to God's attributes he has, in conformity with his «*bi-lā takyīf*», explicitly pointed out that

[45] *Bayān* (1943), p. 79,6 f.: *'iḏā kāna l-lafẓu muštarika l-ma'nà, waǧaba t-tartību wa-'iḍāfatu mā yalīqu fī l-maḏkūri l-muḍāfi 'ilayhī 'alà ḥasabi mā yalīqu bihī*. (The verb '*'aḍāfa, yuḍīfu, 'iḍāfah*' here means «to ascribe», i.e., to ascribe a description or attribute to something; connotationally, however, it retains its grammatical meaning, in that the analysis of the description will present a construct phrase in which the noun or *maṣdar* of the descriptive term will appear in construct (as *muḍāf*) to the term which names the subject (the *muḍāf 'ilayhī*) as, e.g., '*'alima Zayd*' or '*Zaydun 'ālim*' asserts the fact or Zayd's knowing: *'ilmu Zayd*.) Cf. also AL-BAYHAQĪ, p. 459,20-23. Thus al-Ḥallāǧ, in a passage which treats the problem in its most acute form, says «*at-tašbīhu lā yalīqu bi-'awṣāfi l-Ḥaqq*» (likening to creatures is not appropriate to the descriptions of the Truth [sc., of God]): *Ṭawāsīn*, § 10,9, ed. P. NWYIA, in *MUSJ*, 48 (1972), p. 214.

when we have asserted that these attributes belong to Him as is shown by the mind's reasoning and by language[46] and by the consensus of the Muslims, it is not necessary that they be temporally contingent, since He (the Exalted) is qualified by them eternally; nor is it necessary that they be accidents, since He (the Mighty, the Glorious) is not a body (*ğism*) and accidents exist only in bodies[47].

Among the problematic descriptions he takes up are those which seem to predicate motion of God, e.g., the verse «And [when] God comes and the angels, rank upon rank» (Q 89,22) and the hadîth, «He descends every night to the lowest heaven...». Concerning these he says,

[The Muslims] are agreed that God will come on the day of the resurrection... as He has said. It is not, however, a going or a movement or a leaving. A going is a movement and a leaving only when that which goes is a body or an atom and since it is certain that He (the Mighty, the Glorious) is neither a body nor an atom, His going must not be a local transference or a movement. Note that when they say «the fever came to Zayd» they do not mean that it was transferred to him or that it has moved from a place in which it had been, since it is neither a body nor an atom; its coming to him is simply its existence in him. ... Nor is God's «descending» a transference, since He is neither a body nor an atom[48].

[46] What he means by the phrase «and by language» is this: since 'knows' must be true of God, then it must be true that an act of knowing (*'ilmun*) belongs to Him, since an act of knowing is the implied referent of 'knows' and is thus the ontological basis of the truth of the description; this is discussed in *at-Taghr*, p. 95,5 ff. It should be noted here that the Aš'arites consistently list the sources of theological knowledge in order of priority as the Scripture, the Sunna, the consensus of the Muslims, and reasoning (*al-'aql*: where '*al-'aql*' stands in the list in the position analogous to '*al-qiyās*' in the list of the sources of juridical knowledge). Since the question in this passage of *at-Taghr* is not that of theology in general or that of the basic dogmas as a whole and as such, but rather of the understanding and interpretation of certain secondary and subordinate elements of the revealed sources within a context which already accepts the truth of the basic dogmas and of the Koran and the Sunna, the sequence «the mind's reasoning and language and the consensus of the Muslims» in no way calls into question the basic authority of the Koran and the Tradition; «language» here stands for the formal, i.e., reasoned analysis of the language of the revealed sources (cp. the text cited in n. 68 below).

[47] P. 95,18-21, reading *'idā 'atbatnā* for *'idā bayyannā* in line 18 and *dalla* for *dallahu* in line 19; see generally *ibid.*, p. 95 f.

[48] P. 97,4-9; this or a parallel text of al-Aš'arī is cited by AL-BAYHAQĪ, p. 448 f., q.v. The topic is not treated in the published recension of *Luma'*. The purpose of the philological remarks concerning 'come' is simply to show that in its normal use in everyday language the verb is also employed in a way in which it is not understood to refer local motion, wherefore the text under discussion need not be understood to assert that God moves from one place to another. Since the usage mentioned is common it is not considered to be metaphorical; see below n. 54. For the later Aš'arite discussion of these hadîths see, e.g., *Ta'wīl*, f. 157v (the text here is incomplete), *Bayān* (1943), p. 75 ff. and 247 ff. and *Šāmil* (1969), p. 557 ff.

This, of course, is fully consistent with what he has already said in arguing that corporeality necessarily entails contingency and that God is not similar to any creature. Note that al-Aš'arī does not here deny that '*an-nuzūl*' names a distinct attribute of God. Quite to the contrary; he insists only that the attribute so named in the revealed text cannot be understood to be a spatial motion of God[49].

The Ḥanbalites, however, treat these texts quite differently. Characteristically, al-Barbahārī includes the «hadîth of the descent» along with several others, all of which speak of God anthropomorphically, in a group of which he says,

Grant the truth of any tradition you hear which your mind cannot fully understand and affirm it...; do not interpret (*fassara*) any of these reports according to your personal inclination (*'ahwā'*), for it is obligatory that one believe in them and whoever interprets any of these according to his own inclination and rejects it is a Ǧahmite[50].

What al-Barbahārī means by «personal inclination» and «rejecting» is clear enough:

When you hear a man say «We exalt God's magnificence» when he hears the reports of God's Apostle (God's prayer and peace be upon him), know that he is a Ǧahmite. Has he not in fact rejected the report of God's Apostle (God's prayer and peace be upon him) when he said, «We consider God too magnificent to descend from one location to another»? He thinks he knows better about God than any one else. Beware of him[51].

Ḥanbalite doctrine is, in the words of abū Muḥammad 'Abdūs (d. 251/865), that «hadîths are to be taken literally (*'alā ẓāhirihī*) just as they have come from the Prophet; to discuss them (*al-kalāmu fīhī*) is an innovation»[52]. Thus, in an *'aqīdah* ascribed to ibn Ḥanbal and reported by his disciple, abū l-'Abbās al-Iṣṭaḫrī, we read that «God is ... near: He is not neglectful; He moves, He speaks, He looks, He sees, He laughs ...»[53]. Al-Aš'arī's treatment of «the report of the descent» and

[49] That he held (at least in the early post-conversion period of his career) that there is in fact a «revealed attribute» named by '*an-nuzūl*', cf. the statement of ibn 'Abd al-Malik in IBN 'ASĀKIR, p. 150,12f. God's being, however, transcends spatiality: «He needs no place; He is, after the creation of place, just as He was before its creation» (*ibid.*, lines 5 f.; cp. AL-QUŠAYRĪ, *Luma'*, p. 61,4-7).

[50] *Ṭabaqāt*, 2, p. 23,4-11. Among the traditions cited here is that according to which God created Adam «in his own form» (*'alā ṣūratihī*). According to one Ḥanbalite formulation «any one who does not say that God created Adam in the form of the Merciful is a Ǧahmite» (*ibid.*, 1, p. 212,19; see also *ibid.*, p. 313, 2f. and 1, p. 29).

[51] *Ṭabaqāt*, 2, p. 39,9-14; cp. IBN ḤANBAL, *Radd*, p. 106,6f.

[52] *Ṭabaqāt*, 1, p. 242,15f.

[53] *Ibid.*, p. 29,6. Note that al-Barbahārī's 'moves' (*yataḥarraku*) is, strictly speaking, an interpretation (*tafsīr, ta'wīl*) of 'comes' (*ǧā'a*), and so violates his own injunction against

the like, his analysis and interpretation[54] of them, is, to the Ḥanbalite view, sheer heresy (*bid'ah*). To the extent that they consider such interpretations to be equivalent to Ǧahm's teaching, indeed, they regard it as a kind of unbelief (*kufr*)[55].

tafsīr. This doing interpretation while abjuring it is one of the things that the Aš'arites object to on the part of the Ḥanbalites.

[54] The words '*tafsīr*' and '*ta'wīl*' are sometimes ambivalent. Basically the two are synonymous and mean simply interpretation: any explanation or clarification or a word, expression, or sentence, which is accomplished by the use of another word, expression, or sentence; and frequently '*ta'wīl*' refers to and describes the substitution or paraphrase as such; cf. the citations of Ṯa'lab and ibn Fāris in my *Meanings are said in Many Ways*, in *Le Muséon*, 94 (1981), p. 268 and for examples of '*ta'wīl*' used to designate a simple paraphrase or substitution of an equivalent expression, cf., *ibid.*, p. 294 f.; for a clear example of this common use of '*ta'wīl*' in an Aš'arite context see the text cited in n. 68 below. Frequently, however, the terms are distinguished, as, e.g., al-Ghazālī says that *ta'wīl* «is the explanation (*bayān*) of its meaning after one has excluded its literal meaning (*ẓāhiruhū*)»: *Ilǧām*, p. 7 f. In the Ḥanbalite condemnation of interpretation, thus, one most commonly finds '*ta'wīl*' (though note the occurrence of '*fassara*' in the text cited in n. 50 above), which is often rendered by 'metaphorical interpretation'. What underlies this, for the Ḥanbalites pejorative connotation of the word, is the use of interpretation and paraphrase in cases where the original expression is not taken «literally» and at face value as it is used in its most common occurrences. Nevertheless, any substitution of different words, even if they are «literal equivalents» is an interpretation: *tafsīr, ta'wīl*. Sometimes, but not always, the interpretation does involve the unpacking of figurative language, the reduction of a figured expression to what, in part at least, the speaker literally meant by what he said. It should be noted, however, that in their *ta'wīl* of the Koran and the Tradition, the Aš'arites seldom recognise the presence of what we should consider live metaphores in the strict sense. That is to say, in works such as abū l-Ḥasan aṭ-Ṭabarī's *Ta'wīl* and ibn Fūrak's *Bayān* (the latter an extremely popular work to judge by the number of copies), the term '*ta'wīl*' rarely refers to the interpretation of what they would call a metaphore (*maǧāz, isti'ārah*). Where we might feel that they are treating an expression as metaphorical, they quite plainly feel that they are merely making explicit the contextual sense of a polysemic word or expression. In short, they construe distinct lexical items or meanings wherever the for us apparently metaphorical use of the word (which may most likely have originated in a now defunct metaphore) can be shown to be common in ordinary literary usage, as is the case with '*ǧā'a*' in the passage of *aṯ-Ṯaghr* translated above. Thus it is that ibn Ḥanbal condemns what he considers an errant and heretical interpretation, not as *ta'wīl* simply, but saying (*Radd*, p. 104,6 f.) that they propose an interpretation of the Koran that is not *its* interpretation (*ta'awwalū l-Qur'āna 'alā ghayri ta'wīlihī*), which is to say that the paraphrase proposed as an equivalent of what the text says is not rightly equivalent in his view. So too, where al-Mutawallī (p. 13 f., translated below) speaks of «avoiding *ta'wīl*» he plainly means avoidance by offering no paraphrase at all: leaving the verses as they stand (*kamā ǧā'at*).

[55] The Ḥanbalites, following a number of tendentious traditions, often acuse their opponents of «unbelief» (*kufr*; e.g., ibn Baṭṭa in the text cited in n. 79) and they appear to take this quite seriously. Al-Fuḍayl b. 'Iyād (d. 187/802), for example, says that one may not marry his daughter to such an «innovator» nor should a Muslim attend his burrial (cited in *Ṭabaqāt*, 2, p. 43,1-4; cp. *al-Ḥaṯṯ*, § 2.322, p. 150a). Similarly abū Ǧa'far aṭ-Ṭabarī, who was not a Ḥanbalite but tended to follow their teachings (see n. 93 below), takes an equally rigid position (SOURDEL, p. 194,6-13), stating that such people are unbelievers whose blood it is legitimate to shed. Most commonly, the Ḥanbalites term those of their opponents who were *mutakallimūn* 'Ǧahmites' (followers of the doctrine of,

In at least some of his works, al-Aš'arī holds that God has a real and distinct attribute which is named by 'hands', a knowledge of which we could not have were it not for the revelation, even though, given the revelation, a somewhat indistinct and general idea concerning them can be attained through reason and logical inference (*bin-naẓari wal-istidlāl*)[56]. Thus it is that he affirms the consensus of the Muslims as holding that «to God belong two outstretched hands» in *aṯ-Ṯaghr* (p. 96 f.), arguing from Q 38,75 («what I have created with my hands»)[57]. As we have already noted, al-Aš'arī insists that such problematic descriptions of God are not to be understood in such a way that one ascribes physical characteristics to Him, and accordingly he notes here (p. 96, *ult.*) that the attribute referred to by 'hands' cannot consist in bodily members (*ǧawāriḥ*). This is a fundamental thesis of the Aš'arite school: «it is commonly agreed that God cannot be described as having bodily members»[58]. This explicit insistence on *tanzīh*, i.e., that God is utterly

Ǧahm ibn Ṣafwān, who was executed in 128/746), implying thereby that they are unbelievers whose errors are systematically rationalised. More moderate traditionalists, however, take a less rigid position and soften the sense of 'unbeliever' as it occurs in authoritative texts and in the sayings of respected traditionalists. Thus abū Sulaymān al-Ḫaṭṭābī (a Šāfi'ite) is quoted as saying, «The statements eminating from religious leaders of the first generations and from the traditionalists in which those who interpret (*ta'awwala*) traditions concerning God's attributes are called unbelievers and in which those who hold the Koran to be created, etc., are called unbelievers, are simply a castigation of them and a repudiation of their opinions; the intention is not to predicate unbelief of them formally and to exclude them from the community» (*Ghunyah*, f. 11ʳ,4-6, citing al-Ḫaṭṭābī's, *R. an-Nāṣiḥiyyah*; cf. also *Šarḥ al-Iršād*, f. 116ᵛ and the statement of ibn Qutayba, who distinguishes between the basic articles of faith (*al-'uṣūl*), to deny any of which is to be an unbeliever, and the secondary dogmas (*al-furū'*), amongst which he includes the doctrine of the uncreatedness of the Koran and God's visibility, to deny which is not to be an unbeliever: *Iḫtilāf*, p. 14,17-20 and p. 81 f.

[56] Cf. *Muǧarrad*, p. 22,13-21 and *Šāmil* (1969), p. 332,5 f.

[57] The argument, much abridged in this passage, is that the preëminence of Adam in virtue of which the angels were commanded to prostrate themselves before him can only be explained if 'hands' in this verse is taken to name a particular attribute (or attributes; the dual, '*yadayn*', is problematic for the Aš'arites) in respect to which Adam is related to God in a unique way. The argument is standard with those who hold that there is a distinct attribute called 'hands' and which is a «revealed attribute»; cf., e.g., *Ta'wīl*, f. 128ᵛ,8 ff., *Tamhīd*, § 438 (p. 259), *Bayān* (1943), p. 154 ff., AL-MUTAWALLĪ, p. 32 f., and *Iršād*, p. 156 (whose wording appears to follow that of al-Mutawallī, *loc. cit.*). Whether or not by 'outstretched hands' in this passage al-Aš'arī means here to allude to Q 96,20, either as a basis for asserting the reality of God's «hands» or simply as a verse in which the attribute is referred to, or whether he is merely employing a commonly used phrase is uncertain; on this verse see below. He does seem to have discussed the attribute in some detail as ibn Fūrak reports (*Muǧarrad*, p. 214,11 ff.) that he held that «the hands» cannot be said to be alike or unlike even though both are subject to the same description because as eternal attributes they cannot, by definition, be said to be each of them other than the other, just as God's power cannot be described as other than his knowledge.

[58] *Al-ǧāriḥatu lā yaǧūzu fī waṣfihi bil-ittifāq*: AL-MUTAWALLĪ, p. 33; cf. also AL-BAYHAQĪ, p. 330 f. *et alibi pass.* and AL-QUŠAYRĪ, cited below.

transcendent, even though it does not pretend to interpret the revealed text, is yet sufficient to offend many of the Ḥanbalites[59].

Moreover, while al-Aš'arī held that some verses of the Koran do (or may) refer to God's «hands», he never interpreted in this way all verses in which the word 'hand' (or 'hands') occurs in speaking of God. It is reported, for example, that he said that the expression 'hands' in Q 5,64 and 36,71 is to be understood as referring to God's power of creative action (*al-qudrah*)[60], and al-Bāqillānī says with regard to 36,71 that this is the universal opinion of the exegetes (*'ahl at-tafsīr*)[61].

At some point in his post-conversion career, however, he seems to have changed his mind with regard to God's «hands» in Q 38,75, for it is reliably reported that he also taught another position, according to which 'hands' in all contexts where God is described is to be taken as referring to His power[62] and the school is divided on whether or not

[59] That the denial of *tašbīh* and «*kayf*», from one perspective at least, is not considered to be an interpretation (*ta'wīl, tafsīr*) of the sacred text, cf., e.g., AL-MUTAWALLĪ, p. 13 f., partially translated below.

[60] E.g., *Ghunyah*, f. 99r,20 ff. and *Šarḥ al-Iršād*, f. 142r,17 ff.

[61] *Tamhīd*, p. 258, *ult.*; cf. also *Šarḥ al-Iršād, loc. cit.* Some Aš'arites, however, take 'hands' here as a figurative expression referring to God's «Self» (*nafs, ḏāt*), i.e., '*'amilnā bi-'aydīnā*' = '*'amilnā naḥnu*'; cf. e.g., *Tawīl*, f. 128v,6 f. and *Bayān* (1943), p. 153. In some other verses 'hand' is taken as equivalent to 'blessing' (*ni'mah*); cf., e.g., *Tawīl*, f. 128v ff., *Bayān* (1943), p. 153 ff. and also AL-BAYHAQĪ, p. 319 f. This latter is the position of al-Ǧubbā'ī with regard to most, if not all, occurrences of 'hands' where God is described. We cannot be certain whether al-Aš'arī's rejection of the interpretation of 'hands' as 'blessing' in (p. 96 f.) represents an early position in which, rejecting both the doctrine and the exegesis of al-Ǧubbā'ī, he held that all such occurrences of 'hands' in the Koran are to be understood as referring to the «revealed attribute» or whether it is directed simply at the Mu'tazilite interpretation of Q 38,75 (and 5,64?), though the latter would seem more plausible perhaps.

[62] Cf., e.g., *Šarḥ al-Iršād*, f. 143r f., *al-Ghunyah*, f. 99r f. (translated below), and *Milal*, p. 165,9 f. This position is not reported in *Muǧarrad*, however, and in *Iḥtiṣār* (f. 125r) we read that many of the school's leading authorities (*'a'immah*) interpret 'hands' as equivalent to God's power (*al-qudratu aw-kawnu llāhi qādiran*), while the position of al-Aš'arī is that «they are two revealed attributes that are distinct from His essence». It is to be noted that ibn Fūrak holds the position he reports as that of the Master (see the following note), wherefore his failure to report the second position may well be tendentious, either because of his desire to report the Master's teaching as invariant in its consistency or because he did not want to attribute to him a position at variance with his own teaching, or both. Nor need the report of *Iḥtiṣār* be taken as evidence against the statements of *Šarḥ al-Iršād* and *al-Ghunyah* since the author plainly means only to present and discuss the two basic positions, naming al-Aš'arī alone, since he is the founder of the school, and stating his initial and most commonly recognised teaching; «another position», that is, need to refer to no more than one or two later works in which he states the position as his own. Aš-Šahrastānī's remark (*loc. cit.*) that al-Aš'arī tended to follow the *salaf* (by which he may mean the Ḥanbalites; cf. *Nihāyah*, p. 113 f.) and to avoid *ta'wīl* but nonetheless «had a position in which he allowed it» is taken by Makdisi (1, p. 51 f.) as a general statement regarding al-Aš'arī's attitude towards *ta'wīl*. We have seen, however, that he always insisted on *ta'wīl* for verses which describe God as coming or descending

God has a distinct attribute named by 'hands'[63]. The principles cited to support the validity of reading these texts as not referring to a distinct attribute, over and above the basic seven, are stated by al-Anṣārī in the following way:

What confirms our position is that what our Master, abū l-Ḥasan (al-Aš'arī) and the Qāḍī (al-Bāqillānī) say, i.e., their assertion of the reality of two attributes distinct from [God's] power, does not arrive at definitive certitude. Even though for our part we do not find it theoretically repugnant that there be a revealed attribute (*ṣifatun sam'iyyah*) which the demands of reason do not indicate and knowledge of which can be arrived at only through revelation, the condition for this is that the revealed text be definitively conclusive in such a way as to necessitate knowledge. There is, however, no definitive conclusiveness in the texts on which they rely. The literal words of the texts which are subject to interpretation do not necessitate knowledge; and the Muslims are agreed that one may not posit, simply on the basis of his own personal judgement (*iǧtihād*), the existence of an attribute which belongs to God, definitive knowledge of which cannot be attained either by reason or revelation. According to our Master [al-Aš'arī], there is no text concerning the «hands» which is not subject to interpretation; nor is there any consensus or any theoretical premise (*qaḍiyyatun 'aqliyyah*) [which definitively requires that one assert the existence of this attribute], wherefore this must be revealed, as we have said. The basic, literal use of 'hands' is to refer to two bodily members and if it is impossible that it be so used here and is excluded that it refer to creative power or to blessing or to dominion, even then the thesis that it refers to two eternal attributes belonging to God (He is exalted) and distinct from the rest of His attributes is wholly arbitrary[64].

Al-Anṣārī's argument here has good credentials, both in the Aš'arite school and among some traditionalists. Al-Bayhaqī, in the course of discussing a tradition which speaks of «God's finger» (*op. cit.*, p. 335 f.), says the following:

The earlier fellows of our school did not occupy themselves with the interpretation (*ta'wīl*) of this and analogous traditions. From this and ones like it they understood simply the implied manifestation of God's power and His grandeur. The more recent fellows, however, have discussed (*takallamū*) the interpretations to which it is subject. Abū Sulaymān al-Ḫaṭṭābī (God rest him) holds the

(*al-maǧī'u wan-nuzūl*) (cf. also the remarks in *Iḫtiṣār*, f. 125ᵛ,8 f.) and the context of *Milal* here makes it altogether clear that the author is speaking only of al-Aš'arī's position with regard to «the face and the hands».

[63] Cf., e.g., *Šāmil* (1969), p. 523,8 ff. Al-Mutawallī (p. 32 f.) cites both positions without stating any preference of his own. Others, however, e.g., abū l-Ḥasan aṭ-Ṭabarī (*op. cit.*, f. 128ᵛ ff.), al-Bāqillānī (*op. cit.*, p. 258 ff.; cp. also *Šarḥ al-Iršād*, f. 142ʳ), ibn Fūrak (*Bayān* [1943], p. 153 ff. *et alibi*) take the «hands» as a distinct attribute (or attributes), while al-Ǧuwaynī (e.g., *al-Iršād*, p. 156) prefers the contrary position.

[64] *Ghunyah*, f. 99ʳ f. The same text, with a number of variants is found also in *Šarḥ al-Iršād*, f. 142ʳ f. For the alternative interpretations of 'hands' mentioned at the end of the passage, see *Ta'wīl*, *loc. cit.* and *Bayān*, *loc. cit.*

position that the principle with regard to the assertion of [divine] attributes on the basis of this and similar traditions is that this may not be done except on the basis of an explicit passage of scripture or of a report whose validity is conclusively established; if there are no such, then on the basis of reported traditions which have a foundation in the Scripture and in the Sunna whose validity is conclusively established or whose meanings conform to them. One is obliged to suspend judgement concerning the predication of the name whenever these criteria are not met. In this case, one interprets (*ta'awwala*) the tradition in a way that is appropriate to the meanings of the commonly agreed on, basic dogmas (*'uṣūl*) found in the statements of religious, learned men, while denying that God resembles creatures (*tašbīh*). This is the foundation on which we have constructed our theology (*al-kalām*) and on which we rely in this section.

When he says that one must interpret problematic traditions in a way that is consistent with the commonly recognised religious tenets — the fundamental articles of faith — which are explicitly formulated by men who are both pious and learned (*'aqāwīlu 'ahli d-dīni wal-'ilm*), al-Bayhaqī does not suggest that one should adopt an attitude of *taqlīd* towards their teaching with regard to such verses and traditions. What he means, rather, is that one is bound by the community's consensus with regard to those basic dogmas or articles of belief which do not rest on the interpretation of problematic verses and traditions.

The position according to which God has an attribute which is distinct from the seven and in the canonical sources is called 'hands' clearly belongs to the early post-conversion period of al-Aš'arī's life. He asserts the existence of such an attribute in *aṯ-Ṯaghr*, which was written quite soon after his conversion[65]. In the *Luma'*, a later work, the question of God's «hands» is not even mentioned, though one would expect that if, at the time he composed this latter work as a compendium in which he intended «to make the truth clear and to overcome falsehood» (§2), he still held that God has «hands», he should have taken the trouble to refute the Mu'tazilite counter-thesis[66].

We must take it that al-Aš'arī speaks quite seriously when he says that the authoritative consensus of the Muslims is that the canonical sources, in their obscure and problematic descriptions of God, state

[65] It is also mentioned in the traditionalist *'aqīdah* to which al-Aš'arī, evidently at the time of his conversion, declared his own adherence in *Maqālāt*; on this see below. It is thus that the evidence of the available sources, as we shall see more clearly in what follows, indicates that his denial of a distinct attribute called 'hands' is not a holdover from his earlier, training, but is, on the contrary, an element of his mature, post-conversion doctrine.

[66] It is impossible to be sure on the basis of the present evidence that the problem of the «hands» was not treated in the longer recension of the *Luma'*. Its omission in the shorter version is noteworthy in any event.

what is true of Him and that we must «remand to God» anything which we do not understand. He does not mean by this, however, that the words of the text are to be taken literally or that they are to be read with utter incomprehension. The texts whose sense is obscure are read and what they say is heard, even if vaguely, as coherent with the sense of others whose meaning is clear and which are understood within the limits of what we can clearly know about God. This is the main point of the passage of al-Bayhaqī which we just looked at. Instructed by the Scripture and the teaching of the Prophet, we know that the existence of the world depends unconditionally on God's eternal will and that every entity which exists in the world is, insofar as it is an entity (*šay'*, *ḏāt*), an action of God's. We know also that God has at least seven basic attributes: life, knowledge, the power to create, will, speech, hearing, and sight. We know that in His Self and in His eternal attributes He is in no way similar to any creature. Hearing, then, an obscure description of God one follows the words, anticipating a meaning that is coherent with this context, even if it points beyond what we may understand clearly and express in conceptual terms.

To «remand the meaning to God» entirely will mean that one shall have to refrain from any attempt to clarify the meaning of problematic descriptions found in the revelation. With regard to passages where the Koran speaks of God's «hands», for example, one could not say in what respect the obscure description truly describes Him. He may not, that is, suggest how perhaps it describes Him in His essential being (*aḏ-ḏāt, an-nafs*) or with respect to one of the seven eternal attributes, or that it describes Him with respect to some additional, «revealed attribute», or, finally, how it may describe Him with respect to one or more of His actions (i.e., that it is the description of a creature as and insofar as it is a particular action of God). Even the «*bi-lā kayf*» may not be used if the meaning is to be remanded to God altogether, for within the Aš'arite context to add such a qualification requires that one know the meaning of the text at least enough to say that it describes God as He is eternally, not in terms of one of His actions. Al-Aš'arī doubtless allowed that one may and in some cases, indeed, must remit the meaning of a text to God, since a given text is often subject to more than one theologically plausible and coherent interpretation[67]. In any

[67] Al-Bāqillānī held that to affirm a proposition to be true one has to understand it and so says that one cannot believe in the truth of the Koran and submit to it «without knowing its meaning and its interpretation» (*dūna ma'rifati ma'nāhu wa-ta'wīlihī*): *Hidāyah*, f. 143^{v},12 f. Contrast the attitude of al-Barbahārī in the text cited in n. 50.

event, however, both he and his followers in practice take the position that, in the words of al-Bayhaqī,

> you will not, with the praise of God and His graciousness, find any report which is validly transmitted from the Prophet save that it has some interpretation (*ta'wīl*) compatible with the form of expression and a meaning which is not contradictory to reason or to anything known [about God][68].

That is to say, taking the words of the text as they are normally and correctly employed in Arabic, one is always able to restate the sentence (or the portion of it in question) in a form which is lexically and syntactically a valid paraphrase of the original and which is, at the same time, such as to exhibit the original meaning as one which is both logically and conceptually consistent with the basic tenets of Islam. Thus it is that the Aš'arites generally offer an interpretation — often several — of obscure descriptions of God, not as definitive or final (and to this extent the meaning is ultimately remanded to God), but as reasonable and plausible: as compatible with the established usage of the Arabic words of the text and logically consistent with basic Islamic doctrine. What they object to on the part of the Ḥanbalites and others of the radical traditionalists is in part that while claiming not to go beyond the texts themselves they do in fact interpret them, but most especially that by refusing to clarify their dogmatic assertions they seem to say, and lead simple and ordinary people to believe, that God has the characteristics of a corporeal, manlike individual[69].

We should note, finally, that al-Aš'arī does not, as he sees it, interpret the revealed texts «according to his personal inclination» (*al-'ahwā'*) and simply by the exercise of his private judgement (*iğtihād*), but in accord with the Koran and the Sunna and on the basis of rigorous, logical and theological principles which are exemplified in, and so sanctioned by, the authority of the revealed texts[70].

* * *

[68] Al-Bayhaqī, p. 298,3 f.

[69] It is on these grounds that ibn Fūrak explicitly attacks ibn Ḫuzayma (*Bayān* [1943], p. 180 ff.) and aṣ-Ṣibghī (*ibid.*, p. 216 ff.).

[70] For an explicit statement of this, cf. e.g., that of ibn 'Abd al-Malik: «These paths which [al-Aš'arī] followed he did not follow out of blind desire and willfulness nor did he initiate them as an heretical innovation and something he personally felt to be suitable (*bid'atan wa-stiḥsānan*), but rather he confirmed them by rationally tested demonstrations, thoroughly examined, revealed evidences (*'adillah*), and guideposts that point to the Truth (*al-Ḥaqq*, sc., God), and sound arguments that are conducive to what is correct and true (*aṣ-ṣawābu waṣ-ṣidq*); they are the pathways to God»: Ibn 'Asākir, p. 152,5 ff.

The question concerning the createdness of the Koran and of the status of the text as materially realised in our oral recitation of it differs from those of God «hands» and of His «descending» in that it does not arise immediately from the revealed texts themselves. It originates, rather, in a secondary or derivative way from the consideration of a set of prior dogmatic theses, sc., that God's speaking (*kalāmu llāh*) is eternal and that the Koran is God's speaking.

Debates over the createdness of the Koran seem to have arisen as early as the time of 'Umar ibn 'Abd al-'Azīz (d. 101/720)[71]. The discussion of the issue in the works of the Aš'arites in the classical period is quite elaborate, involving a number of necessary and well conceived distinctions. The word 'speaking' (or 'speech': *al-kalām*), according to al-Aš'arī, is employed lexically to name both the mental intention of the speaker and its material expression (*al-'ibārah*)[72]. The latter consists of «sounds and syllables» (*'aṣwātun wa-ḥurūf*) which signify the speaker's interior or mental intention. The latter he seems to have understood as «the striking together of the particles [sc., the atoms] of bodies»[73]. Speaking, in the strictest or primary sense, is the interior speaking, i.e., the intention of the speaker, not the sounds which are its semiotic expression (*ad-dalā'ilu 'alayhī*)[74]. In speaking of the Koran, therefore, he distinguishes between the oral reading or recitation (*at-tilāwah, al-qirā'ah*), which is our material action, and that which is read or recited aloud (*al-matlūw, al-maqrū'*), i.e., that which is brought to expression, is heard and understood: the originating intention of the transcendent speaker. This distinction is one that is found already in the teaching of ibn Kullāb[75], even though according to aš-Šahrastānī, the Ḥanbalites consider it to be an innovation (*bid'ah*) introduced in opposition to the consensus by al-Aš'arī[76].

[71] See J. van Ess, *Umar II and his Epistle against the Qadarîya*, in *Abr Nahrain*, 12 (1971), p. 23.

[72] Cf. *Šarḥ al-Iršād*, f. 87ᵛ,16 ff. It is not our intention to enter into a detailed discussion of al-Aš'arī's treatment of this problem here. It is discussed by al-Aš'arī and his followers with considerable nuance and insight. For a general outline of his teaching concerning «God's speaking» and of the Koran as God's speech, see *Muğarrad*, p. 59 ff.

[73] Cf. *Šarḥ al-Iršād*, f. 102ʳ, where al-Aš'arī's *Egyptian Responsa* is cited, *al-Ghunyah*, f. 74ʳ,1 ff., and *Muğarrad*, p. 68 and 207. Vocal speaking is a complex event; cf. *ibid.*, p. 114 and 64. He also distinguishes «the Scripture» (or «the Book») as something that is written, from God's speaking in the strict sense; *ibid.*, p. 63,8 f. See also the citation of ibn 'Abd al-Malik in Ibn 'Asākir, p. 150,15-20 and note the occurrence of the phrase «*al-ḥurūfu wal-'aṣwāt*» in *al-Ḥaṯṯ*, § 2.321.

[74] E.g. *Muğarrad*, p. 192,4 ff. and *Šarḥ al-Iršād*, f. 87,15 f.

[75] Cf. *Maqālāt*, p. 484 f., *Šarḥ al-Iršād*, f. 115ʳ and *Ghunyah*, f. 83ᵛ.

[76] *Nihāyah*, p. 113; on the distinction, see *Milal*, p. 154,1 ff. In the formulation of al-Mutawallī, «We hold that the recitation is the sounds of the reciters and their intonations

Al-Aš'arī does not make this distinction explicitly in *aṯ-Ṯaghr* or in the section of *Luma'* in which he discusses the eternity of God's speaking (§ 27 ff.). It is clearly implied, however, insofar as he holds that sounds and motions are accidents and is certainly to be understood where he argues (*ibid.*, § 45) that «it is impossible that God create His speech in another»[77]. The core of this argument — what is meant by «impossible» — is that the subject term, 'God's speech' refers to something which is eternal, while the predicate term 'is in another' must refer to a created entity, wherefore the proposition is self-contradictory. Sounds and motions exist in material subjects, sc., in the atoms which make up bodies.

That God's essential attribute of speaking is eternal while the sounds made when the text of the Koran is read aloud, like the letters written on the page of the copy, are created, contingent beings, would seeem to be a simple and straightforward sort of distinction. The Ḥanbalites, however, tended to reject it out of hand. Ibn Ḥanbal is reported to have said, «Whoever holds that our voicing of [the Koran] and our oral recitation of it is created, while the Koran is the speaking of God, is a Ǧahmite»[78]. This he states more fully in a letter quoted by ibn Baṭṭa:

> What is in the Cherished Tablet and what is in the copies of the Koran and people's reciting it aloud, however it be recited and however it be described, is God's speaking and is uncreated. Those who say «it is created» are unbelievers in God, the Magnificent, and whoever does not call them unbelievers is himself an unbeliever[79].

*
* *

It would seem apparent from the foregoing that *aṯ-Ṯaghr* and *al-Luma'* are, together with *al-Ḥaṯṯ*, fully consistent in their teaching and that there is no plausible ground, at least from this perspective, to question their being, all three, works of one and the same author. What

and their actions, while what is understood during the recitation is God's speaking...»: p. 30. For a good summary of this thesis see AL-ǦUWAYNĪ, *Luma'*, §§ 12 f.

[77] This is cited in *Ghunyah*, f. 61ʳ and 82ᵛ. It would seem likely that this problem was treated explicitly with respect to the Koran in ibn Fūrak's *Commentary on the Luma'* (cf. *Ghunyah*, f. 72ᵛ,21 ff.), if not in the longer version of the *Luma'* itself.

[78] *Ṭabaqāt*, 1, p. 29,16 f.; cf. also *ibid.*, p. 32,20 f. and p. 343,3.

[79] Cited *ibid.*, p. 342,18-20 (with which cp. the statement of abū Ǧa'far aṭ-Ṭabarī in SOURDEL, p. 194,6-113); see also *Ṭabaqāt*, 1, p. 343,2 ff. and concerning al-Barbahārī, see below. This position is referred to as that of the « *'ahl aẓ-ẓāhir*» e.g., *Šarḥ al-Iršād*, f. 113ᵛ and *Ghunyah*, f. 86ᵛ, on which see n. 20 above). Not all the *ahl al-ḥadīṯ* refused the distinction, however; al-Buḫārī is said to have accepted it (e.g., SUBKĪ, 2, 228 ff., AL-BAYHAQĪ, p. 260,2 ff., and *Šarḥ al-Iršād*, f. 115ʳ) and al-Anṣārī even tries to absolve ibn Ḥanbal of opposing it (*ibid.*; cf. also AL-BAYHAQĪ, p. 265,9 ff.).

we have to do now is to ask how these works may be consistent with the *Ibānah*, by looking at how the several questions we have been discussing are treated there. In doing this two things must be kept in mind: firstly, the circumstances of the writing of the works in question and secondly, the differences between the tradionalist argumentation and that of the *mutakallimīn*.

In ibn abī Ya'lā's *Ṭabaqāt al-ḥanābilah* we read the following:

When al-Aš'arī came to Baghdad he went to al-Barbahārī and began telling him, «I have refuted al-Ǧubbā'ī and abū Hāšim and have shown the error of the Jews and the Christians and the Zoroastrians; I said [thus and so] and they said [thus and so]»; and he went on at length in this vein. When he stopped talking, al-Barbahārī said, «I don't know what it is you have said, neither the short of it nor the long of it. We only recognise what has been said by abū 'Abdallāh Aḥmad ibn Ḥanbal». Al-Aš'arī then left him and wrote the *Ibānah*, but [al-Barbahārī] did not accept it from him[80].

Several things would seem clear from this. Al-Aš'arī expected to receive the approbation and support of the Ḥanbalite master for his defense of orthodox doctrine. His account of this defense and the description of it to al-Barbahārī was doubtless set out as a series of theses outlined somewhat according to the pattern of a *kalām* disputation. This was rejected by al-Barbahārī, following which, to demonstrate his orthodoxy to the Ḥanbalite master, al-Aš'arī composed the *Ibānah* and presented it to him, hoping that this work, written in the style and form of a traditionalist tract, would find acceptance. It too was rejected, however. It would seem evident that it was after this, chagrined and angered by the second, preëmptory rebuff, and taking his clue from the final statement made by al-Barbahārī when he first dismissed him, that al-Aš'arī composed *al-Ḥaṯṯ*, condemning the practice of *taqlīd* in matters of theology and insisting not only on the legitimacy but also on the religious necessity of *kalām*[81]. Whether he wrote it immediately or after

[80] *Ṭabaqāt*, 2, p. 18,11-16; concerning this and the text of the *Ibānah*, see ALLARD, *Opposition*, p. 94 f. and *Problème*, p. 51 ff.

[81] One must assume that ibn abī Ya'lā's report presents the substance of what transpired between al-Aš'arī and al-Barbahārī on these two occasions. Examining the evidence in the broader context which we are here trying to establish, it may be plausible to suggest that al-Aš'arī moved to Baghdad not at the end of his career, as is usually supposed, but quite early in the post-conversion period of his life. *Aṯ-Ṯaghr*, written from Baghdad, is dated 297/909 (see the references in n. 9 above) and, as we shall see, conforms closely enough to what is said in the *Ibānah*, while it appears that the two may differ in a few significant respects from his later, more mature teaching. It would appear that the first encounter with al-Barbahārī could not have taken place very late in the post-conversion period of al-Aš'arī's life for the following reasons as well. Ibn 'Asākir states (p. 127) that al-Aš'arī's works (sc., his writings which contained his «orthodox» *kalām*)

a period of time (during which there may likely have been other confrontations with the followers of ibn Ḥanbal) makes no difference. The address in both the *Ibānah* and of *al-Ḥaṯṯ* is clear: their are directed to the Ḥanbalites and the latter specifically at the intransigent form of Ḥanbalism represented by al-Barbahārī.

With regard to *aṯ-Ṯaghr* and *al-Luma'* we know next to nothing concerning the circumstances of their composition. The former, as was noted earlier, is apparently a very early work of al-Aš'arī's post-conversion period and the latter somewhat later. Both are formally cast as responses to appeals for theological instruction against various heresies (seemingly the Mu'tazila in particular), but these introductory remarks may be largely formal and so of little significance. In any case, they are clearly addressed to an audience who are presumed to find *kalām* reasoning acceptable and enlightening.

The reasoning and argumentation of *kalām* proceeds by means of conceptual and logical analysis of the terms of the questions, as is seen in both *aṯ-Ṯaghr* and *al-Luma'*. This remains true even when, as is often the case in both works, the author employs citations of the Koran as encapsulating his formal argument in terms of an exegesis which is presumed to be known or immediately recognisable to his readers. The basis of this use of the revealed text is explicitly set forth both in *aṯ-Ṯaghr* and in *al-Ḥaṯṯ*. The traditionalists, as witnessed, for example, by ibn Ḥanbal's *Radd 'alā l-Ǧahmiyyah* and ibn Ḫuzayma's *Kitāb at-Tawḥīd*, proceed by a quite different method. They simply amass a great number of citations of the Koran and of hadīths as well as of

had become quite well known and recognised by the year 300/912-3. Now, on the assumption that al-Aš'arī was not altogether naïve, if any notable period had elapsed between his conversion and his unhappy encounter with al-Barbahārī, his new teaching should not only have had time to be well known and discussed in Ḥanbalite circles, but he should have gotten wind of its reception in those circles and so ought to have anticipated Barbahārī's reaction. This, however, he plainly did not do, as is clear in the report. Ibn abī Ya'lā presents al-Aš'arī as approaching the Ḥanbalite master full of enthusiasm for his new-found orthodoxy and fully expecting to find a hearty approbation of his success in refuting the errors of the Mu'tazila and others. It would seem, thus, that no serious traditionalist opposition has as yet developed to al-Aš'arī's «orthodox» *kalām*, or at least none so vocal and public that he had gotten wind of it. Whether or not the *Ibānah* is later than *aṯ-Ṯaghr* we cannot say for sure. In any case, it is to be noted that some elements of *al-Ḥaṯṯ* so closely reflect or parallel statements attributed to al-Barbahārī that it would seem almost certain that the work was composed specifically with al-Barbahārī in view. Ibn Fūrak (*Muǧarrad*, p. 61) cites al-Aš'arī's *Misceleaneous Responsa*, which was composed at Baghdad, as making somewhat conciliatory remarks concerning the intention of «some sheikhs and traditionists» when they talk about the Koran (they don't want to confuse the common folk who can't make formal distinctions), but he continues to insist on the validity and the necessity of making a distinction between the *qirā'ah* and the *maqrū'*.

statements ascribed to various Companions and other «leading authorities of earlier generations» so as to show, by the sheer quantity of authoritative witnesses that what is proposed is to be asserted and is to be expressed according to the words of the texts and the reports. Orthodoxy is to affirm as true the statements cited and the multitude of citations establishes the community's consensus. Seldom, if ever, does one find in these works any formal analysis at all and never any suggestion that in matters of theology distinctions are to be made in formally conceptual terms.

Now, that a tract such as al-Aš'arī's *Ibānah* is written much in the style of a traditionalist tract does not, of itself, indicate that the author necessarily understands the dogmatic assertions made in it to be either entirely or even primarily grounded in the authority of the texts and reports he cites and even less does it prove that he does not consider them subject to further clarification in conceptual terms and to explanation by systematic, theological reflection and in a formal terminology that is not to be found either in the Koran or in the Tradition. It is particularly important to recall that al-Barbahārī did not accept the *Ibānah* from al-Aš'arī. By implication he did not see it as a traditionalist work which he could accept, but recognised it rather as the composition of a man who wished to pose as — and who maybe actually fancied himself to be — an adherent of true tradionalist doctrine though he was not, at least not of the strict observance as defined by the leaders of the Ḥanbalite school. Al-Barbahārī knew al-Aš'arī and his views through personal aquaintance. It is for us to ask what there may be in the *Ibānah* to justify al-Barbahārī's reaction, i.e., what evidence the text may present that the author does not wholeheartedly share the convictions of the Ḥanbalite school.

We may note at the outset one or two conspicuous features of the *Ibānah* which may be taken as indicative of the author's attitude. First, the work contains no condemnation of *kalām*. Al-Aš'arī censures the Mu'tazila for their *taqlīd* to the doctrines and opinions of the masters of their own school (p. 6,21 ff.), but nowhere does he renounce or abjure *kalām* either as such or for his own practice[82]. Nor does he

[82] This is noted by ALLARD, *Opposition*, p. 93 ff.; see also SOURDEL, p. 179 f. A number of arguments contained in the *Ibānah* would, moreover, appear plainly to require, and so implicitly to embody, a formal *kalām* analysis in order to be fully understood. Allard gives an example (*op. cit.*, p. 102). As another we may suggest the argument (p. 20) against the thesis that the statement «He merely says to it 'Be' and it is» does not imply that God's speaking is distinct from His action and therefore is uncreated. The argument is that if the phrase «He merely says to it 'Be'» is simply a figure of speech meaning that God creates the object, then all entities will be properly described by 'God's speaking', since the descriptions given in the Koran are authoritatively sanctioned by God. For its sense and

declare himself in favor of *taqlīd* in matters of theology. This one would certainly expect if al-Aš'arī's conversion from the teaching of the Mu'tazila had been entirely and without reservation to the traditionalism of the Ḥanbalites. In rejecting the *Ibānah* and disassociating himself from al-Aš'arī, al-Barbahārī is simply following his own dictum: "When a man manifests to you any innovation (*bid'ah*) at all, beware of him, for what he hides from you is more than what he shows»[83]. Since al-Aš'arī holds that *kalām* is legitimated and has its foundation in the Koran and the teaching of the Prophet, as we have seen, we should not expect to find him renouncing it here[84].

As we have seen, the Aš'arites universally distinguish between God's eternal «speaking», which is read, recited, and understood (*al-matlūw, al-maqrū', al-mafhūm*) and the temporally contingent action of reading and reciting (*at-tilāwah, al-qirā'ah*) which we perform, i.e., the vocal sounds made by the human reader in forming the syllables that express the eternal meaning. This distinction, we have already seen, is preëmptorily rejected by the Ḥanbalites. In the words of al-Barbahārī, «Any one who says his voicing of the Koran (*lafẓuhu bil-qur'ān*) is created is a Ǧahmite»[85].

The question of the createdness of the Koran is raised in the *Ibānah*. In the introductory section he says simply that «those who hold the Koran to be created are unbelievers» (p. 9 f.), without offering any clarification of what exactly he means by this. Subsequently, however, he takes the problem up once again (p. 30 f.) and there raises the question of the «recitation», though only obliquely. What he does in this latter passage is to reject the use of the expression '*lafẓ*' (uttering, voicing, vocally sounding) as a description of what we do when we read the Koran aloud. One may not speak of «*lafẓu l-qur'ān*», he says, because the verb '*lafaẓa, yalfiẓu*' basically means to eject something from one's mouth, to spit it out, and this is neither semantically appropriate (i.e., it is unseemly to speak thus of the recitation of the Koran) nor is it lexically authorised by the canonical sources whose

consistency the argument here depends on the Aš'arite understanding that the act of creating is itself the being of the entity that is created. If the Koranic «says to it 'Be'» is equivalent to 'creates it', then 'says' = 'creates' here and, since the action of creating is the speaking, the speaking is the being of the entity which is created.

[83] *Ṭabaqāt*, 2, p. 37,23 f. For the Ḥanbalite condemnation of generally, cf. *ibid.*, p. 38 ff. and also 1, p. 241 f. *et alibi*.

[84] Cf. also, AL-AŠ'ARĪ, *Luma'*, § 10 f., concerning which see the remarks of al-Ǧuwaynī in *Šāmil* (1969), p. 287,9 ff. (where read *yaḏkuruhu* for *tarakahu* in line 12 and *al-kalām* for *kalāmanā* in line 13 with *Tehran University Central Library MS*, no. 350).

[85] *Ṭabaqāt*, 2, p. 30,1.

usage is normative for religious language. This is all he has to say on the subject. Within the context one understands that the use of the verbs '*talā, yatlū*' and '*qara'a, yaqra'u*' to refer to and describe the reading of the Koran is perfectly valid, being sanctioned by the usage of the Koran itself. What he does here, in effect, is simply to reject the use of the word '*lafẓ*' to designate what we do when we recite the Koran and so also as an expression for one of the terms of the distinction between the act of reciting and what is recited. He says nothing, in short, that would suggest that the distinction itself is to be rejected, as is done by the Ḥanbalites, and moreover leaves the words '*talā, yatlū, tilāwah*' and '*qara'a, yaqra'u, qirā'ah*' as words by which to formulate the distinction[86]. This should be sufficient indication, if any be needed, that the proximate context in which the *Ibānah* is to be read and interpreted is not that of the writings and teachings of the Ḥanbalites but rather that which is supplied by al-Aš'arī's two available dogmatic works, *aṯ-Ṯaghr* and *al-Luma'*, together with the accounts of his teaching presented in the works of later Aš'arites.

Against the Mu'tazila al-Aš'arī asserts in the *Ibānah* that God has «hands». In the introductory section he simply states the thesis (p. 9,4 f.) citing Q 38,75 and 5,64 and adding «*bi-lā kayf*», which, as we have seen is to say that 'hands' in these texts is not to be understood in any anthropomorphic sense. Subsequently (p. 37 f.) he argues the thesis from Q 38,75, just as he does in *aṯ-Ṯaghr* (p. 96 f., cited above) and as there remarks here also (p. 38,18) that these «hands» cannot be bodily members[87]. The doctrine of the *Ibānah* with regard to God's «hands» is, in brief, fully in accord with that of *aṯ-Ṯaghr* and is stated in a way that would not likely be found acceptable to al-Barbahārī and his followers, since it goes beyond the words of the text so as to clarify what is asserted (see n. 31 above).

Finally, al-Aš'arī mentions also texts which describe God as «going» and «descending» (p. 11,5 ff. and p. 33 f.) and says that he holds these verses and reports to be true (*ṣaddaqa*) as transmitted. In neither of these passages does he include an explicit statement of *tanzīh*, i.e., a denial that God can have place and so be subject to local movement. To do so, however, would be redundant, since immediately before this,

[86] Cf. also *Muǧarrad*, p. 60 f., where the use of '*lafaẓa, yalfiẓu*' is similarly rejected.

[87] At the same time he rejects the thesis of al-Ǧubbā'ī that «hands» in these texts is to be taken as equivalent to '*ni'matān*'. In translating *al-Ibānah*, p. 9,4 f. and *Maqālāt*, p. 290,5 f. (cited below), McCarthy, *Theology*, p. 237b, § 9 follows Wensinck and renders «*bi-lā kayf*» by «without asking questions»; as we have seen, however, the expression has other, quite formal connotations for al-Aš'arī and his followers.

in the course of the discussion of «the Throne verse» against the thesis of Ǧahm that God is «in every place» (p. 32 f.), he insists that to describe God as having location in any sense at all «implies that He be below whatever is above Him and above whatever is below Him, *and this is what is impossible and self-contradictory*». The sense of the final phrase (*al-muḥālu l-mutanāqiḍ*) is that if a term which refers to God is the subject and the predicate is either explicitly or implicitly equivalent to 'is located in …', then the proposition is self-contradictory. The language and the intention here are those of *kalām*[88].

Several parallels may be worth noting. Al-Qušayrī mentions the verses which describe God as «coming» and «descending» in his *Luma'* (p. 60,5 ff.) and, like al-Aš'arī in the *Ibānah*, says, «We entrust the knowledge of this to God», but leaves no place for any anthropomorphic reading of the text[89]. The position is characteristically stated by al-Mutawallī where he notes (p. 13,21 f.) that

Our fellows [sc., the school of al-Aš'arī] have two ways of dealing with this; one is to avoid interpretation (*ta'wīl*) and to believe [the texts] as they are presented. (Belief in them is valid even though one does not know their meaning). This way is safer. Some of our fellows, however, choose to interpret them.

He goes on then to note that for his part he prefers the former course and speaks (p. 14,8 ff.) of

avoiding the interpretation of these verses while believing in the literal truth of the texts (*ma'a l-'īmāni bi-ẓawāhirihā*) and believing (*al-i'tiqād*) at the same time

[88] The formal implications of this passage are more extensive than may be apparent on a superficial reading. For al-Aš'arī, any true description of God asserts either (1) His «Self» or (2) an essential (eternal) attribute of His «Self» or (3) the existence of an entity which He has created (sc., *ṣifatu fi'l*). Accordingly, to say that 'sits in majesty' refers to some attribute of God means that it refers either to some essential attribute or to «an action attribute» (a created entity which exists as an action of God's). When he suggests, then, that 'sits in majesty' has to have a meaning (sc., a referent) «which is particular to the Throne and not to anything else» (p. 32,23), al-Aš'arī plainly indicates that he understands «sitting in majesty» here as an action attribute, i.e., a property (*'araḍ, ma'nā*) created by God in the outermost heaven. That he did so interpret '*al-istiwā*'', cf. AL-BAYHAQĪ, p. 410,2, AL-BAGHDĀDĪ, p. 113,3 ff., *Šāmil* (1969), p. 555 f. and the citation of ibn 'Abd al-Malik in IBN 'ASĀKIR, p. 150,13 f. Others took *al-istiwā'* to be an essential attribute; see generally, AL-BAYHAQĪ, p. 409 f., AL-MUTAWALLĪ, p. 13 f., *Šāmil*, *loc. cit.* and *Šarḥ al-Iršād*, f. 143^{v} ff.; on the interpretation of these verses, see also *Ta'wīl*, f. 131^{v} ff. and *Bayān* (1943), p. 193 ff. (where read *at-tamakkun* for *at-tamkīn* at p. 193,7), where the author argues against ibn Ḫuzayma's treatment of them (*at-Tawḥīd*, p. 101 ff.). Al-Qušayrī cites ḏū n-Nūn al-Miṣrī as holding that '*al-istiwā*'' describes God essentially: «God's sitting in majesty on the Throne: He asserts the reality of His essential being and denies His [being in] a place» (*Risālah*, 1, p. 58,4 ff.). We have thus interpretations which refer this description to all of the three possible categories of descriptions of God.

[89] *Luma'*, p. 60,17-20, translated above, n. 37. Ibn Ḥanbal rejects such language outright as «Ǧahmite»; cf. *Radd*, p. 105,9-12.

that He is not in every place.... We avoid interpretation and take the position that we believe (*i'tiqād*) in the text as presented while believing (*'īmān*) that the Truth (He is exalted) transcends place (*munazzahun 'ani l-makān*).

As we have seen, to hold that the text is in some way literally true and to take it so «without interpretation» is not to avoid all clarification by refusing even to assert that it may not mean what the words would mean literally in ordinary usage when employed to talk about the beings presented in our normal experience. For al-Aš'arī and his followers, God transcends place absolutely; this is what it means to read these verses «without any how»[90]. In sum, al-Aš'arī and his followers, while insisting on the truth of the Koran and the Sunna and while feeling themselves fully bound by the truth of these texts, simply do not mean the same thing the Ḥanbalites mean when they talk of avoiding interpretation and of accepting the literal truth of the text as presented.

It would appear to be clear, then, that if one reads the *Ibānah*, as we must, in the context of *at-Taghr* and *al-Luma'*, al-Barbahārī's rejection of it as basically non-traditionalist is well justified; there is in it nothing which is in conflict with these two works and, accordingly, nothing which conflicts with *al-Ḥatt*. Differences of form there certainly are between the *Ibānah* and the other works, but allowing for this there is no evidence in the texts on the basis of which to question al-Aš'arī's having written both the *Ibānah* and *al-Ḥatt*, and perhaps, moreover, to have written them at approximately the same time.

* * *

Near the end of the first part of his *Maqālāt*, al-Aš'arī introduces a section in which he summarises «the position of the *'aṣḥāb al-ḥadīṯ* and the *'ahl as-sunnah*»[91], at the end of which he says (p. 297,7-9),

[90] Thus also abū Sulaymān al-Ḫaṭṭābī says that «the only people who find such traditions repugnant are those who construe them analogously (*yaqīs*) with the local descending that we experience, which is a descending from higher to lower and a transference form above to below; but this is an attribute of bodies and corporeal individuals» (cited in AL-BAYHAQĪ, p. 453,15 ff.). The Aš'arites cite a tradition according to which 'Alī b. abī Ṭālib said, «One does not say 'where' of Him Who whered the where and one does not say 'how' of Him Who howed the how ...» (*al-laḏī 'ayyana l-'ayna lā yuqālu lahū 'anya wal-laḏī kayyafa l-kayfa lā yuqālu lahū kayfa* ...), cited in AL-FŪRAKĪ, f. 11r,2 f. and *Guhnyah*, f. 8v,18 f.

[91] P. 290-297 (translated in MCCARTHY, *Theology*, p. 236-254 and KLEIN, p. 31-35). This is sometimes referred to as an *'aqīdah* (McCarthy calls it a «creed»). I should suggest, however, that in the general context it is more properly viewed not as a summary of their doctrine as a whole, but simply as an outline of what is distinctive in the doctrine of the traditionalists; on this see below.

This is the sum of what they command and observe and view as right. We hold and follow their position which we have presented. Our help is in God alone; He is our sufficiency and the best of patrons. We pray for His help; in Him we trust and to Him is our return.

Now, whereas there is no problem in seeing the basic consistency of al-Aš'arī's teaching as it is presented in the works we have looked at thus far and in the reports of his followers, there are difficulties in integrating some of the positions stated here in the *Maqālāt* coherently with what we find in the other works. The basic problem may be seen by reviewing briefly what he says here with regard to the questions we have been using to illustrate his teaching.

Regarding God's «hands», the position outlined in the *Maqālāt* states simply (p. 290,5 f.) that He has them «*bi-lā kayf*», citing Q 38,75 and 5,64. Given the context, i.e., since he states here that he is reporting the doctrine of the traditionalists, there may be some question as to how one should understand '*bi-lā kayf*'. Prima facie there is no basis on which to assume that he means by this phrase to go beyond what is found in the works of the traditionalists.

When he introduces the texts which describe God as «coming» and «descending» (p. 294 f.), again he cites hadîth and the Koran, adding that where there is a dispute one should entrust the question «to God and to the Apostle» (Q 4,59). To this, however, he adds that «they [sc., the traditionalists] hold that it is right to follow the leading religious authorities of the earlier generation and that they not introduce into their religious doctrine innovations which God has not permitted» (p. 295,4 f.) He does not, to be sure, state in such uncompromising terms as do the Ḥanbalites whom we cited earlier that *taqlīd* is the rule which one must follow without any deviation, but nonetheless the statement he makes does not seem to accord with the position taken in *al-Ḥaṯṯ* and perhaps not with that of *aṯ-Ṯaghr* either.

Concerning the Koran, the matter is more complex. He says (p. 292,9-11),

They hold that the Koran is God's speaking and is uncreated. What they have to say with regard to systematic discussion (*al-kalām*) concerning *al-waqf* and the voicing (*al-lafẓ*)[92] is this: those who hold the thesis of the voicing or that

[92] This passage is translated in WATT, *Formative Period*, p. 284 f. as well as in MCCARTHY, *Theology*, p. 241a, § 22 and (poorly) in KLEIN, p. 32, § VIII. By «*al-waqf*» he refers to a position which deliberately refuses to say whether or not the Koran is or is not created. «*Al-lafẓ*» is ostensibly a neutral term meaning oral recitation [of the Koran], but «those who hold the thesis of the voicing» (*man qāla bil-lafẓ*) here is equivalent to '*al-lafẓiyyah*' and refers to a group who held that the oral recitation of the sacred text is

one should take no position [regarding the question of whether or not the Koran is created] are innovators in their view. One says neither that the voicing of the Koran is created nor that it is uncreated.

This, on the surface at least, does not seem to conform to what we know of al-Aš'arī's post-conversion teaching concerning the oral recitation of the Koran. Again, one should keep in mind that most likely here, as in the rest of the section, he is not employing a formal vocabulary of his own but follows rather the usage of his traditionalist source or sources. (He speaks in his own voice only at the end of the section.) An analogous formulation is found in a short work of abū Ǧa'far aṭ-Ṭabarī (d. 310/922-3), in which he cites «a group of our fellows whose names I do not recall» as reporting that ibn Ḥanbal held a position to the effect that «whoever says 'My oral recitation of the Koran is created' is a Ǧahmite and whoever says 'It is not created' is an innovator»[93].

created (for the condemnation of whom by the Ḥanbalites see the text cited in n. 78 f. and 85 above as well as *Ṭabaqāt*, 1, p. 32,20 f. and p. 343,2 f., where the doctrine of the createdness of the *lafẓ* is associated with «those who suspend judgement» concerning the createdness of the Koran; on these disputes generally see WATT, *Formative Period*, p. 280-285). In this and analogous contexts '*al-lafẓ*' thus generally carries the connotation that the recitation is created and it is against this background — against the condemnation of the doctrine of the Lafẓiyyah — that al-Aš'arī rejects the use of the expression outright (see the discussion of *Ibānah*, p. 30 f. above). It seems, however, that despite these connotations, some of the *'ahl al-ḥadīṯ* nonetheless employed '*al-lafẓ*' alongside '*al-qirā'ah*' as a neutral term to designate the oral recitation of the Koran (cf. e.g., *Maqālāt*, p. 292,10 f. and 602,9 f.). The history of these terms would seem to have been something like this: '*Qur'ān*' is taken by some authorities as a grammatical and (in origin) lexical equivalent of '*qirā'ah*' (e.g. AL-FARRĀ', *Ma'ānī l-Qur'ān, ad 20,114 and cf.* AL-BAYHAQĪ, p. 272,8 ff.); both words, thus, as *maṣdars* or *nomina actionis* for '*qara'a, yaqra'u*', may ambivalently designate either the text as such (i.e., the text as original and so as God's speaking) or its recitation by a human reader. In order to state the distinction of the sounds which are the oral recitation of the Koran from God's (original and eternal) speaking, then, '*al-lafẓ*' was chosen as an unambivalent expression for the latter term. When the conservative traditionalists insist, without further explanation and clarification, that «the *qur'ān* is the word of God and is uncreated» the statement is, and is deliberately left, unclear as to whether or not it means to assert that the recitation as well as the original «speaking of God» which is expressed in it is uncreated. Pushed on the point when the expression '*al-lafẓ*' was introduced in order to force the distinction, some refused to take a position (e.g., al-Barbahārī, cited in n. 85 above), while others said (since the recitation is the *qur'ān*: '*al-qirā'ah*' = '*al-qur'ān*') that it is uncreated (e.g. *Maqālāt*, p. 602,9 f.) As we have seen, Ibn Kullāb, along with others, restated the distinction using '*al-qirā'ah*' and '*al-maqrū*'', but the Ḥanbalites went on refusing to come clean on the question.

[93] SOURDEL, p. 198,9-11. This work is not properly speaking either «a profession of faith» or *'aqīdah*, since it deals with only a limited number of disputed questions which are not given the larger form of a general creed. It should be noted that in this work aṭ-Ṭabarī says (p. 198,13) that ibn Ḥanbal is «the imam who should be followed». Aṭ-Ṭabarī's general attitude, like that of abū Sa'īd ad-Dārimī (a Šāfi'ite), is plainly more

Whether or not the attribution of this formula to ibn Ḥanbal is valid or not we cannot say; I know of no such statement regarding the question by any of the Ḥanbalites of the period and suspect that it might not be acceptable to most of them. In any case, the formula is reminiscent of that employed by ibn Kullāb and adopted by al-Aš'arī with regard to God's eternal attributes, i.e., that «one says neither that they are He nor that they are other than He»[94]. Like this latter formula, that cited by aṭ-Ṭabarī is no doubt based on definitions and distinctions made in a formal analysis of the terms. Presumably the distinction underlying it is something like that made by ibn Qutayba in his *al-Iḫtilāf fī l-lafẓ war-radd 'alā l-ğahmiyyah wal-mušabbihah*, according to which '*al-qirā'ah*' is an equivocal expression, employed both to name the human action of reciting the Koran and to name the speech of God which is recited[95]. Even to make this distinction would doubtless agitate most of al-Aš'arī's (and aṭ-Ṭabarī's) Ḥanbalite contemporaries. Where this distinction may fit within the development of al-Aš'arī's post-conversion thought we shall see later.

Finally, then, he seems to speak ill of *kalām* in this section of the *Maqālāt*, even if only obliquely. He says (p. 294,4-8).

[The traditionalists] abhor dialectical disputation and contention concerning religious doctrine (*ad-dīn*) and quarreling about [God's] determination of human affairs and disputing formally about those matters about which dialecticians dispute and about which they contend with regard to their religious doctrine. [The traditionalists choose, rather,] to concede the truth of the valid reports and what is presented by the traditions which are transmitted by trustworthy men, one upright man from another, until this reaches the Apostle of God (God's prayer and peace be upon him); they say neither «how?» nor «why?», for this is an innovation.

The statement about conceding the truth (*taslīm*) of authenticated

conservative than that of the Aš'arites (cf. e.g., the citation in n. 31 above), but nonetheless is less rigid than that of the Ḥanbalites. He explicitly acknowledges the actually of new questions (*ḥawādiṯ*) not treated by the Prophet and the Companions and speaks of the obligation of learned men to «dispel the gloom of darkness» from the ignorant by means of the superior knowledge they have «either by means of a hadîth or by means of systematic reasoning» (*'immā bi-ḥadīṯin wa-'immā bi-naẓar*: p. 193). This is precisely the argument of al-Aš'arī in *al-Ḥaṯṯ* (§ 2.325). Sourdel notes (p. 177) that aṭ-Ṭabarī at the time of his death was himself condemned by the Ḥanbalites.

[94] For the origins and the early history of this formula see J. VAN ESS, *Ibn Kullāb und die miḥna*, in *Oriens*, 18-19 (1967), p. 109 ff.

[95] Ed. AL-KAWTHARĪ, Cairo, 1349, p. 63,7 ff. (Concerning the ambivalence of '*al-qirā'ah*' see n. 92 above.) In this he also indicates, though without spelling out so delicate a matter, that '*al-qur'ān*' is also ambivalent. Ibn Qutayba likely avoids the expression '*al-lafẓ*' because of its association with the teaching of individuals commonly held to be unorthodox by the traditionalists whom he follows.

reports is fully compatible with the known teaching of al-Aš'arī. It is stated explicitly in *aṯ-Ṯaghr*, as we have seen. Further, the position here presented condemns formal, dialectical disputation (*al-ǧadal, al-munāẓarah*) about theological questions, but does not condemn, even by implication, the formal use of systematic reasoning (i.e., the valid role of rational reflection) in matters of fundamental theology. (The immediate context here, it should be noted, concerns obscure or problematic verses and hadîths.). The absence of any specific reference to *qiyās* or to *kalām* is conspicuous[96].

From the foregoing it would appear that the traditionalist position presented here by al-Aš'arī is not meant to reflect the attitude of the radical Ḥanbalites but is, on the contrary, formulated, if not after, then at least so as to include the more reasoned and more moderate approach of individuals such as al-Buḫārī (d. 256/870), ibn Qutayba (d. 276/889), and abū Ǧa'far aṭ-Ṭabarī (d. 310/922-3), and of the later abū Sulaymān al-Ḫaṭṭābī (d. 388/998). Even so, what are we to say about al-Aš'arī's unequivocal acceptance of this traditionalist position as his own? How does it fit with what we know of his thought from his other works and from the reports of his followers?

It is generally recognised that the work we know as al-Aš'arī's *Maqālāt* is made up of two originally distinct treatises[97]. There is good internal evidence which points to the second part's having been composed after the author's conversion and some reason to infer that

[96] Cf., for example, the condemnation of *qiyās* by al-Barbahārī in *Ṭabaqāt*, 2, p. 29,4 and 14. Allard suggests (*Opposition*, p. 93 ff.) that the use of *qiyās* is at the very core of the Ḥanbalite opposition to al-Aš'arī. Probably because of the disapprobation of *qiyās* in traditionalist circles, the Aš'arites, unlike some of the Mu'tazilites, do not commonly employ the word '*qiyās*' to speak of their own reasoning. Whatever may be the origin of the distinction, al-Ǧuwaynī, among others, seems to take *qiyās* as a kind of reasoning which assimilates God's attributes to those of creatures (note the use of the word in n. 90 above) and so rejects it while insisting on the validity of drawing inferences by logical rule from what is known of the phenomenal world (*aš-šāhid*) to the nature of the transcendent (*al-ghā'ib*), cf. the citation in *Ghunyah*, f. 20ʳ,19-21 and for a formal discussion of the question see, e.g., *Šāmil* (1969), p. 412-420 and (1981), p. 61-72. Note also that in this passage al-Aš'arī avoids the expression '*al-kalāmu fī d-dīn*', a more general expression which contextually might be heard as equivalent to the somewhat more specific '*al-munāẓaratu fī d-dīn*'; concerning the semantic range of '*al-kalām*' in this and analogous contexts see the analysis in *al-Ḥaṯṯ*, p. 115 ff.

[97] See Makdisi, II, p. 26 ff. and Allard, *Problème*, p. 58 ff. The second part begins at p. 301 of Ritter's edition. Although the two sections are largely redundant, they are organised according to different principles. Allard thinks that the last major section of the second part (beginning p. 483) may represent a third, distinct work, but this would seem to be unnecessary if one consider carefully the organisation of the second half of the overall work. I shall refer to the two parts of the work in what follows as *Maqālāt*, I and *Maqālāt*, II.

the first part was likely completed prior to that time[98]. On this basis Fr. Allard suggested that the paragraph in which al-Aš'arī proclaims his adherence to the teaching of the *'aṣḥāb al-ḥadīṯ*, if not the whole section dealing with their teaching, was added after the work had been completed. Whether or not the whole section is an addition, there is very good reason to suppose that the work was substantially complete by the time of al-Aš'arī's conversion from Mu'tazilism and to conclude, therefore, that his declaration of adherence to the traditionalist position he outlines was made at or about the time of his definitive rejection of the theology of al-Ǧubbā'ī and the Mu'tazila.

If we accept this dating for the passage of the *Maqālāt* that is in question and for al-Aš'arī's statement of assent to it, we should be able to place the traditionalist position appropriated there plausibly within the overall development of his «orthodox» or post-conversion thought in roughly the following way. The statement of the doctrine of «the masters of the tradition and the people of the Sunna» presented in *Maqālāt*, I was originally formulated not as al-Aš'arī's own, newly adopted view, but as a faithful recording of what the traditionalists generally held. It is not, thus an extraneous intrusion into *Maqālāt*, I, but belongs integrally to the general plan of the work[99]. That the section maintains a somewhat moderate tone and avoids the more radical positions and vehement rhetoric of the leading Ḥanbalite masters of the day reflects this desire to present an objective summary of the basic views and tenets of the traditionalists as a whole rather than of a single faction who were wholly intolerant of any deviation from the detail of their own teaching and practice in matters of theology. It is to this general or common traditionalism that he states his allegiance. The unity of the community's belief which is founded in the teaching of the Koran and the Sunna is contrasted to the clash of conflicting theories and opinions which, formed and argued without the benefit of divine guidance, reflect the inevitable diversity of merely human opinions and judgements[100]. The summary thus condemns (and by implication al-

[98] See Allard, *Problème*, p. 66 ff.

[99] It is thus that no such section is found in *Maqālāt*, II, since the work is organised not according to «sects», schools and individual thinkers, but by topics and questions.

[100] Ibn Qutayba's principal grief against the *mutakallimīn* (sc., the Mu'tazila) is that relying, each of them on his own reasoning and judgement, they neither elucidate or even come to the truth (not even to a common view of it), but rather perpetuate and propagate within the Muslim community that natural conflict of disparate opinions concerning God, the world, and the good of human action which the revelation should reduce to harmony (*Ta'wīl muḫtalif al-ḥadīṯ*, p. 12-14 and p. 46, 7 ff.). The sense of that unity of belief which is to be achieved through the guidance of the Koran and the teaching of the Prophet should be seen as perhaps the primary factor in al-Aš'arī's conversion to the traditionalist creed.

Aš'arī accepts the condemnation of) the aggressive and contentious dialectic of the Mu'tazila without renouncing the use of formal (i.e. *kalām*) reasoning altogether. Similarly, he states that one is bound by the teaching of the great religious teachers (*al-'a'immah*) of the earlier generations without insisting on *taqlīd* as a formal principle to which one is obligated in matters of theology.

Al-Aš'arī, thus, as is clear from his own works and the testimony of the Aš'arites of the following generations, was converted from the dogma of his master, al-Ǧubbā'ī and that of the Mu'tazila generally to that of the tradition. What this required of him was a basic reëvaluation and reïnterpretation of the Koran and the Tradition. At one level it involved a set of fundamental theological propositions: he rejected, e.g., the proposition 'God speaking is created' and affirmed the contrary, as also he rejected the notion that the basic principles of ethics are known intuitively and are absolute for all intelligent agents and that they are therefore binding on God as well as on men and asserted that the ethical valuations of human actions are grounded unconditionally in God's command and prohibition. On another level it involved his rejection of the basic Mu'tazilite assumption that autonomous human reason is the original and primary source of theological knowledge and the arbiter of the truth of theological propositions and his acceptance of the Koran and the teaching of the Prophet as the original and primary sources of theological knowledge. Though he found this new evaluation of the canonical sources and his revised reading of them in the teaching of the *'ahl al-ḥadīṯ*, it was to the authority of the sources themselves that he felt himself primarily bound, not to that of their traditionalist interpreters. That he took as his own the basic dogma of the traditionalists does not have to mean that he became a traditionalist in the Ḥanbalite sense. It is conspicuous that none of our sources reports anything about his having studied under a traditionalist master. His subsequent theological exposition of the dogmatic content of the traditionalist creed would seem, indeed, to have been chiefly influenced by the teaching of ibn Kullāb (d. 240/854)[101], whose system of formal analysis and method of reasoning were essentially identical to that in which al-Aš'arī had been schooled while a disciple of al-Ǧubbā'ī. We cannot know to what extent, if any, the teaching of ibn Kullāb and his

[101] This was doubtless available directly through the teaching of ibn Kullāb's disciples who, though apparently neither very numerous nor very prominent, were to be found in Basra and elsewhere. They are cited in *Maqālāt* and the active significance of the school's teaching appears to have continued into the time of abū Isḥāq al-Isfarā'īnī.

followers may have contributed directly to al-Aš'arī's conversion, but it is plain enough that, if it was not an antecedent factor in his conversion, it at least furnished the foundation and core of his thought once he began to reflect systematically on the dogma which he had appropriated in his conversion. However this might be, al-Aš'arī's conversion was, as he states in the *Maqālāt*, to the teaching of the traditionalists; it was not to that of ibn Kullāb. It was to the teaching of the Koran and the Prophet as witnessed by the Muslim community that he turned. The publicly recognised bearers of the authenticated teaching of the Prophet are the traditionists (*'ahl al-ḥadīṯ*) and it is they who constitute the core and leadership of the traditionalists. Ibn Kullāb is simply a theologian, a *mutakallim*, i.e., an interpreter who clarified the teaching that is originally contained and expressed in the Koran and the Sunna. To have bound himself to the teaching of a theologian would, in effect, have been to have changed allegiance merely, not to have undergone a conversion. Having rejected the Mu'tazilite *taqlīd* to their masters, it would have been simply to replace one *taqlīd* with another. Al-Aš'arī's change of heart was more radical than this and, being more radical, he could not, at least in principle, bind himself to the theological doctrine of the Ḥanbalites or to that of any other school.

There may well have been a brief period, including no doubt that which led up to this definitive, public break with the Mu'tazila, during which al-Aš'arī would have been shy of formal theological reasoning and so would more or less have limited himself, at least formally and explicitly, to the general teaching of the leading traditionists, particularly the followers of aš-Šāfi'ī and ibn Ḥanbal. We find him, thus, going no further in *Maqālāt*, I than to state his adherence to the position which he reports in the routine course of the work[102]. Though he was a highly trained and intellectually sophisticated theologian, naturally inclined to seek conceptual clarification of theological statements, it would inevitably take some time, however brief, after having rejected both the content and the foundation of views acquired and refined over years of study, for him to find an independant voice of his own in which to set forth and explain his new position formally. When he began to articulate his own theology, then, it was along the lines

[102] Even if al-Aš'arī had begun to work out his own views, this would have no public status as one of the «doctrines» (*maqālāt*) of the Muslims and so would not appear in *Maqālāt*. I take it, however, that if he had made any progress in the elaboration of his own theology as it was to develop, he would not have subscribed so unequivocally to the entire position which he outlines at the end *Maqālāt*, I.

laid down by ibn Kullāb[103]. With this he acquired an ever greater independance from the teaching of the more radical traditionalist masters. Evidence for this is found even in the few questions that we have examined.

In the earliest period of his conversion al-Aš'arī held that God has an attribute (or attributes) called «hands» in the revelation, though this attribute is not to be thought of a consisting of bodily members. For this he cites in *aṯ-Ṯaghr* Q 5,64 as well as 38,75. Later he came to interpret 'hands' in the former verse as an extended use of the word, contextually employed to refer to God's power. Subsequently, however, he ceased to be convinced that any of the texts has to be read as asserting a «revealed attribute»[104].

So too with the matter of the oral recitation of the Koran. In *Maqālāt*, I al-Aš'arī subscribes to a view which says neither that it is created nor that it is uncreated. Most likely he understood this on the basis of a distinction made, as we have seen, by ibn Qutayba. Subsequently he ceased to follow the practice of the more rigid traditionalists who, in formulating their dogmatic theses concerning the Koran stadfastly refused to analyse the subject term; recognising two distinct lexemes in '*qur'ān*', the one equivalent to '*qirā'ah*' and the other to '*maqrū*'', he abandoned the «neither created nor uncreated» thesis and took up the position of ibn Kullāb, which he further elaborated.

Though formal *kalām* reasoning played a central role in the progressive development of al-Aš'arī's theology, he never gave up his central belief in the divine authority of the Koran and the Sunna. At no point, however, did he bind himself uncritically to the authority of any school's or any individual's particular interpretation of the sources and of the basic teaching which he found in the revealed sources. Having freed himself from the authority of the masters of the Basrian Mu'tazila, he was not about to enter into intellectual bondage to a new master. In reply, then, to al-Barbahārī's insistence on unquestioned conformity to the views of ibn Ḥanbal, al-Aš'arī insists in *al-Ḥaṯṯ* that

[103] Similarly he adopted from another context the notion of «performance» (*kasb*) as distinguished from «action» strictly speaking and made use of it in order to work out the logic of the ontological status of voluntary human actions as events created by God.

[104] That he read 'hands' as an equivalent of 'power' in every case is not certain. There is on the other hand, no evidence that he any where read it as an equivalent of 'blessing' as was done by his former master for Q 5,64 and elsewhere. (That some Aš'arites did read it so far some verses see above, n. 61.) We may note here that 'Abd al-Ǧabbār (*al-Mughnī*, 7, p. 223) takes the expression '*bi-yadayya*' in Q 38,75 as simply rhetorical emphasis (*ta'kīd*) for the preceding «*ḫalaqtu*»; this may represent al-Ǧubbā'ī's exegesis of the verse, but this is uncertain.

in matters of dogma one *taqlīd* is no more admirable and no more serviceable to the community than another and that, moreover, none is authorised either by the Koran or by the teaching of the Prophet, while formal theological reasoning (*kalām*), on the other hand, is not only authorised but is necessary to the religious life of the community.

Al-Aš'arī's achievement is that he established a system of theology (*kalām*) that was doctrinally bound to the tradition: one in which the basic dogmas (the *'uṣūl*) recognised by the general consensus of the majority of sunnî Muslims who were formally educated in the religious sciences were accepted as given and, most importantly, as originally and primarily given in the Koran and the Sunna. Having the conceptual and logical discipline of *kalām*, the system furnished a theoretical framework in which traditional dogma could be reflected on systematically, rigorously formulated and analysed in such a way as to give it cognitive clarity and logical consistency; and thereby too it supplied the requisite elements for an effective apologetic and polemic against the opponents of sunnî orthodoxy. The formal elements of al-Aš'arī's *kalām*, though to some extent modified and adapted, were drawn, almost all of them, from earlier thinkers. The critical contribution of al-Aš'arī himself would seem, thus, not to much to have been that he brought these elements together into a new, systematic whole, important as this may be, but rather that he tied this formally elaborated system directly to the Scripture and the Tradition. That is to say, he presented his *kalām* as rooted in the Koran and the *Sunna* and argued its bond to these sources — its authorisation by them and its conformity to their essential teaching[105] — with sufficient conviction that the system came to be accepted by a significant number of traditionalist scholars. The need for a formal, systematic theology in the service of conservative, sunnî orthodoxy was evident to many and the trend towards its formation already under way. In the persecution of their

[105] This is argued explicitly and at length in both *aṯ-Ṯaghr* and *al-Ḥaṯṯ* and is plainly to be understood in many passages of *al-Luma'* where premises or arguments are stated in the form of quotations from the Koran which are to be understood and analysed in the formal and systematic terms of *kalām*. We should also note here that one finds in the *K. at-Tawḥīd* of al-Māturīdī no evidence of any such concerted effort to establish and maintain the foundation of theological theses and arguments directly in the Koran and the Tradition as there is in the writings of al-Aš'arī. Being a Ḥanafite and addressing a Ḥanafite audience, al-Māturīdī would feel no pressing need to do this. Furthermore the way al-Māturīdī cites and employs the statements and theses of other writers, both in *at-Tawḥīd* and in his Koran Commentary would be out of place in the writing of al-Aš'arī, given the latter's insistence on the relationship which *kalām* must have to the Koran and the Sunna if it is legitimately and efficaciously to serve its necessary function in the religious and intellectual life of the Muslim community.

founder under the *miḥnah*, the Ḥanbalite school had, so to speak, suffered a trauma which would largely preclude their acceptance and adoption of any system of *kalām*. It was, therefore, within the non-Ḥanbalite schools that the Aš'arite theology was received, taken up, and cultivated, as it attracted large numbers of adherents among the Mālikites and the Šāfi'ites. Both schools claim al-Aš'arī as one of their own. For the latter, his theology came soon to be so widely taught and accepted as to constitute what might be regarded as in effect the official theology of the school[106]. Al-Aš'arī, in sum, succeeded in creating a sort of traditionalist *kalām* which, although never perhaps accepted by all traditionalist scholars — not even universally in the Mālikī and the Šāfi'ī schools — came nevertheless to be the most important and influential tradition of systematic theology in Sunni Islam.

REFERENCES

ALLARD, *Opposition* — M. ALLARD, *En quoi consiste l'opposition faite à al-Aš'arī par ses contemporains hanbalites*, in *REI*, 18 (1960), p. 93 ff.

ALLARD, *Problème* — M. ALLARD, *Le problème des attributs divins dans la doctrine d'al-Ash'arî et de ses premiers grands disciples*, Beyrouth, 1965.

AL-AŠ'ARĪ, *al-Luma'* — ABŪ L-ḤASAN AL-AŠ'ARĪ, *al-Luma' fī r-radd 'alā ahl az-zaygh wal-bida'*, edited in MCCARTHY, *Theology*, p. 1-83.

AL-BAGHDĀDĪ, *Uṣūl* — 'ABD AL-QĀHIR AL-BAGHDĀDĪ, *Uṣūl ad-dīn*, Istanbul, 1346/1928.

Bayān (1941) — ABŪ BAKR IBN FŪRAK, *Bayān muškil al-aḥādīṯ, Auswahl nach den Handschriften von Leipzig, London, und dem Vatican*, ed. and tr. R. KÖBERT (*Analecta Orientalia*, 22), Rome, 1941.

Bayān (1943) — IBN FŪRAK, *K. muškil al-ḥadīṯ*, Hyderabad, 1943 (this edition contains only a much abridged version of the

[106] It would seem likely that the seemingly more pervasive adoption of al-Aš'arī's theology by the Šāfi'ites than by the Mālikites may be in part due to the educational systems. Concerning the organisation of the educational system see G. MAKDISI, *The Rise of Colleges*, Edinburgh, 1981.

	authors's introduction, which is published in its complete form by Köbert).
al-Bayhaqī	Abū Bakr al-Bayhaqī, *al-Asmā' waṣ-ṣifāt*, Cairo, 1358.
ad-Dārimī	Abū Sa'īd ad-Dārimī, *ar-Radd 'alā l-ğahmiyyah*, ed. G. Vitestam, Lund/Leiden, 1960.
al-Fūrakī	Abū Bakr al-Fūrakī, *an-Niẓāmī fī uṣūl ad-dīn, MS Ayasofya* no. 2378.
Gardet and Anawati	L. Gardet and G. Anawati, *Introduction à la théologie musulmane*, Paris, 1948.
al-Ghazālī, *Ilğām*	Abū Ḥāmid al-Ghazālī, *Ilğām al-'awāmm 'an 'ilm al-kalām*, printed in the margins of 'Abd al-Qāhir al-Ğilānī, *al-Insān al-kāmil*, Cairo, 1386/1949.
al-Ghazālī, *Maqṣad*	Abū Ḥāmid al-Ghazālī, *al-Maqṣad al-asnā fī ṣarḥ asmā' Allāh al-ḥusnā*, ed. F. Shehadi, Beyrouth, 1982.
al-Ghazālī, *Munqiḏ*	Abū Ḥāmid al-Ghazālī, *al-Munqiḏ min aḍ-ḍalāl*, ed. G. Saliba and K. Iyar, 9th edition, Beyrouth, 1980.
Ghunyah	Abū l-Qāsim al-Anṣārī, *al-Ghunyah fī uṣūl ad-dīn, MS III Ahmet*, no. 1916.
al-Ğuwaynī, *Luma'*	Abū l-Ma'ālī al-Ğuwaynī, *Luma' fī qawā'id ahl as-sunnah wal-ğamā'ah*, ed. and tr. M. Allard, in *Textes apologétiques de Ğuwayni*, Beyrouth, 1968, p. 116 ff.
al-Ḥaṯṯ	al-Aš'arī, *al-Ḥaṯṯ 'alā l-baḥṯ*, ed. R. Frank, in *MIDEO*, 18 (1988), p. 83 ff.
Hidāyah	Abū Bakr al-Bāqillānī, *Hidāyat al-muštaršidīn*, a portion of the section on prophecy contained in *MS al-Azhar, at-Tawḥīd* no. (21)242.
al-Ibānah	al-Aš'arī, *al-Ibānah 'an uṣūl ad-diyānah*, Cairo, 1348/1957.
Ibn 'Asākir	Abū l-Qāsim ibn 'Asākir, *Tabyīn kaḏib al-muftarī*, Damascus, 1347.
Ibn Ḥanbal, *Radd*	Aḥmad ibn Ḥanbal, *ar-Radd 'alā l-ğahmiyyah waz-zanādiqah*, Riyad, 1397/1977.
Ibn Ḫuzayma	Abū Bakr ibn Ḫuzayma, *K. at-Tawḥīd*, ed. H. abū Harrās, Cairo, 1387/1968.
Ibn Qutayba, *Iḫtilāf*	Ibn Qutayba ad-Dīnawarī, *al-Iḫtilāf fī l-lafẓ*, ed. M. al-Kawthari, Cairo, 1349.
Ibn Qutayba, *Ta'wīl*	Ibn Qutayba ad-Dīnawarī, *Ta'wīl muḫtalif al-ḥadīṯ*, Beyrouth, n.d.
Iḫtiṣār	*al-Kāmil fī iḫtiṣār aš-Šāmil*, author unknown, *MS III Ahmet*, no. 1322.
Iršād	al-Ğuwaynī, *al-Iršād fī qawāti' al-adillah fī uṣūl al-i'tiqād*, ed. M. Mūsā and A. 'Abd al-Ḥamīd, Cairo, 1369/1950.
al-Isfarā'īnī	R. Frank, *al-Ustādh abū Isḥāq, an 'aqīda together with selected fragments*, in *MIDEO*, 19 (1989), p. 129 ff.

AL-KALĀBĀḎĪ	ABŪ BAKR AL-KALĀBĀḎĪ, *at-Ta'arruf li-maḏhab ahl at-taṣawwuf*, ed. A. MAḤMŪD and T. SURŪR, Cairo, 1380/1960.
KLEIN	W. C. KLEIN, *abū l-Ḥasan 'Alī ibn Ismā'īl al-Aš'arī's al-Ibāna 'an Uṣūl ad-Diyāna*, a translation with notes, New Haven, 1940.
MAKDISI	G. MAKDISI, *Ash'arī and the Ash'arites in Islamic Religious History*, in *Studia Islamica*, 17 (1962), p. 37-80 and 18 (1963), p. 19-39.
MAKDISI, *Ibn 'Aqīl*	G. MAKDISI, *Ibn 'Aqīl et la résurgence de l'Islam traditionaliste au XIe siècle*, Damascus, 1963.
Maqālāt	AL-AŠ'ARĪ, *Maqālāt al-islāmiyyīn*, ed. H. RITTER, Istanbul, 1929-30.
MCCARTHY, *Theology*	R. MCCARTHY, *The Theology of al-Ash'arī*, Beyrouth, 1953.
AL-MUTAWALLĪ	ABŪ SA'D AL-MUTAWALLĪ, *al-Mugnī*, ed. Marie BERNAND (*Supplément aux Annales islamologiques*, Ch. no. 7) Cairo, 1986.
AL-QUŠAYRĪ, *Fuṣūl*	ABŪ L-QĀSIM AL-QUŠAYRĪ, *Fuṣūl fī l-uṣūl*, ed. R. FRANK, in *MIDEO*, 16 (1984), p. 59 ff.
AL-QUŠAYRĪ, *Luma'*	ABŪ L-QĀSIM AL-QUŠAYRĪ, *Luma' fī l-i'tiqād*, ed. R. FRANK, in *MIDEO*, 15 (1982), p. 53 ff.
AL-QUŠAYRĪ, *Risālah*	ABŪ L-QĀSIM AL-QUŠAYRĪ, *Risālah ilā ğamā'at ahl aṣ-ṣūfiyyah*, contained in the Commentary of Zakariyā al-Anṣārī, printed in the margins of AL-'ARŪSĪ, *Natā'iğ al-afkār* (4 vol's), Bulaq, 1290.
AL-QUŠAYRĪ, *Taḥbīr*	ABŪ L-QĀSIM AL-QUŠAYRĪ, *at-Taḥbīr fī t-taḏkīr*, ed. I. BUSYŪNĪ, Cairo, 1968.
AŠ-ŠAHRASTĀNĪ, *Milal*	*al-Milal wan-niḥal*, ed. M. BADRĀN, (2 vol's), Cairo, 1370/1951-1375/1955.
AŠ-ŠAHRASTĀNĪ, *Nihāyah*	*Nihāyat al-aqdām fī 'ilm al-kalām*, ed. A. GUILLAUME, Oxford, 1934.
Šāmil (1969)	AL-ĞUWAYNĪ, *aš-Šāmil fī uṣūl ad-dīn*, ed. A. AN-NAŠŠĀR, Alexandria, 1969.
Šāmil (1981)	AL-ĞUWAYNĪ, *aš-Šāmil fī uṣūl ad-dīn*, some Additional Portions of the Text, ed. R. FRANK, Tehran, 1981.
Šarḥ al-Iršād	ABŪ L-QĀSIM AL-ANṢĀRĪ, *Šarḥ al-Iršād, Princeton University Library, MS ELS* no. 634.
SOURDEL	D. SOURDEL, *Une Profession de foi de l'historien at-Tabarî*, in *REI*, 36 (1968), p. 177 ff.
SUBKĪ	ABŪ NAṢR AS-SUBKĪ, *Ṭabaqāt aš-šāfi'iyya al-kubrā*, ed. M. AT-TANĀḤĪ and A. AL-ḤULW (10 vol's), Cairo, 1964-1976.
Ṭabaqāt	IBN ABĪ YA'LĀ, *Ṭabaqāt al-ḥanābilah* (2 vol's), Cairo, 1371/1952.
aṯ-Ṯaghr	AL-AŠ'ARĪ, *Risālah ilā ahl aṯ-ṯaghr fī Bāb al-Abwāb*, in *Ilahiyat Fakültesi Mecmuası*, 9 (1929), p. 80 ff.
Tamhīd	ABŪ BAKR AL-BĀQILLĀNĪ, *at-Tamhīd*, ed. R. MCCARTHY, Beyrouth, 1957.

Ta'wīl	ABŪ L-ḤASAN AṬ-ṬABARĪ, *Ta'wīl al-āyāt al-muškilah, MS Dār al-Kutub al-Miṣriyyah, Ṭal'at Maǧ.* no. 490, f. 108r-162v.
WATT, *Formative Period*	W. M. WATT, *The Formative Period of Islamic Thought*, Edinburgh, 1973.
WENSINCK	A. J. WENSINCK, *The Muslim Creed*, Cambridge, 1932.

VII

THE STRUCTURE OF CREATED CAUSALITY ACCORDING TO AL-AŠ'ARÎ

An Analysis of the *Kitâb al-Luma'*, §§ 82-164

The attention of many scholars has been turned to the study of the general problem of God's predetermination of events and man's freedom of action and causation as it was treated by the various authors of the early kalâm, sometimes with considerable penetration and insight and often without going beyond the mere collection and collation of formulae. W. M. Watt, in particular, has made a number of significant contributions to the elucidation of this problem and its history in his *Free Will and Predestination in Early Islam.* Generally speaking however, the whole problem remains somewhat obscure, both in regard to the position of individual authors and in the general outline of its development through the diverse schools of kalâm in the first four centuries of Islam.

Central to the history of this question in muslim thought is al-Aš'arî's understanding of human causality. Though his system may not have been altogether new and unique, his formulation and organisation of the detail was so and the triumph of his theology marks a pivotal moment in the history of islamic religious speculation. His conception of the ontological structure of the human act however, and the theory of *kasb* has been a rather thorny problem for western scholarship and one about which there seems yet to be no real concensus. A number of writers have taken the position that al-Aš'arî allows for no really human, moral act. For example, Fr. Richard McCarthy, to whom we are indebted for an excellent edition and translation of the *Kitâb al-Luma'*, flatly denies that the author admitted any secondary causation, saying (1) that "for al-Ash'arî there was no such thing" and that the author's " 'acquired' motion seems to be quite as ineluctable and inevitable as his 'necessary' motion." (2) Even upon a cursory examination of the pertinent evidence, however, it is clear that both al-Aš'arî and the main body of even the most conservative of Islamic thinkers intended at least to allow for some kind of really human causality and true moral responsibility in man's performance of his acts, however clumsy their formulation of and proposed solutions to the question may appear to the contemporary reader, steeped as he is in the habits and traditions of classical and western thought. The universal condemnation by orthodox Islam of the so-called *muǧabbira*, those who truly meant to deny all proper human and secondary causality is well known (though again, even here, one should beware of reading their apparently absolute denial of secondary causality in too simplistic a fashion, because most of them were neither simpletons nor prepared to deny all the evidences of experience). One need only note the violent support of man's genuine responsibility for the realisation of his own acts and the bitter comments about the doctrine of the *muǧabbira* by the ultra-conservative Ibn Taymîya in his *Iḥtiǧâǧ bil-Qadar* (3). Again, the *'aqîda* which is attributed to Aḥmad ibn Ḥanbal or which purports, rather, to give an account of his teaching and which without doubt reflects common ḥanbalite doctrine, clearly sets him in opposition to the absolute determinism of the *muǧabbira*, setting forth its teaching in a form which is basically aš'arite (4) ;

(1) *The Theology of al-Ash'ari* (Beyrouth, 1953), 58, n. 15 (*ad* § 91 of the translation).

(2) *Ibid.*, 59, n. 16.

(3) *Maǧmû'at ar-Rasâ'il al-kubrà* (Cairo, 1323) 2, 80 ff.

(4) Cf. Ibn abî Ya'là, *Ṭabaqât al-ḥanâbila* (ed. M. H. al-Faqî, Cairo, 1371/1952) 2, 291 ff, esp. pp. 299f, where there is cited an ḥadîth attributed to 'Alî expressing the aš'arite formula that human action proceeds "from men as act and from God as created." In its present form this *'aqîda* would not seem to belong to Ibn Ḥanbal; the general usage is not in conformity with his *Radd 'alà l-ǧahmîya* and, though not so in every detail, some good part of what is said would seem to show some dependence upon al-Aš'arî. The *isnâd* goes back to 'Abd al-Wâḥid b. 'Abd al-

and the same is true of the preface to the *'aqîda*, written by the ḥanbalî, Rizq Allâh ibn 'Abd al-Wahhâb ibn 'Abd al-'Azîz (d. 488/1095) (1). According to both tracts, man is the true moral agent of his own acts.

Al-Aš'arî may not have been altogether successful in maintaining the truly moral character of the human act. He is polemically accused of being a determinist in the writings of his opponents, both the Mu'tazila and Ibn Taymîya, but these accusations however subtly argued must be read as polemical. W. M. Watt pointed out some time ago that the notion of *kasb* or *iktisâb* is meant to designate "man's share in human acts" (2) and one should be very cautious of taking al-Aš'arî's formulation of the problem as a mere piece of casuistry, his understanding of *kasb* as *merely* "God's juridical attribution" of the human act to the apparent agent or as man's simply "taking on" the responsibility for his acts. No doubt one central factor in the popularity of al-Aš'arî's theology is that the principal formulae in which he expressed his teaching are couched in the vocabulary of the *Koran* and read often like the sententiae of the most radical traditionalists. Nevertheless, one can only assume, from the outset of the inquiry, that his proposed solution to the problem of human causality was indeed intellectually satisfying to all that great body of Muslim theologians who did in fact take it up and that it could not have been so accepted had it not made some coherent theological and philosophical sense.

The insistence that God is, in the final analysis, the sole creator and true cause of all that is, all other causality being completely and absolutely dependent upon it, is common to a far broader area of Islamic speculation than the orthodox kalâm. Al-Kindî, for example, states quite bluntly in his *Risâla fî l-fâ'il al-ḥaqq al-awwal al-tâmm* that all causes other

'Azîz (d. 410/1020) and it may well be that the greater part of the formulae contained in the work date no earlier than the time of al-Aš'arî.

(1) Cf. *ibid.*, 265ff, esp. p. 269; this again is quite aš'arite in its general appearance and though it may perhaps be not altogether so it betrays some influence of the 'aš'arite solution to the problem.

(2) *JRAS* 1943, p. 237 ; cf. also his *Islamic Philosophy and Theology* (Edinburgh, 1962), 87.

than God "are called agents only metaphorically" (1), and this doctrine receives its classic formulation in the work of Avicenna, for whose entire system it is fundamental. He says, for example, in the *Kitâb al-Išârât wat-Tanbîhât* (2) that "every being other than [God] belongs to Him as His possession" and in the *Kitâb an-Naǧât* quite unequivocally sets forth the absolute determination of every aspect of every being as it proceeds ultimately from God, including all acts of the will on the part of man (3). As with Avicenna, in the case of al-Aš'arî, the fundamental assumptions from which he derives his understanding of the detail of the problem may be quite simple (as are most elemental insights) but his conception of the whole is not thereby simplistic. The question with al-'Aš'arî, as with any other great author, is how he understood the implications of the formulae.

What I propose therefore to do in this study is no more than this: to examine the terms and structure of the problem according to which al-Aš'arî came to and formulated his understanding of the question of human causality and to set out the basic philosophical structure of his solution of it.

There can be little doubt as Watt has shown (4), that there is already a long history to the terms which al-'Aš'arî uses and the basic form of his doctrine. The exact relationship of his thought, however, to that of his predecessors, particularly Ḍirâr b. 'Amr and an-Naǧǧâr must wait for any adequate treatment until their teaching has been fully examined in detail and for this reason I shall here restrict myself quite closely to the position of al-Aš'arî himself as it is presented in the *Kitâb al-Luma'*. Though keeping the discussion as general as precision will allow in order to avoid having to take up individually the diverse theories of al-Aš'arî's contemporaries and predecessors,

(1) *Rasâ'il al-Kindî*, ed. M. abû Rîda, 1 (Cairo, 1369/1950), 183; cf. also *ibid.*, 162. The same sort of thing is found in the *Theology of Aristotle*, expressed always in the passages which have no correspondent in the *Enneades* and which may, perhaps, be of Muslim origin.

(2) Ed. J. Forget (Leiden, 1892), 159.

(3) *K. an-Naǧât*[2] (Cairo, 1357/1938), 302.

(4) *Op. cit.*

I should like first to outline briefly the general structure of the problem within whose specific context the precise meaning and significance of al-Aš'arî's achievement must be seen. Once the basic outline of the problem and system is made, the organisation of the sections of the *K. al-Luma'* in which the questions relating to *qudra* and *istiṭâ'a* are treated becomes quite clear and, surprisingly perhaps, the work shows itself to be not only very precise in the order of its exposition, but also very tight and almost scholastically consistent in its argumentation.

One of the chief sources of difficulty in interpreting the *Luma'* is unquestionably that of its style, which is almost algebraic in its conciseness and abstractness. This quality seems to have made it subject to misunderstandings quite early in its history, since al-Ğuwaynî, whose style of exposition and argumentation is frequently not altogether free of its own obscurities, is put to some effort to expand and explain its meaning in several passages (1). The work is a kind of *summa* of several central theological questions and, like any compendium, sets forth both questions and arguments in the briefest possible form. In all cases the question under discussion is very precisely defined; that is, it is assumed that the very strict limitation of the problem is known to the reader as well as the exact definition of the terms in question, as they are used. All matters which are in any way considered by the author as extraneous or marginal to the immediate discussion of his central theme are omitted entirely. As this is coupled with the greatest brevity of exposition, the whole effect then is one of an abstractness and precision which is truly remarkable. Because of this quality however, it is of the utmost importance that the reader keep the exact meaning of the terms always precisely in mind as well as the exact delimitation of the point in question (2).

(1) Cf., for example, *Kitâb aš-šâmil*, pt. 1, ed. H. Klopfer (Cairo, 1959) 131ff and 154ff.

(2) In a number of instances where Fr. McCarthy, the editor, remarks in his notes that the argument seems weak or inconsistent the real problem is that he has fallen afoul of the abstractness of the text. For example, where he suggests that the author is "begging the question" (p. 78, n. 5, *ad* § 126) he has simply failed

The basic terms and the general structure of the problem of the nature of the human act were already well defined in the kalâm tradition by the time of al-Aš'arî; quite briefly it was that of the nature of man's power to realise his own acts and the relation of this "power" to the universal causality of God as the ground of all Being. The central concept to be defined and explained was that of *qudra*, the power of efficient causality (used both of God's power and of man's) and though the term was used in a number of quite different basic meanings as a technical term by several authors, both before and after al-Aš'arî, its general content, as defining the question, was commonly recognised in a quite precise manner. The question of *qudra* and *qadar* does not however, as conceived and formulated by the mutakallimîn, coincide exactly with any single term or any one question which had been the subject of extensive treatment and elaboration in its own right as an isolated locus of speculative debate in either Greek philosophy or Christan theology before Islam. While it becomes ever more apparent that the kalâm is closely related in its origins to the whole classical and Christian tradition of philosophy and theology, nevertheless its uniqueness of perspective and the originality of its contribution to this tradition become also more evident.

Though perhaps the point may seem only too obvious in some respects, it should be noted at the outset that though meaning fundamentally the "power [to act]", the term *qudra* (or *istiṭâ'a*) in its proper and native meaning is in every respect opposed to the normal meaning and the content of Greek δύναμις, as it is usually used in Greek philosophy. Basically, in its Aristotelian use, the term δύναμις, whither δύναμις τοῦ ποιεῖν or δύναμις τοῦ πάσχειν designates the potentiality to become other (1). Whereas δύναμις has thus "no sense save in the interior of a being in movement and has none at all in God" as P. Aubenque remarks (2), the Arabic term *qudra* in a Muslim context (like, indeed, the expressions and terms for God's power

to grasp the fact that it is by definition of the term *qudra* as al-'Aš'arî uses it, that the objection is invalidated and cannot stand; there is no argument thus.

(1) P. Aubenque, *Le Problème de l'être chez Aristote* (Paris, 1962), 440.

(2) *Ibid.*, n. 1.

in Christian thought) is not only exclusively active ([1]), but is understood as primarily and most properly applicable to God, who, in the words of the *Koran*, "holds power over all things". Most importantly, this active quality of *qudra*, which we shall discuss below, is not strictly taken in the kalâm as a power or potentiality to become other but as an "accident" *('araḍ)* or attribute, and so designates the actuality of a state of being in the subject, viz., the actuality of being able to effect the realisation of some act. This remains true even with the diversity of particular significations which it takes on with various authors. For some, Ghaylân, Bišr b. al-Mu'tamir, for example ([2]), and even for Aḥmad b. Ḥanbal ([3]), it was taken as the physical strength and well-being of the body as forming the potential for acting, while for the majority of the Mu'tazila, it was understood rather as a distinct "accident" which forms the state of being a potential agent. In the latter sense it does, in effect, refer to the future and a kind of possibility of becoming; but nevertheless, most strictly understood and in its primary sense, it represents the actuality of a state of being. In short, the *qudra* of the mutakallimîn is a fulfilled actuality not an imperfection relative to a perfection in a state of becoming ([4]). Again, parallel and consistent with this basic understanding, the state of actuality of being for the kalâm is, in general, a finite and discrete moment of being, not, as it is for Aristotle, an actuality or reality achieved out of a becoming ([5]); it is rather the present

(1) Even the usual construction of the verb *qadara* with *'alà* is incompatible with the common uses of δύναμις; note also that while the term *quwwa* (which is used in the *Luma'* several times as the equivalent of *qudra*) in the expression *bil-quwwa* is used as the equivalent of δυνάμει, this is purely a translation usage and the proper Arabic term for potentiality in the Greek sense is *imkân* (according to whose grammatical use, that for which the possibility or potentiality exists is grammatically the object!).

(2) Al-Aš'arî, *Maqâlât al-Islâmîyîn* (ed. H. Ritter, Istanbul, 1929-30), 229.

(3) Cf. *'aqîda, loc. cit.*

(4) From the standpoint of the ontology of the "accidents" as such, this is true even when—as is the case according to most of the Mu'tazila—the individual act of *qudra* is always relative to an act to be performed, to whose realisation the actuality of the *qudra* is prior.

(5) Cf. Aubenque, *op. cit.*, 441.

state of being, perfect and complete in the fulness of its being, discrete and without inherent reference to any past state.

The question of becoming in terms of the inherent principles of things to become other is not a problem which was of central concern to most of the kalâm. Insofar as it treated of material beings, the chief orientation of the kalâm was to the investigation of the ontological or metaphysical structure of the being of material creatures in the createdness of their Being, not τὰ φυσικά, i.e., not the ultimate structure of material beings considered in their materiality as the constitute the world and the principles of its order as world. If one excludes an-Naẓẓâm and Muʿammar, who are quite tangential to the main-stream of kalâm thought, things, for the earlier kalâm—material beings—can hardly be said to contain within themselves any principle of becoming. No being, in and of itself, by virtue of the inherent principles of its being, is oriented towards a becoming-other than it is; for most of the early mutakallimîn, all things are no more than they are and their being is complete and fulfilled at any given moment of their existence. No being has in itself any intrinsic "potentiality" to change or alteration except the knowing, willing, and intending agent; its becoming other is entirely dependent upon and resides in the potentiality of an exterior agent who is capable of effecting the change. The production of being thus is not traced chiefly, as with Aristotle and the Greeks, to principles inherent in the thing, as to the "matter" and the "form" which it contains *in potentia*, but rather rests in the agent, since material being, as such, is no more than it is in the created fulness of its actuality. In the concrete order of the world, matter is completely determined by the "accidents" *(aʿrâḍ)* which together constitute the content of the present reality of the particular being. Whatever alteration it may undergo, whatever "change of form" it may suffer, exists, in its potentiality, entirely and exclusively in the intention of the agent who is capable of producing the change through his own power of causality. The whole problem thus becomes shifted to one of efficient causality; the significant "causes" of being become almost exclusively the "moving" cause, as the intending agent, and the "final" cause, as his intention in his knowing what he intends, the nexus of action and change residing in his power of efficient causality *(qudra)*. In this way, all Being, save God, is absolutely finite in that ontologically it is realised exhaustively in the actuality of its present, as created by God, having intrinsically and by virtue of itself, no potentiality to become other.

Avicenna, in his *Kitâb al-Išârât* attacks precisely this notion that potentiality consists entirely in being *maqdûr 'alayhi* (i.e., subject to the efficient causality of an agent), in that it does not allow in any way for the real potentiality of the existent prior to the actuality of its presence in the world, insisting on the actuality *(ḥuṣûl)* of its potentiality in itself, in the potentiality of the substrate (1). However, it is precisely this non-existence of any true potentiality outside the agent which al-Aš'arî, for example, wished to insist upon. Al-Ğuwaynî notes that, in the *Luma'*, his proof of the existence of God on the basis of the argument of the growth and development of the "drop of sperm" *(nuṭfa)*, is

(1) *Išârât*, 151 *(išâra)*; concerning the priority of matter, cf. *Nağât*, 219 and also Ṭûsî's comment on *Išârât, loc. cit.* (ed. S. Dunya [Cairo, 1958]), 507ff. Avicenna's position on this whole question is not entirely unlike that of the kalâm however, if one consider in his thought the absolute determination of the *muraǧǧiḥ* (that which determines the actualisation of the cause) in the production of being and the total indifference of orientation towards being and non-being of the potential as such, apart from the determination of the *muraǧǧiḥ*. For the kalâm likewise, the cause of the being of the thing is determined in its causality, with the exception of the ultimate cause; cf. also *infra*, p. 31, n. 1. Despite the several tempting analogies and the quasi semantic equvalence of the terms, I hesitate to agree with van den Bergh when he suggests (*Averroes' Tahafut al-Tahafut* [Oxford, 1954] 2, 38) that the term *maqdûr* is the equivalent of the Stoic "εἱμαρμένον, that which is decreed." From the outset, the term *maqdûr* is common throughout the kalâm and shows no such resonance. It is short for *maqdûr 'alayhi*, i.e., that which is subject to the power [of causality] of an agent who is *qâdir 'alayhi* and even in the earliest authors (e.g., abû l-Hudhayl) the expression *maqdûrât Allâh,* as a technical term designates those things which are subject to the power and causality of God (which, for some of the Mu'tazila includes those things which He will never create) not what He has decreed, even though the two may well prove upon examination of a particular author to be equivalent because of the peculiar relationship which is understood to exist between God's power and knowledge and will (as is the case with abû l-Hudhayl). Van den Bergh's rendering of the sentence of Šahrastânî *(ibid.)* is forced and incorrect, since what it says is that "the *muktasab* is that which is subject to the created act of causality and actually exists according to the created act of causality;" the expression "have been decreed" would have to be *muqaddara* in Arabic, not *maqdûra*.

directed against those who hold the potential existence of things in matter *(aṣḥâb al-hayûlà)*: "those who say that the world exists in matter potentially, the date palm in the date stone, the man in the drop of sperm", etc. (1) For the earlier kalâm, the true cause of the being of any thing is the agent who intends its being and realises it according to a knowing act of the will. In this way, the realisation of all being is dependent not only on the efficient causality *(qudra)* of the agent but is wholly determined (pre-determined) in his knowledge and his intention. In this respect the whole construction is somewhat neoplatonic (2).

Within such a framework as this all change involves, in one sense or another, a kind of creation, since whatever change or Being is effected represents the realisation of new being entirely out of the efficient causality of the agent, in that no proper potentiality of the thing is held to precede its realisation, outside that of the agent's power of causality.

This then is the central core of the problem of *qudra* and man's potentiality to perform his own acts, as it was debated in the earlier kalâm. Though in its origin, no doubt, the question was primarily one of the validity and structure of man's moral responsibility for his own action and tends to remain seated in this context for most of the Mu'tazila, it is not, as it ultimately came to be formulated and refined, essentially a question of "free will". For most kalâm authors, the question of the spontaneity

(1) Al-Ǧuwaynî, *op. cit.*, 132; this statement however, against the *aṣḥâb al-hayûlà* (whether made by the 'aš'arites or the Mu'tazila as represented by al-Ǧubbâ'î, abû Hâšim and his followers, etc.) is not to be taken as denying natural processes but rather as opposing the notion of Naẓẓâm and others that matter itself, in virtue of the nature of its materiality, contains any inherent "nature" or principle of self-determination, active or passive; cf. 'Abd al-Ǧabbâr, *Šarḥ al-uṣûl al-ḫamsa* (ed. A. Ousman, Cairo, 1965), 387f.

(2) This, like almost any global statement about the kalâm, requires some qualification; the relationship between the knowledge and intention of the agent and the structure of his act and the degree of his causation is not identical for all writers and is notably "looser" for the school of al-Ǧubbâ'î than for al-Aš'arî and his followers. On the relationship which al-Aš'arî sees between God's knowing all beings and his being the absolute ground of the being of all beings, cf. *infra ad* § 107. It is significant that the earliest muslim system of theology about which we have much information is in fact based on a neoplatonic model, viz., that of Ǧahm b. Ṣafwân; cf. R. Frank, "The Neoplatonism of Ǧahm b. Ṣafwân," *Le Muséon* 78 (1965), pp. 395ff.

and freedom of the will *(irâda)* is another and distinct question and as such is treated separately. More closely allied in the matter of the determination or non-determination of human acts, but still distinct, is the question of the existential transcendence of human existence; but although this would appear to be a scarcely avoidable concomitant to the problem of human causality (and was, in fact, central to the conception of the problem by abû l-Hudhayl), al-Aš'arî, in refining and delimiting the question, eliminated it, as we shall see, altogether from his discussion of *qudra*. The question of *qudra* is thus chiefly if not exclusively one of the metaphysical structure of efficient causality and, insofar as it treats of man and his causation, the ontology of the created cause (1).

The causality of any agent inevitably involves creation, in one way or another; this is a primary conception for most of the kalâm. The problem then is how one is to explain man as the true cause of his own acts, for which he is responsible before God. That he is the morally responsible agent in the eyes of God is a datum of revelation and as such is beyond debate, so that it is the character and nature of his agency which must be understood and explained. The question thus for al-Aš'arî, as for the rest of the mutakallimîn, is not to grasp the process and structure of the human act as process but rather to understand the metaphysical structure and validity of the human act as truly the act of the human agent within the general context of the universally creative omnipotence of God: what is the nature and structure of human causality if all action on the part of a "knowing, intending, and willing agent" *(fâ'il 'âlim qâṣid murîd)* does in fact involve the production, out of and by means of his own potentiality of causation, of new Being, when creation or the bringing into existence of Being belongs to the Creator (2).

(1) That causality was in a unique sense the central problem of Islamic philosophy and theology was long ago pointed out by J. Obermann in his "Das Problem der Kausalität bei den Arabern," *WZKM* 29 (1915), 323ff and 30 (1916-17), 37ff. The Mu'tazila, because they tended always to keep their argumentation of the question within the context of the problem of God's justice, give the impression of not having achieved the precision and abstractness of thought which one finds in the work of al-Aš'arî and his followers.

(2) I would not belie the real complexity of this question in the history of the

The problem which al-Aš'arî sets about to solve is a formulation of human causality which would leave God as the sole and unique creator of all Being without at the same time vitiating the reality of human causation.

The immediate background against which al-Aš'arî wrote is that formed by the Mu'tazila and most particularly the system of his master, al-Ǧubbâ'î and his school, for whom human causality was truly creative. Though allowing that man's potential of causality was indeed created in him by God, al-Ǧubbâ'î nevertheless held that man was the agent of his act by way of "creating and producing new being" *(ḫalqan wa-ibdâ-'an)* (1). Fleeing, as it were, anything which might smack of God's determination or domination of the free human act, al-Ǧubbâ'î and his fellows tended to let man's efficient causality become rather completely free and independent of God's

development of Muslim thought, for the notion of Being in the kalâm is variously understood in a number of quite subtle significations, which are of real importance for the history of philosophy. The kalâm distinguishes, almost from the very beginning, between the thing *(šay')* and the actuality of its presence in the world *(wuǧûd)*, and from the time of Šaḥḥâm a number of authorities held that the two are really distinct. Within this framework the debate concerning the nature of created causality and the respective rôles of God and man in causation of events in the world becomes very complexly nuanced as various authors set forth their different views of the problem. For some of the Mu'tazila, the human agent is the cause of the thing's Being (in the sense of its presence in the world) wherefore they would allow the application of the term "creation" *(ḫalq, iḥdâṯ)* to man's performance of his act (cf. *infra)*. The form of the question during and before the time of al-Aš'arî is difficult to follow in its detail because of the lack of adequate citations of many authors in the available sources. However, since al-Aš'arî, like abû l-Hudhayl and a few others of the Mu'tazila, did not allow the distinction, we need not go into the question here. On the function of al-Aš'arî's position on this question within his understanding of the structure of created causation, cf. *infra ad* § 87.

(1) Šahrastânî, *Kitâb al-Milal wan-niḥal* (ed. M. Badrân, Cairo, 1328/1910-1375/1955), 120; this bald a statement of the question in these terms may well be original with al-Ǧubbâ'î, having been avoided by earlier writers (cf. al-Ǧuwaynî, *Iršâd* [ed. M. Mûsà and A. 'Abd al-Ḥamîd, Cairo, 1369/1950], 187f, the reference to the *muta'aḫḫirîn*, and also *infra ad K. al-Luma'* § 90 and §§ 120f, though al-Ǧubbâ'î is not mentioned by name in the latter); cf. the discussion of the terms *ḫalq* and *ḫâliq* in 'Abd al-Ǧabbâr, *op. cit.*, 379ff. At any rate, that this was indeed the center of the question as clearly understood by al-Aš'arî and his opponents is manifest in the whole discussion of the problem of what is subject to God's causality *(maqdûr Allâh)* in its relation (or opposition) to what is subject to man's causality *(maqdûr al-'abd)*, on which see below.

creation as the source of its actuality, so that in the question of whether something can be subject to the causality of two agents, *scil.*, God and the human agent, they, together with other mu'tazilî authors, held that only one can be said to be the cause (1). In this way, man's independence as a creative cause became in some degree absolute within the limits of the range of his potential activity. Such a notion however, was not generally congenial to the most basic understanding which the principal body of Islamic thinkers had of the ultimate structure of the universe (2).

Al-Aš'arî's solution to the question is, on the whole, quite simple and certainly not at all obtuse, as some have suggested. In outline it is this: man's power of causation, like every other "accident" of his being, is created by God. In this way then, since God is in reality the cause of man's generated causality *(qudra muḥdaṯa)*, He is in the strictest sense the creator of the event which is brought about through that causality, as the creator of the immediate act of causation. This is in notable contrast to the common mu'tazilite position, mentioned above, according to which God is in no sense ontologically the cause of the human act. Al-Aš'arî's position however, should not be taken in any simplistic sense either as a denial of secondary causality or of the reality of the human agency in the performance of the act, as indeed has been done (3). Furthermore, it should be noted that al-Aš'arî does not deny the reality of "natural" causes or of secondary causality other than man's; but rather, since such causality does not fall within the range of the problem of *qudra* as it was universally understood, he simply does not discuss it (4). Insofar as man is the agent *(fâ'il)* of the event

(1) Cf. *Maqâlât*, 549ff and al-Ǧuwaynî, *op. cit.*, 187f and also the remarks *ibid.*, 196f.

(2) This is witnessed not only by the triumph (ultimately almost absolute) of the system of al-Aš'arî but can also be seen in the thoroughly deterministic system of Avicenna, which itself, no doubt because of the basically Islamic character of its fundamental orientation, came in subsequent centuries to have so profound an influence in almost all areas of Muslim speculation.

(3) Cf. for example, McCarthy, *op. cit.*, p. 58, n. 15, *ad* § 91.

(4) Cf. *infra ad* § 98 and § 107; it may be noted that the question is likewise omitted by 'Abd al-Ǧabbâr in his treatment of the problem of *qudra*.

which proceeds from his power of causation, he is the true cause of the entire event (cf. *infra ad* §§ 92f). Man is created in the totality of his being, of which consequently there is no aspect which is not utterly dependent upon God's universal creation at any moment, but God does not perform the human act even though He is the creator of man's power of causation. The act is entirely the agent's insofar as it is determined by him, but his existence, the actuality of his Being as agent *(fâ'il qâdir)* and also the existence of the effect come to be and subsist in Being through the creative causality of God (1).

The term for the free human act in al-Aš'arî's works is *fi'l muktasab*, while the term *iktisâb* is used to describe the relationship between the created agent and his act. Al-Aš'arî, as we noted above, clearly recognised the fact of more than one kind of secondary causality. However, for the kalâm, the only true efficient causality is that of the agent who knowingly intends and wills his act and *kasb/iktisâb* is thus used to describe the relationship of such a created agent to his act, as opposed to those events which belong to no such agent (*lâ yaktasibuhâ aḥadun;* cf. *infra ad* § 98). Watt is no doubt correct in his analysis of the origin of the word as a specialised term for the free human act and that as such it is based on the koranic use of the words, (2) though as a technical term it is more highly

(1) It is to be noted that there is nothing here concerning God's determination of the human event or of the "freedom of the will"; in the *Luma'*, all discussion of the will of the human agent in the structure of the act is omitted, as has been noted. Again, though ultimately all Being proceeds from God's creative power of causation *(qudrat al-qadîm)*, according to His will, the author says nothing about God's wilful determination of human acts of the will, since that is not a part of the probelm of *qudra* as he construed it. Generally on the aš'arite conception of the will, cf. *Šarḥ al-Mawâqif* (Cairo, 1325/1907) 6, 64 and 71f. Though our sources say little on the subject, I doubt that al-Aš'arî would allow an absolute determination of the will any more than does Ibn Taymîya, even though such a conclusion may be rather difficult to avoid within the overall structure of his system.

(2) The term was used much in this sense well before al-Aš'arî, as M. Watt has pointed out (cf. references cited above, p. 15, n. 2) by Ḍirâr and an-Naǧǧâr and may well have been used as a general term for the act for which the human agent was himself fully responsible, by others as well, who did not hold to the theory of *kasb* to explain the ontological structure of the human act; as for example the term *'ilm iktisâb* seems to have been used by abû l-Hudhayl in the sense of knowledge which

specified than this. A careful examination of the text of the *Luma'* shows quite clearly that the basic sense of "acquire" is itself central to al-Aš'arî's understanding; i.e., it does basically refer to the "acquisition" from God of a created power of efficient causality by the human agent. The term does not occur in §§ 122ff, where he discusses human causality in itself as the act of the agent, until he introduces the question of its ground in God's creative act in § 128 (cf. *infra ad loc.*). On the other hand, it also includes the relation between the agent and his act insofar as he is a moved mover whose being is othered by the realisation of his act (cf. *ad* § 96 and § 127) and so designates a specific relationship between agent and act. In this, it expressly excludes and distinguishes the causality of the material, human agent from God's transcendent causality; God, being world-transcendent, is not "involved" in the acts of which He is the ultimate cause and agent *(fâ'il qâdir)*. He cannot, to use an example of al-Aš'arî, be called an "impregnator of women" even though it is He who creates the pregnancy (1). In the terminology of the *Luma'*, He creates the act for or in another, a formula whose meaning we shall take up in detail below (*ad* §§ 97f).

The tale does not end here however, for if we take the general structure of the problem of created causality as seen by the Baṣra school of the Mu'tazila as the point of departure, al-Aš'arî's shift of perspective is yet more thoroughgoing. Again leaving aside those who held, like an-Naẓẓâm, that the principle of man's action and causality was his "nature" *(kiyân/ṭabî'a)* as constituted by the "natures" *(ṭabâ'i')* of the material elements of his body and soul and also those who held that it lay in the physical well-being of the body, although most of the Mu'tazila

a person acquires through experience or reflection, as opposed to *'ilm iḍṭirârî/ ḍarûrî*, innate or necessary knowledge.

(1) *'Abd al-Qâdir al-Baġdâdî, al-Farq bayn al-firaq*[2] (ed. al-Kawthari, Cairo, 1367/1948), 110. This is against al-Ǧubbâ'î (cf. *Maqâlât*, 194f); for the interpretation of the statement by the Mu'tazila cf. 'Abd al-Ǧabbâr, *op. cit.*, 354. The question is probably very old, as the creation of the child begotten in adultery is mentioned in the *risâla* to the Caliph 'Abd al-Malik attributed to al-Ḥasan al-Baṣrî (cf. *Der Islam* 21 [1933], p. 74).

took *qudra/istiṭâ'a* as a more or less permanent attribute *('araḍ)* of man's being, it is defined generally in terms of the single event towards which it is directed, so that one speaks in terms of the single act of *qudra.* This is reflected most clearly in the arguments concerning whether the act of *qudra* is terminated immediately before the event ("in the first moment") or whether it perdures through the actualisation of the act ("in the second moment"), most of the Mu'tazila holding that it perdures through the second moment, because the occurence of the concomitant act through a power of causality which is not actually present is impossible (1). The same basic thesis is also reflected in the discussions of the secondary result which takes place outside the agent *(fi'l mutawallid)* (2). For most of the Mu'tazila, *qudra* is the power to effect the act and as such stands in "an indifferent relationship to the two poles of the act" (*scil.* the performance of the act or its omission) until the act of the will determines which of the two contraries will be effected (3), at which moment the actual event is accomplished through it (4). Whatever the disagreements, *qudra/istiṭâ'a* is the *power through which the individual act is brought to realisation.* For most of the Mu'tazila (including al-Ǧubbâ'î), the actuality of the *qudra* precedes the realisation of the specific act, being equally, in the subject, the power to perform it or leave it undone *(qudratun 'alà l-fi'li wa-tarkihi).* To the extent that man's generated power causation precedes his act and that, as already present *(mawǧûd)* in him, the determination of its actualisation is subject simply to his act of the will, it is his in a quite absolute sense. This is quite in harmony with their notion that man alone is the efficient cause of his act, "that there cannot be two efficient causes [*qâdirân*] for a single event" (i.e., God cannot also be the agent or creator of the effect). If the efficient causation of the event lies within man's free potential of deter-

(1) *Maqâlât,* 232.
(2) *Ibid.*
(3) Cf. *Šarḥ al-Mawâqif,* 6, 64.
(4) Cf. generally *Maqâlât,* 234f; there is some disagreement about the "employment of the *qudra*" in the actual performance of the act, but it is almost entirely a verbal disagreement over the definition of terms.

mination and action, then the realisation of the event is uniquely man's.

As I tried to suggest above, the notion of *qudra* for most of the early mutakallimîn is not at all that of a "potency" in the Aristotelian sense of the word, not a "power to act" which is actualised at the moment of the realisation of the act; rather it is the power of efficient causality which is subject to the determination of the agent and, so determined, is the power of efficient causality through which the event takes place. Again, though for many of the Mu'tazila the concept may come quite close to involving the physical force employed in the realisation of the act, it is clearly not so for al-Ǧubbâ'î, who held that although the event takes place "through it", it is nevertheless "not employed" *(lâ tusta'malu)* in the act (1). It is important to keep in mind here that one does not speak of the *potentiality* of the power of causation before the realisation of the act and of its *actuality* in its realisation. This is due in no wise to any kind of naïveté on the part of the earlier mutakallimîn, for naïve or simplistic in their philosophical and theological thought they were not, nor to their ignorance of the classical terms and their meanings. Rather, the notion of potency and act, as they are formulated and understood by Aristotle and in the Greek tradition, simply have no place in the metaphysics of atoms and "accidents"; (2) the "accident" *('araḍ)* or attribute either exists as actually present *(mawǧûd)* in the subject or does not (3) and if it does not, its potentiality (to the extent that we can speak of such) to exist in the thing resides neither in it nor in the thing in which it may inhere, but in the actual power of efficient causality

(1) *Maqâlât*, 235. The reasoning given is that the act of "employment" *(isti'mâl)* comes to inhere in the thing employed and this, from his standpoint, would involve the inherence of one "accident" in another. Had he wished, however, to speak of the use and transfer of energy, it would have been easy enough to speak of the force in the efficient member *(ǧâriḥa)* (which is mentioned in *Maqâlât*, 232) and somehow to have avoided the problem.

(2) Later, the possibility of existence *(imkân al-wuǧûd)* of things, their necessity or impossibility, comes to be a central question for the kalâm, but this is a period when the kalâm had begun to come under the influence of the falsafa.

(3) The debate, already prominent in the time of al-Aš'arî, regarding the status of the non-present in existence *(ma'dûm)* does not affect this question.

(qudra) which belongs to the agent who can effect its presence. *Qudra*, in short, is the actuality of the *qâdir* as such.

Al-Aš'arî then (though he was not the first to do so) limits the presence in the human agent of the power to act to the moment of the realisation of the act (cf. *infra*). Where for most of the Mu'tazila *qudra* was indifferently a power to perform the act or not, for al-Aš'arî it becomes the "attribute which specifically determines [*ṣifa muḫaṣṣiṣa*] the realisation of one of the two poles of the *maqdûr*" (1). Thus, at the moment of the realisation of the act, God creates in the human agent "a generated power of causality" through which the act is realised. The efficient causality is not God's however, for it is created as an "accident" belonging to the human agent and it is from this created causality that the event takes place. The notion of man's *qudra* is thus restricted to the actuality of the agent in the act of his causation of the event; it is the "power of causation" in act at the moment of the realisation of the event (2). In

(1) *Šarḥ al-Mawâqif*, 6, 71.

(2) R. Brunschvig suggests (« Devoir et Pouvoir », *Studia Islamica* 20 [1964], 9ff), following van den Bergh (*op. cit.*, 37ff), that in the debate between al-Aš'arî and the Mu'tazila on the question of whether the act of *qudra* precedes the realisation of the act or is simultaneous with it, the position of the former is to be compared to that of the Megarians. The analogy is indeed tempting, especially since the kalâm shows many dependencies upon the Stoa and the Greek atomists (some of which, in regard to this question, are brought out by van den Bergh, *loc. cit.*). Regarding the question of *qudra* however, one should not be misled into reading the analogy too broadly. *Qudra* as I have tried to indicate, is in no wise a δύναμις in the Aristotelian sense and where the overall, basic attitude towards the conception of prior potentiality which one finds through an analysis of the kalâm authors is very much like that of the Megarians, Stoics, and Greek atomists (cf. N. Hartmann, « Der Megarische und der Aristotelische Möglichkeitsbegriff », *Sitzbr. d. Preussischen Akad. d. Wiss., phil.-hist. Kl.*, 1937, 51ff), *qudra* is not primarily involved. The systems of the chief authors of the Mu'tazila (abû l-Hudhayl, al-Ǧubbâ'î, etc.) were as opposed to the Aristotelian notion of δύναμις as the basis of the ontology of change and becoming as were al-Aš'arî and his followers. *Qudra* as an "accident" *('araḍ)* is pertinent only in the discussion of the "knowing, willing, intending agent" and is, like all other "accidents", fundamentally "atomic" and discrete in its being. The Mu'tazila insisted on its being prior to the event and relative to both the posited act and its contrary in order to preserve the freedom and spontaneity of the human act but never looked upon it as a "potentiality" towards becoming, even though such a conception may well be an inescapable concomitant of the question, if it be viewed from another perspective. Even as a freedom of determination, the degree of spontaneity allowed the human agent is minimal (cf.

that God creates it at the moment of the act, He is, in a sense, the creator of the act, but in that the *qudra* through which the event takes place is in every respect a determinant attribute of the being of the human agent (for as a created accident inhering in him it does not differ ontologically from the others which constitute his being at the moment) the causality is his and he is in a true sense the agent of the act.

A great part of the misunderstanding of al-Aš'arî's position on this whole question and the tendency of some scholars to see in it a merely verbal (and not altogether honest) affirmation of human causality while at the same time upholding a conservative notion of the universal creativity of God, would seem in great part to find its source in a failure to grasp distinctly and clearly the meaning of the terms of the problem as the author construed it and a parallel failure to restrict the problem to the limits within which it was conceived and formulated.

*
* *

With this introduction then, we can proceed with the analysis of the sections of the *Luma'* in which the author deals with the question of *qudra*.

The organisation of this portion of the work is thus (1):

§§ 82-121 : HUMAN CAUSALITY IS CREATED.

generally my forthcoming *Metaphysics of Created Being according to abû l-Hudhayl al-'Allâf*). In short, the early kalâm, mu'tazilite as well as aš'arite, was quite "megarian" in its fundamental outlook and, taking islamic atomism as a whole, al-Aš'arî, by his restriction of the act of *qudra* to the moment of the realisation of the act, produces, in a certain sense, a more self-consistent and homogeneous system that that of his mu'tazilî opponents.

(1) The basic division of the question of *qudra* into two sections, treating first that of the relation between God's causality and man's and second the character of created causality considered in itself, would seem to be traditional. The same division is found in the *Iršâd* of al-Ǧuwaynî (pp. 187ff and pp. 210f) and also in the *Šarḥ al-uṣûl al-ḫamsa* of 'Abd al-Ǧabbâr (pp. 323ff and pp. 390 ff). Within the general conception of the whole context, common to their respective schools, the latter places these within the larger section on divine justice *(al-'adl)* while the former treates them as altogether separate questions previous to this taking up the question of God's justice.

§§ 82-84 : Affirmation of Creation of Human Acts on the basis of the *Koran*.

§§ 85-86 : That the true efficient cause determines the being of the caused in its total reality.

§§ 87-95 : God's causality and the createdness of human causality:
§ 87: That God alone is the true efficient cause of any act or event;
§§ 88-90: That God is not the immediate agent who performs the act (88f); the place and degree of human causality in relation to the act (90);
§§ 91-94: That all events are alike created, those which are freely performed by the created agent as well as those which are not.
§ 95: Summary on God's creation of human causation.

§§ 96-100 : God as Transcendent Creator:
§ 96: The Creator of a thing is not altered by the act of creation;
§ 97: The relationship of the transcendent creator to the created act of the human agent;
§ 98: The relationship of the transcendent creator to the created event which does not depend upon the causality of a created agent.
§ 99: Corollary regarding the *Koran* as the uncreated word;
§ 100: Affirmation of the efficacy of human effort and action.

§§ 101-107 : God's Goodness and the Problem of the Existence of Evil:
§§ 101-5: In what way it can be said that God's Decree involves evil;
§§ 106-7: God's goodness and providence and the question of the existence of created evil.

§§ 108-118 : Interpretation of disputed verses of the *Koran*, involving God's decree, the universality of His providence, the "Truth" of creation.

§§ 146-149: *Qudra* and *'ağz* and man's relationship to God's command; moral obligation;
§§ 150-157: That man has no causality but what God wills to create in him;
§§ 159-164: General summary.

* * *

HUMAN CAUSALITY AS CREATED

His basic thesis al-Aš'arî first enunciates (§§ 82-4) through the citation of *Koran* 37.94/96, "God has created both you and what you do." (1) This verse has been widely used by orthodox thinkers as a "proof-text" for the universality of God's creation and is introduced here as a kind of *sed contra*. To this then he adds immediately the citation of 46.13/14 ("... as a reward for what they did") in order first to confirm the validity of his having taken the *mâ ta'malûna* of 37.94 in its most general sense and secondly to affirm that it is precisely their acts *(mâ kânû ya'malûna)* which God has created for which men are rewarded, the justice of God's judgement being assumed. The parallelism of wording is sufficient to validate the connection of the two verses (cf. also § 84). This is significant not simply because al-Aš'arî wishes to put on as resoundingly conservative a traditionalist dress as possible, but more especially because the chief effort of the following paragraphs (§§ 82-121) will be to show that the fact of God's creating those events which are most properly the acts of the human agent neither robs the agent of his true and proper causality nor alienates from him his real possession of or responsibility for his actions.

What follows then (§ 83f) is simply to confirm the validity of his interpretation of this first citation, viz., that "what you do" is to be taken in the sense of "your action" and should not be read to mean the thing which you have made or the material

(1) The same verse occurs in the preface to the *'aqîda* of Ibn Ḥanbal (*cit. supra*, p. 15, n. 1), p. 268 to prove the same point and, again, is cited by al-Baġdâdî (*Uṣûl ad-dîn* [Istanbul, 1346/1928], 135) to prove against the ğahmîya that although God is the sole creator, man does have his own proper actions *(a'mâl)*.

object of your act. That the argument is casuistic need not concern us since he is not here trying to prove his thesis but to prove the applicability of the citation and the meaning of the koranic text (1). So also his citation here of the distinction between the material upon which the agent acts and the act which resides in the material and the act of the agent which takes place in him, is only to support the validity of the application of 37.94 (2), and will be taken up separately and discussed in the following paragraphs.

In the following section (§ 85f) al-Aš'arî begins the formal analysis and argumentation of his overall thesis. He states that the total, essential content of the Being of any event or act, considered as an essential unity (its *ḥaqîqa*—the fullness of its Being in being what it is) is produced by some agent *(fâ'il)* who determines it in its totality through his knowing intention. The example which he has chosen, faith *('îmân)* and unbelief *(kufr)*, though superficially "loaded", is altogether appropriate from the author's standpoint. It should be noted in this regard that although the matter is never formally treated in the *Luma'*, al-Aš'arî limits the direct effect of human causality to those acts which take place in the agent (cf. *infra*, § 127), i.e., to motion (specifically the movement of his members—*ǧawâriḥ*) and those other acts which are realised in him, such as lying, believing, thinking, speaking, etc. (3) Faith or unbelief, which

(1) On the philological difficulty in reading the verse in this way, cf. Râzî, *Tafsîr* (ed. M. M. 'Abd al-Ḥamîd, Cairo, 1352/1933), 26, 149.

(2) The grammatical issue of the use of the term *mâ* in *mâ ta'malûn* (treated by Râzî, *loc. cit.*) is not explicitly raised and may well have been specifically and intentionally avoided (cf. al-Aš'arî's apparent neglect of one crucial aspect of an argument regarding the grammatical structure of 2.184/180 in §§ 141-3); where Râzî points out that one cannot properly read "you and your action" (as opposed to "you and what you have made") al-Aš'arî argues from the more general sense of the phrase in its use in the *Koran* and herein on the wider possibility and limits of its possible meaning. It should be noted however that in isolation one may easily hear the verse in the sense upon which the author insists and that the arguments detailed by Râzî represent a much later and perhaps more refined state of the casuistry of koranic verses. The grammatical issue is also skipped altogether by 'Abd al-Ǧabbâr in his discussion of the verse *(op. cit.,* 382) as he treates only the *mâ tanḥitûn*.

(3) Most of the mutakallimîn, in one way or another, restricted the immediate human act *(fi'l mubâšir)* in some such fashion, the results which follow from the

are the just basis of man's reward or punishment in the next life, are human acts according to which the human agent determines himself in his attitude towards God. In the present context belief (as also unbelief) is taken not as reduced to the minimal "affirmation" as it is in the *Luma'* (§§ 180f), but in the broader sense given it elsewhere by al-Aš'arî according to which it includes both the verbal affirmation and works (1). Faith and unbelief, though complex, represent single acts in the being of the believer or unbeliever. He is a believer or unbeliever as he determines himself in his action. As elements which qualify the reality of the individual who is *mu'min* or *kâfir*, belief and unbelief have their own essential reality (which is not relational) as distinct attributes or qualities. Each is something in itself, having its own essential nature as a particular reality (cf. *infra ad* § 90). His argument then is this: the presence of faith comes to be immediately in and from him who is *mu'min* as also unbelief from him who is *kâfir* (2). He is unable, however, to determine the total content and nature of his faith or unbelief; as for example faith causes certain hardships upon the believer which are inherent in its nature *(ḥaqîqa)* but which the believer does not and cannot himself will as such, just as also the unbeliever does not himself intentionally will the real evil of his unbelief (3), of which, indeed, he is essentially ignorant. Human knowledge, in fact, does not encompass the totality of the Being of anything in its every aspect. Neither faith nor unbelief, in the total content of its essential reality can be determined by the will of the immediate human agent from whom its real and concrete existence in the world comes to be; nor, on the other hand, can material reality, considered in itself as material,

act and are altogether outside and apart from the subject being discussed under the question of *tawallud;* the nature of the restriction of the immediate act varies considerably from author to author according to the general structure of his system; cf. generally *Maqâlât,* 410ff.

(1) Cf. *Ibâna* (Cairo, ND), 10 and *Maqâlât,* 293.

(2) Cf. also § 181.

(3) The goodness or evil of a thing is in all cases determined by God, according to al-Aš'arî. McCarthy however is wrong in saying that things are not objectively good or evil, since either quality is inherent in the total structure of a thing's being as this Being is determined by God's creation of it.

be the cause of the reality of anything (cf. § 86 at the end). God must therefore be the agent who has determined the reality of faith and unbelief in the full content of their Being.

Al-Aš'arî denied, against al-Ǧubbâ'î, that a being has in itself any Being other than the individual act of its real presence in the world *(wuǧûd = huwîya)*, so that to be the true cause of the coming to be *(iḥdâṯ)* of any thing is to be its cause in the fullness and totality of its Being. On this basis then (though the principle is not formally enunciated in the *Luma'*) and on the basis of §§ 85f, he then affirms (§ 87) that in the strictest sense, even in the case of events which are performed by a created agent and realised through his causality ("the occurence of the act which is *kasb*"), God alone can be the true agent *(fâ'il)* responsible for the realisation out of non-being *(iḫtirâ')* of the event as it exists in the fullness of its essential Being *('alà ḥaqîqatihi)*. He goes on (§§ 88f) to say that although God is the creator and in the fullest sense agent *(fâ'il)* also of the act of the creature, it does not not follow that God must perforce be the one who actually performs the act (the *muktasib*). This affirmation he establishes (§ 89) by showing that by definition the terms *fâ'il* and *muktasib* are not coëxtensive. The distinction is here quite clear and not merely terminological: the event takes place through or by the created power of the one who actually performs the act and not through some other power (cf. also *infra ad* § 92) but, on the other hand, the causality of the created agent is not sufficient to determine the entire reality of the event. From these two premises the conclusion follows quite easily. In the case of "necessary motion" (i.e., that not effected and determined by the will and intention of a created agent) the true cause or the mover need not be himself moved (something impossible in God) nor need the moved be the true agent of the motion. So also, he goes on to say, in the case of an act which the human agent performs according to his own will and intention *(kasb)*, the fact that the act takes place (comes to *be*) indicates that there must be some agent ultimately responsible for the realisation of the existence of the act in the fullness of its Being but it does not thereby indicate either that this agent is the created agent who performs the act (the *mukta-*

sib) or, on the other hand, that the created agent who performs the act is the one who determined the total reality of the Being of the act. God cannot be the *muktasib* since by definition the event takes place through a created power of efficient causality *(qudra muḥdaṯa)*, while God's power of causation is trancendent, an absolute and uncreated attribute of His Being (cf. also *infra ad* § 96).

This further specification of *kasb* and *muktasib* in terms of a created power of efficient causality he then takes up in § 90, saying that in his performance of the act, the human agent does not produce the thing in its total content. The true sense of the statement that "he has acquired [*iktasaba*] an act of unbelief" is that "he has disbelieved through a created power of causation [here *quwwa*]" (1). To say that he disbelieves is not to say that it is he who has brought into existence the reality of unbelief in its essential nature, independtly and entirely through a causality whose realisation and determination resides exclusively in himself, dependent upon his knowledge and intention (cf. also *infra ad* §§ 120f). The act of unbelief is realised through the causality of the unbeliever but the essential nature of unbelief is something determined by God. The same analysis is applied to the acts of lying and moving: the one who lies and by this act is a liar even though it is through his own intrinsic causality that the act of lying has come to exist in him and for him, is not the one who determined the essential nature of lying as it exists in him, as also the one who moves and in whom therefore motion exists in the fullness of its essential nature, is not the agent who has ultimately determined the essential nature of the movement as movement. To say thus that "it is hard to escape the conclusion that the liar, according to Ash-'arî, is under the same compulsion to lie as he is in any of his involuntary acts" (McCarthy, n. 14, *ad loc.*) is to miss the whole point which the author is trying to make. The question of the freedom or contingent spontaneity of human acts has not been raised at all, but only the ontological order of causes of Being

(1) On the use of *quwwa* as the equivalent of *istiṭâ'a* cf. the remarks of 'Abd al-Ǧabbār, *op, cit.*, 393.

and the place of human causality within this order. The relationship of God's causality to the act as an act of the human agent al-Aš'arî will take up in a subsequent paragraph.

Createdness is a fact of all Being other than that of God Himself, and again the author goes back to his insistence on the fact that the voluntary human act whose realisation proceeds in its entirety immediately from the causality of the human agent is no less created than his involuntary acts or those events which do not involve any created agent.

His initial argument (§ 91) is again based on the principle of sufficient cause and, though here much abbrieviated, is one which in one form or another, is common to the discussion of the question of causality and the necessity of the result through its cause in almost all Islamic speculation, whether that of the kalâm or the falsafa. It should be kept in mind here that in speaking of the Being of movement, belief, or unbelief, etc., in their essential nature or in the fullness of their being what they are (their *ḥaqîqa)* al-Aš'arî in no wise means to indicate any universal or anything like "essence" as opposed to the thing's actual existence. The *ḥaqîqa* of a thing is the total content of the reality of the individual existence *(huwîya)* in its actual existence *(wuǧûd)* as that particular act which it is. Again, he has here omitted—not denied—any mention of secondary causes (*asbâb*, in the formal terminology), since his problem is here that of the willing agent as cause, not of the physics of natural causes. The act or event which does not depend upon the will, knowledge, and intention and therefore upon the causality of a created agent (here movement is the example: *ḥarakat al-iḍṭirâr*) must exist at a particular time and in a particular substrate; and the reality of its Being, which is its existence in time and place, is specifically determined not by itself or any other purely material cause (cf. § 86) but by the cause which knows and wills its existence in the particular time and place. Such a cause can only be God. So also, he says, is the case of man's voluntary act. The actuality of the Being of any created being is dependent upon the cause which specifically determines its individual existence in all the particular determinations which constitute its Being. The human agent, as he is not himself the cause of his own Being, cannot in any way be said to be, of and by himself, the total cause of the event. Thus, regarding the Being of any event, considered within the totality of causes and determinents of its being, intrinsic and extrinsic, God alone is the sufficient cause in that it is He alone who knows exhaustively the total order of Being and the place of every being within this universal order and it must be He therefore who has created the human agent and his particular act of efficient causality (1).

In the following three paragraphs (§§ 92-4) the author further details his thesis that, by definition, involuntary acts and those subject to the determination of the human agent are alike created by God and that the fact of their creation does not vitiate the distinction between the two categories. As if to answer the objection that, as he construes the problem insisting that all acts are equally created by God, that is, if one act is "necessary" (involuntary and in no way subject to determination by the will of the person in whom and from whom it takes place), then all must be so and that if one act is voluntary and subject to the free determination of the agent *(kasb)*, then all must be alike subject to his determination, al-Aš'arî remarks that the distinction between the two categories of action is immediately self-evident, as for example between the movement of a person afflicted with partial paralysis or palsy and the voluntary acts of walking, fleeing, etc. In the former case the act is characterised by the fact of the absolute incapacity *('ağz)* of the person to determine the act, so that it does not in any real sense take place through his free causal determination and in the latter "the essential character of the act which is freely determined by the agent [*kasb*] is that the thing *take place from the one who performs it* through a created act of efficient causality [*bi-quwwatin muḥdaṯa*]". Again here, as throughout the *Luma'*, although he does not go into what we might consider sufficient detail in explaining the full implication of what he says, it is quite apparent that he means that the event takes place fully and

(1) This argument is drawn out in detail in many later works; cf. for example, Baġdâdî, *Uṣûl ad-dîn,* 133 and Šahrastânî, *Nihâya* (ed. A. Guillaume, Oxford, 1934) 73. However, one must be very cautious in reading back into the thought of al-Aš'arî the elaborations of his later followers, particularly those of Râzî.

exclusively through the "created act of efficient causality", God's creating the act consisting precisely in that He creates the total reality of the human agent, including the actuality of his being as agent and cause. Strictly then we should say that God creates the event through the generated causality of the human agent (1). From the standpoint of the human agent the acts are thus distinguished through a function of *qudra/kasb* (proper causality/ free realisation of voluntary act) on the one hand and of *'ağz/ ḍarûra* (total absence of willed causal determination/necessity) on the other, not in the fact of their being created, since they share this in the very fact of their existence in time and place, just as the fact of existence is common to motion and body (i.e., accident and substrate) alike, even though they are totally different in the mode of their Being (§ 93).

In no wise, thus, is his distinction "in the last analysis, a matter of extrinsic denomination" (McCarthy, *ad loc.* n. 17) (2), but on the contrary a completely valid ontological distinction. If, he says (§ 94), any being which comes to be through the immediate causality and according to the determination of an agent other than God *(waqa'a maqdûran li-ġayri llâh)* has its existence in complete exclusion of God's act of creation, then the principle that God creates and determines all things in the fullness of their Being is vitiated, not simply in regard to human acts but also in regard to all other areas of Being. Metaphysically this position is unassailable; God is either the transcendent source and cause of all Being or is a being among beings, a cause among causes (3).

(1) Cf. *Šarḥ al-Mawâqif,* 6, 85.

(2) Cf. the position of 'Abd al-Ğabbar who asks (*op. cit.*, 372) whether al-Aš'arî's distinction between acquired and necessary motion is anything more than verbal (cf. also *ibid.*, 423)! In his argumentation however (372f and 427), the Qâḍî steadfastly refuses to recognise the ontological distinction which al-Aš'arî makes and so does not really take the problem up on the level on which it is posed. (Cf. also McCarthy, *op. cit.*, p. 57, n. 11 and 59, n. 16.)

(3) From the standpoint of the polemics of § 94 it might be noted that just as his opponents are unwilling to give any recognition to al-Aš'arî's distinctions concerning the total, sufficient causality of the Being of anything, so also he refuses to allow the distinctions which al-Ğubbâ'î and his school made regarding the causation of Being *(iḥdâṯ)* on the part of the created agent (cf. references *supra*, n. 24, n. 1). The question is however, much more than simply one of polemical intransigence, since

In sum, to paraphrase the text (§ 95), "God is more strictly the cause of that of which we are the cause, since it is through His causality that we are causes;" what proceeds from our causality He has created and what does not take place, as not resulting from our causality, He has left uncreated.

There follows then a series of *questiones disputatae (masâ'il)*, in replying to which al-Aš'arî takes the opportunity to further elucidate his position.

Against an objection, based on the position of al-Ğubbâ'î (cf. *supra*) to the effect that if the realisation of an act by a human agent, according to his own will and determination, does in reality involve an act of creation *(ḫalq)*, why should we not thus consider the human agent the creator of the act, he notes first that strictly he did not say that the free human act *(kasb)* is an act of creation but rather that the act of creation which is involved is that God create the causality of the human agent. Then, since the thesis that the realisation of the free human act involves an act of creation in total exclusion of God's creative causality is altogether excluded (cf. *supra*, § 90 and *infra*, §§ 120f), al-Aš'arî argues that if we were to say that while the act of creation belongs to God, the human agent is strictly the creator of the act, then it would follow therefore that the relationship between the creator and the act is inevitably that of the agent who actually performs the act (i.e., a relationship of the structure of *iktisâb*), so that we shall be forced to hold that in those acts which do not come into being through the agency of a created agent, who freely wills and intends them, God is the performer of the act [1]. However, as will be brought out later (§ 127), the *kasb* act, most strictly understood, takes place within the agent *(muktasib)* so that consequently, if in the case of involuntary motions, etc., God must be considered *muktasib*

it involves on either side, the detailed structure of the entire system. Al-Aš'arî's absolute refusal to consider the mu'tazilite distinctions in the term "creation" *(ḫalq)* and to allow the use of the term *iḥdâṯ* of the act of the human agent considered in himself, is intimately bound together with his conception of the nature of the Being of beings as well as of the structure and place of the knowledge of the cause in relation to the caused; cf. *supra ad* §§ 86f.

(1) For the polemical assertion by the Mu'tazila that God would have thus to be called *muktasib*, cf. 'Abd al-Ğabbâr, *op. cit.*, 369.

of the act, He cannot be the transcendent ground and source of all Being, but will, on the contrary, be a moved mover, whose being is altered through and in the performance of the act.

By way of further elucidation of his meaning, he notes then (§ 97)—formulating what is the core of his understanding of *kasb/iktisâb*—that the act is the act of the material agent or subject in which it is realised as an act. If, in virtue of His creating them, we were to predicate of God the acts which He creates in the world, then no act could properly be predicated of any material creature as being truly the act of that creature: "if God were unjust for the reason that He is the ground of the Being of injustice, then no creature would be unjust", i.e., if the act of injustice were to exist in God then it could not exist in any creature. As the ultimate ground and creator of all Being, however, God is world-transcendent. Thus al-Aš'arî says that "God creates [for example] injustice as belonging to another"; that is, He creates the act in that He is the ground of its Being, but the act is the act of the Being of the subject in which it has its existence *(wuǧûd)*. If created acts and events were to belong to and to be predicated of God on the basis of His being the true and sufficient cause of their Being, we should then have to predicate of Him all acts as such and He would be willing, desiring, moving, etc., through and in the temporal acts of willing, desiring, moving, etc., which belong to and take place in material creatures.

The same objection is then renewed (§ 98) in a slightly different form as one asks regarding injustice which takes place but of which there is no agent who performs the act—no *muktasib*. Here again is involved God's creation of events in terms of the problem of *ta'dîl*, i.e., of the possibility of God's doing wrong or injustice to his creatures, something which the Mu'tazila denied absolutely and made a central theme of their polemics. The question is very important, albeit taken up but briefly, since it involves events which cause difficulty or misery to human beings and for which there can be said, according to the principles of al-Aš'arî's theology, no proper agent (no agent who has determined the event through the intention of his will—no *fâ'il qâṣid murîd*) other than God himself. To be included would be "natural" events as well as harm or injury inflicted through the involuntary act of another person.

God is not the *muktasib* of the act; His being is not qualified or altered by its realisation, wherefore He cannot be called unjust on its account. The quasi causality of purely material causes is a subject which does not fall within the framework of the problem as here posed, since they cannot be considered as true efficient causes, having no knowledge or intention of their effects. Consequently they are omitted from the discussion. It is nevertheless quite clear that al-Aš'arî does recognise the fact of the operation of purely material causes. Where there is no willing, intending agent intervening between God and the immediate realisation of the act, the event does in fact take place through secondary causes; but since the determination of its realisation cannot be ascribed to material, secondary causes, the act of efficient causality belongs to God alone, in that it is He alone who can be said to have willed them and determined their being in a knowing intention. Such events however cannot be ascribed to God as "His acts", i.e., as qualifying His Being insofar as He is the cause of their existence, since He cannot be *muktasib* of any created act (§ 96f). Such acts are said to have no *muktasib.*

In § 99 again we find another objection based, from the author's standpoint, on the failure to make the distinctions set forth above (particularly in §§ 96f) and reflecting some of the disputes regarding the createdness of the *Koran:* if God created the act in the fullness of its Being, can He not be said to speak through the utterance of the created speaker"? The reply is as above, viz., that the act is created as belonging to another, not by God as His own act. His own utterance *(qawl, kalâm)* whereby He is called "speaking" *(mutakallim)* is, like His power of efficient causality, an uncreated attribute of His Being ([1]).

In the following three questions al-Aš'arî then takes up

(1) Regarding the thesis of God's speaking through the utterance of a created speaker (which is more or less that of the ğahmîya) and the opposition to it of the orthodox thinkers, cf. R. Frank, "The Neoplatonism of Ğahm b. Ṣafwân,", 419.

objections regarding God's providence and man's attitude towards it.

In § 100 the objection assumes the inefficacy of human action: "can man be other than subject to God's blessing for which he must give thanks or a trial under which he must bear up"? In reply the author insists on the real efficacy of human effort and action and man's ability to effect events, distinguishing between those stituations about which man can do nothing and those which he must strive to ameliorate. Al-Aš'arî gives no argument to support his position here, since the objection is captious in that it would eristically identify his position with that of the *muǧabbira* and since, on the other hand, against a mu'tazilî opponent he no doubt feels little need to establish the point. Further, since his central theme is the structure of *qudra* and not of man's freedom or spontaneity of action, the specific objection is not altogether pertinent to the discussion.

The following paragraphs (§§ 101-116), though ostensibly containing merely the treatment of a number of detached *quaestiones*, centering in §§ 108-116 around the interpretation of several disputed verses of the *Koran*, form a quite remarkably structured unit, centered on the question of the nature of creation and God's providence. Though the whole section follows the established pattern and conventional form of argumentation used throughout the *Luma'*, the unity of purpose is quite apparent in the order in which he passes from the admission of the existence of evil in creation as dependent ultimately upon God's will and "decree", affirming both the universality of His providence and His absolute transcendence as creator, to the affirmation that the Truth *(ḥaqq)* of each and every being in Being is grounded in God's creation of it, according to His eternal knowledge. The basic structure is quite "Greek" and specifically neoplatonic, although the general understanding as well as the detail of the exposition is uncompromisingly Islamic.

Falling quite properly into place after the introduction of § 100, the following two groups of paragraphs (§§ 101-3 and 104-5) involve the sense of the term "God's Decree" *(al-qaḍâ')*. In both cases the objection is set so as to place the author and his supporters in the position of having to say that God decrees evil and that, to this extent, His decree is evil (§§ 101ff) or that "we are not satisfied or content with what God decrees" (§§ 104f). Al-Aš'arî says that we may say that God has decreed and determined *(qaḍà wa-qaddara)* evil or disobedience, in the same sense that He is the Creator of all Being and that nothing comes to be but what He wills to create but not in the sense that He specifically commands and approves such acts. Taking thus the term "God's decree" in the broadest sense, he allows that God's decree involves evil as well as good, but the terms evil, unbelief, etc., are not coextensive with the term "decree". To say that we are content with God's decree is not to say that we are content with the unbelief of the unbeliever (cf. also § 100). The whole question, posed thus, is, he notes (§ 103 and § 105), terminological or rhetorical and some of the more conservative, orthodox authorities are more restrictive in the use which they will allow of the terms.

The real question involved here, that of the justice and goodness of God and the implication that evil is to be attributed to God Himself if He is responsible for the existence of evil in the world, al-Aš'arî takes up in the following two paragraphs (§§ 106f) which, although indicated in the text as separate *quaestiones*, form but a single unit. The framework within which the problem is to be understood has already been set out, wherefore in reply (§ 107) the author merely reasserts the distinction made in §§ 96-99, that God does not Himself do evil but rather "evil is from God in that He creates evil belonging to another, not to Himself". Here again he notes that some of his fellows *(aṣḥâb)* distinguish between the universal attribution of creation, as a general providence *(bil-ğumla)* and His creation of the isolated particular. This statement is of especial interest. The author quite clearly finds nothing in it which is in basic opposition to his own doctrine and, on the contrary, would seem to approve it. It is, in fact, to be noted that where al-'Aš'arî cites his *aṣḥâb* elsewhere in the *Luma'*, their opinions would seem generally to have a more conservative formulation than his own. His treatment of the question of God's decree in the preceding paragraphs, as also in § 98 where he made allowance for the results of natural and involuntary events, would seem to point to some such distinction, even though perhaps, al-Aš'arî was not himself altogether satisfied with the particular formulation, because it might tend to make it appear that there were events which escaped in some degree from God's omniscience and will. Since the question is not discussed, it is impossible to determine precisely what was the position of al-Aš'arî or of his companions. Given however the possibility suggested above (cf. note 2, p. 22) that there is some indication of a neoplatonic structure to his conception of sufficient causality, one may be justified in speculating that there is found here a reflection of something like the notions set forth in the two chapters περὶ προνοίας of the *Enneades* (for no being, it should be noted, is omitted from the content of νοῦς) (1).

The following paragraphs, which are divided into three sections (§§ 108-15, 116, 117f), all involve the interpretation of disputed verses which are put forth by the objector in order to establish the common mu'tazilite conception of *qudra* against that of al-Aš'arî. In considering the content and the argument of these paragraphs one should keep in mind the importance of the *textus litteralis* of the *Koran* in muslim theology, for the book was held by all alike, the Mu'tazila as well as al-Aš'arî and also the ḥanbalî traditionists, to be the paradigm of all truth: the Creator's revelation of the Truth of all Being *(al-ḥaqq)*, of Himself and of His creation. For this reason it was of the utmost importance for the mutakallimîn to establish the sense of any verse

(1) I do not in any way wish to suggest that there is any kind of direct influence of Plotinus or of Christian neoplatonism on al-Aš'arî or his immediate sources and predecessors, but simply want to suggest that the background is quite complex and contains many significant elements besides the frequently cited dependencies upon the Stoa and the atomists. The kalâm's formation of its own terminology and the unique way in which many questions were formulated and treated in isolation tended to obscure and cover all the traces of its background and the non-islamic sources of some of its basic philosophical theses and presuppositions. There was also, without doubt, at the outset, a purposeful burying of whatever non-islamic sources were consciously used, because of the generally poor standing of any teaching which belonged to the infidel and was not ostensibly based on the koranic revelation. There is therefore no reason to believe that al-Aš'arî was aware of using any sources which were not strictly the property of the kalâm, but we may have in this paragraph, along with the other indications cited above, some hint or reflection of a part of his intellectual background.

which is to be used to support or confirm any theological assertion. In this context, then, when al-Aš'arî simply sets aside a particular verse as not pertinent to the argument and apparently would seem thereby to avoid the point at issue, he is not dodging the question at all but following what was in reality a valid procedure, well established by his predecessors.

In the first instance (§ 108) his mu'tazilî opponent cites 3.72/78, which he will take as meaning that since the falsification of the revelation is "not from God", God did not create the acts whereby the Jews make false statements about the scriptures. The structure of the creation of human acts al-Aš'arî has already dealt with, so that here he simply says that the verse means that God did not reveal what they claim (cf. also § 99). There is here no problem of *qudra*. Al-Aš'arî will however, though having disposed of the verse as the basis of the argument, take up the intended force of the objection in § 114. Much the same technique is followed in the following paragraphs (§§ 109-115), all of which deal with the mu'tazilite argument that we cannot say that God creates and so is responsible for any thing which is vain or evil *(bâṭil)* and so form a fairly cohesive unit.

Thus in § 109 he says that *Koran* 67.3 f, which the *qadarîya* used as a proof text to show that God does not create unbelief, makes no reference to unbelief or any other kind of human act, since in its context it refers properly to the creation of the heavens (though he notes further that their use of the text, regardless of the context, can have no validity as the basis of the argument). So also he says (§ 110) that they have misinterpreted 32.7/6 which refers not to the goodness of what God creates but to the perfection of His own action and knowledge [1].

In §§ 111-5 then (which the text designates as a single *quaestio*), having set aside the " objections" raised, he takes up anew the problem mentioned in regard to the verses cited in the foregoing paragraphs, in terms of the universality of God's creation, begining with an objection raised on the basis of 38.26/27 ("We did not create the heavens and the earth and what

(1) For the mu'tazilite use of the verse, cf. 'Abd al-Ǧabbâr, *op. cit.*, 357f, where al-Aš'arî's interpretation of it is challenged on philological grounds.

is between them *bâṭilan*"). Stating first that their understanding of the sense of the verse is not valid in its proper context, since it refers properly to God's creation of punishments and rewards in the next life (§ 111), he returns (§ 112) to the distinctions set out above (§§ 103-7) regarding the application of the term *bâṭil* to God's creation and, to confirm the universality of creation (§ 113), cites 25.60/59: "He created the Heavens and the Earth and what is between them in six days". This would, he insists, have to be taken into consideration if one would read 38.26/27 as his opponents interpret it (i.e., as refering primarily to His creation of the world and the things in the world). Returning then (§ 114) to 3.72/78 (cited above in § 108) and the argument about God's creating what is *bâṭil*, he notes that if you will allow the opponent's objection and interpretation of that verse, reading it conjointly with 67.3f (taken up in § 109), you will have to allow that He does create acts of obedience *(ṭâ'ât)*; but this only raises anew the problem of God's justice and the determination of acts (cf. also § 121). Thus one is forced, he says, to allow his own interpretation of 32.7/6 (v. *supra* § 110), just as one does with 13.16/17 ("The Creator of everything"), which is explicitly universal.

Finally (§ 115), to make an end of these arguments based on a casuistry of the term *bâṭil*, he places alongside this last citation, that of 15.85: "We have not created the Heavens and the Earth and what is between them save with Truth" *(bil-ḥaqq)*. His interpretation of this, which must have been well established in conservative circles, since it is given also by Ibn Ḥanbal (1), is that *al-ḥaqq* here refers to God's command "be", through which all things come to exist. The Truth *(ḥaqq)* of all Being—of every being in Being—resides in the act whereby God creates it; the truth and rightness *(ḥaqq)* of the whole order of creation is grounded in the act of the Creator.

This section of the discussion is closed then with an argument (§ 116) which, although formally based on no more than the

(1) Cf. *Radd 'alà l-ǧahmîya* (*Ilahiyat Fakültesi Mecmuasi*, 1927), 321; it may be that the term *ḥaqq* has, in such usage, retained something of the sense of Hebrew *ḥuqqâ*. At any rate, al-Aš'arî's interpretation of this verse conforms exactly to his treatment of 32.7/6, cited above in § 110.

evidence of two common koranic phrases, is central to al-Aš'arî's understanding of the structure of God's omnipotence and the universality of His creation. The form of the argument, abbreviated as it is to the citation of two texts of the *Koran*, so as to give the appearance of a purely "traditionalist" type of argument from authority, should not obscure the profoundly philosophical character of its theoretical basis. Al-Aš'arî cites first the frequent expression that God "knows all things" *(bi-kulli šay'in 'alîm)*. According to the long established usage of the term *šay'* (thing) this will mean in the technical language of the kalâm that He knows each and every *being* (1). Then in view of the universality of this statement, he goes on to say that one will have to read the same universality in the likewise frequent koranic affirmation that God is "powerful over all things", i.e., that his power of action and efficient causality extends to all beings. As was suggested above, there is for al-Aš'arî a necessary and inevitable connection between knowledge and efficient causality: the determination of the Being of any being follows from the knowing intention of the causal agent, being first and essentially determined in the knowledge of the agent. Since therefore God alone knows exhaustively the fullness of the Being of all beings (cf. *supra*, §§ 85-87) we must take the statement that His power of causation extends to all beings to mean that there is no being which is brought into Being save that God is ultimately the true agent and creator who causes its being *(muḥdiṯun lahu, fâ'ilun, ḫâliq)*. In short, while there can be no doubt that secondary causes play their rôles in the events of the world, both human and natural, the fulness of the essential reality of all beings, separately and within the universal order of creation, is determined by and in the knowledge and intention of God, Who is the first and ultimate source of all Being (2). We need not further insist here upon the neoplatonic character of this conception nor its parallels in later Islamic thought.

(1) The sense is clearly established and commonly taken in this meaning already in the work of Ǧahm b. Ṣafwân.

(2) In taking up this argument, 'Abd al-Ǧabbâr (*op. cit.*, 375 and 377) refuses to allow the connection which al-Aš'arî and his followers find between the knowledge of the agent and his causality and treats it as if they would simply conclude from the universality of the first statement to that of the second. Regarding al-Aš'arî's argument here, cf. also *Maqâlât* 550, ll. 4-6.

The following paragraphs (§§ 117f) contain an "objection" based upon the sense of the term *barî'* (to be free of, have nothing to do with) as it occurs in *Koran* 9.3f: "God, indeed, and His Apostle have naught to do with the idolators". As the author points out, the immediate reference of the verse is to the invalidation of such covenants as exist with them, so that the verse is not really pertinent to the discussion of *qudra*. As used by the "objector" however, the verse is taken in isolation and the term *barî'* read in the sense that God is free of any relationship of responsibility to the acts of the idolators, whence it is argued that He did not create their acts. Having then pointed out the proper meaning of the verse in context, al-Aš'arî goes on, as he does above in regard to 3.72/78 (§§ 108 and 114) to take up (§ 118) the sense of the objection despite the non-cogency of the verse, and to raise the same difficulty as with 3.72/78 in § 114, viz., that if God does not create the idolatry of the idolators but nevertheless does create the belief of the believer, the question of His justice is in no way solved (1). For his own resolution of the difficulty he cites again the distinction made above regarding the creation of an act as belonging to another. Although these paragraphs (§§ 117-8) would seem to be possibly more in place between § 115 and § 116, it may be that the objection based on 9.3f is taken up as a kind of final shot, on the basis of the term *barî'*.

In § 119 we find the author's final case in which he will show that although God is the unique Creator and ground of all Being, He is transcendent and so not involved in the events of the world in such a way that He can be spoken of as the immediate responsible agent of an act. The example is carefully set so that, from the standpoint of the objector (al-Ğubbâ'î?) either al-Aš'arî will have to admit of a true spontaneity of self-determination, to be explained in terms of the subject alone,

(1) Involved here is an argument based on the fact that the Mu'tazila did evidently allow that He should be praised on account of the faith of the believer (cf. 'Abd al-Ğabbâr, *op. cit.*, 332f), though al-Aš'arî polemically distorts their intention. It should be noted that we must assume that this verse was important in the polemics of the Mu'tazila whom al-Aš'arî knew (cf. *infra ad* § 126), even though it would seem not to have been so used by the later followers of the school, probably because its adaptation was so obviously far removed from the proper context.

or that God's action excludes all existential spontaneity, with all the problems which follow from such a position. Two twins live alone in the desert (and so are free of outside suggestion and the pressure of the social group), one of whom comes to believe that God is one and the other that He is three. The problem then is set in two questions: is what God "put into the heart of the first man true?" Then: did He tell him the truth in what he put into his heart? The questions are then repeated *mutatis mutandis* regarding the second man.

The second question is purely polemical and the author disposes of it immediately as such. God's truthfulness and integrity *(ṣidq)* are not involved since we have not here to do with what is in any true sense a communication or inspiration of His own word. God's *ṣidq* is a divine attribute, His Word, and so cannot be predicated in any way of what is a purely human conception (an accident inhering in a material substrate or creature). In reply to the first question then, he returns to the distinctions made above: "it does not follow that He lies when He creates the act of lying belonging to another and lying in the heart of another, just as also it is not necessary that when He creates the act of efficient causality in another or the act of willing in another or movement in another that He be the immediate efficient agent [*qâdir*] or that He be thereby willing or moved". Here again, adhering strictly to his central problem and avoiding any description of the process, and any question of the existential spontaneity of the human act, he insists that the events belong properly to the men involved, as taking place through and in terms of their attributes and actions; albeit these are in every respect created, they belong as created to the human individual and it is from him, as belonging to him, that the event takes place. Al-Aš'arî refuses to be drawn onto his opponents ground and take up the question of the contingent spontaneity of the human act, just as his opponents generally refuse to remove the discussion from the context of freedom and justice onto the plain of a purely metaphysical analysis.

In the final paragraphs of the section on *qadar* (§§ 120f), where he defines the term *qadarîya*, al-Aš'arî makes his position clear in its contradistinction to that of al-Ǧubbâ'î and to that of the *muǧabbira.* Here again, as throughout the work his position gives the impression of being far more radical than it in fact is. The *qadarî* is, he says (§ 120), he who claims to be the complete agent of his acts, as they are determined immediately through his own causality *(muqaddaratan lahu)*, in exclusion of the causality of God, and thinks that God has no part whatsoever in the acts which he (the human agent) performs (cf. § 90). In contrast, the position of the *muǧabbira* (who are not named), which he also rejects (§ 121), is that God is the agent of all his acts as determined immediately through His own causality (without any intervention of the created agent). His own position is intermediate: "God determines our acts and creates them as they are determined immediately through our causality". We must beware, however, of reading "God determines our acts" in a deterministic sense. Al-Aš'arî will no more allow an absolute determinism (no matter how hidden under whatever rhetorical screen) than will Ibn Taymîya, Rather, as the essential content of the Being of all beings is determined through God's knowledge and intention, and as He is the source of all Being, "God is more strictly the cause of that of which we are the immediate cause, since it is through His causality that we are causes (§ 95)". His position is analogous to that of St. Thomas who says that *omnis causa secunda dans esse, hoc habet in quantum agit in virtute primae causae creantis* (*de Potentia*, 3.8 *ad* 19).

*
* *

HUMAN CAUSALITY CONSIDERED AS THE ACTUALITY OF THE AGENT

Throughout this section it must be kept in mind that al-Aš'arî understands *istiṭâ'a* or man's created *qudra* as the actuality of his power of causation, i.e., the «accident» *('araḍ)* which defines the actuality of the being of the agent insofar as he is the agent of the particular act, and has thereby departed from the common understanding of the term as it was used by his master Abû 'Alî and most of the Mu'tazila. This is purely a matter of definition and as such is not debatable. The question of the spontaneity of human action and those functions within the overall structure of the human act as are covered by the term *qudra/isṭiṭâ'a* as it is used by various mu'tazilî authors and which al-Aš'arî eliminates from it, he will have to take care of in some other way, if and when he might choose to take up the more general problem. Since he does not do this in the *Luma'* however, it need be of no concern to the present investigation.

In the present section al-Aš'arî is not so much arguing to prove a point against the Mu'tazila as he is trying to elucidate and describe the structure of human causality in terms of his conception of *iktisâb* and *qudra muḥdaṯa.* Most of the propositions which he sets forth follow almost directly from his definition of created causality and his chief effort therefore is to clarify and to validate the detail of his understanding on the basis of the theses which were enunciated in the preceding section and the definition of created *qudra* which he will set forth in the paragraphs which immediately follow. In regard to these initial paragraphs it is to be noted that what the author is doing is no more than fixing the definition of the term *qudra/isṭiṭâ'a.* From one standpoint the definition might be quite briefly stated as the actuality of the agent insofar as he is the cause of his act. Al-Aš'arî however does not give any such concise definition, with what brief elaboration would be necessary to allow the grounding of his later theses. From one standpoint the purely literary or stylistic conventions which impose themselves upon him have certainly a considerable part in determining the way in which his thought is set out. More importantly however, as a determinent factor in the way he sets about defining his meaning, is the fact that the correlated concepts of actuality and potentiality, act and potency (which were unquestionably known to him) are deliberately excluded from the system and so from any discussion of the problem, as has been noted above. Since these concepts are not considered to have any ontological validity, the author must then perforce delimit his meaning of the term *qudra/isṭiṭâ'a* in a dialectic in which the sense of the definition, its inclusions and exclusions, are made manifest through an argumentation which assumes the understanding of the definition, against the meanings which it excludes.

It is also interesting to note that al-Aš'arî does not here, as at the beginning of the other major sections of the work, state his position initially on the authority of a text of the *Koran*, though he does later, after he has elaborated his thesis (§§ 133f), cite several texts to confirm what he has said. So highly technical and abstract a conception could hardly be indicated or suggested by the revelation. That the structure of the act of *qudra* could not be demonstrated from revelation *(bis-sam')* was probably a doctrine of the school of al-Ǧubbâ'î (1). Again, it is notable that when the author does come to the point of citing several texts to support his position, by showing that it conforms with the usage of the *Koran* their cogency is quite tenuous.

In the first paragraphs (§ 122 and §§ 123-5) al-Aš'arî defines his understanding of human *qudra* against and in contrast to that of the Mu'tazila. Against the position of an-Naẓẓâm and 'Alî al-Aswârî (2) he says (§ 122) that *qudra* is not an essential and inevitable determinent of the Being of man as such. This follows immediately from the assumed definition of the term, since the human individual is not at every moment of his existence the consciously intentional and willing agent of every act which defines his Being at the moment. Rather, his actuality as the cause of a particular event is, like a particular act of knowing, an accident of his Being.

In §§ 123-4 then, against the position of the great majority of the Mu'tazila, he says that the act of *qudra* exists simultaneously with the realisation of the act; it is «with the act and of the act». Though the question is set out (§ 123) as to whether it can precede the act or not, the author does not take up the problem first from this direction, in view of the fact that, considered as the actuality of the being of the agent insofar as he is the cause of the act, *qudra* cannot possibly precede the realisation of the act. This assumption is made quite clear later in § 125 where a part of the argumentation

(1) Cf. 'Abd al-Ǧabbâr, *op. cit.*, 401.

(2) Cf. *Maqâlât*, 229; al-Aš'arî does not take up the real sense of an-Naẓẓâm's understanding of the notion of *qudra*, which in the full context of his system differs radically from that of most of the mutakallimîn.

is based on the thesis that the act of *qudra* cannot be already present in existence at the moment it comes to be *(bâqiyatun fî ḥâli ḥudûṯihâ)*. The question here is one of definition. The act of *qudra*, he says therefore (§ 123), must either be simultaneous with the realisation of the event or follow it, and clearly it cannot follow since this would entail the existence of a result prior to the actuality of its cause. As a kind of lemma to §§ 123f then, he argues in § 125 that the causality of the human agent cannot perdure in existence. The thesis of the majority of the Mu'tazila that *qudra* precedes the realisation of the act is eliminated because, within the limits of al-Aš'arî's definition of the term, this would mean that a being should precede the actuality of its own being, i.e., that the actuality of the cause, insofar as it is the cause of a particular being, should exist *per se* prior to the existence of that of which it is the cause or that an «accident» should inhere in an «accident».

In §§ 126-7 then, he goes on to insist that the single act of *qudra* can be the causality of only a single event. He takes up first (§ 126) the common Mu'tazilite thesis that the single act of *qudra* extends to both of a pair of contraries (i.e., that it is the power to perform the act or not to perform it). This thesis was, in effect, formally excluded in the previous paragraphs, in that it demands that the actuality of the *qudra* precede the realisation of the act or, by al-Aš'arî's definition of the term, would necessitate the simultaneous existence of a pair of contraries in the same subject (this last proposition being noted briefly at the end of § 126). Where all this might easily have been said in the foregoing paragraphs, however, he uses § 126 in order further to contrast the nature of human causality to that of God. It is this which justifies the presence of a distinct question here, as he continues delimiting his understanding of human *qudra* which, though the same term is used, is of altogether a different order; God's *qudra*, an attribute of His transcendent Being, is perpetually in act and can have no temporal relationship to the existence of its object *(maqdûr)*, whose existence is defined by the temporal and spatial dimensions of the material world. Al-Aš'arî says therefore that the actuality of God's eternal power is not such that it necessitates the simultaneous actuality of its objects. To say this, in any sense whatsoever, would imply that things *(ašyâ')*, beings other than God, had some transcendent mode of being, and this he will allow under no circumstances. No being is immaterial *(lâ fî maḥall)* or is in any way eternal *(qadîm)* (1) other than God Himself. Thus also is the case with God's knowing *('ilm)* which, as was remarked, is closely associated in a quite platonic way with His causality; albeit God knows, in an eternal act of knowing, all beings and their place in the universal order of being, one cannot say, according to al-Aš'arî, that they pre-exist and have Being in His knowing, for the only Being which creatures have consists in the actuality of their material presence in the world (2). In contrast to the neoplatonists, al-Aš'arî denies categorically that the world or any of the beings which exist in the world in any way share or participate in any kind of immaterial and eternal existence. God's *qudra*, like His knowing, is altogether transcendent from the existence of material beings. From the standpoint of their coming into existence in the finite, temporal sequence of material events we can however say that God's *qudra* precedes the realisation of its objects. Human causality on the other hand, which is the causality of a cause whose Being is in every respect a material Being, can exist only in an immediate and simultaneous, temporal correlation to its effect.

In reply to the question of whether from a single act of *qudra* there can result two similar effects, he mentions (§ 127) for the first time explicitly that, most strictly understood, the act of causation co-exists with its effect not merely in time but also in the same subject *(maḥall/mawḍû')* (3), and

(1) The sense of the term *qadîm* (already well developed as a central concept in the theology of al-Ǧubbâ'î) would seem, as used by al-Aš'arî in the *Luma'*, to contain some important analogies to the sense of the term *al-wâǧib bi-ḏâtihi* (the necessary *per se*) as used by Avicenna and the philosophers; cf. *Luma'*, § 6 and § 36 and also al-Baqillânî, *at-Tamhîd* (ed. M. el-Khodeiri and M. Abû Rîda, Cairo, 1366/1947), 49 and on the use by al-Ǧubbâ'î and the Mu'tazila cf. *Maqâlât*, 529, 'Abd al-Ǧabbâr, *al-Muǧnî*, pt. 4 (ed. M. Hilmî and A. al-Ghanîmî, Cairo, ND) 250f and Šahrastânî, *Milal*, 125.

(2) Cf. *supra* and *Šarḥ al-Mawâqif* 2, 127 and 152, *et alibi*.

(3) The opposition of human causality in its relation to its effect and God's in

then denies the possibility that more than one effect follow a single act of *qudra*, saying that if there were more than one, they will either have to take place successively, in which case one of them will be an effect which does not co-exist with its immediate cause (and so be the result of a non-existent causality) or they will have to exist simultaneously, as two distinct effects and this, in turn, will involve the simultaneous existence of contraries in a single substrate. This paragraph, succinct and modest at it is, is quite important in making explicit several aspects of al-Aš'arî's understanding of the structure of created causality, which are central to his whole conception of the general problem and to his reduction of it to its minimum terms.

To end the first division of this section, confirming what has gone before, he remarks briefly (§ 128) that man's power of efficient causality (here *istiṭâ'a)* is so related to the act resulting from it that it can only exist simultaneously with the act as the immediate causation thereof. Where, in the discussion which preceded, the problem was approached almost exclusively from the analysis of the notion of *qudra*, this last additional evidence he raises from the consideration of the act, which, as it depends upon the actual causation of the agent, cannot be separated from it. More importantly perhaps from the standpoint of the author, he here brings up for the first time in this section, i.e., since § 121) the creation of the human act by God and makes clear the point that the act which is realised through the causality of the human agent takes place simultaneously with God's creation of the agent's power of causation. The effect then of the paragraphs is to tie the present discussion (§§ 122ff) together with the matters discussed in the previous section. Also it is to be noted that here (§ 128) he uses the term *kasb/iktisâb* for the first time in this section. This is important to the proper understanding of the meaning of these terms as al-Aš'arî uses them. Where in §§ 122-127 the discussion of the relationship between man's causality and his act was carried out in isolation from that of God's

relation to what He creates, has been dealt with above (§§ 85f) so that the author feels no need to take it up again here.

creation of man's causality, the only terms used were *qudra* and *istiṭâ'a; kasb* is brought up only here in § 128 when the question of God's transcendent causality is introduced. It is therefore quite clear that the term, most strictly understood, implies the acquisition of the act through God's creation of the act of causation in the agent. This does not, it should again be noted, vitiate the notion that the human agent is the cause. On the contrary, it is evident from §§ 122-127 that human causality can be discussed in and of itself within its own order of being. The introduction of the question of God's creation of human causality and the «acquisition» of the act by the human agent sets the problem within the fuller context, against the framework of another dimension and order of Being and relates the Being of the act which is entirely within the world to the ground of its Being which is world-transcendent.

The use of *kasb* in the previous section—especially, for example in § 116—as defining the relation of the created agent to his act, follows from an extension of its basic meaning (as in § 128) to cover the realisation of the human act in all its dimensions: the relationship between the agent (as moved mover) and his act, as well as his relationship as an agent to the ground of his Being as agent. *Kasb* thus becomes a term for the relationship between the agent and his act as an extension of the primary designation of the createdness of his efficient causality and remains distinct from *qudra/istiṭâ'a* in that these terms denote his efficient causality as such (cf. *supra ad* §§ 92f). Although the single term, *qudra* is used both of God's causality and of man's, the two are not understood as analogous in any way.

In the following paragraphs (§§ 129-132) the author takes up the relation of the causation of the act to those elements and qualities of the Being of the agent without which no act is possible. It is clear enough that from the author's standpoint the closer delimitation of the central problem, which he makes at the outset, is sufficient to cover each of the several items discussed, but given the more general context of the structure of human existence as it was understood, analysed, and discussed by the mutakallimîn, he was constrained to take up each factor as a separate question in order to make his meaning unequivocally clear in respect of each.

The first question (§ 129) is that of the relationship between the act which takes place and the member of the body *(ǧâriḥa)* which is its instrument and locus. There is no question at all of the thesis of some of the Mu'tazila, cited above, that *qudra* consists in the strength and physical well-being of the body, but rather the intention of the author is further to refine and delimit the question of created causality by removing from the discussion all extraneous elements. From the point of view of al-Aš'arî's ontology, the distinctions made here and in the following paragraphs are most important, as again we witness another step in the reduction of the problem to the most basic terms, which characterise its treatment in the later kalâm.

He notes thus that with the absence (in whatever sense) of the efficient member, there can be no act, for the reason that there can be no efficient causality in the absence of the instrument through which and in which the event must be realised. Most strictly speaking, the impossibility of the act is not due immediately to the absence of the efficient member but rather to the absence of the act of efficient causality *(qudra)*, which is the immediate ontological ground of its realisation; that is, the absence of the efficient member may, in the particular case, be the immediate circumstance of the impossibility of the presence of the act of causation, but ontologically the non-realisation of the act is due to the non-actuality of the cause as cause: the non-presence *('adam)* of the act of causation in the cause.

In regard to the relationship between the realisation of the act and the presence of the «accident» of life in the agent, al-Aš'arî makes the same distinction (§ 130) as in the preceding paragraph. This is taken up as a separate question because life was held by most of the mutakallimîn, including al-Aš'arî, to be the condition of the presence in the living being of those attributes associated with it (knowing, willing, perceiving, etc.) and so also of the possibility of the existence of *qudra*. Ontologically, the non-realisation of the act is due immediately to the absence of the causality from which it should have taken place, not to the absence of life as such, even though this necessarily excludes the possibility of the presence of the act of causation. Here again he is not, I think, trying to make a point against the position, such as that of Abû l-Hudhayl, that the realisation of the act can take place in the absence of life (since according to him, the power of causality from which the act proceeds precedes its realisation and does not perdure into the moment of its realisation); this question was adequately dealt with above. Rather, as in the previous paragraph, his intention is to elucidate further the structure of the act of causality and the event in the context of the being of the agent.

Such also is the case in § 131; within the strict limits of the notion of human causality as understood by the kalâm, the agent is the cause of the act only insofar as he knows and freely intends it, wherefore there can be no act, as the true act of the particular agent, in the absence of such knowledge and skill *(iḥsân)* as are prerequisite to it. Al-Aš'arî notes that the realisation of the act is immediately dependent upon the act of causation, not the presence of the prerequisite knowledge or skill, even though the latter constitute a precondition of the possibility of the act.

In § 132 then he summarises the position which he has set forth in the previous three paragraphs, saying that the absence of any internal or external constraint or impediment to the freedom of action (1) is the necessary condition of the realisation of the act. So also the physical organism, as a unified, organic whole, in being the substrate of both the *qudra* and the resulting act, forms a necessary condition of the possibility of the act (2).

(1) For the meaning of the terms *taḫliya* and *iṭlâq* cf. 'Abd al-Ǧabbâr, *Šarḥ al-uṣûl,* 404 and 393; the former I take to refer to the absence of any constraint to or restraint from the performance of the act (cf. the use of the expression *al-qâdir al-muḫallà* in *al-Muġnî,* pt. 6, 1 [ed. A. el-Ahwani and I. Madkur, Cairo 1382/1962] 18 and 26) but not specifically to an external hindrance to its performance, this being covered by the term *iṭlâq* (cf. the addition of the reference to *al-mâni', ibid.,* 18) though perhaps no fine distinction was made between the two.

(2) Al-Ǧubbâ'î used the term *binya,* which al-Aš'arî employs here, as a technical

Accepting the formula of al-Ğubbâ'î but taking it within the framework of his own understanding of *qudra* (as in act at the moment of the realisation of the action), al-Aš'arî allows that the actual realisation of the act is concommitant with «the organism's bearing the act» *(wuğûdu ḥtimâli l-binyati liš-šay')* since «the organism is the subject only of that which subsists in it». Allowing this however, he notes that in both cases, as in the instances mentioned above (§§ 129-31), the immediate ontological ground of the act in the agent is the actuality of the power of efficient causality, not the condition of its actuality.

Having then completed the outline of his basic position on the question. he proceeds to cite several passages of the *Koran* as proof-texts in support of his thesis of the simultaneity of the act of *qudra* and the realisation of the event. The texts (18.66/67 in § 133 and 11.22/20 and 18.101 in § 134) do in fact little more than give some justification for his use of the terms. That their support of his argument is weak (in that they all involve negative statements) the author would seem to be aware, in that he introduces them here, after his meaning is fully established, rather than at the outset of the section.

The question of absolute incapacity *('ağz)* is first introduced (§ 135) in terms of the classical problem of God's imposing upon a person an obligation to that of which he is incapable *(taklîf mâ lâ yuṭâq)* [1]. In both this and the following paragraphs, al-Aš'arî's aim is primarily to make clear several important distinctions regarding the terms. He has already mentioned in the preceding paragraph the principle that the act of leaving an action unperformed *(tarkuhu)* constitutes the realisation of its contrary. This is a matter of perspective, *scil.*, of which act is taken as the point of departure, since whichever act is realised in the agent defines the actuality of his being at the moment. On the basis of this principle

term for the human body in its unity as an organism which, in its structure as such, forms the condition of the presence of life and so of all other attributes for whose presence life is itself the condition (cf. *Milal*, 120); note however, that they did not identify *qudra* and the soundness or physical well-being of the body *(ibid.)*. Cf. also *muğnî* 4, 333.

(1) On this question generally cf. Brunschvig, *op. cit.* (where al-Aš'arî's treatment of the problem is discussed pp. 18ff).

therefore, and of the understanding of *qudra* already established, his first reply to the question of whether the unbeliever is capable *(musṭaṭî‘)* of faith is clear enough: since *qudra/isṭiṭâ‘a* defines the actuality of the agent in his being the cause of the particular act, it cannot, within the limits of the terms be said that the human agent has *qudra* or is *musṭaṭî‘* of the contrary of the act which defines his Being at the moment. The actuality of unbelief in the unbeliever excludes the possibility of the simultaneous actuality of belief in him. In this sense then, al-Aš‘arî allows that the unbeliever can be said to be «incapable of belief» *(‘âǧiz ‘anhu)*, while at the same time God imposes the obligation of belief upon him. This is not in any sense however to say that it is impossible that he become believing at another moment.

To say however, that the unbeliever is incapable of belief involves what for al-Aš‘arî is strictly an improper use of the term «incapability». According to the limitation of the term which he set forth earlier, the contrary of an act can only be properly predicated of one for whom the act is intrinsically possible, so that for example, what is immovable or absolutely incapable of movement cannot properly be said to be at rest *(sâkin)* nor can one who is totally incapable of speaking be properly described as «non-speaking» (*ġayru mutakallim*—§ 43). Thus the «incapacity *(‘aǧz)* of the one who is absolutely incapable of the act cannot be due to the actuality in him of the presence of the contrary» *(istaḥâla an ya‘ǧuza l-‘âǧizu ‘ani š-šay’i li-tarkihi lahu*—§ 136).

As opposed to *qudra*, which is the act of efficient causality of the free agent who is in the full sense morally responsible for the realisation of the act, *‘aǧz* denotes the total absence of such causality. It is therefore, as he noted earlier (§ 38), the contrary of *qudra*: *‘aǧz* is the absolute absence of all causality (understanding causality strictly within the limits of *qudra/ isṭiṭâ‘a* as defined). Consequently where *qudra*, in the human agent, implies a prior freedom of conscious and deliberative choice and in a sense the prior possibility of the realisation of the contrary (1), *‘aǧz* implies the absence or impossibility

(1) Although al-Aš‘arî does not allow *qudra* or any other term in the sense

of any such deliberate determination on the part of such an agent. Consequently, whereas the human agent is morally responsible for the realisation of the act which is realised through his created *qudra* and thereby is also responsible for the non-realisation of its contrary (cf. also § 146), *'ağz* denotes the total absence of responsibility (as the absence of any bond of efficient causality), both for the act whose actuality defines the present being of the subject and concomitantly for the non-realisation *(tark)* of its contrary, in that its presence excludes the existence, in the agent, of the conditions of his free and deliberate performance of the act. *'Ağz*, in other words, as the absence of any relationship of efficient causality (*'adamu l-qudrati kullihâ*—§ 137) between the subject and the act, directly implies the absence of any relationship of causal responsability between the agent and the type or class *(ğins)* of the act involved; as the absence of all true efficient causality, *'ağz* is the absence of the possibility of all causal responsability of the subject to both the posited act and its contrary. In this way then, *'ağz* is not analogous to (*qiyâsan 'alâ*—§ 136) *qudra*, since the latter represents the actuality, in the agent, of the efficient causality of the act and, in the strictest sense, is relative therefore only to the act of which it is the causality. It is this lack of analogous reciprocity between *qudra* and *'ağz* which the author details in § 136, insisting that *'ağz* is, for this reason, not of the same class *(ğins)* as *qudra*.

As was mentioned however, he does say in § 38 that *'ağz* is the contrary *(yuḍâddu)* of *qudra* and this should, if consistent with the normal usage of the kalâm, imply a complete analogy between them. This inconsistency became later the subject of some disagreement and is discussed in detail in the *Šarḥ al-Mawâqif* (1). There the authors say that al-Aš'arî held two positions regarding *'ağz:* the first (and more valid of the

of the potentiality to perform the act nor, as we mentioned above, allow strictly of any potentiality as an indetermination within the Being of the agent, he does quite clearly assume (cf. e. g., § 137) a prior possibility of the realisation of either the act or its contrary. In what terms he discussed this question, however, we cannot tell, since it is not treated formally in any of the sources.

(1) *Šarḥ al-Mawâqif*, 6, 107f.

two according to al-Ǧurǧânî) is that *'aǧz* is the strict contrary of *qudra*, wherefore it is related only to the real, present act *(al-fi'l al-mawǧûd)*, which defines the actuality of the subject, so that strictly we should say only that the palsied person is «incapable of his present act of sitting» *(al-qu'ûd al-mawǧûd)*. That is, within the technical formulae which we have been using, we should say that he has no true relationship of efficient causality to his present act; but we may not, within the strict sense of the terms, say that he is «incapable of the non-existent act of standing». According to this use, *'aǧz* defines only the present actuality of the subject in relation to a particular present act of his Being, «without any allusion whatsoever» to the contrary which is non-existent in the actual Being of the subject. The second position, which al-Îǧî regards as weak, is, he says, that «*aǧz* is relative only to the non-present act», i.e., that of which, in the common, non-technical use of the words, we say that the person is incapable *('âǧiz)*. This position, which he says is followed by a number of Aš'arites, is that of the Mu'tazila. The authors go on then to say that from this position is derived the thesis that *'aǧz* extends to both of a pair of contraries, even though *qudra* does not, since *'aǧz*, in contrast to *qudra*, involves what is not actually present in Being *(al-ma'dûm)*. Since, however, the union of contraries is only possible in what is not actually present in Being, the thesis that *'aǧz* is relative to both of a pair of contraries demands that the actuality of the act of *'aǧz* precede the realisation in the person of the act of which he is incapable *(al-ma'ǧûz 'anhu)*. That is, the act of *'aǧz* is the impossibility in the subject that he realise through his own efficient causality either of a pair of contraries and as such exists in him prior to the realisation in him of one of the pair as a «necessary act» *(fi'l iḍṭirâr)* through an efficient causality other than his own.

Though the first position described by the author of the *Šarḥ al-Mawâqif* would certainly seem to be implied by al-Aš'arî when he says that *'aǧz* is the contrary of *qudra*, since it would be fully consistent with his understanding of the formal structure of *qudra/istiṭâ'a*, the second position described would seem to bear little relationship to anything in the *Luma'*, for in it al-Aš'arî expresses quite a different position and says neither that *'ağz* is relative *only* to the contrary which is not realised in the subject, nor that it precedes the realisation of the act to which it is primarily relative. It is possible, perhaps, that al-Ğurğânî misunderstood al-Aš'arî's meaning and went on to elaborate the matter of the priority of *'ağz* to the *ma'ğûz 'anhu* following the formulation and doctrine of those who did hold such a position. For al-Aš'arî, whereas *qudra* denotes the positive and actual causality of the act which the agent realises in himself and connotes therefore also his moral responsibility for his act, it involves the contrary only insofar as the realisation of the act can be regarded as the non-realisation of its contrary. *'Ağz* on the other hand, as the complete negation of any relationship of efficient causality between the subject and the act which is realised in him, implies correspondingly the total absence of any responsibility whatsoever for the non-realisation of the contrary. Since he does not set forth explicitly his reasons for taking the position stated in § 136, but rather assumes it and argues only to validate it, we cannot say with certainty what may have been the full reason for his apparently abandoning the position taken or at least impled in § 38. In part, no doubt, the denial that *qudra* and *'ağz* are analogous and of the same class was important to his argument with al-Ğubbâ'î regarding the structure of *qudra* (1). Beyond this and more significantly perhaps, it is clear that al-Aš'arî had to take such a position in order to ground the initial statement of § 136 and that of § 135, viz., that *'ağz* is not strictly applicable to the non-causality which exists between the agent and the contrary of the act of which he is properly the agent *(muktasib)*, so that consequently we may not say that the unbeliever is absolutely incapable *('âğiz)* of belief, since the very fact of the realisation in him of the act of unbelief constitutes a positive relationship to the class *(ğins)* constituted by the contraries belief/unbelief. This is in

(1) 'Abd al-Ğabbâr notes (*Šarḥ al-uṣûl al-ḫamsa*, 430) that his «masters» proved that *qudra* precedes the act through the analogy with *'ağz*, whence al-Aš'arî's insistence on the fact that they are not analogous.

conformance with the position stated in § 43, in that neither of the pair of contraries is excluded in the sense of having been absolutely impossible *(mustaḥîl)* of realisation in him, but rather the one is excluded simply by the present actuality of the other. In trying to make his position clear regarding the structure of *'ağz* he is brought by the traditional topology of the question to the necessity of describing at this point the difference between the relationships which exist on the one hand between the responsible agent and the non-realised contrary of the act which is present in him through his own causality and on the other, between the subject in which is realised an act that does not proceed from his own proper causality (the «necessary act») and the non-realised contrary of that act. The problem is to distinguish, within the terms of the system (i.e., within the limits imposed by the exclusion of any notion of prior potentiality within the subject) two types of impossibility and non-actuality as they qualify the actuality of the Being of the subject in its relationship to the non-realised contrary of its present actuality. This is crucial to the elucidation of the difference between the position of al-Aš'arî and that of his mu'tazilî opponents.

Since later (§ 139) he extends the range of the act of *'ağz* to cover far more than the individual act and its contrary, it may well be that his statement in § 38 that *'ağz* is contrary to *qudra* is not to be taken in the strict technical sense of contrariety as it is generally used in the kalâm. He does not explain it there nor is there any other text of al-Aš'arî himself which offers any light on the problem. At any rate the importance of the distinctions made in § 138 becomes quite obvious in the following paragraphs.

The question (§ 137) is then posed as to whether it is possible «that God impose an obligation to something in the absence of the efficient member and the concomitant impossibility of the act [*'ağz*]». Any command, he replies, assumes perforce the possibility of its acceptence or rejection, and since the absence of the efficient member required to carry out the particular act commanded necessarily entails the absolute impossibility of the free acceptence or rejection of the command (i.e., of the realisation of either the act commanded or its contrary), there can be no command. Further elaborating the distinction made in §§ 135f he notes that *'ağz* taken as simply the impossibility of the act which is due to the presence of the contrary is not the same as the absolute exclusion of its possibility due to the total absence of any *qudra* relative to the particular act. The contrary belongs to the same class as the act but *'ağz* in the strictest sense, such as that arising from the absence of the efficient member, involves the total exclusion of all *qudra* relative to the particular act; that is, it precludes the presence of all *qudra*—of any *qudra* whatsoever—both that which determines the present realisation of the act commanded as well as that of the present realisation of the contrary, since it excludes the possibility of the realisation of the class and, indeed, extends to all classes of acts which would require the presence of the particular member for their realisation through the proper causality of the agent (§ 139). So also (§ 138), as in the case with the absence of the efficient member, is that involved in any other type of physical impossibility: the command to *zakât* in relation to him who has no wealth, etc.

Further elaborating the extension of *'ağz* to cover both the act and its contrary (§ 139), al-Aš'arî says that the act of absolute impossibility of action cannot be relative simply to a single, posited act, since this would involve an infinity of incapacities *(a'ğâz)* in the subject. *'Ağz* like all other «accidents» is a positive attribute of the being of the subject. It arises in terms of a particular structure in the subject and involves all classes of action whose possibility or realisation through his true efficient causality are excluded in terms of that structure. Death, whose presence as an «accident» within the subject excludes absolutely the possibility of all action, determines a single, structured act of incapacity relative to all acts.

There follows a series of *quaestiones*, based for the most part on disputed verses of the Koran, by which the Mu'tazila attempted to argue to the necessity of *qudra's* preceding the realisation of the act. Here, as throughout the sections dealing with this problem, the author does not in most instances argue to demonstrate the basis of his teaching but rather, in those cases in which he allows any validity to the objection in terms of the particular verse as bearing on the question, he clarifies the understanding of the particular question within the framework established in the preceding paragraphs.

Thus in § 140 the objector would make his point by playing on the opposition between the everyday use of the verb *qadara* and the Mu'tazilite understanding of *qudra*, as opposed to the technical sense in which al-Aš'arî uses it: can a man be said to be «capable of» divorcing her who, at the moment of the divorce, is not his wife. Al-Aš'arî's reply is simply to insist upon the technical meaning of *qudra* as the agent's act of efficient causality at the moment of the realisation of the act.

The arguments of the remaining paragraphs add little to the understanding of what the author has already said and we can, consequently, deal with them quite briefly.

The arguments of §§ 141-3 are of some interest in that they illustrate quite clearly the importance which proof-texts held for al-Aš'arî and the consequent seriousness with which their interpretation—though it seems often to the modern reader a kind of tactical exercise in polemics and casuistry—was undertaken. The objection, to show that *qudra/istiṭâ'a* precedes the realisation of the act, is proposed on the basis of *Sûra* 2.180/184: «... obligatory upon those who are able to do it [i.e., to fast] is a redemption, the feeding of a poor man...» The verse was used by al-Ǧubbâ'î to show that *istiṭâ'a* precedes the act, since it refers to the capability of fasting at a time when the subject is not actually fasting (1). Al-Aš'arî is unwilling to accept the obvious meaning of the text precisely because the interpretation then would be unavoidable and because he is, in fact, too honest and consistent a theologian to try to escape from the dilemma, once having allowed the literal sense of the text, through some fakery of purely casuistic distinguos. Furthermore, any such distinction as would solve the dilemma would probably have to allow some kind

(1) Râzî, *Tafsîr*, 5, 89.

of prior potentiality in the *istiṭâ'at al-badan* (cf. § 144) and this also is excluded on principle. His only recourse then he takes, namely that of denying that the pronoun of *yuṭîqûnahu* refers to the antecedent «fasting»; he insists therefore that it anticipates the following «redemption» *(fidya)* and so refers to the actual presence of sufficient wealth belonging to the subject to allow the redemption. Philologically, his case is extremely weak, for though he tries to support himself by the citation of a number of other verses in which the pronoun does in fact refer to a following noun (§ 143), the disagreement of gender between the pronoun in question and the word to which al-Aš'arî would have it refer, renders his interpretation most unlikely.

In § 144, where there is no grammatical problem, he makes the same distinction in the mode of the *istiṭâ'a*. The objection is raised on the basis of 3.91/97 regarding the obligation to make the ritual pilgrimage to Mecca for him «who is able to make his way there»; and al-Aš'arî's reply is simply that the reference is to the availability of money and the means of transportation and not to the *qudra* or *istiṭâ'a* which exists as an inherent attribute of the subject *(istiṭâ'at al-badan)* and whose actual presence entails the actuality of the result. The same distinction is made in § 145 regarding the interpretation of 9.42 and in § 148 regarding 65.7.

In §§ 146 and 147 two citations are introduced which the author does consider pertinent to the question. The former («Fear God insofar as you are able»—64.16) is of some interest since his interpretation of it throws some light on the distinctions made in §§ 135f. Whereas the Mu'tazila had evidently understood the verse as supporting their thesis of man's complete posession of his own *qudra* and the consequent implication of its actuality before the act, al-Aš'arî remarks that the meaning is that if they are actually «capable» *(mustaṭî'în)* of fearing God (i.e., within the technical terminology of the system: are actually fearing God) then it is to this that they are obliged and that if they are *mustaṭî'în* of the contrary (i.e., are actually the contrary of fearing God) they are likewise obliged to fear God since «it is not obligatory upon them unless they are capable of it or its contrary». That is, if they have a positive relationship of freely determined efficient causality to the class of the act involved, then they are subject to the command *('amr)* and to the obligation, under penalty of sin *(taklîf)*, since the impossibility *(istiḥâla)* of their performing the act is *de facto* excluded; there is no inherent impediment to their becoming godfearing (cf. *supra ad* § 132 and § 137 and *infra ad* § 149).

With this introduction then he persues the same problem in §§ 147-9, reviewing the opposition of *qudra* and *'ağz* in the fuller context of the command *(amr)* and obligation *(taklîf)*. The question of *'ağz* is introduced in terms of 58.5/4 («He who is unable to [fast]...») which the Mu'tazila evidently used to argue that *qudra* precedes the act on the basis of the analogy between *qudra* and *'ağz*. Here al-Aš'arî simply insists upon his own technical understanding of *'ağz*. Then in § 149 he returns to the distinctions set forth in §§ 135ff, in taking up the interpretation of 2.286: «God imposes no obligation upon a soul save according to its capacity». In treating this text he introduces for the first time the classical problem of Islamic moral thought concerning the unreflected impulse to action *(al-ḫâṭir*, pl. *ḫawâṭir)*, good or evil, a problem which we must assume formed a central question in the traditional topology of the interpretation of this verse in the school of al-Ğubbâ'î (1). In reply he says that in regard to the content of his immediate and unreflected temptation or impulse to disobey God's commands, man is not obliged under penalty of sin so long as he does not follow the impulse and commit the sinful act, since the *ḫawâṭir* are not subject to his will and deliberate intention. God does not, he says, command his servants that of which they are absolutely incapable *('âğizûn)*. Rather, the term capacity *(wus')* refers in this verse to those things over which God gives the human agent the actual power of efficient causality, subject to his own will and determination *(mâ yuṭîquhu 'alayhi)*. The meaning of this last phrase rests

(1) This can be, I feel, generally assumed in regard to all the verses which he introduces as «objections»; cf. for example al-Ğubbâ'î's interpretation and use of 40.33 and 3.104, cited *infra ad* § 162.

upon the distinctions of §§ 135-7 and § 146; «that over which God has given him the actual power of efficient causality» includes thus the class *(ǧins)* of acts and consequently both the thing commanded and its contrary. If the agent, through his own free determination, is the actual cause of either, he is then subject to the law and under obligation to obey it because of his actual capacity to be the agent of acts falling within the class.

The following paragraphs (§§ 150-7) then treat of the problem of human causality in the context of the question of God's willing all that He creates and the fact that nothing exists which He has not willed. The general question of God's will and the dependence of all creation upon it was taken up separately in §§ 49ff, so that the effect of the discussion in the present section is simply to place the general understanding of created causality within the broader context of al-Aš'arî's theology. Here the question is first raised in §§ 150-2 in terms of *Koran* 27.39, where an *ifrît* says to Solomon, «I am strong enough to do it and can be trusted [to do it]». Though al-Aš'arî does not approve the exegetical principles upon which the Mu'tazila arrive at their conclusion concerning the significance of the statement (§ 151), he goes on to say (§ 152) that the assertion of the *ifrît* is invalid unless the intended meaning is that «I am strong enough and can be trusted to do it, if God wills». In following paragraphs then, he introduces four more texts to support his analysis and confirm that no event takes place— there is no act of efficient causality— unless God wills it. The discussion in these paragraphs is mostly polemical and adds little to the understanding of the structure of human causality as al-Aš'arî conceives it.

As a kind of appendix to the discussion of 27.39, because of the parallelism of wording and, no doubt, a similar use of the text by the Mu'tazila to show that *qudra* precedes the act of creation on God's part, in § 157 he analyses 28.26, according to which the daughters of Jethro speak of Moses as «strong and trustworthy» *(qawîyun amîn)*. Al-Ǧubbâ'î took this to mean that he was « capable of whatever work her father needed» (§ 157). In contrast to his treatment of 27.39, al-

Aš'arî says that this text can be used against his master to show that *istiṭâ'a* is, in fact, simultaneous with the realisation of the act since the girl's reference is to Moses' strength of body *(quwwa)* and trustworthiness *(amâna)* of which she was witness (1). So also, he goes on to say, we know that a man's efficient causality of prayer is actualised in him when we see him standing in prayer, even though we do not know the exact moment at which it came into being for him.

The final paragraphs (§§ 159-64) form a kind of summary of a number of the principal questions which he has taken up in regard to *qudra/istiṭâ'a*, in which confirmatory texts and interpretations are introduced with a minimum of explanation and exposition: § 159—the universality of God's creation of what He wills; § 160— misinterpretation of the *Koran* about the lies of the unbelievers concerning God's activity on the part of the Mu'tazila (cf. *supra ad* § 108 and § 117); § 161—*taklîf mâ lâ yuṭâq;* § 162—the creation of evil and injustice; § 163—the affirmation of man's genuine moral responsibility for his action against the *muǧabbira;* and § 164—God's solicitude for man's comfort and welfare.

Though these paragraphs shed no new light on al-Aš'arî's understanding of the problems involved, since in every case his reply to the objection consists in no more than the briefest allusion to the structure of causality already outlined, § 162 is nevertheless of interest in that we have some information on the background of the use of both the verses cited, as they were interpreted by the Mu'tazila and particularly by al-Aš'arî's master, al-Ǧubbâ'î, so that we can see something of the real complexity of argumentation which underlies the apparent simplicity and brevity of much of the *Luma'*. The first verse cited is 40.33/31: «God does not will injustice to human beings». According to the Mu'tazila, two theses can be demonstrated from this verse, first «that God does not will that some men wrong others and secondly that He does not will to wrong any human being. If He were to create unbelief *(kufr)* in them and then to punish them on the basis of this unbelief,

(1) For the story involved, cf. Ṭabarî, *Tafsîr* (Cairo, 1321), 29.36f.

He would be doing injustice. Consequently, since it is established that He does not will any wrongdoing at all, it is confirmed that He does not create human acts *(af'âl al-'ibâd)* since, if He created them, He would will them (1)». The interpretation of the second verse (3.104/108: «God does not will any injustice to the worlds») follows much the same lines as that of 40.33: «Al-Ǧubbâ'î says that this verse shows that He does not will any [wrongdoing]. Were He the agent of any of the various kinds of wrongdoing, He would will it, and this is impossible. [The Mu'tazila] also say that one can verify on the basis of this verse that He is not the agent of wrongdoing nor the agent of the acts of human beings, and that He does not will the evils of human acts. ... They gleefully assert that this one verse is sufficient to confirm all the principles of the Mu'tazila which have to do with the question of God's justice (2).» In view of the significance of these verses for the polemics of the Mu'tazila, the fact that al-Aš'arî takes them up here at the end of the tract on the creation of human causality is noteworthy in respect of his organisation of the *Luma'*, for in summarising his own position he takes off, for the particular question, from a verse on the basis of which his opponents made a similar summary proof of their own position. Again, from a purely rhetorical standpoint, he takes up two central proof-texts of his opponents and in reply does nothing more than to rely upon a distinction which al-Ǧubbâ'î and his school explicitly rejected, when he says that «the meaning of the texts is that He does not will that He wrong them, even if He does will that they wrong one another». The disdain embodied in the reply is remarkable in itself, though the sense of what he means is quite clear from the distinctions made in §§ 96ff, on account of which he feels no need to go further into the matter here. Basically the two systems—that of al-Ǧubbâ'î and that of al-Aš'arî—are in fact so divided on a number of funda-

(1) Râzî, *Tafsîr*, 27.60; the citation of the Mu'tazila goes on to hold that one can also prove that God is nevertheless capable of doing injustice if He should will to do so, etc., but this is not pertinent to the present discussion of human causality; on the same verse, cf. also 'Abd al-Ǧabbâr, *op. cit.*, 359f.

(2) Râzî, *Tafsîr*, 8. 186.

mental principles that there can be no dialogue between them; neither will allow the validity of the primary assumptions of the other. What al-Aš'arî means here is that the acts of wrongdoing can be said to be willed by God in that He has created the efficient causality for them in the human agents. He has however, created the act not as His own act but rather has created it «for another». The wrongdoing is immediately willed and performed by the human agent by whom it is realised through a causality which God has created for him at the moment of the realisation of the act. It is thus the human agent who wills to do wrong to another, to whom the act of injustice is properly imputed and it is he whose act it is, in that it is through his act of causation, which God has created for him, that the act is performed.

VIII

Al-Aš^{c}ari's conception of the nature and role of speculative reasoning in theology

Since the days of al-Aš'arî himself there has been no dearth of discussion concerning his attitude towards the function and role of speculative reasoning in theology. Even among his partisans apparently different positions seem to be proposed as, for example, Ibn 'Asâkir and as-Subkî go to some length to depict him as almost rigidly traditionalist while his followers amongst the *mutakallimîn* such as al-Juwaynî cite an Aš'arî who is profoundly engaged in the discussion of the most abstruse and refined questions of a purely philosophical nature.[1] Gardet and Anawati find an "anti-intellectualism" in his writing and "a more rigid literalism" than is evident in the work of his successors[2] but assert that there is a real problem for him and for his school concerning the integration of theoretical speculation in the theological system. In a more recent study, G. Makdisi has suggested that "the question of whether Ash'arî adopted *kalâm* as a method remains to be proved".[3] That while allowing the traditionalist and Ḥanbalite thesis of the supreme authority of the *Koran* and the traditions, al-Aš'arî does employ theoretical reasoning to argue his dogmatic positions is beyond question;[4] that he does use it and takes it quite seriously is at the heart of the conflict between him and the Ḥanbalites.[5] The real question, thus, is not whether or not al-Aš'arî used the methodology of the *kalâm* theologians in his writing but what he conceived to be its role in explicating, grounding, or determining theological and dogmatic theses and its relationship to the canonical sources and its value and function for the faith of the community and the individual believer.

The question has almost become a commonplace but a brief reexamination of some of the most pertinent data may yet not be uncalled for since the matter is somewhat unsettled. What I wish to do in these few pages is to examine closely what al-Aš'arî has to say on this topic and most particularly what he has to say in the prefatory section of his "Epistle to the People of the Fronteer",[6] for in the beginning of this *risâla* he treats the general question of the sources and method of theological knowledge at some length.[7]

The author's purpose in this work is to outline "the principles on which our forebears relied and by virtue of which they and the later righteous men of our own generation who follow them turned to the Scripture and the Tradition".[8] These principles (*'uṣûl*), as he sets them forth,[9] prove to be the basic propositions of the Muslim faith: the *'uṣûl ad-dîn*, and accordingly the main body of the work is a kind of glossed *'aqîda*[10] or, as the author has it, a statement of "the principal dogmas together with some bits of argumentation that will manifest to you the rightness of our position and the error of the *ahl al-bida'*."[11]

Prefatory to his exposition of these fundamental theses of Islamic dogma al-Aš'arî goes to some considerable length to show that the whole of the faith, "what is required to believe and what is required to do",[12] is given fully and explicitly in the canonical sources and that these, viz., the *Koran* and the traditions, are the completely sufficient and only altogether reliable guide in all matters of the faith. "The reports from him (prayer and peace be on him) turn out to be the proofs of the validity of all that he has called [men] to."[13] The Prophet "has shown the validity of every act to which he summoned them with the proofs and clear evidences of God ..."[14] This, he says, is confirmed in the words of Scripture: "*al-yawma 'akmaltu lakum dînakum wa'atmamtu 'alaykum ni'matî*"[15]

Muḥammad, he says, found the world divided into various sects and beliefs[16] and "to all the sects to whom he was sent[17] he made plain the error of their situation with the conclusive proofs of God and His clear explanation and he demonstrated the validity of that to which he called them with the proofs of God and His signs so that to none of them did there remain a counter argument (*šubha*) concerning the matter nor was there any need therein for any supplement to what was had from him (prayer and peace be on him)."[18] Accordingly one finds in the transmitted reports "no supplement to the arguments that he pointed out to them".[19]

The question, then, is how al-Aš'arî understands these assertions. This is of signal importance if one is to grasp his conception of his own activity as a theologian or *mutakallim*, for what he is at in this preface to his exposition of the *'uṣûl ad-dîn* is, in effect, to establish the basis of "the science of the fundamentals of religion" (*'ilm 'uṣûl ad-dîn*), to identify the sources and show their nature and their use. In following al-Aš'arî's exposition of his thesis[20] one may gain a superficial impression that he takes a kind of fideist position, viz., that since the communications of the Prophet are in fact from God, the mind must, from the outset, acknowledge the divine authority of the Scripture and the *sunna* and that there can be no judgement concerning the content of the revelation and no reflection concerning its plausibility, truth and meaning that are prior to the Scripture and the Tradition and that are based on criteria or evidence extraneous to the canonical sources as such.[21] Such an interpretation, however, is too facile. What is required is to examine the principal theses that he here enunciates and employs in articulating his understanding of the preëminent role of the Scripture and Tradition in theology. For the sake of both brevity and clarity we may omit all direct consideration of his position on individual dogmas as well as of his specific arguments concerning them.

At the outset al-Aš'arî divides the teaching of the Prophet into four major areas or topics which, taken in order, form a sequence that develops through a logical progression.[22] According to this conception, the Prophet called his auditors to the faith by leading them through progressive stages of understanding until they came to recognize the origin and nature, and so the authority of his teaching. The stages are essentially these: first, to acknowledge the contingency of the world and that of one's own being; second, to acknowledge that the world and each individual are subject absolutely to the will of an omnipotent and provident God; third, to recognize that Muhammad is a true emissary of God; and lastly, in consequence of this, to believe all that the Prophet says is to be believed and to do all that he has commanded to do.[23] The importance of this sequence in the author's mind is evident in that, with minor variations of wording, it is repeated several times[24] and in that it underlies the whole argument of the preface of the *risâla*. What we have here is al-Aš'arî's conception of what may be termed the rational order of the progress of faith.

One notes that here within this order there is no appeal to the authority of the Prophet—of the Scripture and the traditions—until after one has achieved the third stage. The expressions that al-Aš'arî uses to denote the activity of the Prophet regarding the first three stages are noteworthy; the terms *nabbaha*, *bayyana*, *dalla*, and *ḥujja* occur over and over again. Thus he says that "Muḥammad was sent to all men ... *to point out to them* (*liyunabbihahum*) that they are created ... and *to make plain to them* (*yubayyina lahum*) the way to recognise [their creator] through the effects of his action in them."[25] The Prophet "set forth conclusive arguments" (*'aqâma ḥujajan*);[26] "he gave demonstrations from evidence (*'adilla*) for the truth of everything to which he called them either to believe or to do".[27] The expressions *dalla*, *istadalla*, and *dalâla* are found no less than fifty-one times in the twelve pages of the preface. There can, in fact, be no question that he means by these expressions that the Prophet gave, in whatever form, rationally probative arguments. The Prophet, he says, "through the alternation of form and disposition that occur in their persons (*bimâ fîhim mini ḫtilâfi ṣ-ṣuwari wal-hay'ât*) and through the differentiation of languages pointed out to them the contingency of their being".[28] In outlining these proofs of the createdness of the world, man's dependence on the creator and the unity of God in His attributes,[29] al-Aš'arî bases his reasoning on texts of the Koran[30] but the form of his expression is to be noted: the Prophet "made known to them the way to recognise their maker through the evidence found in themselves and elsewhere that requires His existence and demonstrated his will (*'irâda*) and His Providence (*tadbîr*), where He says, '...' and he explained this by saying,

'...'."[31] Here quite clearly the Koran is not cited as giving authority to the argument but only to confirm that this is the argument that was used by the Prophet. That is, within the perspective of the topical order of the Prophet's teaching set out at the beginning of the work, the Koran does not, at this stage, confer any authority on the argument or confirm the validity of the analysis but rather it is cited only to establish that these arguments, whose validity is to be granted entirely in terms of their coherence with the nature of things as given to human understanding in the experience of being, are those found in the canonical sources and reflect the true form of the teaching of the Prophet. Al-Aš'arî subsequently asserts that these demonstrations that are found in the Scripture and the traditions are addressed "to all who indulge in theological speculation" (*li-sâ'iri l-muta-kallimîn*)[32] and goes to considerable pains to show that they are the best and most conclusive arguments, to which no counter argument (*šubha*) can be raised.[33] They are, he says, clearer and more conclusive than those of "the philosophers or of the Qadarîya who follow them, or of the innovators and those who turn away from the prophets;"[34] the argument for the contingency of the world that is found in the Scripture (*sc.*, that based on the changeable character of corporeal being: *taġayyur al-ajsâm*) is better than that based on accidents (*al-istidlâl bil'a'râḍ*) because, he says, the latter is founded on premises that are difficult to establish and is, consequently, inconclusive being readily open to the challenge of a counter position.[35] In brief, the demonstrations found in the canonical sources (as read by al-Aš'arî) are better on purely theoretical grounds and are, within the framework of the rational order of the progress of faith—i.e., according to al-Aš'arî, the topical order followed by the Prophet in his teaching—prior to any consideration of the authority of the revelation given by the Prophet.

The veracity of the Prophet (and so the validity of his claims and of his authority) is established by signs and miracles (*'âyât wa-mu'jizât*), Muhammad having had a special sign, *sc.*, the Koran, just as Moses and Jesus had each his characteristic sign.[36] Within the topical order of teaching attributed by al-Aš'arî to the Prophet, the consideration of the miracle follows that of the "conclusive arguments" (*ḥujaj*) and the demonstrations (*dalâ'il*) which ground the first two stages; "the miracles that demonstrate his veracity (prayer and peace be on him) *after* he has shown to all those who practice theological speculation the contingency of their being and the existence of their creator, necessarily establish the validity of his statements and show (*dalla*) that the Scripture and the Tradition which he has given you are from God (the Mighty and the Glorious)."[37] The consideration of the miracle must be posterior to that of the propositions that are the subject of the first two stages of belief to which the Prophet called his audience because the miracle is intentional and for its sign value requires, on the part of the one to whom it is addressed as a demonstrative sign, the prior recognition and understanding of the context of its interpretation, *viz.*, of his own contingency and essential dependency upon an allpowerful and provident God who may, if He so wills, address him some word or command. Within this context al-Aš'arî conceives the miracle itself as an evidence that is addressed to rational understanding as a call to further reflection: "after setting forth the valid arguments, God (the Mighty and the Glorious), by overpowering signs and mighty miracles, then stirred the thoughts of all of them to investigate (*naẓara*) what he called them to and what he had pointed out to them".[38] "The signs (*'âyât*) and demonstrations (*'adilla*) ... stirred up their minds and aroused their thoughts to investigate (*naẓara*) the validity of that to which he was calling them and to reflect (*ta'ammala*) on that which he asked them to take as witness of his veracity" (*ṣidquhû*).[39] The miracle is, thus, an appeal to rational understanding that must itself take place in the context of a framework that is founded in rational understanding. That this is al-Aš'arî's teaching is made fully explicit when, at a later point in the work, discussing the obligation of the unbeliever to become a believer, he says that the unbeliever (*kâfir*) is so obliged "because the Prophet has made the demonstration (*dalâla*) clear to them ...; and the way for them to know this is through the native intelligence (*al-'uqûl*) that was given them as an instrument of discrimination (*'âlat at-tamyîz*), in that they have reached intellectual maturity prior to their refusal[40] to reflect on the evident demonstrations (*'adilla*) on which they were called to reflect— demonstrations that he made the way to their recognising the necessity of investigating ... the signs which, by interrupting the normal sequence of events, aroused their minds and motivated them to enquire."[41] If, says al-Aš'arî, the Prophet's teaching—that of the *Koran* and the *sunna*—were not complete and sufficient as conclusive demonstrations (*ḥujaj*) of the Prophet's authority, obedience to him would not be encumbent upon them, since, being incomplete they would be open to refutation and one could not know with certainty that Muhammad is a true Prophet.[42]

Having arrived at this stage, however, i.e., having recognised and acknowledged the divine authority of the Prophet, one comes to know that there is no need to seek for any authority other than that of the transmitted sources, "for in all of it he made clear to them the methods of the demonstrations so that their minds were content with it and they had no need of developing further proofs of the matter".[43] "The reports from him (prayer and peace be on him) turn out to be demonstrations ...; the reports from him (prayer and peace be on him) concerning this turn out to be a way of grasping it and a method of knowing its truth."[44] Accordingly, one learns "the way to use the reports of the Prophet as a demonstration."[45] At no point does al-Aš'arî deprecate the use of speculative reason; on the contrary, one must adhere "to what reason demands".[46] It is, rather, that the false claims of the "philosophers" and their followers are to be rejected because they do not use reasoning correctly and "what they claim to be the judgements demanded by reason" are not as they say.[47]

Thus is it, al-Aš'arî says, that the first generations of Muslims and their righteous followers of his own generation, having come by rational stages to recognise the authority of the Prophet, hold exclusively to the Scripture and the traditions[48] and that they go to great pains to collect and authenticate the traditions[49] because they have come to know, not simply by a blind act of faith but through the evidence of reason, that these are the infallible guide to what is essential for man to know and to do. "In what we are called to believe we have no need to develop new proofs other than the proofs that the Prophet (prayer and peace be on him) has pointed out and called his community to consider, since it is impossible that anyone produce any thing that is a surer guide than he has."[50] Essentially the case of the authority of the Koran and the *sunna* is closed definitely by the evidence of the miracles[51] but this requires the hermeneutic context of the previous questions.

The order of al-Aš'arî's exposition (which he insists throughout in the repetition of the expression "thereupon"—*ṯumma*—is that of the teaching of the Prophet) follows and reaffirms his stated understanding of the logical progression of the mind to the full acceptance of the Scripture and the traditions. He begins, having listed the four stages of the Prophet's teaching,[52] by setting forth the arguments for the creation of the material universe and of mankind in particular, together with those for the existence of the creator and his chief attributes (pp. 82, 1–84, 29).[53] Following this, he argues that God may and does send messengers to men, saying that the Prophet "*then* pointed out to those who deny the proposition that God sends apostles" that he has done so in the past (85, 11 ff.). He goes on to note[54] that God, having conclusively established the foregoing theses, *then* aroused their minds, by means of miracles, to examine and reflect upon the Prophet's claim to be an emissary of God. Significantly this passage (86, 2–87, 1) which deals with the sign value of the Koran as Muhammad's chief and characteristic miracle, is framed, at the beginning and at the end, with the expression *'iqâmat al-ḥujaj*,[55] the first referring to the foregoing establishment of the first two stages of the Prophet's teaching (i.e., the hermeneutic context mentioned above) and the second to that of the third stage, viz., that Muhammad is truly an emissary of God. To this point al-Aš'arî has yet made no real appeal to authority but only contended that these arguments are conclusive (that they are genuinely *ḥujaj*) and cited the sources to show that these are the arguments that were employed by the Prophet. It is *then*, after all these things have been established, says al-Aš'arî, that "the Prophet (prayer and peace be on him) called upon them to recognise God and to obey himself in what he enjoined upon them in bearing the message, citing His statement: 'Obey God and obey His apostle'."

This deserves particular attention because of the sense that emerges from its situation within the context. The Prophet, he says, *then*, at this point in the progression of his teaching, called upon them to recognise God and to obey God and himself as a duty: an absolute moral obligation. The previous appeal to recognise the existence of an allpowerful and provident creator was a reasoned appeal to any and all intelligent men to recognise and acknowledge an objective state of affairs as such. The appeal now, the authority of the Prophet as an emissary of God having been conclusively established (again as simply a factual state of affairs plainly to be acknowledged by any reasonable man who has considered the evidence), is to recognise and acknowledge that there is a moral obligation to know God and, in recognition of His absolute will and command, transmitted by the Prophet, to obey Him and His messenger. Only after the divine authority of the Prophet has been recognised can one know, through his transmission of the command (*fîmâ kallafa bi-tablîġihî ʾilayhim*), that to know God is obligatory (*wâjib*).[56]

As we noted at the beginning, al-Ašʿarî's conclusion in this preface to his outline of the fundamental dogmas of Islam is that a thorough examination of the evidence is sufficient to show beyond all doubt that one needs no guide in questions of religion other than the transmitted sources,[57] sc., the Koran and the *sunna*, and that it is for this reason that the first generations of Muslims and their followers have devoted themselves exclusively to the study of these sources[58] and to seeking "the valid methods" of using them.[59] A careful reading of his argument here allows us to see quite clearly his conception of the nature of the "science of the fundamentals of religion". The first generations of Muslims and their righteous followers have come to rely exclusively on the transmitted sources in recognition of the authority of the prophet, *baʿda mâ ʿarafû min ṣidqihî*;[60] that is, they have accepted the authority of the teaching of the Prophet because they have gone through the several stages of his teaching, a process of stages within which the acceptance and so, utilization of the authority of the Scripture and traditions as authority is the last of four.[61] Clearly then the authority of the Scripture and the traditions is not the point of absolute beginning;[62] if the prophet had not first demonstrated "the contingency of their existence, the knowledge of their creator and the unity of His being ... and his own veracity in the message he transmitted to them" there would have been no valid ground for their acceptance of his message.[63]

One notes here two points: first, that these three fundamental stages for which, al-Ašʿarî insists, the transmitted, canonical sources give the most conclusive demonstrations and arguments, embrace most of the questions that are commonly treated in the *kalâm*;[64] and second, that, according to al-Ašʿarî, the recognition, on the basis of these demonstrations, of the truth of what they mean to show is essentially prior to the acceptance of the authority of the Prophet. It is, he repeats several times, because the Prophet's arguments and demonstrations were not merely complete and adequate, but absolutey conclusive and beyond challenge, that the first generations of Muslims never tried to augment them or find new ones;[65] and for this reason also one finds, in the transmitted sources, no report of any disagreement among them concerning these proofs and arguments.[66] As was pointed out above, he goes to some length at this place in the discussion to show that on purely theoretical grounds these arguments of the Prophet are less open to challenge by a counter position than are those of the philosophers and others who try to demonstrate these same theses by other methods.

The function of the science of the *'uṣûl ad-dîn* is systematically to recapitulate and, so doing, to explain the teaching of the Prophet. To follow the way or method (*ṭarîqa*)[67] of the Prophet is "to learn to use the reports as a demonstration"[68] and to carry out the investigation (*naẓar*)[69] that he sought to provoke on the part of those who heard and saw him and thereby to understand the truth of his teaching as beyond all question. For the theologian, the situation is a kind of dialectical or reflexive one: the arguments and demonstrations of the first three stages of the Prophet's teaching, which contain a major portion of the central dogma of Islam (viz., God and His attributes, man's relationship to God and the validity of the claims and teaching of Muhammad as a prophet)[70] must, following the example of the Prophet and the reasonable order of things, be essentially theoretical. Their claim to conclusive persuasiveness is the claim of "what reason requires" (*mâ qtaḍathu l-'uqûl*). On the other hand, however, if the authority of the *Koran* and the *sunna* is, as was suggested, not the point of absolute beginning, it is nonetheless the point of beginning for the student of the *'uṣûl ad-dîn* or *mutakallim*, for he is already a believer; he knows and acknowledges the authority of the canonical sources and his method accordingly is that of demonstration through the transmitted sources (*al-istidlâl bil-'aḫbâr*).[71] To chase after other arguments is wrong because it is, in effect, to reject the guidance of God and His Prophet: what is known to be certain for what is questionable.[72]

Reason and revelation in the doctrine of al-Aš'arî are, thus, inseparably bound together. The rudimentary outline of a single example will clarify the point. Al-Aš'arî says that as the second stage of his teaching, the Prophet "showed them the methods of the demonstrations whereby one may know God's most beautiful names, His exalted attributes, and His justice" (*'asmâ'ahu l-ḥusnà wa-ṣifâtihi l-'ulyâ wa-'adlahû*).[73] Because of his recognition of the authority of the Scripture and the Tradition, the theoretical examination of these attributes by the theologian is not a speculative inquiry that is altogether unrestrained and free to follow any course whatsoever, ὡς τὰ ἴχνη τῶν λόγων φέρει, to use Plato's phrase; on the other hand, however, the arguments (*ḥujaj* and *'adilla*) of the Prophet are, according to al-Aš'arî, the best possible arguments and demonstrations attainable by reason, so that reason itself, for its own perfection, demands its self-restriction to these arguments and conclusions. Consequently, the attributes of God that are theoretically discoverable are limited to precisely "those by which He has described Himself, by which He has named Himself in His Scripture, of which the Prophet has informed them, and which are evidenced by His acts,"[74] and the surest reasoning that leads to the most certain knowledge of these is exclusively that which is found explicit or implicit in the canonical sources.[75] The foundational assumption, however, remains, viz., that the reasoned arguments are probative and complete on the grounds of theoretical reason alone, for if they are not so, then the Prophet's claim to authority cannot be reasonably accepted.

The position that al-Aš'arî enunciates here in the preface to his "Letter to the People of the Fronteer" is clearly reflected in his usage both in the body of this work and in the *Kitâb al-Luma'*.[76] It is, furthermore, fully consistent with the position set forth in his *Risâla fi stiḥsân al-ḫawḍ* which in fact, if one will abstract from its immediate polemical aim, does little more than explain and clarify certain of the implications of the preface of the earlier *risâla*.[77] Having insisted in the latter that the Prophet gave rational demonstrations of the theses enunciated in the first two stages of his teaching and that it is uniquely upon this explicit teaching that the student of the *'uṣûl ad-dîn* must rely, he remarks that the first generations of Muslims "troubled themselves with such investigation and inquiry (*al-baḥṯ wan-naẓar*) as they were obliged to carry out on their own only in dealing with new situations (*ḥawâdiṯ al-'aḥkâm*) as they chanced to arise and occur among them, treating them on the basis of the principles that [the Prophet] had taught them"[78] and goes on to note that no one of them demanded *taqlîd* on the part of the others, i.e., that the others be bound exclusively to his particular use of the sources.[79] In similar fashion, he says in the *Istiḥsân al-ḫawḍ* that some people disapprove of "inquiry and investigation" (*al-baḥṯ wan-naẓar*) and insist on *taqlîd*,[80] claiming the authority of the Koran and the *sunna*[81] whereas, however, the truth is that the Koran sets forth rational arguments embodying, at least implicitly, the same concepts as are found in the analyses of the *kalâm* and similar arguments are found in the traditions.[82] It is these principles, al-Aš'arî says, that the theologians of his own persuasion employ.[83] In short, the fundamental philosophical concepts and presuppositions (*'uṣûl*) of his system of *kalâm* are implicitly and in some instances explicitly found in the *Koran* and the traditions, the difference being simply that the Prophet did not use the technical analysis and terminology that is peculiarly characteristic of the *kalâm* since the issues were not raised and defined in those terms by those to whom he immediately addressed his teaching; had they been so he would have employed the terminology and technique of the *kalâm.*[84] Because of the specific question to which he addresses himself in the *Istiḥsân al-ḫawḍ*, al-Ašʿ*arî* is obliged to divide the question of treating new problems in terms of the principles given in the revelation (*radduhâ* ʾ*ilà l-*ʾ*uṣûl*) so as to spell out in explicit detail what is assumed as obvious in the preface to the earlier work. That is, where in the earlier *risâla* he simply stated that in dealing with new situations (*sc,* the reformulation and recasting of the problems raised in the basic issues to which the Prophet had addressed himself) the first generations of Muslims applied the principles given in the teaching of the Prophet (*raddûhâ* ʾ*ilâ l-*ʾ*uṣûl*), in the later work he explicitly distinguishes those matters the understanding of which rests on the foundation of theoretical reason (*al-*ʿ*aqlîyât*) and those that are founded on the authoritative sources of the law (*aš-šar*ʿ*îyât*), noting that in dealing with new situations (here ʾ*aḥkâm ḥawâdiṯ*)[85] in which there is a different casting of the problem (*ta*ʿ*yîn al-mas*ʾ*ala*), the two separate kinds of problems must be handled each according to its own distinctive principles: those of the *kalâm* or of the *fiqh.*[86] In terms of the exposition of the earlier *risâla*, if one is to follow the example of the Prophet and his "method" (*ṭarîqa*), the matters that form the subject of the first three stages of his teaching are to be understood, studied, and, if need be, explained and argued in theoretical terms (ʿ*aqlan*) and the law (what one is obliged to do, in whatever sphere) according to the principles of authority and the commands of the lawgiver. In the one case as in the other the principles are given in the *Koran* and the *sunna*; that the ʿ*aqlîyât* are distinct from the *šar*ʿ*îyât* and have their own characteristic ʾ*uṣûl* does not mean for al-Ašʿarî that the basis for their correct use is not given in the canonical sources or that the theologian or *mutakallim* is less bound, in following the principles found in these sources, than is the *faqîh.*

Al-Ašʿarî's position, then, is this: the transmitted canonical sources—the Koran and the *sunna*—are complete, sufficient and adequate in themselves for the believer to demonstrate and grasp any essential doctrine of the faith and so may be used alone as sufficient evidence of their own truth. This is the underlying principle and explicit thesis of the *Ibâna*. Furthermore, regarding a large number of primary and central dogmas, the sources contain more or less explicitly speculative or theoretical arguments and explanations based upon a specifically defined understanding of the physical and metaphysical structure of being and the world. In the expositon of the teaching of the Koran and the Prophet concerning these matters, the speculative theologian—the *mutakallim* or ʾ*uṣûlî*—may simply cite the appropriate texts, assuming the systematic exegesis;[87] in some circumstances, however, in order to address himself to a particular formulation or conception of the question or simply to make the content of the sources unambiguously clear in the truth they contain, the may expand, explain and elaborate their sense in the language and analysis of the *kalâm*. To do so, however, is not an innovation or departure from the sources but only an elaboration, from a particular perspective, and an explicitation of the reasoning that is contained in the canonical sources. The rational argumentation of the *kalâm* analysis (his own system, of course) is thus for al-Ašʿarî to be taken with unqualified seriousness as a speculative demonstration of what it means to show, for it is the reasoning of God and the Prophet and if it is not absolutely probative on strictly theoretical grounds then, given his understanding of the ordered progression of the teaching of the Prophet and the basis of the recognition of the obligation to believe, the whole edifice, including the authority of the revelation, must collapse because of the unsoundness of its initial foundation in the point of absolute beginning. It is plain from this that, contrary to the suggestion of some authorities, the primary argumentation employed to establish the doctrines that fall under the scope of the first two topical areas (sc., creation, the creator and his attributes) cannot be conceived by al-Ašʿarî as no more than a series of ad hoc arguments concocted simply in response to one or another objection or counter thesis, each being drawn up individually and separately against a particular opponent with little or no regard for the theoretical consistency and conceptual coherence of the whole system.

One should note also that nowhere does al-Ašʿarî say explicitly that the purpose of *kalâm* is simply one of apologetics. In the "Letter to the People of the Fronteer" he replies to questions posed by friends who adhere strictly to the Koran and the *sunna*, to show them the rightness of their position as opposed to that of those who do not[88] and in the *Istiḥsân al-ḫawḍ* he speaks of the use of technical analysis and its terminology in terms of the casting or framing of questions (*taʿyîn al-masâʾil*). In the one as in the other, he notes that the Prophet addressed himself to an audience of (originally all of them) unbelievers of various stripe whom he taught giving various demonstrations of the truth of his teaching and of the error of their original belief. Throughout both works he strives to show that the prophet *demonstrated* the truth of his teaching in specific terms, explicit or implicit, that rest upon and so point to a coherent theoretical conception of the physical and metaphysical structure of the world and of being in general. He says, furthermore, that one may, and in some instances is obliged to reformulate and elaborate these arguments of the Koran and the Prophet,[89] as circumstances demand. Though these "changing circumstances", quite obviously, are characteristically determined, in part at least, by the questions posed by opponents of the faith or those who raise objection to particular dogmas, al-Ašʿarî does not allude directly to the role of any such opponent or suggest any apologetic function for the *kalâm* in the paragraphs where he raises the specific issue of dealing with new circumstances. Since, according to his claim, *kalâm* (sc., his own system) is the true and literal teaching of the Prophet, he needs not apologize for it on any such pragmatic grounds. Indeed, the development of *fiqh* and *kalâm* he seems to see as effected by analagous conditions.[90]

In summary, al-Aš'arî does not deprecate or denigrate the use of reason or rational argumentation in theology in favor of a fideist conception of the canonical sources. He sees it, in fact, whether as embodied in the Koran and the traditions or as elaborated in the technical analyses of his *kalâm*, as the true ground for the authentic understanding and realisation of the faith of the believer. The topical order of the exposition of the preface of the "Letter to the People of the Fronteer" follows essentially that of the *kalâm* compendia (cp., e.g., al-Aš'arî's *Luma'* or al-Mâturîdî's *Tawḥîd*); nowhere, however, does al-Aš'arî argue that this is the logical or rational order of the questions but rather he reiterates over and again that this is the method of the teaching of the Prophet. Similarly he insists that his formal analysis is literally that of the teaching of the Prophet.

In a sense, al-Aš'arî's conception of the relationship that exists for the theologian between reason and the faith-given authority of the canonical sources is intermediate between the claims made for the primacy of the one or the other by the Mu'tazila on the one side and the more extreme traditionalists (*al-ḥašwîya*) on the other.[91] In taking the position specifically as he does he puts between the authority of revelation and the mind's innate claim to autonomous judgement a bond of reciprocity by which each simultaneously grounds the functional authority of the other: the one serves as the prior ground for the theologian's validation of his use and understanding of the other; the probative use and intelligent understanding of either can be achieved with certainty only through guidance of the other. Within the system, however, this conception of the nature of theology is mightily confined; in bestowing canonical authority upon a particular analysis with its distinctive conceptions and presuppositions and in binding it in a particular way to the canonical texts, al-Aš'arî produced a system that, for all its acuity, is in many ways inflexible and in some respects restrictive as a tool of intellectual understanding.[92]

Corrigenda to the printed text of *R. ilà ahl aṯ-ṯaġr*, pp. 80-91.

80, ult.: ابرتموها for انذرتموها

82,16: بالاتفاق for الا باتفاق

82,18: على for الى

85,9: خالق for خلقا

87,2: omit الصلاة والسلام

87,12: وحدته (with ms.) for وحده

87,16: له for لهم (at end of the time).

88,3: لم يخبر for لم يوجد (ms. = لم يجد)

88,4: omit السلام

88,8: عليها for عليه

88,19 بسائر for لسائر

89,18: على مايدل عليه for ماهى له (ms.= على ماهى له له عليه)

89, ult.: add الى following حواسنا

90,5: مخالفتهم for مخالفهم

90,9: لما for فما

91,4: omit الجواهر (see n. 35)

Notes

1. Cf. e.g., the many citations in the *Šâmil fî 'uṣûl ad-dîn* (ed. A. Naššâr, Alexandria 1969; this work, it should be noted, is a commentary (*taḥrîr*) on al-Bâqillânî's Commentary (*šarḥ*) on al-Aš'arî's *K. al-Luma'*, though citations of the latter work are sparce indeed and do not, such as they are in the limited portion of the *Šâmil* that is presently available, reflect verbatim the published recension of the *Luma'*). One should, however, be cautious in using the elaborated positions attributed to al-Aš'arî since al-Juwaynî openly admits on several occasions (e.g., op. cit., pp. 458, 649 f., 656) that the position he attributes to the master is only a conjecture made by earlier authorities. Though many works are attributed to al-Aš'arî even al-Bâqillânî and Ibn Fûrak, among others, appear to have lacked adequate information concerning some important areas of his teaching; cf. *Šâmil*, loc. cit. and also as-Suyûṭî, *al-Muzhir fî 'ulûm al-luġa*, 1, 24.

2. Introduction à la théologie musulmane (Paris, 1948), pp. 56 f. This judgement is based on the assumption (cf. *ibid.*) that the most typical exponents of his work are the *Ibâna* and the *Maqâlât al-Islâmîyin*. (The *Luma'* had not yet been published.)

3. "Ash'arî and the Ash'arites in Islamic Religious History", Studia Islamica 18 (1963), p. 30; Makdisi speaks of the image of "a two way Ash'arî" (ibid., 43 f.).

4. Cf. J. van Ess, die Erkenntnislehre des 'Aḍuddadîn al-Icî (Wiesbaden 1966), p. 319.

5. Ibid., 23 f.

6. *Risâla ilà ahl aṯ-ṯaġr bi-Bâb al-abwâb*, published in the Ilahiyat Fakültesi Mecmuasi 8 (1928), pp. 80–108. A question may be raised concerning the authenticity of the work (cf. generally M. Allard, le Problème des attributs divins selon al-Aš'arî et ses premiers grands disciples (Beyrouth 1965), pp. 53 ff.) but the evidence is predominantly in favor of its being genuine (cf. ibid., p. 58). It is clearly mentioned by Ibn 'Asâkir in his list of al-Aš'arî's writings (cf. R. McCarthy, The Theology of al-Ash'arî, Beyrouth 1953, pp. 228 f. (§ 99) and p. 230 (§ 103)) and the only major problem would seem to be that of the date, *sc.*, A.H. 297 (cf. Allard, op. cit., p. 58, n. 2, where he notes that the 267 found in the ms. is clearly to be emended) which is earlier than that most commonly ascribed to his "conversion", *viz.*, 300/912–13 (cf. generally ibid., pp. 35 ff.) and several years prior to his definitive residence in Baghdad (cf. ibid., 45). The traditional date of A.H. 300 for his "conversion" is probably a little late (Allard suggests that it may have been as early as 292; cf. ibid., p. 42); by then, according to the testimony of Ibn 'Asâkir (*Tabyîn kaḏib al-muftarî*, Damascus 1347, p. 127, cited by Allard, op. cit., 42) his "post conversion" writings were already gaining some notariety. The traditional date, then (if the "forty years of age" is not just too convenient a figure within this context) may represent only the point of his public declaration of the breach with his former fellows, an act that became increasingly

necessary as his "new" position became known more widely. *Corrigenda* to the printed text of the prefatory section of this *risâla* are listed at the end of the present study.

7. Fr. Allard suggests that the first part of the risâla is a general apologia for Islam (op. cit., pp. 54 and 189); the direct purpose, however, as will become clearer in the following analysis, is to show that the Koran and the traditions are the supreme and unique guide to all the *'uṣûl ad-dîn*. To take this preface as merely a general apologetic "addressed to unbelievers" (ibid., p. 54) neglects the primary evidence of the work itself: it is, in the first place, addressed expressly to believing Muslims whom the author recognises as firm adherents to the *Koran* and the *sunna* with, in the second place, the explicit intention of confirming them in their adherence to these as the sole sources and sure guides to the fundamentals of the faith; the conclusion, finally, that he draws in the preface (and to which he devotes a relatively considerable space) is precisely that the canonical sources contain everything whatsoever that is needful for the understanding of the Muslim faith. His explicit argument with the *falâsifa* here is only that their argument for the creation of the universe is less conclusive than that of the *Koran*. If the preface is an apologia it is, thus, an apologia for the *Koran* and *sunna*. In that the work was composed quite early in the "post-conversion" period of al-Aš'arî's career a preoccupation with this matter is scarcely unexpected. I would insist here, as elsewhere before, that the more one studies the writing of al-Aš'arî the more one is impressed with its acuteness and precision; nothing is extraneous and the further one pursues the implications of any expression or formulation taken in its strictest formal sense, the more apparent becomes the inner consistency and conceptual discipline of his thought and his exposition of it. This remarkable economy of his style requires that it be read very closely.

8. 81,4 f.

9. 93 ff.

10. That it is essentially an *'aqîda* has been noted by Allard, op. cit., p. 202.

11. 81,8 f.

12. Cf. 87,4 f., 92,11 ff. and below.

13. 89,9 f., cited below n. 23.

14. 87,14 ff.: دلهم على صحة جميع ما دعاهم الى اعتقاده وفعله بحجج الله وبيناته ولم يؤخر عنهم بيان شئ مما دعا اليه عن وقت تكليفه لهم. Cf. also p. 92,11 ff.

15. Sûra 5,3, cited p. 92,2 f.

16. P. 81,16 ff. The groups are listed as the People of the Scriptures, the philosophers, the *Barâhima*, the dualists, and the idolators.

17. I.e., all men universally; cf., e.g., 81,17.

18. 86,15 ff.; cf. also 86, ult. f.: واذا كان هذا على ما ذكرناه علم صحة مذهبنا اليه في دعوته عليه الصلاة و السلام الى التوحيد واقامة الحجة على ذلك وايضاحه الطرق اليه.

19. 88,4 f., cited below, n. 43.

20. Especially pp. 89–92.

21. Cf., e.g., 89,8 ff.: واذا ثبت بالايات صدقه قد علم صحة كل ما اخبره به النبى صلعم عنه وصارت اخباره ادلة على سائر ما دعا اليه. . .

22. E.g. 81,16–82, 1; see following note.

23. E.g. 81,21 ff.: لينبههم على حدوثهم ويدعوهم الى توحيد المحدث لهم ويبين لهم طرق معرفته . . . ودلالته على صدقه . . . ويوضح لهم سائر ما تعبدهم الله عزوجل من شريعته.

24. E.g. 87,17–20: ومعلوم عند سائر العقلاء ان ما دعا اليه النبى صلعم من واجهه من امته من اعتقاد حدوثهم ومعرفة المحدث لهم وتوحيده ومعرفة اسمائه الحسنى وما هو عليه من صفات نفسه وصفات فعله وتصديقه فيما بلغهم من رسالته مما لا يصح ان يؤخر عنهم البيان فيه.

Besides the preceding note cf. also 88,13 ff. and 90,13 ff. (cited below n. 48) and see below concerning the function of the miracle.

25. P. 81,17–23 (cited n. 23 above). These expressions recur throughout the section; cf. e.g., 82,2 f.: نبههم على حدوثهم بما فيهم من اختلاف الصور والهيئات وغير ذلك من اختلاف اللغة

88, 5: وجوه الادلة التى نبههم عليها .88,7 f.: لا زيادة على ما نبههم من الحجج

90, 14 f.: . . . ما دعاهم اليه من العلم بحدوثهم ووجود المحدث لهم بما نبههم عليه من الادلة. Cf. also below n. 48.

26. Cf. 87,1, cited above n. 18; 87,14, cited above n. 14; 86,2 ff., cited below n. 38 and 88,5, cited in the preceding note.

27. Cf. 87,14 (cited above, n. 14); see also 85,3, 88,7 f. and 90,14 f. (both citẹd above n. 25) and 101, 8 and 11 (cited below) and also 101,18 f. and 93,8. On the technical sense of the expression *dalâla*, *ʾadilla*, see J. van Ess, "The Logical Structure of Islamic Theology" in Logic in Classical Islamic Culture (ed. G. von Grünebaum, Wiesbaden 1970), pp. 26 f.

28. Cf. 82,2 f. (cited n. 25 above); the second, a reference to the Koran 30,22, al-Ašʿarî does not pursue in this work.

29. Pp. 82 ff.

30. Viz., 51.21 (cited 82, 4 f.), 23.12–14 (cited 83,13 f.); for the oblique allusion to 30.22, see above.

31. 82,3 f.

32. 89,7 (cited below n. 37).

33. Cf., e.g., 86, 16 ff. and 88,5 as well as below.

34. 89,12 ff.

35. 89,11–20; the term *al-jawâhir* is probably to be omitted at 91, 4 since the question from p. 89 is of *al-istidlâl bil-ʾaʿrâḍ*.

36. Cf. 86,2 ff. and 90,3 ff. Other miracles were given to reinforce and emphasise (*'akkada*) the primary and characteristic one; cf. 87,1 ff.

37. 89,6 ff.: ان ما دل على صدق النبى صلعم من المعجزات بعد تنبيهه لسائر المتكلمين على حدوثهم ووجود المحدث لهم قد اوجب صحة اخباره ودل على ان ما اتاكم من الكتاب والسنة من عند الله عزوجل.

Cf. also 86,2 ff (cited in the following note) 81,17 ff. and 90,13 ff.

38. 86,2 f.: ثم ان الله عز وجل بعد اقامة الحجج ازعج خواطر جماعتهم للنظر فيما دعا هم اليه ونبههم عليه بالايات الباهرة والمعجزات القاهرة.

39. 89, ult. ff.: لان اياته والادلة على صدقه . . . قد ازعجت القلوب وبعث الخواطر على النظر فى صحة ما يدعو اليه وتامل ما استشهد به على صدقه.

40. This he explains (p. 102,4–7) saying that ليسر يجب اذا كلفوا مفرقة مالا يعلمونه فى حال التكليف لاعراضهم ان يكلفوا الفعل مع عدم جميع علومهم اذ كان عدم جميع علومهم يخرجهم عن صحة عقولهم ويصيرهم الى الجنون الذى لا يصح تكليف الاستدلال معه (reading *y'lmwnh* for *y'mlwnh* in line 5. In the same passage omit '*alayhî* in line 2).

41. 101,7–12: قد كلف الكفار الايمان والتصديق بنبيه . . . لان النبى قد اوضح لهم الدلالة . . . وطريقة معرفتهم بذلك العقول التى جعلت الة تمييزهم وانهم اتموا فى ذلك من قبل اعراضهم عن تامل ما دعوا الى تامله من الادلة التى جعل لهم بها السبيل الى معرفة وجوب ما دعوا اليه من النظر فى اياته التى ازعج بخرق العادات فيها قلوبهم وحرك بها دواعى نظرهم . . .

42. Cf. 86,18 ff.: لم يبق لاحد منهم شبهة فيه . . . لو لم يكن ذلك كذلك لم يكن له عليه الصلاة والسلام حجة على جماعتهم ولا كانت طاعته لازمة لهم.

Cf. also 87,14 ff. and 88,1 ff. This is the basis for the exegesis of Q. 5.3 cited above n. 15.

43. 88,14 f.: قد تبين لهم وجوه الادلة فى جميعه حتى ثلجت صدورهم به واستغنوا عن استئناف الادلة فيه. Cf. also nn. 18 and 19 above and 43 below. The similarity of the expression *ṯalaja ṣudûruhum* (which occurs several times) to abû Hâšim's *sakana n-nafs* may, given the early date of the work, be significant.

44. 89,9–11: صار اخباره ادلة . . . وصار خبره عليه الصلاة والسلام عن ذلك سبيلا الى ادراكه وطريقا الى العلم بحقيقته

45. 90,7: طرق الاستدلال باخبارهم. See also 89,7 f.

46. 93,21 f. (on this passage see JAOS 88, 1968, p. 301, n. 1); cf. also n. 40 above.

47. Cf. the discussion above nn. 33 f. and his comment that the philosophers, at the time of the prophet, قد تشعبت لهم الاباطيل فى فنون تدعيها بقضايا العقول (81,18 f.)

48. 90,13 ff.: فأخلد سلفنا رضى الله عنهم ومن اتبعهم من الخلف الصالح بعد ما عرفوه من صدق النبى صلعم فيما دعاهم اليه من العلم بحدوثهم ووجود المحدث لهم بما نبههم عليه من الادلة الى تمسك بالكتاب والسنة وطلب الحق فى سائر ما دعوا الى معرفته منهما والعدول عن كل ما خالفهما لثبوت نبوته عليه السلام عندهم وتبينهم بصدقه فيما اخبرهم عن ربهم لما وثقته الدلالة لهم فيه.

49. Cf. 91,7 ff.

50. 88,19 ff.: ... من غير ان يحتاج ... فى العرفة لسائر ما دعينا الى اعتقاده الى استئناف ادلة غير الادلة التى نبه النبى صلعم عليها ودعا سائر امته الى تاملها اذ كان من المستحيل ان ياتى بعد ذلك باهدى مما اتى به.

51. Cf. 88,16 ff. and 89,6 ff.

52. 81,21 ff. (cited n. 23 above).

53. This is followed (84,20–85,1) by the argument for the possibility of the resurrection. The position, in view of the common order of topics in the later *kalâm* tracts, may appear peculiar but the same basic order is found in the *K. al-Luma*ʿ (§§ 9 f.; cf. JAOS 86, pp. 302 f.). It is as if al-Ašʿarî feels that the "creation a second time" should be treated in conjunction with the "first creation". It is probable that he feels simply that this is the order of the original teaching of the prophet (see below). Al-Juwaynî in the *Šâmil* (p. 401) postpones his treatment of *Luma*ʿ §§ 9 f. in order to follow the more common order.

54. 86,2 ff.; see nn. 38 f. above.

55. Ibid. and 87,1.

56. This is the essence of the Ašʿarite thesis that the obligation to know God is known only through the Scripture and traditions; whereas the Baṣra School of the Muʿtazila hold that this obligation arises existentially, as it were, from human nature itself and prior to any knowledge of the createdness of the universe, al-Ašʿarî and his followers, since they hold that all obligation has it source uniquely in God's command (*bi-ʾîjâbi llâh*; cf. 102, 4 ff. cited above), insist that it cannot be known as an obligation until one knows the express command and recognises it as authoritative and binding. For the Muʿtazilite rejection of the extraneous imposition of the fundamental moral imperatives cf. G. Hourani, Islamic Rationalism, Oxford 1971, passim and esp. 115 ff. and Studia Islamica 33 (1971) n. 2.

57. Cf. nn. 12–15 above and generally pp. 87–92. One interpretation of "the straight path" is that it is the Koran (cf., e.g., Ṭabarî, Tafsîr 1, 56) and some interpreted the expression *mustaqîm* as *al-qâʾimu bi-maʿnà ṯ-ṯâbiti bil-barâhîni wal-ʾadillati lâ yuzîluhû šayʾun wa-lâ yanquḍu ḥujajahû kaydu l-kâʾidîna wa-lâ ḥiyalu l-murîbîn* (cf. al-Mâturîdî, Taʾwîlât ahl as-sunna, Cairo 1391/1971, 25

58. Cf. esp. 90,13 ff.

59. Cf. 89,1 ff.

60. 90, 13 ff., cited above; see also the following note.

61. Cf. 88,5 f.; 87,16 ff.; and 90,13 ff.

62. They do, quite obviously, constitute an absolute point of departure in that there can be no awareness or knowledge of the Prophet's claims and precise teaching apart from the transmitted sources and in that the Koran embodies the primary miracle; this is not, however, initially as authority but as evidence.

63. Cf. 87,17–88,3 (cited partically above n. 24) and n.b. also 101,7–12 (cited above n. 41).

64. Thus he says explicitly that these arguments are addressed to all the *mutakallimîn* (cf. n. 37 above).

65. Cf. 88,3 f., 88,15 and 89,3 f.

66. 88,3 ff.

67. That the Prophet showed the way or method is repeated several times, e.g., 81, 22 (cited above n. 23); 87, 1 (cited above n. 18) and 101,7 ff. (cited above n. 41); likewise he gave the *wujûh al-ʾadilla* (cf. 88,7 and 88,14).

68. Cf. n. 45 above.

69. Cf., e.g., 86,3 (cited above n. 38); 90, 1 (cited above, n. 39) and 101, 11 (cited above n. 41).

70. It is for this reason that the sections against the Christians, Jews and the other *firaq* are found in the *kalâm* tracts, as in the preface here, in the first part and not elsewhere.

71. Cf., e.g., 90,7 and 89,7.

72. Cf. 81,9 ff. and 89,13.

73. 88,13 f. (the occurrence of the term *'adluhû* in this position in this context, reflecting as it does the order of subjects in the Muʿtazilite *summae*, may be significant given the early date of this epistle among al-Ašʿarî's post-conversion writings); cf. also n. 24 above. The arguments are outlined here pp. 82 ff, 93 ff. and in the *K. al-Lumaʿ*, §§ 3 ff.

74. 92,24 f.

75. Al-Ašʿarî's understanding of the role and function of reason and its relation to the revelation thus categorically precludes the conception of his Muʿtazilite master, al-Jubbâ'î, and his followers in the Baṣra school, according to whom, as autonomous reason discovers the attributes of God it is bound to apply such predicates (*ṣifât*) as it knows to be conceptually appropriate and fitting and, accordingly, to apply such names as, according to the conventionally established usage of the language, denote those concepts. Thus too, the conflicting doctrines of the two schools in regard to the origin and nature of language are integrally tied to the fundamental tendencies of the systems.

76. A full analysis of his argumentation, though highly desirable, is excluded from the present study for reasons of space. The matter, of which a very brief outline is to be found in JAOS 88, 301 ff. (where at 306B, 2 correct "abû l-Hudhayl" to read "an-Naẓẓâm"), would appear to be reasonably clear. Again, to the extent that one can draw any conclusions concerning al-Ašʿarî's conception of the character and method of theology from the last written portions of the *Maqâlât al-Islâmîyîn* (cf. Allard, op. cit. 184 ff.) they also would appear to conform to the evidence of the present study.

77. Superficially the two works differ considerably but most of these differences are easily explained in terms of the different addressees and the circumstances under they were written. The first is an early work of the period of his "conversion" while the second is most probably much later, having been composed, as Fr. Allard has pointed out (op. cit., 206 ff.), in consequence to the hostile Ḥanbalite response to his *Ibâna*. In the *Istiḥsân al-ḫawḍ* he is brought to argue against an intransigent opponent what he took as self-evident in addressing his friends in the earlier work. The *Ibâna* in no way at all questions the concept of the role of reason set forth in the two epistles but, on the contrary, is fully compatible with them and with the practice of the K. al-Lumaʿ (see below). In the light of the present study I continue to find Prof. Makdisi's contention that the *Risâla fî stiḥsân al-ḫawḍ* is spurious (cf. Studia Islamica 18, 1963, 22 ff.) unconvincing; cf. also van Ess, Erkenntnislehre, 318 f. and JAOS 88, 308, n. 31.

78. 88,8–10: انما تكلفوا البحث والنظر فيما كلفوا من الاجتهاد فى حوادث الاحكام عد نزولها بهم وحدوثها فيهم وردوها الى معان الاصول التى وقفهم عليها

79. 88,11 f.

80. § 2, p. 87,19 f.

81. §§ 3 f.

82. Cf. e.g., 92,1 f,; 93,6 f.; 93,8 f.; and generally §§ 6 ff.

83. Cf. e.g., 92,9 f: *wahuwa 'aṣlun lanâ.*

84. Cf. §§ 20 f.

85. 92,5: *'aḥkâm ḥawâdiṯ* (see generally §§ 21 f.) paralleling the expression *ḥawâdiṯ al-'aḥkâm* in the earlier *risâla.*

86. § 22 (note again the expression *ar-radd 'ilà l-'uṣûl*); cf. JAOS 88,308 f.

87. As I have pointed out elsewhere (cf. JAOS 88, 302 f.) this is a common practice of al-Aš'arî and one must take care to distinguish those instances wherein he cites the sources merely as statements of the argument from those where he cites them as authority. Regarding al-Aš'arî's assumption of a specific, rational analysis implicit in many verses of the Koran it is interesting to note that al-Dhahabi reports that al-Aš'arî was still an adherent of the Mu'tazila when he wrote his *tafsîr* (though al-Subkî denies the report); cf. al-Subkî, *Ṭabaqât aš-šâfi'iya al-kubrà* (Cairo 1384/1965) 3, 355 (bottom).

88. Pp. 81 f.

89. Cf. the expression *mâ kullifû mina l-ijtihâd* (see above n. 78) in *R. ilà ahl aṯ-ṯaġr,* 88 and cf. *Istiḥsân al-ḫawḍ,* § 22,

90. The same position is stated by al-Ijî (cf. al-Jurjânî, *Šarḥ al-mawâqif* (Cairo 1325) 1, 266, 1 ff.; translated in van Ess, Erkenntnislehre, 317, § 146; see also ibid., 319). The analogy with the *fiqh*, i.e., that the *kalâm* develops in response to circumstances, though certainly including an "apologetic", implies at the same time that it is somehow equally needful to the faith of the community, i.e., needful to the community as it must explain to itself its faith in the *aḥwâl ḥawâdiṯ.*

91. This, in a sense, parallels the "intermediate position" that he takes in matters of dogma; cf. Ibn 'Asâkir, op. cit., 149 ff., Gardet and Anawati, op. cit., 57 ff. and generally L. Gardet, "Raison et foi en Islam", Rev. Thomiste 43 (1937), 457 ff.

92. The comparison with the theology of al-Mâturîdî is particularly revealing of the rigidity of al-Aš'arî's thought.

IX

AL-ASHᶜARĪ'S "KITĀB AL-ḤATHTH ᶜALĀ L-BAḤTH"*

The text which I shall present here is not that of a hitherto unknown work of al-Ashᶜarī. It has been published several times under the title *Risālat Istiḥsān al-khawḍ fī ᶜilm al-kalām,* first in Hyderabad in A.H. 1323 and again in 1344, and subsequently republished by the late Fr. Richard McCarthy, S.J. in his *The Theology of al-Ashᶜarī* (Beyrouth, 1953, pp. 87–97) together with an English translation (*ibid.*, pp. 119–134).

The new text of the *Kitāb al-Ḥathth ᶜalā l-Baḥth* is furnished us by abū l-Qāsim Salmān ibn Nāṣir al-Naysabūrī al-Anṣārī (d. 512/1118)[1] in his *al-Ghunya fī l-kalām,* which is found in MS III Ahmet n° 1916. Cited in full, the Ashᶜarite text forms the bulk of a subsection of a chapter devoted to "the obligation to [theological] enquiry" *(wujūb al-naẓar)*. Having first examined the question in a general way (foll. 5v°f.), al-Anṣārī then takes up the thesis that to carry out formal, theological speculation is an obligation of the community *(wujūb al-kifāyah),* not one which is incumbent on each individual Muslim *(wujūb al-aᶜyān)* (foll. 6r° ff.). The text of *al-Ḥathth ᶜalā l-baḥth,* following an introduction of some twelve lines, constitutes virtually the whole of the next and final subsection of this chapter, in which he deals with the contention that "to occupy one's self with *kalām* is an innovation" (fol. 9r° ff.).

Besides the text contained in al-Anṣārī's *al-Ghunya* (A) and that of the Hyderabad edition (H), we have utilised in the preparation of the present edition of *al-Ḥathth* that contained in Landberg n° 1030, foll. 4v°–6v° (= Ahlwardt n° 2162) (B)[2] and that contained in Feyzullah n° 2161/2, foll.

* I wish to express my gratitude to Manuscript Institute of the League of Arab States, which furnished me the copy of al-Anṣāri's *K. al-Ghunya* and also to the directors of the Süleymaniye Kütüphanesi and the Staatsbibliothek preussicher Kulturbesitz, who supplied me with photocopies of the texts of *al-Ḥathth* held in their collections and who kindly granted permission for their publication.

49v°–52r° (F). Witnessed in these four copies, however, are two distinct versions of the work, which I shall refer to as T–1 and T–2. The former is contained in A and the latter in B, F, and H. Where T–1 and T–2 are essentially identical I shall present a single text; where they differ the two are presented in parallel columns.

Regarding the title of the work, that given in A is confirmed as original by its occurrence in Ibn ᶜAsākir's supplement to Ibn Fūrak's list of al-Ashᶜarī's writings and in that of Ibn Farḥūn.[3] The title given in the Hyderabad edition is plainly spurious, a descriptive pseudo-title made up by some one, a copyist or perhaps the editor, who was either ill acquainted with the vocabulary of al-Ashᶜarī and his followers or was fundamentally opposed to the position set forth in the tract and wished to label it in a disparaging manner. The expression "*istiḥsān*" would never have been used by al-Ashᶜarī in speaking of something of which he approved nor likely "*al-khawḍ*" either, since both have essentially negative connotations for him and for most of the tradition.[4] The catalogue entry for F, "*Risālah fī l-radd ᶜalā man ẓanna anna l-ishtighāl bil-kalām bidᶜah*" is interesting in that it closely parallels the wording employed by al-Anṣārī at the beginning of the passage in which he presents the text of *al-Ḥathth,* but it is not found either at the beginning or at the end of the text in the manuscript. In B likewise the work is untitled.

Since we have the work in two different forms there is a question as to which of the two is primary and in what sense. Does one form represent the author's own revision of an earlier writing presented by the other or is one of them a recension, produced by one of his disciples?

For T–2, F and H furnish an almost identical *isnād* according to which the F text is based on a copy executed in Rabīᶜ I, 677 (August/September, 1278) by the Mālikite *muqri*ʾ.

1. abū l-Qāsim ᶜAbd al-Raḥmān b. ᶜAbd al-Ḥalīm b. ᶜImrān Saḥnūn (d. 4/X/695 = 6/VIII/1296) from a copy of

2. abū Ṣādiq Muḥammad, the son of the famous Mālikite traditionist abū l-Ḥusayn Yaḥyā b. ᶜAlī l-Rashīd al-ᶜAṭṭār (584/1188 – 662/1264), which was made from a copy of

3. abū l-Ḥasan ᶜAlī b. Ibrāhīm al-Qurashī, made on 8/X/600 = 9/VI/1204 from a copy of the Shāfiᶜite *muqri*ʾ,

4. abū l-Maᶜālī l-Mawṣilī (539/1144–5 – 621/1224), made in 573/1177–8 from a copy of

5. abū Manṣūr al-Mubārak al-Baghdādī, made in 542/1147–8 from a copy of the Shāfiᶜite traditionist,

6. abū l-Faḍl Ibn al-Ukhuwwa (d. 547/1153) from a copy of

7. abū l-Faḍl Muḥammad b. Yaḥyā l-Nātilī from a copy of

8. abū Naṣr ᶜAbd al-Karīm al-Shīrāzī from (a text transmitted by)

9. ᶜAlī ibn Rustam from (a text transmitted by)

10. abū l-Ḥasan ᶜAlī b. Muḥammad b. Mahdī l-Ṭabarī, a direct disciple of al-Ashᶜarī.

H lacks the first two names of this *isnād*. It is explicitly stated for numbers 1–7 that each copy was orally collated with the one from which it was made. Though no date is given for al-Nātilī's copy, it was executed at dictation in the residence of al-Shīrāzī, wherefore it is apparent that between this and the time of Ibn Mahdī l-Ṭabarī there is a span of at least four generations — maybe a century and a half — for which we have only the name of ᶜAlī b. Rustam, whom I have been unable to identify. The presence of this gap does pose a problem,[5] but one need not, on this basis alone, impugn the validity of the *isnād* altogether. There is, that is to say, no prima facie evidence on which to doubt that Ibn Mahdī is the first transmitter of T–2, at least as represented in F and H. Even so, however, the question remains as to whether this text represents the primary and original form of the tract or a secondary recension, and if so by whom.

The A text, copied in Rabīᶜ I, 592 (February, 1196) bears no *isnād*. It is, however, given to us directly by abū l-Qāsim al-Anṣārī, a disciple of abū l-Maᶜālī al-Juwaynī and so belongs to a line of transmission which lies within the tradition of the foremost masters of the Ashᶜarite school. In this the A text stands in sharp contrast to that of FH, none of whose transmitters, after Ibn Mahdī, is a recognised Ashᶜarite master. As we shall see, in addition to this there is some evidence to suggest that more than one copyist of the manuscripts representing T–2 was not in the habit of copying *kalām* texts. Nonetheless, even though the association of the A text with the leading theologians of the Ashᶜarite school would indicate that it has a pedigree such as to claim considerable respect, it is yet not sufficient to indicate whether it represents the original form of the work or not.

With respect to T–2 the A text contains several clear additions which were inserted by al-Anṣārī and are plainly indicated as such, being introduced by "I say" (as contrasted to "the master, abū l-Ḥasan said"). Besides these, T–1 has one short paragraph (§2.225) which is not found in T–2. In general, however,

T–2 is longer, fuller in its expression, and more detailed than T–1 and in some places very conspicuously so. On the principle that the simpler and shorter form of a text is generally the primary one and the longer secondary, we should take it as likely that T–1 is primary. General rules, however, do not of themselves allow any certainty concerning particular individuals, wherefore we shall have to look more closely at some of the differences between the two text forms. I shall examine several of the more notable elements in which T–1 and T–2 differ from one another and which would seem to confirm the hypothesis — some of them more clearly than others — that T–2 does in fact represent a secondary revision of T–1 or of a text closely resembling it. Following this it will be opportune to look briefly at the relationship between the three witnesses to T–2.

T–2 shows a number of elements which appear as additions with respect to T–1. In several cases these additions are relatively long. One such passage, found in §2.2131, would seem unquestionably to have originated in a gloss, possibly brought in from the margin of the archetype.[6] By contrast with this, the long sentence which stands at the end of §2.323 in T–2 seems in no way out of place. It forms a kind of coda which sums up the argument of §2.23, if not of §2.22 and §2.23 together, and anticipates the issues raised in §2.31. One may, therefore, plausibly suggest that this sentence (treated as a separate section or paragraph in McCarthy's edition) most likely was introduced as a part of a more general effort of redaction, evidence of which we shall look at below.

We find an awkward intrusion into the text in §2.223 where, following the sentence "and it is impossible to enumerate an infinity" (*wa-muḥālun ʾiḥṣāʾu mā lā nihāyata lahu*), T–2 adds "and it is impossible that a single thing be divisible, since this requires that it be two things" (*muḥālun ʾan yakūna l-shayʾu l-wāḥidu yanqasimu liʾanna hādhā yūjibu ʾan yakūna shayʾayn*). The addition of T–2 is clearly out of place, since the following sentence, "but He has made it known that they are denumerable" refers to the earlier citation of Q 36.12 and 72.82 and has, for coherence sake, to follow the statement "it is impossible to enumerate an infinity". The inserted sentence would seem originally to have stood in the margin of the archetype of T–2, where it was to be read after the "*waqaʿa l-ʿadadu ʿalayhā*" which concludes the paragraph. In order to adjust the syntax HF has altered the final *ʿalayhā* to *ʿalayhimā*, making it agree with the dual, *shayʾayn*, but the conclusion, even with this, remains meaningless.[7]

An insertion of analogous material is made in §2.221 where, following "and no day but that it is preceded by another day" T–2 adds "and the discussion against those who say that there is no particle *(juz')* save that it has a half limitlessly". The context, however, deals with the question of the denial of an infinite temporal regression and the added element is wholly out of place. The ḥadīths cited in the refutation of the position of those who hold that the world is eternal are read as asserting God's absolute initiation of the being of things, not as having to do with infinite divisibility. Here, as also with the insertion in §2.223, it would seem that at least one copyist involved in the formation and transmission of T–2 was not well schooled in *kalām* and was not used to copying *kalām* texts.

In §2.2132, following *"al-ḍiddāni lā yajtami^cāni ^calā maḥallin wāḥid"* (two contraries cannot be conjoined so as to qualify a single substrate), T–2 shows an addition to the text which is corrupt in all three manuscripts. In its original form it would seem to have read *"wa-lā ^calā l-jumlati wa-lā fī l-mawjūdi lā fī maḥall"* (nor so as to qualify the composite whole nor in what exists in no substrate). The addition is pointless in the context, since the argument involves the possibility of the bodily resurrection of the dead and specifically an objection which claims that to posit such a possibility requires that one posit the possibility of the conjunction of contrary properties or accidents (dry and damp, hot and cold) in one and the same material substrate. The sense of the addition, in fact, if its original form is as I have suggested, is not immediately clear. The phrase *"al-mawjūdi lā fī maḥall"* could, in principle, be a description of the atom, but if this is the case it stands here redundantly with the preceding *"maḥallin wāḥid"*.[8] It could, on the other hand, be a description of God, but such a reference makes no sense at all in the context.[9] Again, the phrase *"wa-lā ^calā l-jumlah"* might reflect the teaching of abū Hāshim, but this would seem pointless in the context, since (a) al-Ash^carī, together with all the Ash^carites of the classical period, denies that any accident can qualify more than its single substrate and (b) though abū Hāshim does recognise a class of accidents which effect a quality (or state) which belongs to the composite whole (sc., a living being as a unitary whole), he denies that accidents such as those mentioned belong to that class.[10] It would seem, therefore, that this pair of phrases originated as a marginal note which perhaps meant to generalise the statement regarding contraries so as to make it cover all conceivable cases, even ones which would not be considered conceivable by al-Ash^carī, and was subsequently copied into the body of the text.[11]

Apart from these elements, which seem more or less clearly to be extraneous additions to the text, the most general and conspicuous characteristic of T–2 with respect to T–1 is that it is longer, whether the lengthening be by addition or simply by the employment of more expansive forms of expression. In a number of places T–2 has filled out the text by stating explicitly what is merely alluded to or implied in T–1. Thus, for example, in §2.221 T–2 supplies the contextual detail for a ḥadīth which in T–1, evidently under the assumption that the reader both knows it and knows al-Ashʿarī's exegesis of it, is only alluded to. Again, for example, in §2.212 and §2.2131 T–2 explicitly indicates the arguments which the Ashʿarite exegesis discovers in the verses cited, while T–1 feels no need to state them. Likewise at the end of §2.321 T–2 adds "which are themselves derivative matters that are accessible only through revelation and [God's] apostles", making fully explicit a thesis which, though important to the overall argument of §2.31, is a commonplace for the *mutakallimīn* and so is left unstated in T–1.

In other places T–2 tends to give more explicit and formal indication of the divisions of the work and its topical structure. Thus in §2.20 the simple "*dhālika*" of the A text is represented in T–2 by "*mā dhakartumūhū mina l-kalāmi fī l-jismi... wal-ṭarfah*", recalling by outright repitition most of the terms found in §2.12, which are only alluded to in T–1. At §2.211, then, with "*wa-ʾammā l-ḥarakatu wal-sukūn...*", T–2 not only recalls some of the terms previously mentioned in §2.20, but structurally introduces, as it were, a formal heading where none appears in T–1. The same sort of thing occurs again in §2.221, the beginning of the next major section of the second response, where he introduces "*wa-ʾammā mā yatakallamu bihi l-mutakallimūna min ʾanna lil-ḥawādithi ʾawwalan...*". Analogously, T–2 introduces a formal parallelism of "heading" in both §2.223 and §2.224 by means of "*ʾammā l-ʾaṣlu*", which is taken up from §2.231 and §2.232, where it occurs in T–1 as well.

It should be noted that the effect of this rhetorical "tidying up" or, if you will, literary formalisation of the text is not entirely neutral. If one considers the first three subsections of the second response, they involve by way of example **1.** the proof for the existence of God (§2.211) **2.** the thesis that there is only one God (§2.212), and **3.** the thesis that the bodily resurrection of the dead is possible (§2.213). The topical sequence is identical to that found in al-Ashʿarī's *al-Thaghr* (pp. 82–84) and his *K. al-Lumaʿ* (§§3–9).[12] By the introduction of the "heading" at §2.211, T–2 tends to narrow the focus of the reader's attention; where T–1 focuses on *kalām* arguments in general and, by implication, through the examples chosen in §§2.211–3, shows that they are foundational to Islamic belief, T–2 at the outset focuses narrowly on a set of formal concepts and argues their particular validity through the examples. The heading in §2.20, moreover, partially vitiates the function of the section as an introduction to the entire second response, since a wider diversity of topics is in fact discussed than is suggested in the "heading". Again, T–2's introduction of the phrase "*wa ʾammā l-ʾaṣl*" in §2.223 and §2.224 tends to mitigate the rhetorical effect of its occurence in §2.231 and §2.232, about which we shall have something to say later in the structural analysis of the tract. Similarly, the continuation of the second person address in §2.332 diminishes the rhetorical effect achieved by the shift to the third person in T–1.

Analogous to the introduction of introductory formulae in §2.223 and §2.224 so as to parallel §2.231 and §2.232 is the parallelism introduced in §2.313, where T–2 inserts the words "*ʾuṣūlu l-ᶜaqli l-latī ṭarīquhā*" so as to parallel the preceding "*ʾuṣūlu l-sharᶜi l-latī ṭarīquhā*".[13]

This apparent work of expansive redaction in T–2 is perhaps most conspicuous in §2.322 and §2.323. In the first of these sections the author raises the question of one's attitude towards erroneous and unseemly descriptions of God. This is treated simply and succinctly in T–1, where the question is introduced by "And one says to them: If some one were to say 'God's knowledge is created' or were to say in describing Him anything which is inappropriate to Him, then would you...?". Here, however, T–2 divides the question so as to present two distinct questions, each with its own answer and response. The first is introduced by "Tell us, if some one were to say 'God's knowlege is created' would you...?" and is followed by the opponent's answer and the author's response, which are virtually identical to those found in T–1. The second question in T–2 is, by contrast, much longer and is formally different from that of the first paragraph. The introductory "If some one were to say" presents a lengthy list of rather preposterous descriptions of God which is followed immediately by the author's response, "then it would be the case that you ought to... or you would...". Several things should be noted here. Firstly, the pattern according to which the author responds to the opponent's answer to the question, found in the first paragraph as also in §2.323, is not followed here. Secondly, in the first paragraph the author's opponent is addressed in the plural, "Would *you all* refrain from taking a position on the matter? If *they* say..." and this plural is implicitly carried over into the statement of the second question in the "*your*" (pl.) of "your Lord" *(rabbukum)* and is, moreover, continued in §2.323. In the second paragraph, however, the opponent is addressed in the singular in both verbs, "you ought to remain silent" *(yanbaghī ʾan taskuta)* and "you would not remain silent" *(kunta lā taskutu)*. The singular would here appear to follow and to agree with that of the introductory *"law qāla qāʾilun"*, just as does the second person singular of §2.3212, where the context involves *al-tawaqquf*. Here in the second paragraph of §2.322, however, the singular is not contextually coherent, since the section begins with a plural address to the author's opponents *(khabbirūnā..., ʾa-kuntum...)*, which ought to be carried over across the "so also" which introduces the second paragraph. It would seem highly plausible that this second paragraph of §2.322 may perhaps have been originally composed as a substitute for the first, in which case the inconsistency is simply the result of the redactor's failure to eliminate the first paragraph. Also consonant with the hypothesis that the second paragraph is here intrusive is the fact that the author's second "response" (the second alternative in the apodosis: "or you would not remain silent...") would seem to suggest that in taking a position the opponent will give a theoretically reasoned argument for his position. To the extent that this is implied the second "response" would appear to be out of place in the present context in that it formally goes beyond the scope of the immediate question in such a way as to anticipate and, to a certain degree, to pre-empt the author's response which will be given in §2.331. It certainly tends to mitigate the rhetorical force of §2.331. Thus again it would seem that T–2 is a secondary rewriting of T–1.

In what follows, T–2 is again considerably expanded with respect to T–1 and once more the sequence of questions and responses is not without some problems. Here the topic is *takfīr*, the author's opponents' contention that certain heretics, particularly those who hold the *Qurʾān* to be created, are "unbelievers". As in the preceding section T–1 raises the question (§2.323) in the simplest terms and gives a response which is at once brief and effective. In the statement of the problem, the phrase *"kaffarnā l-qāʾila bi-khalqi l-Qurʾān"* is ambiguous, since it can be taken in two ways. It can be read, "we hold those who say the *Qurʾān* is created to be unbelievers" in the sense "we consider them unbelievers in the strict and formal sense", i.e., as having the juridical status of unbelievers: they are not Muslims. On the other hand, it can be read to mean simply "we call them 'unbelievers'", i.e., we use the term 'unbeliever' but do not mean by this to ascribe the juridical status of non-Muslims to them. The former position is characteristic of the Ḥanbalites, while the latter is that of some Shāfiʿites.[14] Accordingly, the general context of the work, sc., that it is composed against al-Barbahārī and the Ḥanbalites, would suggest that it is the former reading which is correct. This would seem moreover to be confirmed by the author's response, for after having noted that there is no precedent in the documented teaching of the Prophet for any such *takfīr* against those who hold the *Qur'ān* to be created, he goes on to cite as an analogue and precedent against his opponents the Prophet's attitude towards the *munāfiqīn*. It will be recalled that in the *Qur'ān* (63.3) it is stated that "they believed and afterwards became unbelievers". This notwithstanding, the Prophet accorded them the status of believing Muslims *(ḥukmu l-muslimīn)*, i.e., he treated them not as unbelievers but as members, not perhaps wholly respectable but nonetheless legitimate members, of the Muslim community. Since it occurs in the *Qur'ān*, 'unbelievers' may be used to describe them, but it is not used in a formal, juridical sense, but rather as a term of opprobrium. By citing the precedent of the Prophet's action with regard to the *munāfiqīn*, thus, al-Ashᶜarī implicitly takes the position of some of the Shāfiᶜites with regard to those who say the *Qur'ān* is created.

In T–2 this section is introduced by *"fa-'in qālū"*, where the plural picks up the plural *(wa-yuqālu lahum..., fa-'in qālū)* of §2.3211, which is continued in the *"'a-tatawaqqafūna"* of §2.322.

In the treatment of the question of *takfīr*, T–2 once again presents a problem, since it consists of two distinct paragraphs which are not wholly consistent with one another nor with the overall context. It begins "If some one says, 'I shall refrain from speaking about the matter and shall give him no response' or 'I shall shun him' or 'I shall get up and go away from him' or 'I shall neither salute him [when we meet] nor visit him when he is sick nor attend his funeral when he dies',...". In this one has to hear the pronouns of *"askutu ᶜanhu"*, *"lā 'ujībuhu"*, etc., as referring contextually to the question and to the holder of the heretical theses suggested in the preceding paragraph, the first alternative of whose response it apparently takes up but qualifies.[15] Consistently thus the author's response here continues to employ the second person singular: "One replies to *him*, 'Then it follows that in all these forms of action which *you* have mentioned *you* are an innovator and in grave error, for the Prophet neither said... nor did he say anything at all of this". At this point, however, the text continues in the second person plural: "So *you all* are innovators since *you all* do this". This last sentence, as it occurs here, is not altogether coherent in the context. It appears to pick up and to continue the second person plural of the first paragraph of §2.322, but there has been, up to this point, nothing to suggest that the opponents there addressed do in fact take such an attitude towards those who hold the position mentioned in the immediately preceding paragraph. The sentence containing the plural could be read coherently with the preceding statement concerning the Prophet, but not when the latter is taken as integral with the opening portion of the section. Plainly something is amiss.

Moreover, the second person plural is continued immediately by a pair of questions which introduce what is clearly a new paragraph, in which the question of *takfīr* is taken up anew: "So why have you people not kept silent with regard to those who say that the *Qur'ān* is created? Why do you consider them to be unbelievers?". In his edition of the text Fr. McCarthy here inserts an introductory *"wa-yuqālu lahum"*, but there is no support for this in the manuscript witnesses to T–2; nor, indeed, would its presence solve the larger question of the origin and relationship of the various elements. Because of the plurals, this new paragraph clearly belongs with the preceding sentence *(fa-'antum... fa'altum)* and is most likely another element of the redaction which, like some of the others, was never fully integrated editorially into the whole.

Whatever may be the textual problems concerning the redaction of T–2 the first paragraph dealing with *takfīr* is concise and follows the simple pattern of question and response found earlier in §§2.3211, 2.3212, and the first paragraph of §2.322. The second paragraph. by contrast, presents a much more elaborate "dialogue", in which the argument is drawn out at length through the dialectical repetition of the question with a series of responses which progresses backwards through four generations of religious authorities beginning with Ibn Ḥanbal and ending with the Companions. Since the rhetorical strategy of the polemic is different from that employed elsewhere in the tract it will be instructive to look at it more closely. The sequence of questions and responses is as follows:

Q. 1: Why do you not keep silent with regard to those who hold that the *Qur'ān* is created?

R. 1: Because Aḥmad ibn Ḥanbal didn't.

Q. 2: Why didn't he keep silent on the matter?

R. 2: Because al-'Abbās al-'Anbarī, Wakī', et al. didn't.

Q. 3: Why didn't they keep silent?

R. 3: Because 'Amr ibn Dīnār, Sufyān ibn 'Uyayna, et al. didn't.

Q. 4: Why didn't they keep silent?

R. 4: It is impossible that all the Companions have done so. (I.e., though we cannot cite any particular authority, Ibn ᶜUyayna and the rest must have been following the usage of some of the Companions).

Q. 5: Why did they not keep silent, since they had no warrent from the Prophet for doing otherwise?

The argument here is plainly focused on the Ḥanbalite doctrine of *taqlīd,* drawing out by concrete example their notion of each generation's imitation of the belief and practice of the one preceding until the series rests finally on the foundation of the Companions' imitation of the Prophet. The sequence of questions and responses terminates not in a formal statement or conclusion by the author but by posing to the Ḥanbalite opponent the simple query of why those Companions who allegedly spoke against the thesis that the *Qur'ān* is created, accusing those who held it of unbelief *(kufr),* did not keep silent on the subject "given that the Prophet neither discussed the matter as such nor said 'call those who hold it *kāfir*'". To this question there is no response because there is no report that the Prophet had anything to say on the matter. Not only is al-Ashᶜarī's Ḥanbalite opponent vanquished by his inability to respond, but by implication all the pious forebears on the authority of whose teaching and practice the Ḥanbalites found the validity of their own are "innovators", for they do not follow the practice of the Prophet in this matter. The Ḥanbalites, in brief, are *muqallid* to men who are guilty of precisely that which they consider the root of all religious error (and of which they accuse al-Ashᶜarī), namely innovation *(bidᶜah).*[16]

We should note here that McCarthy's division of the text would appear to indicate that his understanding of the structure of this passage is different from that which we have presented. He indicates the beginning of a new paragraph (his §27) whith the words "If they say that it is impossible" (the response to the fourth question in our analysis) and includes in this section our §2.331, beginning "And if they say, 'the learned have to...'". As McCarthy divides the passage, the fourth question is left without any response on the part of the opponent and the section is terminated before the series of religious authorities is exhausted. Given the formal significance of the sequential pattern of questions and answers to the argument, however, it would seem clear that one has to carry the series one step further into the generation of the Companions, and this is precisely what is done when he says "If they say that it is impossible...". This answer, which involves on "their" part an assumption gratuitously made without any historical evidence, is essentially inadequate from al-Ashᶜarī's standpoint and so leads up to the final question at which, unable to find any response at all, the opponent is reduced to silence.[17] Furthermore, the topic under discussion in the sentence "If they say that it is impossible..." continues to be that which was introduced at the beginning of §2.323 (McCarthy's §26), viz., the claim that those who hold the *Qur'ān* to be created are to be considered as unbelievers. This is clear enough from the end of the response. Finally, if one follows McCarthy's division, the passage beginning "If they say 'The learned have to...'" will stand as a distinct alternative to "If they say that it is impossible..." and this is inappropriate. That is to say, the assertion that the learned have to take up such "recent questions" and deal with them by means of formal, systematic reflection could not be understood as a reason or explanation for why it is not conceivable that all the companions have remained silent on the issue of the unbelief of those who hold that the *Qur'ān* is created (in which case one would require *li'annahu* or *fa'innahu* in place of *'in qālū*), but it cannot be understood as an alternative response within the context. As an alternative response, §2.331 is an alternative not to the fifth and concluding question of §2.323 but to §2.32 as a whole.[18]

The basic recensional differences between T–1 and T–2 are clear enough. As one might expect, there are also, even in passages where T–1 and T–2 are substantially identical, numerous variants in which T–2 differs from T–1, e.g.,

1.12 *al-jismi wal-ᶜaraḍi wal-ḥarakati wal-sukūn* A
= *al-ḥarakati wal-sukūni wal-jismi wal-ᶜaraḍi* BFH

1.222 *tamassakū* A = *iḥtajjū* BFH

2.1 *bi-taḍlīlikum* A = *wa-ḍallaltum* BFH

2.311 *fī l-kitāb* A = *fī l-Qur'ān* BFH

It remains to examine briefly the relationships between B, F, and H, the witnesses to T–2. F and H belong to one and the same basic line of transmission and so show frequent agreement against B. For example,

2.2130 *naḥwa hādhā l-kalām* HF: + *al-ladhī 'akhbara llāhu taᶜālā bihi ᶜanhum* B

2.2130 *fī l-Qur'ān* FH: + *al-ᶜaẓīmi ᶜalā dhālika... l-ᶜazīz* B

2.222 *yanqasim* FH = *munqasiman* B

2.224 *yaqūlū bi-ḥujjah* FH = *yuqawwimū l-ḥujjah* B

2.232 *'ilā qawlihi khasimūn* FH: + *wa-hādhā naṣṣun...* B

2.223 *fa-qawluhū ʿazza wa-jalla* FH: + *wa-ʾaḥṣā... qawluhu* B (lost in FH by homoiotel.)

2.232 *taʿyīnuha* FH = *muʿayyanan* B

2.313 *al-ʿaqliyyāti wal-maḥsūsāti* FH: + *ʾan taruddahā ʾilā ʾuṣūli... wal-qiyās* B (lost in FH by homoiotel.)

In passages where T–1 and T–2 are fundamentally alike one finds a number of instances in which FH stands with A against B; for example,

1.10 *ṭāʾifah* AFH = *qawman* B

1.21 *ʾilayhi ḥājah* AFH = *ḥājatun ʾilayhi* B

1.222 *fī tarki l-naẓari fī l-ʾuṣūl* AFH: lacking in B

2.0 *thalāthati ʾawjuh* AFH = *wujūhin thalāthah* B

2.1 *wa-takallama* AFH = *ʾaw-takallama* B

2.2132 *raṭbatan ḥārrah* AFH = *ḥārratan raṭbah* B

2.222 *ʾashbahahu* AFH = *ʾashbahahā* B

2.222 *yakūna l-muḥdath* AFH = *takūna l-muḥdathāt* B

2.222 *al-makhlūqāt* AFH = *al-makhlūqīn* B

2.231 *ʾilayhim... yuʾminu... yaʾtiyahum* AFH = *ʾilaynā... nuʾmina... yaʾtiyanā* B

2.311 *muʿayyanah* AFH: lacking in B

2.313 *yarudda ḥukmahā* AFH = *yaruddahā* B

There are, on the other hand, a number of instances in which we find A and B in agreement against FH; for example,

1.21 *wa-rushdan* A(B) = *wa-rashādan* FH

2.0 *qāla l-shaykhu abū l-Ḥasan raḍiya llāhu ʿanhu* AB: lacking in FH

2.1 *yuqālu lahum* AB = *yuqālu* FH

2.2131 *wa-bi-qawlihī* AB = *wa-qawluhu* FH

2.2132 *al-ḍiddān* AB = *ʾinna l-ḍikkayn* FH

2.2132 *al-ʿahḍari nāran* AB: + *fa-ʾidhā ʾantum tūqidūn* FH

2.222 *al-shabah* AB = *al-shabīh* FH

2.311 *al-nabiy* AB = *rasūlu llāh* FH

2.312 *kulli wāḥidah* AB = *kulli wāḥid* FH

2.312 *al-nabiy* AB = *rasūli llāh* FH

2.312 *bi-jtihādihim* AB = *wa-jtihādihim* FH

2.3212 *man qāla bi-khalqihī* AB: + *wa-man qāla bi-nafyi khalqihi* FH[19]

There are a few places in which it would seem that B is witness to a corruption which appears corrected in FH. For example, we find in § 2.2131, where A correctly reads *fiᶜlan lā ᶜalā mithāl* that B has lost the negative *lā*, probably by haplography with the *lam alif* of *fiᶜlan*. In FH, then, the phrase was corrected by introducting *ghayr* so as to read *fiᶜlan ᶜalā ghayri mithāl*[20] Similarly at § 2.313 where A correctly reads *ʾuṣūli l-sharᶜi l-latī ṭarīquhā*, B reads *ʾuṣūli l-sharᶜi l-latī ṭarīquhu*, which is then made grammatically coherent in FH were we find *ʾuṣūli l-sharᶜi l-ladhī ṭarīquhu*.

In several places, again, it would seem that a corruption of the text witnessed in B likely underlies the reading of FH. For example, in § 2.232 B reads *fa-qaraʾahā l-nabiyyu ṣlᶜm*, while H reads *fa-qaraʾa l-nabiyyu ṣlᶜm dhālika* and F *fa-qaraʾa l-nabiyyu ṣlᶜm ᶜalayhi dhālika*. Here it would appear that the *hā* of the original reading was lost in the succession of three *alifs*, following which *dhālika* was added in order to supply an object for the verb and then the *ᶜalayhi* inserted for good measure. In § 2.232 B reads *ʾaṣlun lanā wa-huwa ḥujjah...*, while FH read *ʾaṣlun lanā wa-ḥujjatun lanā....* Here it may be suggested that the *huwa* was lost following the preceding *wāw* and *lanā* then introduced in the archetype of FH.

B and FH are in some places independently corrupt and in § 2.2132 this would seemed to have happened because the copyists were not used to dealing with *kalām* texts. Here B has introduced, following *yushāhidūnahū*, the phrase *lil-shajari l-ʾakhḍari ᶜalā burūdatihi wa-ruṭūbatihi dalīlan ᶜalā ḥārrihā wa-yabasihā*. The first part of this is a phrase which occurs towards the end of the section, but the line is corrupt and makes no sense at all in the place it is inserted in. Following this, the copyist has managed also to loose the words *al-ʾūlā dalīlan ᶜalā jawāzi l-nashʾati* because of the homoioteleuton with *jawāzi l-nashʾah*. The archetype of FH, on the other hand, has lost *fī maᶜnāhā wa-jaᶜala fī mujāwarati l-nāri ᶜalā ḥārriha wa-yabasihā lil-shajari l-ʾakhḍari ᶜalā bardihi wa-ruṭūbatihi*, changing then the following *dalīlan* to *dalilun* in order to restore the grammatical coherence of the sentence. By contrast with all this, A, whose transmission took place in the circles of the leading masters of the Ashᶜarite tradition, manifests no confusion at all.

Where T–1 and T–2 are the same I have, in almost all places preferred the reading of A, even when it is unique. So too, where they are substantially the same, I have, unless there seemed good reason to do otherwise, followed the indication of A, particularly where the reading of A is supported by any of the witnesses to T–2. Given the relative independance of B from the archetype of FH it is clear that where T–2 differs from T–1 a reading supported by BF or by BH is, barring solid grounds for the contrary, to be considered the better witness to T–2. Where, as witness to T–2, B reads against FH I have tended, for reasons indicated above, to follow the reading of B.

The assumption that for T–2 the combination BF is prima facie a better witness to the original form of the recension than is H and BH than F, when the readings thus diverge, presents us with a difficult problem in §2.232, which is worth citing as a likely example of how corruptions may become hidden. In the first part of this section the author recounts an incident in which ᶜAbdallāh ibn al-Zibaᶜrā came to the Prophet and argued with him. In the A text the argument is very briefly put and begins, "He [Ibn al-Zibaᶜrā] said, 'the angels are worshipped *(ᶜubidū)* and so also Jesus; do you then, Muḥammad, say that they are *the fuel of Jahannam* (Q 21.98)?' The Apostle of God was silent...". In the corresponding portion of T–2, H reads, "he said, O Muḥammad, do you not claim that Jesus and ᶜUzayr and the angels are worshipped *(ᶜubidū)* ? The Prophet was silent...". In B, however, we find a very different form, one in which Ibn al-Zibaᶜrā's statement is much longer and in which the text is plainly corrupt. "He said, 'O Muḥammad, do you not claim that Jesus and ᶜUzayr and the angels are righteous worshippers?' He replied, 'Indeed'. He said, 'But the Christians worship Jesus and a group of the Jews worship ᶜUzayr and the Banu Ljm [sic, *lege* Luḥayy?] here worship the angels, they be *the fuel of Jahannam'*. The Prophet was silent...". Here not only is the form of the dialogue very different than in A and in H, but a subjunctive, "they be" is introduced which has no connection with the preceding sentence.[21] In F, following "do you not claim that Jesus and ᶜUzayr and the angels" there is a blank space encompassing the end of one line and the first part of another, in total about two thirds of a line — enough for maybe a dozen words, not all of B's addition — at the end of which the text recommences "that they be *(ʾan yakūnū) the fuel of Jahannam'*. The prophet was silent...". Here the subjunctive is governed by the particle, but still we do not know what preceded it. It is evident that the copyist of F (or his archetype) had before him something which either he could not read or which made no sense to him and which, on the evidence, we should assume should have represented something like what we find in B. On this assumption, then, H will present a corrected text, one in which the copyist restored the sense of the text by omitting or cancelling much of the plus of B and inserting *ᶜubidū* either conjecturally and on his own or on the basis of something like the A text. The H form of the text will, thus, albeit it reads coherently against B and F, represent a secondarily corrected version of T–2. It is not unlikely that, like some of th additions found in T–2 which were noted earlier, the longer form of this "dialogue" shown in B and partially represented in F, stood originally in the margin of the archetype of T–2 and was not coherently incorporated into the body of the text.[22] The problem of the H reading remains, however, since it is difficult to see how, given the association of H with F and their relationship to B, it might be possible that H have independently preserved the pristine reading of T–2. *W-Allāh aᶜlam.*

We may summarise the evidence regarding the text and its two forms as follows. The A text is given us by abū l-Qāsim al-Anṣārī and presumably derives, directly of indirectly, from a copy belonging to his master, al-Juwaynī. On this basis we should reasonably assume that T–1, as we have it in A, was transmitted through a series of leading Ashᶜarite masters. This is confirmed in that the title under which al-Anṣārī presents the work is found in the lists of al-Ashᶜarī's writings. Compared to T–1, T–2 manifests a number of aspects (even excluding those elements which are plainly intrusive) which would indicate that it represents a secondary redaction or revision of T–1.[23] Concerning the transmission of T–2 there is some uncertainty.

Of the transmitters of T–2 other than abū l-Ḥasan al-Ṭabarī named in the *isnād* of FH I have managed to identify only four: **1.** abū l-Qāsim Saḥnūn, who was a Mālikite muqriʾ (see al-Dhahabī, *al-Qurrāʾ*, p. 555), **2.** abū Ṣādiq Muḥammad, the son of al-Rashid al-ᶜAṭṭar, who was one of the most famous Mālikite traditionists (see, e.g., al-Suyūṭī, *Ṭabaqāt,* p. 505 and al-Tinbuktī, *Nayl,* p. 354), **3.** abū l-Maᶜālī l-Mawṣilī, a Shāfiᶜite jurisconsult and *muqriʾ* (al-Dhahabī, *op. cit.,* p. 489), and **4.** Ibn al-Ukhuwwa (al-Dhahabī, *Mīzān* 2, p. 124 and al-Zikirlī, *al-Aᶜyān* 3, p. 343). We have, thus, to do with a series of important scholars and it is apparent that at least from the copy made and collated by Muḥammad b. Yaḥyā al-Nātilī, probably in the last quarter of the 5th/11th century, through that of Saḥnūn, in 677/1278 the text was transmitted with considerable care. The variants between F and H will, consequently, derive from a date posterior to 600/1204. Passages in which B contains material lost in FH (certainly those lost by homoioteleuton, since the others may perhaps be additions in B) indicate that the immediate antecedent of BFH must antedate the copy belonging to abū Naṣr al-Shīrāzī, from which al-Nātilī worked and it is to this period (the century immediately following the death of Ibn Mahdī) that the major corruptions of T–2 must derive, e.g., the insertions of extraneous material found in §§2.2132, 2.221, and 2.223, which, as we noted above, were most likely incorporated into the body of the text from the margins of the archetype. These additions are somewhat curious.[24] One thing, however, they do indicate clearly, sc., that since they are common to BFH and since their incorporation into the text would hardly have been the work of a specialist, or of any one well versed in *kalām*, Ibn Mahdī was not himself responsible for the nearest common ancestor of BFH.

In conclusion, then, we may suggest, even if with some hesitancy, that minus the intrusive elements of which we have spoken (and however the corruption of §2.232 is to be resolved) the text presented in BFH substantially represents the original of T–2 and is likely the text of abū l-Ḥasan ibn Mahdī al-Ṭabarī. The question of whether it was Ibn Mahdī or was al-Ash^c^arī himself who is ultimately responsible for the revision of T–1 which resulted in T–2 as witnessed in our manuscripts and that of what possible sequence of steps the process of revision may have taken we shall not address; the available data are not such as to give firm support to any conclusion in this regard. It would seem, however, that the work of revision was never completed.

* * *

The *Kitāb al-Ḥathth ^c^alā l-Baḥth* is more subtly constructed and more thorough and rigorous in its polemic argumentation of the author's position than many of the scholars of al-Ash^c^arī's writings seem to have been aware. All too often, indeed, the formal structure of *kalām* works is neglected, with the result that secondary theses and arguments are treated as if they were primary and the systematic character of their reasoning consequently ignored. It will be useful therefore to present a schematic analysis of *al-Ḥathth* outlining its main topical divisions and their subsections.[25] Following this I shall present a few remarks concerning the rhetoric of the work and its structure. It was written against al-Barbahārī, one of the foremost Ḥanbalite masters of the period, after he had preëmptorily refused to accept al-Ash^c^arī's *Ibāna fī uṣūl al-diyāna* as evidence of its author's claim to follow the doctrine of the *ahl al-sunna*.[26] Even a brief consideration of the rhetorical structure of the tract is sufficient to reveal both how sharply al-Ash^c^arī was stung by the Ḥanbalite's refusal to accept him as a supporter of traditionalist orthodoxy and to demonstrate the masterful skill with which he was able polemically to counter their attack and argue his own attachment to the *sunna*.

A Schematic Outline of "al-Hathth"

1. INTRODUCTION:

1.10 THE OPPONENT'S POSITION

1.11 One should adopt the Principle of *Taqlīd* in all Matters of Religion.

1.12 Those who formally (i.e., rationally) investigate the basic articles of faith are guilty of innovation *(bidᶜah)* and of grave religious error *(ḍalāl)*, because to discuss in formal, speculative terms *a)* the nature of created beings and *b)* the nature of God is an innovation and grave religious error.

1.20 ARGUMENT ADDUCED BY THE OPPONENT IN SUPPORT OF § 1.12:

1.21 If *kalām* were an authentic element of Muslim practice *(al-dīn)* the Prophet would have practiced it and would have made it known to the community; but he did not do this.

1.220 It must be the case either that

1.221 The Prophet knew *kalām* but kept silent on the matter, in which case *a)* we need not practice it and *b)* it is not an authentic element of *al-dīn*; or that

1.222 The Prophet did not know *kalām* , in which case *a)* we need not practice it and *b)* it is not an authentic element of *al-dīn*.

2. THE AUTHOR'S REFUTATION: THREE RESPONSES

2.1 THE FIRST RESPONSE: The Prophet did not command that one consider those who practice *kalām* to be innovators who are in grave religious error; therefore, given the principles on which you base your argument (§ 1.21) you are yourselves innovators who are in grave religious error.

2.2 THE SECOND RESPONSE: That the Basic Principles, Theses, and the Practice of *kalām* are authorised by the *Qur'ān* and the Sunna:

2.20 General Statement: Individual elements of *kalām* and the discussion of particular questions are found in the *Qur'ān* and in the Sunna, though only in a vague or general form, not in formal detail.

2.21 Examples to show that the basic principles and theses and practices of *kalām* are witnessed in the *Qur'ān* and the Sunna:

2.211 That no corporeal being can be a God.

2.212 That there is only one God.

2.213 That the bodily resurrection of the dead is possible:

2.2130 General Statement: *a)* Presentation of Qur'ānic formulations of pagan opposition to this thesis and *b)* that the *Qur'ān's* counter arguments emphasise rational grounds for asserting the thesis against two classes of opponents, viz.,

2.2131 Against those who acknowledge the original creation of the world but deny the possibility of the resurrection;

2.2132 Against those who hold that the world is eternal.

2.22 Several Theoretical Principles and Theses Found in the *Qur'ān* and the Sunna:

2.221 Against the thesis that there exists no motion which is not preceded by another motion.

2.222 The Principles of similarity and dissimilarity: the rules of analogical reasoning.

2.223 Atomism.

2.224 The formal connotations of 'create'.

2.225 That all contingent events (including human actions) occur in conformity with God's determination and will.

2.23 The Basic Methods of Disputation and Argumentation are Sanctioned in te *Qur'ān:*

2.231 Demonstration of the counter thesis *(al-munāqaḍah).*

2.232 Showing the fallacy of an opponent's argument *(al-mughālaṭah).*

2.3 THE THIRD RESPONSE: Concerning Problems and Questions which are not treated either in the *Qur'ān* or in the Sunna.

2.31 That to Deal with New Theological Questions is Juridically Authorised.

2.311 The elements needed in order to deal with the problems mentioned in §1.12 are found in the *Qur'ān* and the Sunna, even though the questions were not explicitly and formally discussed as such during the lifetime of the Prophet.

2.312 The Companions and their successors did investigate, dispute, and argue their own solutions to juridical problems whose treatment is not attested in the *Qur'ān* or in the Sunna.

2.313 The sources and principles of juridical reasoning are distinct from those of theoretical reasoning; the former are discovered exclusively in revelation while the latter are founded in reason.

2.314 If the questions of the creation of the *Qur'ān* and the questions mentioned in § 1.12 had arisen during the lifetime of the Prophet, he would have dealt with them explicitly.

2.32 On the Condemnation of Recently Formulated Heresies and their adherents.

2.3210 The opponent holds that the *Qur'ān* is uncreated, a thesis which is not authoritatively attested either in the *Qur'ān* or in the Sunna;

2.3211 If they ascribe this thesis to one of the Companions or Successors, then such a Companion or Successor is guilty of innovation.

2.3212 If one *a)* explicitly refuses either to affirm or to deny the thesis that the *Qur'ān* is created but at the same time *b)* condemns those who affirm it as unbelievers, neither *a)* nor *b)* is explicitly authorised by the example of the Prophet.

2.322 There is no explicit warrent in the teaching of the Prophet for taking any position with regard to the truth or falsity of any particular, erroneous or misleading description of God whose initial formulation is subsequent to the death of the Prophet.

2.323 If the opponent says that in condemning those who hold the *Qur'ān* to be created he follows the example of earlier religious leaders, it can be shown that such leaders did not follow the example of the Prophet, wherefore the opponent's action has, on his principles, no authoritative warrent.

2.33 CONCLUSIONS

2.331 That *kalām* is necessary in at least one case, sc. that the community know the truth with regard to questions which have arisen since the time of the Prophet.

2.332 In his condemnation of *kalām* the opponent is *muqallid* to one whose action is not based on sound juridical reasoning.

2.333 On the opponent's principles the foremost masters of Jurisprudence will have to be judged guilty of innovation.

★ ★ ★

The divisions between the various sections and their subsections may not in every place appear so sharply drawn in the rhetorical flow of the author's discourse as they seem in this schematic analysis of the text. The analysis does, nonetheless, represent the elements and structure of the text quite exactly. Since *al-Ḥathth* is not a didactic work but is essentially polemical, its formal organisation and rhetorical structure deserve particular attention. Upon examination, indeed, the work appears to be much more carefully structured, more carefully crafted in the ordering of its parts and in its use of language, than are most of the polemical writing s of the *mutakallimīn*. It is important that one keep in mind the intentionality of the tract and of its arguments. Nowhere is the purpose to demonstrate as such the truth of any theological or philosophical thesis taught by the *mutakallimīn*. The focus of the work is, rather, to refute the Ḥanbalites in their denial of the juridical legitimacy of *kalām* and of the need for it within the Muslim community. In §2.2, thus, he cites various texts of the *Qurʾān* and the *ḥadīth* not to prove the truth of the theses which they may be employed to support but simply to demonstrate the precedent for the *kalām's* reasoning and argumentation with regard to those theses. Similarly in §2.321 where he introduces by way of example a question his treatment of which is at variance with that of the Ḥanbalites, he avoids the discussion of the substance of the issue, even though he does allude to their doctrine.

The overall symmetry of the tract is conspicuous. In the final sections of the conclusion (§§2.332–3) he deals with the opponent's insistence on *taqlīd*,[27] mentioned in §1.11, noting in §2.333 that if it is rigorously followed the Ḥanbalites will have also to condemn the leading juridical authorities and in §2.332 that the *taqlīd* they claim with regard to the basic doctrinal tenets of Islam (*ʾuṣūl al-dīn*)[28] as justification for their condemnation of those with whom they disagree (§1.12) has no sound juridical basis. In §2.331, following the arguments of §2.23, he asserts the counter thesis to their contention that *kalām* contains no element of right guidance, stated in §1.21, while §2.2 is employed to answer the argument of §1.22. Al-Ashᶜarī's justification for the procedures employed in the tract occurs at the very center, in §§2.231–2.

The first response (§2.1) is a summary refutation of the Ḥanbalites' contention that those who investigate matters commonly treated in *kalām* are "innovators" *(mubtadiᶜūn)* and that they are "in grave error" *(ḍullāl)*.[29] The argument of this section is purely dialectical and intends to indicate a kind of paradox in his opponent's reasoning, viz., that his argument is based on and explicitly enunciates a principle which, if accepted as universal, must exclude the legitimacy of the thesis it is meant to support. Al-Ashᶜarī will return to the same basic form of argument in the third response where he argues for the validity of his own position against the Hanbalites. Lying between these two responses §2.2 forms the central element of the text. Here he presents the evidence to show that the argument put forth by his opponents (§1.2) in order to support their condemnation of *kalām* is based on a fundamental error of fact. He argues, that is, that the constitutive principles and elements of *kalām* are witnessed in, and therefore sanctioned by, the *Qur'ān* and the Sunna. This section of the work is not theoretical; it does not proceed by means either of a theoretical or of a dialectical argument but simply calls attention to the material evidence of the *Qur'ān* and the ḥadīth, citing a series of texts and reading them in such a way as to insist that the Ḥanbalites ignore or misconstrue the historical facts and thereby fail to recognise their significance. The witness of specific texts *(nuṣūṣ)* is central to the nature of the overall argumentation of the tract, since it is on the texts of the *Qur'ān* and the Sunna that the juridical validity of any judgement must ultimately rest. At a later point al-Ashᶜarī will make a point of his opponent's inability to cite an authoritative text *(naṣṣ)* in support of the Ḥanbalite position. Here in §2.2 he cites specific examples of various elements that are constitutive of *kalām* theology and which appear in the *Qur'ān* or are documented and authenticated as belonging to the teaching or to the practice of the Prophet. He begins by citing arguments concerning major theological issues (§2.21) and proceeds then to cite arguments concerning more detailed theses and principles on which arguments are based (§2.22) and closes the section by citing texts which furnish canonical precedent for the methods or argumentation employed in *kalām* in order to refute erroneous theses (§2.23). In this way §2.2 serves both to demonstrate the canonical precedent for some elements of *kalām* and to supply the foundation on which his final argument for the validity of *kalām* (§2.3) will be based. It is to be noted that, accepting the binding authority of the *Qur'ān* and the Sunna, al-Ashᶜarī validates in §2.23 the dialectical procedures he employs here against his opponents and so justifies the writing of the tract. Noteworthy here is the rhetorical emphasis placed on this section by the "*'ammā 'aṣlunā*" which stands at the beginning of both §2.231 and §2.232.

The third response (§2.3) presents the main point and climax of al-Ashᶜarī's attack and with this his sharpest polemic against his Ḥanbalite opponents. Although the third response does recall (in §2.324) the formal argument presented in §2.1, it remains nevertheless fully distinct and as such is essential to the purpose of the tract. In §2.1 he points to the inconsistency of the opponent's reasoning and in §2.2 exhibits some of the precedents which authorise formal reasoning concerning theological questions and formal argumentation against erroneous doctrines. The science of *kalām*, as a formal discipline, however, is relatively new. It was not known or practiced during the lifetime of the Prophet. Some of the topics and questions with which it deals are, moreover, themselves of recent origin and so are not witnessed as such in the canonical sources. Most importantly, within the context of this tract, the question of taking a position (of discovering, formulating, and arguing for a thesis) with regard to theological questions which are not treated, either directly or indirectly, in the *Qur'ān* or in the hadīth is a materially distinct issue from those mentioned in §§2.1 and 2.2, and it is this which forms the focal point of §2.3, as the proper supplement and completion of the first two responses.

The third response, like the second, is complex both in content and in structure. It is divided into two parts. In the first (§2.31) he argues that the exercise of independent reasoning in order to resolve new questions is valid in theology, just as it is in jurisprudence. With this he notes that as the two differ in the subject matters they treat, so also they differ formally in their principles, since the principles appropriately employed in the one are not the same as those which are appropriate to the other discipline. These differences, he insists, must be recognised and respected in their legitimacy. In the second part (§2.32), then, he argues *a)* that the formal theology *(kalām)* condemned by the Hanbalites is not only legitimate and valid but also necessary to the religious life of the Muslims and *b)* that to describe those who practice *kalām* and hold that the *Qur'ān* is created by the name "unbeliever", as do the Ḥanbalites, is canonically illegitimate and so invalid.

These two sections (§2.31 and §2.32) are rhetorically more subtle and more thorough in their argumentation than may appear on first reading, wherefore some further analysis of them may be useful. In §2.31 the fundamental argument is that just as the use of *ijtihād* (the independant use of reason in order to achieve conclusions or judgements not already presented authoritatively in the canonical sources) is legitimate and valid in jurisprudence, so also an analogous *ijtihād* is legitimate and valid for dealing with theological questions which had not been explicitly posed *(taᶜayyana)* or were not clearly resolved in the *Qurʾān* or in the documented teaching of the Prophet. Accordingly al-Ashᶜarī distinguishes in §2.311 and §2.312 two kinds of "recent questions",[30] theoretical (theological) and practical (juridical). Specific examples of the former are alluded to in §2.311 simply as "these [aforementioned] questions", referring to the list set out in §1.12 and later to be recalled in §2.314. Examples of the latter are detailed in §2.312, sc., *al-ᶜawl,* etc.[31] Both kinds of questions are "pertinent to the religious life" of the Muslim community *(lahu taᶜalluqun bil-dīn).*[32] Concerning the first set of questions al-Ashᶜarī notes in §2.311, which forms the introduction to the section, simply that though the Prophet was fully cognizant of them they had not been thematically posed during his lifetime, wherefore there can be no question of his having said something about them or not having said something about them *(...fa-yatakallama fīhā ʾaw-lā yatakallama fīhā).*[33] Where no precedent can claimed there can be no question of following the example of the Prophet exactly or not following it. By this he expressly denies the assumed foundation of the Ḥanbalite argument stated in §2.21. When, at the end of the paragraph, al-Ashᶜarī says with regard to "these questions" that their "principles *(ʾuṣūl)* are found in the Scripture and the Sunna" he plainly means to indicate that as the "principles of jurisprudence" *(ʾuṣūl al-fikh)* are founded in the canonical sources, so analogously are those of *kalām,* its elements (concepts) and methods, as was shown in §2.2. The second kind of questions, sc., those of jurisprudence, are dealt with at greater length (§2.312) because the facts are uncontested and he wishes to bring the full weight of their significance to bear when he applies the analogy. Here al-Ashᶜarī notes that his opponents and other universally respected legists employ systematic reasoning in a rigorous way in order to come to conclusions concerning problems which are not witnessed and authoritatively dealt with in any canonical text *(naṣṣ).* Both "*qiyās*" and "*ijtihād*" occur here (§2.312) as terms for systematic reasoning.[34] The implications are clear enough. The sources and foundations *(ʾuṣūl)* of juridical science are the *Qurʾān,* the Sunna, the consensus of the Muslims *(ʾijmāᶜ),* and systematic reasoning according to specific rules *(al-qiyās).* The list is not explicity given but is implied where he mentions the "*ʾuṣūl al-sharīᶜah*" at the end of §2.312. By implications within the context, then, the same is true for theology. The sources of religious knowledge, in short, and the order of their priority are analogously the same in both disciplines, *fiqh* and *kalām*. Because of the essential differences in the two disciplines, however, the role of rational understanding as well as the basis and the mode of reasoning differ in the two, wherefore in the *ʾuṣūl* of theology one substitutes *"al-ᶜaql"* (the mind's understanding, theoretical reasoning) for *"al-qiyās"* as the last term in the list when giving the "sources" of theological knowledge and science. The significance of this substitution, its origin in the intrinsic, formal differences of the two disciplines, will be made fully explicit in the following subsection.

The opening of §2.313 appears initially to be simply a more explicit statement and summary of what was said in §2.311, made in the light of §2.312: as al-Ashᶜarī's opponents deal with recent and secondary questions of law by the rigorous application of the *ʾuṣūl al-sharīᶜah,* analogously the theologian *(al-mutakallim)* deals with recent and with derivative and secondary questions of theology, such as those alluded to in §2.311, on the basis of principles analogously founded in and authorised by the revealed texts. The expression *"ʾan yarudda ḥukmahā ʾilā jumlati l-ʾuṣūl"* (that he determine their character and status by considering them in the light of all the principles/sources) directly reflects the wording of §2.312. Rhetorically, however, al-Ashᶜarī makes a very decisive move at this point. In the preceding paragraph he referred to "the secondary matters" *(al-furūᶜ)* of the law and to the "primary elements and principles of the law" *(ʾuṣūl al-sharīᶜah)*. Contextually, then, one hears the implication that *kalām* questions of the nature of the atom and of accidents, of motion and rest, etc.,[35] are secondary matters *(furūᶜ)* with respect to others not mentioned.[36] Like the juridical questions mentioned in §2.312, they too are "recent" *(ḥawādith)*. He speaks in the opening of §2.313, however, of "new questions which have arisen concerning the *ʾuṣūl*", "the *ʾuṣūl*" tout court, simply and without qualification. What al-Ashᶜarī means by *"ʾuṣūl"* here is, of course, the *ʾuṣūl al-dīn,* the basic tenets of Muslim belief, which form the principle subject of *kalām*. By his omission of the qualifying *"al-dīn"* he plainly suggests that these *ʾuṣūl,* dealt with in *kalām,* are *ʾuṣūl* in some absolute sense; they are as such prior to any question of jurisprudence or ethics.[37] To put it conversely, all juridical matters are *furūᶜ* with respect to the basic theological dogmas of Islam; jurisprudence *(fiqh)* itself is secondary, posterior to fundamental theology and its sourses, as the sources of juridical knowledge, are as such posterior to the sources of theological knowledge as such. It is only after one has appropriated the truth of the basic doctrines concerning the nature of God as creator and judge, of the world and mankind as creatures, and of the status of the Prophet as God's

Apostle to mankind, that he recognizes, and recognizing submits to, the authority of the *Qur'ān* and the Sunna and so finds himself in a position that he must consider the questions of the fundamental principles of the Sharīʿah as ethical and juridical principles. One must, in brief, believe in God as the one who reveals himself in the *Qur'ān* before he can reasonably recognise God's commands as binding; jurisprudence is an element, one of the constitutives of the totality of *al-dīn,* but not as such of its *'usūl. Kalām* as such is prior to *fiqh.* This is not the primary topic of the work and so is not spelled out here, but merely suggested. Subsequently (§2.32) al-Ashʿarī will bring up the thesis of the uncreatedness of the *Qur'ān* which, though a "recent" topic of debate, is nonetheless a fundamental tenet *('aṣl)* for the Hanbalites as it is for al-Ashʿarī himself.

The main point of §2.313 is to distinguish the domains of fundamental theology and of jurisprudence and most particularly to insist on the difference of the principles *('uṣūl)* which found and govern the reasoning appropriate to and characteristic of each. Both are religious sciences and for the one as for the other the significance of the *Qur'ān* and the ḥadīth is recognised and accepted. Both, moreover, are "new" disciplines: neither had been known to the community or needed during the lifetime of the Prophet. (To this he will return). Disputed questions *(masā'il)* of law arise and are dealt with systematically within a context which not only presupposes the authority of revelation as such but begins from the authoritative data of revelation as such. Its principles which are required in order to make appropriate distinctions and to arrive at valid judgements are presented and discovered exclusively in the texts of the revelation *(al-samʿ).* The basic distinctions and principles are themselves initially presented in the revelation; the rules of systematic reasoning and inference *(al-qiyās)* simply allow the *faqīh* to apply these distinctions and principles validly to particular cases. In fundamental theology the situation is different. The principles of the fourth source *(al-ʿaql)* required in order to make appropriate distinctions and to arrive at true conclusions are prior to and independent of the revelation as such. These distinguishing principles *('uṣūl)* consist in "the principles universally accepted on the basis of reason, sense, immediate intuition, et cetera".[38] It is on the basis of these 'principles" that *kalām* grounds its recognition and acceptance of the truth and the authority of the revelation and, having thus recognised the divine origin of the *Qur'ān* and the Sunna, it proceeds systematically to the theological exegesis of these sources on the basis of the same principles. It is incumbent *(yanbaghī)* on every adult Muslim of sound mind to understand these sources on the basis of these universal principles. In essence, what al-Ashʿarī does here is to specify the distinctive foundations which underlie the difference of *al-ʿaql* as the fourth "source" of theological science from *al-qiyās* as the fourth "source" of juridical science and thereby to characterise the fundamental difference of the two disciplines. In each it is the fourth source which allows one to recognize and to appropriate the truth presented in the other three sources, sc., the *Qurʾān,* the Sunna, and the consensus of the Muslims. Al-Ashʿarī concludes §2.313, then, by insisting that matters which are properly the subject of theoretical inquiry *(al-ʿaqliyyāt)* must not be confused with those which can be known, understood, and elaborated only on the basis of authoritative report *(al-samʿiyyāt),* viz., through the teaching of God and the Prophet as authentically and publicly witnessed in the canonical sources. It belongs to the very nature of the latter *(al-samʿiyyāt)* that a kind of rigorous adherence to the teaching and practice of the Prophet and his Companions and of the religious authorities of earlier generations is necessarily required from the outset and at every level in studying, elaborating, and extending their application; the contrary is true of the former *(al-ʿaqliyyāt).* By implication, al-Ashʿarī's opponents, since they insist on *taqlid* in matters of theology, fail to distinguish the two kinds of questions. Because of this error they are unable to deal properly with "new questions" which arise in the area of theology. This will be the subject of the ensuing section (§2.32).

In §2.314, then having asserted on the evidence presented in §2.2 that the "principles" of *kalām* are found in the Scripture and the Sunna and that they were known to the Prophet (§2.311), and having indicated the characteristic difference between theology and jurisprudence (§2.313), al-Ashʿarī concludes by stating that "If the discussion *(al-kalām)* of the creation of the *Qurʾān* and the question of atoms and bodies, etc., had arisen in the time of the Prophet, he would have discussed them *(la-takallama fīhā)* and made the matter clear...". The basic assumption which underlies the argument and is presumed to be conceded by al-Ashʿarī's opponents is that the Prophet left the community every thing which is necessary to, and constitutive of, "the [Muslim] religion" (*al-dīn;* cf. Q 5.3), both with regard to belief and to action. That is to say, what was left by the Prophet is complete as containing every thing which the community then needed and that it would need in time to come in order to meet and to deal with whatever contingencies might circumstantially arise with regard both to belief and to practice. The assumption is not, however, that the Prophet left to the community in the *Qurʾān,* in his words, and in the example of his action specific instructions and explicit formulations as to how to deal with every contingency or to resolve every dispute which would eventually arise. It is rather that the perfection and completeness *(al-kamāl)* of what he left them are that it embraces all of the principles needed to deal with them and to resolve them. Taking, then, the primary focus or topic of the tract to be the juridical legitimacy of *kalām,* al-Ashᶜarī's argument is fundamentally this: he establishes the presence of the "principles" *(ʾuṣūl)* of *kalām* in the *Qurʾān* and the Sunna. His opponents recognize (concede) the legitimacy (sanctioned by consensus) of drawing new judgements in juridical matters by the exercise of systematic reasoning. Given this, al-Ashᶜarī proceeds to set forth the evidence in order to draw a conclusion by formal rule of analogy *(qiyās)* for the legitimacy of *kalām.*

By mentioning the question of atoms and bodies and saying that the Prophet "would have discussed them" had occasion arisen, he alludes directly to §2.311, thereby closing the section. By raising the question of the creation of the *Qurʾān* he anticipates the following section (§2.32). The function of the expressions *"al-kalām"* and *"takallama"* which occur in §2.311 and §2.314 we shall examine later.

In §2.31 the argument was focused on al-Ashᶜarī's own position; he set forth a positive argument to show that the practice of *kalām* is in fact juridically authorised by the canonical sources according to a validly drawn juridical judgement. In §2.32 he proceeds to show that the practice of *kalām* is furthermore necessary to the religious life of the Muslim community. In contrast to §2.31 the argument here follows a kind of reductio, as he shows the internal inconsistency of his opponent's position. The same negative element of the reduction is repeated in each of the four subsections, as he moves from a particular case to the generalisation of it as a type. The first two subsections (§§2.321–2) could be read as being materially focused on three theses all of which were condemned by the Ḥanbalites as "Jahmite", sc., **1.** that the *Qurʾān* is created, **2.** that one should refuse to assert either that it is created or that it is uncreated, and **3.** that God's knowledge is created. Though this is obviously not without significance for the rhetorical force of al-Ashᶜarī's polemic, it would nonetheless seem more appropriate to analyse the section in the following way.[39] In §2.321 he raises as an example the question of the createdness of the *Qurʾān,* taking up in §2.3211 both *a)* the "Jahmite" (and Muᶜtazilite) thesis that it is created and *b)* his opponents' (and his own) thesis that it is uncreated; in §2.3212, then, he considers *c)* a third position (that of the *"wāqifah"*) which refuses to affirm either *a)* or *b).* In §2.322 he generalises the issue by considering any "inappropriate" description of God's attributes which, not having been explicitly proposed during the lifetime of the Prophet, is not authoritatively dealt with either in the *Qur'ān* or in the canonically authenticated teaching of the Prophet. Finally, in §2.323 he takes up the contextually correlated issue (already adumbrated in §2.321) of the Ḥanbalite thesis according to which those who hold either *a)* or *c)* are validly called "unbelievers". This is appropriately treated here, by itself in a separate subsection, since the matter of names and status is properly juridical and is accordingly distinct from the material issues considered in the foregoing subsections.

The argument is founded on, and re-inforces, the dichotomy between the juridical and the theoretical, *al-samᶜiyyāt* and *al-ᶜaqliyyāt*, set out in the preceding section (§2.313). If *taqlīd*, as strict conformance to the teaching and practice of the Prophet, and his Companions, is a principle that must be rigidly adhered to in forming judgements concerning theoretical or theological matters, then both the "Jahmite" theses and their condemnation must alike lack legitimacy.

Al-Ashᶜarī's polemic is not directed at the "Jahmite" positions mentioned in §§2.3211–2 and the argument, accordingly, is not ordered to them but to the denial of the difference between juridical and theoretical reasoning and the principles on which they are founded. In §2.3211 he addresses his opponent's position in holding that the *Qur'ān* is uncreated. Pointing to the lack of any clear authorisation for this position either in the *Qur'ān* or in the attested teaching of the Prophet, he addresses the Ḥanbalites directly (i.e., in the second person plural) for the first time in the tract saying "So why do you people hold that it is uncreated?".[40] To a reply which, presuming the principle of *taqlīd*, claims the precedent of "certain of the Companions and Successors", al-Ashᶜarī insists that, since there is no documented authorisation for holding such a position, any Companion or Successor who said that the *Qur'ān* is uncreated is "according to your view" himself "an innovator and is in grave religious error" *(mubtadi'un ḍāll)*. The expression *"mubtadi'un ḍāll"* hearkens back to the *"bidᶜatun wa-ḍalālah"* of §1.12 and §1.21 and so turns the charge directly against the Ḥanbalites: if one follows their principles rigorously, then those on whom they rely for their opinions are heretics. This will be repeated in more explicit and more forceful terms at the end of the section (§2.323) and again at the end of the tract.[41]

In §2.3212 al-Ashᶜarī takes up the *tawaqquf*, i.e., the position which refuses to assert either that the *Qur'ān* is created or that it is uncreated but does nevertheless condemn the thesis of its creation and call those who hold it "*kāfir*" and "*ḍāll*". Here again, the context assumes that the opponent holds *taqlid* to be a principle to which one is obligated to adhere strictly and accordingly al-Ashᶜarī's response is essentially identical to that which he gave in the preceding paragraph: there is no canonical authorisation for the opponent's position regarding either the *Qurʾān* or for the status of those who say it is created. This section (§2.3212) is somewhat curious, however. The formal address is to the "Wāqifah". By the contextual assumption that the opponent holds *taqlīd* as a universal principle in religious matters (theoretical as well as practical) and by the implication that he describes those who hold the *Qurʾān* to be created as "unbelievers"[42] the real address is to the Ḥanbalites. That the explicit and formal address is to the Wāqifah is not without rhetorical effect here. It occurs as a matter of course, given the question and the form in which the fictive "dispute" is presented ("If some one says..., then we reply, 'You...'."). The effect of this, in view of the direct address to the Ḥanbalites in the immediately preceding paragraph, is rhetorically very sharp: the Ḥanbalites are put on the same level and are addressed in the same terms as the Wāqifah, whose doctrine they condemn and whom they term "unbelievers".

As we noted earlier, §2.322 is employed to generalise what has been said in the two foregoing subsections. Here al-Ashᶜarī formally addresses the Hanbalites once again, as is clear from the form of the introductory expression "*wa-yuqālu lahum*" ("One says to them" — plural in contrast to the singular of §2.3212), which parallels that of §2.3211: "If some one says, 'God's knowledge is created' or describes Him by any predicate which is inappropriate to Him, will you people refuse to say either that it is true or that it is false?" (*ʾa-tatawaqqafūna fīhi*)). In conclusion al-Ashᶜarī says that if they answer in the negative, i.e., as the Ḥanbalites in fact do, and will condemn any such description of God, their reply has no basis in the canonical sources: neither the Prophet nor any of his Companions said anything to support it.[43] Here al-Ashᶜarī is doing more than merely repeating in a more generalised form what he has already said in the previous paragraphs. In passing from the particular case presented by the class of questions which it represents he implicitly raises a point — the principal point at issue — which will be more directly indicated in the conclusion (§2.331). If, as needs must be the case, one is able to recognize that a newly proposed description of God (or of one of His attributes) is in fact such that it is inappropriate[44] or false, then there must be some criterion or means by which it can be known to be inappropriate or false; there must, even in the absence of any direct or explicit indication of the

Qur'ān and the Sunna, be some means of discovering the appropriate or true proposition in contrast to which that which is inappropriate or false can be manifestly seen as such.

One returns thus to the distinction between the modes of reasoning in jurisprudence and their foundations and the modes of reasoning in theology and their foundations, made earlier in §2.313. If one refuses the validity of the latter, arguing that it is not juridically authorised in the canonical sources, then he cannot consistently hold that any description of God which has been recently formulated is erroneous or heretical, however absurd it may be; one has no authorisation to say anything at all concerning it if he practicises *taqlīd* as the Ḥanbalites insist.

Al-Ashᶜarī proceeds then (§2.323) to focus directly on the question of calling those who teach that the *Qur'ān* is created by the title "unbeliever" *(kāfir)*.[45] His Ḥanbalite opponents claim that one is authorised to consider them as unbelievers by the practice of "the leading religious authorities of the earlier generations" *(a'immat al-salaf)*. One notes that here the description of those to whose authority al-Ashᶜarī's opponents bind themselves is not the same as at the beginning of the section. Whereas in §2.321 they claimed the authority of "certain of the Companions and Successors" he has them here claiming the authority of a category of individuals which extends beyond the first two generations. This is important to the sense of the argument. The question here posed is not theological or theoretical, but rather judicial: what names (descriptions and titles: *'asmā' wa-'aḥkām)* are to be applied to what sorts or classes of people; what judgement is juridically authorised in the canonical sources according to the principles and procedures commonly recognized as valid for their interpretation? In such juridical questions the authority of the Companions and the Successors is universally recognised; but what authority has the practice of such "leading religious authorities" as here are referred to when that practice has no foundation in the *Qur'ān* and in the teaching or practice of the Prophet and in the documented practice of the Companions? There can be no claim of consensus *('ijmāᶜ)* in the present case. Accordingly, al-Ashᶜarī notes first that "no judgement *(ḥukm)* is transmitted from the Prophet concerning this". Given, then, no positive precedent concerning those who hold the *Qur'ān* to be created, al-Ashᶜarī turns to the Prophet's practice in another matter as a valid basis for arriving at a judgement by analogy *(qiyās)*, citing the Prophet's silence with regard to whether the *munāfiqūn* were or were not really unbelievers, i.e., to his treating them publicly as formal members of the Muslim community rather than as unbelievers. The example is apt and in conclusion al-Ashʿarī comes by *ijtihād* to the decision *(ḥukm)* that what the "leading religious authorities" cited by his opponents ought to have done, "what was incumbent upon them" *(al-wājib)* given the precedent cited, "was to imitate the Prophet", sc., by keeping silent with regard to the name to be applied to those who say that the *Qurʾān* is created and with regard to their status. By implication the Ḥanbalites bind themselves to the authority of individuals who have no authority of their own and whose practice in this case is plainly an innovation *(bidʿah)* which, since it is at variance with the action of the Prophet in an analogous situation, is also religious error *(dalālah)*.[46]

One should note here how the subsections of §3.2 are linked to one another and to the general context of the tract by the repetition of analogous phrases which reinforce the author's polemic: "There is no valid tradition from him [sc., the Prophet]" *(lam yaṣiḥḥa ʿanhu ḥadīthun:* §2.3211), "because God's Apostle neither said... nor did he say..." (*liʾanna rasūla llāhi lam yaqul... wa-lā qāla...:* §2.3212), "God's Apostle did not say..." *(lam yaqul rasūlu llāhi:* §2.322), and "since no decision is transmitted from the Prophet..." (*ʾidhā lam yurwa ʿani l-nabiyyi ḥukmun...:* §2.323). The expression *"lam yurwa"* of §2.323 directly recalls the wording of §1.21, where the Ḥanbalites are cited as saying, "So since no discussion *(kalām)* is transmitted from him concerning anything of what we have mentioned, we know that to discuss it is an innovation and to investigate it is a religious error".[47] It is within this context that al-Ashʿarī states his major conclusion (§2.331). Since **1.** no conclusion regarding theological theses which have been first proposed only since the death of the Prophet and have become topics of controversy can be drawn by following the rules and procedures of juridical reasoning or by adhering strictly to the stated principles of the Ḥanbalites and since **2.** it is evident that the Muslim community has to take a position with regard to whatever "new" theological questions may arise,[48] one must conclude that not only is *kalām* juridically authorised, as was shown in §2.31, but that it is also necessary for the religious life of the community.

As we have noted, the argument of §2.32 is directed to the fallacy, i.e., the internal inconsistency, of the Ḥanbalite position with regard to *kalām:* the procedure is juridically authorised by the precedent cited in §2.232. In the conclusion (§2.331), then, al-Ashʿarī presents what is in effect, and what he explicitly claims as, his own position: the religious scholars *(al-ʿulamāʾ)* have to employ *kalām* in order to deal with theological questions that have arisen since the death of the Prophet and which will subsequently arise in order that the ignorant — the unlettered and unlearned of the community — may know the truth with regard to them.[49] *Al-Ḥathth* was not, however, composed simply in order to demonstrate the legitimacy of *kalām*. It was written chiefly as an attack on the intransigency of the Hanbalites in their doctrine.[50] This becomes clear in §2.331, for al-Ashᶜarī does not terminate the discussion with his *quod erat demonstrandum*. On the contrary, the "this is what we wanted you to admit" leads directly into a question: "So why then do you people shun the science of *kalām* and prohibit it?". The discourse, in brief, passes on through the assertion of the author's own position in order to continue the polemic against his opponents' positions set forth at the beginning of the tract. We have already noted how the concluding paragraphs of the work pick up symmetrically the elements of the introduction. Before examining them more closely, however, it will be opportune to consider briefly the range and usage of the word '*kalām*' and of the verb '*takallama, yatakallamu*' and to note the rhetorical use to which al-Ashᶜarī has here put them.

As a formal name for fundamental theology, the expression '*al-kalām*' is an abridgment for 'ᶜilm al-kalām'.(the science of *kalām*), just as '*al-fiqh*' is for '*ᶜilm al-fiqh*' and '*al-naḥw*' for '*ᶜilm al-naḥw*'. In this sense '*ᶜilm al-kalām*' is synonymous with '*ᶜilm ʾuṣūl al-dīn*' (the science of the basic articles of faith), a more properly descriptive expression already used in al-Ashᶜarī's time. The occurrences of '*al-kalām*' by itself in their formal sense are generally such that the specific sense is clear from the context. So too is the use of the verb '*takallama, yatakallamu*' in the formal sense "to practice theology" *(kalām)* and of its participle, '*mutakallim*' where it means "a theologian". This is not inevitably so, however, and al-Ashᶜarī employs the potential ambiguity of these terms with great rhetorical skill in *al-Ḥathth*.

The verb '*kallama, yatakallamu*' means basically to speak or to talk, to talk (with another) about *(fī)* something, and so also to discuss something. '*kalām*' is commonly employed as the *maṣdar* or *nomen actionis*, though not in all contexts (one has, e.g., to employ '*takallum*' where the full verbal force has to be retained). Contextually the meaning of '*takallama, yatakallamu*' is often more closely specified with particular connotations as it is used in the sense of "to discuss something formally" or "to enquire into a matter and reflect on it" or "to debate a question" or "to carry on a formal disputation". It will be useful to begin with several examples which do not involve theology as such, in order to illustrate these usages.

1. *'Takallama'* is frequently employed in the sense to express and explain one's opinion or considered judgement. A story is told, for example, that Jamīla (a famous singer of the early Umayad period) contemplated giving up her profession since poetry and the singing of it *(al-ghinā')* were held by many to be contrary to the religious ethic of Islam. She told this to a large assembly of her friends and admirers whom she had invited to her house expressly for this purpose and a lengthy discussion ensued. Finally "a sheikh among them, an elderly man of learning, wisdom,[51] and experience said, 'The gathering have spoken [*takallamati l-jamāᶜah:* have expressed their opinions] and each group *(ḥisb)* is happy with their own views *(mā ladayhim)*. Listen now to what I have to say *(qawlī)*...'. The assembly fell silent and the sheikh spoke *(takallama)*...". I.e., he gave them his considered view of the matter, explaining at length why she should not give up her art.[52]

2. The terms refer to a learned discussion and inquiry where we are told of an encounter between abū Hāshim al-Jubbā'ī (the Muᶜtazilite theologian) and abū l-Ḥasan al-Karkhī (a Ḥanafite legist, d. 340/952) in which they had a heated discussion concerning ritual prayer (al-ṣalāh). "They began to discuss *(yatakallamāni)*... and went on discussing until abū l-Ḥasan claimed that the discussion *(al-kalām)* had reached a point of agreement" *(ijmāᶜ)*.[53] Here plainly *'takallama'* indicates a serious and learned dialogue, i.e., an inquiry in which disparate views are resolved.

3. So also we find the noun *'kalām'* employed in a slightly more formal sense. It is reported that some one said to Yaḥyā b. Khālid al-Barmakī introducing Sībawayh, who wished to be presented to the scholars of the ᶜAbbasid court, "The outstanding grammarian of Basra here is very eager to have people hear what he has to say" *(ishtāqat nafsuhu 'ilā samāᶜi kalāmihi)*.[54] That is, he wants people to give his grammatical theories a hearing; he wants them to listen to a formal presentation of them as he expounds and argues them.

4. Even closer to a formal use of the verb is that which we find where al-Nāshi' says that the science of medicine at first "simply happened piecemeal and afterwards was brought together *(jumiᶜa)* and made the subject of formal discussion" *(tukullima ᶜalayhī)*, i.e., of formal study and scientific enquiry.[55]

5. Finally, *'takallama'* is sometimes used in the sense to debate or dispute. Thus the grammarian, al-Māzinī (d. 248/862) says, "I was present one day in the company of al-Mutawakkil and Yaᶜqūb ibn al-Sikkīt (d. 243/857) was there too. Al-Mutawakkil said, 'you two debate *(takallamā)* concerning a grammatical question'. I said, 'I'll ask the questions' and he said, 'you ask the

questions', so I said,...".[56] Here we have to do with what is clearly a formal disputation.[57]

In (1)–(3) the terms plainly refer to and describe the formal presentation of the speaker's opinion, his view or judgement, as presented in dialogue with others who hold differing or contrasting views. In (1) and (2) a resolution of the question is achieved. In (3) the ensuing dialogue takes the form of a disputation; this was expected, given the situation and the custom, though "*kalām*" here refers to and describes only the formal presentation of one speaker's position, i.e., his own grammatical theory, which would be debated. In (4) and (5) different connotations of the foregoing become primary so that '*takallama*' takes on more specific senses as determined by the contexts. In (4) the presentation of points of view is understood as a process of deliberation and takes on the sense of formal inquiry or investigation *(baḥth)* in order to know and understand. This is closely akin to (3), since "*kalāmuhu*" there indicates a formally elaborated theory. In (5) it has unambiguously the sense of formal disputation, not in order to resolve an issue or question but in order to see who wins: for sport. Albeit the precise historical background may not be altogether clear, it is nevertheless certain that the formal use of '*kalām*' to name a specific discipline originates out of these uses of '*kalām*' and '*takallama*'.[58]

Usage of '*kalām*' and '*takallama*' semantically analogous to that of (1)–(3) are also found where one has to do with theologically very conservative contexts.

6. In his notice on al-Barbahārī, Ibn abī Yaᶜlā cites the following from the former's *Sharḥ Kitāb al-Sunna:* "Consider with particular care (God have mercy on you) every one of your contemporaries to whose discourse *(kalām)* you listen and do not go along with any of it until you ask and see whether one of the Companions of the Prophet (God's prayer and peace be upon him) or one of the learned has had anything to say on the subject" *(takallama fīhī)*.[59]

7. So too in al-Ashᶜarī's *Ibāna* there is a reported conversation between al-ᶜAbbās ibn ᶜAbd al-ᶜAẓīm al-ᶜAnbarī (d. 246/860) and Ibn Ḥanbal concerning the controversy over the createdness of the *Qur'ān*, more specifically concerning the position of those who refuse to say either that it is created or that it is uncreated. In the course of the discussion, after Ibn Ḥanbal has condemned the doctrine of the Wāqifa as more pernicious than that of the Jahmiyya, we read the following: "Al-ᶜAbbās said 'abū ᶜAbdallāh, What is your own position?',

to which he replied, 'What I believe and hold and about which there is no doubt, is that the *Qur'ān* is uncreated'. Then he said, 'And who has any doubt about this?'. Then abū ʿAbdallāh [ibn Ḥanbal] spoke *(takallama)* stating that to doubt this is a very heinous thing...".[60]

'Takallama' in (7) refers to and describes the formal expression of the speaker's view or judgement, set forth at length in the dialogue, the substance of which was that it is a grave and, indeed, heinous thing *(ʿaẓīm)* to have any doubt in this matter. (He continues, in al-Ashʿarī's account, to present his argument for the *Qur'ān's* uncreatedness). The *"kalām"* of (6) refers, again, to the expression of theological views or doctrinal position encountered in discussion (and by extension, in writing), while *"takallama"* there refers to the formally expressed views of the Companions and of "the learned" *(al-ʿulamā')*, viz., those experts in tradition who follow the Sunna.

'Takallama' is also employed in similar contexts with the preposition *'bi-'* with the sense to speak for a given doctrine, to set it forth as one's own or arguing for it.

8. Thus we read in Ibn Saʿd's *Ṭabaqāt* that "Asʿad ibn Zurāra and abū l-Haytham al-Tayyihān spoke in Yathrib in favor of the doctrine that there is but one God" *(yatakallamāni bil-tawḥīd)*.[61] That is to say, in Medina prior to the Hejira they spoke of, and tried to make others believe in, Islam and the teaching of Muḥammad that there is only one God.

9. Al-Barbahārī is reported as saying, "Between a man and his being a believer there is nothing prior to his becoming an unbeliever save his rejecting something of what God has revealed... or his denying something of what God has said *(qāla)* or something of what God's Apostle (God's prayer and peace be upon him) has taught" *(takallama bihi)*.[62]

In both (8) and (9) the term describes a speaking as the expounding of a doctrine in dialogue in order that others shall appropriate it and undertstand it: to set it forth, expound it, teach it, urge it.

10. Finally, al-Barbahārī is reported to have said, "Know that discussion about the Lord (He is exalted) *(al-kalāmu fī l-rabbi taʿāla)* is an innovation *(muḥdath)*; it is a heresy and an error *(bidʿatun wa-ḍalālah)*. One speaks about the Lord *(yutakallamu fī l-rabb)* only in those terms by which He has described Himself in the *Qur'ān* and which the Prophet made clear *(bayyana)* to his Companions."[63]

In its basic sense, thus, the use of *'takallama'* and its noun, even by the most conservative authors, does not necessarily carry any prejudicial connotations with regard to the legitimacy of presenting one's view (or teaching) or concerning the soundness of the view expressed. The verb is used with the Prophet and with his Companions as subject as also of Ibn Ḥanbal.[64] This remains true also of *"al-kalām"* in (6): since the speaker of this *kalām* has no authority of his own, the view expressed has to be scrutinised in order to verify its conformity to the authoritative statements of the Companions. Contextually one hears in (6) that in a time when many heretical doctrines are being taught one must be cautious, but there is no automatic condemnation or rejection of this *kalām*. When, however, we get to (10), *"al-kalām"* plainly has a surcharge of pejorative connotations which are not wholly explained by the compliment *'fī l-rabb"*, though this does clarify the context. On a more general semantic level the use and sense of the word here may be compared *a)* to that in (3): *"al-kalām"* here denotes the dialogic discussion and exposition of one's own understanding or theory, the result of his own systematic inquiry and reflection. This al-Barbahārī will condemn as *bidᶜah wa-ḍalālah* precisely because, in his view, such reflection and theory cannot, by definition, conform appropriately to the tradition. Or *b)* it may be compared to (4), in which case *"al-kalām"* denotes the dialogical examination and consideration of differing views so as to arrive at agreement on what is correct. This al-Barbahārī will condemn since the limits of what can be known and correctly stated concerning God is definitively presented in the *Qur'ān* and the Sunna and about these there can be no debate. Or, finally, *c)* it may be compared with (5), in which case *"al-kalām"* denotes the formally speculative investigation of the nature of God which is beyond the reach of human understanding save insofar as it grasps what is authoritatively presented in the canonical sources. It were idle to attempt to restrict the sense of the expression in (10) to one of these three; we should, rather, hear all of them. *"Al-kalām"*, in brief, here refers to and names that activity which is constitutive of "the science of *kalām*". With this look at the background of the terms we can now examine al-Ashᶜarī's rhetorical exploitation of *'takallama'* and *'kalām'* in *al-Ḥathth*.

Al-Ashᶜarī begins his tract by speaking of his adversaries as a group of people who find "systematic reasoning and investigation" *(al-naẓaru wal-baḥth)* about theological questions too difficult. The association of *kalām* with "systematic reasoning and investigation" (and the association of the expressions) is immediate in the context, wherefore, by implication, they are incompetent in, and uncomprehending of, *kalām*, i.e., of theology as a formal activity and discipline. In (§1) the usage is plain and in accord with what we find in Ḥanbalite sources. "They allege that the formal discussion of bodies, accidents... *(al-kalāmu fī l-jismi wal-ᶜaraḍi...)* is an innovation and a religious error" (§1.12). Here *"al-kalām"* not only denotes formal discussion and inquiry, but implies that this is carried out in a theological context. If to do this were a matter of true guidance and direction *(hudan wa-rushd)* "the Prophet, the [rightly guided] Caliphs, and the Companions would have had something to say on the subject" *(la-takallama fīhi)*, i.e., would have expressed their judgement for the instruction on the community. "Since no formal discussion *(kalām)* is reported from him about any thing of what we have mentioned, we know that to discuss it formally *(al-kalāmu fīhi)* is an innovation and to investigate it *(al-baḥthu ᶜanhu)* a religious error" *(ibid.)*. *"Al-kalām"* in §1.21 and in the first paragraph of §1.12 may be taken simply as "to have said something", but in its juxtaposition with *"al-baḥth"* in the last paragraph one clearly hears the connotation of a formally speculative activity (as in (4) above). The same is true of *"takallama"* in §2.1 and likely in §2.20. Up to this point one hears first the usual, non-formal sense of the word with the overtones of the formal sense (of "theological speculation"). We find the term *'kalām'* next in the heading of §2.212: *"ʾammā l-kalāmu fī l-tawḥīd"*. Here the polemical thrust of the phrase, even though it is conventional as a heading (The Discussion of the Topic...), is clear enough in the context: the formal exposition *(kalām)* of the evidence for the thesis. The same is true of the heading of §2.2130. In the opening and in the closing subsections of §2.31 *"takallama"* occurs in a place in which it is basically neutral: one cannot speak of the Prophet's having had something to say on the subject or of his not having had anything to say—of his having spoken on the subject or not having spoken (where deliberate silence would constitute a basis of sunna). In §2.312, however, the verb occurs with the *fuqahāʾ* as the subject and in a "heavy" sense: they "discuss formally, investigate, dispute, and offer probative arguments [against counter positions]" with regard to recently raised juridical questions. The more formal use of the term here anticipates te analogy he draws in this section between systematic reasoning in jurisprudence and in theology in order to establish the legitimacy of the latter, taking "systematic discussion" as legitimate in either of the modes which he distinguishes in §2.313. Given this, the occurence in §2.314 (the Prophet "would have discussed") takes on more pregnant overtones.

All of this is brought to a head when he reaches his conclusion in §2.331 and §2.332. *"Al-kalām"* occurs twice in §2.331 and twice again in §2.332, in both of which one passes from *"al-kalām"* to *"ᶜilm al-kalām"*. "The learned have to undertake the formal discussion *(al-kalām)* concerning recent questions..., so why do you people shun the science of *kalām...?*" (§2.331). To claim to know the truth with regard to recent theological questions and to shun *kalām* is inconsistent. That is to say, one can only make a judgement of what is true or false—valid or invalid—by a kind of theological *ijtihād,* which requires the discipline of *kalām.* Whoever lacks competence in "the systematic reasoning and investigation concerning theological matters" *(thaqula ᶜalayhimu l-naẓaru wal-baḥthu fī l-dīn:* §1.10), since he can form no judgement of his own, requires the guidance of the learned, sc., of one who has mastered the science of *kalām.* At this point al-Ashᶜarī's opponents are reduced to silence, vanquished in the disputation. In §2.332 accordingly, he does not address them directly, either by continuing the second person of §2.331 or by continuing the *"yuqālu lahum"* of §2.32, but speaks rather to the audience (the reader) about them: "Those people[65] speak [i.e., make formal pronouncements] concerning *kalām (yatakallamūna fī l-kalām)* until, when they are unable to proceed any further, they say 'we have been forbidden the science of *kalām*'...". Again, speaking and reduction to silence, though here with an allustion to the charge of incompetence brought in §1.10. Here, as al-Ashᶜarī addresses the reader concerning his opponents, he presents what he considers the origin of their difficulty: "...they bind themselves uncritically to one who came before them without any conclusive argument or demonstration [of the validity of the position taken]" (§2.332). The two final phrases here, *"man kāna qablahum bi-lā ḥujjatin wa-lā burhān",* are wonderfully ambivalent in the context. Taking the *"man"* of *"man kāna"* as implicitly plural in the context one could understand the reference as to "the leading religious authorities of the earlier generations" whose practice the Ḥanbalites cited as authoritative precedent for their own in §2.323. Taken as singular, however, it must refer to Ibn Ḥanbal. Again, the phrase *"bi-lā ḥujjatin wa-lā burhān"* (without any conclusive argument or demonstration)[66] can be read with *"yuqallidūn"* (they bind themselves uncritically) or it could be heard either as a qualifying element to *"qablahum"* (taking "before them" as the predicate of the *"kāna"*) or as a predicate ("who before them was without any conclusive argument or demonstration"). That the reference of the *"man"* is singular and is to Ibn Ḥanbal would seem clear, since it is to his doctrine that al-Barbahārī and his followers explicitly bind themselves in their *taqlīd.*[67] The statement of §2.332 is very strongly put as al-Ashᶜarī underlines the inconsistency of the Ḥanbalite position in the first sentence and the unsoundness of the juridical reasoning on which it is based in the second. That Ibn Ḥanbal is not named is noteworthy.

This may indicate that al-Ashᶜarī does not wish to attack him so much as his followers and their interpretation of his doctrine.[68] If this is the case, then one will interpret the final sentence of §2.332 as "with neither conclusive proof nor demonstration they bind themselves uncritically to one who was before them". That is, they claim to follow his doctrine strictly but do not do so in a valid manner. If, on the other hand, he means to attack Ibn Ḥanbal directly, we shall read "They bind themselves uncritically to one who before them had neither conclusive argument nor demonstration". Here as elsewhere, we must take it that the ambivalence of expression is deliberate and intentional. The primary and immediate butt of the polemic is al-Barbahārī, to whom the tract was addressed. Ibn Hanbal is a respected and venerable master, but one whose attitude towards systematic theology was irrationally biased, at least in al-Ashᶜarī's judgement.

In §2.333 al-Ashᶜarī addresses his Ḥanbalite opponents for one last time, but not to ask a question. He tells them, in a final polemical thrust, what judgement they must reach, if they are to be consistent, concerning the great masters of Sunnite jurisprudence, sc., that they are all guilty of innovation and error. Though it may seem to be a somewhat otiose appendix, the primary points of the tract having been quite adequately made in §2.331 and §2.332, this final paragraph has a structural function and so is not really redundant. The central focus of the argument in most of the work, beginning with the opening section, has been on the juridical legitimacy of the science of *kalām*, a new discipline. In §2.333 he tells his opponents that they have, in order to be consistent, to condemn abū Ḥanīfa, Mālik, and al-Shāfiᶜī as innovators "since they have done things which the Prophet did not do".[69] The topic recalls materially and formally the juridical context of the earlier arguments. The inconsistency of the Ḥanbalites' theory and practice is again suggested as also by implication that they are themselves guilty of innovation. *Taqlīd* is at best a juridical principle, but if followed rigidly as al-Barbahārī insists, then the foremost jurists also be condemned as innovators. The last sentence of the tract states what the Prophet did not do—non-action in which no binding precedent is to be seen (cf. §2.311 and §2.314). Everything is there and the last phrase of the tract is "the Apostle of God (God's prayer and peace be upon him)". Rhetorically the work is a masterpiece.

The manuscripts

A– III Ahmet n° 1916 (= *al-Tawhīd* n° 176 of the microfilm collection of the League of Arab States), 26 × 19 cm, written in a clear, regular *naskhi* hand,

24 lines to the page. The copy was completed on 11/III/592 = 7/IX/1196. *Al-Ḥathth* is found of foll. 9r° 18 – 11r° 1. It begins

وقد قال أبو الحسن رضي الله عنه في كتابه المترجم بالحث على البحث أن طائفة...

and ends

إنتهى كلام أبي الحسن رضي الله عنه [١١ و] في هذا الباب.

B– Landberg n° 1031, foll. 4v° - 6v° (= Ahlwardt n° 2162, 18.5 × 13.5 cm, executed in a hastily written, untidy *taᶜlīq* hand, 20 to 22 lines to the page. The last leaf of the tract is missing; the text ends in §2.322 (see note 253 to the text). The copy, according to Ahlwardt, was completed about 1150/1737. The text begins, fol. 4v° 1.

بسم الله الرحمن الرحيم قال الإمام أبو الحسن علي بن اسمعيل الأشعري رضي الله عنه
أعلموا وفقكم الله أن قومًا...

and ends, 6v° ult. مقرور أو صفراوي.

F– Feyzullah n° 2161, foll, 49v° – 52r°, 26 × 17 cm, written in a small, carefully executed *maghribī* hand, 30 lines to the page. I have not seen the manuscript itself but should judge that the copy is probably no earlier than the 12th/18th century.[70] The text begins fol. 49v° 1

بسم الله الرحمن الرحيم وصلّى الله على سيدنا محمد وعلى ءاله وصحبه وسلّم تسليمًا
قال أبو صادق محمد بن يحيى بن علي القرشي انبأنا الشيخ الإمام جمال الدين أبو الحسن
علي بن ابراهيم بن عبْد الله القرشي إجازة بخطه[٧١]...

It ends fol. 52r° 9:

وفيما ذكرنا كفاية لكل عاقل غير معاند. – ءاخره والحمد لله وحده وصلى الله
على سيدنا محمد وعلى ءاله وصحبه وسلم وبعقبه ما صورته سمعت جميعه بقراءتي على الشيخ
المحدث أبي صادق محمد بن الحافظ الرشيد أبي الحسين يحيى بن علي بن عبد الله بن
مفرج القرشي وفقه الله تعلى ورحم سلفَه بمنزله بمصر كتبه عبد الرحمن بن عبد الله
ابن عبد الحليم بن عمران في ربيع الأول سنة ٦٧٧ عابدًا مصليًا.

H– The edition of Hyderabad 1344, republished by R. McCarthy in *Theology*, pp. 87–97. Note that to the formula *Ṣallā llāhu ᶜalayhi wa-sallam* this text consistently adds *wa-ʾālihi* following *ᶜalayhi*, which I have omitted from the apparatus.

NOTES

1. Cf. Ibn ʿAsākir, p. 307.

2. The text is incomplete in B whose final leaf is missing.

3. Ibn ʿAsākir, p. 136, 8 (see also McCarthy, *Theology*, p. 228, n° 94) and Ibn Farḥūn, p. 195, 1. Concerning these lists see also below.

4. Not only is *istiḥsān* considered to have no legal validity but, more significantly al-Ashʿarī's argument in the text is that the practice of *kalām* has authorising precedents in the life of the Prophet and in the *Qurʾān*. (Concerning the Ashʿarite attitude towards such private or personal judgements of what is right and their sense that the school's *kalām* is not founded in *istiḥsān*, see e.g., the remarks of abu l-Maʿāli ibn ʿAbd al-Malik (d. 494/1100) cited in Ibn ʿAsākir, p. 152, 5ff.). "*Khāḍa, yakhūḍu, khawḍan*" does occasionally, though rarely, occur in a more or less neutral sense, but even then some negative overtones appear to be present. For example, in his *al-Maqsid al-asnā* (ed. F. A. Shehadi, Beyrouth, 1982, p. 36) al-Ghazzālī introduces a chapter concerning "Whether names which are approximately the same may be synonymous, signifying but a single meaning, or whether they must also differ in intension" and begins, "*ʾaqūlu: al-khāʾiḍūna fī sharḥi hādhihi l-ʾasmāʾi lam yataʿarraḍū li-hādhā l-ʾamr*" (Those who have undertaken to explain these names have not considered this matter). Here the use of "*al-khāʾiḍūn*" would seem to imply that they undertook it rashly and without sufficient preparation. (Al-Ghazzālī, here as elsewhere, seems to have taken on some of the pretentiousness of the *falāsifa* along with their teaching while at the same time having too little appreciation of the work of his predecessors).

5. Cf. G. Makdisi, "al-Ashʿarī and the Ashʿarites" 2, p. 24. In this article (pp. 21ff.) the author contends that *al-Ḥathth* is in all probability not an authentic work of al-Ashʿarī but on the contrary dates from a much later period. Concerning the authenticity of the tract and its place among the writings of al-Ashʿarī which are presently available, see my "Elements in the Development of the Teaching of al-Ashʿarī" where it is suggested that both *al-Ḥathth* and the *Ibāna* are probably early works. Since *al-Ḥathth* is found in the supplementary list of Ibn ʿAsākir and not those given by Ibn Fūrak we have no direct evidence concerning the date of its composition. Ibn Farḥūn's list (*op. cit.*, pp. 194f.) follows a somewhat different order from those presented by Ibn ʿAsākir and is probably therefore independant of them. Here *al-Ḥathth* is the tenth item and occurs among works composed, according to Ibn Fūrak's information, prior to 320/932. (Most of those cited by Ibn Farḥūn belong to this period). The *Risāla ilā ahl ath-thaghr*, it should be noted, is almost certainly a very early work of al-Ashʿarī's post-conversion period, and it too is given in Ibn ʿAsākir's supplementary list. None of these lists is complete; conspicuously, for example, *al-Ibāna*, found in Ibn al-Nadīm as well as Ibn Farḥūn and concerning the circumstances of whose composition we are informed by Ibn abī Yaʿlā (*Ṭabaqāt* 2, p. 18), is not mentioned—not at any rate by this title—in any of the lists given by Ibn ʿAsākir.

6. McCarthy, in his translation, p. 124, n° 20, remarks that "this paragraph is an exegetical note which is almost independant of the text".

7. It is perhaps worth noting that following the "*hādhā*" of this addition B shows a short blank space, about enough for one word, while the editor of H says that there was a space also in the manuscript from which he prepared the edition. Nothing seems to be missing, however,

and no emendation plausibly suggests itself. The space would, even so, indicate that the copyist of the archetype of T–2 had some problem at this point, perhaps something (in the margin?) which he was unable to read in the copy from which he was working.

8. One might suggest that the reading of H, "*lā fī jihatin wāḥidatin wal--lā fī l-mawjūdi fī l-maḥall*" is correct, but 'that which exists in a substrate" is the accident and no *mutakallim* holds that there is such a thing as an accident inherent in another accident. Here also the reading *lā fī jihatin* of H is surely a corruption of *lā ᶜalā l-jumlah* (found in both B and F) to which *wāḥidah* has been added, since *lā fī jihah* (with or without *wāḥidah*) is substantially synonymous with *lā fī maḥall* and so would be wholly redundant.

9. The expression "*mawjūdun* (or, more commonly, *muḥdathun*) *lā fī maḥall*" is employed by al-Jubbāʾī and abū Hāshim as a description of God's volitions, but such a reference here is altogether implausible.

10. Cf. R.M. Frank, *Beings and their Attributes*, pp. 95ff.

11. It could, to be sure, be suggested that this element, sc., the "*wa-lā ᶜalā l-jumlati wa-lā fī l-mawjūdi lā fī maḥall*" was lost in A by a quasi homoioteleuton with the preceding "lā fī maḥallin [wāḥid]", but this is unlikely. First, the final word of the preceding text is *wāḥid* and not *maḥall;* secondly, the inclusion of so pointless a remark would be contrary to the overall economy of the tract's style and to that of the writings of al-Ashᶜarī in general.

12. Note that this is not the usual sequence of topics found in the classical compendia, where the treatment of God's unity normally follows the thesis that there is only one eternal creator; see the remarks of al-Juwaynī in *al-Shāmil,* p. 401.

13. The concomittant substitution of "*al-naẓaru wal-ḥissu wal-qiyās*" for the "*al-bidāyatu wal-maḥsūsātu wal-ḍarūriyyāt*" of T–1 is noteworthy. It is possible that the purpose of the alteration may be simply to spell out more clearly what is implicit in the more basic terms given in T–1, though it may have some greater significance wich is not immediately clear.

14. Concerning the uncompromising attitude of the Ḥanbalites and the milder attitude of some other (Shāfiᶜite) traditionalists on this question, see my "Elements" n. 59.

15. Note also that the expression "I shall keep silent on the matter" (*ʾaskutu ᶜanhu*) is itself ambiguous; it can be understood to say "I shall keep silent on the question of the creation or non-creation of the *Qurʾān* (implied in the "*la-kāna yanbaghī ʾan taskuta ᶜanhu*" of the preceding paragraph) or "I shall keep silent with regard to the question of the status (or title) of those who hold that the *Qurʾān* is created". The final statement of § 2.323 in T–2 takes care of both interpretations.

16. The argument is not *tu quoque,* since the author has shown earlier, at least to his own satisfaction, that *kalām* is founded on the teaching of the Prophet.

17. McCarthy seems to take it that the clause "given that the Apostle of God did not state it" contained in the fourth question is sufficient to make the author's point and so to close the section. This clause, however, simply parallels the "*ᶜammā sakata ᶜanhu*" of the previous question and the "*wa-lam yatakallam... wa-lā qāla...*" of the final question which terminates the whole sequence. The sequence ends (*if* the text is correct and complete insofar as it goes) with a question because the opponent has no further response. This is not the case with the fourth question, since there remains a yet earlier generation of pious ancestors.

18. Concerning the structural place and function of § 2.331 see the discussion below.

19. One might suggest that this phrase has been lost in A and B by homoioteleuton, but the

conjunction of AB is a strong indication of an original reading and moreover the additional phrase is not pertinent to the immediate polemic.

20. Both forms, "*lā ʿalā mithāl*" and "*ʿalā ghayr mithāl*", occur in this formula (cf. e.g., al-Bayhaqī, *al-Iʿtiqād*, p. 34,6 [*ʿalā ghayri mithāl*] and pp. 16f. and 56, 14 [*lā ʿalā mithāl*]); one notes, however, that "*lā ʿalā mithāl*" occurs in al-Ashʿarī's *Lumaʿ*, §9. p. 8, 15.

21. This cannot be adjusted by the mere addition of a "*fa-*", wherefore it is clear that something more than a conjunction has been lost. I have added "*fa-yajibu*" in the present edition in order to make the passage coherent.

22. The text of B here is quite similar in its wording to the account of the story found in abū l-Ḥusayn al-Wāḥidī's *Asbāb al-nuzūl* (Cairo, 1379/1959, p. 175) and Ibn al-Jawzī's *Tafsīr* (vol. 6, Damascus, 1385/1965, pp. 394f.) and may well be based on the same source. In this version Ibn al-Zibaʿrā says that banū Mulayḥ worship the angels, wherefore the "*ljm*" of B is probably to be corrected to Luḥayy, since they were a subgroup of Mulayḥ. Though it may account for the first part of this passage in B, the account given by al-Wāḥidī and Ibn al-Jawzī is of no help with regard to the corruption at the end where the subjunctive "*yakūnū*" occurs.

23. One has to recognize that it might, and not impertinently, be suggested that the reasoning that underlies this conclusion may beg the question or that it is, viewed from another angle, maybe circular, since it is also, if not equally, plausible that a fuller form of the work have been shortened by revision and tightened up. This hypothesis might be argued for several passages (particularly, perhaps, for the shorter form of §2.323), but it would be most unlikely that in revising the text the author or redactor should have omitted already present formulae that mark off sections of the text such as the "*wa-ammā l-ʾaṣlu*" found at the head of §2.223 and §2.224 in T–2 and the others we indicated. Quite to the contrary. Nor does it seem likely, given the problem mentioned above, that for §2.323 a redactor would have substituted the form in T–1 for that of T–2, while the inverse seems altogether plausible.

24. It would seem to me, indeed, that these additions were originally marginal notes made by a student not far progressed in his studies, particularly those found in §§2.2132, 2.221, and 2.223, which are not even pertinent to the contexts in which they occur.

25. There is a brief analysis of the content of the work in M. Allard's *Le Problème des attributs divins dans la doctrine d'al-Ashʿarī et de ses premiers grands disciples* (Beyrouth, 1965), pp. 206–211, but he fails to see the multiplicity of distinct topics and arguments presented.

26. Concerning this see *Allard, op. cit.* and the further discussion in my "Elements".

27. The Ashʿarites generally condemn *taqlīd* in theology as the following of the opinion or judgement of another without knowing its foundation (or lack of foundation). Although in the present tract *taqlīd* is viewed from a juridical standpoint (as involving a judgement concerning an action rather than a theological thesis), the basis of al-Ashʿarī's condemnation remains the same, as he insists in §2.332 that his opponents follow the judgement and practice of individuals (or of an individual) which are not based on sound juridical reasoning; they do not themselves understand the issue and the facts and therefore neither do they know the basis or lack of it for their own position.

28. Though we shall have shortly to return to the rhetorical use and the sense of these terms as they occur in *al-Ḥathth*, it is advisable to say something about their lexical basis here. '*ʾAṣl*' (pl. *ʾuṣūl*) is primarily the base or foundation on which a thing rests (v. Ibn Fāris, *Maqāyīs al-lughah*, s.v.) and is commonly used to designate the roots of a plant or the stem of a tree, as opposed to the branches *(furūʿ)* or crown *(farʿ)*. In its formal use it means generally the basic

element, constituent, principle, or foundation of a thing. This Ibn ᶜAbbās is cited as saying, "[God] created water first (or water together with whatever He wished), not from any *ʾaṣl* [i.e., not out of any already existent material] nor on the basis of any preëxistent pattern; then He made it an *ʾaṣl* [i.e., a basis, material foundation or principle] of what He subsequently created" (al-Bayhaqi, *al-Iᶜtiqād*, p. 56). Similarly in a *kalām* context, "the atoms are the *ʾuṣūl* [i.e., the basis, constitutive elements] of composites and composites are bodies (*ʾajsām*): abū l-Qāsim al-Anṣārī, *al-Ghunyah*, fol. 13v, 12. The word is commonly employed in *kalām* contexts in the sense of "a thesis" (sometimes "topic"). E.g., al-Juwaynī says (*Irshād*, p. 6, 8) that he will take up the thesis (or topic) of antecedent causes (*ʾaṣlu l-tawallud*) in its proper place and al-Bāqillānī speaks of "this thesis" (*hādhā l-ʾaṣl*) (*Hidāya*, fol. 4r°, 12) referring to the thesis or topic of the immediately preceding section (beginning fol. 2r°). More narrowly, however, the term is used of the basic theses, i.e., doctrines, dogmas, or articles (*articuli fidei*) of Islamic belief (taking "dogma" here in the older sense, as equivalent of "*articulus fidei*", not in the narrower, 19th century use). Thus Ibn Qutayba says that the ahl al-ḥadīth are unanimous in holding "that the *Qurʾān* is God's speech and is uncreated, and that He will be visible on the day of resurrection..." and goes on to say that "they do not differ on these *ʾuṣūl*", i.e., on these basic doctrines (*Taʾwīl*, p. 14, 17–20; see also *ibid.*, p. 14, 2). So too Ibn Fūrak speaks of the "*ʾuṣūl* which are the universals which embrace the doctrine of God's unicity and the *Sunna*" (*Bayān* [1941], §11, p. 15, 10f., where "God's unicity"—*al-tawḥīd*— denotes the basic theological doctrines of Islam, not simply God's uniqueness or unity). These are commonly referred to as *ʾuṣūl al-dīn* (the basic doctrines of the [Muslim] religion), as when al-Qushayrī, at the end of his *Lumaᶜ*, a short *ᶜaqīda*, says, "These are the *ʾuṣūl al-dīn* which one has to know" (p. 63, 6). Taking "*ʾuṣūl*" in this contextually specified sense, then, the *ahl al-ʾuṣūl* are the *mutakallimīn:* they are, that is, those who study primarily the (basic) dogmas and those matters whose investigation is directly pertinent to understanding them (cf. e.g., al-Mutwallī, fol. 1v°, 13ff. and al-Juwaynī, *al-Shāmil*, p. 105, 13.). Accordingly al-Anṣārī speaks of the superiority of the "science of the *ʾuṣūl*" (i.e., of fundamental theology or *kalām*) over all the other sciences (*al-Ghunyah*, fol. 7v°, 10). Which dogmas are explicitly included among the *ʾuṣūl al-dīn* and which not may vary by author and most often simply, it would seem, on the basis of the length and detail of the tract, though the list is generally constant. Distinctions are made, in any event; as the stem (*ʾaṣl*) of a tree is contrasted to its crown (*farᶜ*) and its branches (*furūᶜ*), so the basic dogmas are termed "*al-ʾuṣūl*" in contrast to secondary, derivative or simply less important, doctrines which are called "*furūᶜ*". Ibn Qutayba, e.g., contrasts the doctrines of the existence of God and of the resurrection as *ʾuṣūl*, not to believe in which makes one an unbeliever (*kāfir*) to that of God's determination of human events (*al-qadar*), which is a *farᶜ*, a secondary doctrine concerning which Muslims may disagree (*op. cit.*, pp. 81f.; see also *ibid.*, p. 13, 17ff.). In a wider sense, finally, "*ʾuṣūl*" may refer to the (thematically presented) principles, axioms, presuppositions, and formal procedures which found and govern systematic reasoning in a given discipline, as al-Ashᶜarī speaks of "the *ʾuṣūl* universally agreed upon through rational undertanding, sense perception, and immediate intuition" (*al-Ḥathth*, §2.313, concerning which see below).

29. For the phrase "*mubtadiʾūn ḍullāl*" (also §2.1) cp. al-Barbahārī, cited below in n° 63.

30. The canonical precedent for *kalām* reasoning with regard to questions which are treated in the *Qurʾān* and the ḥadīth al-Ashᶜarī has already treated in §2.2, where the use of reasoning from creation to God was taken up as a separate question (§2.222) (cp. al-Ashᶜarī, *Lumaᶜ*, §10). One should note in this regard that in dealing with such questions, e.g., that of the contingency of the world, al-Ashᶜarī's own argumentation follows the *Qurʾān* very closely (e.g., *al-Lumaᶜ*, §3, with which cp. al-Bayhaqi, *Iᶜtiqād*, pp. 24f.), rejecting the more common *kalām* argument based on

the nature of atoms and their inherent accidents (cf. *al-Thaghr*, pp. 89f.). In this he differs from the practice of the leading Ashᶜarite masters of later generations. Note that the term *ḥādithah* (pl. *ḥawādith*), which occurs several times here would appear to have been a normal expression for new questions in both law and theology; cf. the use in abū Jaᶜfar al-Ṭabarī, "Profession", p. 193, 11 and 198, 14f. and in Ibn ᶜAqīl, *K. al-Jadal*, ed. G. Makdisi in *BEO* 20 (1967), p. 203, §6.

31. *Al-ᶜawl* is a method for adjusting the fractions assigned in the distribution of an inheritance where the normal divisions would entail a sum greater than the whole; see art., *ᶜawl* in *E.I.*².

32. This he says explicitly only with regard to the juridical questions: "new questions which arise concerning matters pertinent to religion *from the standpoint of the law*" (*min jihati l-sharīᶜah:* §2.312), but this is understood contextually as true of theological questions not explicitly raised in the canonical sources (concerning which he has noted in §2.312 that their "principles are found in the Scripture and the Sunna"). "Pertinence to religion" is mentioned explicitly only in §2.311. Al-Ashᶜarī shows reserve at this stage so as to make his major point more effectively later. Similarly he mentions *ijtihād* explicitly only in §2.312 but understands its extension also to §2.311; concerning this see below.

33. Note that in §2.311 the statement "he [the Prophet] was not ignorant of any one of them in its detail" *(lam yajhal minhā shayʾan mufaṣṣalan)* constitutes an essential presupposition of the argument. Only if the Prophet knew the question and the truth about it as well as how it could be proven does the argument hold, for if he did not, then to deal with the question could not be an element of *al-dīn*, sc., an authentic element of valid religious practice (cf. the opponent's argument in §1.22). Concerning the connotations of "*takallama*" here and the rhetorical use of the word in *al-Ḥathth*, see below.

34. "*Qiyās*" does not itself occur but as the *maṣdar* of "*qāsū*" it is understood as implicitly expressed. J. Schacht (*The Origins of Muḥammadan Jurisprudence*, Oxford, 1953, pp. 127ff.) says that the two terms, "*ijtihād*" and "*qiyās*" are basically synonymous in context and that both connotationally exclude the notion of one's following his own whim or personal preference *(al-ʾahwāʾ)*. Properly speaking, however, "*qiyās*" is narrower in extension; "*al-qiyās*" (the definite, employed to designate a particular instance) means "the (logical) rule", i.e., the rule or form to be followed in reasoning about the particular case or the application of the rule; when the term is used generally (to designate the class) it refers to logical rules (or rules of analogical reasoning) in general and their application. The Ashᶜarites, it should be noted, do not normally employ '*qiyās*' for the reasoning employed in *kalām*, but rather '*al-naẓar*'.

35. The list of questions is given in §1.12: "bodies, accidents, motion, rest, colors, the *ʾakwān*...". (The divine attributes are not pertinent to the context of §2.31). It is significant that the *ʾakwān* appear in this list to be distinguished from motion and rest. Concerning the coneption of the *ʾakwān* by the Ashᶜarites and the development of the concept in the school, see my "Bodies and Atoms", pp. 44f.

36. In §2,212 al-Ashᶜarī speaks of "*furūᶜu l-tawḥīd wal-ᶜadl*" but gives no indication of what questions he will include among them. The expression, sc., "*al-tawḥīd wal-ᶜadl*" is itself noteworthy in that it is, though certainly nor their exclusive property, characteristic of the Muᶜtazila. One suspects that its occurrence here may be based chiefly, if not entirely, on polemical grounds.

37. This is made fully explicit in the descriptive clause which T–2 adds at the end of §2.312. Al-Ashᶜarī's insistence on *ʾuṣūl* in the present context is anticipated in §1 where he speaks of "*ʾuṣūl al-dīn*" (§1.12) in outlining his opponents' attitude towards *kalām* and of "*ʾuṣūl*" at the end of §1.222 where he concludes the statement of their argument.

38. Note that when he says that these are the principles (or sources) of theoretical reasoning and so of the basis of *kalām* he does not mean to deny the place of the *Qur'ān*, the Sunna, and consensus in fundamental theology, but rather to indicate that principle which is unique in *kalām*. It is, in each discipline, this fourth "source" which allows one to employ the other "sources" coherently and validly. Accordingly he says here concerning the concrete possibility of the resurrection that what is given in the revelation is presented so as to "reinforce what is [or can be] known by speculative reasoning" (*ta'kīdan li-mā fī l-ᶜuqūl:* §2.2130). What he is doing, in short, is to specify the distinctive foundations which underlie the difference of *al-ᶜaql* as the fourth "source" of theological knowledge and judgement from *al-qiyās* as the fourth "source" of juridical judgement. The *ᶜaqliyyāt* remain fully distinct from the *samᶜiyyāt* and within their own sphere are independent; cf. the use of the phrase "what is required by speculative reasoning" *(mā qtaḍathu l-ᶜuqūl)* in *al-Thaghr*, p. 93, 22.

39. That §2.3211 and §2.3212 are subdivisions of a single unit is evident by the fact that *"Yuqālu lahum"* stands at the beginning of §2.3211 and of §2.323 but not of §2.3212, where the *" 'in qāla qā'ilun"* indicates a sub-question to the previous paragraph.

40. The comment "there is in your view no *qur'ān* apart from the syllales and the sounds" is added to point *a)* to the Ḥanbalites' stubborn refusal to make the kinds of distinctions which must be made in theology and thereby *b)* to another example of the inconsistency of their thought. Here one says that the *Qur'ān* is uncreated while at the same time identifying anything which is correctly described by '*Qur'ān*' as consisting of "syllables and sounds", which are material, contingent entities.

41. The context throughout this section assumes (both on the part of al-Ashᶜarī and of his opponent) that there is no ḥadīth from the Prophet or one of the Companions which states that the *Qur'ān* is uncreated and which is properly authenticated in terms of the usual criteria. (The H text plays this out in an elaborately built argument, which we examined earlier). No such Ḥadīth is found in any of the "Six Books" or in the *Musnad* of Ibn Ḥanbal, and this alone, within the formal framework of al-Ashᶜarī's reasoning here is sufficient to ground the assumption and so the argument too. Al-Ghazzālī in his *Iljām al-ᶜawāmm ᶜan ᶜilm al-kalām* (in the margins of al-Jīlānī, *al-Insān al-kāmil*, Cairo, 1368/1949, p. 66) alleges that the Prophet said, "The *Qur'ān* is God's speech and is uncreated" *(qawluhu ṣlᶜm al-qur'ānu kalāmu llāhi ghayru makhlūq)*. Where he might have gotten this, or whether his attribution of the formula to the Prophet is the result of enthusiasm (the *ᶜawāmm* wouldn't know!), we cannot tell. He gives no *isnād* nor any other suggestion of what might be the origin of such an ḥadīth. Al-Bayhaqī cites Ibn Dīnār as saying that the *Qur'ān* is uncreated (*Iᶜtiqād*, p. 64 and *Asmā'*, p. 245) but has no earlier authority; as he notes in connection with a similar statement from Anas b. Mālik, the issue did not arise in the first generation (*ibid.*, 243f.). There are in abū Saᶜīd al-Dārimī's *Radd ᶜalā l-Jamiyyah* (p. 88) several ḥadīths which state that the *Qur'ān* is uncreated in the same common formulation employed by al-Ghazzālī. All are reported by Muḥammad b. Manṣūr al-Ṭūsī (d. 255/869); the formulation, however, is ascribed not to the Prophet or any of the Companions but to a number of individuals all of whom died towards the end of the second century. (Ibn Manṣūr claims himself to have heard this formula directly from the Prophet in a dream during dhū l-ḥijja 232; *ibid.*, pp. 88f.) Abu Saᶜīd al-Dārimī studied ḥadīth with Ibn Ḥanbal (al-Subkī, *Ṭabaqāt* 2, p. 303 and Ibn ᶜAsākir, *cit.* Vitestam in al-Dārimī, p. 53) and was considered by some Ḥanbalites as a follower of their school (Ibn abī Yaᶜlā 1, p. 221); he was, however, a Shāfiᶜite in law, having studied *fiqh* with Yūsuf b. Yaḥyā al-Buwayḍī, a direct disciple of al-Shāfiᶜī (v. al-Subkī 2, pp. 162f.): see the notice on al-Dārimī, *ibid.*, pp. 302f.

42. To my knowledge none of the so-called Wāqifa (or Mutawaqqifa) held that those who teach that the *Qur'ān* is created should be called (or considered as) unbelievers. The issue is introduced as a juridical matter correlated to the question of the createdness of the *Qur'ān* and for this reason is appropriately introduced here at the end of §2.321 in anticipation of its formal treatment in §2.323.

43. The text here (T–1) does not consider the alternative of a positive reply, since the Ḥanbalite opponent's response is determined by the school's practice. (The alternative will be given as the author's position in §2.331). As we noted earlier, T–2 does introduce two paragraphs here (the second forming the beginning of what is §2.323 of T–1) in which the affirmative reply is considered, though this is contextually unnecessary. It is possible, to be sure, that something other than (or more than) a simple "*lā*" has been lost in A following *'in qālū*, but this would seem unlikely. One might, on the other hand, conjecturally suggest that the text is correct as it stands and is to be interpreted, "If they reply [i.e., if they give any reply whatsoever], then one says to them...". This is theoretically coherent and grammatically possible, but would be highly unusual; I know of no parallel for such a form and should think its occurrence most improbable, especially since 'qālū' expects a direct quotation.

44. The expression "does not befit" (*lā yalīqu, ghayru lā'iq,* etc.) is extremely common in Ashʿarite writings in contexts such as this. Cf., e.g., abū l-Ḥasan al-Ṭabarī, *Ta'wīl,* foll. 147v°, 10 and 118r°, 5; Ibn Fūrak (1943), pp. 76, 12 and 15, 79, 6f., 91, 8, *et alibi passim;* and also al-Bayhaqī, *al-Asmā',* p. 459, 21.

45. Concerning the ambivalence of "*kaffara*" here see the discussion of §2.232 above where the differences between T–1 and T–2 were treated.

46. That the terms "*bidʿah*" and "*ḍalālah*" are evoked by allusion to an earlier passage see above.

47. With this cp. the formulation of al-Barbahārī in Ibn abī Yaʿlā 2, p. 19; 17 cited in n° 63 below.

48. This second premise (or antecedent) is neither explicitly stated nor argued since by their very practice the Ḥanbalites acknowledge it.

49. Note that for al-Ashʿarī the function and purpose of *kalām* is not, in this instance, apologetic. With this compare the statement of abū Jaʿfar al-Ṭabarī ("Profession" p. 193) that the learned should enlighten the ignorant with regard to religious truths by means of knowledge which they have achieved "either through a ḥadīth or some systematic reasoning" (*bi-ḥadīthin 'aw bi-naẓarin).* Similarly, abū Saʿīd al-Dārimī, though very much a traditionalist in spirit, is not opposed to *kalām;* with regard to the Jahmiyya he says, for example, "*wa-ʿalayhim ḥujajun kathīratun mina l-kalāmi wal-naẓar*" (*Radd,* p. 82, 12).

50. It should be noted that the attitude of Ibn Ḥanbal and most of his followers towards *kalām* is altogether different from that of al-Ghazālī. The former was hardened in the crucible of the *miḥna* which was brought on by *kalām* (at least in the eyes of Ibn Ḥanbal). Al-Ghazzalī, by contrast, simply lost his confidence in the value of speculative theology, partially on theoretical grounds and partially, no doubt, in reaction to the success of the philosophically elaborated religious propaganda of the extreme Shīʿa. Generally speaking, al-Ghazzālī seems to have looked upon *kalām* as a more purely rational (more exclusively self-grounding) theology than it was, or had been, for most of the Ashʿarites; having lost confidence in the demonstrative certainty of human reasoning regarding the basic theological doctrines he had to give up any notion of the primary value of *kalām*. Consistently then, he felt that though incapable of demonstrating the trugh of the basic religious dogmas of Islam, *kalām* can

nonetheless demonstrate the error of some counter theses or, at least, the inconclusiveness of te reasoning used to support them. (Note that within this framework *al-Tahāfut* can only be considered a *kalām* work; that philosophers read it and wrote against it does not make it something it wasn't originally). Unable to achieve the degree of cognitive certitude (*^cilm yaqīn*) he desired by rational inference (*iktisāban*), he concluded that it has to be attained without inference as *^cilm ḍarūrī* (sc., *kashfī*).

51. "*Shaykhun dhū... ^cilmin wa-fiqh*"; note the multiple connotations of "*^cilm*" and "*fiqh*" in this context.

52. *Al-Aghānī* 8 (Beyrouth, 1948), pp. 224f.

53. ^cAbd al-Jabbār, *Faḍl al-i^ctizāl*, p. 307, 9–11.

54. Ibn al-Qifṭī, *Anbāh* 2, p. 348, 3f.

55. *Kitāb al-awsaṭ*, in J. van Ess, *Frühe mu^ctazilische Häresiographie* (Beyrouth, 1971), §204. Van Ess translates "dannn würde sie gesammelt und theoretisch begründet" (p. 116).

56. Ibn al-Qifṭī, *op. cit.* 1, p. 250.

57. Concerning formal disputations see van Ess, "Disputationspraxis in der islamischen Theologie, eine vorläufige Skizze", *REI* 44 (1976), pp. 24–60.

58. In none of these examples does '*kalām*' or '*kallama, yatakallamu*' specifically denote or refer to a discipline, i.e., to that theological discipline which is distinguished from *fiḳh*, etc. The same is true also of the ensuing instances. In (6) and (7) the terms signify the expression of one's reflected consideration or view concerning the topic referred to, while (8) and (9), because of the preposition, signify the urging of a position or doctrine upon those who are addressed. In (10) "*al-kalām*" signifies speculative discussion, but again does not name, save by contextual implication or allusion, the discipline of the *mutakallimīn*. In these and similar cases, thus, '*al-kalām*' and '*kallama, yatakallamu*' may be seen as general expressions employed to designate and describe an acitivity which is carried on in various modes and to various ends and which, accordingly, may be viewed in diverse ways, depending on the context of the discourse and the perspective of the primary voice. It is an activity (*the* activity) which, in its various modes (reflection, inquiry, exposition, discusssion, debate, dispute or disputation), is characteristic of the larger practice and exercise of "the science of *kalām*," "*al-naẓaru wal-baḥthu ^cani l-dīn*: §1.10). The semantic range of '*kallama, yatakallamu*' in the examples we have cited is closely parallel to that of Greek ' διαλογίζομαι ' and similarly the range of '*al-kalām*' in these and analogous instances parallels that of ' διαλογισμός ' as used in both pagan and in Patristic texts. (Cp. also the occurrences of ' διαλογισμός ' in the New Testament). With this one may also compare the uses of '*disputatio*' and '*disputare*' in medieval Latin where the earlier use is more of reflection or thinking than of disputing over "*quaestiones*" (see H. de Lubac, *Exégèse médiévale* I/1, Paris, 1959, pp. 88ff.). Even though '*al-kalām*' has beeen associated with ' διάλεξις ' there is no more probable ground to seek for a "calque" in the use of '*kalām*' as the name for Muslim theology than there is to look for such behind the use of '*fiqh*' and '*naḥw*' as the names of disciplines. For other examples of '*takallama, yatakallamu*', etc., in religious contexts in early Muslim contexts, see J. van Ess, "The Beginnings of Islamic Theology" in J.E. Murdoch ad E.D. Sylla (eds.), *The Cultural Context of Medieval Learning* (Dortrecht, 1975), pp. 87ff. A.Pines in his "A Note on an Early Meaning of the Term *Mutakallim*", *IOS* 1 (1971) pp. 244ff. suggests that in the beginning the *mutakallimin* were basically and essentially religious propagandists and public disputants, the institutional champions of Islam. In this he follows the line laid out by al-Fārābī, which, he suggests, "springs from his knowledge of the history and original nature and function of

the *mutakallimīn*" (p. 228). Here, however, he seems not only to ignore the self-serving character of al-Fārābī's construction of the nature and role of *kalām* within the hierarchy of disciplines, but also to oversimplify the historical situation, even as it is witnessed in the sources he cites. Disputations were staged in the ʿAbbasid court and elsewhere (often in the homes of scholars) on almost all subjects, including grammar; and it was the material subject to be debated which determined who should participate. That is, before one could rightly and appropriately be called upon to serve as a participant in a public disputation he had, in principle at least, to be an expert in the particular subject. Before becoming a disputant in a theological debate one had first to be a theologian (or at least, presumably, competent in the subject). Abū Saʿīd al-Sīrāfī enters the debate with abū Bishr Mattā concerning *manṭiq* precisely because he is an expert in grammar and language, which is what abū Bishr and his fellow logicians claimed to have surpassing knowledge about. A far better indication of the nature of *kalām* and of its function within the historical context, whether seen by its proponents or by its opponents, is presented in al-Ashʿarī's *al-Ḥathth* than in the writings of al-Fārābī.

59. Ibn abī Yaʿlā, *Ṭabaqāt* 2, pp. 18f.

60. *Ibāna*, p. 27, 3–5: *thumma takallama abū ʿAbdillāhi mustaʿẓiman lil-shakki fī dhālika.*

61. *K. al-Ṭabaqāt al-kabīr* (ed. E. Sachaw, Leiden, 1917) 1, p. 146, 19. One or the other of these two is said to have been the first to pledge allegiance to the Prophet at ʿAqaba prior to the Hegira; see Ibn Hishām, *al-Sīra* (ed. M. al-Saqā, *et al.*, Cairo, 1355/1936) 2, p. 89

62. Ibn abī Yaʿlā, *Ṭabaqāt* 2. pp. 33, 4–6.

63. *Ibid.*, p. 19, 17–19; with the expression *bidʿatun wa-ḍalālah*, cp. *al-Ḥathth* §1.12 and with *takallama wa-bayyana* here cp. *al-Ḥathth* §1.21 and 2.314.

64. One has here, of course, to pay attention to the contextual connotations. The Prophet does not put forth his *own* (i.e., private) teaching, but that of God; the Companions, where they do not cite the Prophet, are understood to speak in conformity with that which they have learned from the Prophet and thus do not express merely their private views. Ibn Ḥanbal in (7) implicitly argues his own view, but again, he would insist, as conforming strictly to that of the Prophet and the Companions; he does not, that is, claim to go beyond what is given in the *Qurʾan* and the Sunna. So too, "the learned" of (6) are understood to belong to the ahl al-ḥadīth.

65. Note that the deictive '*hā-*' of this form gives it an almost contemptuous resonance in the context. T–2 here continues the second person address of §2.332 and thereby vitiates somewhat the rhetorical force of the section.

66. Note the juridical connotations of "*ḥujjah*" and "*burhān*" here.

67. That the text is to be understood thus is confirmed by the occurrence of Ibn Ḥanbal's name at the head of the sequence of authorities in T–2's version of §2.323. Cf. also the statement of al-Barbahārī, "We only recognise what has been said by abū ʿAbdallāh Aḥmad ibn Ḥanbal", cited in Ibn abī Yaʿlā 2, p. 18, 15.

68. Note that Ibn Ḥanbal is cited several times in the first section of al-Ashʿarī's *Ibāna* and is thereby recognised as an authority whose teaching is valid. That the tract was not read as an unqualified condemnation of the tradition and of the traditionists as a whole is apparent from the occurence of Ibn al-Ukhuwwa, abū l-Maʿālī al-Mawṣilī, Ibn abī l-Ḥusayn al-Rashīd al-ʿAṭṭār, and abū l-Qāsim Saḥnūn in the isnad of F.

69. Ibn Ḥanbal's name does not appear in this list of jurists since he is implictly included in the "you" of "*yalzamukum ʾan taḥkumū*". One understands, nonetheless, that if Mālik, etc., are guilty of innovation, then Ibn Ḥanbal is guilty of analogous innovations in the instances cited.

70. The copyist has simply repeated the colophons from the exemplars he copied without noting the date of his own work. That for *al-Ḥathth* is, as we noted earlier, Rabiᶜ I 677; that for the preceding tract (Ibn Ḥajar al-ᶜAsqalānī's *Bulūgh al-marām fī adillat al-aḥkām*, ending fol. 49r°) is 1063/1653.

71. For the remainder of this up to the beginning of the text itself see the Hyderabad edition.

REFERENCES

ᶜAbd al-Jabbār: *Faḍl al-iᶜtizāl*, ed. F. Sayyid, Tunis, 1393/1974

al-Anṣārī: *al-Ghunya fī l-kalām*, MS III Ahmet n° 1916

al-Ashᶜarī: *al-Ḥathth:* the text here published
al-Ibāna ᶜan uṣūl al-diyāna, Cairo, 1348/1957
al-Lumaᶜ, published in McCarthy, *Theology*
Risāla ilā ahl al-thaghr, in *Ilahiyat Fakültesi Mecmuasi* 8 (1929) pp. 80–108.

al-Bāqillānī: *al-Hidāya*, MS al-Azhar n° (21) 242.
al-Tamhīd, ed. R. McCarthy, Beyrouth, 1957

al-Bayhaqī: *al-Asmāʾ wal-ṣifāt*, Cairo, 1358
al-Iᶜtiqād wal-hidāya, Beyrouth, 1403/1983

al-Dārimī: *al-Radd ᶜalā l-Jahmiyya*, ed. G. Vitestam, Lund/Leiden, 1960

al-Dhahabī: *Maᶜrifat al-qurrāʾ al-kibār*, ed. M. Jād al-Ḥaqq, Cairo, 1969
Mizān al-iᶜtidāl, 3 vol's, Cairo, 1325

Ibn abī Yaᶜlā: *Ṭabaqāt al-Ḥanābila*, 2 vol's, Cairo, 1371/1952

Ibn ᶜAsākir: *Tabyīn kadhib al-muftarī*, Damascus, 1347

Ibn Farḥūn: *al-Dībāj al-mudhahhab*, Cairo, 1351

Ibn Fūrak: *Bayān taʾwīl mushkil al-aḥādīth, Auswahl nach den Handschriften in Leipzig, Leiden, London und dem Vatikan*, ed. R. Köbert, Rome 1941
Bayān taʾwīl mushkil al-ḥadīth, Hyderabad, 1943

Ibn al-Qifṭī: *Anbāh al-ruwāh*, ed. M. Ibrāhīm, 4 vol's, Cairo, 1050–1973

Ibn Qutayba: *Ta'wīl mushkil al-ḥadīth*, reprint, Beyrouth, n.d.

al-Juwaynī: *al-Irshād*, ed. A. ᶜAbd al-Ḥamīd, Cairo, 1950
al-Shāmil, ed. A. S. al-Nashār, Alexandria, 1969

al-Mutawallī: *al-Mughnī fī 'uṣūl al-dīn*, MS al-Baladiyya, n° 2014D/1

Q.: *al-Qur'ān al-karīm*

al-Qushayrī: *Lumaᶜ fī l-iᶜtiqād*, ed. R. Frank, in *MIDEO* 15 (1982), pp. 59-63

al-Subkī: *Ṭabaqāt al-shāfiᶜiyya al-kubrā*, 10 vol's, Cairo, 1964–76

al-Suyūṭī: *Ṭabaqāt al-ḥuffāẓ*, Beyrouth, 1403/1983

al-Ṭabarī, abū l-Ḥasan: *Ta'wīl mushkil al-āyāt*, MS Ṭalᶜat, maj. n° 491, foll. 108r°–162v°

al-Ṭabarī, abū Jaᶜfar: «Profession», a short theological work published in Sourdel

al-Tinbuktī: *Nayl al-ibtihāj*, in margins of Ibn Farḥūn

Frank, R.M.: *Beings and their Attributes*, Albany 1978
«Bodies and Atoms, the Ashᶜarite Analysis» in M. Marmura (ed.), *Islamic Theology and Philosophy: Studies in Honor of George F. Hourani*, Albany, 1984

McCarthy, Richard: *The Theology of al-Ashᶜarī*, Beyrouth, 1953

Makdisi, George: «Ashᶜari and the Ashᶜarites in Islamic Religious History» pt. 1, *Studia Islamica* 17 (1962) pp. 37–80, pt. 2, *ibid.* 18 (1963), pp. 19–39

Sourdel, Dominique: «Une Profession de foi de l'historien al-Ṭabarī», in *REI* 36 (1968) pp. 177–199

كتاب الحث على البحث
للشيخ ابي الحسن علي بن اسمٰعيل الأشعري

A 9r°

بسم الله الرحمن الرحيم[١] B 4v°

F 49v°

1.10 إن طائفة[٢] من الناس جعلوا الجهل رأس مالهم وثقل عليهم النظر والبحث عن الدين.

1.11 ومالوا إلى[٣] التقليد.

1.12 وطعنوا على من فتّش عن أصول الدين ونسبوه إلى الضلال فزعموا[٤] أن الكلام في الجسم والعرض والحركة والسكون[٥] والألوان والأكوان والجزء والطفرة وصفات البائ تعالى[٦] بدعة وضلالة.

1.21 قالوا[٧]: لو كان ذلك[٨] هدى ورشدًا[٩] لتكلم فيه النبيء عليه السلام[١٠] وخلفاؤه وأصحابه. قالوا ولأن النبيّ عليه السلام[١٠] لم يمت حتى تكلم في كل ما يحتاج إليه في[١١] أمور الدين وبيّنه بيانًا شافيًا ولم يترك لأحد من بعده[١٢] مقالاً فيما بالمسلمين[١٣] إليه حاجة[١٤] من أمور دينهم[١٥].

فلما لم يرو[١٦] عنه الكلام في شيء مما ذكرناه[١٧] علمنا أن الكلام فيه بدعة والبحث عنه ضلالة، لأنه لو كان فيه خير[١٨] لما فات النبيّ ﷺ وأصحابه[١٩] ولتكلموا فيه[٢٠].

(١) في اختلاف أوائل المخطوطات أنظر ما تقدم في وصفها؛ – (٢) إن طائفة ا: فإن طائفة ح ف. إن قوما ب؛ – (٣) + التخفيف و ب ح ف؛ – (٤) فزعموا ا ب: وزعموا ح ف؛ – (٥) الجسم والعرض والحركة والسكون ا: الحركة والسكون والجسم والعرض ب ح ف؛ – (٦) تعالى ا: عز وجل ب ح ف؛ – (٧) قالوا ا: وقالوا ب ح ف؛ – (٨) ذلك > ب؛ – (٩) ورشدًا ا: ورشد ب. ورشادًا ح ف؛ – (١٠) عليه السلام ا: صلّى الله عليه [+ واله ح] وسلّم ب ح ف؛ – (١١) في ا: من ب ح ف؛ – (١٢) لأحد من بعده ا: لأحد بعده ب. بعده لأحد ح ف؛ – (١٣) بالمسلمين ا ب: للمسلمين ح ف؛ – (١٤) إليه حاجة ا ح ف: حاجة إليه ب؛ – (١٥) + وما يقربهم إلى الله [+ عز وجل ح ف] ويباعدهم عن سخطه ب ح ف؛ – (١٦) يرو ب ف: يرد ا. يرووا ح؛ – (١٧) ذكرناه ا ح ف: ذكرنا ب؛ – (١٨) فيه خير ا: في ذلك خير ب. خيرا ح ف؛ – (١٩) وسلّم وأصحابه ا. ب. ف: وأصحابه وسلم ح؛ – (٢٠) فيه > ب؛ – (٢١) + أحد ب؛ – (٢٢) نحن

1.220	قالوا : ولأنه ليس يخلو ذلك من وجهين :	قالوا : ولأنه ليس يخلو ذلك من[٢١] وجهين : إما أن يكونوا علموه فسكتوا عنه او لم يعلموه بل جهلوه.
1.221	إما أن يكونوا [أ : ٩ ظ] علموه فسكتوا عنه ، فكذلك يجوز لنا السكوت عنه ولأنه لو كان من الدين لما وسعهم السكوت عنه .	فإن كانوا علموه ولم يتكلموا فيه ، وسعنا أيضًا نحن[٢٢] السكوت عنه كما وسعهم السكوت عنه ووسعنا ترك الخوض[٢٣] ، ولأنه لو كان من الدين لما[٢٤] وسعهم السكوت عنه .
1.222	وأما إن لم يعلموه بل جهلوه ، فوسعنا جهله كما وسع أولئك جهله ، ولأنه لو كان من الدين لم يجهلوه .	وإن كانوا لم يعلموه وسعنا جهله كما وسع أولئك جهله ، لأنه لو كان من الدين لم يجهلوه . فعلى كلا الوجهين الكلام فيه بدعة والخوض فيه ضلالة .
	فهذه جملة ما تمسكوا به في ترك النظر في الأصول .	فهذه جملة ما احتجوا به في ترك النظر في الأصول[٢٥] .

2.0 والجواب[٢٦] عنه من ثلثة أوجه[٢٧] :

2.1 أحدها قلب السؤال عليهم بأن يقال لهم : فالنبيّ[٢٨] ﷺ [ف : ٥٠ و] لم يقل أيضًا[٢٩] أن من بحث عن ذلك وتكلم[٣٠] فيه فاجعلوه مبتدعًا ضالاً : فقد لزمكم أن تكونوا مبتدعة ضلالاً[٣١] بتضليلكم[٣٢] من لم يضلله النبيّ ﷺ .

2.20	الوجه الثّاني في الجواب أنّا لا نسلم أن النبيّ ﷺ وأصحابه لم يعلموا ذلك على الجملة ، وإن لم ينقل عنهم	الجواب[٣٣] الثاني أن يقال لهم : أن النبيّ ﷺ لم يجهل شيئًا مما ذكرتموه من الكلام في الجسم والعرض والحركة

> ف ؛ – (٢٣) + فيه ح ف ؛ – (٢٤) لما ب : ما ح ف ؛ – (٢٥) فهذه... الأصول ب ؛ – (٢٦) والجواب ا ب : قال الشيخ أبو الحسن رضي الله عنه والجواب ح ف ؛ – (٢٧) ثلثه أوجه ا ح ف : وجوه ثلاثة ب ؛ – (٢٨) لهم فالنبي ا ب : النبي ح . والنبي ف ؛ – (٢٩) أيضًا ف ؛ – (٣٠) وتكلم ا ح ف : أو تكلم ب ؛ – (٣١) + إذ قد تكلمتم في شيء لم يتكلم فيه النبي ﷺ ب ح ف ؛ – (٣٢) بتضليلكم ا : وضللتم ب ح ف ؛ – (٣٣) تلجواب ب ف : والجواب ح ؛ – (٣٤) إن > ف .

الكلام في احادها ؛ كيف وهذه الأشياء التي ذكرتموها معينة أصولها موجودة في القرآن والسنة جملة غير مفصلة.

والسكون والجزء والطفرة وإن[٣٤] لم يتكلم في كل أحد من ذلك معيّنًا وكـذلك[٣٥] الفقهـاء والعلمـاء مـن الصحابة غير أن هذه الأشياء التي ذكرتموها معينة أصولها موجودة في القرآن والسنة جملة[٣٦] غير مفصلة.

2.211 فقال سبحانه خبرًا عن ابراهيم عليه السّلام في قصّة أفول الكواكب وزوالها وانتقالها من مكان إلى مكان مما دلّه أن ربّه لا يجوز عليه شيء من ذلك وإن من جاز عليه الحركة والسكون والإنتقال من مكان إلى مكان فليس باله[٤٧].

فأمّا[٣٧] الحركة والسكون والكلام فيهما فأصلهما[٣٨] في القرآن[٣٩] وهما يدلان[٤٠] على التوحيد وكذلك الإجتماع والإفتراق. وذلك في قول الله تعالى[٤١] مخبرًا عن خليله إبراهيم عليه السلام[٤٢] في قصة أفول الكوكب والقمر والشمس[٤٣] وتحركها[٤٤] من مكان إلى مكان[٤٥] ما دله[٤٦] على أن ربّه عزّ وجلّ لا يجوز عليه شيء من ذلك وإنّ من جاز [ب : ٥ و] عليه الأفول والإنتقال من مكان إلى مكان فليس باله.

2.212 وأمّا الكلام في التوحيد فمأخوذ من الكتاب كما تلونا من الآيات مثل آية

وأما الكلام في أصل[٤٨] التوحيد فمأخوذ من الكتاب أيضًا[٤٩]، قال الله

وهي في الهامش ؛ – (٣٥) وكذلك ح ف : ولذلك ب ؛ – (٣٦) جملة ح ف ا : لجملة ب ؛ – (٣٧) فأما ب ف : أما ح ؛ – (٣٨) + موجود ح ف ؛ – (٣٩) + والسنة ف ؛ – (٤٠) يدلان ح ف : يدخلان ب ؛ – (٤١) وذلك في قول الله تعالى ب : قال الله تعالى ح ف ؛ – (٤٢) عليه السلام ب : صلوات الله وسلامه عليه ف. صلوات الله عليه وسلامه ح ؛ – (٤٣) القمر والشمس ب : الشمس والقمر ح ف ؛ – (٤٤) تحركها : تحركهما ب. تحريكها ح. تحريكهما ف ؛ – (٤٥) إلى مكان > ب ؛ – (٤٦) دله ب : دل ح ف ؛ – (٤٧) وبعد هذا في ا زيادة لابن القاسم الأنصاري : قلت وقوله عليه السلام لا أحب الأفلين أي لا أرتضيه فيما أطلبه وأبغيه ولا يقع به الكفاية. قال أبو الحسن رضي الله عنه ؛ – (٤٨) أصل ب : أصول ح ف ؛ – (٤٩) من الكتاب أيضًا ب : أيضًا من الكتاب ح

التمانع ومثل قوله ﴿أَمْ جَعَلُوا لِلّٰهِ شُرَكَاءَ خَلَقُوا كَخَلْقِهِ : ١٣ ، ١٦﴾ الآية.

وكذلك سائر الكلام في تفصيل فروع التوحيد والعدل إنما هو مأخوذ من القرآن.

وكذلك الكلام في جواز البعث 2.2130
واستحالته الذي قد اختلف فيه مشركو العرب ومن قبلهم من الأمم حتى تعجبوا من جواز ذلك ، فقالوا ﴿أَئِذَا مِتْنَا وَكُنَّا تُرَابًا وَعِظَامًا أَئِنَّا لَمَبْعُوثُونَ : ٣٧ ، ١٦﴾ وقالوا ﴿ذَٰلِكَ رَجْعٌ بَعِيدٌ : ٥٠ ، ٣﴾ و ﴿هَيْهَاتَ لِمَا

عز وجل[٥٠] ﴿لَوْ كَانَ فِيهِمَا آلِهَةٌ إِلَّا اللّٰهُ لَفَسَدَتَا : ٢١ ، ٢٢﴾ وهذا كلام[٥١] موجز منبّه على الحجّة بأنه واحد لا شريك له. وكلام المتكلمين في الحجاج في التوحيد بالتمانع والتغالب إنما[٥٢] مرجعه إلى هذه الآية وقوله عزّ وجلّ ﴿ما اتَّخَذَ اللّٰهُ من وَلَدٍ وَمَا كَانَ مَعَهُ من إِلٰهٍ إِذًا لَذَهَبَ كُلُّ إِلٰهٍ بِمَا خَلَقَ وَلَعَلَا بَعْضُهُمْ عَلَى بَعْضٍ : ٢٣ ، ٩١﴾ وإلى قوله تعالى[٥٣] ﴿أَمْ جَعَلُوا لِلّٰهِ شُرَكَاءَ خَلَقُوا كَخَلْقِهِ فَتَشَابَهَ الْخَلْقُ عَلَيْهِمْ : ١٣ ، ١٦﴾. وكلام المتكلمين[٥٤] في توحيد الله إنما مرجعه إلى هذه الآيات التي ذكرناها[٥٥].

وكذلك[٥٦] سائر الكلام في تفصيل فروع التوحيد والعدل إنما هو مأخوذ من القرآن.

وكذلك[٥٧] الكلام في جواز البعث واستحالته الذي[٥٨] قد اختلف فيه[٥٩] عقلاء العرب ومن قبلهم من غيرهم[٦٠] حتى تعجبوا من جواز ذلك فقالوا ﴿أَئِذَا مِتْنَا وَكُنَّا تُرَابًا ذَٰلِكَ رَجْعٌ بَعِيدٌ : ٥٠ ، ٣﴾ وقوله تعالى[٦١] ﴿هَيْهَاتَ هَيْهَاتَ لِمَا تُوعَدُونَ :

ف ؛ – (٥٠) عز وجل ب : تعالى ح ف ؛ – (٥١) كلام ب ف : الكلام ح ؛ – (٥٢) إنما ب : فإنما ح ف ؛ – (٥٣) والى قوله تعالى ب : إلى قوله عز وجل ح ف ؛ – (٥٤) + في الحجاج ح ف ؛ – (٥٥) ذكرناها ح ف : ذكرنا ب ؛ – (٥٦) وكذلك ب ح : فكذلك ف ؛ – (٥٧) وكذلك ب : فكذلك ح ف ؛ – (٥٨) الذي > ب ؛ – (٥٩) اختلف فيه : اختلفت فيه ب. اختلف ح ف ؛ – (٦٠) + فيه ح ف ؛ – (٦١) وقوله تعالى ب : وقولهم ح ف ؛ – (٦٢) وقوله ب ف : وقولهم ح ؛ +

تُوعَدُونَ : ٢٣ ، ٣٦ ﴾ و﴿ مَنْ يُحْيِي الْعِظَامَ وَهِيَ رَمِيمٌ ٣٦ ، ٧٨ ﴾ ونحو هذه الشبه.

فورد في القرآن الدلالة على جوازه تأكيدًا لجواز ذلك من العقول. وعلّم الله نبيّه تثبيت الحجاج عليهم في أنكادهم البعث من وجهين على طائفتين منهم ، طائفة أقرّت بالخلق الأول وأنكرت الثاني وطائفة جحدت ذلك وقالت بقدم العالم.

٢٣ ، ٣٦ ﴾ وقوله[٦٢] ﴿ مَنْ يُحْيِي الْعِظَامَ وَهِيَ رَمِيمٌ : ٣٦ ، ٧٨ ﴾ وقوله تعالى ﴿ أَيَعِدُكُمْ أَنَّكُمْ إِذَا مِتُّمْ وَكُنْتُمْ تُرَابًا وَعِظَامًا أَنَّكُمْ مُخْرَجُونَ : ٢٣ ، ٣٥ ﴾ ونحو[٦٣] هذا الكلام منهم الذي اخبر الله تعالى[٦٤] به عنهم[٦٥].

وإنما ورد الحجاج[٦٦] في جواز البعث بعد الموت في القرآن[٦٧] تأكيدًا لجواز ذلك في العقول. وعلّم الله تعالى[٦٨] نبيّه عليه السلام[٦٩] وأمته[٧٠] الحجاج عليهم في إنكارهم البعث من وجهين على طائفتين ، طائفة اقرّت بالخلق الأول وأنكرت الثاني وطائفة جحدت ذلك[٧١] وقالت[٧٢] بقدم العالم.

2.2131 فاحتجّ على المقرّ منهما[٧٣] بإلحاق الأول بقوله تعالى[٧٤] ﴿ قُلْ يُحْيِيهَا الَّذِي أَنْشَأَهَا أَوَّلَ مَرَّةٍ : ٣٦ ، ٧٩ ﴾ وقوله[٧٥] ﴿ وَهُوَ الَّذِي يَبْدَأُ الْخَلْقَ ثُمَّ يُعِيدُهُ وَهُوَ أَهْوَنُ عَلَيْهِ : ٣٠ ، ٢٧ ﴾ وغير ذلك من نظيره[٧٦] فنبّههم بهذه الآيات على أن من قدر على[٧٧] أن يفعل فعلاً لا على[٧٨] مثال سبق[٧٩] فهو أقدر على[٨٠] أن يفعل فعلاً محتذيًا[٨١] وهو[٨٢] أهون فيه فيما بينكم وتعارفكم.

تعالى ب ؛ – (٦٣) ونحو: في نحو ب ف : وفي نحو ح ؛ – (٦٤) تعالى : متكررة في ب ؛ – (٦٥) الذي... عنهم > ح ف (ولعله قد سقط من الأصل من أجل تكرار «نهم») ؛ – (٦٦) وإنما ورد الحجاج ب : إنما ورد بالحجاج ح ف ؛ – (٦٧) + العظيم على ذلك وألزمهم بذلك في كتابه العزيز ب ؛ – (٦٨) الله تعالى > ح ف ؛ – (٦٩) عليه السلام ب : ﷺ ح ف ؛ – (٧٠) وامته ب : ولقنه ح ف ؛ – (٧١) ذلك > ب ؛ – (٧٢) وقالت > ح ؛ – (٧٣) منهما ا ب : منها ف ح ؛ – (٧٤) تعالى > ح ف ؛ – (٧٥) وقوله ا : وبقوله ب ح ف ؛ – (٧٦) وغير ذلك من نظيره ا : وبقوله كما بداكم تعودون ب ح ف ؛ – (٧٧) على > ب ح ف ؛ – (٧٨) لا على ا : على ب. على غير ح ف ؛ – (٧٩) سبق ا : سابق ح. وكاتب ب قد كتب «سابق» أولا ثم شطبها فكتب «سبق» ، > ف ؛ – (٨٠) على > ب ح ف ؛ – (٨١) محتذيًا ا ب : محدثًا ح. متحذيًا ف ؛ – (٨٢) وهو ا : فهو

ثم قال ﴿وَلَهُ الْمَثَلُ الْأَعْلَى : ٣٠ ، ٢٧﴾ الآية ، أي فليس خلق شيء بأهون عليه من خلق الآخر.

وقال ﴿أَوَ لَيْسَ الَّذِي خَلَقَ السَّمَوَاتِ وَالْأَرْضَ بِقَادِرٍ عَلَى أَنْ يَخْلُقَ مِثْلَهُمْ : ٣٦ ، ٨١﴾ وقال ﴿لَخَلْقُ ٱلسَّمَوَاتِ وَٱلْأَرْضِ أَكْبَرُ مِنْ خَلْقِ النَّاسِ : ٤٠ ، ٥٧﴾.

وأما[٨٣] البارئ تعالى[٨٤] فليس خلق شيء بأهون عليه من الآخر.

وقد قيل إن الهاء في «عليه»[٨٥] إنما هي كناية عائدة إلى الخلق[٨٦] ، تقديره[٨٧] إن البعث والإعادة أهون على أحدكم وأخفّ عليه من إبتداء خلقه لأن ابتداء خلقه إنما يكون بالولادة والتربية وقطع السرة والقماط وخروج الأسنان وغير ذلك من الآيات الموجعة المؤلمة وإعادته إنما تكون[٨٨] دفعة واحدة ، ليس فيها شيء من ذلك[٨٩] فهو أهون عليه من ابتدائه.

فهذا ما أحتج به على [ف : ٥٠ ظ] الطائفة المقرّة بالخلق الأول.

2.2132 وأما الطائفة الثانية حيث قالت بقدم العالم وأنكرت الخلق الأول والثاني[٩٠] [ب : ٥ ظ] فشبهتهم أن[٩١] قالوا : وجدنا[٩٢] الحيوة رطبة حارة[٩٣] والموت باردًا يابسًا من[٩٤] طبع التراب ، فكيف يجوز أن يجمع بين[٩٥] الحيوة والتراب والعظام النخرة فيصير خلقًا سويًا ، والضدّان لا يجتمعان. فأنكروا البعث من هذه الجهة. ولعمري

ب ح ف ؛ – **(٨٣)** وأما ب ح : فأما ف ؛ – **(٨٤)** تعالى ب : جل ثناوه وتقدست أسماؤه ح ف ؛ – **(٨٥)** عليه ب ح : أهون عليه ف ؛ – **(٨٦)** عائدة إلى الخلق ب : للخلق ح ف ؛ – **(٨٧)** تقديره ب : بقدرته ح ف ؛ – **(٨٨)** تكون ح ف : يكون ب ؛ – **(٨٩)** شيء من ذلك ب : من ذلك شيء ح ف ؛ – **(٩٠)** الثانية... الثاني ا : التي أنكرت الخلق الأول والثاني وقالت بقدم العالم ب ح ف ؛ – **(٩١)** فشبهتهم أن ا : فإنما دخلت عليهم شبهة بأن ب ح ف ؛ – **(٩٢)** + أبانا ا وقد شطبها الكاتب ؛ – **(٩٣)** رطبة حارة ا ح ف : حارة رطبة ب ؛ – **(٩٤)** من ا : ومن ب. وهو من ح ف ؛ – **(٩٥)** بين ب ح ف : من ا ؛ – **(٩٦)** الضدان ا ب : أن الضدين ح

الضدّان[٩٦] لا يجتمعان على[٩٧] محل واحد[٩٨] ؛ بل صحّ[٩٩] وجودهما في المحلين[١٠٠] على سبيل المجاورة . وأحتج الله[١٠١] عليهم بأن قال ﴿أَلَّذِي جَعَلَ لَكُمْ مِنَ الشَّجَرِ الْأَخْضَرِ نَارًا : ٣٦ ، ٨٠﴾[١٠٢] فردّهم الله[١٠٣] في ذلك إلى ما يعرفونه ويشاهدونه من خروج النار على حرها ويبسها[١٠٤] من الشجر الأخضر على بردها ورطوبتها ؛ فجعل جواز النشأة الأولى دليلاً على جواز النشأة[١٠٥] الآخرة[١٠٦] لأنها في معناها وجعل في[١٠٧] مجاورة النار على حرّها ويبسها للشجر الأخضر على برده ورطوبته[١٠٨] دليلاً[١٠٩] على جواز مجاورة الحيوة التراب[١١٠] والعظام[١١١] وجعلها خلقًا سويًا[١١٢] .

2.221 وفي قول النبي عليه السلام «كان الله ولا شيء معه» دليل على بطلان قول من قال لا ليل [أ : ١٠ و] إلّا وقبله نهار ولا حركة إلّا وقبلها سكون .

وفي قوله عليه السّلام «لا عدوى ولا طيرة» وفي جوابه للأعرابي «فمن

وأما ما يتكلم به المتكلمون من أن للحوادث[١١٣] اولا وردهم على الدهرية في[١١٤] أنه لا حركة إلّا وقبلها حركة ولا يوم إلّا وقبله يوم والكلام على من قال ما من جزء إلّا وله نصف لا إلى غاية فقد وجدنا اصل[١١٥] ذلك في سنّة رسول الله ﷺ حين قال «لا عدوى ولا طيرة» ، فقال أعرابيّ «فما

ف ؛ – (٩٧) على ا : في ب ح ف ؛ – (٩٨) + ولا على الجملة ولا في الوجود ولا في محل ب : ولا في جهة واحدة ولا في الموجود في المحل ح . ولا على الجملة ولا في الموجود ولا في المحل ف ؛ – (٩٩) بل صح ا : ولكن يصح ب . ولكنه يصح ح ف ؛ – (١٠٠) في المحلين ا ب (وكاتب ب قد كتب أولا حرف «على» ثم شطبها فكتب «في محل») ، في محلين ح ف ؛ – (١٠١) واحتج الله ا : فاحتج الله ب ح ف . + تعالى ح ؛ – (١٠٢) + فإذا أنتم منه توقدون ب ح ف ؛ – (١٠٣) + تعالى ب . عز وجل ح ف ؛ – (١٠٤) + للشجر الأخضر على برودته ورطوبته دليلاة على حرها ويبسها ب ؛ – (١٠٥) الأولى ... جواز النشأة > ب (لأجل تكرار «جواز النشاة») ؛ – (١٠٦) + مثلها ب ؛ – (١٠٧) في > ب ؛ – (١٠٨) في معناها ... ورطوبته > ح ف ؛ – (١٠٩) دليلاً ا ب : دليل ح ف ؛ – (١١٠) التراب ا ح ف : للتراب ب ؛ – (١١١) + النخرة ب ح ف ؛ – (١١٢) سويا + [وقال ح] كما بدأنا أول خلق نعيده (٢١ ، ١٠٤) ب ح ف ؛ – (١١٣) للحوادث ب : الحوادث ح ف (وقال محقق ح إن بعد أو لا بياضًا في النسخة) ؛ – (١١٤) في > ح ف ؛ – (١١٥) أصل > في نصر ف وهي في

أعدى الأول؟» دليل على ما قلناه.

بال الإبل كأنها الظبياء يدخل فيها الجمل الأجرب فيجر بها؟[١١٦]» فقال النبي ﷺ «فمن أعـــدو الأول؟» فسكت الأعرابي لما أفحمه[١١٧] بالحجة المعقولة.

ولو كان الأمر على ما قالوا من أنه لا حركة إلّا وقبلها حركة لاستحال حدوث واحدٍ منهما لأن ما لا نهاية له لا حدوث له.

فكذلك[١١٨] نقول[١١٩] لمن زعم أنه لا حركة إلّا وقبلها حركة لو كان الأمر هكذا لم يحدث[١٢٠] منها واحدة لأن ما لا نهاية له لا حدوث[١٢١] له.

2.222 وكذلك لما قال الأعرابي[١٢٢] إن امرأتي ولدت غلامًا أسود وغرض[١٢٣] بنفيه، فقال عليه السّلام[١٢٤] له هل لك من إبل؟ فقال نعم. قال فما ألوانها؟ فقال[١٢٥] حمر. فقال عليه السلام[١٢٦] هل منهما[١٢٧] من أورق؟ قال نعم إن فيها أورق[١٢٨]. قال فأنّى تراه[١٢٩] ذلك؟ قال لعل عرقًا نزعه. فقال عليه السلام لعل[١٣٠] ولدك نزعه عرق.

فهذا ما علمه الرسول عليه السّلام[١٣١] من رد الشيء إلى شكله ونظيره فهذا[١٣٢] أصل لنا في سائر ما يحكم[١٣٣] به من الشبه[١٣٤] والنظير. ولذلك[١٣٥] نحتج[١٣٦] على من قال إن الله[١٣٧] يشبه المخلوقات[١٣٨] وهو جسم بأن نقول[١٣٩] له لو كان يشبه شيئًا من الأشياء لكان لا يخلو إما[١٤٠] أن يشبهه من جميع جهاته[١٤١] أو يشبهه من بعض

هامشه؛ – (١١٦) يدخل فيها... فيجربها ب: تدخل في الإبل الجربي فتجرب ح ف؛ – (١١٧) أفحمه ب ف: أفهمه ح؛ – (١١٨) فكذلك ب: وكذلك ح ف؛ – (١١٩) نقول > ب؛ – (١٢٠) يحدث ب: تحدث ح ف؛ – (١٢١) حدوث ب: حدث ح ف؛ – (١٢٢) الإعرابي ا: الرجل يا نبي الله ب ح ف؛ – (١٢٣) غرض ا: عرض ف. عرّض ب ح؛ – (١٢٤) عليه السلام له ا: [له ب] النبي ﷺ ب ح ف؛ – (١٢٥) فقال ا: قال ب ح ف؛ – (١٢٦) عليه السلام ا: النبي [رسول الله ف] ﷺ ب ح ف؛ – (١٢٧) منها ا: فيها ب ح ف؛ – (١٢٨) أورق ا ب ح: وُرقًا ف؛ – (١٢٩) تراه > ب ح ف؛ – (١٣٠) عليه السلام لعل ا: النبي ﷺ ولعل ب ح ف؛ – (١٣١) علمه الرسول عليه السلام ا: علمه [علم ح] الله نبيه [ﷺ ب] ب ح ف؛ – (١٣٢) فهذا ا: فهو ب. وهو ح ف؛ – (١٣٣) يحكم ب: حكم ا. نحكم ح ف؛ – (١٣٤) الشبه ا ب: الشبيه ح ف؛ – (١٣٥) ولذلك ا: وبذلك ب. وبذلك ح ف؛ – (١٣٦) نحتج ا ح ف: يحتج ب؛ – (١٣٧) + تعالى وتقدس ح ف؛ – (١٣٨) المخلوقات ا ح ف: المخلوقين ب؛ – (١٣٩) نقول ا ح ف: يقول ب؛ – (١٤٠) أما ا: من ب ح ف؛ – (١٤١) جميع جهاته ا: كل جهة ب. كل

جهاته ؛ فإن كان يشبهه من جميع[١٤٢] جهاته وجب أن يكون محدثًا من كل جهاته ، وإن كان يشبهه من بعض جهاته وجب أن يكون[١٤٣] محدثًا[١٤٤] من حيث أشبهه[١٤٥] ، لأن كل مشتبهين حكمهما واحد فيما اشتبها فيه[١٤٦] ويستحيل أن يكون المحدث[١٤٧] قديمًا والقديم محدثًا[١٤٨].

2.223 وأما قولنا أن للجسم نهاية وأن الجزء لا ينقسم فدليل ذلك من التنزيل قوله تعالى ﴿كُلَّ شَيْءٍ أَحْصَيْنَاهُ فِي إِمَامٍ مُبِينٍ : ٣٦ ، ١٢﴾ وقوله ﴿أَحْصَى كُلَّ شَيْءٍ عَدَدًا : ٧٢ ، ٢٨﴾ ويستحيل إحصاء ما لا يتناهى وما لا نهاية له.

وأما الأصل بأن للجسم نهاية وأن الجزء لا ينقسم فقوله[١٤٩] عز وجل[١٥٠] ﴿وَأَحْصَى كُلَّ شَيْءٍ عَدَدًا﴾ وقوله[١٥١] ﴿وَكُلَّ شَيْءٍ أَحْصَيْنَاهُ فِي إِمَامٍ مُبِينٍ﴾. ومحال إحصاء ما لا نهاية له ومحال أن يكون الشيء الواحد ينقسم[١٥٢] لأن هذا[١٥٣] يوجب[١٥٤] أن يكون[١٥٥] شيئين. وقد خبّر[١٥٦] أن العدد وقع عليها[١٥٧].

2.224 ومن الدليل على أن الخالق هو من يتأتى المخلوقات منه على حسب قصده. وأما من يكون مقدوره واقعًا على خلاف قصده أو دون قصده

وأما الأصل في أن المحدث[١٥٩] يجب أن يتأتى له[١٦٠] الفعل على حسب[١٦١] قصده[١٦٢] وينتفي عند[١٦٣] كراهته[١٦٤] فقوله[١٦٥] تعالى ﴿أَفَرَأَيْتُمْ

جهاته ح ف ؛ – **(١٤٢)** جميع ا : كل ب ح ف (قارن لمع الأشعري ، # ٧) ؛ – **(١٤٣)** محدثًا من كل ... يكون > ا ؛ – **(١٤٤)** + مثلها ب ف : مثله ح (قارن لمع الأشعري ، # ٧) ؛ – **(١٤٥)** اشبهه ا ح ف : اشبهها ب. (قارن لمع الأشعري ، # ٧) ؛ – **(١٤٦)** اشتبها فيه ا : اشتبها له ح ف ، اشبهها له وقديمًا من حيث خالفها ب ؛ – **(١٤٧)** يكون المحدث ا ح ف : تكون المحدثات ب ؛ – **(١٤٨)** + وقد قال تعالى [+ وتقدس ح ف] ليس كمثله شيء [+ وهو السميع البصير ب] وقال [+ تعالى وتقدس ح ف] ولم يكن له كفو أحد ب ح ف ؛ – **(١٤٩)** فقوله ح ف : بقوله ب ؛ – **(١٥٠)** + اسمه ح ف : – **(١٥١)** وأحصى ... قوله > ح ف (من أجل تكرار «قوله») ؛ – **(١٥٢)** ينقسم ح ف : منقسمًا ب ؛ – **(١٥٣)** في ب بعد «هذا» بياض مقداره مقدار كلمة واحدة وقال محقق ح أن فيها بياضًا بعد «ينقسم» ؛ – **(١٥٤)** يوجب ح ف : موجب ب ؛ – **(١٥٥)** يكون ب : يكونا ح ف ؛ – **(١٥٦)** خبر ب : اخبر ح ف ؛ – **(١٥٧)** عليها ب : عليهما ح ف ؛ – **(١٥٨)** + وقلت ومن هذا القيل قوله أفرأيتم ما تحرثون أنتم تزرعون الآية ؛ – **(١٥٩)** للعالم ب ح ف. لكنها قد سقطت في مطبوع مكارثي ؛ – **(١٦٠)** له > ب ؛ – **(١٦١)** على حسب ب : نحو ح ف ؛ – **(١٦٢)** + واختياره ح ف ؛ – **(١٦٣)** ينتفي عند : ينتفي عن ب. تنتفي عن ح ف ؛ – **(١٦٤)** كراهته ب ف : كراهيته ح ؛ – **(١٦٥)** فقوله ح ف : بقوله ب ؛ – **(١٦٦)** وأنتم ح ف : الأنتم ب ؛ – **(١٦٧)** يقولوا بحجة ح

144

فليس بخالق له ولا المقدور مخلوقًا له قوله تعالى ﴿أَفَرَأَيْتُمْ مَا تُمْنُونَ ءَأَنْتُمْ تَخْلُقُونَهُ أَمْ نَحْنُ الْخَالِقُونَ : ٥٦ ، ٥٨ ، ٥٩﴾[١٥٨].

مَا تُمْنُونَ ءَأَنْتُم[١٦٦] تَخْلُقُونَهُ أَمْ نَحْنُ الْخَالِقُونَ﴾.

فلم يستطيعوا أن يقولوا بحجّة[١٦٧] أنهم يخلقون مع تمنّيهم الولد فلا يكون ومع كراهتهم له ، فيكون[١٦٨] فنبّههم أن الخالق هو من تتأتى منه[١٦٩] المخلوقات على حسب[١٧٠] قصده .

2.225 وأما الدليل على أن الكائنات على وفق تقديره سبحانه ومشيئته من التنزيل فقوله ﴿لَوْ شِئْنَا لأَتَيْنَا كُلَّ نَفْسٍ هُداهَا : ٣٢ ، ١٣﴾ و﴿لَوْ شَاءَ اللهُ لَجَمَعَهُمْ عَلَى الْهُدَى : ٦ ، ٣٥﴾ و﴿لَوْ شَاءَ اللهُ مَا أَشْرَكُوا : ٦ ، ١٠٧﴾ إلى غير ذلك من الآيات .

2.231 قال أبو الحسن رضي الله عنه :

وأما أصلنا في المناقضة على الخصم في النظر فمأخوذ من الكتاب والسنة . وذلك أن النبي عليه السلام قال لمالك بن الصيف ، وكان حبرًا سمينًا من أحبار اليهود ، نشدتك الله ، هل تجد فيما أنزل الله من التورٰة أن الله يبغض الحبر السمين؟ فغضب الرجل

وأما أصلنا من المناقضة على الخصم في النظر فمأخوذه من سنة النبي[١٧١] ﷺ . وذلك تعليم الله عز وجل إياه حين لقي الحبر السمين فقال[١٧٢] نشدتك بالله ، [ف : ٥١ و] هل تجد فيما أنزل الله[١٧٣] تعالى من التوراة أن الله تعالى يبغض الحبر السمين؟ فغضب الحبر حين عيّره

ف (وقارن لمع الأشعري ، # ٥) : يقوموا الحجة ب ؛ – (١٦٨) ومع كراهتهم (كراهيتهم ف) له فيكون ب ف (وقارن لمع الأشعري ، # ٥) : مع كراهيته له ح ؛ – (١٦٩) تتأتى منه ف : يتأتى منه ح ، تتأتى ب ؛ – (١٧٠) حسب> ح ف ؛ – (١٧١) النبي ب : سيدنا محمد ح ف ؛ – (١٧٢) + له ح ف ؛ – (١٧٣) الله> ب ؛ – (١٧٤) وقال ب : فقال ح ف ؛ – (١٧٥) وهدى للناس> ح

وقال ﴿مَا أَنْزَلَ اللهُ عَلَى بَشَرٍ مِنْ شَيْءٍ : ٦ ، ٩١﴾ ؛ فناقضه عن قرب لأن التورٰية شيء وموسى بشر. فعلمه الله تعالى حتى قال ﴿مَنْ أَنْزَلَ الْكِتَابَ الَّذِي جَاءَ بِهِ مُوسَى : ٦ ، ٩١﴾ .

بذلك ، وقال[174] ﴿مَا أَنْزَلَ اللهُ عَلَى بَشَرٍ مِنْ شَيْءٍ﴾ . فقال الله تعالى ﴿قُلْ مَنْ أَنْزَلَ الْكِتَابَ الَّذِي جَاءَ بِهِ مُوسَى نُورًا وَهُدًى لِلنَّاسِ[175]﴾ الآية . فناقضه عن قرب[176] لأن التوراة شيء وموسى بشر ، وقد كان الحبر مقرًا بأن الله تعالى أنزل التوراة على موسى .

وكذلك ناقض الذين زعموا أن الله[177] عهد إليهم أن لا يؤمنوا برسول[178] حتى يأتيهم[179] بقربان تأكله النار ، فقال تعالى ﴿قُلْ قَدْ جَاءَكُمْ رُسُلٌ مِنْ قَبْلِي بِالْبَيِّنَاتِ وَبِالَّذِي قُلْتُمْ فَلِمَ قَتَلْتُمُوهُمْ إِنْ كُنْتُمْ صَادِقِينَ : ٣ ، ١٨٣﴾ ؛ فناقضهم بذلك وحاجّهم .

2.232 وأما أصلنا في مغالطة الخصوم فذلك مأخوذ من القرآن ، فإن الله تعالى لما قال ﴿إِنَّكُمْ وَمَا تَعْبُدُونَ مِنْ دُونِ اللهِ حَصَبُ جَهَنَّمَ : ٢١ ، ٩٨﴾ . أراد ابن الزبعرى أن يناقض رسول الله ﷺ فقال : إن الملائكة عُبدوا من دون الله وكذلك عيسى ، أفتقول يا محمد أنهم حصب جهنم؟ فسكت رسول الله ﷺ تعجبًا من جهله . وذلك أن الله تعالى قال ﴿وَمَا تَعْبُدُونَ مِنْ دُونِ اللهِ﴾ ولم يقل «ومن تعبدون» فلم يدخل فيه عيسى ولا الملائكة .

وأما أصلنا في استدراكنا مغالطة الخصوم فمأخوذ من قوله تعالى ﴿إِنَّكُمْ وَمَا تَعْبُدُونَ مِنْ دُونِ اللهِ حَصَبُ جَهَنَّمَ أَنْتُمْ لَهَا وَارِدُونَ﴾ إلى قوله[180] ﴿وَهُمْ فِيهَا[181] لَا يَسْمَعُونَ : ٢١ ، ١٠٠﴾ فإنه[182] لما نزلت هذه الآية بلغ ذلك عبد الله بن الزبعرى وكان جدلاً خصمًا فقال خصمت محمدًا ورب الكعبة فجاء إلى النبي[183] ﷺ فقال : يا محمد ، ألست تزعم أن عيسى وعزيرا والملائكة عباد صالحون؟ قال أجل . قال : فإن النصارى تعبد عيسى وطائفة من اليهود تعبد عزيرا وهذا بنو

ف ؛ – (١٧٦) قرب ح ف : قريب ب ؛ – (١٧٧) + تعالى ح ف ؛ – (١٧٨) برسول ا : لرسول ب ح ف ؛ – (١٧٩) إليهم ... يومنوا ... يأتيهم ا ح ف : إلينا ... نؤمن ... يأتينا ب ؛ – (١٨٠) + تعالى ب ؛ – (١٨١) وهم فيها > ح ؛ – (١٨٢) فإنه ب : فإنها ح ف ؛ – (١٨٣) إلى النبي ب : إليه رسول

لجم[١٨٤] تعبد الملائكة <فيجب> أن يكونوا حصب جهنم[١٨٥] فسكت النبي ﷺ لا سكوت عي ولا منقطع[١٨٦] ، تعجبًا من جهله ، لأنه ليس في الآية ما يوجب دخول عيسى وعزير والملائكة فيها ، لأنه قال ﴿وَمَا تَعْبُدُونَ[١٨٧]﴾ ولم يقل «وكل من عُبد[١٨٨] من دون الله» . وإنما أراد ابن الزبعرى مغالطة النبي ﷺ ليوهم[١٨٩] قومه أنه قد حاجّه .

فأنزل الله تعالى[١٩٠] ﴿إِنَّ الَّذِينَ سَبَقَتْ لَهُمْ مِنَّا الْحُسْنَى[١٩١] أُولَئِكَ عَنْهَا مُبْعَدُونَ﴾ فقرأها[١٩٢] النبي ﷺ[١٩٣] فضحكوا[١٩٤] عند ذلك لئلا يتبين[١٩٥] انقطاعهم وغلطهم . فقالوا ﴿ءَأَلِهَتُنَا خَيْرٌ أَمْ هُوَ﴾ يعنون عيسى فأنزل الله عز وجل[١٩٦] ﴿وَلَمَّا ضُرِبَ ابْنُ مَرْيَمَ مَثَلاً إِذَا قَوْمُكَ مِنْهُ يَصِدُّونَ : ٤٣ ، ٥٧﴾ إلى قوله[١٩٧] ﴿خَصِمُونَ﴾[١٩٨] .

فقال سبحانه بيانًا لذلك ﴿إِنَّ الَّذِينَ سَبَقَتْ لَهُمْ مِنَّا الْحُسْنَى أُولَئِكَ عَنْهَا مُبْعَدُونَ : ٢١ ، ١٠١﴾ فقالوا ﴿ءَأَلِهَتُنَا خَيْرٌ أَمْ هُوَ : ٤٣ ، ٥٧﴾ يعنون عيسى أرادوا مغالطة رسول الله ﷺ فقال سبحانه ﴿مَا ضَرَبُوهُ لَكَ إِلَّا جَدَلاً بَلْ هُمْ قَوْمٌ خَصِمُونَ : ٤٣ ، ٥٨﴾ ، لأنه لو قال «عيسى خير» فقد أثبت لالهتهم خيرية . فقال سبحانه ﴿إِنْ هُوَ إِلَّا عَبْدٌ أَنْعَمْنَا عَلَيْهِ : ٤٣ ، ٥٩﴾ .

الله ح . إلى رسول الله ف ؛ – (١٨٤) لجم : هكذا في ب ويحتمل أن يكون الصحيح لحيّ ؛ – (١٨٥) عباد... أن يكونوا ، هكذا في ب . ولكنه في آخره «الملائكة يكونوا» : عبدوا ح ، وليس في ف شيء من ذلك بل في موضعه بعد «عزيرا والملائكة» بياض طويل هو منقسم بين سطرين ، مقداره مقدار ثلثي سطر . وفي القراءة أنظر كلامنا الوارد في المقدمة ؛ – (١٨٦) عي ولا منقطع ح ف : منقطع ولا عي بل ب ؛ – (١٨٧) تعبدون ح ف : يعبدون ب ؛ – (١٨٨) من عبد ب : ما تعبدون ح ف ؛ – (١٨٩) ليوهم ح ف : لتوهم ب ؛ – (١٩٠) تعالى ب : عز وجل ح ف ؛ – (١٩١) يعني من المعبودين ح . يعني من المعبود ف ؛ – (١٩٢) فقراها ب : فقرا ح ف ؛ – (١٩٣) + ذلك ح ، عليه ذلك ف ؛ – (١٩٤) فضحكوا ب : فضجوا ح ف ؛ – (١٩٥) يتبين ب ح : يبين ف ؛ – (١٩٦) عز وجل ب ف : تعالى ح ؛ – (١٩٧) قوله ح ؛ – (١٩٨) + وهذا نص عليه على مجادلتهم ومحادلته إياهم بالوحي وما علمه

وكل ما ذكرناه من الآي وما لم[١٩٩] نذكره أصل لنا[٢٠٠] وهو حجة[٢٠١] في الكلام فيما نذكره من [٢٠٢] تفصيل الكلام في المسائل[٢٠٣]، وإن لم يكن كل[٢٠٤] [ب : ٦ ظ] مسئلة معينة في الكتاب والسنة، لأن ما حدث معيناً[٢٠٥] من المسائل العقليات في أيام النبي ﷺ والصحابة قد تكلموا فيه على نحو ما ذكرناه[٢٠٦].

2.311 قال أبو الحسن[٢٠٧] :

والجواب[٢٠٨] الثالث أن هذه المسائل التي ذكروها وسألوا[٢٠٩] عنها قد علمها النبي[٢١٠] عليه السلام[٢١١] ولم يجهل منها شيئًا مفصلاً، غير أنها لم تحدث في أيامه معينة[٢١٢] فيتكلم فيها [أ : ١٠ ظ] أو لا يتكلم فيها، وإن كانت[٢١٣] أصولها موجودة في الكتاب[٢١٤] والسنة.

2.312 وما حدث من شيء فيما له تعلق بالدين من جهة الشريعة فقد تكلموا فيه وبحثوا عنه وناظروا فيه وحاجّوا، كمسائل العول والجدّات من مسائل الفرائض وغير ذلك من أحكام الميراث وعدّة الحامل والمتوفّي عنها زوجها. وكذلك في قول من قال لامرأته أنت

وما حدث من شيء فيما[٢١٥] له تعلق بالدين من جهة الشريعة فقد تكلموا فيه وبحثوا عنه وناظروا فيه[٢١٦] وجادلوا وحاجّوا كمسائل[٢١٧] الفرائض وغير ذلك من الأحكام كالحرام[٢١٨] والبائن والبتة وحبلك[٢١٩] على غاربك وكالمسائل في الحدود والطلاق مما يكثر

الله إياه ب ؛ – (١٩٩) وما لم ب ف : أو لم ح ؛ – (٢٠٠) لنا > ح ؛ – (٢٠١) وهو حجة ب : وحجة لنا ح ف ؛ – (٢٠٢) من ح ف : في ب ؛ – (٢٠٣) الكلام في المسائل ح ف ؛ – (٢٠٤) يكن كل ب : تكن ح ف ؛ – (٢٠٥) معينًا ب : تعيينها ح ف ؛ – (٢٠٦) تكلموا... ذكرناه ب ح : تكلمنا فيه ف ؛ – (٢٠٧) قال أبو الحسن > ب ح ف ؛ – (٢٠٨) والجواب ا ح ف : وأما الجواب ب ؛ – (٢٠٩) ذكروها وسألوا ا : سألوا ب ح ف ؛ – (٢١٠) النبي ا ب : رسول الله ح ف ؛ – (٢١١) عليه السلام ا : ﷺ ب ح ف ؛ – (٢١٢) معينة > ب ؛ – (٢١٣) وإن ب ح ف : فإن ا ؛ – (٢١٤) الكتاب ا : القرآن ب ح ف ؛ – (٢١٥) فيما ح ف : مما ب ؛ – (٢١٦) فيه ح ف : فيها ب ؛ – (٢١٧) مسائل > ف ؛ – (٢١٨) كالحرام ب : وكالحرام ح ف ؛ – (٢١٩) حبلك ح

عليّ حرام وغير ذلك من الحدود والمعاملات ، فتكلموا فيها من غير أن وجدوا فيه نصًّا عن النبي ﷺ ، إذ لو وجدوا فيها نصًّا لما اختلفوا فيها . وبقي الإختلاف إلى الآن .

ذكرها مما قد حدثت في أيامهم ولم يجيء في كل واحد[٢٢٠] منها نصّ عن النبي ﷺ لأنّه لو نصّ على جميع ذلك لما اختلفوا فيها[٢٢١] وبقي الخلاف إلى الآن .

وهذه المسائل ، وإن لم يكن[٢٢٢] في كل واحدة[٢٢٣] منها نصّ عن النبي[٢٢٤] عليه السلام[٢٢٥] ، فإنهم ردّوها وقاسوها على ما فيه نصّ من كتاب الله[٢٢٦] أو سنة نبيه عليه السلام[٢٢٧] باجتهادهم[٢٢٨] ؛ فهذه أحكام حوادث الفروع ردوها إلى أصول[٢٢٩] الشريعة[٢٣٠] .

2.313 فأمّا الحوادث التي[٢٣١] تحدث في الأصول من تعيين مسائل فينبغي لكلّ مسلم عاقل[٢٣٢] أن يرد حكمها[٢٣٣] إلى جملة الأصول المتفق عليها بالعقل والحسّ والبديهة وغير ذلك ، لأن حكم مسائل الشرع التي طريقها السمع أن تكون مردودة إلى أصول [ف : ٥١ ظ] الشرع إلى طريقها[٢٣٤] السمع ؛ وحكم مسائل العقليات[٢٣٥] أن تردّ[٢٣٦] إلى البداية والمحسوسات والضروريات ليرد[٢٣٧] كل شيء من ذلك إلى بابه ولا يختلط[٢٣٨] العقليات بالسمعيات ولا السمعيات بالعقليات .

ف : حملك ب ؛ – (٢٢٠) واحد ب ف : واحدة ح ؛ – (٢٢١) فيها > ب ؛ – (٢٢٢) يكن ح ف : ىكن ا . تكن ب ؛ – (٢٢٣) واحدة ا ب : واحد ح ف ؛ – (٢٢٤) النبي ا ب : رسول الله ح ف ؛ – (٢٢٥) عليه السلام ا : ﷺ ب ح ف ؛ – (٢٢٦) + تعالى ح ف ؛ – (٢٢٧) أو سنة نبيه عليه السلام ا : أو السنة ب ف . والسنة ح ؛ – (٢٢٨) باجتهادهم ا ب : واجتهادهم ح ف ؛ + وقلت ولما قال مسهب بن مخرمة لعلي رضي الله عنه فيما جرى له في حرب الجمل من القتال والقتل هل عهد إليك رسول الله ﷺ ذلك فقال على رضى الله عنه لا والله خاب من افترى ولكنا القرآن خرابنا فيه دايا قال أبو الحسن ا ؛ – (٢٢٩) أصول ا : أحكام ب ح ف ؛ – (٢٣٠) + التي هي فروع لا تستدرك أحكامها إلّا من جهة السمع والرسل ب ح ف ؛ – (٢٣١) الحوادث التي ا : حوادث ب ح ف ؛ – (٢٣٢) مسلم عاقل ا : عاقل مسلم ب ح ف ؛ – (٢٣٣) يرد حكمها ا ح ف : يردها ب ؛ – (٢٣٤) التي طريقها ا : التي طريقه ب . الذي طريقه ح ف ؛ – (٢٣٥) + والمحسوسا ب ح ف ؛ – (٢٣٦) أن ترد ا : تردها ب . أن يرد ح ف ؛ وقراءة ح ف هذه لأن فاعل «يرد» قد صار «كل شيء» بعد ما سقط القول المشار إليه في هـ ٢٣٧ ؛ – (٢٣٧) إلى البداية ... ليرد ا : إلى أصول العقل التي طريقها النظر والحسّ والقياس ليرد ب . وهذا القول قد سقط من ح ف ؛ – (٢٣٨) يختلط : تخلط ا : يخلط ب ح . تخلط ف ؛ –

2.314 ولو حدث في زمان النبيّ ﷺ في خلق القرآن وفي مسئلة الجزء والجسم وغير ذلك لتكلم فيه وبيّن كما بين ما حدث في زمانه وأيامه.

فلو حدث في أيام النبي ﷺ الكلام في خلق القرآن وفي الجزء والطفرة بهذه الألفاظ لتكلم فيه وبيّن[٢٣٩] كما بين سائر ما حدث في أيامه من تعيين المسائل المذكورة[٢٤٠].

2.3211 ويقال لهم : فالنبي ﷺ لم يصح عنه حديث في أن القرآن غير مخلوق ولا هو مخلوق ، فلم قلتم أنه غير مخلوق؟

ثم يقال لهم : فالنبي[٢٤١] ﷺ لم يصح عنه حديث في أن القرآن غير مخلوق أو هو مخلوق ، فلم قلتم أنه غير مخلوق؟

فإن قالوا قد قاله بعض الصحابة والنابغين ، قلنا : فلزم الصحابي والتابعي عندكم مثل ما يلزمكم من أن يكون مبتدعًا ضالاً ، إذ قال ما لم يقله النبي عليه السلام ، لا سيما ولا قرآن عندكم إلّا الحروف والأصوات وقد قلتم إن من قال أنها مخلوقة فقد كفر.

فإن قالوا قد قاله بعض الصحابة والتابعين[٢٤٢] ، قيل لهم : فيلوم[٢٤٣] الصحابي والتابعي مثل ما يلزمكم من أن يكون مبتدعًا ضالاً ، إذ قال[٢٤٤] ما لم يقله النبي[٢٤٥] ﷺ.

2.3212 فإن قال قائل أنا متوقف فيه فلا أقول مخلوق أو غير مخلوق ، قلنا : فأنت من توقفك في ذلك مبتدع ، لأن رسول الله لم يقل إذا حدثت هذه الحادثة فتوقفوا فيها ولا تقولوا فيها شيئًا ، ولا قال كفّروا وضللوا من قال بخلقه.

فإن قال قائل فأنا أتوقف في ذلك فلا أقول مخلوق ولا غير مخلوق ، قيل له : فأنت في توقفك في ذلك مبتدع ضالّ ، لأن النبي ﷺ يقل إن حدثت هذه الحادثة بعدي توقفوا فيها ولا تقولوا[٢٤٦] فيها شيئًا ، ولا قال ضللوا وكفروا من قال بخلقه[٢٤٧].

2.322 ويقال لهم : لو قال قائل علم الله مخلوق أو قال في وصفه ما لا يليق به أتتوقفون فيه؟

وخبرونا لو قال[٢٤٩] قائل أنّ علم الله[٢٥٠] مخلوق أكنتم تتوقفون فيه[٢٥١]؟

(٢٣٩) وبين ب ف : وبينه ح ؛ – (٢٤٠) المذكورة ب : وتكلم فيها ح ف ؛ – (٢٤١) فالنبي ب : النبي ح ف ؛ – (٢٤٢) والتابعين ب : وبعض التابعين ح ف ؛ – (٢٤٣) فيلزم ب : يلزم ح ف ؛ – (٢٤٤) إذ قال ح ف : إذا قالوا ب ؛ – (٢٤٥) النبي ب : الرسول ح ف ؛ – (٢٤٦) تقولوا ح ف : يقولوا ب ؛ – (٢٤٧) + ومن قال بنفي خلقه ح ف ؛ – (٢٤٨) لا > ا ؛ – (٢٤٩) قال : متكررة في

فإن قالوا لا[٢٤٨] قلنا : فلم يقل رسول الله ﷺ ولا صحابته في ذلك شيئًا .

فإن قالوا لا قيل لهم فلم[٢٥٢] يقل النبي ﷺ ولا أصحابه في ذلك شيئًا .

وكذلك لو قال قائل هذا ربكم شعبان أوريان أو مكتسي أو عريان أو مقرور أو صفراوي[٢٥٣] أو مرطوب أو جسم أو عرض أو يشمّ الريح او لا يشمّها أو هل له أنف وقلب وكبد وطحال وهل يحجّ في كل سنة وهل يركب الخيل او لا يركبها وهل يغتمّ أم لا ونحو ذلك من المسائل لكان ينبغي أن تسكت عنه لأن رسول الله ﷺ لم يتكلم في شيء من ذلك ولا أصحابه أو كنت لا تسكت فكنت تبين بكلامك أن شيئًا من ذلك لا يجوز على الله عز وجل وتقدس[٢٥٤] بحجة كذا وكذا .

فإن قال قائل أسكت عنه ولا أجيبه بشيء أو أهجره أو أقوم عنه أو لا أسلم عليه ولا أعوده[٢٥٥] إذا مرض ولا أشهد[٢٥٦] جنازته إذا مات ، قيل له : فيلزمك أن تكون في جميع هذه الصيغ التي ذكرتها مبتدعًا ضالاً ، لأن رسول الله ﷺ لم يقل من سأل عن شيء من ذلك فاسكتوا عنه ولا قال لا تسلموا عليه ولا قوموا عنه ولا قال شيئًا من ذلك ، فأنتم مبتدعة إذا فعلتم ذلك[٢٥٧] .

ف ؛ – **(٢٥٠)** + تعالى ب ؛ – **(٢٥١)** فيه > ب ؛ + أم لا ح ف ؛ – **(٢٥٢)** فلم ب ف : لم ح ؛ – **(٢٥٣)** إلى هاهنا انتهى ب ؛ – **(٢٥٤)** + كذا وكذا ح ؛ – **(٢٥٥)** ولا أعوده ف : أو لا أعوده ح ؛ – **(٢٥٦)** ولا أشهد ف : أو لا أشهد ح ؛ – **(٢٥٧)** قد أدخل الأب مكارثي «ويقال لهم»

2.323 فإن قالوا إنما كفّرنا القائل[٢٥٨] بخلق القرآن لأن أئمة السلف كفروه قلنا : إذا لم يرو عن النبي عليه اسلام حكم في ذلك فلم كفّروه ، وهلا سكتوا عنه كما سكت عنه رسول الله ﷺ ؟ كان عالمًا بالمنافقين بأعيانهم ، ومع ذلك كان يجري عليهم حكم المسلمين. فإذا لم يتكلم في خلق القرآن ولا في نفي خلقه كان الواجب على أئمة السلف أن يقتدوا به في ذلك .

ولم لم تسكتوا عمن قال بخلق القرآن ولم كفرتموه ، ولم يرد عن النبي ﷺ حديث صحيح في نفي خلقه وتكفير من قال بخلقه؟

فإن قالوا لأن أحمد بن حنبل رضي الله عنه قال بنفي خلقه وتكفير من قال بخلقه قيل لهم : ولم لم يسكت أحمد عن ذلك بل تكلم فيه؟

فإن قالوا لأن عباسًا[٢٥٩] العنبري ووكيعًا وعبد الرحمن بن مهدي وفلانًا وفلانًا قالوا أنه غير مخلوق ومن قال بأنه مخلوق فهو كافر قيل لهم : ولم لم يسكت أولئك عما سكت عنه رسول الله[٢٦٠] ﷺ ؟

فإن قالوا لأن عمرو بن دينار وسفيان بن عيينة وجعفر بن محمد رضي الله عنهم وفلانًا وفلانًا قالوا ليس بخالق ولا مخلوق قيل لهم : ولم لم يسكت أولئك عن هذه المقالة ولم يقلها رسول الله ﷺ ؟

فإن أحالوا ذلك على صحابيّ[٢٦١] أو جماعة منهم كان ذلك مكابرة ، فإنه يقال لهم : فلم لم يسكتوا عن ذلك ولم يتكلم فيه النبي ﷺ ولا قال كفّروا قائلة ؟

2.331 فإن قالوا لا بدّ للعلماء من الكلام في الحادثة ليعلم الجاهل حكمها ،

وإن قالوا لا بد للعلماء[٢٦٢] من الكلام في الحادثة ليعلم الجاهل

هنا قبل قوله ولم لم تسكتوا ؛ – (٢٥٨) القائل : القائلين ا ؛ – (٢٥٩) عباسًا ف : عباس ح ؛ – (٢٦٠) رسول الله > ح ؛ – (٢٦١) صحابي ف : الصحابة ح ؛ – (٢٦٢) للعلماء ح : للعالم ف ؛ –

قيل : فهذا أردنا منكم فلم أضربتم عن علم الكلام ومنعتموه ؟

2.332 وهؤلاء يتكلمون في الكلام حتى إذا انقطعوا قالوا نُهينا عن علم الكلام ويقلدون من كان قبلهم بلا حجة ولا برهان .

2.333 ثم يقال لهم : فالنبي ﷺ لم يتكلم في الدور والوصايا ولا في حساب المناسخات ولا صنَّف في ذلك كتابًا كما صنف مالك وأبو حنيفة والشافعي رضي الله عنهم ، فيلزمكم أن تحكموا عليهم[٢٦٥] بالبدعة إذ فعلوا ما لم يفعله رسول الله ﷺ .

انتهى كلام أبى الحسن رضى الله عنه [أ : ١١ و] في هذا الباب .

حكمها ، قيل لهم[٢٦٣] : فهذا[٢٦٤] الذي أردناه منكم ، فلم منعتم الكلام ؟

فأنتم إن شئتم تكلمتم حتى إذا أنقطعتم قلتم نُهينا عن الكلام ؛ وان شئتم قلدتم من كان قبلكم بلا حجة [ف : ٥٢ و] ولا بيان ؛ وهذه شهوة وتحكم .

ثم يقال لهم : فالنبي ﷺ لم يتكلم في الدور[٢٦٦] والوصايا ولا في العتق ولا في حساب المناسخات ولا صنَّف فيها كتابًا كما صنعه مالك والثوري والشافعي وأبو حنيفة فيلزمكم أن يكونوا مبتدعة ضلالاً ، إذ فعلوا[٢٦٧] ما لم يفعله النبي ﷺ وقالوا ما لم يقله نصًّا بعينه وصنّفوا ما لم يصنّفه النبي ﷺ وقالوا بتكفير القائلين بخلق القرآن ولم يقله النبي ﷺ . وفيما ذكرنا كفاية لكل عاقل غير معاند .

آخره[٢٦٨]

(٢٦٣) لهم ح : له ف ؛ – (٢٦٤) فهذا ف : هذا ح ؛ – (٢٦٥) عليهم : عليه ا ؛ – (٢٦٦) الدور ف : النذور ح ؛ – (٢٦٧) يكونوا ... فعلوا : تكونوا ... فعلتم ف * . وقد شطب الكاتب نقطتي تاء تكونوا وكتب فعلوا في الهامش ؛ – (٢٦٨) آخره ف : نجز ح .

INDEX OF NAMES AND SUBJECTS

Diacritical marks of letters are disregarded in the alphabetical order. The Arabic article is also disregarded. Transliteration of Arabic words has been made uniform for the purpose of these indices in accordance with the German convention (with the exception of j for ǧ, and aw for au and ay for ai for the diphthongs). The indices were prepared by Alexander Treiger.

INDEX OF ARABIC WORDS

INDEX OF GREEK AND SYRIAC TERMS